DATE DUE

JE 19 02			
NO			
DE			
DE 17 02			

DEMCO 38-296

A Nation of Peoples

A NATION OF PEOPLES

A Sourcebook on America's Multicultural Heritage

Edited by
ELLIOTT ROBERT BARKAN

Greenwood Press
Westport, Connecticut • London

Library of Congress Cataloging-in-Publication Data

A nation of peoples : a sourcebook on America's multicultural heritage
  / edited by Elliott Robert Barkan.
       p.   cm.
    Includes bibliographical references and index.
    ISBN 0–313–29961–7 (alk. paper)
    1. Minorities—United States.   2. Immigrants—United States.
  3. Pluralism (Social sciences)—United States.   4. United States—
  Ethnic relations.   5. United States—Race relations.   I. Barkan,
  Elliott Robert.
  E184.A1N2866   1999
  305.8'00973—dc21   98–41061

British Library Cataloguing in Publication Data is available.

Library of Congress Catalog Card Number: 98–41061
ISBN: 0–313–29961–7

First published in 1999

Greenwood Press, 88 Post Road West, Westport, CT 06881
An imprint of Greenwood Publishing Group, Inc.
www.greenwood.com

Printed in the United States of America

The paper used in this book complies with the
Permanent Paper Standard issued by the National
Information Standards Organization (Z39.48–1984).

10 9 8 7 6 5 4 3 2

Copyright Acknowledgment

The editor and publisher are grateful to the following for granting permission to reprint from
their material:

Excerpts from Yukuo Uyehara, ''The Horehore-Bushi,'' in *Social Process in Hawaii*, Volume 28
(1980–1981), appear courtesy of the University of Hawaii.

CONTENTS

PREFACE

FRAMING THE ISSUES FOR THIS BOOK

This reference work presents a series of twenty-seven new essays that, collectively, represent an effort to provide within one volume what I believe to be the most up-to-date, comprehensive overview of America's ethnic peoples since the publication of the *Harvard Encyclopedia of American Ethnic Groups* in 1980. While present length limitations precluded any effort to achieve quite the same breadth in terms of the number of groups covered (or to include separate thematic essays) as in that earlier work, it is hoped that the many peoples this volume does treat will provide both a telling portrait of Americans and their very diverse ethnic roots and compelling stories of the peoples, past and present, who have played varied and often vital roles in the nation's development.

In 1964, sociologist Milton Gordon published what is now regarded as a classic exploration of ethnicity and assimilation, *Assimilation in American Life*, in which he defined *ethnicity* as embracing racial, religious, and nationality groups that met his set of common criteria. He also offered a model of the stages through which ethnic group members *might* proceed—and, indeed, through which they would need to move—if they aspired to complete assimilation. Those stages included cultural, identificational, civic, marital, and especially structural assimilation by minority group individuals as well as attitudinal and behavioral assimilation with respect to dominant group beliefs and behaviors involving those minority individuals. Gordon's model (particularly his emphasis on structural assimilation, involvement in organizations, and activities outside the ethnic group) and his inclusive definition of *ethnicity* provided the initial premises underlying my approach to the breadth of the essays selected for this reference book and the issues I asked contributors to consider. This volume focuses on America's multicultural heritage with respect to its racial, religious, and nationality groups. Having begun with Gordon's approach and criteria, I, too, offer all three types under the umbrella term of *ethnic* groups. However, while for me that definition originated with Gordon's seminal work, it is now based on three decades of research and instruction focusing on an interdisciplinary, comparative approach to American ethnicity. Indeed, the orientation here also implicitly rests on a premise serendipitously contained in a remark made by a local teacher: "If you know only your own culture, you do not know your own culture." Thus, if you know only the history of your own ethnic group, you do not really know your own group's history. For example, its "cultural baggage," the treatment accorded it, the experiences its members have enjoyed or endured, and their impact on America, and vice versa, can all be fully appreciated only through the perspective gained by comparison with the experiences of others. Consequently, I am aware that much has occurred since Gordon's book appeared—changes dramatically underscored by the multicultural movement—and that we are compelled to incorporate more facets into his criteria of ethnicity and to refine his original model of assimilation—not so much by altering its specific features (i.e., cultural versus structural assimilation) but by modifying its implication that assimilation is a relatively linear process.

Seven broad points will set out the issues underlying this reference work.

First, as I detail in my own model of the American ethnic experience (1995), assimilation is now better understood as something that *may* be possible—*if* it is mutually acceptable (to those in both the minority and majority groups)—but it is not, and has not been, an *inevitable outcome* in American history. For some groups it has not been a desirable goal; for many others, it has only been partially attainable.

Second, the triple reference of "ethnic" remains valid. I have here intentionally included ethnic groups identified by their race, religion, or nationality because all three types do share a number of commonalities in their group dynamics. Yet it must be emphasized that they have diverged considerably in the quality of their historical experiences and in the outcomes of those experiences. Therefore, while there has been no one path into the mainstream, no one time line, and no one outcome, these divergent experiences do not nullify the presence of other, basic commonalities that ethnic groups do share.[1]

Third, we have long been told that we are a nation of immigrants. But that, we now recognize, is no more fully accurate than the Kerner Commission's ominous declaration in 1968 (concerning the riots during the prior five years) that we were becoming two nations, one black and one white. Where Latinos, Asians, American Indians (or Native Americans or "First Nations"), or even Hawaiians fit in was never clarified, but the violent multiethnic events of the next quarter century would demonstrate the narrowness of that original assessment. We are not a Nation of Immigrants, nor are we simply descending into a nation of two societies cut by one racial divide, be it black versus white or black versus all others.

Americans are beginning to understand and accept that their country is a *Nation of Peoples*—some indigenous and others resident for centuries; many arriving voluntarily and many brought by force; still others compelled to migrate without much choice and many who originally planned to return home; and large numbers who have entered legally along with similarly large numbers who have not. We are composed of those who have gone to the countryside and others who have gathered in the cities. We are peoples who have been here many centuries, and we are peoples whose newcomers have been here but days. Only by knowing some of those remarkably varied stories can we begin to comprehend that the story of America, America's multicultural heritage, embraces the impact of conquest and enslavement; indenture and labor contracts; internment and deportation; flight and asylum; settlement in the name of God and migration in pursuit of security; entry legally and entry covertly; migration with few women versus settlement as families; adaptation to a new culture and agony over the clash of cultures; confinement within one's community and integration among others; citizenship with political rights versus ineligibility for citizenship; transplantation of gender roles as against accommodation to a more open environment; and invisibility by choice versus invisibility without choice.

Fourth, the long turmoil over how we interpret our multiethnic, multicultural society has not been merely over academic issues. On the one hand, it has been enmeshed with fundamental issues of power and rewards: jobs; political office; government contracts; public funding; and desegregation of education, housing, and public accommodations. On the other, it is inseparable from the visions we have long held of American society, in particular of our public schools and their role in the preparation of future citizens for participation in a common civic culture. In most time periods (except wars), the ethnic differences that had persisted alongside that shared core culture have usually been viewed as temporary and secondary to the minority group's commitment to the civic core. That this core culture proved flawed—marred by racism and bigotry—was only slowly acknowledged and understood. Americans only gradually appreciated the scope of its adverse impact on minorities.

Fifth, because of both its continued openness to newcomers and its failures in dealing with its diversity, this nation has had periodically to reevaluate and redefine its image and purpose as part of its ongoing process of self-definition. And as long as there are groups who continue to feel excluded or marginalized by others from mainstream America and as long as the nation continues to allow substantial numbers of new immigrants to be admitted, the process of redefinition itself is likely to continue. Furthermore, the particular strategies, goals, and values that people embrace in their quest for inclusion need periodic reformulation because the larger context of economic and societal conditions is changing continuously. Consequently, in academic terms, we are still seeking a fuller understanding of the nature of the historical interplay between this nation's multicultural heritage and its common civic heritage.

Sixth, the nature of the debates over this history—bitter or amicable—depends on how that history is framed, how the resulting information is used, how inferences are drawn and words employed. Through one frame the debate can produce good-faith reassessments; through another it may yield a postmodern deconstruction and disassembly that leaves littered the remnants of a core culture—with little left in its stead. For all of its imperfections, the American core culture unlocked for the world the doors of a nation that did not possess an ethnic/racial homogeneity. More and more Americans now recognize that, for all its shortcomings, the core culture's success was all the greater because it provided the nation with the foundation of a multiethnic, multicultural heritage and enabled the peoples of the world who journeyed to America to enrich the nation with their labors and cultures while pursuing a mixture of ancestral traditions and newfound hopes and dreams.

In that light, the purpose of the essays in this collection is to address the many efforts of diverse peoples seeking to determine their place in American society, to analyze the obstacles they have encountered and the extent to which they have overcome them (and the ways they have done so), to account for those they have not surmounted, and to evaluate the groups' impact on America. The intention is to provide readers with information and interpretations that encompass the principal ethnic groups in American society throughout the nation's history (and even before) so that readers can determine what has worked and what has not; what choices groups have made or not made or have been unable to make (and why); and what men and women in those groups have been able to do (or not do) because of the culture of their group and/or the "context of reception"—the conditions and treatments encountered with mainstream America. The thrust here is also to demonstrate, as part of America's multicultural heritage, that (1) many peoples, from many backgrounds and cultures, have partaken of the building of this nation; (2) most of them have benefited in the short or long run by settling in America—and not a few at the expense of others; and (3) millions of Americans, including those in groups that have suffered at the hands of other Americans, have embraced and supported the goals and ideals of the national culture. And those ideals have remained within the collective conscience of the nation—serving as an inspiration for generations of new Americans.

Seventh, I do believe that the whole has been greater than the sum of its parts but not infrequently at the considerable expense of some of those parts. What America's multicultural heritage imparts on one level is that the nation cannot succeed in ensuring the maximum potential of its citizens if it continues to permit the unequal treatment of its constituent members. This is not simply a question of social justice, although the nation's ideals warrant that. It is also a fact that the nation's minorities have become far better and more rapidly informed and mobilized than ever before and possess higher levels of expectations. Moreover, as suggested above, newer groups now seeking the same kinds of success that their predecessors have achieved are compelled to do it within a significantly altered, postindustrial, increasingly technological context and that necessitates changes to ensure that the structural prerequisites (the "opportunity structure") for pursuing success remain viable.

On a second level, the cumulative multiethnic histories suggest certain patterns likely to continue: Many immigrants will enter America, and they and their children will, in all likelihood, adapt rather effectively, enjoying the nation's promise; some newcomers will choose not to remain, others will but will choose not to integrate or not to seek assimilation, and still others will encounter resistance, even rejection, from the mainstream or obstacles too formidable to overcome. There is no one path in America and no one outcome, but there are many stories.

On a third level, although anthropologists have made it quite clear that "race" in biological terms is an unreliable and misleading marker of group differences, the legacy of the societal concept of race—as viewed through the accounts presented here—suggests, on the one hand, that the color line will indeed continue to be an issue in the twenty-first century—with uncertain consequences. On the other hand, its recent manifestations also indicate that, in the absence of a profound reversal of fortunes, more and more persons of all "races" will cross that line, significantly increasing the population of mixed-race Americans.

FRAMING THE ORGANIZATION OF THIS BOOK

The selection of the groups and topics to include in this volume entailed some of the agony and debate that have enveloped the whole field of multiculturalism and ethnic studies for the past quarter century. Its coverage could not be complete, only, hopefully, richly representative, and limitations on length necessitated finding a balance between the number of essays and adequate lengths for them. The solution lay in selecting those groups that are indigenous, those long resident, and from among those sharing the more traditional immigrant experiences of the past three centuries, in other words, the principal peoples past and present. They are representative of the world's major sending regions; they are the groups particularly associated with all the key phases of the nation's history and development (and some peoples that tend to get overlooked, such as Hawaiians and Puerto Ricans); and, in nearly a dozen of the essays, they are related groups that have been combined to ensure as much coverage as possible.[2]

While the following listing might imply that many of these groups are being presented as an array of single peoples—that is, as single ethnic groups (notably American Indians, to use Alice Kehoe's term)—the extensive diversity within them is fully discussed by the various authors. Ethnic groups are rarely homogeneous entities. Regionally, eleven essays cover Europeans (British, Dutch, East Europeans, French, Germans, Greeks, Irish, Italians, Jews, Poles, and Scandinavians); eight treat the Americas (Central and South Americans, Cubans, French Canadians and Cajuns [along with the French], Mexicans, Mormons,[3] American Indians, Puerto Ricans, and other West Indians/Caribbeans [besides Cubans and Puerto Ricans]); seven present Asian and Pacific peoples (Chinese, Filipinos, Hawaiians, Japanese, Koreans, South Asians, and Southeast Asians); and one focuses on African Americans (but not contemporary African migration) and another on peoples from the Middle East (principally Muslims).

In an effort to achieve some comparability in the essays (as was done for the

Harvard Encyclopedia of American Ethnic Groups, edited by Stephan Thern-strom, Ann Orlov, and Oscar Handlin [1980] and for a previous volume published by Greenwood Press, *Multiculturalism in the United States: A Comparative Guide to Acculturation and Ethnicity*, edited by John D. Buenker and Lorman A. Ratner [1992]), all prospective contributors were given a set of guidelines as to the key issues I hoped to see covered as well as my goal of having essays that were as current as possible in terms of the literature, available statistical data, contemporary developments, and the major topics and controversies concerning the particular groups. At the same time, however, given the expertise of these authors, I encouraged them to define the scope/focus and interpretation of their respective essays as they individually saw fit. This was particularly important for those eleven essays involving multiple groups and/or concentrating on peoples from particular regions (e.g., Central and South America, Middle East, South Asia, Southeast Asia, the Caribbean, Eastern Europe, and North America's First Nations, to use Alice Kehoe's other phrase). Several of these essays are understandably longer than others, either because of the group's exceptionally long history (e.g., Native Americans and African Americans) or because of the number of peoples covered (notably East Europeans, Central and South Americans, and Middle Easterners).

The six areas that the authors were asked to consider (insofar as it was appropriate) were (1) *immigration/entry* into America—including secondary migration after arrival or incorporation; (2) adjustment, obstacles, adversities—*first-generation adaptation*—hurdles encountered, degree of success, impact on America, and vice versa, plus gender-and class-related topics; (3) the ethnic group and American material culture—*economic integration*—their impact on the economy and it on them; (4) the ethnic group and American politics—*political integration*—issues of citizenship and the impact of the group as voters, candidates, and officials; (5) the ethnic group and American culture—*cultural integration*—contributions to American education, arts, literature, religion, norms, values, and so on, and the impact of American culture and society on the group in terms of its culture, institutions, identity, intergenerational friction, intermarriage, assimilation of individuals, and the like; and (6) the ethnic group in *contemporary American society*—overall legacy and impact, the current status of the group, the intensity and extent of its members' ethnic identity, and its place in America's multicultural heritage. In addition, given length limits and limits on the number of endnotes with which we had to work, each contributor was asked to provide a "Bibliographic References" section, a few pages discussing the principal (and particularly the most current) works related to the respective group(s).

In view of the fact that the *Harvard Encyclopedia of American Ethnic Groups* appeared nearly twenty years ago (1980) and that Buenker and Ratner's collection was more limited in terms of the number of groups included and the extent of their coverage of the past three decades, it is my modest hope that readers will find that the present collection significantly and qualitatively updates many of the group-specific essays that appeared in those earlier volumes. It is my hope, too, that readers will find these essays to be comprehensive, given their length; comparable in terms of addressing common issues; up-to-date in their coverage of data, issues, and literature; and yet distinctive in their individual emphases and interpretations.

ACKNOWLEDGMENTS

I would like to thank Gary Nash, David Reimers, Lawrence Fuchs, and especially John Higham for their comments on the introduction. Of course, I remain responsible for the final results. I would also like to thank California State University at San Bernardino for a grant to complete the preparation of this book and the remarkable and invaluable typing assistance of Paula Tilton-Molocznik. Crucial, too, has been the invaluable support of my editor at Greenwood, George Butler, who appreciated our efforts and the high quality of what my many contributors have provided, as well as the assistance of my production editor, David Palmer, and the exceptional copyediting by Susan E. Badger. Finally, along with my gratitude to my wife Bryn for her forebearance during the last, "manic" stages of completing this work, I would like to dedicate this volume to our children in my wish that all their dreams and hopes materialize—Ari, Liana, and Yoni Barkan and Eric Hoffmann (and wife Cheryl) and Gabe Hoffmann (and wife Mazie)—and first grandchild, Garrett Hoffmann. Books are a challenge to produce, and then they are done; children are a challenge to raise but can give us a joy that goes on and on. This they do.

NOTES

1. These include, within each group, principally a shared sense of peoplehood, identification with particular historical experiences, common values, cultural traditions, holiday observances, foods, often a common language and/or religion, preference for in-group friendships and endogamy, and usually communal centers or geographic concentrations. Since almost no ethnic group is homogeneous, not all members share their group's characteristics to equal degrees but do so enough to identify with their ethnic groups. The degree of intensity will usually vary, depending on the recency of migration, the quality of treatment by the dominant group, the presence of any special goals binding members together, and how integrated the individuals are within the larger society.

2. East Europeans, Scandinavians, French/French Canadian and Cajun, Central and South Americans, South Asians, Southeast Asians, Middle Easterners, Native Americans/American Indians, and West Indians, as well as—to a somewhat lesser extent—Germans and British.

3. The debate over whether Mormons constitute a comparatively unique, indigenously developed, religiously based ethnic community has continued for some time. For that reason, I have included them, and Steven Epperson directly addresses the issue in his essay.

INTRODUCTION: AMERICA—A NATION OF PEOPLES

Elliott Robert Barkan

MULTICULTURALISM: THE ISSUES

How did the often heated and acrimonious debates over multiculturalism arise, and in what direction have they been moving, particularly now, in the late 1990s? Addressing these matters will provide the context for describing the conclusions I have drawn from the essays that follow and their potential contribution to the discussions about multiculturalism in America and the nation's multicultural heritage.

In 1975, while walking with one of the nation's leading historians, I asked why, well into the 1960s, there was virtually nothing in his text about ethnic minorities and women. "We didn't think it was important," was his candid response. Ethnic groups and women would finally challenge such invisibility and, in so doing, radically transform our study of history. But the issue was not one confined merely to the realm of scholarship and college texts. In 1989 I was invited to Washington, D.C., by the U.S. Bureau of the Census to participate in the review of the ancestry question for the 1990 census. I raised the following issue. Because the race question asked Asian Americans to check off if they were Chinese, Japanese, Filipino, and so on, it implied that these were racially distinct populations, thus perpetuating even more misleading notions about race in America and especially about Asians. I was told that it had to remain that way, for the race question was asked of everyone and such tabulations were vital for groups seeking federal funding. In other words, for practical (that is, pecuniary) reasons, such complete-count data were more important to Asian Americans than the implications of the stereotyping format of the question. Sure enough, the Census Bureau's *1990 Profiles of Asian and Pacific Islanders* (CPH-L-151) is broken down by "Chinese Race," "Filipino Race," "Korean Race," "Hmong Race," and so on.

Some such government categories—devised for their simplistic convenience—

have influenced how other agencies, the media, and even scholars have subsequently categorized those peoples, most notoriously "Hispanics" and "Asian and Pacific Islanders." They shape the nature of the debate because so much in this contentious realm of ethnicity is a matter of perception and interpretation and the stake one has in the particular issue. For example, around 1980 I was caught up in a fierce argument with a colleague who insisted that racial groups were *not* ethnic groups. A decade later, I was confronted by a large group of ethnic studies faculty (whom I had invited to a statewide seminar on ethnic studies) who even more intensely insisted that *only* racial groups were entitled to the label *ethnic*! In effect, they were embracing James Banks's earlier notion that multicultural education focus on groups that were "victims of oppression." They were therefore insisting that white ethnic populations did not fall into that category and were indistinguishably part of the "dominant" society. Hence, they were not ethnic. Furthermore, they said, I was a racist, for I had agreed to coordinate this "Ethnic Studies Seminar" even though I was neither Latino nor a person of (nonwhite) color.

It was more than coincidental that that year, 1991, was about the time that the fiery debates over multiculturalism and its place in school curricula were escalating in intensity. The popular press and academic meetings and publications teemed with discussions and articles on political correctness, ethnic groups and multiculturalism in the curriculum, and the meaning and relevance of American history and culture—anxious expressions of a polarizing debate, which Todd Gitlin has described as America's "culture wars."

It soon became apparent to me that this particular multiethnic conclave had adopted an extremist and academically unsupportable definition of *ethnicity* that denied the continuing experiences of many quite viable ethnic groups, from Armenians and Dutch to Poles, Russian Jews, and Ukrainians. Nor did they consider the extent to which discussions of the multiplicity of cultures in America were frequently acknowledging the distinctive (even cross-ethnic) roles and impact of social classes and gender or the persistence of America's regional cultural variations. Moreover, my critics, in their ideological fervor, had also lost sight of the practical strategy necessary for a successful program of ethnic multiculturalism: collaboration with interested whites, not simply an adversarial approach that spurned them. And in their determination to control the dialogue, they had subscribed to the fallacy on which Nathan Glazer has recently focused: "There is no necessary equivalence between a person's race or ethnicity and the views that person holds. It is one of the errors of the more extreme version of multiculturalism to believe there is."

What had happened to the dialogue on multiculturalism? Was the letter writer to the *New York Times* in October 1991 correct in declaring that "the proponents of multiculturalism have little interest in the elements in American ideology that bond us together[?] . . . [T]heir emphasis on race and ethnicity as the most important elements of a person's identity augurs a new apartheid in which one's racial and ethnic qualifications are scrutinized carefully to determine fitness for a job or inclusion in the curriculum.'' Indeed, with respect to multiculturalism, the direction of curricular development was not clear. Only a few months before that letter appeared, Ronald Takaki, a leading scholar of American ethnic history, had echoed the question over which many had been agonizing: ''What is an educated, culturally literate person?'' and ''What should be the content of education and what does cultural literacy mean?'' The old formats would no longer be acceptable. Certainly, conceded Nathan Glazer at about the same time, ''the kind of Americanizing experience that those of my generation underwent in the New York City schools would be considered an outrageous exercise of hegemonic Eurocentrism today.''

The multiculturalists had in fact altered the nature of the debate by deemphasizing the common core culture and the merits of assimilation and concentrating on overcoming the previous invisibility many groups had experienced. While the term *multicultural* might appear to be only a semantical variation on pluralism, or multiethnicity, its advocates were actually pursuing—with varying degrees of intensity and militancy—an educational approach that advocated American diversity as a permanent feature not only of the nation's heritage but of its future. Its legitimation lay in the contention that multiethnicity and multiculturalism were not merely a passing phase of American history and, hence, needed to be fully (and explicitly) incorporated throughout as much of the school curriculum as possible. For some, their agenda also involved economic and political opportunities for ethnic group members, not just educational reforms.

Prompting a good deal of discussion at that time was the publication in June (1991) of New York State's Social Science Review and Development Committee's report, *One Nation, Many Peoples: A Declaration of Cultural Interdependence.* Although it emphasized pluralism over assimilation and called for a ''more tolerant, inclusive, and realistic vision'' of American identity, it also stressed the importance of ''educating toward citizenship in a common polity while respecting and taking account of continuing distinctiveness.'' As a challenge to the melting pot notion of American society, it was viewed by some as advocating more division than unity. Particularly dissenting from the report was Arthur Schlesinger, Jr., who, in his talks and in his later widely reviewed work *The Disuniting of America* (1991), lamented the curricula trend toward putting so much stress on multiculturalism. ''The point of America was not to preserve old cultures, but to forge a new *American* culture.'' In his view a nation of individuals was being supplanted by a nation of groups that would ''cherish [their] own apartness'' and, in so doing, dismiss the European origins of American common culture and its constitutional history. ''Instead of a transformative nation,'' America was being ''seen as preservative of diverse alien identities.'' And, that was, he claimed, the result of a mythmaking arising from ''the cult of ethnicity,'' propounded by ''militants of ethnicity.'' Sounding somewhat like Harold Isaacs, who had decried ''The Idols of the Tribe'' sixteen years earlier, Schlesinger focused on ''the virus of tribalism'' that was spreading globally. He, too, deplored those emphases on ethnic loyalties that were promoting separatism and argued that a multicultural education that reflected such a bias was fostering fragmentation. He was particularly alarmed because "the debate about the curriculum is a debate about what it means to be an American." Thus, it was quite significant for the debate when, a half dozen years later, Glazer began his new book, *We Are All Multiculturalists Now* (1997), with the observation, "Multiculturalism in education . . . has, in a word, won . . . [In schools] a new dispensation prevails and it will not change for a long time."

But exactly what won—and to what extent? And will that multicultural victory—if such it is—be good or bad for Americans—for American education, for American society, business, politics, and for America's intergroup relations? During that especially frantic and feverish year of 1991, Henry Louis Gates, Jr., one of the nation's leading African-American scholars, responded to the charges that tribalism and fragmentation would be the outcome by pointing out that "the cultural diversity movement arose partly because of the fragmentation of society by ethnicity, class, and gender. To make it the culprit for this fragmentation is to mistake effect for cause." Yet "fragmentation" was exactly the word used by many who were likewise expressing their concern about the direction that multiculturalism had taken. On the academic level, some of its more ardent advocates had manifested what was labeled postmodernism, in effect a deconstructive approach to American history that repudiated the claims of a common culture. That alarmed many persons who perceived this as a frontal assault on the traditional role of public education: the transmission not only of knowledge but also of shared values, goals, and ideals—the civic culture. Others maintained the view that the conflict was basically a struggle "over shifts in dominion in our society."

The Black Power movement of the mid-1960s and the black cultural efflorescence of the late 1960s and early 1970s, accompanied by militant demands for Black Studies programs in universities across the country, generated heated debates over ethnicity. By the early 1970s they had sparked the white ethnic revival in a number of European-American communities, as well as comparable activities among Asian and American Indian groups (and then among feminists). By the late 1970s and early 1980s, the curriculum discussions—perhaps in an effort to move beyond the polarization of the 1970s debate and to acknowledge the many groups that had struggled for recognition—expanded to "multiethnic" and "multicultural" dimensions. Accompanying that has been a swirl of issues involving identity, race, class, immigrants' impact, and the civic culture. The quest for a resolution has compelled Americans to address the larger question, Just who *does* comprise the "peoples of the United States"? Todd Gitlin, in his recent study of the "culture wars," *The Twilight of Common Dreams* (1995), made a perceptive observation on this matter: "In retrospect, it is difficult to believe that a nation of immigrants, a nation run by Europeans but claiming a universal mission, a nation ostensibly liberal in its belief that people make their own destinies yet subjecting whole categories of people to special oppression and humiliations, could have postponed forever a protracted convulsion over the question, 'Who Are We?' " But precisely part of the problem is what Gitlin's statement actually skims over. It is at the heart of the contemporary debate and at the heart of this volume: Despite the popularized image, America is more than a nation of immigrants; it is a nation of peoples, many of whom, it is true, are of immigrant origin, but there are many others, as well, whose roots are essentially here in America.

During the past four decades, in particular, Americans have had to confront the implications of that reality, but the discussions surrounding it have been going on for much of this century. James A. Banks, a specialist on multicultural education, and Philip Gleason, John Higham, and Gary Nash—three of the foremost historians of American ethnicity—have, in various works, detailed the steps taken this century to formulate and present the answers to the questions of who are we and whose history is America's history. They lead from the initial exploration of cultural pluralism (1910s–1920s) to intercultural education in the 1940s, to ethnic studies and multiethnic studies in the late 1960s–1970s, and then, with ever more groups demanding recognition, to multiculturalism in the 1980s (and 1990s). Each phase broadened the scope of the debate and the breadth of groups to be taken into account. In a recent essay, Gary Nash has pointed out how, beginning in the 1960s, a new generation of scholars—young white men and then a growing cadre of Latino, African, Asian, Native Americans, and especially women—of different social backgrounds and experiences from their predecessors began to confront the Eurocentric, consensus-driven portrayals of the nation's past: "People whose histories have never been written," wrote Nash, were "now challenging the dominant paradigm by recovering those histories." For critics who saw the results as chaotic—history without coherence—Nash pointed out that the previous coherence had only been possible "as long as scholars emphasized the experience of dominant groups in American society and grounded all historical generalizations in the Western experience."

James Banks emphasized that the explosion finally took place because certain ethnic groups were long "denied the opportunity to attain the attributes and behaviors that were needed to assimilate in the mainstream society" and that the "widespread discrimination, racism, and structural exclusion [that they] experienced . . . served as a vehicle for political mobilization." The revitalization and mobilization by more and more ethnic groups also were responses to the rising expectations of the 1960s and early 1970s, prompting these various groups to demand, first, equitable incorporation within the mainstream society and economy and, then, inclusion in key aspects of the culture and its symbols—particularly its public school curriculum. If I might play off of a famous line: The lesson they advocated was: *We have seen America, and it is all of us.*

For many persons—especially within those active groups—the articulation of this perception prompted more challenges to the conventional understanding of the cohesive character of American society. During the 1970s, with the "severe weakening of confidence in the American system—in the principles on which it was based" (as Gleason put it)—both Higham and Gleason grappled with the

implications of the heightened ethnic awareness and strident emphases on pluralism, especially as they were being expressed in the intense, often angry,
militancy of blacks, Chicanos,[1] Native Americans, Puerto Ricans, and a number
of agitated white ethnic groups. The "etiquette of public discourse" on pluralism, it was obvious, was still in a rather formative state. Higham recognized
that the debate had become lopsided—what he would thereafter describe as a
"reign of an unchallenged pluralism." As an alternative to the divisiveness of
the pluralists, who emphasized rigid ethnic group boundaries that "put the individual at the mercy of the group," Higham focused on the elements of social
integration. He offered an approach that acknowledged both diversity and unity,
stressing the need for "a decent multi-ethnic society" that would "rest on a
unifying ideology, faith, or myth." He also argued for a pluralistic integration
wherein groups do have a temporary solidarity and do value their "ethnic nu-
clei," but their boundaries are permeable. That orientation would recognize that
eventually members of most groups identify with their ethnic groups with varying degrees of intensity while also pursuing some aspects of integration—and
more extensively with each succeeding generation.

Gleason, writing for the *Harvard Encyclopedia of American Ethnic Groups*,
likewise tried to sound a balanced note in terms of the strident demands of
ethnic groups in relation to the needs of the nation:

To affirm the existence of American nationality does not mean that all Americans are
exactly alike or must become uniform in order to be real Americans. It simply means
that a genuine national community does exist and that it has its own distinctive principle
of unity, its own history, and its own appropriate sense of belongingness. . . . American
nationality, so understood, does not preclude the existence of ethnicity in the subgroup
peoplehood-sense, but neither does the existence of the latter preclude the former; nor
should subgroup ethnicities be regarded as more privileged . . . over American nationality.

However, the voices of the white, liberal scholars were drowned out by the
din of contention. The struggles and discoveries by myriad ethnic groups had
produced successes for some but frustrations for many others. Together with the
impact of the Vietnam War, the growing disillusionment "on the streets" (so
to speak) inspired a crescendoing assault on the nation's traditional civic culture—values and ideals now seen by their critics as hypocritical subterfuges for
perpetuating white power. Ironically, during this same period, federal programs
had been enacted to facilitate the education of low-income children (1965), to
provide for bilingual instruction (1968), and to promote the teaching of ethnic
heritages (1974). Yet within the context of the growing controversies over
busing, desegregation, affirmative action, curriculum reform, and so on, it all
seemed too little too late. At that point, as Michael Omi and Howard Winant
have argued, the African Americans' "rearticulation" of their goals and ideals,
which had undergirded the "Great Racial Transformation"—the civil rights
movement—but which had fragmented by the end of the 1960s, was, in the

1970s, confronting a neoconservative backlash. That countermovement proceeded with its own skillful rearticulation of many key civil rights objectives and phrases. Some ethnic advocacy leaders argued that the countermovement employed code words for the retrenchment and reversal of the civil rights movement, particularly objecting to their opponents' disarming use of the goal of "a color-blind society."[2]

While the multicultural revisionist reconstruction was taking form on all educational levels, and scholars were trying to gain perspective and thereby make sense of the transformation under way, the political climate was undergoing a rapid, backward change. The conservative backlash was strengthened by the Reagan Revolution of the 1980s, which lured white, suburban, working-class Democrats out of that party's half-century coalition. The climate of the 1980s also spurred some scholars to reemphasize the need for a curricular balance, wherein the experiences and roles of various minorities and women might complete and even enlarge the unifying factors that had created the nation. These unifying factors were now recognized as flawed but important and salvageable. As German historian of American Studies Willi Paul Adams put it in 1991, "The integration of 50 million immigrants . . . from various parts of the world would have been impossible without the strong insistence on the primacy of a clearly defined Anglo American core."

The quest for redefinition was actually occurring on two levels simultaneously. On the first, in international terms, President Ronald Reagan had aroused Americans by articulating who they were in terms of who the common enemy was, but the end of the Cold War marked the beginning of the end of Americans defining themselves by what they were not. On the second, in domestic terms, issues of identity were no less in flux. As we have seen, opposed to the ardent multiculturalists were more and more persons who viewed the "new identity orthodoxy"—or "cant of [ethnic] identity"—as a form of rigid, "binary thinking" (us versus them), which they perceived as a major flaw in the multiculturalist movement. During the mid-1980s, the search was on for viable alternatives. The end of the Cold War at the end of the decade "left America [in Todd Gitlin's phrase] with an enemy crisis" around which to unite the nation, whereas the mounting uneasiness stemming from the controversies over the politics of multiculturalism had likewise exposed a void where a national consensus had once existed: Faced with such abrasive and divisive ethnic demands and the novel absence of a common foe around which to rally, many Americans were disconcerted by the lack of readily apparent cohesive forces that could provide the foundation of a needed leadership. Then, following Desert Storm in 1991, adds Gitlin, "we fell, and what we fell into were culture wars."

In reaction to what has been labeled "a promiscuous pluralism" that attacked the common culture and put a primacy on the multitude of individual group experiences, the countertrend gained more ground in the public's mind. The divide was substantial: Ardent supporters of multiculturalism feared a return to invisibility and hoped their educational reforms would lead to larger societal gains from the explicit recognition of various ethnic groups and women. Their critics feared that the multiculturalists would teach their children a false or distorted history and, in so doing, undermine civic harmony and threaten national unity without increasing the achievement levels of minority children. Some of the latter group also associated the demands for recognition by advocates of feminist and gay rights with what they already perceived as the extreme objectives of certain ethnic groups and then lumped them all together as the sins of multiculturalism.

The controversy was still more complex, argued John Higham once more, in 1993. "Multiculturalism fosters cultures of endowment while drawing a veil over the cultures of class. The new curricula have made a fetish of 'diversity.' " The great post–World War II "renewal of American democracy" that had generated so much prosperity and mobility had run "out of steam" by the early 1960s, leaving behind "the poorly organized segments of certain endowment groups, notably lower class blacks, middle class women, and uncared-for children." Since the late 1970s, Higham wrote, "the multicultural movement has tried to carry forward the great campaigns of the mid-twentieth century against racial and ethnic inequalities without reviving the wider outcry of that earlier era against class inequalities." But, he added, if race were being used "as an antidote to class divisions," young Americans needed to recognize that race and ethnicity must not be allowed "to seem intractable or class to remain invisible." Moreover, he maintained, multiculturalism was still "a movement without an overall theory," dwelling not on goals but on group needs. Returning to his earlier theme and sharing a growing sentiment, he advocated the need to preserve what he now labeled "our egalitarian ideology [of] 'American universalism' " against "the acids of modernity." Like Schlesinger, Glazer, and others, he was calling for balance, for a return to a notion of the "common good," one that recognized that American culture embraced a "reality of assimilation as well as the persistence of difference." Four years later, in the spring of 1997, Higham remained convinced about the need to address class as well as ethnicity and optimistic that a common ground could be found but concerned that it had not yet been achieved. He once again observed (and rather sadly, I suspect), "For 30 years nation building [has] virtually disappeared from the agenda of academic historians."

Indeed, by the latter part of the 1990s, the debate over multicultural issues had not waned. In fact, it was reported that press references to the topic had gone from 33 in 1989 to 600 in 1991 and then had leaped to 1,500 in 1995 and 1,200 the following year. Certainly, there is evidence that this debate can still wax rather hot. In a relatively recent work (1995), Sandra Jackson and José Solís chose to state their concerns in the following terms: "If multiculturalism is to travel beyond the comfort zones it must come to terms with the criminal acts committed by the United States against [Mexicans and Puerto Ricans] and other peoples." In another example from the opposite perspective, one from a 1994 polemic published by a mainstream company, Seymour W. Itzkoff described the United States as "enveloped in an orgy of 'multiculturalism' " and then proceeded to decry "the tide of recent immigration" (from the south) threatening the nation's "genetics of European intelligence"—a consequence of America's mistaken "myth of [various groups'] intellectual uniformity." Citizens from "the nations of the north" (Northern Hemisphere) needed to take measures so that immigration would "continue to reflect, to a degree, the existing composition of the peoples of the United States."

In their recent book *Mapping Multiculturalism* (1996), Avery Gordon and Christopher Newfield present a considerable collection of essays from a 1992 conference that explored a variety of aspects and dimensions of this topic and, based on them, they offered their own perspective. They called attention to the fact that more Americans were (1) coming to see the pluralism espoused by some multiculturalists as "a dangerous thing" and (2) perceiving the common culture as "a defensive barrier" against the excesses of the more militant multiculturalists (an idea that had been germinating since the 1970s). However, Gordon and Newfield drew from the conference papers a different measure of multiculturalism and suggested that a more moderate version of it was also present. They contended that (beyond the deconstructionism) many observers had also noted that "multiculturalism had a secret longing for the kind of commonality it pretended to replace" and that behind multiculturalism's celebration of diversity has "lurked an ambivalent attachment to *e pluribus unum*, with *unum* regaining command when the majority rule was disrespected or challenged." Although they suggest that there has been a shift from ambivalence to retrenchment and a renewed prestige for the nation's common culture, they also suggest that had the "core American values" all along possessed an unambiguous antiracism and commitment to democratic equality, Americans would not still be struggling after fourteen decades "toward racial Reconstruction of an America without slavery." Or, as Glazer put it in his 1997 study, "Multiculturalism has now become a contested term, an epithet to some, a banner to others. Multiculturalism of some kind there is, and there it will be . . . [for] we now pay for our failure to realize ideals, while ignoring the realities that contradict them."

Robert K. Fullinwider also recently edited a collection of conference papers from the early 1990s—*Public education in a multicultural society: Policy, theory, critique* (1996)—and he eloquently presented what would seem to be a sensible conclusion about this increasing prevalence of multiculturalism in school curricula across the country:

Here is the germinal idea of multicultural education. Multicultural education is what good schools do in the face of extensive "cultural" differences among students and teachers. Multicultural education is what good schools do to assure that "cultural" factors do not get in the way of equal educational opportunity and high student achievement.

Yet that is a surprisingly incomplete statement, for Gary Nash points out (in his essay in Fullinwider's volume) that a narrow curriculum (that is, a more traditional one) narrows the students' vision and constricts the likely scope of their future achievements by ill preparing them "for satisfactorily adult lives in the twenty-first century." So Fullinwider ought to have included a third admonition, that "multicultural education is what good schools do to prepare all their students for effective participation in a remarkably diverse nation and a still more diverse world."

Notwithstanding Glazer's remark (quoted above) that multiculturalism "has won," it is not easily determined to what extent multiculturalism with respect to ethnic groups has actually been effectively incorporated in the educational experiences of students around the country. The debate persists about the meaning of multiculturalism, the groups to be included under its rubric, and the objectives of such curricula reforms in terms of the balance between the preservation of ethnic subcultures and the transmission of the common civic culture. Nevertheless, some are seeking to shift the very terms of the debate. Thus, whereas in their 1996 books Gordon and Newfield and their contributors and Fullinwider and his were engaged in the efforts of mapping multiculturalism and exploring the policies and theories of multicultural education, David Hollinger, in his own 1996 work, argued for defining a *Postethnic America: Beyond Multiculturalism*. Among the many issues he addresses, quite possibly reflecting the tempo and temperament of the late 1990s, are six that bear on the collection of essays in this volume.

First, he discusses the cultural pluralist ideas of Horace Kallen and Randolph Bourne and noted the differences between them and multiculturalism in that the latter emphasized political and economic inequalities and the former had "overlooked" them. Second, he points out that government agencies have channeled our thinking of American ethnicity into a "pentagon" of official classifications—white, black, Indian, Asian, and Latino—although these subdivisions are neither entirely culturally distinctive nor internally homogeneous in almost any respect. However, the ethnic pluralist and then the multicultural movements have acknowledged so many groups that we have experienced a "diversification of diversity." That, in turn, has intensified the challenges by many more peoples seeking inclusion politically and economically as well as within the studies of American history and culture. Third, like many others, notably Lawrence Fuchs and John Higham, Hollinger raises a question regarding the civic character of the nation-state, inquiring if it actually possesses one or if it is merely "a container of groups." His own position clearly leans in a nationalist direction, as did Adams's, Higham's, and Fuchs's.

Fourth, Hollinger then advances his principal argument. We are faced with a dichotomy between pluralism and cosmopolitanism. In his view, the former emphasizes a particularist approach and inherited boundaries regarding ethnic groups. The latter represents a universalism and a common ground that includes a "recognition, acceptance and eager exploration of diversity" along with a stress on individuals being members of (and identified with) several communities. Fifth, in terms of group identification, he perceives America as having gone from nationality to postnationality to the threshold of postethnicity, wherein he posits a sharp distinction between the fixedness of identity and the flexibility of "affiliation." The latter implies "revocable consent," a blurring of boundaries, and independence of peoples from identity by ascription and one logical outgrowth of the mixed-race movement of the 1990s that has spotlighted the growing number of Americans of multiracial origins. As evidence of that particular development, he points to that expanding subgroup (over 2 million in 1990) and their now successful campaign (through such organizations as the Association of Multiracial Americans) to persuade the Census Bureau to acknowledge the increasing extent of race mixing by allowing respondents to make more than one racial choice on the census 2000.[3] Finally, reiterating the idea of ethnicity as "surprisingly fluid" (to use Higham's phrase), Hollinger urges consideration of comparability between ethnic/racial groups and religious ones, which could underscore both their similarities in orientation and the possibility of flexibility in a person's ethnic identity.

Now, there remain several key issues that link these explorations with the essays in this volume. While class factors could be worked into Hollinger's proposed model, race is another matter, possibly one he treats somewhat too optimistically. Glazer, for one, agreed with much of Hollinger's position except, in a reversal of his view thirty years ago, Glazer now recognizes that the intractable opposition of a significant percentage of white Americans to the full inclusion of African Americans has not only perpetuated significant barriers in the way of the group's progress but has also compelled many African Americans to develop and preserve cultural and attitudinal differences that are not fading away (or merging) as they have for others. He now maintains that it is not just that blacks are *not* like the immigrants of yesterday nor like those of today; those new immigrants—as those before them—are becoming more like white Americans, and more rapidly so, than are African Americans who have been here nearly four centuries. We are therefore not becoming two nations, one black and one white, Glazer concludes, but two nations: "blacks and others." Not all would agree with that analysis, either (Juliet Walker in this volume surely does not), because it too readily blurs nonblack racial lines, implies a homogeneity of views and experiences among African Americans, and too readily assumes an extensive multiracial assimilation under way—a point applicable to both Glazer and Hollinger.

Another issue involving Hollinger's model concerns the dichotomy he sets up of fixed identity versus flexible affiliation. Perhaps the objectives of multiculturalism (in terms of recognizing diversity and the salience of ethnic identities) are not incompatible with an acknowledgment that "fluidity" and "affiliation" are also characteristics of ethnic group life. Although Hollinger's proposal rests on something of an either/or situation—moving from pluralism to his notion of cosmopolitanism—the essays in this volume make it very clear that various options with respect to ethnic identity have actually long been part of America's multicultural heritage. Within most ethnic communities there have been countless men and women who have opted for a variety of adaptive or accommodative strategies. As noted earlier, there has never been any one pattern, nor any one route, nor any one outcome. Nor will there be. For some groups treated here, the intentional preservation of an ethnic identity is paramount and, for some, usually inescapable; it is therefore their predominant pattern. Among others, ethnic identity has been less entrenched and the boundaries more permeable because group members have been receptive to the idea of integration, and persons outside that community have been willing to accept those individuals. These variations in patterns of integration and assimilation are the consequences of the dynamic interplay of cultures, goals, societal conditions, the reception accorded minority groups, and their responses to that reception.

CONCLUSIONS FROM THIS VOLUME

What other general conclusions can be drawn from the twenty-seven essays in this reference volume besides those already described? I would hope that readers draw many and that they are enriched by the opportunity to assess the experiences of many different peoples. I would like to put forth twenty points that I have gathered from reading each of these essays several times. I know that the list is nowhere near exhaustive, but it is the product of thinking multiculturally about the many peoples who comprise America's nation of peoples.

1. Not all nations or peoples have equally strong traditions of outmigration. Those who did leave did pull up their roots for (in their minds) compelling reasons, even when their original intention was to return home. While conditions in their homeland may have persuaded them of the necessity to choose migration, many persons have also been drawn to America because of its promise, its image as a land of hope and opportunities.

2. Among many, if not most, there have been successive waves of migration (including among native populations of Indian and African Americans), producing chain migrations and sometimes (especially as modes of transportation improved) patterns of circular migration. A common consequence of migration has been the indispensable networks among newcomers, between newcomers and their homelands, and more recently, between compatriots who have resettled in America as well as in other countries. Not only have these developments intensified the trends toward circular migration, but they have also contributed to the crystallization of transnational identities transcending nation-state boundaries.

3. Most immigrants either mold or strengthen an ethnic identity after migration or prolonged contact within a minority status in America, and that occurs along with their community and institutional development. On the one hand, among groups that were minorities in their native land (with some few exceptions)—and increasingly among twentieth-century peoples—newcomers have arrived with well-defined national or religious identities that have accelerated

the evolution of their identity and community formation. On the other hand, such ethnic identities have, in many (but not all) cases, proven over time to be fluid and susceptible to changes and redefinition, and the ethnic group boundaries permeable, especially across the generations.

4. Nearly universally, immigrants and native populations have wanted to maintain their cultures, and those cultures have invariably had an impact both on how they responded to the changes following migration and on how they were perceived by outsiders. Part of the preservation efforts has involved keeping contacts with the homeland and/or an interest in its affairs and, more recently, ties with it for economic purposes. For one and a half centuries populations from nearby homelands (e.g., French Canada, Mexico, the Caribbean, and some Indian reservations) have particularly experienced the impact of proximity in terms of the nearby homelands enabling them to more readily preserve their social and cultural ties. In recent decades, however, dramatic improvements in transportation and communications have also permitted migrants from more distant lands to maintain such connections.

5. Acculturation has been difficult to avoid, particularly in the twentieth century. A pervasive American culture, functioning through schools, media, consumerism, and the expectation expressed that newcomers will adopt the civic culture, has posed great challenges for groups struggling for a balance between cultural preservation and cultural adaptation. Lapses in immigration, such as during wartime, have deprived newcomers of their cultural reinforcement, thereby hastening their groups' acculturation.

6. From the Dutch to the Hmong, immigrants have sought to preserve traditional language usage, while the children have been far less committed to language retention, just as homeland issues have less salience for them. Except for physically isolated groups and those where the language maintenance is inseparable from the maintenance of the religion, language shift has invariably occurred by the second and certainly by the third generation.

7. Adaptation by the children has quite commonly produced intergenerational conflicts. In addition, multiple waves of immigrants may sharpen differences between generations within an ethnic community because they are likely to be at different stages of acculturation and integration than those who arrived before them or those who are American-born.

8. Family adaptation has frequently produced conflict over gender roles between husbands and wives, although, in more enclave circumstances (where groups are self-contained and/or isolated), such issues have often been played out within the second generation.

9. Groups bringing or nurturing a strong (often orthodox or even fundamentalist) religious identity have had the most success in mitigating acculturative (cultural assimilation) pressures, just as peoples that settled in rural or otherwise ethnically concentrated/relatively homogeneous settings have collectively slowed the acculturation processes. For most groups, religious institutions have been at the center of their community life, yet, in not a few instances, it

is those same institutions that have made changes in order to accommodate to the American religious environment.

10. Eligibility for citizenship and subsequent participation in politics have varied considerably. Blacks were denied citizenship until 1866. Not all Native Americans received it until 1924. And all racial barriers to acquiring citizenship were not entirely dropped until 1952. Whereas refugees have generally been among those most eager for citizenship, people intent on returning home, those with strong national attachments, and those from nearby homelands have been more ambivalent about acquiring another citizenship.[4] However, national crises, especially war, have spurred applications, as have recent welfare policy and immigration reforms. In the same manner that groups have varied in their receptivity to changing citizenship, so has their interest in political participation (voting, office holding, participation in campaigns). Socioeconomic levels (class factors), cultural backgrounds, and the nature of their homeland political experiences have also been important variables influencing the extent of different ethnic groups' participation.

11. At each stage of American development the economic transformation of the nation affected, and was affected by, the presence of so many available laboring ethnic groups (from the unskilled to the entrepreneurial). At the same time, the groups' own modes of cultural and economic adaptation have similarly had to be modified with each changing stage of the nation's economic and cultural orders, notwithstanding the persistence over time of certain basic similarities in the patterns of accommodation by most ethnic groups.

12. With few exceptions, socioeconomic mobility has been a major objective of most groups, one that has more frequently than not been attained, especially as immigrants compare their condition in America with life in their homelands. Not infrequently, however, significant mobility has been realized only across several generations. The record of a number of racial and Latino groups has been more uneven than that of European and (non-French) Canadian ones, but, along with other factors, recency of arrival is a key variable accounting for some of the lesser mobility.

13. Most strangers (especially among peoples of color) have at least initially encountered resistance and perhaps even discrimination by native Americans, but none more severely than Native Americans, African Americans, and Mexican Americans: Expulsion, enslavement, exploitation, deportation, and untold numbers of murders fill the pages of their respective histories. Thus, while hostility to religious minorities, such as Catholics, Jews, Mormons, and Muslims, has at times been intense, racial groups have endured the most severe hardships and the most persistent mistreatment. Such rejection has usually provoked the affected groups to resist acculturation and certainly integration (while some do strive to "pass").

14. Often overlooked is the fact that, in different ways, Native Americans and African Americans profoundly influenced the course of American spatial expansion and economic growth up through the late nineteenth century (and

aspects of American culture and language, too). Obvious but also frequently denied or underappreciated in "the multicultural wars" is the fact that, in differing degrees and ways, virtually all ethnic groups have made contributions to the nation's social or economic or cultural growth.

15. Over time, significant degrees of integration, intermarriage, and even assimilation have occurred among members of nearly all ethnic groups, but to a lesser extent among peoples of color[5] and among religiously devoted populations determined to preserve their isolation and exclusivity. A pattern of racial mixing has significantly intensified over the past three decades, as has that among persons of different religious groups. Nonetheless, many of the authors make it quite clear that assimilation has neither been an inevitable outcome of the American experience nor, where it has occurred, something that has taken place in any uniform manner over a predictably consistent period of time.

16. Given the postindustrial changes continually under way, significant socioeconomic challenges will continue to obstruct the mobility of less educated or less trained newcomers and those groups with members who have hitherto lagged in their educational and occupational advancement and/or have encountered more resistance or inferior educational opportunities. While the long-term consequences are difficult to determine, the short-term ones involve substantial numbers of persons who remain economically marginal and/or susceptible to deviant activities (particularly gangs, drugs, crime, and family disorganization). The costs to society and the ethnic communities cannot easily be exaggerated as the riots of the past thirty-five years have repeatedly shown.

17. Although the nation has been committed to the principles of equality in theory, and subsequently in law, some ethnic groups continue to encounter difficulties, discrimination, exclusion, and hate crimes, usually in informal and noninstitutionalized ways.

18. Considering the sweep of the nation's history, Americans have periodically been more, rather than less, ambivalent about immigration and continue to be so. Periodically they have been anxious about the changing composition of American society—and its effect on the culture, polity, and the unity of the nation. And even more than concerning immigrants, Americans have frequently been preoccupied with the issue of race, consistently demonstrating more reservations about the integration of peoples of color than about most other matters. Although those attitudes have softened during the past four decades, swings in public sentiments are seen by many racial group members and advocates of civil rights reforms as potentially threatening those gains.

19. Essays such as those in this volume, examining the experiences of an array of groups from five continents and lands in between, enable us to develop a comparative perspective so that we can better understand why and how great numbers of persons among so many groups have been able to enter mainstream America but far fewer among particular other ones—sometimes by their own choice but most often regardless of their choice.

20. Finally, if we define America's multicultural heritage as one that is social,

economic, and political as well as cultural, then most ethnic groups have contributed substantially to various aspects of America's multicultural heritage. Therefore, that heritage cannot be fully appreciated in the absence of a full appreciation of how the parts have formed the whole and, in the process, made it greater than the sum of those parts.

NOTES

1. The preferred term used by Mexican-American activists at that time; the term is still used but far less frequently, and *Latino* and *Hispanic* have become more commonly used umbrella terms in recent years.

2. Many liberals and members of racial ethnic groups (and white women) would also become disenchanted with some of the more strident demands of certain advocates for affirmative action programs and policies. The difference lay, for example, in how far the neoconservatives would wish to go in dismantling them, despite the persistence of patterns of informal discrimination.

3. In July 1997, a special task force recommended against any changes in the format of the race question (such as having an additional choice of "multiracial") but in favor of allowing individuals to check off more than one racial identification. It was adopted for census 2000. However, despite the growing numbers of such mixed-race persons, mainstream ethnic groups saw this proposal as a threat to their numbers-based funding, and the U.S. Office of Management and Budget, charged with monitoring compliance with the 1977 Statistical Policy Directive 15 (which defines the acceptable four racial classifications for all federal policies), opposed the change.

4. In some cases, the continued possession of property in people's homelands is contingent on their retention of their original citizenship, unless dual-nationality laws have been enacted by those home countries.

5. Not including here the involuntary intermixing forced on slave women.

BIBLIOGRAPHIC REFERENCES

The literature related to the debates over ethnicity and multiculturalism is vast, and I can here only refer to a small portion of it, especially from among the multiple works of some of the leading scholars. Most of those listed below are selected because those particular ones are cited or quoted in the introduction. I group these into general items discussing issues of ethnicity in America; works that more specifically dealt with the course of the debates over pluralism and multiculturalism; those pieces that more heavily engaged the debates themselves; a few examples that addressed the specifics of incorporating multiculturalism into the curriculum and other educational facilities; and an example of literature on multiculturalism in Canada, where this issue has been confronted and dealt with for many years (although not entirely resolved).

One of the most impressive analyses of race relations in America, one that proposes a model of Racial Formation which enables us to conceptualize earlier developments and to anticipate the steps in which events are likely to proceed (which is not the same as predicting the outcome), is Michael Omi and Howard Winant, *Racial Formation in the United States: From the 1960s to the 1990s*, 2nd ed. (New York: Routledge, 1994). Another seminal work that shaped my thinking and much of the discussion about ethnicity for many years in the 1960s and 1970s, and whose terminology regarding assimilation is still used currently, is Milton Gordon, *Assimilation in American Life: The Role of Race, Religion, and National Origin* (New York: Oxford University Press, 1964). In an effort to update Gordon's model and to incorporate our greater understanding of the multiple avenues and outcomes of assimilation, an alternative approach is offered in Elliott R. Barkan, "Race, Religion, and Nationality in American Society: A Model of Ethnicity—From Contact to Assimilation," *Journal of American Ethnic History* 14.2 (Winter 1995): 38–75, 95–101. A major study of the development of the American civic culture and the course of racial/ethnic history in America, emphasizing many of the policy issues and arguing forcefully for the central role of a common civic culture, is Lawrence H. Fuchs, *The American Kaleidoscope: Race Ethnicity, and the Civic Culture* (Hanover: Wesleyan, 1990). The "bible" for nearly the past two decades for anyone seriously examining ethnicity in America and the intellectual and policy issues related to that, and which was at the time (and substantially remains) a remarkably comprehensive collection of essays, is Stephan Thernstrom, Ann Orlov, and Oscar Handlin, eds., *Harvard Encyclopedia of American Ethnic Groups* (Cambridge: Harvard University Press, 1980). An interdisciplinary overview of immigration and ethnicity in America that covers the period between 1920 and 1995 is Elliott R. Barkan, *And Still They Come: Immigrants and American Society, 1920 to the 1990s* (Wheeling, IL: Harlan Davidson, 1996).

A number of fine works have examined contemporary issues of pluralism, the evolution of the multiculturalism debate/wars, and the struggle to find a balance between the centrifugal forces of the multiculturalist movement and the important centripetal role of the nation's core culture. Certainly among the foremost has been the work of John Higham, a few of whose pieces I use here: *Send These to Me: Immigrants in Urban America*, rev. ed. (Baltimore: Johns Hopkins University Press, 1984); "Current Trends in the Study of Ethnicity in the United States," *Journal of American Ethnic History* 2.1 (Fall 1982): 5–15; "Multiculturalism and Universalism: A History and Critique," *American Quarterly* 45.2 (June 1993): 195–219, 249–255; and "History in the Culture Wars," *OAH Newsletter* [Organization of American Historians] 25.2 (May 1997): 1+. Another truly fine scholar, whose works here examine quite effectively the course of many issues related to the integration of minorities into American society in this century and even earlier, is Philip Gleason, *Speaking of Diversity: Language and Ethnicity in the Twentieth Century* (Baltimore: Johns Hopkins University Press, 1992), and his essay in the *Harvard Encyclopedia of American Ethnic Groups*, "American Identity and Americanization" (pp. 31–58). James A. Banks is preeminent for his essays on the history of the movement, his proposals for reforming the curriculum, and his editing of outstanding essays on various aspects of "multiethnicity" and multiculturalism. See James A. Banks and James Lynch, eds., *Multicultural Education in Western Societies* (Westport, CT: Greenwood Press, 1986); *Multi-Ethnic Education: Theory and Practice*, 2nd ed. (Boston: Allyn & Bacon, 1988); and, edited with Cherry A. McGee Banks, *Multicultural Education: Issues and Perspectives* (Boston: Allyn & Bacon, 1989). These collections contain many fine essays. Two recent collections of articles providing a rather intriguing array of views as well as most useful introductions is Avery F. Gordon and Christopher Newfield, eds., *Mapping Multiculturalism* (Minneapolis: University of Minnesota Press, 1996), and Robert K. Fullinwider's *Public Education in a Multicultural Society: Policy, Theory, Critique* (Cambridge: Cambridge University Press, 1996). The latter contains Gary Nash's essay, "Multiculturalism and history: Historical perspectives and present prospects" (pp. 183–

202). Also quite recent and outstanding for its quality of writing and its perceptive analysis of contemporary culture and the "culture wars" is Todd Gitlin, *The Twilight of Common Dreams: Why America Is Wracked by Culture Wars* (New York: Henry Holt, 1995). A brief survey of the development of the core culture and its enduring relevance is in Willi Paul Adams, "U.S. Fears of Multiculturalism Are Unfounded," University of California, Institute of Governmental Studies, *Public Affairs Report* 32.2 (March 1991).

Obviously, many authors have joined the fierce debate over the direction of the multicultural movement, including Higham, Gleason, Banks, Gordon and Newfield, and Gitlin (cited above). A few other works that directly enter the fray and are worth noting include Ronald Takaki's brief article, "The Value of Multiculturalism," *Liberal Education* [Association of American Colleges] 77.3 (1991), special issue, "Engaging Cultural Legacies"; of Nathan Glazer's many pieces, a "Comment" on Gary Pellis's "Race against Integration," *Tikkun* 6.1 (1991): 66–67, and *We Are All Multiculturalists Now* (Cambridge: Harvard University Press, 1997); Martin E. Marty's different approach in *The One and the Many: America's Struggle for the Common Good* (Cambridge: Harvard University Press, 1997); a more contentious one in Sandra Jackson and José Solís, eds., *Beyond the Comfort Zone in Multiculturalism: Confronting the Politics of Privilege* (Westport, CT: Greenwood Press, 1995), versus Fred Siegel, "The Cult of Multiculturalism," *New Republic* (February 18, 1991): 34–39, and Seymour W. Itzkoff, *The Decline of Intelligence in America: A Strategy for National Survival* (Westport, CT: Praeger, 1994). Coming at this topic from somewhat opposing viewpoints are Harold Isaacs, *The Idols of the Tribe: Group Identity and Political Change* (New York: Harper and Row, 1975), and Arthur Schlesinger, Jr., *The Disuniting of America: Reflections on a Multicultural Society* (New York: W. W. Norton, 1992 [1991]), versus Henry Louis Gates, Jr., "Whose Culture Is It, Anyway?" *New York Times*, May 4, 1991. David A. Hollinger proposes still another approach to get past some of the limits, as he sees them, in hanging on to the rigid categories of ethnicity—not unlike some of Higham's arguments twenty years earlier—in *Postethnic America: Beyond Multiculturalism* (New York: Basic Books, 1996).

A few examples of teachers and administrators who have tried to propose ways of incorporating multiculturalism into the curriculum, besides Banks and his essayists, are Rosemary R. DuMont, Lois Buttlar, and William Caynon, *Multiculturalism in Libraries* (Westport, CT: Greenwood Press, 1994); Marilyn Lutzker, *Multiculturalism in the College Curriculum: A Handbook of Strategies and Resources for Faculty* (Westport, CT: Greenwood Press, 1995); and especially, Christine E. Sleeter and Carl A. Grant, "An Analysis of Multicultural Education in the United States," *Harvard Educational Review* 57.4 (November 1987): 421–444, and Sleeter's *Empowerment through Multicultural Education* (Albany: SUNY Press, 1991) and *Keepers of the American Dream: A Study of Staff Development and Multicultural Education* (Washington: Falmer, 1992).

Finally, one of the outstanding Canadian scholars who has written much about the multiculturalism and Canadian attitudes related to it is John W. Berry. I cite only two items to draw the reader's attention to this important area: John W. Berry and Jean A. LaPonce, eds., *Ethnicity and Culture in Canada: The Research Landscape* (Toronto: University of Toronto Press, 1994), and, with Rudolph Kalin, "Multicultural and Ethnic Attitudes in Canada: An Overview of the 1991 National Survey," *Canadian Journal of Behavioural Science* 27.3 (1995): 301–320.

AFRICAN AMERICANS

Juliet E. K. Walker

American history has been distinguished by two worlds of race, white and black. Virtually since the arrival of the first Africans in English colonial America in 1619, racial societal practices and economic policies have been shaped by an aggrieved and uneasy coexistence of people of African and European descent. As Cornell West emphasizes, race has long mattered in America in that "anti-black racism is integral, not marginal, to the existence and sustenance of American society." It is ironic, then, as historian Edmund Morgan notes, that "America bought its independence with slave labor." Moreover, the facts are that the civil rights movement of the 1960s represented a long and persistent tradition in African Americans' historic struggle for freedom, social justice, and equality and that that struggle has provided the basis for the expansion of liberties for all Americans, even whites. Despite those facts, observed West, "race remains the most explosive issue in the country today." Thus, revisionist efforts to challenge the place and agency of blacks in the American experience cannot change four centuries of historical reality.

THE AFRICAN BACKGROUND, RACE, AND SLAVERY

In 1918, southern historian Ulrich B. Phillips set the tone for the history of blacks in America when he claimed that slavery for Africans in America provided the basis for the civilization of a group of primitive people. In actuality, the West and West Central African victims of the transatlantic slave trade had lived in complex, organized, structured market economies in which they participated as producers, traders, brokers, merchants, and entrepreneurs. Indeed, the African slave trade was a business of "kings, rich men and merchants," not only in Europe but also in Africa. In fact, what made Africans invaluable as slaves was precisely their expertise in the cultivation of subtropical agricultural commodities. Without the exploitation of African labor in the new land, sub-

Table 1
African Imports in the United States, 1620–1870

Years Imported	to	Colonies/ USA	Louisiana	Total
			Numbers	
1620-1700		20,500		20,500
1701-1720		19,800	1,200	21,000
1721-1740		50,400	8,300	58,700
1741-1760		100,400	8,500	108,900
Total 1701-1760		**170,600**	**18,000**	**188,600**
1761-1770		62,668		62,668
1771-1780		14,902		14,902
1781-1790		55,750		55,750
1791-1800		79,041		79,041
1801-1810		114,090		114,090
1761-1810			10,200	10,200
1811-1870		51,000		51,000
Total 1620-1870		**568,551**	**28,200**	**596,751**

Sources: Compiled from Philip D. Curtin, *The Atlantic Slave Trade: A Census* (Madison: University of Wisconsin Press, 1969); Roger Anstey, "The Volume of the North American Slave Carrying Trade from Africa, 1761–1810," *Revue Française d'Histoire d'Outre-Mer* 62 (1975); and James A. Rawley, *The Trans-Atlantic Slave Trade: A History* (New York: Norton, 1981).

stantial profits could not have been realized. The multiangular trade that developed from the sale of slave-produced commodities enriched the American colonies, as did the transatlantic shipment and sale of Africans.

Before 1700, only 20,500 Africans were brought into the struggling English American colonies. By the time of the legal end of the transatlantic slave trade to the United States in 1808, about 546,000 Africans had been brought to this country, although they comprised only 5 percent of the 10 to 12 million brought to all the Americas and the West Indies for enslavement (see Table 1). Thus, in Virginia in 1625, there were 23 blacks and 300 whites in 1649. By 1708, there were 12,000 blacks and 18,000 whites; in 1756, 120,156 blacks and 173,316 whites. In South Carolina, the wealthiest colony, blacks were in the majority as early as 1715, when there were 10,500 blacks and 6,250 whites. In contrast, in New York the proportion of blacks remained the same, with 2,170 blacks and 18,067 whites in 1698 and, by 1771, 19,883 compared to 168,000. By the time of American Independence in 1776, people of African descent comprised 21 percent of the nation's population. With the first U.S. census in 1790, African Americans ranked second in number, after the English, who comprised almost 50 percent of the nation's population. The Germans ranked third, with 8.7 percent. For four centuries, African Americans would remain the nation's largest minority.

In colonial American history, the initial focus has been on the question of whether racism preceded slavery, or vice versa, or whether both developed simultaneously, mutually reinforcing each other. Even before the initial confrontation with Africa, indicates historian Winthrop Jordan, there was an English cultural bias against blackness. It pervaded their religion, popular culture, and linguistic symbolism. Yet the historical reality, argues economist Eric William, is that "slavery was not born of racism, rather, racism was the consequence of slavery." With the first blacks in America in 1619, presumably only their labor, as opposed to their person, was sold. However, the selling of human labor in English colonial America was not limited to Africans. In the English colonies, large numbers of the white population began their life in the new land as unfree, unpaid servile laborers. In the period from 1680 to 1775 almost two thirds, some 350,000 to 375,000, of the white population from Britain and Europe immigrated to the American colonies with such an initial status.

However, race, as opposed to class, would make the difference in determining a racial group's future. Societal presumptions, increasingly supported by judicial decisions and statutory enactments, established that, with the exception of some Indians, only people of African descent would be enslaved. The initial institutionalization of African slavery was an economic decision. Distinctions were made based not only on the recognized invaluable labor of Africans but also on fear of black resistance to their forced enslavement. From the beginning, colonial laws made it illegal for blacks, slave or free, to own weapons. One of the early legislative acts in Virginia, passed in 1639—only twenty years after the arrival of the first blacks—stipulated: "All persons except Negroes are to be provided with arms and ammunition or be fined at the pleasure of the governor and council." With the exception of Virginia and, to a lesser extent, Maryland in the seventeenth century and Georgia in the eighteenth century, African slavery was instituted almost from the point of origin in many of the colonies. Even in Virginia and Maryland, de facto slavery preceded de jure slavery, and it was not until 1662 that slavery was statutorily enacted into Virginia law, with the provision that a child's status would be determined by that of the mother.

Life was brutal, and Africans quickly found that their survival beyond mere sustenance as well as any improvement in their material lives would depend on their own initiative. It was not unusual for slaves to have provision grounds, which they used not only for their own food cultivation but also to produce surplus that was used for trade and marketing. As plantation slavery developed, field slaves worked under two kinds of labor systems. Under the task system, used especially in rice cultivation, which Africans introduced to the colonies, slaves were assigned one job. After completing that task, most by early afternoon, they had the remainder of the day to work their provision grounds. In this informal slave economy, profits were limited, often negligible, but it appears that independent slave-initiated enterprise was much more extensive than the historical record has acknowledged. Consequently, while blacks were denounced as people of a "wild and barbarous nature," colonial laws declaring it illegal for slaves to participate in any independent economic activity proved the contrary. On the other hand, in contrast with the task system, under the plantation gang slave labor system, the traditional practice established was to allow slaves part of Saturday and all day Sunday off for them to pursue self-maintenance activities, including food production. However, at harvest time, field slaves were required to work every day, and house slaves were on call literally every moment for both domestic work and fieldwork. Only the very large plantations had the specialization of labor that allowed for full-time slave domestics and craft artisans.

Some slaves who participated in the emerging formal economy were able to profit from their independent economic activities, save their money, and purchase their freedom. While their numbers were comparatively limited and the profits earned substantially small, a free black population emerged, and some achieved a degree of economic success. Once manumitted, most continued in developing the enterprises they had established independently while in slavery. The first free Africans, though limited in number, rather quickly began to acquire property. The patriarch of the first free black family of record, Anthony Johnson, and his wife were among the first Africans brought to the English colonies in 1619. By the 1640s, they had acquired freedom and participated in the colonial economy as commercial farmers, with an extensive livestock operation in Northampton, Virginia. In acquiring land, the family took advantage of the headright system by paying the passage of a new immigrant to the colony. In the mid-1600s the Johnson family acquired 900 acres under the headright system for importing a total of eighteen people as servants and slaves, one of whom petitioned the court for his freedom. Meanwhile, blacks in New Amsterdam were already demanding freedom. In 1644, eleven African slave men petitioned for freedom on the grounds that "they are burdened with many children so that it is impossible for them to support their wives and children, as they have been accustomed to do." These men had been brought to the Dutch-owned colony in the 1620s, contraband seized from either Spanish or Portuguese prizes by the Dutch and then made company employees in much the same way as were Jamestown's black and white settlers.

The free black population expanded slowly in the eighteenth century, and not all had come involuntarily or as slaves. Some of the first free immigrants of African descent came from the French colonies, and most settled in Louisiana. Jean Pointe Baptiste DuSable (c. 1750–1819), from Santo Domingo, established his trading post on the Chicago River and thus was the founder of that city. His settlement was noted by a British commandant in a 1779 report. The market for DuSable's trading post extended 200 miles into Michigan, Indiana, and Wisconsin, in addition to servicing fur traders in the Mississippi River Valley. In the English colonies, free blacks, many of whom purchased their freedom, also participated in the economy by establishing businesses. Some even became slaveholders, including black plantation holders, black craftsmen, and especially blacks in the construction trades. Nonetheless, most free blacks who established businesses experienced financial difficulties, for in 1788, a European visitor writing on the black American businessman said: "Those Negroes . . . never augment their business beyond a certain point. The reason is obvious: the whites . . . like not to give them credit . . . [nor] even give them means of a common education."

By the Revolutionary War era the black presence in this nation already extended over 150 years. In the initial draft of the reasons for the revolt of the colonies, the Continental Congress deleted the denunciation of King George for the slave trade. It is ironic, therefore, that the first American to die in the Revolutionary War was a black man, Crispus Attucks, in what became known as the Boston Massacre of March 1770. Five years later, blacks participated in the first battles of the Revolutionary War at Lexington and Concord. However, American military policy initially excluded blacks until after November 1775, when the British governor of Virginia, Lord Dunmore, issued a proclamation that promised freedom to all slaves who joined the British Army. One month later, General George Washington, commander of the Continental Army, rescinded his orders and allowed the enlistment of free blacks. Owners were paid for their slaves; slaves were promised freedom, and some were promised land. South Carolina and Georgia were the only two states that did not sanction the enlistment of blacks. Eventually, some 1,000 blacks fought with the British, and after the war, 20,000 left the new nation with the British forces. Some went to Canada, while others went to the British West Indies or England. Others fled and launched their own armed resistance against both British and American forces. During the Revolutionary War era, almost 70,000 slaves escaped from South Carolina, Virginia, and Georgia, the latter losing 75 percent of its slave population.

Among the total of 300,000 American soldiers, there were 5,000 blacks, serving continuously throughout the war, whereas many white soldiers served briefly, primarily when the battles reached their home state. There were also two all-black regiments, one in Rhode Island, the other in Massachusetts. In addition, one fourth of the American navy during the Revolutionary War was black. Besides combat service, blacks filed freedom suits in the courts and submitted group petitions to state legislative bodies in a plea for freedom. The

Revolutionary War era marked the beginning of the First Emancipation, the beginning of the end of slavery in the North through new state constitutions, judicial decisions, and gradual emancipation laws. Yet slavery was not abolished in the 1787 Federal Constitution, although there were three provisions that referred to the existence of the institution because the priority for the Framers of the Constitution was to "form a more perfect union" and, at the same time, guarantee the protection of private property. Otherwise, the southern states would have refused to ratify the Constitution. The Continental Congress had, however, established precedent by demolishing slavery in the 1787 Northwest Ordinance.

INSTITUTIONAL DEVELOPMENT OF THE BLACK COMMUNITY

The institutional development of the black community began during the Revolution and included both mutual aid and benevolent societies, fraternal organizations, schools, churches, and cultural improvement societies. Included in the late eighteenth-century vanguard were Phillis Wheatley, a black poet, whose works were published in both the United States and England during the Revolutionary War era; Benjamin Banneker, a mathematician, astronomer, and inventor, who participated in the building of Washington, D.C.; and Prince Hall, founder of the Black Masons, Africa Lodge #1, the first of the fraternal orders of which blacks would become members. But the most significant black institution that had its origins in the late eighteenth century was the independent black church. Its leaders were Richard Allen and Absalom Jones, two former slaves who had purchased their freedom. In 1787 they formed the Free African Society, a mutual aid society. In 1792, the society disbanded, and its funds were used to establish a black church. The African Methodist Episcopal (AME) Church was also founded by Richard Allen. From its origins the black church and its leaders have been in the forefront, a bulwark of survival materially and spiritually, promoting the rights of black Americans, while providing social services for the homeless, impoverished, widows, orphans, and the aged. Because it was the center of community life, especially in the slave quarters, religious services were carefully scrutinized by whites.

ANTEBELLUM SLAVES AND FREE BLACKS

Out of 8 million whites in the fifteen slave states, only 385,000 owned slaves, and only 47,000 of them owned more than 20 slaves. By 1860, of the African-American population of 4.5 million, only 10 percent were free. Of the almost 4 million slaves, 1.8 million worked on cotton plantations in Alabama, Mississippi, Georgia, South Carolina, Texas, and Florida. Some 350,000 worked on tobacco plantations in Virginia, Kentucky, Tennessee, Missouri, and North Carolina. In addition, about 125,000 slaves labored on rice plantations in South

Carolina and Georgia and 80,000 on sugar plantations in Louisiana and Texas, whereas 60,000 worked on hemp farms in Kentucky and Missouri. In addition, there were 400,000 urban slaves and 200,000 industrial slaves who worked in internal improvements (building railroads, canals, and roads), factories (producing tobacco, iron, textiles, and hemp), and in other industries (including the extractive ones). In addition, on plantations there were skilled slaves, carpenters, blacksmiths, wheelwrights, masons, and plantation slave women who had skills as seamstresses, dressmakers, and nurses and some who worked in a management capacity supervising cloth making, nurseries, and "hospitals." But few in rural areas escaped field labor. Indeed, in the history of the African-American woman, the most prevalent and persistent themes in their lives have centered around multiple forms of oppression: slavery, sexual exploitation, economic and labor exploitation, marginalization, and societal racism.

Yet, as noted earlier, the slaves' bare subsistence level and a tradition of self-help provided the basis for slaves, both men and women, to develop further independent economic activities, which expanded in antebellum America. Besides those who simply produced food, there were urban slave vendors (predominantly women) and hawkers and itinerant peddlers; some became slave entrepreneurs, men and women, who hired their own time from their owners, and still others hired other slaves as their employees. The fact that more than 92 percent of plantation slaves lived in nuclear two-parent households meant that familial obligations inherent in the roles of husband-wife, mother-father, were powerful incentives. For example, Free Frank McWorter (1777–1854) was taken to Kentucky in 1795, where he established a saltpeter manufactory during the War of 1812 and used his profits to purchase his wife's freedom in 1817 and then his own. Over a period of forty years, and at a cost of $15,000, he purchased sixteen family members from slavery. His sons later became conductors on the Underground Railroad (UGRR), leading slave fugitives to Canada. With respect to free black women, while most worked as laundresses and domestics, a few were also involved in self-employed enterprises as dressmakers, boarding house keepers, and caterers. The wealthiest antebellum black businesswoman was New Orleans merchant Madame Eulalie "CeCee" d'Mandeville Macarty, who sold "fancy goods" imported primarily from France. She was also a slaveholder and, by the 1840s, was worth more than $150,000.

Meanwhile, free blacks, both men and women (especially those in business), were establishing self-help organizations. For example, in 1793, the first black women's organization was founded, the Female Benevolent Society of St. Thomas, a black church. Along with their cultural and literary societies, women also formed mutual aid societies. These men and women financed the building of churches and schools and were actively involved not only in the abolitionist movement but also in the temperance, moral reform movements, women's rights, and even the peace movement. The wealthiest black American in the early nineteenth century, James Forten, who owned a sail-making company and subsequently accumulated a fortune of $100,000, used much of his wealth to support the abolitionist and other social reforms. The slave-born Frederick Douglass, who escaped to freedom, was known both nationally and internationally for his leadership in the abolitionist movement. While exemplifying the spirituality that sustained many women, Harriet Tubman, the escaped slave and a conductor on the UGRR, led almost 500 slaves to freedom.

Among the important institutions, there was an antebellum black press that stood in the forefront of the protest against slavery. The first black newspaper was founded in 1827, *Freedom's Journal*, and by the Civil War, more than forty-five had been established. In addition, one of the leading black organizations before the Civil War was the National Negro Convention. It first met in 1830, and by 1860, some thirteen conferences had been held. Besides the major goal of bringing about the end of slavery, the convention supported proposals to increase black business participation, including a national black bank and the equivalent of rotating credit unions.

In terms of employment, racism and discrimination were factors that limited access to jobs and contributed to the impoverishment of free blacks, which led many to become self-employed. The leading black businesspeople, however, were those who served wealthy whites, and the three ranking "high-status" occupations (barbering, catering, and tailoring) provided the basis for the developing profitable enterprises. Antebellum blacks were also wholesale and retail grocers and dry goods merchants. Others owned transportation enterprises, whereas some were inventors and manufacturers and a few real estate speculators and developers. One of the wealthiest antebellum free blacks was the former slave Stephen Smith, a Pennsylvania lumber and coal merchant who was a leading real estate holder. In 1850 his wealth was reported to be $250,000; in 1860, it exceeded $500,000. Nonetheless, by far the wealthiest antebellum blacks lived in Louisiana, notably the Soulié brothers, and Lacroix brothers, with fortunes matching Smith's.

THE CIVIL WAR AND RECONSTRUCTION

In America's Civil War 180,000 black soldiers served in the U.S. Colored Troops (USCT) and took part in some 499 Civil War battles. A total of 67,178, one third, died in the war. Another 20,000 served in noncombatant positions. These 200,000 blacks made up 10 percent of Union forces, whereas black sailors again comprised one fourth of the navy. When the war began in 1861, however, the American military had initially continued its practice of rejecting black participation. The Emancipation Proclamation, however, changed the focus of the war, and it now became a war to free the slaves. Ironically, two months before the war ended, the Confederate States approved the enlistment of slaves.

Before his assassination, Abraham Lincoln also signed the Freedmen's Bureau Bill, which established an agency to aid the freedmen. In its seven-year operation, the Bureau built 4,300 schools. This was also the founding era of historically black colleges and universities. Some of the schools founded between 1866 and 1876 included Fisk University, Lincoln University, Morehouse College, Howard University, Talledega, Morgan State, Johnson C. Smith, St. Augustine College, Clark College, and Dillard and Meharry Medical School. Meanwhile, the end of the Civil War did not bring immediate freedom, that is, civil and political rights to black Americans. In the summer of 1865, the South passed black codes, which were particularly harsh in limiting the economic activities of blacks. In a racist society that propagated myths and stereotypes, which asserted that blacks were lazy and lacked initiative, it is ironic that most of the black codes in force, as during slavery, were designed to suppress independent black economic initiative. In fact, while planters were required to negotiate sharecropping contracts with the freedmen, these contracts routinely exploited blacks. As sharecropping developed, the refusal (or failure) of the sharecroppers to comply with all stipulations could mean that they would "forfeit all His or Her [half] interest" in the crop.

Freedmen had hoped only for "forty acres and a mule." For the 90 percent of the African-American population who were slaves in 1860, farm ownership, even at a virtually self-subsistence level, could have provided the foundation for black economic independence and the expansion of black business activities. However, Congress did attempt to provide freedmen with civil and political rights. The Thirteenth Amendment, ratified in December 1865, abolished slavery. The 1866 Civil Rights Act granted citizenship, with the provision that the federal government would intervene to ensure that "citizens of every race and color," except Indians, were given the same legal rights as white men. Attempting to ensure that these rights of blacks would be protected, Congress drafted the Fourteenth Amendment, ratified in 1868. (A century later it provided the constitutional support for the 1964 Civil Rights Act.) Then, in 1867, Congress acted to provide for black political participation with the first Reconstruction Act. Southern states were required to convene constitutional conventions. All men, black and white, except those who held high offices in the Confederacy, could vote and participate. The newly elected delegates, including blacks, drafted new constitutions and instituted progressive social changes. Free public schools were established, and new public works programs were initiated to provide roads and bridges for a new economic infrastructure. Congress also required that the new state constitutions guarantee black suffrage and that the Fourteenth Amendment be ratified before readmission to the Union. When voting registration in the southern states was complete, 700,000 blacks, compared to 663,000 whites, were registered.

In 1868 Ulysses S. Grant was elected president, but he won only 53 percent of the popular vote, some 700,000 more than his opponent. The Republicans carried six southern states with the black vote. From then until the 1930s blacks continued to support the Republican ticket. The significance of the black vote was clearly recognized by the Republican Party, which pushed through the Fifteenth Amendment (ratified in 1870), guaranteeing that no one could be deprived of the right to vote because of race, color, or previous condition of servitude. At the national level, between 1869 and 1880 sixteen blacks were elected to Congress, including two from Mississippi, who served in the Senate. Hiram Revels served an incomplete term in the Senate from 1870 to 1871, filling the seat held formerly by Jefferson Davis. Blanche K. Bruce, elected in 1874, was the first black to serve a full term. These were the last two blacks to serve in the U.S. Senate until 1966, when Edward Brooks (Massachusetts) was elected, and 1992, when the first black woman, Carol Mosely Braun (Illinois), was elected.

Blacks were also elected to various state and local offices. Two served as acting governors in Louisiana. South Carolina, Mississippi, and Louisiana had black lieutenant governors. Blacks were also elected senators and representatives in southern state legislatures. Florida's secretary of state was black, and in South Carolina, there was a black state supreme court judge. They also served as superintendents of education and state treasurers and, at the local level, became municipal judges, sat on juries, were elected mayors, and appointed postmasters and policemen. To note the exceptional background of a few of the more illustrious leaders: South Carolina's state treasurer Francis L. Cardozo had been educated at Glasgow and in London; Robert Brown Elliot, a brilliant lawyer elected to Congress in 1870, had attended Eton College in England; J. Wright, a state supreme court justice, studied at the University of Pennsylvania; and Florida's secretary of state, Jonathan C. Gibbs, graduated from Dartmouth and had been a Presbyterian minister. Others were ministers, teachers, farmers, artisans, and lawyers.

The admission of each state, however, marked the beginning of white conservative rule in the South and the decline of black political participation. Moreover, literally, from the beginning of Reconstruction, white terrorists groups, inspired by the Ku Klux Klan, embarked on a devastating reign of terror and violence, first to force black subordination and compliance to unjust laws and then to force blacks out of electoral politics. In the Exodus of 1879, many blacks fled the South, including those who subsequently established black towns. Before 1900, more than eighty had been started, primarily in Oklahoma and the Great Plains states. Unfortunately, the federal government supported the South in its black civil rights retrenchment movement, and the Supreme Court took the lead with its strict construction of the Fourteenth and Fifteenth Amendments. Thus, in the 1883 civil rights cases decision, the 1875 Civil Rights Act (which allowed blacks equal access to places of public accommodation) was declared unconstitutional. In the 1890 *Texas Railroad v. Mississippi* case, the Court ruled that a state could require segregation on transportation carriers, whereas in the infamous 1896 *Plessy v. Ferguson* case, the Court established the separate but equal rule, which provided the legal basis for the expansion of Jim Crow. New state constitutions in the South disenfranchised blacks through poll taxes, literacy tests, good character and property qualifications, the grandfather clause, and the Democratic white primary. In Louisiana, as an example, there were 130,334 black voters in 1896; by 1904, only 1,342 could vote. It seemed that blacks had no choice but to capitulate. In fact, this was the message Booker T. Washington had given blacks in 1895 in his infamous Atlanta "compromise" speech, when he urged blacks to accommodate to the rise of Jim Crow. He warned African Americans that "agitation of questions of social equality is the extremist folly," and he emphasized, regarding race relations between the blacks and whites, that "in all things that are purely social we can be as separate as the fingers, yet one as the hand in all things essential to mutual progress." He then advised blacks, "Cast down your bucket where you are. . . . Cast it down in agriculture, mechanics, in commerce, in domestic service, and in the professions." By arguing so, Washington was catapulted into national and international prominence by the nation's white power structure, emerging as the leader of black America.

THE AGE OF BOOKER T. WASHINGTON, 1895–1915

Some three years later, at the 1898 Fourth Atlanta Conference, W.E.B. Du Bois, soon to be known more for his promotion of the "Talented Tenth" and his emphasis on civil rights protest, stressed the importance of black business and called for "the organization in every town and hamlet where colored people dwell, of Negro Business Men's Leagues, and the gradual federation." In 1900 Washington organized the National Negro Business League (NNBL). By 1915 membership was estimated from 5,000 to 40,000, with over 600 chapters in thirty-four states and in West Africa on the Gold Coast. While Washington's philosophy of promoting political accommodation was quite well known, few people knew that, behind the scenes, he supported the fight against segregation and discrimination, a policy that Du Bois, however, pursued openly.

Still, both men viewed the business activities of blacks as taking place within the existence of a separate economy, and both promoted cooperative efforts for the survival of black economic life. Fraternal orders founded both insurance companies and banks, and then black insurance companies also founded banks. From 1888 to 1934, some 134 black-owned banks were established. Moreover, in this age of segregation, besides starting businesses, including transportation, leisure, and entertainment enterprises, other black responses included individual acts of protest, mass demonstrations, and legal challenges in the courts. Blacks also built parks and recreation centers and opened resorts. They constructed hotels, theaters, and other buildings that provided public space for black civic and cultural activities. In addition, by 1910 blacks also owned 20 million acres of farmland. All these economic activities represented the continuation of the tradition of self-help that has distinguished the black historic experience in America.

Furthermore, in the period of America's greatest economic growth, black inventors contributed significantly to the nation's industrial growth, securing over 1,000 patents. Several were distinguished by their productivity. In 1872 Lewis Latimer (1848–1928) worked on Alexander Graham Bell's 1876 patent applications for the telephone and then, in 1880, was hired by Thomas A. Edison and made improvements on the incandescent lightbulb. Latimer headed the team that installed the municipal electric light systems for New York City, Philadelphia, and London. John E. McWorter had several patents for his helicopter inventions from 1911 to 1921. In 1923 Garrett Morgan patented the traffic light, having earlier, during World War I, patented a gas "breathing" mask—his "national safety helmet," as it was called—"used by the United States and the Allies to combat poisonous gases and as a safety device on submarines." Blacks during this period also made significant advances in science. George Washington Carver's experiments with peanuts and sweet potatoes subsequently provided the foundation for several new food-processing industries. While such inventors and scientists failed to become wealthy, that was not the case with the largest and fastest-growth profitable industry for blacks, the hair care and beauty aids business. The pioneers in this industry, Madame C. J. Walker, Mrs. Violet Turbo-Malone, and Anthony Overton, all achieved millionaire status before 1920. Nonetheless, although black businesses relied primarily on a black consumer market, blacks did not exist in a wholly separate economy, since white businesses captured most of the black consumer dollar.

THE GREAT MIGRATION AND THE RISE OF THE URBAN BLACK GHETTO

The period from 1910 to 1920 is known as the Great Migration in African-American history. The era marked the beginning of the black urban ghetto, but it was not until 1940 that more than 50 percent of blacks lived in places of more than 2,500 people. The push-pull factors that contributed to the Great Migration were (1) the intensification of racism in the South; (2) the differential in wages in northern industries' salaries, which were $3.00 to $5.00 a day, compared to southern wages of $.75 to $1.00 (there were higher wages for domestics in the North, too); (3) better health care in the North; and (4) the wartime decline in European immigration. Indeed, many industries, notably meatpacking, auto, and steel, sent labor agents to the South to recruit black workers, while the leading black newspaper with a national circulation, the *Chicago Defender*, encouraged migration. Many said they were heading for "the Promised Land," and for black women, this meant a chance to escape not only the oppressiveness of agricultural field labor but also their lack of protection from sexual assaults. In 1910, there were 10 million blacks, with 90 percent living in the South and 80 percent living in rural areas. Between 1917 and 1920, an estimated 700,000 to 1 million blacks left the South, followed by another 800,000 to 1 million during the 1920s. (In addition, there was also the immigration of blacks from the West Indies—most of whom settled in New York or Florida.)

Black migration patterns followed the lines of least resistance. Those from Georgia, the Carolinas, and Virginia migrated to the Northeast cities of New

York, Philadelphia, and Boston. Blacks from the Cotton Belt—Louisiana, Mississippi, and Alabama—using the Illinois Central Railroad, migrated to Chicago and Milwaukee, and those from Kentucky and Tennessee migrated to industrial centers in Ohio and Indiana. Black migration to the Midwest, however, was greater than to the Northeast. Detroit's black population rose from some 6,000 in 1910 to 120,000 by 1930; Cleveland's leaped from 8,500 to 72,000; and St. Louis's increased from 45,000 to 94,000. At the same time, Los Angeles's black population went from 7,600 in 1910 to almost 40,000 by 1930. The three cities with the greatest jumps were Chicago, where the black population increased from 44,000 in 1910 to 234,000 by 1920; New York, whose black population more than tripled from 100,000 to 328,000; and Philadelphia, which saw a jump from 84,500 to 220,000. Nevertheless, more southern blacks migrated to southern cities between 1900 and 1920 than to northern cities. In some southern cities they soon comprised from 25 to 50 percent of the total population, whereas in northern cities they never exceeded 10 percent.

Once settled in the North, recent migrants wrote back telling of their success, including one black man who wrote: "I should have been here twenty years ago . . . I just begin to feel like a man." Yet black migration to northern urban centers also resulted in the development of an urban black physical and institutional ghetto. Contributing factors included racism; zoning laws (municipalities zoned industrial areas that surrounded black residential areas to keep blacks contained in those areas); private sector discrimination in the housing market (redlining); restrictive covenants—where property deeds stipulated that the property could not be sold to a certain racial or religious group; and most important, the refusal of financial institutions, banks, and savings and loan companies to approve mortgage loans for blacks. These concentrated racial ghettos contained both slum-infested housing occupied by the impoverished urban black masses and the well-kept homes of the black middle class and the wealthy. At the same time, black churches, clubs, and social and civil organizations were located there. Moreover, it was the Great Migration that made possible the election of blacks in northern cities to municipal offices as well as the election in 1928 of the first black congressman from a northern state, Oscar DePriest (R) from Chicago.

In response to the debilitating conditions of blacks not only in urban centers but also in rural areas, many black self-help organizations were founded. Black women of all classes were in the forefront. In 1896, the National Association of Colored Women was organized, and by 1929, its membership numbered over 300,000, with branches located both in the United States and abroad. Local branches concentrated on specific problem areas. Thus, one of the most successful organizations of black community clubwomen was the Neighborhood Union in Atlanta, Georgia, organized in 1908. Its purpose was to provide playgrounds, improve the sanitation of homes and streets, promote better health care, and force the municipality to provide street lights, pave streets, and suppress vice and crime. As with other black women's groups, they established kindergartens and day nurseries for working mothers, sponsored homemaking classes, founded orphan and old folks homes, and promoted women's suffrage.

When the United States entered World War I, blacks once again literally had to fight to be allowed to fight in defense of their nation. Regrettably, the efforts of the Allied Powers to make the world safe for democracy did not extend to blacks, and the summer of 1919 saw more than forty race riots in America. The Chicago race riot was one of the most serious in what became known as the "Red Summer." Now urban race riots have long plagued American cities since the two in New York in 1712 and 1741, when both black slaves and free blacks threatened to burn down the city. In the early twentieth century, the Atlanta race riot in 1906 and the Springfield race riot of 1908, especially, had shocked the nation. The latter lasted for two days until the National Guard was called out. By then, two men were lynched, hundreds assaulted, several beaten to death, and another tortured. Indeed, it was in response to that riot that the National Association for the Advancement of Colored People (NAACP) was founded in 1910 to attack segregation and discrimination in the courts. It would emerge as the legal arm of the black civil rights movements. Following the East St. Louis, Illinois, riot of 1917 and those during the "Red Summer" of 1919, there were others from 1920 to World War II. But it was the 1921 Tulsa riot that truly shocked the nation. The economic success of blacks, again, was the precipitating factor, and the black business section was totally devastated, attacked not only by mobs of armed whites but also by air. The National Guard was called out, and some 6,000 blacks were marched to detention camps, allowed to leave only when their badges were signed by their white employers. The business district never recovered its prewar economic vitality.

The resurgence of racial violence in postwar America was also reflected in the new Ku Klux Klan, an organization that no longer confined its activities to the South and its racial hostilities to blacks. The new Klan was now also anti-immigrant, anti-Catholic, and anti-Semitic. The black response was reflected in their support for black nationalist leader Marcus Garvey and in the cultural nationalism of the Harlem Renaissance. Jamaican-born Marcus Garvey had founded the Universal Negro Improvement Association (UNIA) in 1914. He came to America in 1916 and established his UNIA headquarters in Harlem. By 1920, with branches not only in America but also throughout the African Diaspora, Garvey claimed a membership of 3 million, but even the most conservative estimates acknowledge that at least 500,000 belonged to his organization. Garvey was popular because he sensed the mood of the black masses, glorified the African past, exalted blackness, and emphasized race pride. "Up You Mighty Race, Accomplish What You Will." The UNIA established factories, businesses, and the Black Star Steamship Line, but Garvey also called for a "Back to Africa" movement and the independence of Africa from white colonial rule. However, in 1923, accused of using the mails to defraud in selling stock in his steamship line, Garvey was convicted, jailed in 1925, and, two years later, pardoned and deported.

Pride in race was also expressed in the arts in the 1920s in a black cultural movement known as the Harlem Renaissance. It proceeded in three phases. The literary polemic of the black intelligentsia, who announced themselves as the "New Negro," signaled the beginning of this movement by expressing their disillusionment with racist America. But it was the new musical and dance forms created by blacks that pervaded all areas of American life: the 1920s "Jazz Age." New York was the center of American culture and black music, including blues and black dance forms, such as the cakewalk, which spread nationwide, aided by the radio and the new record industry. Then, while some writers were celebrating black life, despite the despair of racism, others were expressing the black rage, such as poet Claude McKay in his poem "If We Must Die." Even throughout the 1930s, the literary works of Columbia-trained anthropologist Zora Neal Hurston, the poetry of Countee Cullen, the great acting and singing of Paul Robeson, the novels of Richard Wright, and the music of Duke Ellington and Louis Armstrong continued to electrify America.

THE GREAT DEPRESSION AND NEW DEAL

Already in the 1920s, there were factors that contributed to the depressed economic state of black America. First, during the war blacks had made economic gains in industrial employment, primarily as unskilled workers, but in the postwar demobilization white soldiers replaced many blacks in the heavy industries. Second, at the same time, there was an economic slump in industries that traditionally employed blacks, such as the mining, textile, shipping, and shoe industries. Third, in the 1920s, agriculture was in a depressed state, due especially to the loss of grain markets and greater competition internationally in the sale of tobacco, cotton, and cane sugar. This agricultural recession particularly affected blacks, since 80 percent of the black population still lived in the South, and most had remained farmworkers. When the stock market crashed in 1929, a substantial proportion of black workers in agriculture and industrial employment had for some time been living a depressionlike existence.

Moreover, President Herbert Hoover did very little for the nation, much less for blacks, which marked the beginning of a massive political shift of blacks from the Republican to the Democratic Party. In the 1932 election, 20 percent of blacks voted for Franklin Delano Roosevelt. Sixty-four percent of blacks voted the Democratic ticket in 1936, but only 50 percent did so in 1940, a response to the evident racism in FDR's New Deal programs. Notwithstanding that, FDR's New Deal administration was the first to include a substantial number of blacks, and several served as advisers for what was termed *Negro affairs*, including Robert Weaver, Judge William Hastie, Robert Vann of the *Pittsburgh*

Courier, and Mary McLeod Bethune, who founded the National Council of Negro Women in 1935.

Even so, by 1934, 38 percent of blacks were unemployed compared to 17 percent of whites. While unemployment had declined by 1940, still 22 percent of all black workers remained unemployed, compared to only 13 percent of whites. During the 1930s, 36 percent of blacks were agricultural workers, 27 percent personal-service workers, only 2 percent professionals, and some 6 percent self-employed business owners. Consequently, virtually any black person who had a steady job had status and was a member of the black middle class, particularly those with protected steady jobs, such as civil servants, mailmen, and teachers, as well as Pullman porters, many of whom were college graduates. On the other hand, historically, blacks have been criticized by white unionists for being scabs, strikebreakers, but it was these same white union members who had staunchly long opposed the admission of blacks to their unions. Therefore, among the few opportunities that blacks ever had to secure employment, which was especially critical during the 1930s, was to become a scab and work as a strikebreaker. However, in 1925, A. Philip Randolph had founded the Brotherhood of Sleeping Car Porters, and, in 1925 and 1929, the union obtained recognition as the bargaining agency for porters and maids employed by the Pullman Company. While relatively few blacks were employed in that industry, there was other labor success in the 1930s with the founding of the Congress of Industrial Organizations (CIO). Its membership was open to anyone employed in an industry.

Meanwhile, in urban areas, efforts to find employment were particularly degrading for black women domestic workers, for there were "slave markets" where black women would go to wait for white women to look them over and hire them for day work at unbelievably low wages: $1.87 for an eight-hour day, often without food or carfare home. The Social Security Act did not protect them, for the employers of the almost two-thirds of black workers who were domestic and agricultural workers were not required to contribute to Social Security. Subsequently, when in need of financial aid, they had to rely on public assistance, which was administered by the state. Although this was the first instance of some federal funds "trickling down" to blacks, the majority of funds went to white Americans, particularly in the South. Thus, even in farm areas, black farmers were thrown off the land, notwithstanding the fact that the federal government was providing aid to farm owners. The Southern Tenant Farmers' Union, an interracial organization, was formed to fight for fair treatment.

Necessarily, therefore, self-help activities were once again significant factors enabling blacks to survive the depression. Blacks formed cooperatives and organized "Double Duty Dollar" and "Don't Buy Where You Can't Work" campaigns. As white stores in Chicago with black patronage began to hire blacks, the "Double Duty Dollar" campaign spread to other cities, including New York, Washington, D.C., Baltimore, and St. Louis. At the same time, the independent black churches fed countless thousands of people, most notably the

Harlem-based Divine Peace Mission Cooperatives, a black religious-based organization led by Father Divine.

In large cities, such as New York and Chicago, an important source of employment for blacks during the depression was in the "policy" or "numbers" game, which differed little from state-run lotteries today. Then, however, the "numbers" game was illegal but profitable. Beginning in the 1930s, white gangsters moved in and took control, especially after Prohibition ended their lucrative, though illegal, bootleg operations. In Harlem, the gangster "Dutch" Schultz seized policy operations from blacks. In Chicago, however, blacks became part of the syndicate that controlled the numbers game. Before World War II, there were 500 policy stations in Chicago that grossed $18 million annually. The most successful black policy kings in Chicago in the 1930s and early 1940s were the Jones Brothers, educated sons of a highly respected minister.

Yet there were sources of black pride beyond their sheer survival: Jesse Owens's triumph at the 1936 Olympics in Berlin touched many, and black Americans were ecstatic two years later when heavyweight champion Joe Louis defeated German Max Schmeling, who had knocked Louis out in 1936. Finally, in 1939, when the DAR (Daughters of the American Revolution) refused to allow the great contralto Marian Anderson to sing at Constitution Hall, First Lady Eleanor Roosevelt withdrew her DAR membership in protest, and Anderson gave a concert before a huge crowd at the Lincoln Monument.

THE WAR AND CIVIL RIGHTS

Even before the Japanese bombed Pearl Harbor in 1941 and blacks rushed to join the American military, their leadership stressed that the fight by African Americans would be on both the home front and the battle front: black America's "Double V" campaign. In January 1941, A. Philip Randolph threatened a mass March on Washington in protest against racial discrimination in the nation's defense industries, prompting a reluctant FDR to issue Executive Order 8802, making racial discrimination in defense industries illegal. A Fair Employment Practices Committee (FEPC) was also established. Even so, race riots across the nation in 1943 often reflected whites' opposition to the hiring of blacks in defense industries and public housing for blacks in white communities. In the meantime, although the first black general, Benjamin Davis, had been appointed in 1940, blacks continued to serve in segregated units. Some 500,000 served overseas, and the black community took special pride in the all-black Tuskegee Airmen strike force, which flew bombing raids in Europe. Yet blacks still encountered racism in the military—at home as well as overseas. For example, when German prisoners of war (POWs) were transported across the South to prison camps in Arizona, black soldiers who guarded them were required to eat outside of white restaurants, while the POWs were served inside.

With the postwar commencement of the cold war between the U.S. and the USSR superpowers, the prevailing international question was, What political ideology would win the hearts and minds of the newly emerging colonial nations, democracy or communism? America had reasons for concern, for its racial problems contravened the promise of American democracy as a force in promoting social equality. Consequently, the federal government's expansion of rights to black Americans can also be seen as part of its new international goals and policies. Even so, black America early on had launched the attack against racial subordination. In 1915 the *Guinn v. the United States* decision struck down the grandfather clause. The NAACP's effort to beat down the walls of segregation and second-class citizenship continued with the 1927 *Nixon v. Herndon* decision, which invalidated the Texas Democratic white primary. Then, in the 1930s and 1940s, the NAACP began to attack inequities in public and graduate school education, providing the legal precedents for the landmark 1954 *Brown* decision and establishing that, because of intangible factors, separate facilities could never be equal.

By the 1950s, the NAACP Legal Defense Fund, led by Thurgood Marshall, had decided to directly challenge segregation in public schools with the *Brown v. The Board of Education of Topeka* case. The Supreme Court voted unanimously in May 1954 that separate but equal was unconstitutional under the Fourteenth Amendment. While historian John Hope Franklin provided documented evidence of historical inequities in education, black psychologist Kenneth Clark detailed how segregated education damaged black children and contributed to their negative self-images, which lowered their motivation and aspirations and adversely affected their academic achievement. The infamous *Plessy v. Ferguson* decision was overturned, signaling the end to constitutionally protected segregation and discrimination. While, even before *Brown*, other Supreme Court decisions had advanced the rights of blacks in voting, housing, transportation, and public accommodations, it was three years later, in 1957, that a civil rights bill provided for a U.S. Commission on Civil Rights to investigate discrimination and segregation in violation of the Fourteenth and Fifteenth Amendments.

Still, racism persisted in its most pernicious form. In 1955, a fourteen-year-old Chicago black boy, Emmett Till, visiting in Mississippi, was killed for allegedly making advances to a white woman. The violence of his death was perhaps symbolic of the white resistance that would take place from 1955 to 1964 in response to the new era of black protest.

FROM CIVIL RIGHTS TO BLACK POWER

In the first year after *Brown*, blacks in Montgomery, Alabama, launched a boycott against the city's buses in protest of the arrest of black seamstress Rosa Parks, who had refused to give up her seat to a white man. Leadership was turned over to a young minister, the Reverend Dr. Martin Luther King, Jr. The boycott began in December 1955 and ended the following December, when the Supreme Court ruled that segregated seating on the city's buses was unconstitutional. Throughout that year, blacks in other cities launched municipal bus boycotts and also challenged segregated education.

The Congress of Racial Equality (CORE), an integrated group founded in 1942 by black activist James Farmer, was one of the four major protest organizations in the civil rights movement. In 1942, it had staged a sit-in at a downtown restaurant that refused to serve blacks. In 1947, it sent "freedom riders" to the South to test desegregation in interstate bus travel. The most prominent organization, however, was the Southern Christian Leadership Conference (SCLC), founded in 1957 after the Montgomery bus boycott. King was elected president. In May of that year, he headed a 15,000-participant demonstration in support of a voting rights act. While most participants were black, support came from an increasing number of whites. Several months later, Congress passed the Voting Rights Act of 1957, strengthened three years later with the 1960 Voting Rights Act.

However, as black protest increased, white terrorism intensified in response, with bombings and lynching of blacks; destruction of their churches, homes, and businesses; threats of unemployment; and denial of bank loans—all as measures to force blacks to cease protesting in demand of their rights. In 1957, with the attempted integration of the high school at Little Rock, the federal government did respond. The defiance of the *Brown* ruling by Arkansas's Governor Orville Faubus represented the most serious state's rights challenge to the federal government since the Civil War. President Dwight D. Eisenhower sent federal troops, subsequently followed by the National Guard, to force compliance and to secure the admission of nine black students to the school.

Still, the event that marked the full-scale onset of the civil rights movement was the February 1960 sit-in by young black college students in Greensboro, North Carolina. As sit-ins spread throughout the South, the Student Non-Violent Coordinating Committee (SNCC) was organized in April 1960 to coordinate the movement. Sit-ins took place in restaurants and anyplace else where there were segregated public facilities that refused to serve blacks. The SNCC-led wave of sit-ins continued for more than two years, and both blacks and whites who participated in the sit-ins were subjected to white violence and thrown in jail. In 1961, as segregation continued on interstate buses, CORE escalated its "freedom rides." Its black and white members were also attacked by white mobs. In Birmingham, the April 1963 response by Police Commissioner Eugene "Bull" Connor to civil rights protesters' efforts to end segregation in that city (led by King) was brutality at its worst. As the nation watched on television the scenes of beatings, the use of billy clubs, whips, cattle prods, fire hoses, tear gas, and attack dogs, it was horrified at the extent of southern white resistance to the end of segregation. Despite massive arrests, the protest continued until May 10, when an agreement was reached that called for gradual desegregation of public accommodations. The following month Medgar Evers, an NAACP field secretary in Mississippi, was gunned down; his alleged assailant, a white segregationist, was acquitted by a hung jury.

Throughout June and July of 1963, civil rights demonstrations, protests, and boycotts occurred in almost every major urban area in the country and culminated in the August 28, 1963, March on Washington, the largest single protest demonstration in U.S. history. Some 250,000 blacks and others demanded passage of a civil rights bill, their resolve strengthened by King's historically memorable "I Have a Dream" speech. But white resistance would not abate, and the following month a black church was bombed, killing four black girls. In November, the assassination of President John Kennedy awakened Americans to a nation verging on anarchy, and in early 1964 Congress passed the Twenty-fourth Amendment, prohibiting the denial or abridgment of the right to vote by "reason of failure to pay any poll tax or other tax." The leadership in moving a civil rights bill through Congress passed to the new president, Lyndon Baines Johnson. In July 1964 Congress passed the Civil Rights Act, the most far-reaching legislation to protect the rights of blacks since the 1875 Civil Rights Act. That December, King was awarded the Nobel Peace Prize.

For many black Americans, however, the gains made were a matter of a little bit a little late, especially in the North, where blacks could vote and had access to places of public accommodations. Their civil rights concerns centered on equal economic opportunities. In midsummer 1964, urban rebellions engulfed the nation, beginning in Harlem and followed by riots in Brooklyn, Rochester, Chicago, and Philadelphia. In January 1965 King led a voter-registration drive in Selma, Alabama, that resulted in more violence. Two months later, a fifty-mile protest demonstration march took place in which some 50,000 people participated, including a Michigan white woman, Mrs. Viola Liuzzo, who was then brutally killed, as were several other blacks and whites. Congress responded with the 1965 Voting Rights bill. The right to vote was also extended to Americans unable to read or write English but who could demonstrate they had an eighth-grade education. Yet the granting of these rights still did not address the issues of economics for northern blacks, and in August 1965, the most serious single racial conflict in American history took place, the Watts riot, ending with 34 dead, 900 injured, and 3,500 arrested. The National Guard was called in to quell the riot.

The passage of the 1964 Civil Rights Act and the 1965 Voting Rights Act marked the culmination of the integrationist phase of the Black Revolution of the 1960s. By 1966 the civil rights movement was fragmented. There was now a resurgence of black nationalist and separatist sentiments that challenged the integrationism and legalism of the NAACP and other elements of the integrationist civil rights coalition, which disintegrated as leading civil rights groups embraced the concept of Black Power. The great promoter of Black Power was the new head of SNCC, West Indian–born Stokeley Carmichael, a Howard University student who moved the organization to militancy when he gave a speech in June 1966 denouncing nonviolence and demanding "Black Power." Under Carmichael's leadership, SNCC endorsed independent black political action and challenged the value of alliances with whites. Its Black Power agenda not only alienated white liberals; it divided blacks. CORE also moved toward black nationalism when the militant Floyd McKissick succeeded the integrationist James Farmer as director. Under McKissick, CORE sanctioned the use of violence in self-defense, while advocating black economic boycotts and all-black business and financial institutions in the ghettos. Then, in the fall of 1966, in Oakland, California, the Black Panther Party was founded by Huey Newton and Bobby Seale. It was considered the most extreme example of Black Power in action. They advocated armed self-defense, and their ten-point program called for full employment and restitution for past oppression. They demanded education relevant to black needs and aspirations, decent housing, exemptions from military service for blacks, trial of blacks to be heard only by black juries, and an end to police brutality. Their cry was "Power to the people." Declared enemies of the state by FBI (Federal Bureau of Investigation) director J. Edgar Hoover, the movement was finally suppressed by 1971, with its leaders either dead, jailed, or in exile.

Among King's opponents was the fiery and vociferous Malcolm X, who early on had denounced the integrationist thrust of the civil rights movement. Born Malcolm Little to a West Indian mother and African-American father, Malcolm was six when his militant father was killed by whites. His mother slowly went insane and was put in a mental hospital. Malcolm eventually left home, got involved in drugs and crime, and in 1945 was sentenced to jail, where he was introduced to the tenets of the Nation of Islam. Founded in 1930 by a Wallace Fard, who castigated whites as degenerate devils, the movement was taken over in 1933 by Elijah Muhammad, a former Garveyite. The Nation of Islam advocated racial separatism, black self-determination, economic self-help, and the establishment of an independent black state within the borders of the United States. Members adhered to a strict moral and health code. Respect for black women was requisite, and members could not participate in politics and were required to be conscientious objectors. As Malcolm emerged as the leading spokesman for the Nation of Islam, its membership increased. Many converts were attracted to Malcolm not only because of his condemnations of white racism but also because of his advocacy of retaliatory violence. In 1964, after being censured by Elijah Muhammad, Malcolm resigned and made a pilgrimage to Mecca, where he was impressed by the multiracial character of orthodox Islam. In June 1964, he founded the Organization of Afro-American Unity (OAAU), based on his new philosophy of racial unity, but in February 1965 was assassinated.

In the spring of 1967, King came out against the Vietnam War, stating that racism, poverty, and American militarism and imperialism were interconnected. He was vilified by the white press but continued his plans for a poor people's March on Washington, perhaps given greater urgency by the worst summer of racial disturbance in American history, the five months from May to October 1967. More than forty riots and some 100 racial incidents took place across the country, the most serious in Newark, New York, Washington, D.C., Atlanta,

Cleveland, and Chicago. The 1968 National Advisory Commission on Civil Disorders reported that "white racism" was the principal cause of the 1967 racial disturbances and that the United States was headed toward two communities, one white, one black, separate and unequal. And then, on April 4, 1968, Dr. Martin Luther King, Jr. (1929–1968) was assassinated in Memphis, sparking a week of riots in 125 cities.

Consequently, before 1970, the two prominent male figures in the Black Revolution of the 1960s, King and Malcolm X, were dead. While historical reconstruction of that era has focused primarily on male leadership, black women also participated in the civil rights movement. Even though their activities have been viewed as primarily supportive, several women did emerge as leaders. Daisy Bates, of the NAACP, was instrumental in seeing that the rights of the "Little Rock Nine" students were protected. Activist Septima Clark (1898–1987) began her NAACP activities in the 1930s and joined SNNC in 1961 as its director of education and teaching. Ella Baker, an NAACP field organizer, was the executive secretary of SCLC as well as the catalyst for the founding of SNCC. Fannie Lou Hamer worked with both SNCC and the SCLC and was one of the founders of the Mississippi Freedom Democratic Party. Next to Hamer, Angela Davis, who worked with SNCC, gained the most media notoriety, primarily because of her ties with the Communist Party and the Black Panthers. Kathleen Neal Cleaver, now a law professor, held a national leadership position with the Black Panthers, whereas Elaine Brown was the first and only female chairperson of the Panthers.

THE POST–CIVIL RIGHTS ERA

By the 1970s, economic black nationalism was the focus of black leadership, and both surviving as well as emerging black leaders embraced Black Capitalism, which signaled the end of the Black Revolution of the 1960s. Under President Richard Nixon, the federal government turned its interest in civil rights to promoting black economic development. Yet in the distribution of both prime and subcontract federal dollars, small disadvantaged businesses, including most minority businesses, received only $8 billion out of $246 billion. Thus, while in 1987 there were 424,165 black businesses, which by 1992 had increased to 620,912 enterprises, the black business picture remained comparatively bleak. Black Americans, 12.2 percent of the population, had gross business receipts of only 1.0 percent of all American business receipts. In 1995, the total gross business receipts for the top 100 black businesses listed in *Black Enterprise* amounted to only $7.7 billion.

Moreover, a comparative review of the annual earnings of blacks and whites reveals continuing economic inequities. In 1949, five years before the *Brown* decision, black annual earnings were $6,655, compared to $12,595 for whites, with a per capita ratio of 45.3 percent. In 1984, thirty years after *Brown*, black annual earnings amounted to $13,218 versus $20,457 for whites, with a per capita ratio of 56.1 percent. By 1990, when the median family incomes of all Americans was $39,353, that of black Americans was $21,423. The inequities in the income of blacks are also reflected in the racial disparities in wealth holding: "In 1993, white families in the United States had a mean net worth of $45,740. Black families had a mean net worth of only $4,418." Economic equality had not been achieved.

However, the civil rights movement did result in an increase in black political participation. In 1941, there were only 33 elected black officials, and a decade later merely 82. By 1965, the number had increased to 280; 1,469 in 1970; 4,890 in 1980; and by 1985, 6,016 elected officials, of whom 3,801 were from the South. In 1990, there were 26 blacks in Congress, 108 state senators, 340 state representatives, 810 county officials, 314 black mayors, 2,972 city council members, and 1,561 school board officials—for a total of 6,131 black elected officials.

In particular, the election of black mayors in the nation's largest cities reflected the changing racial composition of urban America, especially in the North. In the three decades from 1940 to 1970, 1.5 million blacks left the South. Consequently, while 70 percent lived in the South in 1940, only 53 percent did so in 1970, representing an increase in the black population outside the South of from 4 million to 11 million during this period. By 1980, the changing racial composition of America's cities was also due to the increasing suburbanization of whites. Having begun in the 1960s, "white flight" was attributed to a fear of declining property values and a lowering of educational standards in the face of federal policies calling for school desegregation. While there has been a reverse migration of blacks to the South since the 1980s, open housing has actually led to an increase in black suburbanization, as well. By the 1990s, some previously white suburbs, particularly those adjacent to cities with large black populations, had become almost 100 percent black.

By the 1990s, too, there was a move toward retrenchment in federally sponsored affirmative action initiatives, supported by several Supreme Court decisions. Equal employment opportunity policies had increased black employment in many areas, and blacks were then blamed for taking jobs from whites and their seats in professional and graduate schools. Statistics show otherwise. In all areas of the economy, the occupational proportion of blacks has never approximated their percentage in the population. In actuality, the civil rights movement has benefited white women more than blacks, men and women. All in all, it is not the black population, with limited employment in white Corporate America and the public sector civil service jobs, that has usurped jobs traditionally available to white men; rather, those jobs have been appropriated by white women or have been phased out and/or transferred overseas. Furthermore, even while there have been significant advancements in black education, racial parity has not been achieved. In 1940, only 11 percent of black men and 14 percent of black women had completed high school, compared to white completion rates of 40 percent. By 1980, 87 percent of whites had completed high school, whereas 76 percent of black women and 74 percent of black men had. As to college graduates, in 1940 less than 2 percent of both black women and men completed college, compared with 5 percent of white women and 7.5 percent of white men. It was not until 1960 that more than 5 percent of blacks had completed college. Yet what was alarming in the post–civil rights era is that there was a loss in the advancements gained in black high school graduates going to college. The rate attending college had increased from 39 percent in 1973 to about 48 percent in 1977, almost equal to that of whites, but dropped to 38 percent through 1983. By 1986, only 36.5 percent of black high school graduates went directly on to college, compared to 57 percent of white high school graduates. Several factors can account for the decline in black college attendance, but the greatest correlation shows that it can be attributed to the reduction of financial aid. On the other hand, there was an increase in blacks in professional schools in business, law, and medicine, but even their numbers declined somewhat in the 1990s.

It is true that the civil rights movement, by providing for greater job opportunities for blacks, had resulted in an expanding black middle class. They could afford better housing, and their move to the suburbs also reflected attempts by parents to provide better education for their children. At the same time, the changes in the American economy, from deindustrialization to high-tech—in addition to the movement of white businesses and industries to the suburbs— were factors that contributed to an expanding black underclass left behind in the central cities. Indeed, the factors of race and class were played out with a vengeance in the 1995 case of football great O. J. Simpson, accused of murdering his white wife and her white male friend. In a convoluted way, the trial provided an example of the degree to which class has taken precedence over race in America. Black Harvard University sociologist William J. Wilson has argued that for blacks in post–civil rights America, class rather than race would determine their life chances. Here, the millionaire O. J. Simpson could afford to hire a "dream team" of lawyers to defend him. When the not-guilty verdict was announced, black Americans felt a sense of victory, perhaps more so for the symbolic value of the decision than for Simpson, who in his celebrity had long ignored the black community. His victory marked one of the few times a black man, accused of the murder of a white woman, was not sentenced to life imprisonment or death.

Besides race and class, the Civil Rights Era and the woman's movement have opened new issues of race and gender and, in so doing, have produced a new wave of black literary figures, with, for the first time in African-American cultural history, black women authors at the forefront: for example, Alice Walker, Maya Angelou, Toni Morrison, Gloria Naylor, Rita Dove, and Terry Macmillan. Moreover, several of the books written by black women were made into movies, including Macmillan's *Exhale*, Walker's *The Color Purple*, and Naylor's *The Women of Brewster Place*, which was produced by leading television talk show host Oprah Winfrey. In fact, by the mid-1990s, Winfrey had emerged as the richest black person in America, symbolic of the inroads blacks have made in several spheres of contemporary American culture.

And other changes involving the broader American culture were evident, too. While several blacks had emerged as movie producers in the 1960s and 1970s, Spike Lee represented a new generation of black film producers, and a new generation of well-paid black movie stars had emerged with tremendous cross-over audience appeal, including Denzel Washington, Whoopi Goldberg, Wesley Snipes, Halle Berry, and in the late 1990s, Will Smith. Yet, even on television, until the 1990s blacks had appeared in roles that primarily reflected the black experience. Most were comedies, including *Good Times*, depicting black life in a Chicago housing project; *The Jeffersons*, on black middle-class life in Manhattan; and *The Cosby Show*, a series on an upper-middle-class black family, starring Bill Cosby, which remained in the top ten TV shows for several years. Others would follow in the mid-1990s.

But much of the media sensation of these successful individuals has masked serious underlying problems. In a sense, symbolically, beginning in the 1980s and into the 1990s, with the emergence of rap and the black youth hip-hop culture, with their baggy pants, combat boots, knit caps, and hoods, the music of young blacks signaled all was not well in America. Their music, nihilistic in its symbolism and despair and filled with the language of the streets, was poetically profane in denouncing police brutality and the devastating effects of drugs on ghetto life. But it was also often filled with disdain and contemptuousness expressed against women. Now, in 1965, the Daniel P. Moynihan report *The Negro Family in America: The Case for National Action* had blamed such pathologies in the black ghetto on the disintegration of the black family. With limited knowledge of the black experience, it was said that, due to slavery, blacks lacked a tradition of two-parent households. Not emphasized was that until the 1930s over 90 percent of black families were headed by two parents, according to historian Herbert Gutman. Even up to the 1960s, over 75 percent of black households were headed by two parents. However, poverty, unemployment and underemployment, the dumping of drugs in the ghettos, and substandard education were taking their toll, together with the deindustrialization of America, which affected blacks and whites. With blacks, however, racism has compounded all these societal conditions. Moreover, by this last decade of the century, two significant historical forces are further compounding these conditions, marking a change in the position of blacks in America that was evident since the 1960s: the retrenchment on affirmative action and the politics of the nation's new immigration.

AMERICAN HISTORY IN THE AGE OF MULTICULTURAL DIVERSITY

In the postmodern world, there is a noticeable trend, as newcomers seek to establish a place for themselves in the American historical experience, of an immigrant vox populi striving to diminish the significance of the black experience in this nation's history. With some, the determining factor of who should and can be a "true" American and who should have a place in this nation's history is premised within the context of who came voluntarily, as opposed to those who came involuntarily. It seems as if the premise is, If the black experience could be erased from the nation's history, then so, too, could the pattern of American race relations; thereby, societal degradation by color would no longer be a factor in American life. This is ludicrous. First, while black slavery attested to the racist nature of American society, the blacks' struggle for freedom and their contributions to this nation have provided the basis for the expansion of freedom and liberties for all Americans, including the nation's new immigrants. Second, the parallels of both the Civil Rights and post–Civil Rights eras with the Reconstruction and post-Reconstruction eras, as well as that between the current retrenchment on affirmative action and the rise of Jim Crowism early in the century, are too great for race to be dismissed or to be ignored by the nation's new immigrants in their deconstruction of American history.

In the late twentieth century, race and racism remain prevailing factors that also militate against the full inclusion of immigrant people of color. In fact, inextricably linked and an inseparable part of the national past, the issues of race, class, and caste will shape—if not determine—the experiences of Asian and Latin American new immigrants on the road to their Americanization. The senseless killings of Asians by white Americans ("hate crimes") and the societal prejudices expressed against both Asians and Latin Americans underscore not just the extent to which racism still permeates this nation's life at the century's end but the existence of strong anti-immigration sentiments, too. Ironically, anti-immigrationism has existed, historically, not only among segments of the white American community but also among some black Americans. In his infamous Atlanta address in 1895, Booker T. Washington addressed the threat of economic displacement that blacks feared from America's late nineteenth-century wave of immigrants and the danger that posed of violent reactions by those blacks. The death, destruction, and devastation of the 1960s riots/civil disorders bear out Washington's counsel, as have the race riots in the 1980s and 1990s, where in New York, California, and Florida immigrant businesses in black communities have been attacked.

Finally, in this closing decade of the century, there has been a move toward a new societal construction of race, especially among the increasing number of children of African descent with mixed racial ancestry, exemplified by young golf star Tiger Woods. In describing his heritage, Woods refers to himself as "Cablinasian." In America, the historical definition of *black* has been anyone of African descent, but in response to Wood's remark, Oprah Winfrey referred to him as "America's child." Indeed, more than 80 percent of African Americans reflect this type of "Caublasian" triracial mixture. But does it really matter? It does not change the reality of the two worlds of race in this nation. In America, either one is white or one is a person of color, which in American race relations means one might as well be black. In 1903, W.E.B. Du Bois said that the problem of the twentieth century would be the problem of the color line. With the "browning" of America, anticipated by 2050, it seems probable that the problem of the twenty-first century in America will continue to be the problem of the color line. Yet in an increasingly competitive global economy, America in the twenty-first century cannot remain a world power by providing preferential treatment and opportunities only to its white population. The "dream" of the Reverend Dr. Martin Luther King, Jr. must become a reality for all Americans.

BIBLIOGRAPHIC REFERENCES

For general studies, John Hope Franklin and Alfred Moss, *From Slavery to Freedom: A History of African Americans*, 7th ed. (New York: McGraw Hill, 1994) provides an extensive bibliography, as does Philip S. Foner, *History of Black Americans*, 3 vols. (Westport, CT: Greenwood Press, 1975). See also, Lerone Bennett, Jr., *Before the Mayflower: A History of Black America*, 6th ed. (Chicago: Johnson Publishing Co., 1987); Mary Frances Berry and John W. Blassingame, *Long Memory: The Black Experience in America* (New York: Oxford, 1982); Benjamin Quarles, *The Negro in the Making of America* (New York: Collier Books, 1964); William Loren Katz, *Black People Who Made the Old West* (Trenton, NJ: Africa World Press, 1992); Leon Litwack and August Meier, eds., *Black Leaders of the Nineteenth Century* (Urbana: University of Illinois Press, 1988); and John Hope Franklin and August Meier, eds., *Black Leaders of the Twentieth Century* (Urbana: University of Illinois Press, 1982). Note also Herbert Gutman, *The Black Family in Slavery and Freedom, 1750–1925* (New York: Pantheon Books, 1976); Eileen Southern, *The Music of Black America: A History* (New York: W. W. Norton, 1971); C. Eric Lincoln and Lawrence H. Mamiya, *The Black Church in the African American Experience* (Durham, NC: Duke University Press, 1990); Forrest G. Wood, *The Arrogance of Faith: Christianity and Race in America from the Colonial Era to the Twentieth Century* (New York: A. A. Knopf, 1990); Harold Cruse, *The Crisis of the Negro Intellectual* (New York: Morrow, 1967); Darlene Clarke-Hine and Kathleen Thompson, *A Shining Thread of Hope: The History of Black Women in America* (New York: Broadway Books, 1998); and Juliet E. K. Walker, *The History of Black Business in America: Capitalism, Race, Entrepreneurship* (New York: Twayne, 1998).

On African Americans, slavery, and race, 1619–1865, see Winthrop Jordan, *White over Black: American Racial Attitudes toward the Negro, 1550–1812* (Chapel Hill: University of North Carolina Press, 1968); T. H. Breen and Stephen Innes, *"Myne Owne Ground": Race and Freedom on Virginia's Eastern Shore, 1640–1676* (New York: Oxford, 1980); and Edmund Morgan, *American Slavery, American Freedom: The Ordeal of Colonial Virginia* (New York: W. W. Norton, 1975). Also see Benjamin Quarles, *The Negro in the American Revolution* (Chapel Hill: University of North Carolina Press, 1961), and Donald R. Wright, *African Americans in the Early Republic, 1789–1831* (Arlington Heights, IL: Harlan Davidson, 1993). For general studies on slavery, see John Blassingame, *The Slave Community: Plantation Life in the Antebellum South*, rev. ed. (New York: Oxford, 1979); Eugene Genovese, *Roll Jordan Roll: The World the Slaves Made* (New York, 1974); Leslie Owens, *This Species of Property: Slave Life and Culture in the Old South* (New York: Oxford, 1976); Michael Angelo Gomez, *Exchanging Our Country Marks: The Transformation of African Identities in the Colonial and Antebellum South* (Chapel Hill: University of North Carolina Press, 1998); and Brenda E. Stevenson, *Life in Black and White: Family and Community in the Slave South* (New York: Oxford University Press, 1996). On slaves and free blacks, see Gary B. Mills, *The Forgotten People: Cane River's Creoles of Color* (Baton Rouge: Louisiana State University Press, 1977); and Juliet E. K. Walker, *Free Frank: A Black Pioneer on the Antebellum Frontier* (Lexington: 1994 [1983]). On free blacks, see Leon F. Litwack, *North of Slavery: The Negro in the Free States, 1790–1860* (Chicago: University of Chicago Press, 1961); Leonard P. Curry, *The Free Black in Urban America, 1800–1850: The Shadow of the Dream* (Chicago: University of Chicago Press, 1981); Ira Berlin, *Slaves without Masters: The Free Negro in the Antebellum South* (New York: Pantheon Books, 1974); James Oliver Horton, *Free People of Color: Inside the African American Community* (Washington, D.C.: Smithsonian Institution Press, 1993). On black women from slavery to freedom, see Deborah Gray White, *Arn't I a Woman? Female Slaves in the Plantation South* (New York: Norton, 1985); Jacqueline Jones, *Labor of Love, Labor of Sorrow: Black Women, Work and the Family from Slavery to the Present* (New York: Basic Books, 1985); Tera W. Hunter, *To 'Joy My Freedom': Southern Black Women's Lives and Labors after the Civil War* (Cambridge, MA: Harvard Univeristy Press, 1997); and Gerda Lerner, ed., *Black Women in White America: A Documentary History* (New York: Pantheon Books, 1972).

On blacks from the Civil War to the present, see Benjamin Quarles, *The Negro in the Civil War* (Boston: Little, Brown & Co., 1953); John Hope Franklin, *Reconstruction* (Chicago: University of Chicago Press, 1961); Eric Foner, *Reconstruction: America's Unfinished Revolution, 1863–1877* (New York: Harper and Row, 1988); C. Vann Woodward, *The Strange Career of Jim Crow*, 3rd ed. rev. (New York: A. A. Knopf, 1974); Louis R. Harlan, *Booker T. Washington, the Wizard of Tuskegee 1901–1915* (New York: Oxford, 1983); Kenneth Marvin Hamilton, *Black Towns and Profit: Promotion and Development in the Trans-Appalachian West, 1877–1915* (Urbana: University of Illinois Press, 1991); Willard B. Gatewood, *Aristocrats of Color: The Black Elite, 1880–1920* (Bloomington: Indiana University Press, 1990); Leon F. Litwack, *Trouble in Mind: Black Southerners in the Age of Jim Crow* (New York: Alfred A. Knopf, 1998); John S. Butler, *Entrepreneurship and Self-Help Among Black Americans: A Reconsideration of Race and Economics* (Albany: State University of New York Press, 1991); Joe William Trotter, *The Great Migration in Historical Perspective* (Bloomington: Indiana University Press, 1991); James Grossman, *Land of Hope: Chicago, Blacks, Southerners, and the Great Migration* (Chicago: University of Chicago Press, 1989); David Levering Lewis, *When Harlem Was in Vogue* (New York: A. A. Knopf, 1981); Richard Kluger, *Simple Justice: The History of* Brown v. Board of Education *and Black America's Struggle for Equality* (New York: A. A. Knopf, 1976); Robert Weisbrot, *Freedom Bound: A History of America's Civil Rights Movement* (New York: Norton, 1991); Aldon D. Morris, *The Origins of the Civil Rights Movement: Black Communities Organizing for Change* (New York: Free Press 1989); Robert Brisbane, *Black Activism: Black Revolution in the U.S., 1954–1970* (Valley Forge, PA: Judson Press, 1984); Robin D. G. Kelley, *Race Rebels: Culture, Politics, and the Black Working Class* (New York: Free Press, 1994); Tricia Rose, *Black Noise: Rap Music and Black Culture in Contemporary America* (Hanover, NH: Wesleyan University Press, 1994).

For contemporary information, note Gerald David Jaynes and Robin M. Williams, eds., *A Common Destiny: Blacks and American Society* (Washington, D.C.: National Academy Press, 1989); Jack Salzman, David L. Smith, and Cornel West, eds., *Encyclopedia of African-American Culture and History*, 5 vols. (New York: MacMillan Library Reference/Simon and Schuster/Prentice Hall, 1996); Darlene Clark Hine, Rosalyn Terborg-Penn, and Elsa Barkley Brown, eds., *Black Women in America: An Historical Encyclopedia* (Bloomington: Indiana University Press, 1994, 1993); Randall M. Miller and John David Smith, eds., *Dictionary of Afro-American Slavery*, rev. ed. (Westport, CT: Praeger, 1997); John N. Ingham and Lynne B. Feldman, *African-American Business Leaders: A Biographical Dictionary* (Westport, CT: Greenwood Press, 1994); and Juliet E. K. Walker, ed., *Encyclopedia of African American Business History* (Westport, CT: Greenwood Publishing, forthcoming).

AMERICAN INDIANS

Alice B. Kehoe

American Indians are not immigrants. America is their ancestral homeland. They were here when Columbus made his landfall; they were here when the Norse sailed into the Strait of Belle Isle; they were here when Polynesians found no more islands but a continent. American Indians are the only Americans whose entire heritage is here, has always been here, and is to be preserved only here. At the outset, it is important to realize that American Indians are the population of a continent composed of many nations. Some originally ruled thousands, whereas others were autonomous communities of a few hundred; population size correlated with density of resources and agricultural potential. America was already multicultural when the first overseas colonizers arrived.

In this chapter, I shall summarize the history of these First Nations of America, both the millennia known primarily through archaeological research and the more recent centuries documented primarily through written records supplemented by oral history. Comprehending the number and diversity of the First Nations is fundamental to understanding their contemporary situations, for much of the tension comes from the unconformity between this fact and the U.S. policy of treating members of the First Nations as a single class. Few Americans are familiar with these long histories.

ENTRY INTO AMERICA

Most of the First Nations consider themselves truly indigenous, descended from humans created here through the agency of transcendental power. Their homelands are the centers of their worlds. Some nations aver they have lived in their homeland from time immemorial; others retain histories of migrations from places of emergence to the divinely appointed abode. Such histories are encoded in landscape features, rendering the homeland a text of revelations.

In the Pleistocene era, before a rise in sea level drowned an immense expanse of coastal lowlands and the steppes now under the Bering Strait, Siberia and Alaska were the west and east regions of ''Beringia,'' where mammoths and giant bison as well as caribou, horses, elk, and sheep grazed. Humans hunting on the Beringian plains, or fishing and spearing sea mammals along Beringia's southern coast, slowly colonized what became America; the evidence for this is a few campsites in eastern Siberia and in Alaska with generally similar, although by no means identical, stone artifacts. Human habitation sites are as early in South America as in North America—around 11,000 B.C.—which suggests to many archaeologists that colonization proceeded southward along the now-drowned Pacific coastal plains, rather than initially southeastward into interior North America and thence south.

Human occupation is demonstrated throughout the United States by 9500 B.C. (central Canada remained under glacial ice for several more millennia). The principal ''signature'' of these ''Paleoindians'' is the expertly chipped Clovis-style stone blade, used for knives and spearpoints. Subsequent stone blade styles, for example, Folsom, Plainview, Agate Basin, and Hell Gap, lend their names to archaeologists' ''cultures,'' that is, assemblages of distinctive and also simpler stone artifacts from campsites and winter villages. Paleoindians successfully hunted big game, particularly through trapping animals in natural corrals such as box canyons or boggy waterholes, where they could not easily escape the spearmen. Paleoindians no doubt also collected berries and other vegetable foods, but little evidence of such perishables has been recovered, contrasted with the stone blades and butchered bones from hunting. America around 9500 B.C. was quite different from its Holocene (i.e., present post–Ice Age) appearance. At the end of the Pleistocene, vast lakes and huge rushing rivers drained the melting continental glaciers, and the Mississippi Valley may well have been impassable for most of its length, channeling west-east human movement south toward the Gulf of Mexico. To what degree Indian management of vegetation to develop and maintain grasslands, forests with ample browse, or groves of preferred trees may have produced the historic landscapes is a question not yet answered outside a few locales.

CULTURAL DEVELOPMENT

Languages and cultural diversity proliferated over the dozen millennia America has been inhabited by populations of the First Nations. There was, of course, adaptation to climates and resources, but continental trade routes and adventuresome journeys crosscut regional specializations. The pre-Columbian pattern strongly resembled economic differentiation in the United States prior to the post–Civil War construction of transcontinental railroads, with highly productive agriculture in the Southeast-Midwest, less productive agriculture in the Northeast, fishing in the Great Lakes, and meat production on the Plains. Rivers were the principal transportation routes and foci of major settlements.

Anthropologists (following Edward Sapir, 1921) classify indigenous American languages into six stocks. Algonkian (also spelled Algonquian) covers much of the Northeast, from Chesapeake Bay through Canada, west to the Rockies, with outliers (or possibly the original homeland) in northern California. Siouan covers much of the Midwest, from the Carolinas to the Rockies and generally bordering Algonkian to the north. Aztec-Tanoan runs from eastern Oregon southward through the Great Basin into northwest Mexico and then east to central Mexico, where one of its languages, Nahuatl, was the language of the Aztec empire. Penutian is mostly along the Pacific from British Columbia through California and to Southwestern Mexico, with a branch in the Plateau. Hokan is primarily Californian. Athabascan (Athapascan, Dené) dominates northwest Canada and interior Alaska, with an outlier in the U.S. Southwest, probably the result of protohistoric migration from western Canada. Each of these great stocks is comparable to Indo-European in comprising dozens of languages grouped into families (comparable to Germanic or Romance). The number of stocks and of languages alike testify to the millennia of cultural development and population movements in America, that is to say, to the long histories of the First Nations.

Languages correlate only roughly with sections of America. A fundamental division of indigenous America is into a Continental Core, comprising Mexico (including its northwestern frontier, the American Southwest) and America east of the Rockies as far north as the St. Lawrence Valley and Great Lakes; Pacific Drainage west of the Rockies, through British Columbia; and High Latitudes (most of Canada and Alaska). Most of the Continental Core societies depended on maize agriculture; Pacific Drainage societies cultivated plants native to the regions rather than Mexican-originated maize; and High Latitude societies perforce depended upon hunting and fishing, since agriculture is not possible in the cold climate. Turkeys and dogs were the only domesticated animals, but regular, controlled burning of habitats managed game and selected for desired plants throughout America. Landscapes met by the first European immigrants were largely modified by First Nations' techniques for enhancing harvests.

Conventionally, America is divided into "culture areas," geographic regions with characteristic indigenous cultural patterns. A standard list of culture areas sets out: Mexico; the Southwest; the Southeast; the Northeast; Prairie-Plains; Intermontane (or Great Basin and Plateau); California; Northwest Coast; Subarctic; and Arctic. The Southeast, Northeast, and Midwest can be subsumed in an Eastern Woodlands culture area. Both adaptation to climate and resources and contacts with neighboring societies influenced societies within a culture area to share its general cultural pattern; and balancing this tendency toward geographic distinctions was the long-distance trade that carried artifact styles, food sources, such as maize, and religious ideas over thousands of kilometers. Long-distance trade appears in Paleoindian sites and has always been significant in America.

Archaeologists recognize an Archaic epoch following the termination of the Pleistocene. From around 7000 to about 1000 B.C.E., populations remained dependent on hunting, fishing, and gathering wild plants, achieving sophisticated knowledge of regional potentials by the third millennium B.C.E. Population density reached levels comparable to most of later millennia, testifying to strategically sound scheduling of efficient harvesting and processing techniques. Health, evidenced through analyses of skeletons, was good, with well-balanced, adequate diets and seasonal movements between camps and villages helping to keep living sites clean. In the Lower Mississippi Valley, earthen mounds were constructed as early as 3000 B.C.E., and an impressive set of platform mounds and concentric earthwork ridges were built in northeastern Louisiana, at Poverty Point, late in the second millennium. In the western Great Lakes region, copper was quarried from rich deposits and worked into a variety of implements and ornaments from the third millennium on. Indigenous grains—chenopods, marsh elder, sumpweed—and a squash native to the Ozarks were cultivated in the Eastern Woodlands. The Archaic period is said to terminate in the first millennium B.C.E., when pottery was introduced, possibly from northern South America.

The late first millennium B.C.E. saw conical burial mounds come into fashion in the Ohio Valley, developing around 2,000 years ago into the Hopewell cultures. These were societies subsisting primarily on indigenous grains and game, planting a little maize, living in hamlets or farmsteads dispersed along river valleys, and constructing remarkable, unique, giant earthen geometric figures as well as burial mounds. In the mounds are log tombs containing, usually, a man with copper, sheet-mica, stone ornaments and carvings, and fine pottery, with a few other bodies, presumably wives and retainers, placed along the sides of the tomb. Such evidence of class stratification is insufficient to explain the practice of building huge geometric circles, squares, and linking causeways. An entire golf course now lies within the Great Circle at Newark, Ohio. Hundreds of these perfectly engineered figures once lined the Scioto River Valley from its confluence with the Ohio. In Illinois, tombs and mounds similar to the Ohio Hopewell are found but not the extraordinary geometric embankments. Hopewell tombs contain obsidian carried from Yellowstone Park in Montana, marine shells, and other proof of continent-wide trade. A few fragments of textiles, preserved by being wrapped around copper objects, demonstrate high expertise in fabrics. Archaeologists are puzzled by Hopewell, a cultural pattern that has many of the attributes of urban societies (monumental architecture, long-distance trade, agriculture, skilled craftsworkers) but seems not to have had cities.

Hopewell went into decline in the fourth century C.E., probably affected by a colder phase of climate that lasted three centuries, until the eighth century. At that time, a new variety of maize appears in both the Southwest and the Eastern Woodlands, utilized in both regions for intensive agriculture supporting urban-style populations. In the Southwest, Chaco Canyon (northern New Mexico) is the scene of several adobe-and-stone apartment-block towns (pueblos) linked to other towns on the plateau above by long, straight roads. In the desert of southern Arizona, Hohokam societies built irrigation canals fed from the Gila and

Salt Rivers. With red-painted brown pottery, rectangular adobe houses and plat-form mounds, and ballgame courts, the Hohokam resemble societies in north-west Mexico and probably were the ancestors of the 'O'dham. Chaco and its allies must have been ancestral to some of the Pueblo nations. In the Eastern Woodlands, the urban societies based on intensive maize agriculture in major river valleys are called Mississippian, made visible by their large pyramidal mounds but with their modest adobe-plastered wooden homes and larger wooden public buildings having decayed.

Cahokia, at the confluence of the Missouri and Mississippi Rivers (present-day St. Louis), was the largest city in pre-Columbian America. Its population was surely over 10,000, although it is difficult to know how many of its satellite villages and outlying farm hamlets ought to be counted as its metropolitan dis-trict. Cahokia is stupendous; its principal mound is still 100 feet high, 1,000 by 790 feet at its base, and its top level larger than a football field. Before it a grand plaza prepared with tons of fine soil stretches 1,000 by 1,300 feet. Dozens of other mounds line the grand plaza and secondary plazas set around the central precinct. Altogether, the city resembles the great cities of Mexico, except that it did not build with stone; Cahokia's principal mound is exceeded in size only by the Pyramids of the Sun and Moon in Teotihuacán, in the Valley of Mexico. The territory ruled out of Cahokia is estimated at 52,000 square kilometers (20,000 square miles). One of its small mounds revealed, upon excavation, the burial of one of the lords of the realm, a man laid upon a blanket, covered with thousands of glittering shell beads in the shape of a hawk. Underneath him and in pits around him were more than 200 human sacrifices, along with tribute from the four corners of his domain.

The relatively swift emergence of urban societies in America during the tenth century C.E. suggests the possibility of trade relations with the Toltec empire in Mexico. Trade between central Mexico and Chaco is proven by New Mexico turquoise found in Mexican cities and tropical Mexican macaws kept in pens in Chaco pueblos, presumably as a source of gorgeous feathers for ritual costumes. Trade between Cahokia and Mexico has not been demonstrated but may have involved such perishables as cloth, leather, and slaves. Chaco and Cahokia de-clined in the thirteenth century as rapidly as they had emerged, and if trade with Mexico was significant to their power, their declines may have been associated with the fall of the Toltec empire in 1168 C.E. In the Southwest, a new pueblo-style town, Paquimé (also called Casas Grandes), expanded in Chihuahua, just south of the New Mexico border during the thirteenth century and became the major entrepôt until about 1500, continuing to export turquoise and import ma-caws and ornamental marine shells as well as fine ceramics (and probably cotton cloth). In the Midwest and Southeast, numerous small kingdoms filled the void left by the decline of the Cahokian state. Spiro, in easternmost Oklahoma on the Arkansas River, was one of these kingdoms; its principal mound contained the tomb of a lord buried with quantities of exquisitely etched chalices made out of conch shells, carved pipes and figurines, embossed copper plates, feather-ornamented cloaks, and textiles including gauze and lace. Many of the decorated objects in this tomb were heirlooms from earlier generations, and some may have originated in Cahokia.

While agricultural-based, urban societies developed in the Southwest and Southeast-Midwest, other sections of the country fostered cultural development maximizing their principal resources. In the northern Midwest, wild rice was (and is) harvested in a manner that maintains the stands year after year, furnishing a reliable staple grain. On the Plains, bison herds were driven into corrals and the meat cut very thin, dried, and pounded with rendered fat and dried berries to make nutritious, long-lasting, pemmican, a balanced food efficiently packed into storage bags; Plains people also regularly used the potatolike prairie turnips. On the Plateau, camas lily bulbs were cultivated, baked, and made into flour; salmon were dried and pounded like pemmican, and the salmon meal and camas flour not only sustained local families but were sold to travelers. California nations processed acorns into meal, and Great Basin people depended on piñon nuts. In the Pacific Northwest, salmon and *wapato*, a tuber called "Indian potato," were the basic foods, served with eulachon fish oil. Throughout America, deer, elk, and smaller game were hunted, often being driven toward bowmen waiting at fences or nets. Waterfowl were important, too, and in the West might be captured in large nets strung across flyways. Weirs extended the principle of efficient hunting to fishing. Thus, both animal and plant resources were managed for high yields in every section of America. These techniques appeared primitive to European colonists bringing their plow agriculture and domesticated livestock, but in fact the First Nations' practices were sophisticated, utilized detailed scientific knowledge of ecology, and aimed for enough diversity to ensure a food supply even if some species did not do well in a particular year.

It is worth pointing out that American Indians did not "worship Mother Earth." That is a notion invented by modern seekers after spiritual wisdom who assume Western conquerors overcame noble savages unchanged for thousands of years. The idea that the First Nations of America retained a primordial religion, one that celebrated a Mother Earth rather than the Judaeo-Christian-Islamic patriarchal God, denies history to the First Nations, debases their many prophets and philosophers, and simplifies into a childish nature worship a number of profound cosmologies. First Nations thinkers generally conceptualized a female reproductive power gifted to women and plants, complementing the power to kill sought by men as hunters and defenders of their communities. As plants grow out of the earth, so female power lies *in* the earth, yet it is not *the* Earth—that is, in fact, a Greek concept.

THE ERA OF EUROPEAN INVASIONS

Western America

Columbus was not the first European to find America. Norse from Greenland tried a settlement in northern Newfoundland 500 years before, and earlier occasional contacts are quite probable. What Columbus heralded was the determined invasion and conquest of American nations. Europeans fought Americans mile by mile across the continent for 400 years and, again and again, won only because First Nations were decimated by epidemics of diseases to which they had no immunity. Europeans died of such illnesses as smallpox, diptheria, measles, and cholera, but after generations of exposure, mortality was not as high as among indigenous Americans, and equally important, in nearly every epidemic among Europeans, some people who had survived an earlier bout of the disease could take care of the sick. Among American nations, the epidemics hit everyone, and an entire community would be sick, with thirst and hunger exacerbating the illness because no one was able to prepare food and go for water. As much as 90 percent of the inhabitants of a region died in these "virgin soil" epidemics; one instance is the 1616–1618 epidemic that killed large numbers of New England inhabitants, leaving untended fields for the Plymouth Pilgrims to expropriate. That epidemic presumably came from the hundreds of European fishing boats off Canada that put into harbors in the Maritimes to pack their catches for the voyage back and trade with the Indians. As early as 1580, there were 17,000 European men in eastern Canada for codfishing and whaling.

Mexico became the main source of the devastating epidemics. The diseases passed northward from the early sixteenth century conquests (Cortés and his Tlaxcalan allies owed their hard-fought victory over the Aztec to an epidemic infiltrating their besieged capital). After the mid-sixteenth century, no Europeans saw Indian nations as they had been before the invasions: Epidemics raged ahead of the armies, missionaries, and traders. Among the last to see indigenous nations in normal strength were Coronado in the Southwest, 1540–1541, traveling as far as Kansas, and De Soto in the Southeast, 1539–1542, traveling in a great circle up into Georgia, over to the Mississippi and up the Arkansas, then back to the Mississippi Valley, where he died of fever. A generation later, when Spain, France, and England resumed attempts to colonize America, indigenous populations were reduced, political power decentralized or in the throes of reorganization, and economic patterns modified. The smaller postepidemic populations in their smaller towns led to estimates of indigenous American population size much less than actually had prevailed. A reasonable estimate of First Nations in America at 1490 is about 5 million people, although arguments have been made that it could have been two or even three times more. And, it must be kept in mind, some earlier towns were larger, political organizations more hierarchical, occupational specialization greater, and trade more substantive, all the concomitants of greater population size and density. The usual picture of American nations is comparable to what observers would have said of Europe if they had seen it only in 1350, after the Black Death had taken one-third to one-half its population, reduced or obliterated communities, and left fields to revert to the wild.

Spain's campaigns of conquest continued to 1697, the fall of the last Mayan kingdom, the Itzás' Tayasal in the Petén lowlands of Yucatán. Northwest Mexico had been reorganized under Spanish domination, carried out principally by Jesuit missionaries until the crown expelled the order from Mexico in 1767. Indigenous nations of the Northwest fought Mexico's appropriations of their lands and water, the settlement of mestizos, the establishment of commercial plantations and ranches, and mining. One of these nations, the Yaqui, claim never to have been conquered nor to have legitimately signed any treaties; Yaqui armed resistance culminated during the Díaz regime, 1905–1910, with the deportation of 5,000 Yaquis sold as slaves into Yucatán, while hundreds fled north into Arizona. In their refugee village on the edge of Tucson, they attracted Anglos with their colorful Easter Deer Dances. The United States granted Arizona Yaquis a reservation in 1964.

Aztec-Tanoans native to the present United States may be classified, linguistically, between Uto-Aztecans and Tanoans. Uto-Aztecans include the 'O'odham (known as Pima and Papago) in the southern Arizona desert, where they were granted a reservation in 1918, and the Paiute, Ute, Shoshoni, and Comanche of the semiarid Great Basin between the Rockies and the Sierra Nevada of California. Probable ancestors of the 'O'odham built hundreds of miles of irrigation canals to farm the Gila and Salt River Valleys, but drought and changes in rainfall patterns in the thirteenth and fourteenth centuries apparently disabled these systems. They lived in extended-family *rancherías*, harvesting cactus fruit, hunting, and farming maize, tepary beans, and squashes where water could be found. This pattern was common among Uto-Aztecans, the northern groups substituting the collection of pine nuts where climate made maize unreliable. Where accessible, fish were channeled into weirs, and waterfowl as well as rabbits and antelope were caught in huge nets. Mormon colonization beginning in 1847, followed after 1859 by other Euro-American mining and ranching protected by military forts, drove Paiutes, Utes, and Shoshoni away from their lakes and streams, forcing many to work as farm and domestic labor and others into scavenging. Descriptions of these parlous times recorded in the late nineteenth century, or taken down by anthropologists in the 1930s, did not take cognizance of the colonial situation, instead assuming that the postconquest poverty represented a pre-European pattern. Paiutes, Utes, and Shoshoni became textbook examples of "primitive foragers," supporting a Social Darwinist ideology that such "primitives" could not resist European domination.

Tanoan is the language stock spoken in thirteen of the twenty-one existing pueblos: Hopi (whose language is Uto-Aztecan), Taos, Picuris, Sandía, Isleta, San Juan, Santa Clara, Pojoaque, San Ildefonso, Nambe, Tesuque, Jemez, and Hano (who live with the Hopi). Seven pueblos speak Keresan languages, unrelated to any of the six major stocks: Ácoma, Laguna, Cochití, Zía, Santo Domingo, Santa Ana, and San Felipe. Zuni (Áshiwi in its own language) speak a language apparently unique. Hopi and Zuni are far to the west of the other pueblos, most of whom live along the Río Grande. There is archaeological evidence that inhabitants of pueblos on the Colorado Plateau emigrated to the Río Grande during the thirteenth-fourteenth-century droughts and climate shift, settling among villages already farming in the Valley. Spanish colonization beginning in 1598 escalated an Indian slave trade, imposed heavy taxes in labor and goods on the pueblos, and endeavored to force entire populations to follow Christianity. The pueblos allied in 1680 to revolt, driving the Spanish out, but by 1696, after four years of hard fighting, the Spanish army reconquered this northern borderland. The pueblos fought again for independence, against Mexico in 1837 and against the United States in 1847. Military setbacks led the pueblos to secretly maintain traditional government and religion while the alien power dealt with front men.

Navajo and Apache—together, Apacheans—are southwestern nations that moved into the region perhaps as late as the fifteenth century. They speak Athabascan (Dené) languages, related to those of western Canada and interior Alaska. Apparently, a few bands shifted to the High Plains along the Rocky Mountain Front and gradually expanded southward, hunting bison and then picking up knowledge of maize agriculture in southern Colorado. Coronado in 1540 encountered nomadic Apaches on the southern Plains, while forebears of the Navajo and western Apache cultivated small fields on canyon floors and hunted in New Mexico and Arizona. Raiding pueblo towns and then Spanish settlements and pack trains was part of the Apachean economy, practices that continued to the end of the nineteenth century for some Apache. Apachean small community size and mobility allowed them to stage quick raids and disappear into rough landscape, while skimming from agricultural peoples enabled them to survive on a rugged terrain too poor for full-scale agriculture. When in 1863 the United States sent troops to guard the Santa Fe Trail route between Missouri and California from Confederate appropriation, the Navajo were systematically rounded up and interned in Fort Sumner in New Mexico, to be released after the Civil War in 1868. Chiricahua Apaches were interned in Florida until 1894, then permitted to move to Oklahoma but not back to the Southwest until 1913.

Spanish America included California up to the Mexican War of 1848. Native nations include Hokan-speaking Pomo, Chumash, Mohave, and Diegueño (Kumeyaay), Penutian-speaking Klamath, Modoc, Maidu, Yokuts, Miwok, and Patwin, Athabascan-stock Hupa and Tolowa, and Yurok and Wiyot distantly related to Algonkian. What had been some of the densest populations in America—living by sowing indigenous seed-bearing grasses and harvesting acorns, fish, and game, including sea mammals along the coast—were decimated between 1769 and the 1870s, first by coerced labor in concentration camp–style missions and then by dispossession from their lands and resources. During the first couple of decades after the U.S. takeover, miners and ranchers shot Indians on Sunday afternoons for sport, openly bought Indians as slaves, and forbade Indians to testify in court against white men. These outrages declined without any mitigation of racism, and a century later, California Indians would be outnumbered in California by an influx of Indians from other First Nations; by 1990, over one fourth of Indians in the state would identify themselves as Cherokee.

Eastern America

Turning to the Anglo-dominated eastern half of America, three centuries of piecemeal appropriations followed Ponce de León's aborted Florida colony of 1521. The standard story is initial dependence on Indian food stores (in 1607 the Powhatan sold Jamestown three large rowboats full of corn), then bloody skirmishes for a generation or two, then wars of extermination once the European incursions reached population and economic strength sufficient to supplant the Indian nation. For coastal Virginia, this happened in 1644; for New England, with the Pequot War of 1637 and King Philip's War of 1676. ("King Philip," Metacomet, was sachem of the Wampanoags, whose territory included Plymouth Colony.) On the colonial frontier, Indian nations were sought as allies, much as Cortés had allied with the Tlaxcala and other enemies of the Aztec. Iroquois especially were integral to shifting balances of power in the Northeast. They were long-distance traders from precontact times, in the vanguard of the fur trade (and were noted working for a trader in Montana as early as 1792) and courted by British agents. In 1649, the Haudenosaunee League of the five Iroquois nations south of the St. Lawrence River destroyed rival Huron towns north of the river. League power was respected until the defeat of their British allies against the Americans in 1781 and, indeed, still in 1787, when Benjamin Franklin used the League to argue the viability of a federal system preserving states' rights.

Hundreds of Iroquois fled after 1781 to British Canada, where they were given reserves, while those remaining in the United States were relegated to marginal reservations, their prime lands made available as homesteads to Revolutionary War veterans. U.S. policy demanded the Iroquois disperse their communities into family farms where men, no longer free to pursue trade, should labor in the fields—traditionally the work of groups of related women—and their wives, isolated from their kin, would carry out European-style household tasks. Iroquois resistance was crystallized in 1799 by the visions of the Handsome Lake, an impoverished sachem who began preaching a gospel of accommodation to U.S. policy concomitant with retention of core Iroquois values and rituals. His longhouse religion is practiced by many Iroquois today and strengthens Iroquois insistence that they remain sovereign although forced to deal with the encapsulating powers of the United States and Canada.

The Southeast, like the Northeast, has both Siouan-stock and Algonkian-stock languages, plus Muskogean, an independent group of languages. Algonkian languages were in regions of early English colonization, for example, spoken by the Powhatan. Cherokee, like Iroquois to the north, is classified within Macro-Siouan. Creek (Muskogee), Choctaw, Chickasaw, Alabama, Koasati, Hitchiti, and Apalachee are all Muskogean, as is the Seminoles' language, Mikasuki. Cherokee, Creek, Choctaw, Chickasaw, and Seminole are known as the Five Civilized Tribes because they quickly adopted many European material practices, from crops and metal tools to brick houses, European clothing, literacy, and the use of African-descended slaves. Thus, it was peculiarly ironic that these five nations bore the brunt of U.S. land appropriation, culminating in the 1830 Indian Removal Act that resulted in the mass deportations to western territory, since called the Trail of Tears. An 1831 Supreme Court ruling by John Marshall in *Cherokee Nation v. Georgia* declared Indian nations to be ''domestic dependent nations''—a new legal concept—subordinate to the U.S. federal government. Along with the following year's *Worcester v. Georgia*, establishing exclusive federal jurisdiction over these ''domestic dependent nations,'' and the 1902 *Cherokee Nation v. Hitchcock*, upholding U.S. power to overrule Indian laws, Marshall's decision legitimated U.S. domination over nations that had negotiated treaties. U.S. perfidy is illustrated by the experience of the Lakota, who agreed in the 1868 Fort Laramie Treaty to cede a substantial portion of their domain, retaining the Great Sioux Reservation in Dakota Territory. In 1876, the Black Hills were removed from the Sioux Reservation so that gold mining could proceed unhampered, and in 1889 Congress cut up the reservation, with five separate sections reserved in South Dakota and the remaining half of the Great Sioux Reservation opened for Euro-American homesteading.

The 1887 Dawes Allotment Act was the single most destructive action of the U.S. Congress against its ''domestic dependent nations.'' This act authorized allotting farm acreage, usually 160 acres, to individual Indians, these allotments to lie within existing reservations and land not required for allotments to be removed from trust status and sold. No provision was made for any increase in reservation populations, nor were allotment acreages generally adjusted for local conditions under which 160 acres could be too little to support a family. The Curtis Act of 1898 strengthened the Dawes Act and specifically enforced it over the Five Civilized Tribes in Oklahoma Territory. In *Lone Wolf v. Hitchcock* (1903) the Supreme Court decided that consent of Indians, such as the Kiowa Lone Wolf, need not be obtained for federal decrees. The Court in *Lone Wolf* repeated Marshall's declaration that Indians are ''a dependent race'' and added that they are ''ignorant,'' needing to be ruled by the ''Christian people'' of the United States. Although a majority had acquired citizenship before that time, not until 1924 were Indians, as a class, considered full U.S. citizens.

Midwest and Plains

Removal of the southeastern nations to west of the Mississippi, of course, impinged upon the nations of the Midwest and Plains. A Sauk leader, Black Hawk, had fought the Cherokee, then returned to his Illinois farm. One day in 1829, coming home from a winter hunt, he discovered a Euro-American colonist had taken over not only his land but his very house. U.S. militia, among whom was a young Abraham Lincoln, waged war against the Sauk until, by 1832, many had been killed and refugees captured and sent across the Mississippi to Iowa, including Black Hawk. A treaty prepared in Chicago in 1833 directed all Indians still east of the Mississippi to remove to the West, although the Menomini and Chippewa (Ojibwe or Anishinabe) along the northern Great Lakes, beyond maize agriculture limits, were permitted to retain portions of their homelands as reservations. As with Cherokee, Creek, and other southeastern nations, some midwestern families of Potawatomi, Ho-Chunk (Winnebago), Miami, and others hid out in hills or forests or remained on the basis of intermarriage with traders.

Plains Indians are the stereotype, one created by nineteenth-century conditions. European colonists introduced horses, principally by employing (or enslaving) Indians to tend stock on New Mexico ranches. Use of horses spread northward through the Plains and to its western and eastern borderlands, reaching southern Canada by the mid-eighteenth century. Packhorses increased the amount of goods families could transport, encouraging more use of tipis and perhaps more reliance on extensive hunting trips; concomitantly, midwestern and prairie communities were pressured to abandon their villages and farms. Nations, such as the Cheyenne in western Minnesota, chose, at the end of the eighteenth century, to live year-round in tipi camps, planting maize, beans, and squashes near spring camps and returning with hopes of harvest in the fall. The Lakota, westernmost of the Sioux neighboring the Cheyenne, were historically more dependent on bison hunting than the Yankton and Dakota Sioux in Minnesota, who harvested wild rice in northern lakes and hunted deer as well as bison. Partly maneuvering to monopolize regional access to European traders fanning out along the Great Lakes and their tributary rivers, partly seeking control of prime bison and horse pasturage, all fought over the western prairies and high Plains. The western prairies and high Plains were contested by Siouan-speaking Lakota and Assiniboin; Algonkian-speaking Cheyenne, Arapaho, Gros Ventres, and Blackfoot; Caddoan-speaking Pawnee and Arikara; and the midwestern Siouan-speaking Ponca, Omaha, Kansa, Osage, Quapaw, Oto, Missouri, and Iowa. Along the Missouri River in North Dakota, the Siouan-speaking Mandan and Hidatsa maintained relatively large towns of domed wooden houses heavily insulated with sod, producing surplus corn in fields in the Missouri trench and trading this, manufactures, slaves, and horses to the nomadic communities.

European traders utilized traditional rendezvous and the established towns, amplifying rather than initiating Indian trade. One significant but neglected historical fact is that the Hudson's Bay Company factor, Peter Fidler, wintering in 1801 at the post he built on the South Saskatchewan River in what is now southeastern Alberta, asked a visiting Blackfoot leader, Ac ko mok ki, to draw a map of the country. Ac ko mok ki's map covered 200,000 square miles, from the Mandan towns on the central Missouri west to Idaho, and from Alberta to central Wyoming. He drew the Missouri River system with its tributaries, the passes and valleys of the Rockies, the locations of dozens of Indian nations, and the Snake River leading to the Pacific. Fidler noted that Ac ko mok ki was personally familiar with most of this immense territory and its nations. A copy of Ac ko mok ki's map, annotated in English, was sent by Fidler to the Bay's

London headquarters and printed, whence it came to Jefferson's hands, and from him to Lewis and Clark. It was this Blackfoot map that guided Lewis and Clark from the Mandan towns to the Columbia River system.

Thomas Jefferson, in common with most Euro-Americans, assumed that "full-blood" Indians could not be assimilated into European-style culture, that children of mixed parentage might be educated but that Indians per se would inexorably be pushed westward by colonists until the frontier halted at the Great American Desert or Spanish California. Creek and Cherokee gentry in handsome plantation mansions somehow could not be recognized, nor were the thousands of midwestern Indian families in log houses that were hardly distinguishable from those of the Euro-American "pioneers." Throughout the nineteenth century, treaty after treaty was debated and signed, sometimes under military threat, sometimes with deliberately inadequate translation from the English, and sometimes despite American negotiators' misgivings over unfair demands. Generally, the Indians who signed treaties represented only themselves and the communities they led but were taken as authorized to sign away enormous territories. Between this lack of true authorization and the pattern of U.S. business interests overruling inconvenient treaty obligations, Indian nations had little opportunity to reconstitute economic bases after their forced moves. No other recourse but war was left to Indian nations, and that finally was gone as a consequence of the 1870s combination of deployment of Civil War armies plus an unexpected rapid decrease in bison herds, the food staple of all the prairie and Plains nations. The 1869 completion of the transcontinental railroad opened an eastern industrial market for bison hide (used for industrial belting), attracting wholesale slaughter for hides alone. Then cattle were introduced onto the Plains, competing with bison (and an increasing number of horses) for pasture. Several years' drought in the early 1880s was the fatal blow, crushing the herds below reproductive capacity. Bereft of food, Indian communities had to accept reservations and the rations promised.

AMERICAN INDIANS AND AMERICAN SOCIETY AND POLICIES

American Indians differ from all post-Columbian immigrants in that they alone can preserve their ancestral cultures. For them, there are no parental lands overseas. Sole guardians of their languages, religions, material creations, and customs, America's First Nations resisted centuries of invaders' determination to obliterate their cultures. The first wave, in the sixteenth and seventeenth centuries, brought European-based armed incursions that were soon amplified by the ravages of epidemics. The second wave ran from the mid-eighteenth through the mid-nineteenth centuries, with Euro-American populations substantial enough to mount well-supported military campaigns along the series of western frontiers until the post–Civil War final conquests. The official position of the United States during its first century of wars was that articulated by Chief Justice

John Marshall in *Johnson v. McIntosh* (1823): "The tribes of Indians inhabiting this country were fierce savages, whose occupation was war and whose subsistence was drawn chiefly from the forest. To leave them in possession of their country was to leave the country a wilderness; to govern them as a distinct people was impossible."

The late nineteenth century was in every sense the nadir of the First Nations of America. The 1890 census recorded 228,000 American Indians in the United States, considerably less than one tenth of the population four centuries earlier. The census figure did, it is true, fail to record some thousands of American Indians living independently of reservations and either avoiding census registration or "passing" in some other census category, and it ignored the hundreds of thousands of residents of some First Nation ancestry mixed with predominating European, African, or Asian ancestry. All over the country, openly racist paternalism, often coupled with venality, kept Indians in dire poverty, malnourished, in shacks, their children torn from families to be kept in boarding schools, forbidden to speak their own languages or practice their religions. Mortality was very high, tuberculosis common. The notion of cultural evolution dictated that Indians had to be trained to be simple peasants before any could "progress" to higher education or businesses. Small-scale farming was enjoined upon Indians whatever their reservation environment, and when Indian farmers were successful—many came from nations with millennia of successful agriculture—they frequently were second-guessed by inexperienced Bureau of Indian Affairs agents. For example, stockmen were instructed to hold calves from market because the price might be higher next year, when feeding the animals over a long winter would surely significantly reduce net profits. Indians were held to a reserve labor pool, coerced to work seasonally, especially as agricultural labor and at wages and in camp conditions well below what Euro-Americans would accept. The Indians' schools put boys to manual and girls to domestic work, graduating young adults with an education level of eighth grade or less. One illuminating case is that of Beloit College, 1871–1884, when the college accepted Dakota youths selected and prepared by the Riggs family of missionaries in Minnesota. Ohiyesa, called Charles Eastman in English, earned top status in mathematics at Beloit, went on to Dartmouth, and took an M.D. from Boston University in 1890. The Bureau of Indian Affairs was affronted at Beloit's efforts to give such opportunities to Indians and cut off support for the program when college officials refused to limit Indian students' academic education and place them in factory work.

The turnaround came with Franklin Roosevelt's New Deal. Roosevelt appointed a crusader for Indian rights, John Collier, commissioner of the Bureau of Indian Affairs (BIA) in 1934. Collier was as paternalistic as his predecessors (other than Ulysses Grant's appointee, the Seneca Iroquois Ely Parker), but instead of believing in the moral superiority of Christians, he thought American Indians were noble children of the earth. Hobnobbing with upper-class bohemians, such as the heiress Mabel Dodge Luhan (who had married a man from

Taos Pueblo), Collier romanticized Indians and was determined to restore their lands and a primitive democracy he imagined had once characterized them. Each federally recognized tribe (this denigrating term was used rather than the colonial period *nation*) was pressured to write a constitution and elect a tribal council to govern the reservation. Traditional "nonrepresentative" forms of government and hereditary leadership were discouraged. Tribal members who protested against the alien ideas of written constitutions and proportionately elected representatives found their boycotts of elections only gave "progressives" apparent victories. Collier's actual reforms, ending persecution of non-Christian religions, encouraging retention of Indian languages and day schooling for children, restoring thousands of acres into tribal trust status, creating craft cooperatives to encourage traditional manufactures and art, and curbing the powers of BIA agents, were perhaps less effective than they might have been had the country not been in the throes of the Great Depression. As it was, economic improvements did not come until World War II called out Indians for war industries and military service.

Two southwestern examples illustrate the uneven consequences of the efforts at reform. First, both tourism, which had earlier been heavily promoted by the Santa Fe Railroad, and the federal Indian Arts and Crafts Board, established during the 1930s, created a market for selected Pueblo products and dance performances. Still, the hordes of gapers were a nuisance, and the increasing popularity of Indian crafts could not offset the greater twentieth-century problem, namely, the steady population growth on limited land bases. An increasing proportion of Pueblo citizens had to find employment either outside or in new occupations, compelling many to move away. Returning to the homeland reservation for holidays would become increasingly common in the last half of the century. Second, efforts to promote economic self-sufficiency among the Navajo during the 1930s produced a paternalistic policy dictating the size of sheep herds that ended disastrously. Overriding Navajo management practices in favor of engineers' prediction that overgrazing would lead to an erosion that would silt up the new Hoover Dam reservoir resulted in the bitterly lamented slaughter of thousands of Navajo sheep. Then World War II military service and industries' need for labor brought thousands of Apacheans into mainstream America (Navajo "code-talkers" became famous, transmitting military information in their own language, which the Japanese thought was an unbreakable code). The Navajo Nation would grow into the largest Indian nation in the United States, and Apacheans would find employment throughout the country, later building reservation schools to prepare their youth for trades and professional education and constructing businesses, but rural poverty would continue to beset the Navajo and many Apache.

The Indians' experiences during World War II had, in 1944, encouraged them to begin taking a more pro-active stance by forming a pan-Indian political organization, the National Congress of American Indians (NCAI). Strengthened by familiarity with the U.S. government and by modes of civil action gained after Collier's Indian Reorganization Act brought many more Indians into federal employment, the NCAI persisted as a moderate but firm voice. Ironically, on the other hand, one result of the wartime was the visibly intensified involvement of American Indians in mainstream economic and citizen activities, which earned them respect but also stirred a postwar government policy to end the Indian's federal status. Consequently, federal laws forbidding liquor in reservations, the sale of guns to Indians, and Indians' buying and selling of livestock, farm implements, and even clothing were rescinded. Then, in accord with the goal of assimilation, the director of the War Relocation Authority was appointed Commissioner of the Bureau of Indian Affairs in 1950, and under Eisenhower's administration, in 1954 Congress began enacting legislation to terminate Indian tribes, one by one. Hearings in Washington ranked federally recognized tribes according to the proportion of educated and economically independent members, on the premise that these qualities indicated assimilation in American society. Not surprisingly, final judgments were influenced not only by such statistics but also by whether state politicians favored termination of particular tribes. That in turn reflected the opinions of representatives' constituents.

Overall, termination was a minuscule sector of a Republican strategy for retracting Roosevelt's New Deal social engineering. Between 1954 and 1964, when the policy was revoked, Congress abrogated traditional Indian status for the Menominee of Wisconsin, Klamath of California, Southern Paiutes of Utah, Catawba of South Carolina, Alabma-Coushatta of Texas, Ponca of Nebraska, and a number of very small bands, including those on California *rancherías*. Jurisdiction over Indian residents belonging to these tribes was given to the states; the Menominee Reservation, for example, became a county. Termination was disaster for the affected tribes, moving their assets into funds administered paternalistically by non-Indian bankers and lawyers and imposing burdens of taxation and municipal services their members could not afford. The Menominee, for example, had been relatively comfortable for reservation Indians until their rural, heavily forested "county" had to suddenly provide education, health, employment training, police, conservation, and other needs. For two decades, the Menominee desperately lobbied to regain reservation status, finally achieving it in 1974.

Concomitant with the policy for termination was one to relocate Indians into cities. Wartime industries had proven Indians' abilities to work in factories, while their armed forces service proved their ability to live integrated with Euro-Americans. The improved education programs instituted by the New Deal had also raised the general level of education on most reservations, so it seemed obvious that younger Indian families ought to be assisted to leave impoverished reservations to join the prospering working class of the 1950s. Recipients were given travel money and enough to rent a place to live and buy necessities for the few weeks they would be seeking jobs. After that, they were on their own. Most Indian relocees encountered discrimination in both employment and housing and returned to their homes, preferring rural to urban poverty. There was some retention, and one effect of the agencies settling Indians in cities was to encourage pan-Indian consciousness through Indian Community Centers in the cities. Minneapolis is the only U.S. city said to have a discrete Indian ghetto; in other cities, Indian families are more dispersed, and the intertribal centers substitute for neighborhood centers. As the Indian population continues to rise (by real increase and by changes in self-identification), and a larger number of Indians live in urban areas, pan-Indian powwows, religious services, and agencies grow in number and respectability. What developed in the later twentieth century was a voluntary internal migration, somewhat similar to overseas migration into the United States, leaving the reservations to be homelands for the national cultures and merging the emigrants into an American ethnic category, American Indian, that had subordinated their original nations' diversity.

Here, then, remained the crux of the status of American Indians: They were members of sovereign nations recognized as such by European invaders and by the United States until 1831 (Marshall's "domestic dependent nations" ruling) and effectively so until 1871, when the Congress decided it would no longer make treaties with groups within its national boundaries. In 1934, the Department of Interior's solicitor (the Bureau of Indian Affairs is within Interior) clarified "Indian sovereignty" by declaring that "those powers which are lawfully vested in an Indian tribe are not, in general, delegated powers granted by express acts of Congress but rather inherent powers of a limited sovereignty which has never been extinguished." The Constitution recognized Indians as members of societies that would engage in commerce with (not "within") the United States, implying they were sovereign vis-à-vis the United States. The serious debate in the mid-twentieth century was whether military conquest had extinguished Indian sovereignty. As late as 1955, in *Tee-Hit-Ton Indians v. United States*, the Supreme Court ruled that "the savage tribes of this continent were deprived of their ancestral ranges by force and that, even when the Indians ceded millions of acres by treaty in return for blankets, food and trinkets, it was not a sale but the conquerors' will that deprived them of their land." Yet the United States had made treaties with a large number of the indigenous nations, undercutting that might-makes-right position. Compounding the murky legal situation, in 1946, the Congress had established an Indian Claims Commission to pay compensation for lands taken more or less by force. The excruciatingly slow judicial process for claims went on for thirty years and cost millions of dollars for legal fees, finally ending with more than half the claims not yet settled but shifted to the regular Court of Claims. Such tribes as the Lakota (who will not take money for the Black Hills) that cannot be satisfied with payment rather than return of land have not been given options for other forms of compensation. Thus, in practice, Indian sovereignty has been acknowledged, but its domain and powers remain confused by divergent legal precedents.

There were yet other long-term outcomes of the changes begun during the New Deal, despite the mixed results of the reforms and the subsequent efforts of congressional leaders to dismantle them. During World War II, Indian veterans demonstrated their abilities and tasted respect. When they returned to reservations, many became leaders in tribal governments. They wanted their people to complete higher education, become lawyers, doctors, and officials. That postwar generation's struggles in colleges that neither remedied poor preparation in Indian schools nor honored non-Western cultures led to programs in the 1970s assisting Indian students' adjustment. Fueled by a high birthrate and, most recently, self-identification as Indians by persons who earlier would have passed as "white," Indian representation in professions and management has significantly increased in the late twentieth century. Yet overall economic improvement has been slower, for most reservations have been remote from commercial hubs and unable to raise the massive capital to exploit mineral resources themselves, whereas sweetheart deals between federal government agencies and major oil, gas, and mining corporations long gave tribes royalties much below those negotiated by private landowners.

Then a younger generation of American Indians decided to draw attention to the needs of American Indians by resorting to more public action. In 1968, when the Civil Rights Act was specifically extended to American Indians, a group of young Indian men in Minneapolis announced the founding of the American Indian Movement (AIM). They quickly established chapters in several cities with relatively large Indian populations and linked with "malcontents" on the two contiguous principal Lakota reservations in South Dakota, Rosebud and Pine Ridge. By late 1969, a coalition calling itself "Indians of All Tribes" demanded that the abandoned prison on Alcatraz Island in San Francisco Bay be "restored" to Indian occupancy, specifically to replace the San Francisco American Indian Center that had just burned down. Inviting news media to broadcast their claim, Indian youth camped in the forbidding buildings on the island. The Alcatraz occupation gradually petered out, while national and international news were given a series of other dramatic protest actions, including rallies for fishing rights illegally abrogated by the State of Washington, a Trail of Broken Treaties cross-country March on Washington in 1972, and then, in 1973, occupation of the tiny hamlet of Wounded Knee on the Pine Ridge Reservation in South Dakota, site of the Indian massacre of 1890.

There were numerous grievances against the Pine Ridge tribal chairman and against police and judges who had twice recently treated lightly Euro-American men who had murdered Oglala Lakota. A mixed group of Pine Ridge Oglala and supporters from the neighboring Rosebud Reservation and young Indian men and women recruited by AIM from other parts of the country initiated a rebellion for two months at Wounded Knee, besieged by U.S. marshals fully equipped with tanks and artillery. Television covered the siege and the deaths of two young Indian men shot during barrages of gunfire. Neither the U.S. government nor the public would concede the rebels' position that they represented the Independent Oglala Nation and that the 1868 Fort Laramie Treaty between the nations must be the basis of any settlement. The United States insisted that the Indians were engaged in political insurrection, inciting to riot, and conspiracy. Finally, a meeting was arranged between presidential aides and Oglala traditional chiefs, and the siege was lifted in early May 1973. The United States prosecuted AIM leaders Dennis Banks and Russell Means and others, but the courts found Federal Bureau of Investigation (FBI) and Department of Justice agents' malfeasance had irredeemably compromised the cases. The Second Wounded Knee, like the massacre there in 1890, gained nothing for either side, but its needless violence deterred further militancy.

Paralleling these events were the developments taking place in Alaska and the impact that they, in turn, would have on American Indian activists elsewhere. Alaska contrasts with the Lower Forty-eight in that nearly all of its native nations remained in their homelands, subsisting primarily on their own faunal resources—hunting, fishing, and trapping—the latter two for commercial as well as home consumption. Neither Russia nor, subsequently, the United States negotiated formal treaties with these nations (the 1867 purchase of Alaska occurring just prior to Congress's 1871 decision to cease making treaties with Indians). A 1936 version of the Indian Reorganization Act brought some of the Alaskan and Aleut communities into line with BIA structure. World War II and its aftermath, cold war radar defense, afforded wage labor to many members of Alaskan First Nations without necessarily keeping them from seasonal traditional pursuits. Statehood in 1958 passed without clarification of First Nations' territories: Nearly one third of the new state was held to be public land, overlapping with native communities. Strong pressure to develop oil production forced the issue. An Alaska Federation of Natives in 1966 demanded recognition of its members' claims. The outcome was the 1971 Alaska Native Claims Settlement Act, creating 13 regional corporations: 12 mapped regions and a thirteenth to incorporate persons no longer actively affiliated with an ancestral native community. Members of the corporations are shareholders, and the corporations use their land, resources, and labor to support the shareholders (i.e., the native nations' territories are wholly converted into capital, regardless of their own cultures' concepts of resources). Within the regional corporations, which hold subsurface resource rights, are 223 village corporations with surface but not subsurface title. The corporations were given twenty years, to 1991, tax free to build their businesses; modifications in 1980 and 1987 somewhat reversed the capitalization of the nations' resource bases. At the end of the twentieth century, a few of the corporations were profitable, with others still struggling to work out means of providing for shareholders' education, health, and welfare needs.

After the invention of the Alaska regional corporations to resolve claims in that state, Indians in the American West allied to improve the income they might derive from mineral resources on their reservations. CERT, the Council of Energy Resource Tribes, was formed in 1975, the year of Congress's Indian Self-Determination and Educational Assistance Act and a year after its Indian Financing Act. CERT copied the recently established and immensely powerful international OPEC, Organization of Petroleum Exporting Countries, but the

CERT tribes' resources were nowhere near as globally crucial as OPEC's. Actually supported in part by the federal Department of Energy, CERT renegotiated unfavorable lease terms and royalties without the clout of OPEC; furthermore, it could not benefit tribes lacking "energy resources" (principally oil, gas, and coal). Water rights, vital to many western reservations, have been individually litigated, sometimes relatively successfully (the Tóhono 'O'odham in Arizona were compensated in 1986 for losses through a dam ruining the arable capacity of their original reservation). Gross inequity, on the other hand, ensued from the massive mid-century Missouri Basin series of dams, their reservoirs flooding most of the arable bottomlands of reservations along the Missouri. Access to irrigation water was promised, but systems to deliver it were never constructed. Paternalistically, the U.S. government invoked the Trade and Intercourse Acts enacted by Congress between 1790 and 1834 to hinder direct sales of land and of water rights from Indians to non-Indians, while permitting its own agencies' appropriations of Indian resources to further economic goals of the dominant society.

Then, quite unpredictably, and in quite another manner, economic capital gushed for American Indians from the 1980s shift in American morality that legalized state lotteries. In the mid-1970s, the Oneida of Wisconsin, an Iroquois nation that had moved there from New York State in 1838, had realized that independence from state jurisdiction ought to allow them to offer bingo games with prizes higher than those permitted to games run by non-Indians. If churches around Wisconsin supported their operations from bingo, why should not the Oneida? Offering high stakes would bring players. Within a few years, the Oneida had built a hall accommodating over a thousand patrons, then an adjoining hotel, then a larger casino with slot machines. Patrons came by the thousands, many in chartered buses from cities 200 or 300 miles away. Within a decade, bingo halls had been transformed into casinos offering most of the betting games once available only in Las Vegas and Reno. Employment was now available for many Oneida as well as funds for a home for the elderly, schools, day care, an industrial park, convenience stores, and a museum.

Gambling—"gaming"—then erupted during the 1980s on other Indian reservations, rapidly becoming a major economic opportunity. Proliferation and promotion of state lotteries set the tone, replacing the image of gambling as vice with one of gambling as wholesome pastime. The Oneida experience has been repeated across the country. But while casino gambling is out of reach for the majority of reservations, being too remote to attract many players, others have promoted outdoor sports activities or invested in enterprises designed to lure tourists, notably the Mescalero Apaches' luxurious Inn of the Mountain Gods. Those unable to devise some such strategy to overcome their physical isolation would likely remain severely impoverished, their people disheartened by lack of employment.

Meanwhile, casinos give employment, directly and indirectly, to hundreds of reservation residents, with popular casinos funding construction of schools, nurs-

ing homes, health clinics, community recreation centers, and housing and producing capital for stores industrial and service businesses. Forty-two tribes
formed the National Indian Gaming Association in 1983, and the Wisconsin
Chippewa, publishers of the newspaper *News from Indian Country*, also put out
a monthly *Bingo and Casino Gaming Magazine*. Concern over contracts between tribes and non-Indian professional casino managers led to Congress passing in 1988 the Indian Gaming Regulatory Act, giving states a standing in
negotiating conditions and limitations on Indian reservation gambling. Gambling
was the cash cow (or, some would say, resurrected buffalo) gushing money.

At the end of the 1990s, gambling fervor seemed to be abating, although
"routinized" is probably a better word for the plateau that was reached. Two
hundred out of 556 federally recognized tribes opened public gaming enterprises,
of which about 20 are close enough to large cities to be really successful. Consumer demand in the Northeast Metropolitan corridor catapulted the Pequots, a
Connecticut nation barely existing since its defeat in 1637, into owners of the
biggest casino in the United States. Marginalized since 1637, they built their
Foxwoods Casino to a scale beyond the commercial casinos of Atlantic City. In
Wisconsin, a Potawatomi community that had resisted removal to Oklahoma in
the nineteenth century petitioned for restoration of a few acres of its village in
what is now downtown Milwaukee to build a bingo hall for revenue. The hall,
soon expanded into a casino, rescued the Milwaukee intertribal urban Indian
Community School from penury and invigorated the upstate Potawatomi, who
began planning sustainable businesses, such as raising European red deer for
meat and antlers (ground into medicinal powder for Asian markets). Milwaukee's Potawatomi Casino magnanimously donates thousands of dollars annually
to local charities. The Pequots sponsor an annual powwow showcasing the country's champion Indian dancers competing for the biggest prizes on the circuit.
"Gaming" looked to be the way out of poverty and into reestablishing Indian
nations, putting at least the 20 or so advantageously situated in an economic
position to command respect. The dark cloud was the invasion of hordes of
people with no better idea of passing the time than commercialized gambling.
Wisconsin Potawatomi did not worry because their restored acreage is hours
away from their actual community, but some New York Mohawk were so troubled that several families moved off the Akwesasne Reservation to protect their
children from the pernicious influence of gamblers.

At the same time that Indian casino gambling was getting under way in the
1970s, another phase of federal reforms built upon those begun during the New
Deal, this time led by President Richard Nixon, who remembered the discrimination suffered by his Quaker college football coach who happened to be an
Indian. The 1975 Indian Self-Determination and Education Assistance Act, the
1978 Indian Child Welfare Act protecting Indian nations' custody of their children, and the American Indian Freedom of Religion Act, also in 1978, at last
explicitly recognized Indian nations' innate rights. From World War I, when
Indians joined other Americans to defend the country from European powers,

through the rest of the twentieth century, step by step the United States has acknowledged the humanity of the indigenous nations it had overcome and gradually accorded more and more recognition of their rights to at least footholds in their original domains. Thus, for example, in northern Wisconsin, a 1983 court decision affirmed the treaty right of Chippewa to continue subsistence hunting, fishing, and plant harvesting in ceded territory. Even the violent protests by non-Indian landowners, especially those operating resorts, lessened over the ensuing decade.

And there remained the issue of federal policy linked to the numbers of American Indians. The 1990 census counted 1,959,234 American Indians, only one-third residing on Indian lands. The federal government officially recognized over 550 tribes and 291 Indian reservations. There had only been 523,600 American Indians listed in the 1960 census but 1,423,043 in the 1980 census, an increase larger than can be accounted for even by the high birthrates in many First Nations. A sample of Americans taken with the 1980 census indicated that some 7 million did not report themselves as "American Indian" but do claim some American Indian ancestry. This represents a large pool of citizens who may choose to identify themselves as "American Indian" in a subsequent census, and it is this increased respectability for Indians that explains the extraordinary jumps in the census lists of "American Indians." It is telling, for example, that the self-identified Indian population of the state of Alabama rose 117.7 percent, from 7,583 to 16,506, between the 1980 and 1990 censuses!

Who has cared about these numbers? Politicians and taxpayers. Indians can vote, and in Arizona and Montana, Indians are approximately 6 percent of the state population; in Oklahoma, 8 percent. Even in Oregon, Minnesota, and North Carolina, Indians are 1.1 to 1.4 percent of the population, enough to swing a vote in some districts. In addition, in 1990 the federal government allocated $1 billion to the Bureau of Indian Affairs—of which one-tenth reached the Indian people it was set up to serve—and an additional $2 billion was provided to other federal agencies targeting American Indian clients. Some of these monies go only to Indians residing on reservations, some to any enrolled member of a federally recognized tribe. Some of the monies are in lieu of state or municipal welfare payments, the recipients being entitled to federal rather than state or local assistance (i.e., entitlements tied to recognized Indian status shift this funding from state to federal taxation). However, those nations that had accommodated Euro-American intrusion without formal treaties were simply out in the cold. Admitting that dozens (at least) of historically attested Indian groups happen not to have made treaties, in 1978 the Federal Acknowledgment Project was instituted to hear claims of Indian status that might allow the plaintiffs entitlements that were specifically Indian.

In one other sphere, that of education for First Nations children, there has also been a long struggle throughout U.S. history with some important successes in recent decades. Dartmouth College, begun as an Indian Charity School, before long addressed itself to Euro-American youth, taking only a small number of

Indian charity pupils. Post–Civil War Indian schools, notably Carlisle in Pennsylvania, aimed only at destroying "the Indian" in children, replacing their heritage with English, Christianity, work discipline, and skills suited to peasants. Repression and regimentation in the boarding schools set up to erase "the Indian" welded the children, usually from a variety of nations, into sodality. Forced to speak English, it became a lingua franca facilitating intertribal friendships and eventual marriages. Memoirs of men and women raised in these boarding schools brim over with fond memories of childish tricks and comradeship, overriding the initial sadness at separation from family and the frequent deaths. Under the Collier reversal of policy in the 1930s, when separation was no longer pursued, boarding schools came to be seen as a haven for some children who might not otherwise have been fed and kept warm and clean in that era of the Great Depression. Collier's policy was to provide day schools for Indian children and to maintain their families and educate them within their own national ("tribal") cultures. Besides creating day schools, his staff commissioned bilingual readers at the primary level, and Interior's Indian Arts and Crafts Board strongly encouraged artists to work in an "Indian" version of Art Deco taught in the Santa Fe Institute of American Indian Arts. World War II curtailed Collier reforms in education as in other activities, but his twin goals of bringing all Indian children into schools and minimizing boarding schools in favor of day ones remained as policy. But reality, in the form of low expectations for Indian pupils and playground scorn, left many Indian parents disenchanted with their children's schools, leading to 1970s activism on two fronts—parent demands for input on public school curricula and administration and creation of Survival Schools run by Indian activists especially for urban Indian children. Of the latter, one in Minneapolis became a magnet school within the public system; the one in Milwaukee, the beneficiary of the wildly profitable Potawatomi Casino.

The postwar upsurge in Indian population, urban and armed forces experiences, and the effect of a generation of parents among whom a significant minority had received a secondary-level education—taught in BIA schools only since the 1920s—raised expectations that Indians would attend college. This of course paralleled the social revolution in the United States tied to the G.I. Bill underwriting college education for hundreds of thousands of working-class veterans who had not considered college feasible. High dropout rates among Indians entering colleges were attributed, in the postwar period, to inadequate academic and social preparation rather than, as in earlier periods, to racial inferiority. Programs were created to tutor Indian students and compensate for homesickness and feelings of alienation. An alternative to hacking it in mainstream universities appeared at the end of the 1960s, with the Navajo Community College, the first of eventually over twenty reservation-controlled colleges. Navajo Community College was in a sense a spin-off from Rough Rock Demonstration School in Arizona, created under a 1966 grant from the Office of Economic Opportunity to the Navajo Tribe.

This venture in bicultural schooling operated by a tribe indicated the value of similarly run postsecondary education. The 1978 Tribally Controlled Community College Assistance Act set off a spate of tribal colleges, the majority in the West. They emphasize retention of local cultural values along with the acquirement of credentialed skills, such as are standard in mainstream two-year technical community colleges. Returning national languages to daily use is a common aim; native-language courses are popular and seen as vehicles for transmitting traditional worldviews. On some reservations, independent language institutes strive for the same objective through adult instruction and children's language-immersion classes. On the Blackfeet Reservation in Montana, the Piegan Institute (Piegan being the Blackfoot language) has been building one-room neighborhood schools in which only Blackfoot is spoken, hoping that the children will grow into teenagers using Blackfoot rather than English as a matter of course. These may reinforce the young adults learning Blackfoot in the Blackfoot Community College and the hundreds of children in the reservation's Head Start classrooms, where aides are encouraged to use Blackfoot. At the college and the institute, staff members with advanced degrees from major universities demonstrate in their own persons the compatibility of their own heritage with dominant-society occupations.

AMERICAN INDIANS AT THE CENTURY'S END

Many books have been written on the image of the American Indian as primeval savage, and "The Indian" continues to be described as the pristine Edenic human, supposedly tenderly loving Mother Earth, honoring Woman, and incarnating true spirituality. Simply to be fully human seems more than other Americans want to grant to Indians. It is instructive to compare Ben Nighthorse Campbell, a Northern Cheyenne elected to the U.S. Senate in 1992 from Colorado, with Charles Curtis, a Kansa-Kaw elected representative from Kansas in 1892 and senator in 1909. Curtis is remembered for the Curtis Act, 1898, extending the Dawes Act of 1887 and ending tribal law and courts in Indian Territory (Oklahoma), and, in 1924, as the principal sponsor of the Indian Citizenship Act. A long career as a politician's politician in Congress was capped by Curtis's becoming vice president of the United States in 1928. In his time, he proved that a man of part-Indian descent could assimilate into American society and earn its highest rewards. Of course, Indians resisting assimilation considered him wholly untrustworthy.

Campbell built up a successful business making jewelry of his own bold design, as much "western" as "Indian" in style. He was first elected to the Colorado legislature and then served three terms as a congressman before being elected to the Senate; he is currently the only American Indian in that body. He owns a ranch in Colorado, rode his big paint horse as grand Marshal of the 1992 Rose Parade in California, and insists on dressing western style, neckerchief instead of tie, even in Washington. In contrast to Curtis, Campbell is seen as an individualist drawing upon Cheyenne culture and the West's freedom of spirit, tempered with business savvy. Unlike Curtis, he has been amenable to speaking for Indian interests. As an artist and Indian, he embodies the American promise of tolerance for individual configurations of heritage and talent.

But American Indians saw a sea change in the 1990s far more pervasive than Nighthorse Campbell's victory. NAGPRA, the Native American Graves Protection and Repatriation Act, was passed by Congress in 1990 and was intended to rectify earlier appropriations of American Indian objects and actual bodies for museums and research collections. Horror stories abounded of graves opened to secure skulls for measurement and ornaments for display cases, religious retreats despoiled of altar icons, and ritual objects surreptitiously bought from thieves. NAGPRA ordered museums and federal agencies to inventory their collections and inform Indian tribes of origin of their human remains and "cultural patrimony." Tribes that can prove original ownership can obtain these forebears' remains and artifacts. But NAGPRA has also raised innumerable questions about affiliations of First Nations to those who lived in their territories centuries or millennia ago.

The larger perspective shows that First Nations' sovereignty is fragmented and regained piece by piece. Thus, the 1978 American Indian Freedom of Religion Act affirmed First Nations' right to practice their religions, but particular practices, such as ritual ingestion of peyote, forbidden by the state of Oregon, and protection of the ritual path up a mountain to a holy lake in northern California, were subsequently denied. The 1975 Indian Self-Determination and Education Assistance Act was enacted to permit tribal decisions and control on economic and political organization and actions, but the 1988 Indian Gaming Regulatory Act keeps the "Bureau Machine" (as Charles Eastman termed the BIA a century ago) grinding on. One-quarter of Indian families in 1990 lived in officially recognized poverty, with median household income for Indians one-third less than median income for the United States as a whole. Thus, First Nations continue, regardless of the rhetoric of "self-determination," to be encapsulated internal colonies, more like Third World than U.S. communities.

The First Nations of North America constitute a peculiar group, the legal anomaly of domestic dependent nations. They stand parallel to states in that it would appear that powers not explicitly delegated to the federal government would be understood to be reserved to the First Nations, but this doctrine was superseded by the dominant society's presumption that American Indians are a less-evolved race incapable of the ordinary political relationships of modern states. At the end of the twentieth century, this unscientific racism is no longer tenable. Based on the visible trend, it would seem that the twenty-first century will witness the continuing resurgence of First Nations' populations and resumption of some sovereign powers, and several hundred homelands will persist to cradle the diverse heritages of the First Nations of America. Indeed, incorporation into mainstream culture has not been, generally speaking, sought by First Nations: Separatism rather than assimilation has been the principle. Recognition that there are many paths to fulfilling lives supports the separatism that seemed the best hope of survival for the many nations caught under Manifest Destiny.

BIBLIOGRAPHIC REFERENCES

The rebound of American Indian nations is accompanied by burgeoning histories. Two comprehensive volumes are Alice Beck Kehoe's *North American Indians: A Comprehensive Account*, 2nd ed. (Englewood Cliffs, NJ: Prentice-Hall, 1992), a survey of North America's First Nations from Paleoindians to 1990, and the *Cambridge History of the Native Peoples of the Americas*, vol. 1 (in two parts), *North America*, edited by Bruce G. Trigger and Wilcomb E. Washburn (Cambridge: Cambridge University Press, 1996). Both offer lists of principal sources for each culture area. Kehoe's book covers all of North America, including Mexico and Canada, overriding European colonial boundaries and providing a comparative perspective. The Cambridge history tends toward conservative interpretations of archaeological data in its three chapters on prehistory, making for disjunction with its twelve colonial and reservation period chapters; the latter vary as is usual in multiauthored books, with the chapter by Trigger and William R. Swagerty on the first major interactions between Europeans and American Indians in the sixteenth century an outstanding discussion.

The Smithsonian Institution Press's encyclopedic *Handbook of North American Indians* was designed to be a primary source covering the continent, although not all of the planned twenty volumes have materialized. Those that have been published are useful for primary references and detailed special topics, with the lists of synonyms for ethnic and personal names being especially valuable. The current series' predecessor, the two-volume *Handbook of American Indians North of Mexico*, edited by F. W. Hodge and published in 1907–1910 as Bureau of American Ethnology Bulletin 30 (reprinted in 1971 by Rowman and Littlefield), remains a good and convenient source.

Particular aspects of First Nations' histories are the focus of a plethora of studies. Prehistory is systematically covered in Brian M. Fagan's *Ancient North America*, rev. ed. (New York: Thames and Hudson, 1995). Federal Indian policy is superbly chronicled in Francis Paul Prucha's *The Great Father* (Lincoln: University of Nebraska Press, 1984), in both two-volume and abridged paperback editions, and U.S. law dealing with Indians in Charlies F. Wilkinson's *American Indians, Time, and the Law* (New Haven, CT: Yale University Press, 1987). Sharon O'Brien's *American Indian Tribal Governments* (Norman: University of Oklahoma Press, 1989) is a well-organized study of the political history of the "domestic dependent nations," with detailed sections on five representative reservation governments. Edward Spicer's *Cycles of Conquest: The Impact of Spain, Mexico, and the United States on Indians of the Southwest, 1533–1960* (Tucson: University of Arizona Press, 1962) is a powerfully written classic. Richard White's *The Roots of Dependency* (Lincoln: University of Nebraska Press, 1983) analyzes the economics of Choctaw, Pawnee, and Navajo efforts to survive U.S. domination in the Southeast, Plains, and Southwest, respectively. Sociologist Joane Nagel's *American Indian Ethnic Renewal: Red Power and the Resurgence of Identity and Culture* (New York: Oxford University Press, 1996) focuses on the extraordinary increase in self-identified American Indians between the 1960 and 1990 censuses, discussing the ambiguities in census data; her emphasis on national political actions, however, slights the diversity of American Indian positions as it fits the American Indian Movement into contemporary ethnic mobilization politics. A much broader perspective can be gained through Olive Patricia Dickason's *Canada's First Nations* (Norman: University of Oklahoma Press/ McClelland and Stewart, 1992), a sophisticated political history worth reading against studies exclusively on U.S. Indian policy.

Among more popularly written books, Jack Weatherford's *Indian Givers* (New York: Fawcett, 1988) and *Native Roots* (New York: Crown, 1991), on Indian contributions to the nation and world, are sound and well written. Peter Nabokov's (edited) *Native American Testimony* (New York: Penguin, 1991) and Brian Swann's (edited) *Coming to Light: Contemporary Translations of the Native Literatures of North America* (New York: Penguin, 1994) are comprehensive collections in English of bona fide written and oral material from a range of First Nations. For teachers, Karen D. Harvey and Lisa D. Harjo's *Indian Country* (Golden, CO: North American Press, 1994) is sound and organized, with lesson plans and resource guides. Finally, Donald B. Smith's *Long Lance: The True Story of an Imposter* (Lincoln: University of Nebraska Press, 1982, paperback) is a moving biography of a man, identified as black in his native North Carolina, who passed as Indian to achieve a career as a film actor and journalist. His tragic struggles from his entrance into Carlisle Indian School in 1909 to his 1932 suicide—or was it murder?— (in a wealthy woman's California mansion) epitomize the burden of race in America.

BRITISH (ENGLISH, WELSH, SCOTS, SCOTCH-IRISH)

William E. Van Vugt

"Here individuals of all nations are melted into a new race of men." So wrote Hector St. John de Crèvecoeur in his familiar *Letters from an American Farmer*, published in 1792. While the extent to which there has been a "melting" of different peoples into a race of "new men" is debatable, the fact that America was built by peoples from many different nations and ethnicities is not.

Yet for several reasons the British (including the English, Welsh, Scots, and Scotch-Irish) had a particularly great impact upon the United States. Most fundamentally, the British planted the first successful colonies in what would become the United States. For 169 years Britain was indeed the "Mother Country" whose language, basic legal institutions and heritage, cultural and economic values, and methods of agrarian and industrial production were adopted, with modifications, by America as her own. Even as an independent nation the United States would continue to be closely tied to Britain with a social and economic relationship that was unique. From 1607 through the twentieth century, it was the British who contributed the greatest numbers of immigrants to America.

COLONIAL PERIOD

From the start, Britain's colonies in what would become the United States were distinct for the type of people who established them and their form of government. The English who founded Virginia colony and made it flourish (after the ghastly mortality rates during the "starving time") were led by people who were essentially businessmen. They had financial backing from London merchants and they raised capital from middle-class investors through joint-stock companies. English colonization and early immigration was thus mainly a profit-minded enterprise, initiated and financed largely by middle-class people, though made possible by the labor of more common folk.

Because the English never found the large silver and gold deposits that the

Spanish did in their empire, they resorted to less dazzling sources of profit—mainly tobacco, naval stores, fishing, and some crops—all of which required long-term investment, many participants, and relatively free economic and political institutions, which the English had. From the outset the dynamic economic ethos of British immigration was evident. Even the Puritan migration to Massachusetts, though inspired by a quest for complete religious freedom, was organized, promoted, and funded through a joint-stock company, backed by investors and energized by a quest for profit and a better material life.

The scale and essential nature of early British immigration were influenced by the fact that the British government was increasingly responsive to a rising middle class, as represented in the House of Commons. James I and Charles I could ignore the interests of this aggressive class only at their peril—Charles would pay with his head in 1649. In 1605 James granted the Virginia Company a royal charter that was repeatedly revised to attract more immigrants and stimulate development through generous incentives, including offers of free land and even more local political control and self-determination than people had in England. At times the colonies were practically self-governing, especially when imperial attention was focused on the more lucrative sugar colonies of the Caribbean. This policy of "benign neglect" indeed attracted many immigrants to the North American colonies; but when tighter controls became necessary a century and a half later, a powerful minority of the colonists would call it "tyranny" and fight to preserve their "English liberties." Thus, America's very conception of freedom was rooted in the English culture that was carried by British immigrants.

The early British immigrants' deep and lasting impact upon American culture is evident in their migratory patterns, which were shaped by the religious and constitutional conflicts of the seventeenth century. The British did not come to America randomly. Rather, they formed four discernible waves: a migration of 21,000 Puritans from East Anglia to Massachusetts during the 1630s; a migration of 45,000 Royalists and indentured servants from southern England to Virginia during the mid-seventeenth century; a migration of 23,000, mostly Quakers from Wales and England's North Midlands, to the Delaware Valley during the late seventeenth and early eighteenth centuries; and a migration of 250,000 people from Northern Britain and Northern Ireland to the Appalachian region during the eighteenth century. Altogether, a third of a million Britons arrived during these years. Farmers and artisans predominated, and most were young, single males who were poor and uneducated.

Although each of these four groups was British, each was also distinct in their religious and social background, their attitudes, patterns of speech, customs, and political beliefs—what some historians call "folkways." The true significance of these distinct groups lies in the fact that their culture not only survived and expanded but also persisted long enough to influence subsequent immigrants, most of whom willingly assimilated and reinforced America's regional differences and British culture with their own distribution patterns. By 1776 about half of the white population in the colonies consisted of English immigrants and their descendants, making what was clearly an English-dominated culture. Much of the remainder were Scots, Scotch-Irish, or Welsh and their descendants. Altogether, late colonial America was overwhelmingly a British world, as one would expect from Britain's successful and dynamic system of colonization.

For example, during the few years immediately preceding the American Revolution, over 8,000 emigrants left England and Scotland for the thirteen colonies. Unusually detailed information about them allows some reasonably accurate generalizations and important insights. Fully a third had come from the Thames Valley, which includes London; a tenth came from Yorkshire. About 40 percent were Scottish (15 percent were from Perthshire, the Scottish Highlands, and the Hebrides), even though the Scots formed a much smaller proportion of the British population. This higher rate of Scottish migration to America persisted throughout much of the nineteenth century and is explained in part by Scotland's greater lack of alternative employment for people who needed or wanted it, as well as a clan structure that encouraged emigration. Differences between the Highland and Lowland Scottish immigrants were rather sharp. Highlanders resembled a rural proletariat, whereas Lowlanders were less impoverished and more similar to the English in their social and economic background. Altogether, the Scots were composed of fewer artisans and more laborers and poor tenant farmers than the English. Roughly a third of the Scots were laborers, compared to only a fifth of the English; another third were craftsmen or artisans, compared to over half of the English, though more of the Scots were textiles workers. The Scotch-Irish included many linen weavers who left after the collapse of their industry in Ulster in the 1770s and helped establish the linen industry in New England.

When the migrants' origins are correlated with their demographic and occupational traits, it becomes clear that the significant surge of British immigration immediately before the Revolution contained two distinct patterns. The "provincial" migrants from the north were very largely families with backgrounds in farming. They were not the poorest members of their class, and they made significant contributions to the economic growth of America—both as producers and as consumers. In contrast, the "metropolitan" migrants from London and the Thames Valley were composed very largely of young single men, many of them artisans whose occupation required apprenticeships. As a group, almost half of the English and Scots were indentured servants or redemptioners, who were typically contracted to labor for four years in America in exchange for their passage. But even these were not as desperate or poor as one might assume. For many, it made economic sense to hang on to their slim resources and buy their passage with an agreement to work for four years—as opposed to spending every last penny on a £4 passage and arriving in total destitution. In fact, many indentured servants were skilled and could negotiate favorable conditions in their contract. Obviously, indentured servants made important contributions to early

American labor and economic development, although their full impact on consumption and population growth was delayed until their years of service were over. Less free were the roughly 20,000 British convicts who were transported to the thirteen colonies; however, most of these also became free Britons in America.

As a whole, British immigrants in the late colonial period were ambitious and enterprising people who made the dynamic growth and expansion of the infant United States possible. Scattered evidence suggests that, in the late eighteenth century and throughout the nineteenth century, British immigrants were more literate than the poorer people who stayed home. Through their letters to and from friends and family who had gone before them, they minimized their risks by becoming well informed and making calculated decisions based on their comparative appraisal of a future in Britain with one in America. Most were poor, but relatively few were truly destitute. They seem to have been reaching for opportunities as much as escaping from desperate situations, perhaps even more so. This was clearly true, for example, of the 150 adults who embarked at Hull for America between 1774 and 1775 and whose backgrounds are known to us. None were being supported at public expense. Most had some property and had experience in one of thirty different trades, and most arrived with family members, which indicates an ability to afford multiple passage tickets. Some even brought along their servants.

The late colonial immigrants from Britain were also composed of disproportionate numbers of Methodists. This fact is especially revealing. As separatists from the officially established church, who sometimes experienced prejudice and lingering forms of religious discrimination, Methodists shared a sense of isolation and separation from the mainstream British culture. Not surprisingly, they were among those who found it more thinkable to break away and leave for America. Furthermore, these Methodists forged links between Britain and America, which became a conduit for greater numbers of English and Welsh Methodists in the nineteenth century. Such links were also forged by Scottish and Scotch-Irish Presbyterians, who brought Presbyterianism to America in the early eighteenth century and remained in contact with their coreligionists in Britain.

The formative impact of British immigration upon early America's culture and institutions is apparent even when looking at just the Scots and Scotch-Irish, who were distinct from the English and Welsh. American medical science was led by Scottish immigrant physicians, or Americans who received their training in Edinburgh. Indeed, the "Scottish Enlightenment," which came to America via educated immigrants as well as books, was a foundation for American intellectual culture. With their curricula more pragmatic and their accessibility more democratic than that of their English counterparts, the Scottish universities became models for America, as exemplified by King's College (Columbia University), Rhode Island College (Brown University), and especially the College of New Jersey (Princeton University). The Scots had a special zeal for education. Accordingly, Scottish immigrants were vital in their influence on

American intellectual institutions, as were such Americans as John Witherspoon, who studied in Scotland and returned.

The impact of Scottish and Scotch-Irish immigration on America's religious culture was no less substantial. Scottish immigrants Thomas and Alexander Campbell founded the Disciples of Christ, also known as the Campbellites, who were an important feature of frontier religion during the Second Great Awakening. More important, of course, was Scottish Calvinism, brought to America by Scottish and Scotch-Irish Presbyterians. Presbyterianism and English Puritanism were very different religious traditions, and yet they shared defining characteristics. Both relied on an educated ministry. Both sought to permeate not just the individual but the entire community and its civic life. Thus, the political implications of this transplanted religious culture were great. The impact of the "democratic" structure of Presbyterianism, like that of the Puritans, should not be exaggerated in an assessment of American political culture, but neither should it be ignored. More significantly, when Scotch-Irish Presbyterians migrated to the colonies, they often took with them a grudge against English- and Anglican-dominated government. And they were less likely to maintain deep feelings of loyalty to the Mother Country if they had also suffered from the rack rents of Anglo landlords. Not surprisingly, the Scotch-Irish were the first group to show a widespread desire for independence from the British crown.

Altogether, British immigrants to colonial America set the tone of white American culture and hastened its inexorable westward expansion. Their acquisitiveness and sense of superiority were of course a disaster for Native Americans, who long ago had established their own culture. But, to the emerging United States, British immigrants were beneficial for bringing valuable labor, skills, experience, some material wealth, and important ideas. Among them, after all, was Thomas Paine himself, an English immigrant of 1774, who more than any other individual converted the Americans from British colonists fighting to protect their "English liberties" to revolutionaries creating a new nation.

THE ANTEBELLUM PERIOD

After a lull during the American Revolution and the Napoleonic Wars, British immigration picked up once again. In the early decades of the nineteenth century the movement came mostly from Britain's rural and less developed regions, and it was largely composed of families. In 1831, for example, more than three-fourths of the English and Welsh traveled with other family members—a greater proportion than for any other immigrant group. Over the century as a whole, British immigrants continued to arrive in significant numbers; but they formed three prominent "waves," or surges, of migration that were ultimately linked to economic conditions in the United States and Britain. The first occurred from the mid-1840s to the mid-1850s, the second from 1863 to 1873, and third and largest from 1879 through the late 1880s. The available data on the total numbers of British immigrants are not clear, but at least 5 million Britons permanently settled in the United States between 1820 and 1930, and the actual numbers were probably much higher, especially when counting those who first came to Canada and then crossed the border.

The American Revolution inherently transformed the nature of the British immigrants; they were no longer loyal subjects building the colonies but rather persons leaving their country, changing their allegiance, and joining what was now a competitor nation. The British government and various publishers and other opinion-makers did what they could to channel British emigrants to the parts of the empire that remained. These efforts, however, had limited effect. As for the Americans, many had unjustified suspicions of the British newcomers. Lingering hostilities from the Revolutionary period flared periodically and caused some ill will. During the War of 1812, which to some Americans was a "second war for independence," English aliens were seen as potential enemies, and males aged fourteen and over were required to register at a U.S. marshal's office. Later, British immigrants were required to sign special oaths of loyalty and to swear an intention to become citizens and "renounce forever all allegiance and fidelity" to Queen Victoria. Those who expressed fondness for their land of birth or were slow to become American citizens (as was common among the British) were confronted with hostile accusations of disloyalty. England's continued overshadowing of American literature and art gave some Americans a sense of colonial inferiority, which was commonly expressed with defensive hostility and zealous patriotism toward British newcomers, as writers and travelers, such as Charles Dickens and Francis Trollope, so vividly recorded.

Still, these disadvantages were insignificant when compared to the unique advantages that Britons had in their ethnicity, which may be the central fact in the history of British migration to the United States. With no language barriers (most of the Welsh and Scottish immigrants spoke English), the British could integrate and participate in American society more immediately and fully than other groups could. They did not have to form ethnic communities (though some chose to do so), and they were among the rare groups of immigrants who did not live in identifiable ethnic neighborhoods in American cities. Nor were they limited to interaction with their fellow countrymen in the United States, as were most other new immigrants. Furthermore, in their new land the British found familiar religious denominations and institutions. Their cultural similarities with Americans were also manifested in the fact that they had the highest rate of intermarriage with native-born Americans and that often their children were impossible to distinguish from white Americans. Generally, the British were not seen as foreigners but rather as cousins who were already Americans. In a sense, they were "invisible immigrants" because they could generally fit right into existing white American society—and did so to considerable advantage.

The more immediate assimilation of the British is evident in their voting behavior. During much of the nineteenth century the Democratic Party had always attracted the support of most immigrants, whereas the Whigs and Republicans, many of whom were wary of increasing immigration and the more egalitarian impulses of the Democrats, were the parties that appealed to the native whites. Revealingly, the British were the only immigrants to show strong support for the Whigs and Republicans, as though the British were already Americans. The Scotch-Irish did support Jackson but mainly because of Jackson's own Scotch-Irish background.

Even though the British knew they could blend in with American society quickly, they still took full advantage of the "chains," or networks of information, formed by Britons already in America. Therefore, there were sometimes "clusters" of Britons in rural areas where the new immigrants joined those who had arrived earlier. This was especially true of the Welsh, who formed small settlements throughout Ohio, Pennsylvania, and Wisconsin. In these and other states in the Old Northwest one could also find small English and Scottish settlements, although they were not long-lived. There were also a number of cases of industrial workers banding together in Britain to form "emigration societies." In these schemes subscribers pooled their meager savings to purchase a tract of land in America, and then lotteries were held to determine who would be funded to emigrate and take up land as an American farmer. The goal was to reduce the supply of skilled labor in Britain in order to raise wages there, as well as to enable artisans to fulfill their dreams of farming their own land.

Such was the plan of the British Emigration Temperance Society, which was organized in Liverpool in 1842 and managed to relocate nearly 700 Britons to southwestern Wisconsin by 1850. There was also the Iowa Emigration Society, which transplanted tradesmen from Hull to Clinton County, in Iowa. The Potters' Joint-Stock Emigration Society, organized by the Staffordshire Potters' Union and an act of Parliament in 1844, purchased land in Columbia County, Wisconsin. Other smaller ventures took place, many of them with a vision based on the ideas of Charles Fourier and other socialists. All of these projects failed because the organizers had underestimated the costs of such projects, or had not found suitable land with access to markets, and because the bickering and lawsuits inherent in such utopian schemes contributed to their dissolution. Those who immigrated through these plans soon mingled with native white farmers, and the colonies quickly faded from the scene. Ultimately, such projects were simply not necessary for British immigrants, notwithstanding that some did use them to get to America in the first place.

IMMIGRANTS FROM INDUSTRY

Also of central importance to British migration to America during the nineteenth century was the fact that Britain was the world's first and leading industrial nation. Therefore, British immigrants had more industrial knowledge and experience to offer America than did newcomers from any other country. The flow of skill and technology from Britain to America was so significant that until 1824 Britain officially banned the emigration of skilled artisans to such competitor nations as the United States. In any event, enforcing that type of a ban was virtually impossible. In most areas of American industry British immigrants were important, if not essential, in their establishment and development.

The transfer of textiles technology took place early and rapidly. Already by the 1820s, thanks to the immigration of textiles workers, the best American producers of woolen goods were as advanced, perhaps more so, than those in Yorkshire. Thereafter, most of the textiles immigrants who were handloom weavers were carrying outmoded and rather limited skills and were, therefore, no longer vital to the modernizing of American industry. Yet, many of these weavers were intending to farm in America, and some worked first in cities like Philadelphia (where handloom weaving carried on well into the 1850s) to earn the capital that farming required.

Textiles workers, especially weavers and spinners, migrated in fairly significant numbers in the 1840s. Many left Lancashire and Scotland in the late 1840s because of miserably depressed conditions and rising unemployment—a time that would be remembered as the "hungry forties." Among them was the family that included the young Andrew Carnegie. But when Britain's textile industry recovered in 1850 and enjoyed the fruits of the "Great Victorian Boom," the numbers of immigrant textiles workers dropped to insignificant proportions. They comprised 9 percent of the British male labor force in 1851 but only 3 percent of the male British immigrants to the United States. Most were handloom weavers, and American factories were offering them less, now that Irish immigrants were flooding in and providing cheaper labor. However, as late as the 1860s Scottish weavers' societies assisted the emigration of their members to America, where wages were still higher than in Scotland. Furthermore, some British textiles immigrants still brought skills and expertise that America lacked, as did Charles Bailey, an expert weaver from Yorkshire, who in 1857 arrived in Little Falls, New York, and was hired to set up the Jacquard looms there. Modern worsted manufacturing was brought to Massachusetts in the 1860s by English workers, who even brought along their own equipment.

Compared to textile workers, ironworkers, engineers, and machinists enjoyed a higher demand for their labor in America. This was especially true of those with the special skills that America still lacked. From the 1830s through the 1850s, specialized workers from Sheffield's steel and toolmaking industries were recruited to such an extent that by 1860 the Americans could compete with the British in the production of most kinds of steel, as well as cutlery, saws, files, chisels, razors, and related tools. The total numbers of these workers were not great, but their impact on the rise of American industry was. Like the textile workers, many ironworkers and engineers who arrived in the antebellum period were drawn to America by its cheap farmland. Few were desperate victims of unemployment in Britain.

More numerous were the various preindustrial craftsmen, or skilled artisans, who comprised roughly a third of the immigrants throughout the period. Building trades workers and miners were usually prominent among them, followed by shoemakers, millers, smiths, and the like. Their numbers were steady in part because they were affected by rural depopulation in Britain and the rise of the railways, which integrated rural and urban markets and put some artisans out of work. Many of the shoemakers suffered from an oversupply of their skill in their villages, or they sensed a stigma for being lowly craftsmen. The growing United States welcomed this additional skilled labor, although again many— probably most who arrived before the Civil War—had come to farm in America. Skilled artisans in American agriculture showed a shrewd adaptability and utilized their skills when it made sense to do so. For many, this meant working at their craft and then employing others to do the backbreaking tasks of clearing land.

The immigration of British miners is especially noteworthy. Throughout much of the nineteenth century a steady stream of them came and introduced the skill of craft mining to the United States. During the 1850s alone about 37,000 British miners came directly to the United States; more arrived via Canada. Most mined coal in the anthracite regions of Pennsylvania, where in the 1830s Welshmen discovered and opened up the most important mines. In Indiana and Illinois, too, British immigrants were instrumental in getting the coal mining industries established. Staffordshire miner Richard Freeman came to Indiana in 1850 and became known as "the father of the coal industry in Knox County" for opening and developing the industry there, and others did the same in other states. In addition, thousands of quarrymen settled in New England and, with their finely honed skills, opened up and developed the region's granite and limestone quarries. In America they enjoyed higher wages and positions in expanding companies, and of course many eyed American land. The closure of limestone quarries in Tenby, south Wales, in the 1840s precipitated a flood of quarrymen to America, but they were joined by other quarrymen from north Wales who were mainly looking for a greater reward for their labor—and farmland. In 1850 a Connecticut quarry company sent a recent English immigrant who worked there back to England to recruit more quarrymen, and he returned with 150 of them.

British miners and quarrymen had skills that could take them almost anywhere that mining opportunities led them. They frequently switched between mining coal and mining other minerals and moved between America's disparate mining regions with ease. Without any language barrier to overcome, they could easily pick up and go to more lucrative mines. The most famous episode is of course the California gold rush, in which Britons participated as much as any group. Many came directly from Britain when they heard about "Eldorado," but most had already been mining in the eastern states and the Old Northwest, especially in the upper Mississippi River Valley in northwestern Illinois, western Iowa, and southwestern Wisconsin, where they mined lead. Many had also worked in Michigan's Upper Peninsula, where iron and copper were being discovered in abundance. From these places it was natural to move to California.

Many of the immigrants heading for California were originally hard-rock miners of tin, copper, and manganese from Cornwall or lead miners from the Yorkshire dales who were already in America. Cornish miners were working in Galena, Illinois, as early as 1820, and by the 1830s, Cornishmen were arriving in large numbers. In 1850, over 13,000 British-born people were living in this lead mining region, and by 1860 that number had more than doubled. Then, when word of the riches of California hit the lead mining regions, thousands immediately trekked west, sometimes to the extent of depopulating lead mining towns in southwestern Wisconsin, Iowa, and Illinois.

The Cornish were especially important for bringing the expertise of how to mine deeper into the hard rock and follow the mineral veins. They also brought along the safety fuse and new smelting furnaces, like the "Scotch hearth" furnace. Because they brought modern mining techniques to America and led the industry's development, British immigrants quickly rose to prominent positions. Priscilla Long, a historian of America's coal industry, has even claimed that before the Civil War "every mine boss in the anthracite region was English, Welsh, or Scottish."

To be sure, the large and steady immigration of British miners was not caused simply by greater opportunities in America. Many of the emigrant miners had left deteriorating conditions in Britain. By the 1830s some of Britain's tin and lead mines were nearing exhaustion, wages were falling, and conditions and wages could be miserably bad. British coal mines were bleak places, where sudden cuts in wages or mine closures led to worker unrest and poverty. Some of these miners went to America. However, it was also true that probably most of the immigrant miners had a history of mobility and an eagerness to move in search of the highest wages they could find. Many claimed that they were acting mainly out of a desire to seek adventure in the New World. So great was the mobility of these miners that, especially after the era of transatlantic steamships had commenced in the 1860s, many miners traveled back and forth between the two countries on an annual basis. In Cornish towns and villages, one could find miners who had never been to London but knew San Francisco like the back of their hand. In their letters and journals some indicated that their desire to live in a land of more equality was also an important reason for their migration.

Nevertheless, it remains true that probably a significant majority of the immigrant miners in the antebellum period were ultimately seeking American farmland. Many had combined farming with mining in Britain and continued to do so once in America. Mining during the slower winter months was also a good way of raising extra capital. And when Wisconsin's lead mines neared exhaustion in the 1850s, the British miners there simply put their full attention into the farms that they had purchased and improved with their earnings as miners. These agrarian ambitions are another indication that they were acting not so much out of desperation but out of a determination to make the most of their lives.

AGRICULTURE: THE LURE OF AMERICAN FARMLAND

British immigrants came from a wide range of occupational backgrounds. During the mid-century period, between a fifth and a quarter of the adult males were agriculturists, close to half of whom were a mixture of farm laborers and unskilled laborers; another third were preindustrial craftsmen; roughly a tenth were industrial workers; and the remainder were clerical and professional workers. Up to the Civil War, as we have seen, even people with nonagricultural occupations were probably dominated by those who intended to take up farming. The fact that British weavers, miners, tailors, merchants, and lawyers joined farmers and laborers in their quest for a life in American agriculture shows the extraordinary appeal that farming had for British immigrants through the first half of the nineteenth century, and it is also a good indication that the great bulk of the migrants were not acting out of desperation. This agrarian aspiration is an especially interesting feature of British immigration during the first half of the nineteenth century—a period associated with rapid industrial growth and socially disruptive technological displacement. For as tempting as it is to blame the very real dark side of Britain's industrial revolution for increased British emigration, industrial and social pressures were a distant second to the appeal of American agriculture as a reason for the movement.

The special appeal that American agriculture had for all types of Britons is understandable in light of the fact that many of Britain's industrial workers and urban laborers had originated in rural areas; they had come to towns and factories in their search for work but had not necessarily shed their love for land and their desire to own some. In this way, the distinction between rural and urban people was often blurred, especially for those who had shown a willingness to move in search of work and opportunity. Many of the Welsh left the farms and the hills for the coal mines of south Wales precisely because there they could earn the money necessary to immigrate to America, mine coal there if necessary, and then buy land. Meanwhile, in America, it was possible to buy land for the cost of renting it for a year or two in Britain, and land was cheaper and easier to get than in Britain's own colonies. As the United States continued to expand across North America, government land was going for a mere $1.25 per acre, and improved land for only a little more. Then, in the late 1840s and 1850s, the U.S. government passed a number of acts that reduced the price of land further and gave 61 million acres to the veterans of America's wars, much of which went on the market. This period was a golden age for Britons who wanted to farm their own land in America.

For another important reason British migration to America in the mid-century period was dominated by agrarianism. In 1846, Britain repealed her Corn Laws, or protective duties on imported grain, which caused British prices to fall as imports from Europe and America flowed in. As a result, many of Britain's small tenant farmers who lacked the capital to invest in their farming operations and raise productivity to compensate for the falling prices decided to emigrate to the United States. Many had long contemplated emigration and now chose to do so before they lost all their capital in the new era of free trade. At the same time, repeal gave American farmers a new market in Britain, and accordingly, American agriculture expanded and provided new places for British farmers to take up land. The repeal of the Corn Laws, and subsequent expansion of agricultural migration from Britain to America, is perhaps the best example of the symbiotic relationship that existed between the United States and Britain, within their shared "Atlantic economy." The building, mining, and some manufacturing sectors of the British and American economies were similarly intertwined. This was the overarching economic context of British immigration to the United States in the nineteenth century.

Thus, the British who came to farm in the United States—to confront its realities—had a wide range of farming experience. Many of those who had little or none would find, to their great frustration, that they had in fact been seduced by the "agrarian myth" that American farming consisted of an idyllic life of leisure and care-free self-sufficiency. The reality could be shocking. The Herculean task of clearing land, of working the soil, of swinging the ax, of living in a log shanty until a proper home could be built, of living isolated in the forest, of working near the point of exhaustion—all of these inescapable realities of pioneering life in America overwhelmed British immigrants from all backgrounds, some of whom either returned to Britain or headed for an American city to take up some other form of work. Such a life was also too much for some British farmers who had limited means and could not afford to buy improved land. But the majority persisted, fought the early temptation to give up, and gradually built up improved farms and became successful farmers in America.

Not all of the immigrants took up uncleared land, of course. Especially as the frontier receded westward, more and more of the immigrants bought cleared or partially improved lands. Skilled Britons and farmers with capital usually took this option, while laborers and poorer artisans often had to buy the cheaper virgin lands or work first in the United States to acquire the necessary capital. The British were especially adept at climbing the "tenure ladder" of American agriculture: buying small parcels, improving them and selling them for a profit, reinvesting in more land, and eventually owning a large, well-developed farm. Indeed, so successful was the adaptation of many British immigrants in American agriculture that they showed a remarkable ability—second only to the native whites—to squat on the best lands and eventually stake out a legitimate claim.

But long-term success as an American farmer was almost always dependent upon making significant adjustments in methods, for most Britons faced a very different agricultural environment in America. In particular, the labor-intensive methods of English "high farming," which entailed extensive manuring, crop rotation, drainage, and so on, and which were often vital for success in Britain, were less appropriate for America, where labor was scarce but land was abundant. Some British newcomers refused to make adjustments at first because they were convinced of the superiority of their own methods and saw American methods as wasteful, even immoral, for the tendency to farm the soil to the brink of depletion. But sheer economic reality compelled most to adopt American methods and attitudes and especially to lower the ratio of labor to land.

Nevertheless, some English farmers managed to hold on to their old methods for a time and in various ways made important contributions to nineteenth-century American agriculture. Although the Scotch-Irish immigrants of the eighteenth century were often known for having messy, poorly managed, and undeveloped farms (especially in comparison with the nearby farms of German immigrants), the English, Welsh, and Scottish farmers of the nineteenth century were often credited with having some of the neatest, best-managed farms in their area. Many earned reputations for being "progressive" or "scientific" farmers, for "elevating the standards of agriculture," and for establishing "model farms" in their county. This should not be surprising, because England was the origin of many of the methods that produced the so-called Agricultural Revolution of the seventeenth and eighteenth centuries. Particularly during the half century following Independence, America received much of its inspiration for innovative agriculture from England. The fact that early clovers were called "English grass" and that advanced farming in America was based on what many called "English methods" attest to the English influence. British immigrant farmers in antebellum America were also important for bringing new methods of drainage and drainage pipe manufacturing, which the British had perfected early because Britain's need for drainage was so extensive. They were even more influential in animal breeding and for introducing many new breeds to America; in fact, for a long time cattle breeding in Wisconsin and other midwestern states was dominated by British immigrants. Finally, British farmers helped Americans discard the old notion that prairie soils were not fertile enough for American farming. Britons were among the first to take up prairie lands and demonstrate their fertility, although in some cases the bleak, flat lands and extreme weather—so unlike that of Britain—induced acute homesickness and caused some to leave for other parts of America or to return to Britain.

Crucial for the success of British immigration to agricultural America were women, who were certainly not passive persons being dragged to the United States but active participants who often helped make the decisions to migrate and whose labor was indispensable in settling in the New World. Although some women resisted emigration, so did men against their wives' wishes from time to time. The women's courage, independence, and effect on British immigration were significant. During much of the nineteenth century, roughly a quarter of the British women arrived as single individuals—some of them to join husbands who had preceded them but many of them to join friends or other relatives or to make their own way in the world. Disproportionate numbers of them were young and had experience as "needlewomen," or seamstresses, which shows that their earnings were often crucial to finance their family's migration and to supplement their family income once in America. Most of the young women with occupations were domestic servants, who suffered from an oversupply of their labor in Britain and found it easier to take up work in America, despite having had increasingly to compete with Irish and other immigrant women. There were fewer women textiles workers than one might expect, given their huge numbers in Britain, because increasing Irish immigration lowered America's demand for their labor, while British textiles factories were expanding and drew in prospective emigrants. There were also considerable numbers of British women who had experience in teaching and medicine and who made valuable contributions to American society. One who contributed to both was Helen McAndrew, a Glaswegian with much experience caring for the sick. After settling with her husband in Michigan in 1849, McAndrew left her family to attend medical college in New York. After she returned to Michigan to practice medicine, she helped lead the effort to admit women to Michigan State University.

RELIGION

For most British immigrants economic factors were ultimately most important in their decision to come to America. However, their migration cannot be explained as a response to purely social, political, or economic forces. Well into the nineteenth century religion continued to influence the numbers and types of Britons who emigrated and their settlement patterns in the United States. As was true in the pre-Revolutionary period, nonconformists were more likely to emigrate to America than conformists (Anglicans). In 1851, for example, the population of England and Wales was quite evenly divided between conformists and nonconformists, and yet the latter appear to have constituted two-thirds of the immigrants to the United States. The majority of these nonconformists were composed of various types of Methodists, although Congregationalists, Baptists, and those attending any Welsh nonconformist chapel were also among them. A small minority were actually victims of religious discrimination. Early in the century, to cite one instance, some English farmers who converted to Methodism suddenly found that the customary leases on their farms were not to be renewed, and so they migrated to America, where there was no established church. Subtler forms of discrimination existed and blocked nonconformists' full political and economic participation in British life, and this made some more willing to consider emigration. But most important were the strong communication links between British and British-American Methodists, which had been established since the earliest days of Methodist immigration and which provided a natural conduit for those who considered leaving Britain. Through these networks prospective British immigrants not only received enticing details about America but also frequently prearranged their place of settlement, their employment, even their land purchases.

A good example of the importance of religious-based migration patterns lies in the history of the Primitive Methodists. Formed in England in 1811 when a number of Wesleyan Methodists were expelled for holding overly exuberant revivals (a practice that they had borrowed from the camp meetings that were being held on the American frontier), the Primitive Methodists grew in number and entered the American Midwest in 1842, when converts settled in Galena, Illinois, to farm and mine lead. Their constant correspondence with the Primitive Methodists back in England naturally piqued the interest of converts and funneled more to America. By mid-century they dominated many lead mining and farming communities of the upper Mississippi River Valley, and they were holding spiritual revivals that were an important part of American religious culture on the frontier.

British Mormons were also important participants in the migration. Only three years after the first Mormon mission was established in Britain in 1837, converts crossed the Atlantic to join the new church. About 5,000 additional converts migrated between 1848 and 1851, and some 16,000 followed between 1853 and 1856. By 1870, their total numbers approached 38,000, and the English formed nearly 20 percent of Utah's population, which was the highest percentage of English-born people anywhere in the United States.

Many Mormons left because of the hostility of their unconverted neighbors and because of the power of their perceived religious mandate to establish a new Zion in the American wilderness. But the economic side of the coin was also there. Like other British immigrants, Mormons from Wales and the industrial northeast of England were recruited to start up industries in Salt Lake City, especially mining and iron production, and their skills were vital to Utah's economic development. The Mormons, however, were generally poorer than non-Mormons: More of them were urban industrial workers or unskilled laborers from poor, low-wage areas. About half of them emigrated with the financial assistance of the Mormon Church, which came in the form of loans to be repaid with labor in Utah. Such assistance, their religious enthusiasm, and the solid links between American and British Mormons explain the large numbers.

SLAVERY AND THE CIVIL WAR

British immigrants in antebellum America had come to a land of unprecedented economic opportunity and political and religious freedom but a land that permitted slavery. All but a small fraction of British immigrants hated slavery and considered it an evil and intolerable violation of America's own principles and ideals, as well as a threat to free labor. Because of it, some Britons refused to join relatives in America—even those in northern states. Sympathy for American slaves was widespread in Britain at the time, as demonstrated by the popular lecture series in Britain by Frederick Douglass in 1847 and the phenomenal success of *Uncle Tom's Cabin*, which in its first year of publication sold seven times more copies in Britain than in America. Revulsion toward slavery was most widespread among Britain's working classes because they saw their own struggle for complete freedom and equality in Britain as part of a larger international movement that included emancipation for American slaves.

Of course, not all British immigrants condemned slavery. Some supported it on biblical grounds or were among the relatively few who settled in the South and bought slaves or adopted pro-slavery views in order to get along with their slaveholding neighbors. But quite a few soon left for the North after being sickened by the spectacle of a slave auction or after simply comprehending the abomination of slavery. In the North, Britons became active abolitionists and worked closely with Wendell Phillips, William Lloyd Garrison, and other leaders of the cause. Frederick Douglass recognized that American abolitionism was "largely derived from England," and for this reason, he said, "It ought to be no disgrace to be an Englishman."

With their deep revulsion for slavery, it was perhaps natural that so many Britons risked their lives to stamp it out between 1861 and 1865. British immigrants were among the earliest and most enthusiastic volunteers for service in the Union Army. At least 54,000 English-born men served for the Union, a much higher rate than any other immigrant group. Remarkably, many served within a very short time of their arrival. Dawson Smith, for example, left his wife and children in Yorkshire in 1864, sailed for America, and immediately joined the army and went to the front. Such cases abound and demonstrate not just a loathing for slavery but also a pressure to prove their patriotism. Such pressure could be considerable for British immigrants because of lingering suspicions of some Americans toward Britons, especially when it appeared that the British government might recognize the Confederacy.

Yet once in the army British immigrants were readily accepted and easily filled a wide range of positions. They were unique among immigrants for not needing to form ethnic regiments. While German and Irish regiments multiplied, there was but one Scottish regiment, and even then its ethnic identity was weak from the start. As they could with American society in general, the British blended in with native-born soldiers, most of whom did not regard the British as true foreigners.

British immigrants served in every major campaign of the war, in almost every imaginable capacity: soldiers, officers, buglers, drummer boys, surgeons, carpenters, blacksmiths, and mechanics. At least two were officers of black regiments: Ebenezer Denny, an immigrant from Yorkshire in 1855 who became first lieutenant of the Fiftieth "Colored Regiment," and John Cartwright, who arrived in 1845, became captain of the Twenty-seventh Colored Infantry, and was killed while leading a charge in the battle of Petersburg. Hundreds of others were maimed or killed, and some ended up in Andersonville Prison and either died there or emerged emotionally and physically scarred for life. The war also devastated British families who came to America only to see their sons sacrificed in a ghastly war to preserve a Union and to end slavery. Thus, the American Civil War meant different things to different British immigrants. For many, it was an opportunity to prove their loyalty, their patriotism, their manhood. Ultimately, the war was an important event in their full assimilation into American culture, and many would remember the war as the event that converted them into true Americans. But the nobler purpose of the war was foremost in the minds of some Britons who fought in it. As William Stockdale wrote from England to his son, who had come to America just prior to the war and had lost an eye and a leg in battle, "You fought in a good cause. . . . You were one that were the means of giving the blacks freedom."

THE LATE NINETEENTH CENTURY

After a slump during the last few years of the Civil War, large-scale British immigration resumed. Increasing numbers of Scottish textiles workers came because of a slump in their industry, which was caused in large part by new American tariffs on imported textiles. Then, after another lull during the American economic depression of the 1870s, the numbers surged once again in the 1880s, thanks to an upswing in the business cycle and increased construction in the United States. Through the rest of the century the average rate of British immigration rose and, in fact, was higher during the 1880s than that of any other European nationality, save the Swedes and Norwegians. And this in spite of the fact that per capita incomes were higher in Britain than on the Continent. Peaks were reached in 1887 and 1888, when about 130,000 English, Welsh, and Scots embarked for the United States. By this time, the rise and fall of British immigration was closely tied to the rise and fall of America's economic activity.

The incentives for migration were changing, too. The rising migration of the 1880s appears to have had little to do with Britain's agricultural depression, even though farmers still came in slightly larger proportions than they constituted in Britain's labor force. Some of these attempted to establish agricultural colonies on the Great Plains, usually on land purchased from railroad companies. These were often cooperative schemes, sometimes led by sons of aristocrats with ample funding, refined tastes, and a yearning for leisure that was out of place on the frontier. Like the earlier attempted colonies, these were doomed to failure because of a lack of farming experience, lavish spending, and unrealistic expectations about American farming. In fact, the ideal of being an independent farmer in America was fading in an era of agricultural overproduction, falling prices, and increasing dependence on railroads, banks, and middlemen. The golden age of easy acquisition of good, cheap land in the United States and the profitable farming of it was virtually over. Now, younger, single men from British towns and cities were attracted to America by construction work and skilled and unskilled jobs in the towns and mining regions. Unskilled laborers were more prominent than ever before, as were building trades workers. Over a third of the Scottish immigrants in the late 1880s were in the building trades, with slumps in building in Britain at that same time contributing to their high numbers. It appears that as more unskilled laborers left Britain for America, the demand for housing in Britain fell accordingly, which in turn prompted the migration of the building trades workers, who could find work more easily in the growing United States. In other words, like the emigrant farmers of the mid-century period, the laborers and building trades workers of the late century were participating in a single, integrated Atlantic economy.

These newer immigrants were dominated by single men: For every male traveling with family members, eight went alone, as compared to two in the early 1850s. These were mobile, unencumbered people. Increasing numbers were "birds of passage," seasonal migrants making repeated trips to America on the faster and safer steamships; they did not necessarily have a firm commitment to settle permanently in America. At the same time, more British women, many of them single, were attracted by domestic service. In this way British migration to the United States was no longer a "folk migration" as much as it was a "labor migration." This shift in the nature of the migration, which happened to other immigrant groups as well, occurred among the British first because of Britain's earlier industrialization and urbanization and because of the closer economic ties between Britain and America.

By the end of the century, American industries were outperforming British ones, but America's need for skilled persons had declined, and hence, more of the immigrants were composed of unskilled or semiskilled people. American industries no longer recruited many skilled British artisans. Indeed, English workers now had the reputation for demanding too much. Because Welsh immigrants had led the first strike committees in the American anthracite region in the 1840s and other Britons organized some of the first American labor unions, British immigrants were seen by some industrial employers as potential troublemakers. Still, there were notable cases of British immigrants bringing skills and technology that the United States lacked. In the late 1870s, the U.S. Encaustic Tile Works of Indianapolis was built on the skills of imported English specialists, and into the 1880s the company continued to recruit skilled workers and their families. Between 1870 and 1893, virtually the entire skilled workforce in the silk industry of Macclesfield emigrated after the industry declined there. In all, over 15,000 of these persons came to Paterson, New Jersey, where their skills and experience helped build America's own silk industry. And, as late as the 1890s, skilled Welsh tin-platers arrived in significant numbers and contributed to the development of that industry in the United States.

THE TWENTIETH CENTURY

In the twentieth century, British immigration to the United States declined. Emigrants were going to the Dominions instead. From 1905 on, Canada, whose economy was booming at the time, took in more Britons than did the United States, while Australia, New Zealand, and other parts of the Commonwealth and empire also increased their share. By World War I, a mere 18 percent of the English and Welsh emigrants came directly to the United States, compared to roughly 75 percent in 1841.

There were several reasons for this shift in destination. Most important, the United States was no longer as attractive as it had been. American industries had plenty of cheap labor from southern and eastern Europe, and skilled British workers could no longer offer much to American industry that it did not already have. Meanwhile, cheap farmland was harder to come by, and farming profitably at a time of continued overproduction and falling prices was harder still. At the same time, the Dominions were having more appeal. Certainly, there was a growing imperial consciousness in Britain and perhaps a greater sense of loyalty on the part of emigrants. But of greater importance were the inducements now being offered to those who would stay within Britain's orbit: assisted passages, prearranged employment and housing, and free or very affordable land. The Empire Resettlement Act of 1922 reinforced and facilitated the movement of labor from Britain's crowded cities and depressed farming districts to the parts of the Dominions that lacked sufficient labor.

As the United States began to shut its doors to massive immigration and discriminated against non-Anglo-Saxon peoples in the National Origins Act of 1924, it left very generous quotas for the British. However, these quotas were never filled. In fact, during the Great Depression more British people returned to Britain than arrived in America. Those who did arrive were responding to some of the same inducements as those who had arrived in the prior century: better work and economic opportunity, a better future for their children, a better home. Yet, as the century wore on, farmers and laborers continued to decline in number, with the result that some skilled workers and especially professional persons became more prominent.

The "special relationship" between Britain and America grew out of the common cultural and political roots that were planted with British colonization, and it was reinforced over time by the steady immigration of millions of Britons and their contact with friends and relatives who stayed behind. In the twentieth century the relationship was forged anew by military alliances, especially during the common struggle in World War II. The war affected British migration to America in important ways. Britons were evacuated to Canada or the United States for safety, and some either stayed or soon emigrated after the war. More dramatically, soon after the war was over, 40,000 British war brides came to the United States with their new American husbands.

After World War II, Britons arrived in America in steady numbers that have accumulated significantly. In the 1980s alone, nearly 160,000 Britons immigrated to the United States, which was by far the greatest number from a developed country. Furthermore, the proportions with professional qualifications were higher than ever before. During the 1950s and 1960s the United States welcomed more surgeons and physicians from England than from any other nation, and during the 1970s and 1980s, about half of the British immigrants to the United States were professional, technical, or managerial workers—mainly doctors, nurses, academics, engineers, and secretaries. Most recently, British experts in financial services, computer software, the media, and entertainment have been prominent. In 1990, for example, almost 16,000 Britons were allowed to immigrate to the United States as ''workers of distinguished merit and ability,'' compared to fewer than 4,000 Germans during the same year. California, especially, has received huge numbers of recent British immigrants. The addition of so many talented, professional, and well-trained people was obviously of great benefit to the U.S. economy and society.

America's culture, too, benefited greatly from the immigration of so many British stage and film actors, play and screen writers, classical and pop musicians, and just about every other person involved with culture and entertainment. One key reason why California today is the home of more British immigrants than any other state is precisely because it is the center of the movie and music industries, in which the British have been far more prominent than any other immigrant group, thanks in part to the language they had in common with Americans but also to their own long tradition of excellence in writing, acting, and music.

Although the most recent British immigrants arrive by jet aircraft, they have some similarities with those who sailed a century or more before them. They, too, are generally ambitious, talented, adventurous people who see a brighter future in America. Many had family members or friends already in America and used these connections to facilitate their move. Economic considerations were the most important, but not the only reason for their migration. Attractive offers to work in companies, laboratories, or universities have more than simple economic appeal. In addition, Americans living in Britain as businessmen, students, or military personnel have brought back British spouses, whereas many British students living in America have met spouses and stayed. Many recent immigrants also were exasperated with the comparatively rigid hierarchical tradition in Britain's society and institutions, and more were simply fed up with high taxes and what they saw as growing dependency in society. And like many immigrants of previous eras, some were just eager for a change and wanted to start over in a new country where there were greater rewards for their work. The shared heritage of Britain and America and the long, continual tradition of migration of people from one to the other made this quite easy to do.

BIBLIOGRAPHIC REFERENCES

There is not yet a comprehensive book on British migration to America from colonial times to the present, although still useful is Stanley Johnson's *A History of Emigration from the United Kingdom to North America, 1762–1912* (London: F. Cass, 1966 [1913]). The most important work on colonial migration is David Hacket Fischer's *Albion's Seed: Four British Folkways in America* (New York: Oxford University Press, 1989.) For a critical discussion of this work, see the published symposium on it in *The William and Mary Quarterly* 48.2 (April 1991): 223–308. For colonial immigration, see also David Cressy, *Coming Over: Migration and Communication between England and New England in the Seventeenth Century* (Cambridge: Cambridge University Press, 1987). British immigration before the Revolution is covered in detail in Bernard Bailyn, *Voyagers to the West: A Passage in the Peopling of America on the Eve of the Revolution* (New York: Knopf, 1986). For the nineteenth century, see Maldwyn Jones's survey in "The Background to Emigration from Great Britain in the Nineteenth Century," in *Perspectives in American History* (Cambridge, MA:Harvard University, 1973), 7:3–92; Alan Conway's "Welsh Emigration to the United States," ibid., pp. 177–271; and Wilbur Shepperson's *British Emigration to North America: Projects and Opinions in the Early Victorian Period* (Oxford: Blackwell, 1957). Gordon Donaldson's *The Scots Overseas* (London: R. Hale, 1966) is also helpful. Indispensable is Charlotte Erickson's *Invisible Immigrants: The Adaptation of English and Scottish Immigrants in Nineteenth-Century America* (Leicester: Leicester University Press, 1972) and *Leaving England: Essays on British Emigration in the Nineteenth Century* (Ithaca, NY: Cornell University Press, 1994).

For agricultural and industrial migration during the mid-century period, see William E. Van Vugt, *Britain to America: The Mid-Nineteenth Century Immigrants to the United States* (Champaign, IL: University of Illinois Press, 1999). The history of diffusion of skills and technology through British immigrants is covered in David Jeremy, *Transatlantic Industrial Revolution: The Diffusion of Textile Technologies between Britain and America, 1790s–1830s* (Oxford: Basil Blackwell, 1981); Geoffrey Tweedale, *Sheffield Steel and America: A Century of Commercial and Technological Interdependence, 1830–1930* (Cambridge: Cambridge University Press, 1987); as well as Rowland Berthoff, *British Immigrants in Industrial America, 1790–1950* (New York: Russell and Russell, 1968 [1953]). The migration of British Mormons is covered in Philip Taylor's *Expectations Westward* (Edinburgh: Oliver and Boyd, 1965). The twentieth century is not yet well researched, but see Kenneth Lines, *British and Canadian Immigration to the United States since 1920* (San Francisco: R & E Research Associates, 1978), along with his short but insightful article, "Britons Abroad," *The Economist* 325.7791 (1993): 86–88.

See also Priscilla Long, *Where the Sun Never Shines: A History of America's Bloody Coal Industry* (New York: Paragon House, 1991).

CENTRAL AND SOUTH AMERICANS

Carlos B. Cordova and Raquel Pinderhughes

For far more than a century, Central and South Americans have continuously immigrated to the United States.[1] Their countries of origin include Costa Rica, El Salvador, Guatemala, Honduras, Nicaragua, Panama, Belize, Argentina, Bolivia, Chile, Colombia, Ecuador, Paraguay, Peru, Uruguay, and Venezuela. These countries vary greatly in size, geography, history, language, levels of urbanization and industrialization, and number of immigrants who have resettled in the United States. Immigrants from these countries have been incorporated into the social fabric of the United States in different ways; the U.S. government has welcomed some groups more than others.

Central and South American immigrants are a very diverse group, for the population includes people from different socioeconomic, ethnocultural, and geographic backgrounds. Although the majority of Central and South Americans speak Spanish, the population also includes indigenous Indians who speak such languages as Quiche or Kanjobal and coastal Central Americans who speak English. Racially and ethnically, Central and South Americans are the descendants of indigenous Indian, African, and European peoples; yet the population also includes people of Asian descent. Although the majority of South and Central Americans are Roman Catholic, they also include many Protestants and a smaller number of Jews and people from other religions. Economic and sociopolitical instabilities are the most important determining factors for South and Central Americans to come to the United States. Overall, their relocation to the United States is the direct result of economic and political stresses in their home countries. According to the U.S. census, in 1990, there were 2,359,432 Central and South Americans from Spanish-language countries living in the United States. It is important to note that due to an undercount of undocumented persons the census figures appear to be a low estimation of the actual Central and South American populations.[2]

IMMIGRATION PATTERNS: FROM SOUTH AMERICA

Immigrants from South America have been coming to the United States since the 1800s. Over the past almost 200 years, over 1.4 million South Americans have legally entered and resettled in the United States, and a smaller, unknown number have entered the country without documents. South Americans have been motivated to immigrate for both socioeconomic and political reasons. In the 1800s, Chilean, Peruvian, and other South American men were drawn to the United States from economic motives. Their extensive experience in the mining industry in their home countries put them in high demand during the gold mining period in such states as California. Throughout the 1900s, South Americans continued to immigrate to the United States. From 1910 to 1930, over 4,000 South Americans entered annually. During World War II, labor demands contributed to increased immigration from South America. As a consequence of these early migrations, there are many second-, third-, and fourth-generation South Americans in the United States. However, the overwhelming majority of South American immigrants entered the United States after 1960, and a large part of the population, about 45 percent, has arrived since 1980.

According to the 1990 census, 87,705 South Americans reported that they had entered the United States prior to 1965. During the 1960s many new South American immigrants entered and resettled in the United States as a consequence of new policies in the Immigration Act of 1965, including a ceiling placed on the Western Hemisphere for the first time. The preference system was extended to the Western Hemisphere in 1977, as well as new labor certification procedures. The 1965 law encouraged professionals and skilled laborers to migrate to the United States and permitted the resettlement of numerous young working-class and middle-class South American families. Recent decades have also been characterized by political instability and the rise of military dictatorships in much of South America, and although many South American immigrants who came to the United States were seeking economic opportunities, others were fleeing political persecution and turmoil in their countries of origin. For example, thousands of Chileans fled their country from the severe military repression of the Pinochet government. As they sought refuge abroad, many selected to resettle in the United States. Moreover, by this time, many U.S. urban centers had well-established Latin American immigrant communities that attracted South Americans to their neighborhoods.

Between 1965 and 1979, about 291,491 persons from Spanish-speaking South America entered the United States. Between 1980 and 1990, almost 400,000 more were admitted, and another 219,500 in the early 1990s (1991–1995). These immigrations were primarily composed of Colombians, Peruvians, Ecuadorians, Argentineans, Venezuelans, and Chileans. Among these groups, the greatest number of legal South American immigrants in the United States immigrated from Colombia. In 1994, Colombia ranked as the nineteenth largest sending nation. In addition, during the past several decades, a smaller number of South Americans entered the United States without immigrant documents. According to the census, 1,035,602 South Americans resided in the United States in 1990.

IMMIGRATION PATTERNS: FROM CENTRAL AMERICA

Central Americans have been resettling in the United States since the 1800s. Between 1820 and 1995, over 1 million Central Americans legally resettled in the United States. More than half of the Central American immigrant population took up residence in the United States after 1980. The post-1980 immigrants also included a very large number of undocumented persons.

The first wave of Central American immigration to the United States can be traced to the mid-1800s, when coffee was introduced as a cash crop in Central America, and a thriving export trade developed on the West Coast, with San Francisco as the chief processing center. Once these links were established, social networks led to migratory movements back and forth, at first limited to the Central American elite. Gradually many Central Americans, both male and female, were recruited to work in coffee factories and other food industries in the United States.

The second wave of Central American immigration to the United States occurred during the 1930s and 1940s. During this period, Central American immigrants established communities in New York, San Francisco, Los Angeles, Houston, and New Orleans. This cohort of Central Americans was composed of men and women from the urban middle classes who had relatively high levels of education—intellectuals, teachers, labor organizers, political dissidents, and exiled military officers who were not in agreement with their national governments. There were also individuals who had direct ties to their governments and/ or who were members of the dominant social class in their countries. Their immigration was motivated by their desire to escape failing economies, political persecution, and a lack of personal freedom.

Unlike subsequent waves of Central American immigrants, the second wave of Central American immigrants relied mostly on family networks established by the first wave rather than on ethnic, neighborhood, village, or national migration networks. It was this cohort of Central American immigrants who became active members of social migration networks and helped to establish the social and economic foundations of U.S.-based Latin American immigrant communities that would benefit future generations of Latin Americans. World War II did create some demand for labor from Central America, and a small number of immigrants resettled in the United States, but the third wave of Central American immigration to the United States can be traced to the 1960s, when over 100,000 were admitted. According to the 1990 U.S. census, 59,737 Central Americans reported that they had entered the United States prior to 1965. Then, in the mid-1960s, Central American immigration began to increase dramatically. The increase was influenced by the new policies of the Immigration Act of 1965, which permitted the resettlement of numerous young working-class and middle-class Central American families. Newcomers resettled in established Latin American neighborhoods, where existing social networks, familiar cultural traditions, and support systems were maintained by the Latin Americans residing there. The new Central American arrivals further developed the economic, social, and cultural structures and networks of Latin American ethnic communities in San Francisco, Los Angeles, Houston, New Orleans, and Washington, D.C., as well as on Long Island, New York, and towns in New Jersey. The impact of the new immigrants on these already established communities was already clearly discernible during the late 1960s and early 1970s.

In the late 1970s and early 1980s, migration patterns from Central America changed as a direct result of sociopolitical and socioeconomic conditions in the region. Political turmoil forced large numbers of Salvadorans, Guatemalans, Nicaraguans, and Hondurans to enter the United States as political asylum applicants or without legal immigration documents. While the pre-1979 migrations had been mostly economic in nature, the post-1979 migrations were generated by severe economic and political stresses faced by most of the nations in the Central American region.

Before the 1970s, most Central American immigrants arrived with legal immigration status as permanent residents or with student visas. After the 1970s, the majority entered the United States without documentation. The U.S. Bureau of the Census reported that the total number of Central Americans counted in the 1990 census was 1,323,830 persons. Of the total, only 277,731 were U.S.-born, whereas 1,046,099 were foreign-born. According to the census data, 59,737 had arrived in the United States prior to 1965; 256,149 came between 1965 and 1979; and 730,213 were admitted between 1980 and 1990. During the early 1990s (1991–1995) another 292,350 from Spanish-speaking Central America also acquired permanent residence. However, there is wide agreement that exact demographic figures of legal and undocumented Central American immigrants are not currently available, for large numbers of Central Americans entered the country illegally after 1979. Presently, Central America ranks as the second largest Latin American region contributing legal and undocumented immigrations to the United States (after Mexico). For example, according to Immigration and Naturalization Service (INS) estimates for October 1992, out of nearly 2.39 million undocumented persons in the United States, one fourth (about 595,000) were from the Spanish-speaking countries of Central America (e.g., El Salvador, 327,000; Guatemala, 129,000), almost three-fifths of whom were believed to be in California. By way of contrast, only 160,000 were estimated to be from all of Spanish South America, principally Colombians (59,000) and Ecuadorians (45,000).[3]

As a direct consequence of widespread political turmoil in the Central American region, Central Americans have been affected by a number of changes in immigration and refugee policy and legislation. The 1980 Refugee Act added distinct classifications for refugee and political asylum applicants, and tens of thousands of Central Americans petitioned for political asylum in the United States; comparatively few applications have been granted. For example, in 1990, the INS received 22,271 asylum applications from Salvadorans; 260 individuals were granted asylum, and 8,648 were denied.[4] The Immigration Reform and Control Act (IRCA) of 1986 was enacted by Congress to grant legalization status to undocumented persons who had entered the U.S. territory prior to, and resided continuously since, January 1, 1982. By 1988 only 168,053 Salvadorans and 70,960 Guatemalans (out of 286,158 applicants from Central America) had applied for amnesty, much lower than the numbers that the INS predicted would apply. The Temporary Protected Status (TPS) Legislation for individuals from designated countries (notably El Salvador) was passed by Congress as part of the Immigration Act of 1990. TPS meant that these individuals could legally reside in the United States for an eighteen-month period that began on January 1, 1991. Deferred Enforced Departure (DED) then extended TPS for an additional twelve months. Although many Salvadorans applied for TPS/DED, many more did not, thinking that TPS/DED was a short-term remedy for their immigration status. The ABC Program was enacted in January 1991 after the U.S. government settled a legal case brought by the American Baptist Churches (ABC) on behalf of over eighty religious and refugee assistance organizations, which claimed that the INS and State Department had a history of discriminatory practices against Salvadorans and Guatemalans applying for political asylum. Consequently, under the ABC Program those individuals who were residing in the United States as of September 19, 1990, and had previously been denied political asylum by a district director, an immigration judge, or the Board of Immigration Appeals could get another opportunity to have their cases reviewed by a newly trained corps of asylum officers hired under regulations that were enacted in November 1990. Because they feared for their personal safety upon their return to their country of origin and were interested in a more permanent solution than TPS/DED offered, many Salvadorans and Guatemalans applied to the ABC Program. Still, the number of applicants denied political asylum is unclear; in the late 1990s many individuals were being deported back to their country of origin. Even greater concern was expressed by those whose temporary status expired in 1996 and early 1997, especially since the September 1996 Illegal Immigration Reform and Immigrant Responsibility Act streamlined deportation procedures. At the end of September 1995, there had been 137,857 Salvadoran asylum cases still pending, along with 125,867 Guatemalan but only 23,364 Nicaraguan ones. In fact, 63 percent of *all* pending cases (464,121) involved Central Americans. Between 1991 and 1995, less than 4,900 had been approved from the three principal countries.

MIGRATION PATTERNS WITHIN THE UNITED STATES, 1970–1990: SOUTH AMERICANS

The majority of South Americans who immigrated to the United States after 1970 were motivated by a combination of economic and sociopolitical conditions in their countries of origin; that is, many came seeking opportunities that would benefit family members who had remained in their countries of origin, and others had left their countries as a result of political instability and the rise of military dictatorships. Most South American immigrants settled in urban areas; very small numbers have settled in rural areas. The majority are concentrated on the West Coast, in San Francisco and Los Angeles, and in the Northeast, in New York and Chicago. In New York, for example, many South Americans resettled in the borough of Queens, where various subgroups live in separate neighborhoods. In all these cities, having found jobs in the professional, service, and manufacturing sectors, South Americans have settled both in and outside of established Latino communities.

The following three examples will illustrate the diversity among South Americans residing in the United States.

Colombians

The Colombian community is concentrated mainly in the Northeast, in New York City and Chicago. Between 1945 to 1955, political instability in Colombia triggered a large-scale immigration to the United States. The community in New York City dates back to the 1940s, when a few hundred white, middle-class, educated Colombians settled in the borough of Queens in a then working-class neighborhood called Jackson Heights. It provided decent housing, good schools, and easy access to Manhattan. These early immigrants formed the nucleus of a now predominantly white, middle-class community into which large numbers of Colombians have settled over many years. After 1960, thousands more of Colombians emigrated in search of economic and educational opportunities not available to them in Colombia, and most settled in existing Colombian and Latino neighborhoods. Throughout these communities, Colombians have established professional, social, business, political, and recreational associations and opened many small businesses, such as restaurants, grocery stores, real estate and travel businesses, and repair shops. The Colombian community in Chicago is smaller and more racially diverse than its New York counterpart, but it includes both a highly educated, middle- and upper-class community, which resides mostly in the suburbs, and a working-class community that is more urbanized. However, both communities (New York and Chicago) are racially diverse, consisting of white Colombians and those whose ancestry is a mixture of Afro-Caribbean, Indian, and European descent. Like New York City's Colombian communities, those in Chicago have established professional, social, business, political, and recreational associations held together by ethnic and regional ties. The 1990 census reported 378,726 Latinos of Colombian origin (see Table 2).

Chileans

Chileans have been immigrating to the United States since the mid-1800s, when Chilean miners came to work in the gold mines in California. The civil

Table 2
Hispanic Central and South Americans: 1990 Census

Country	Total Number	U.S.- born	Foreign- born	Before 1965	1965- 1979	1980- 1990
Central America						
Total	1,323,830	277,731	1,046,099	59,737	256,149	730,213
Costa Rica	57,223	17,785	39,438	7,218	15,424	16,796
El Salvador	565,081	106,405	458,676	11,851	100,883	345,942
Guatemala	268,779	52,783	215,996	6,608	60,500	148,888
Honduras	131,066	30,076	100,990	7,957	25,028	68,005
Nicaragua	202,658	38,363	164,295	12,127	30,118	122,050
Panama	92,013	30,317	61,696	13,437	22,607	25,652
Other	7,010	2,002	5,008	539	1,589	2,880
South America						
Total	1,035,602	259,566	776,036	87,705	291,491	396,840
Argentina	100,921	22,935	77,986	15,950	31,147	30,889
Bolivia	38,073	9,030	29,043	2,874	8,410	17,759
Chile	68,799	18,477	50,322	5,772	23,348	21,202
Colombia	378,726	97,657	281,069	29,373	106,129	145,567
Ecuador	191,198	49,859	141,339	17,253	62,337	61,749
Paraguay	6,662	1,886	4,776	229	1,744	2,803
Peru	175,035	40,530	134,505	11,923	39,387	83,195
Uruguay	21,996	3,785	18,211	1,125	8,838	8,248
Venezuela	47,997	12,783	35,214	2,606	8,861	23,747
Other	6,195	2,624	3,571	600	1,290	1,681

Source: U.S. Bureau of the Census, *1990 Census of Population and Housing. Special Summary Tape File 3, Persons of Hispanic Origin in the United States* (Washington, D.C.: Government Printing Office, September 1994).

war of 1891 provoked Chile's first mass emigration, with large numbers fleeing to Argentina, Europe, and the United States. This population movement was followed by political instability, a parliamentary republic, a military coup (1924), constitutional reform, a brief socialist republic (1932), a return to conservative rule, and the leftist Popular Front coalition (1938). After World War II, Chile's economy deteriorated, and at the same time as European immigration to Chile was increasing, Chilean immigration to other Latin American countries and to the United States also increased. Most of these immigrants were middle-class urbanites. Then Salvador Allende Gossens was elected president in 1970, and his socialist policies, including land reforms and the nationalization of the copper industries, sparked a U.S.-led economic embargo. In 1973, a U.S.-backed military group, led by General Augusto Pinochet, assassinated Allende, dissolved Congress, persecuted dissenting political activists, and declared a state of siege. Pinochet became president in 1974 and banned political parties three years later. Over 1 million people are estimated to have been exiled or forced to flee Chile during Pinochet's rule (1973–1989). About 10 percent of these refugees settled in the United States, with large numbers going to California, New York, and Washington, D.C., and creating a significant cultural impact on the communities in which they settled. Although the flow of immigrants subsided in the early 1980s, the numbers increased again in the mid-1980s as a result of Chile's economic deterioration. However, since the reinstatement of civilian government in 1989, thousands of Chileans have returned to their native land. According to the U.S. census, in 1990 there were 68,799 Latinos of Chilean origin in the United States.

Peruvians

Peruvians have been migrating to the United States since the 1800s. In the contemporary period, the majority of Peruvian immigrants have followed traditional social migration networks when they relocated to the United States. The majority have settled in the following states in order of preference: New York, California, Florida, and Illinois as well as Washington, D.C. Peruvian immigrants are the only Latin American immigrants in the United States who, since 1984, formally have annual conventions of their immigrant and community organizations and cultural associations to address the needs of their community. In 1990, the census reported that there were 175,035 Peruvians in the United States. However, research on Peruvian immigration to the United States suggests that more than 400,000 are currently residing in the United States. In recent years there has been a major influx of Peruvians into the state of California, the majority of whom are young students who have left Peru as a result of economic and political instability.

MIGRATION PATTERNS WITHIN THE UNITED STATES, 1970–1990: CENTRAL AMERICANS

Sociopolitical and economic crises have been the most important determinant factors for the contemporary Central American migrations to the United States. In the post-1970 period, El Salvador, Guatemala, and Nicaragua were affected by armed insurgency against the established governments. During the 1980s, more than 200,000 people were assassinated by right-wing paramilitary groups, death squads, and the armed forces in El Salvador and Guatemala. During this time of war and persecution the most common targets for assassination were labor leaders, Indian leaders, intellectuals, community organizers, Catholic priests, lay preachers, catechizers, agricultural workers, and students. In Nicaragua, the Sandinista revolution against the Anastasio Somoza government in the late 1970s and the Contra war in the 1980s claimed an additional 200,000 victims.

Three different migration patterns have been identified among Central American immigrant populations in the United States. The first has been selected by urban dwellers who choose to relocate to urban centers in the United States. It is assumed that these individuals are accustomed to city life and make every possible attempt to relocate to an urban environment in order to take advantage of the opportunities available in U.S. cities. In general, these immigrants have higher levels of education and possess some of the skills necessary to be successfully incorporated into the U.S. society. The Central American communities in San Francisco and Los Angeles are examples of this migration.

The second pattern is observable in Central American rural populations immigrating to U.S. urban communities. These populations come from lower-working-class backgrounds, have lower levels of education, and are not as well prepared to be successfully incorporated into the U.S. urban environment. Consequently, the majority must accept low-wage jobs in insecure sectors of the labor market. These patterns are observable in Houston, Washington, D.C., and Los Angeles.

The third pattern is followed by Central American rural dwellers who elect to resettle in rural areas and to work as agricultural laborers. The majority earn very low wages, and most live below the poverty level, a pattern commonly observed in the large agricultural fields in California and Florida.

Examples here, too, will convey the variety of patterns and experiences among Central Americans in the United States.

Salvadorans

The Salvadoran immigrant population in the United States is composed of people from a range of socioeconomic and cultural backgrounds who hold diverse political ideologies. In the 1970s, many members of the ruling class in El Salvador left the country to resettle legally in the United States, predominantly in Florida and California. These newcomers had already established economic, cultural, and political ties in the United States; many had been educated in U.S. or European universities. Their socioeconomic status, educational background, bilingual skills, and legal residency helped them to adjust readily to their new lives in the United States. This phenomenon of upper-class migrations is characteristic of Latin American societies undergoing revolutions, as was observable, for example, in the case of Cuba and Nicaragua.

Salvadoran society has been affected by a long history of political upheaval, and the impact of the civil war has been multidimensional. The majority of Salvadorans who fled their country after 1979 did so to escape the civil war and to search for personal safety and a new life. The lack of justice and the constant threats and intimidation by opposing sides not only made life there precarious but also left the refugees with the residual effects of living in a society severely traumatized by a climate of terror. Moreover, most who entered during the 1980s did so without a legal status and originated from middle-and lower-class backgrounds, the majority thus lacking both the economic and social support available to upper-class Salvadorans and recognized rights of legal residency. A significant number also did not have the educational, occupational, and language skills needed to succeed in the United States.

And yet the majority of post-1979 Salvadoran immigrants arrived as part of ethnic and family migration networks that have been shaped by long-standing family, friendship, ethnic, home town, and community ties, which partially eased the immigrants' integration into the host society. These patterns are particularly visible in their communities in San Francisco, Los Angeles, Houston, Chicago, New York City, Washington, D.C., and on Long Island, New York.

Since the early 1980s Salvadorans have made up the largest of all of the Central American groups in the United States; however, exact demographic figures are not available because of the undocumented status of a large percentage of them. The Bureau of the Census estimated the Salvadoran population living in the United States in 1990 to be over the 565,081 people enumerated, of which 106,405 were U.S.-born and 458,676 foreign-born. The *1995 Immigration and Naturalization Service Yearbook* placed the number of undocumented Salvadorans at 298,000 persons, second in the United States only to Mexicans.

Guatemalans

Guatemalans began to arrive in the United States following the 1954 military coup that overthrew the democratically elected government of Jacobo Arbenz. After the coup, many were exiled or fled the country in order to escape political persecution; the majority migrated to California. This early migration was characterized by an urban middle-class population made up of intellectuals, political activists, union leaders, and university students.

According to the 1990 census, only about 6,600 Guatemalans reported that they had entered the United States before 1965. After 1965, the Guatemalan population increased dramatically. The 1990 census reported that 268,779 Latinos of Guatemalan origin lived in the United States: 52,783 were U.S.-born, and 215,996 foreign-born. However, in 1995, the Immigration and Naturalization Service estimated that there were also approximately 121,000 undocumented Guatemalans present. According to the INS, Guatemala ranks third among the ten countries that contribute most to the undocumented population in the United States. In urban centers, the majority of Guatemalans come from urban communities and from middle- and working-class backgrounds. They are mostly Spanish-speaking persons with higher levels of education who are more skilled and better prepared to cope with the U.S. culture and society than are the indigenous Mayans who entered the United States in large numbers in the early 1980s. Nevertheless, Mayans have also settled in such large metropolitan centers as Los Angeles, Houston, and San Francisco.

During the early 1980s, numerous Mayan communities in Guatemala were systematically destroyed as part of a strategic plan of action on the part of the Guatemalan military government. The refugees were subjected to government military actions that massacred the elderly, women, and children, who made up the vast majority of the refugee population. Entire populations were involuntarily relocated in strategic areas or were forced to migrate to Mexico or the United States by the repressive campaigns of terror carried out by the armed forces.

In rural areas in the Southwest, the Central American population is composed mostly of indigenous, rural Mayan people, most of whom had made a living from traditional agriculture, for the Mayan indigenous culture is governed by the rhythm of the corn agriculture and the seasons, and people preferred to reestablish their lives in a rural rather than an urban environment. Large numbers of Guatemalan Mayan immigrants are unskilled young males with low educational backgrounds who can only find employment as seasonal migrant workers in the agricultural farms throughout the Sunbelt states. There are also numerous Guatemalan Mayans working in the agricultural fields of Florida, Texas, Arizona, Oregon, Washington, and California.

Nicaraguans

Nicaraguan migrations to the United States began in the 1930s and were characterized by a flow of people escaping political persecution from the Somoza government. This first wave of Nicaraguans to the United States was composed of middle-class individuals, professionals, intellectuals, university students, labor organizers, and political dissidents. Many of these Nicaraguan exiles resettled in New York, New Orleans, San Francisco, and Los Angeles. During the 1940s, Nicaraguans entered the United States in search of economic opportunities, but many eventually returned to their country after World War II to become part of a new, rising entrepreneurial class. Nonetheless, by the 1960s, the Nicaraguan population in the United States was the largest of the Central American national groups. As the political turmoil in the 1970s escalated to armed conflict, Nicaraguans sought refuge in the United States.

After the fall of the Somoza regime and the Sandinista victory, many of the original immigrants from the 1930s and 1940s (or their descendants) returned to live in Nicaragua. At the same time, Nicaraguans associated with the former government began to arrive in the United States. During the early 1980s, some were members of the upper class that fled because of their ties with Somoza or their political disagreements with the Sandinista government. Others were businessmen who had had economic ties to Somoza, and still others were former members of the National Guard who had escaped from the Sandinista army. Most of these immigrants resettled legally in Florida and California, bringing their wealth and conservative political ideologies with them. By the mid-1980s, however, most immigrants arriving were working-class youth escaping from the Contra war and the military draft.

According to the 1990 census, 202,658 Latinos of Nicaraguan origin were residing in the United States. Of that number, 38,363 were U.S.-born and 164,295 foreign-born. In 1995 the Immigration and Naturalization Service estimated that there were at least 76,000 undocumented Nicaraguans living in the United States and that Nicaragua ranked eighth among the top ten contributing to the undocumented population in the United States.

Costa Ricans and Hondurans

In 1990 the Census Bureau estimated that 57,223 Costa Ricans were in the United States, of whom 17,785 were U.S.-born and 39,438 foreign-born. One can assume that the small number of Costa Ricans in the United States can be attributed to Costa Rica's long history of political stability and democratic tradition. The majority of Hondurans (100,990 foreign-born and 30,076 U.S.-born) reside on the East Coast, from Florida to New York. The social, cultural, and political experiences of both national groups have not been studied in depth.

DEMOGRAPHIC CHARACTERISTICS: SOUTH AMERICANS

Of the approximately 1,035,600 South American immigrants counted in the 1990 U.S. census from Spanish-origin countries, 281,069 had emigrated from Colombia; 141,339 from Ecuador; 134,505 from Peru; 77,986 from Argentina; 50,322 from Chile; 35,214 from Venezuela; 29,043 from Bolivia; 18,211 from Uruguay, and 4,776 from Paraguay. For all of these groups, the population is about equally composed of males and females, with the exception of Colombians, who have more males than females in the U.S.-based population. Overall and within groups, the South American Latino-origin population in the United States is a young population. In 1990 the median age of its members was approximately thirty-one years of age. Fewer than 6 percent of its members were over age sixty-two, whereas 27 percent were under nineteen years of age. In addition, the proportion of foreign-born persons to U.S.-born persons is significantly larger for every South American immigrant group. According to the U.S. census (1990), 776,036 South Americans were foreign-born, compared to 259,566 who were U.S.-born (75 percent–25 percent).

As a group, South Americans in the United States have high levels of educational attainment. On average, in 1990, 71 percent of all South Americans had at least a high school education, 20 percent had a bachelor's degree or more, and only 13 percent had less than a ninth-grade education. Venezuelans appear to have the highest levels among South Americans (in 1990, 86 percent had a high school degree or more; 38 percent had a B.A. degree or more; and only 6 percent had less than a ninth-grade education).

South Americans have been integrated into the U.S. labor market at every level. Their labor force participation rates are high, and their rates of unemployment are relatively low, although higher among women than men. In 1990,

84 percent of South American men and 63 percent of South American women were in the paid labor force, whereas 6 percent of men and 9 percent of women were unemployed. Importantly, naturalized South Americans had lower rates of unemployment than did those who were not citizens. Compared to most Latino groups, South Americans not only have high levels of education, but more are also employed in the managerial and professional sector (21 percent). However, the numbers employed in jobs requiring high levels of education vary among particular South American groups. For example, while one-third of all Venezuelans, Argentineans, and Chileans were in the managerial and professional sectors, only 14 percent of Ecuadorians and 17 percent of Colombians were so employed. There are also large numbers of South Americans employed in the technical, sales, and administrative sectors (21 percent) and as operators, fabricators, and laborers (22 percent). Smaller numbers are employed in precision production, craft, and repair (18 percent) and in the service sector (17 percent). Only 1 percent of South Americans work in farming, forestry, or fishing. Finally, although the majority of South Americans work for others, many South Americans have opened small businesses. A significant proportion of these businesses cater primarily to Latinos and include grocery stores, restaurants, auto, travel, lending, real estate, and taxi businesses.[5]

As a consequence of relatively high levels of education and integration into all levels of the labor market, compared to most Latino subgroups, South American households brought home higher wages. In 1990, 24 percent of South American households were earning more than $50,000 (31 percent of Argentinean households; 29 percent of Uruguayan households; and 28 percent of Chilean households), and 9 percent were earning over $75,000 (16 percent of Paraguayan households; 14 percent of Argentine households). Importantly, South American households whose members are naturalized have significantly higher earnings than those whose members are not citizens: for example, 23 percent verses 12 percent, respectively, among those earning $50,000 or more. However, not all South American households are insulated from poverty. Thus, despite the fact that Venezuelans have high levels of education, high rates of labor force participation, and low rates of unemployment, 15 percent of their families were living below the poverty line in 1990; Ecuadorian and Colombian families also had high rates of poverty. Here, too, rates of family poverty are twice as high among South American immigrant families whose members are not citizens as among those whose members are naturalized, although part of the explanation lay in the fact that many of the former were relatively recent newcomers who had not yet qualified to apply for citizenship.

DEMOGRAPHIC CHARACTERISTICS:
CENTRAL AMERICANS

According to the U.S. census, 1,046,099 Central American immigrants resided in the United States in 1990. The largest group of Central American immigrants were from El Salvador (458,676); next were Guatemalans (215,996), followed by Nicaraguans (164,295), Hondurans (100,990), Panamanians (61,696), and Costa Ricans (39,438). These groups vary in the ratio of men to women in their populations; among El Salvadorans and Guatemalans, there are more men than women; among the other four groups, there are more women than men. The proportion of foreign-born persons is significantly large for every Central American group, reflecting the recency of arrivals. Among the Central American population as a whole, 79 percent were foreign-born (1,046,099).

Compared with other populations, the Central American Latino-origin population is also young, with proportionately more children and fewer elderly. In 1990, the median age of the population was approximately twenty-eight years old. Only 4 percent of the population were sixty-two years of age or over, and 32 percent were nineteen years of age or less. This youthful age structure is a result of a combination of new immigration, which consists mostly of young adults in their reproductive years, and high fertility among the foreign-born.

As a group (and compared to South Americans), Central American immigrants in the United States have relatively low levels of educational attainment. On average, in 1990, more than half of the Central American population (54 percent) had less than a high school degree; 34 percent had less than a ninth-grade education; and only 9 percent of Central Americans had a bachelor's degree or more. Among Central Americans, the Panamanians, Costa Ricans, and Nicaraguans have the highest levels of educational attainment, Salvadorans and Guatemalans the lowest. A significant proportion of the Central American population (60 percent) does not speak English well, and a large majority of them (71 percent) are not U.S. citizens.

While both Central American men and women have high rates of labor force participation, they are poorly integrated into the U.S. labor market, for the vast majority are disproportionately employed in low-wage sectors. The vast majority (approximately 85 percent) are employed in jobs requiring no more than lower levels of education. In 1990, only 9 percent of Central Americans were employed in the managerial and professional sector. A direct consequence of this are the low earnings of many Central American families. The majority would be described as "working poor," since these are families where adults are working full-time, but their wages are not high enough to lift them out of poverty. In 1990, one fourth of Central American families with children were living below the poverty level, with the rates of poverty highest among Honduran, Salvadoran, and Guatemalan families and particularly among families whose members were not citizens. The population also includes a small percentage of families and households whose incomes are substantially higher. In 1990, 15 percent of Central American households had incomes of more than $50,000, and 4.6 percent had incomes of more than $75,000.

Nevertheless, throughout and across various Central American countries, working-class and poor populations have strong similarities in their social and cultural experiences—cutting across ethnic boundaries—and most have little in common with upper-class social and cultural experiences. And yet, despite the poverty many of these newcomers have been experiencing, large numbers of individuals of various Central American origins presently living in the United States do actually come from middle-or working-class backgrounds. They include teachers, high school and university students, secretaries, accountants, homemakers, domestic workers, office workers, and skilled factory workers. They also include large numbers of much poorer, rural agricultural workers, who arrived in the United States in the 1980s, escaping political persecution, forced relocation, or the unsafe political climate in their native rural communities.

OBSTACLES TO INTEGRATION AND ADAPTATION

The most common recurring acculturation problems faced by Central and South American immigrants include language acquisition; lack of employment opportunities; labor market exploitation; low income; educational attainment; access to health care, both physical and psychological; and cultural differences. For those living in the United States without immigration documents, their "undocumented" status is the overarching problem. Undocumented South and Central American immigrants have more difficulties in adapting to their host society than do their legal counterparts. Their undocumented status, constant fear of deportation by immigration officials, and often, psychological problems caused by the repressive political conditions in which they previously lived all affect their daily lives and settlement experiences. Thus, while many undocumented South and Central Americans feel trapped because they are unable to return to their country of origin due to their documentation status, fear of persecution, and lack of personal safety, they are also encountering a series of difficulties that prevent them from becoming fully incorporated into U.S. society and culture.

Language Acquisition

Language acquisition is considered an important priority in the acculturation process. Mastering the English language is necessary if recently arrived immigrants are to improve their socioeconomic status and cultural experience. The higher the degree of proficiency in the new language, the greater the opportunities and skills the individual will possess to enable him or her to effectively interact in the mainstream society. Those holding professional degrees or some formal education demonstrate higher-level language acquisition than do those who are unskilled laborers, and this does improve their labor market opportunities. However, for those without legal status, it is very difficult to find work in their fields, including professionals, university professors, and teachers. Many experience downward social mobility, and many are employed in occupations where they cannot use their training or skills. This generates frustrations and emotional and psychological problems. In addition, their high expectations of opportunities available in the United States and the disappointment of not fulfilling those expectations create a high degree of stress.

Age also plays an important role in the acquisition of language skills. Typically, younger individuals demonstrate higher motivation and capacity to learn English than do older persons. With the exception of individuals with a professional background, middle age and older immigrants often limit their social interaction to their ethnic enclave and demonstrate a preference for retaining Spanish as their primary means of communication. It provides them with social comfort but also functions to constrain their integration into the labor market and American society.

Although all South and Central American immigrants are confronted with cultural differences when they resettle in the United States, indigenous Central and South American peoples face particular challenges in their adaptation to the United States, for many speak neither English nor Spanish; many have never lived outside their rural villages; and many have lived in the cycle of agriculture and the seasons. The situation of Guatemalan Mayan people who have settled in the state of Florida serves as an example. Most of those working in Florida are Kanjobal-speaking people who originate from the town of San Miguel Acatlán, located in the Cuchumatan mountains in the northern province of Huehuetenango. Their adjustment has been difficult because they are mostly monolingual, speaking only Mayan languages, and hold non-Western cultural values. In the United States these refugees work primarily in the citrus fields and are no longer engaged in the cycle of corn agriculture. They encounter situations that disrupt their culture and religion and compel them to discontinue their rituals and cultural traditions. Although the pre-U.S. experiences of indigenous people from Otovalo, Ecuador, are much more urban, they, too, are confronted by a culture and a way of life that are quite different than their own.

Employment Opportunities

Employment opportunities are one of the major factors affecting the social adaptation and economic stability of immigrant communities. Those who immigrate with legal status and high levels of education have been able to integrate into almost every sector of the labor market. Those with legal status but low levels of education have some opportunity to pursue education and training, although programs for adults are limited. Because employment opportunities are so closely dependent on an individual's immigration status, the economic opportunities available to undocumented workers are very limited. While individuals with high education and good English-language skills are sometimes able to find better-paid employment, for educated immigrants who are undocumented, employment is most often found in factories, construction and janitorial firms, the hotel and restaurant industry, or in domestic services, sectors where undocumented workers are especially vulnerable to exploitation and low wages.

Many immigrants find employment within an ethnic enclave, in the secondary labor market, or in domestic labor. Employment is secured through contacts established via the ethnic networks—for example, family and friends who find jobs for new arrivals at their place of employment—or in places known to hire undocumented workers. For Central Americans, church-based groups and non-profit community agencies have provided employment counseling, referral services, and job networks. Under the present-day anti-immigrant climate, their undocumented immigration status is the most serious problem faced by the majority of Central and South American immigrants in this country. Such legislation as Proposition 187 in California and the 1996 federal immigration changes may seriously affect the economic, social, and cultural experience of the undocumented Latino population.

Educational Needs

According to information available on educational attainment from the March 1994 *CPS* (*Current Population Survey*), Latino adults in the United States have a significant disadvantage in educational attainment vis-à-vis other population groups. However, there are significant differences between Latino subgroups, and the contrasting educational profiles of South and Central Americans exemplify some of these differences. As noted, compared to South Americans, Central Americans have lower rates of educational attainment as well as significant differences in rates of educational attainment between naturalized and non-citizen immigrant populations, with citizen populations having much higher levels of educational attainment.

Poverty appears to play a significant role in educational attainment among youth. Poverty forces teenagers prematurely into the labor force, and problems of overcrowded, poorly equipped big-city American schools, which most Latinos attend, also boost dropout rates and discourage continued education. Latinos also suffer from discrimination in U.S. schools and in their communities, but one glaring obstacle to higher education remains the lack of documentation status: Almost all institutions of higher learning require a Social Security number and other evidence of legal status, with recent legislation and policy reforms, such as those curtailing affirmative action by the University of California, further constricting the educational opportunities of undocumented persons. Among Latinos generally, the historically high dropout rate has ranged from two to three times the rate for children from other groups, depending on the measure used.

Access to Medical and Mental Health Care

Many of the medical and health services targeted toward immigrants, and especially those offered to undocumented immigrants, have been threatened by the anti-immigrant hysteria in the early and mid-1990s. One consequence of this has been policy changes that have placed restrictions on the undocumented or their access to food stamps and non-emergency medical services. Many among the Central American population in the United States have special needs in the fields of health and nutrition, as many recent immigrants suffer from a variety of medical problems, including parasitic infections, gastroenteritis, malnutrition, tuberculosis, high mortality rates, and/or mental health problems. Furthermore, until recently, only a small number of social workers, psychologists, and psychiatrists had studied the mental health problems of these immigrants, and most Central Americans are not familiar with U.S. mental health concepts and modes of psychological treatment.

It is a common belief in Central America that healthy and sane individuals do not need the services of psychologists and that only the mentally ill do. Yet the incidence of mental health problems—such as psychosocial trauma, posttraumatic stress disorders (PTSD), alcoholism, and abuse of pharmaceutical drugs—is reportedly high among Central American immigrants, especially among those who are undocumented. Individuals and their relatives who were victims of political violence in their homelands often manifest various forms of psychological problems upon their arrival and settlement in the United States. Torture victims suffer from PTSD symptoms exhibited as severe depression, guilt, nightmares, hyperalertness, insomnia, suicidal tendencies, and withdrawal. Psychiatric evaluations of Central Americans conducted by refugee centers in the San Francisco Bay Area, for example, have concluded that a significantly large number of their clients suffer from psychosocial trauma and PTSD. Reports documenting the impact of psychological disorders on Central American immigrants and their families suggest that marital and family relationships are negatively affected by the above-mentioned mental health problems. Conflicts, depression, alcohol and drug abuse, frustration, domestic violence, separation, and divorce are the recurring conditions reported.

Political Integration

The sociopolitical characteristics of the Central and South American populations are very diverse. Their communities have divergent political ideologies, ranging from conservative right-wing views to orthodox Marxist orientations. A community in a specific geographical location may manifest a wide diversity of political views or a more unified political ideology. In many ways, political diversity in Central and South American communities has constrained the development of social cohesion and political empowerment for all of its members, and as a group, these communities have ended up having limited political power and influence within the U.S. political structure. To date, South and Central American communities have not unified around issues associated with their shared Latino identity, regionalism, political party affiliations, ethnicity, religion, civil rights, and/or socioeconomic status. This lack of cooperation has prevented the social cohesion needed to transform these diverse populations into a strong unified political body that would be able to seek viable political solutions to the problems and realities that its members encounter in American society.

One major drawback to political empowerment has been the common belief on the part of the immigrants that their stay of residence in the United States will be of a temporary nature. Many refrain from seeking U.S. citizenship, and many others are unable to do so, owing to their uncertain refugee/asylum or undocumented status. Consequently, many remain isolated and nonparticipants in domestic political affairs at the community, municipal, state, or national levels. Over the years, some community activists have attempted to persuade South and Central American immigrants to become U.S. citizens and to participate in the electoral process. Until recently, these efforts were fruitless because many believed that if they became U.S. citizens, they would betray their national identity and citizenship. The situation changed rapidly in the 1990s because of the anti-immigrant currents, the passage of Proposition 187 in California in 1994, and the enactment in 1996 of the federal welfare and immigration legislation. These developments motivated thousands of Central and South Americans to apply for U.S. citizenship in order to retain their social service benefits and to protect themselves from INS harassment. For the first time in decades, community activism and political empowerment began to take root in Central and South American communities throughout the country.

Within the Central American population, the undocumented status of many persons has played a role in the community's not achieving formal political power. However, many Central American community organizations have attempted to achieve political power by forming organizations that are closely associated with political parties or organizations in their home country or region. For example, Casa El Salvador, Casa Nicaragua, and some Guatemalan organizations have close ties with Central American revolutionary movements. In California, these groups successfully employed solidarity actions against U.S. policies in Central America. Their success was based on the fact that they did not limit their activities to organizing only with Latin American communities. They reached out to the mainstream and created multiethnic coalitions by working closely with international solidarity coalitions and networks, including Committee in Solidarity with the People of El Salvador (CISPES), Amnesty International, and the Emergency Response Network. Their main objective was to deal with issues that directly affected the Central American region, but they did not place their main emphasis on the empowerment efforts within the local communities.

Such organizations as the Coalition for Immigrant and Refugee Rights and Services work within a local community structure to advocate on behalf of immigrants, especially concerning abuses against immigrant women. Their efforts have been successful in creating bridges between different local immigrant communities. Three Central American refugee organizations have been particularly effective in the internal affairs of the Central American community, while at the same time representing the refugees in the mainstream society and local political structures. They are the Comite de Refugiados Centro Americanos (CRECE), which provides refugees with social services; El Rescate, in Los Angeles, which offers a wide range of services to the Central American population; and the Central American Refugee Center (CARECEN), the legal and immigration services and advocacy agency of the refugee organizations in Washington, D.C., Houston, San Francisco, and Los Angeles. The latter provides legal representation to refugees in political asylum hearings, gives health referral services, trains health promoters, and produces literature for the Central American refugee community. During the mid-1980s and the early 1990s, CARECEN played an important role in the formation of the Central American National Network (CARNET), which included thirty-eight refugee agencies and grassroots organizations in the United States. The development of local leadership is an important priority in the selection and training of low-income Central American refugees who could work as refugee rights promoters and refugee advocates. The promoters provide services to the refugee community, speak in public forums, and both monitor and attempt to influence legislation affecting the Central American refugee community at the municipal, state, and national levels.

In these organizations, refugees work together to empower other refugees and address issues affecting the social experiences and cultural adaptation of Guatemalan and Salvadoran immigrants and refugees. Because of their organizational structure, history, philosophy, and their empowerment efforts, these community groups are recognized as representing the leadership in the Central American refugee and immigrant community. They also work closely with the religious organizations, a network of churches, Catholic Charities, Baptist Ministries, and Quakers, among others. They receive funds and direct services from religious organizations and private foundations. One successful model can be seen in the work done by St. Peter's Church, in the heart of San Francisco's Mission District. Led by refugees working side by side with the local pastor, they have created a Central American refugee program that provides a wide variety of services, such as a long-term shelter for homeless men, mental health counseling, rights advocacy, day laborer advocacy, cultural support, and language classes to the Mayan population in the area.

SUMMARY

The South and Central American population includes people who trace their families' resettlement in the United States to the 1800s, as well as persons who have recently arrived in the United States. It includes people who have all the privileges of citizenship along with those who fear government detection and are most vulnerable to discrimination, exploitation, and violations of basic rights. It includes urban people and rural people. It includes those whose primary language is Spanish and those whose primary language is an indigenous Indian language, among them Quiche, Kanjobal, or Quechua, together with persons whose principal language is English. It includes individuals who wish to stay in the United States as well as those who dream of returning to live in their homelands. It also includes people of all races, many ethnicities, and very diverse socioeconomic backgrounds. It includes those who have been incorporated into American society in very different ways, with some welcomed as workers or refugees and others rejected. These millions of people, who trace their ancestry to countries in Central and South America, have had an important impact on the social, cultural, economic, and political fabric of the United States and will continue to do so in the future.

NOTES

The authors would like to thank Jorge Del Pinal, of the U.S. Bureau of the Census, for providing statistical data on South and Central Americans from the 1990 census summary tape data file on Hispanics.

1. This chapter focuses on Central and South American immigrants who migrated from countries where Spanish is the official language, although the immigrants themselves may not speak Spanish. About 25 percent of South American immigrants who have been admitted into the United States come from Guyana and Brazil. Brazil, Guiana, Guyana, and Suriname are South American countries where French, Dutch, English, and Portuguese are the dominant languages. We have subtracted from our figures the numbers of South American immigrants from non-Spanish-speaking countries. Our text also does not include a discussion of the immigration experiences and settlement patterns of immigrants from Brazil, Guiana, Guyana, or Suriname. Likewise, our treatment of Central America omits Belize. Note: The statistical census data used in this essay have been derived from U.S. Bureau of the Census, *1990 Census of Population. Persons of Hispanic Origin in the United States*, 1990 CP-3–3 (Washington, D.C.: General Printing Office, August 1993).

2. See below for 1992 estimates.

3. The regional/ethnic variations in migration streams and networks are considerable and significant. Thus, whereas 59 percent of Central American undocumented persons were estimated to be in California, only 18 percent of such persons from South America resided there. Although merely 6 percent of the former lived in New York, 37 percent of the latter did. Finally, while undocumented Salvadorans and Guatemalans principally live in California, large percentages of such Nicaraguans and Colombians are believed to be in Florida.

4. Prior to 1980, U.S. immigration law did not have a formal definition of *refugee*, although there was a provision that allowed for the admission of up to 17,400 persons fleeing from persecution in a communist or communist-dominated country or within the general area of the Middle East. After the 1980 Refugee Act, for persons to qualify as a "refugee," they must be residing outside the United States; be able to prove that they have a well-founded fear of persecution because of race, religion, nationality, or membership in a particular social or political organization; and can show that they are unable to receive protection in their country of origin. The act also provided procedures for asylum seekers already present in the United States.

5. In 1982, South and Central Americans already owned approximately 27,000 firms in the United States, but most were quite small.

BIBLIOGRAPHIC REFERENCES

The available literature on South and Central American populations in the United States has been increasing at a slow pace since the mid-1980s. Sources on the demographic, socioeconomic, political, and cultural characteristics of Latinos/Hispanics have increased in recent years. The major sources for the demographic and social history of Central and South American immigrants in the United States are available in the U.S. Bureau of the Census, *1990 Census of Population. Persons of Hispanic Origin in the United States*, 1990 CP-3-3 (Washington, D.C.: Government Printing Office, 1993). The complete set of Hispanic 1990 census data can also be found in a CD-Rom published by the Bureau of the Census, *1990 Census of Population and Housing. Subject Summary Tape File 3, Persons of Hispanic Origin in the United States* (Washington, D.C.: Government Printing Office September 1994). A selected analysis of the 1990 census data with an emphasis on comparative data on Central and South American immigrant and U.S.-born demographic data can be found in Carlos B. Cordova and Jorge del Pinal, *Hispanics-Latinos: Diverse People in a Multicultural Society* (Washington, D.C.: National Association of Hispanic Publications, 1996).

An interesting analysis of early Chilean migration is Carlos U. Lopez, *Chilenos in California: A Study of the 1850, 1852, and 1860 Censuses* (San Francisco: R & E Research Associates, 1973). Another source on the Chilean migrations that took place between 1973 and 1976 is Diana Kay, *Chileans in Exile: Private Struggles, Public Lives* (New Hampshire, 1987). A great resource on the Andean migrations to the United States is Teofilo Altamirano, *Exodo: Peruanos en el Exterior* (Lima: Pontificia Universidad Católica del Peru, 1992). This book, written in Spanish, gives a detailed analysis of the demographics and nature of the Andean and specifically Peruvian migrations to the United States from 1980 to 1992.

The experience of Central American immigrants and refugees in the United States as a multidimensional reality is explored by a series of recent publications. Some of these works analyze a variety of issues, such as the determinant factor causing the migrations out of Central America; the various migration patterns followed by Central American immigrants; the acculturation dynamics of the various Central American populations; the formation and structure of Central American communities; the degrees of political participation of recently arrived immigrant groups and long-established communities; and the transnational cultural experiences of the various Central American groups presently living in the United States and their cohorts still residing in the Central American region.

Sara Mahler's *American Dreaming: Immigrant Life on the Margins* (Princeton NJ: Princeton University Press 1995) gives an interesting account of the migratory experiences of individuals who fled their homelands seeking refuge in the United States as well as a discussion of the experiences of Salvadoran and South American undocumented immigrants in suburban New York. Mahler's *Salvadorans in Suburbia: Symbiosis and Conflict* (Boston: Allyn and Bacon, 1995) also gives an excellent analysis of the living experiences of Salvadorans in New Jersey and also provides an excellent history of U.S. immigration legislation impacting Central American communities since the 1980s. Some excellent resources for individuals working with Central American immigrants are Carlos B. Cordova's "Living in the U.S.A.: Central American Immigrant Communities in the U.S.," in *Community Organizing in a Diverse Society*, 3rd ed., edited by F. Rivera and J. Erlich (Boston, 1977); and Nestor P. Rodriguez, "Undocumented Central Americans in Houston: Diverse Populations," *International Migration Review* 21 (1987): 4–26. This essay provides a history of Central American migrations to the United States and discusses the specific acculturation experiences of the various Central American national groups in the United States. In addition, Nora Hamilton and Norma Stoltz Chinchilla's "Central American Migration: A Framework for Analysis," *Latin American Research Review* 26 (1991): 75–110, provides an excellent theoretical model to work with Central American communities. And Allan F. Burns's *Maya in Exile* (Philadelphia: Temple University Press, 1992) gives a detailed account of the experiences of Kanjobal Mayans working in the citrus fields in Florida and their social and cultural experiences in Indiantown, a Maya community in Florida.

Two important studies that analyze the economic impact of Central American immigrants to the receiving societies in the United States are Norma Stoltz Chinchilla and Nora Hamilton's *Central American Enterprises in Los Angeles*, Special Report to the Mayor's Office (unpublished, 1989) and Terry A. Repak's *Waiting on Washington: Central American Workers in the Nation's Capital* (Philadelphia: Temple University Press, 1995).

A number of studies have been done on Colombian immigrants in the United States. Most important among these are Ines Cruz and Juanita Cantano's "Colombian Migration to the United States," Part I, and Elsa Chaney, "Colombian Migration to the United States," Part II, in *The Dynamics of Migration: International Migration*, edited by Wayne Cornelius, Interdisciplinary Communications Program (Washington, D.C.: Smithsonian, 1976); Ian Rockett's "Immigration Legislation and the Flow of Specialized Human Capital from South America to the United States," *International Migration Review* 10.1 (1976): 47–62; and Alejandro Portes's "Determinants of the Brain Drain," *International Migration Review* 10.4 (1976): 489–508.

CHINESE

Judy Yung

Chinese Americans are the oldest established and largest group among Asian communities in the United States. Because of their immigration pattern since the 1850s, Chinese Americans are also diverse in terms of geographic origin, dialect, generation, political orientation, religious practice, and class background. However, Chinese Americans do share a common cultural heritage and legacy of racial discrimination in the United States. They have the unfortunate distinction of being the first ethnic group in U.S. history to be singled out for immigration exclusion. The Chinese Exclusion Act of 1882, which barred the further immigration of Chinese laborers and denied Chinese in the United States the right to naturalization, was not repealed until 1943. Chinese Americans waited another two decades, until the Immigration Act of 1965, before receiving equal immigration rights like other national groups.

The unique history of Chinese Americans has been shaped by four factors: (1) U.S. immigration and domestic policies, (2) U.S.-China foreign relations, (3) race, class, gender and cultural conflicts within the United States, and (4) political activism on the part of Chinese Americans. Because the historical record has long ignored the experiences and contributions of Chinese Americans in the building of this nation, it is time not only to acknowledge their many contributions but, more importantly, also to examine this group's journey from exclusion to inclusion in their struggle to be treated and accepted as equal Americans. Therein lies the lesson of what it takes for this country to live up to its democratic principles of justice and equality for all.

FREE IMMIGRATION, 1848–1882

There is a saying that "the sun never sets over the Chinese," meaning that the Chinese are all over the world because of their historical pattern of migration. Long before they began immigrating in large numbers to California in response to the gold rush of 1848, Buddhist monks, political refugees, seamen, merchants, and laborers were traveling east of China to Japan, Korea, and North America, possibly as early as the fifth century; southward to India and parts of Southeast Asia in the seventeenth and eighteenth centuries; and westward via the overland route to western Europe around the same time. Chinese were among the servants of Spaniards aboard the galleons that sailed between the Philippines and Mexico after 1565. By 1635 a small Chinese colony had been established in Mexico City. In the late eighteenth and early nineteenth centuries, ships engaged in the China trade brought a few Chinese crewmen and merchants to Hawaii, British Columbia, and the east and west coasts of the United States. As early as 1818, Chinese were studying at the Foreign Mission School in Cornwall, Connecticut.

However, it was not until the mid-nineteenth century that a significant number of Chinese immigrants from the Pearl River Delta of Guangdong Province (close to the ports of Canton and Hong Kong) began going overseas to America in search of a better livelihood. They were but a segment of the Chinese Diaspora and a sliver of the international migration of labor caused by the global expansion of European capitalism, in which workers, capital, and technology moved across national borders to enable entrepreneurs to exploit natural resources and a larger market in less industrially developed countries like China. According to one estimate, after China was defeated in the Opium Wars (1839–1842; 1856–1860) and forced open by European imperialist countries to outside trade and political domination, 2.5 million Chinese migrated overseas during the last half of the nineteenth century. Except for the 250,000 Chinese who were coerced into slave labor in the "coolie trade" that operated from 1847 to 1874, most of those who left answered willingly the call of Western capitalists, immigrating to undeveloped colonies in Southeast Asia, Australia, Hawaii, Peru, the Caribbean Islands, Africa, and North America to live, work, and eventually settle.

There were reasons as to why Chinese immigrants to California in the mid-nineteenth century were predominantly peasants from the Pearl River Delta in southeast China. For one, they were particularly hard hit by imperialist incursions and the inept responses of the Qing dynasty. Aside from suffering increased taxes, forfeiture of land, competition from imported manufactured goods, and unemployment, they also had to contend with problems of overpopulation, repeated natural calamities, bandits, and the devastation caused by peasant rebellions and the ongoing Punti-Hakka interethnic feud. Because of their coastal location and their long association with the sea and contact with foreign traders, they were easily drawn to America by news of the gold rush and by labor contractors who actively recruited young, able-bodied men to help develop the western frontier. Steamship companies and creditors were also eager to provide them with the means to travel to America.

Like other immigrants coming to California at this time, these Guangdong men intended to strike it rich and return home. Thus, although more than half of them were married, most did not bring their wives and families. In any case, because of Chinese cultural mores against women traveling abroad, limited economic resources, and the harsh living conditions in California, it was cheaper and safer to maintain a split household and support the family in China from across the ocean. Later, when Chinese immigrants turned from being sojourners to settlers and wanted to send for their wives and families, they were prevented from doing so by American immigration laws. The absence of women set the patterns of Chinese immigration and community development apart from that of most other immigrant groups until after World War II, resulting in a bachelor society plagued by social vices and a delay in the emergence of a second generation.

From 1850 until 1882, when the Chinese Exclusion Act was passed, over 300,000 Chinese entered the United States. Some were merchants and craftsmen, but the overwhelming majority were unskilled laborers who had obtained passage on credit. In 1852 alone, stories of the gold rush drew 20,000 Chinese to Gold Mountain (as the Chinese came to call California), yet by the time they arrived, the easy pickings were almost all gone. Very few Chinese became rich overnight. However, their physical presence irked white miners, who, imbued with ideas of white supremacy and Manifest Destiny, viewed the Chinese as foreign competitors who had no right to the gold. In 1852 the state legislature reenacted the Foreign Miners' Tax against the Chinese, which, until it was repealed in 1870, accounted for $5 million—or half—of California's revenue. As hostile miners resorted to physical violence to expel the Chinese from the mines and a number of mining counties passed resolutions and taxes to exclude them, Chinese miners fanned out into gold fields throughout the West, reworking left-over claims abandoned by white prospectors or hiring themselves out to work borax deposits and mine coal and quicksilver. Not only did their hard labor reap immense profits for mining corporations, but the Chinese also contributed to the economy by supplying goods and services to miners—hence, the development of Chinese camps throughout the mining areas.

As part of the western expansion to open up new markets in the West and eventually Asia, entrepreneurs pushed for the building of a transcontinental railroad that would link up the country and expedite trade between the two coasts. In this effort the federal government provided railroad entrepreneurs incentives to the tune of $16,000 to $48,000 and one square mile of land for each mile of track laid—land that had been taken from the American Indians. Even so, the Central Pacific Railroad, given the rugged terrain of the Sierra Nevada and the scarcity of reliable labor, made little progress on the western end of the railroad line until they tried Chinese workers. They proved so capable and diligent that some 12,000 to 14,000 Chinese, 4 of every 5 men hired by the Central Pacific, were soon put to work in all phases of construction—leveling roadbeds, boring tunnels, blasting mountainsides, and laying tracks. The work was hard as well as dangerous. To carve a roadbed out of the granite promontory of Cape Horn (1,400 feet above the American River), Chinese laborers were lowered from the top of the cliff in wicker baskets to drill holes and light explosives, then pulled up as the gunpowder exploded beneath them. Working through two severe winters in the High Sierras, the Chinese practically lived underground, buried in snow, and were often victims of snow slides and avalanches. While no record was kept of the number of lives lost in this endeavor, one newspaper reported that there must have been at least 1,200 deaths, based on the 20,000 pounds of bones that were shipped back to China before the completion of the railroad in 1869. Chinese labor was also instrumental in the construction of railroad trunk lines in the Pacific Northwest and the Southwest as well as a major canal in Augusta, Georgia, helping further to stimulate national growth and commerce in these parts of the country.

From the 1860s to the 1910s, Chinese farmers also contributed to transforming California into the nation's premier agricultural state. Chinese labor was used to reclaim swamp lands in the Sacramento–San Joaquin River Delta, increasing the land value from $1 to $3 an acre to $20 to $100 an acre. They also played a role in laying the foundation of the wine industry in Napa and Sonoma by constructing roads, stone bridges, rock walls, wine cellars, and irrigation ditches; clearing land, planting, pruning, and harvesting grapes; and even in the making and tasting of wine. The farming skills that they brought with them from China were put to good use in the growing of citrus fruits, beans, peas, sugar beets, and hops—commercial crops that became the mainstay of the state's agricultural economy. As tenant farmers and truck gardeners, the Chinese specialized in potatoes, garden vegetables, fruits, peanuts, and celery. Chinese vegetable peddlers became a common sight in many towns, and housewives came to depend on their fresh produce. In other parts of the country, Ah Bing, a foreman in Milwaukie, Oregon, developed the Bing cherry, and plant wizard Lue Gim Gong, a frost-resistant orange in DeLand, Florida. In Hawaii, Chinese farmers also introduced many new varieties of flowers, fruits, and vegetables, including jasmine, lychee, longan, pomelo, Chinese cabbage, taro, and water chestnut.

Chinese laborers were equally adept at fishing, working in canneries and factories, and as domestics and laundrymen. In the 1860s and 1870s Chinese fishing villages dotted the California coastline, and Chinese fishermen caught a variety of fish, shrimp, and abalone, which they dried and sold locally or shipped to China, Japan, and the Hawaiian Islands. In fact, it was the Chinese who introduced abalone meat and the decorative shells to white Americans. By the mid-1870s, Chinese workers also made up the bulk of the labor force in salmon canneries in the Pacific Northwest and the factory labor force in San Francisco, dominating those light industries that had the lowest profit margins: woolen mills, cigars, shoes, and garments. Once the Chinese learned the trade, they pooled together capital to start their own factories, specializing in inexpensive lines, such as ready-made clothing, undergarments, slippers, and boys' shoes, to avoid competition with white manufacturers. Also in the mid-1870s, Chinese laborers were recruited as strikebreakers to factories in Belleville, New Jersey, Beaver Falls, Pennsylvania, and North Adams, Massachusetts.

By then, an economic depression in the West had unleashed intense anti-Chinese sentiment and violence among white workers, farmers, and fishermen, who saw the Chinese as unassimilable aliens, unfair competition, and the cause of all their economic woes. Denis Kearney and the Workingman's Party took the lead in scapegoating the Chinese. When hatred flared, bloodthirsty mobs stormed Chinese settlements, looting, lynching, burning, and expelling the Chinese. Their goals to drive the Chinese out of all areas of profitable employment and ultimately out of the country were finally realized with the help of opportunistic politicians who pressured Congress to pass the Chinese Exclusion Act of 1882. The act suspended the coming of Chinese laborers for ten years and was renewed in 1892 and 1902. Only diplomats, students, teachers, merchants, and visitors were exempted. The ban on Chinese labor was applied to Hawaii after it became a territory of the United States in 1898. It was extended indefinitely in 1904.

The message behind the anti-Chinese movement was evident: The Chinese were only welcomed as long as their labor was needed to develop the economic infrastructure of the American West. Racist attitudes, policies, and practices ensured that they would not settle down, own land, establish family life, move up the socioeconomic ladder, become American citizens, or integrate into mainstream society. But the Chinese refused to be driven out of the country. Many moved to eastern and midwestern cities, even to the South, where they could find work and their presence was better tolerated. By the turn of the century, Chinese could be found in every state of the union and were concentrated in agriculture or in domestic and personal services. A quarter of all Chinese men were laundry workers. To meet their social, economic, and political needs, they tended to cluster in Chinatown communities that sprang up in many urban areas. There, Chinese laborers were able to shop for Chinese foods and supplies, look for work, socialize with kinsmen, frequent brothels, attend Chinese operas, worship at temples, observe traditional holidays and customs, and find protection from racial persecution. In the larger Chinatowns, family and district associations, fraternal organizations, and labor guilds were formed for social control, mutual help, and labor arbitration. Tongs, or secret societies, involved with prostitution, gambling, and drugs also thrived. The stiff competition for control of these illegal activities often led to assassinations and fights, notoriously known as tong wars.

Chinese were also known to pool together their resources to start businesses, sustain strikes and boycotts, and hire attorneys to act on their behalf. For although they were politically powerless, they knew how to file petitions of complaint and use the judicial system to defend their civil rights, contributing significantly to the molding of American constitutional jurisprudence. In the 1862 case of *Lin Sing v. Washburn*, the California Supreme Court nullified a law imposing an onerous tax on Chinese immigrants only; an 1885 lawsuit by Joseph and Mary Tape, challenging the exclusion of Chinese children from public schools (*Tape v. Hurley*), resulted in a court order to admit their daughter; and in *Wong Kim Ark v. United States* (1898), the court held that anyone born in the United States was a citizen and could not be stripped of that right.

Because of the sex imbalance, the laws that forbade interracial marriage, and the profits that could be made in criminal activities, the prostitution trade thrived along with gambling and the sale of opium. In 1860, approximately 85 percent of Chinese women in San Francisco were indentured prostitutes, mostly young women who had been kidnapped, lured, or purchased from poor parents in China for as little as $50 and then resold in America for as much as $1,000. Treated as chattel and abused physically and mentally, few could outlive the average contract term of four years. The fortunate ones were redeemed by wealthy clients, ran away with the help of lovers, or sought refuge at Protestant mission homes. It was not until the early twentieth century that organized prostitution declined, owing to the stricter enforcement of antiprostitution legislation and the successful rescue raids led by Protestant missionary women, such as Margaret Culbertson and Donaldina Cameron.

The situation was different for Chinese in the Hawaiian Islands, where racial discrimination was not as virulent as on the mainland. Imported in large numbers beginning in 1852 to work in the sugar plantations, Chinese laborers soon moved on to raise livestock, grow rice, taro, coffee, garden vegetables, and fruits, and eventually become shopkeepers and skilled craftsmen in Honolulu and other towns. Although they had been encouraged to bring their wives to work in the cane fields and were allowed to marry native Hawaiian women, the Chinese in Hawaii still comprised basically a bachelor society. The 1884 Hawaiian census reported 17,068 Chinese males and 871 Chinese females, but the Chinese made up 25 percent of the Islands' total population. In the multicultural climate of Hawaii, prostitution was not an issue, intermarriage was allowed, family life developed, and the Chinese were able to integrate into the larger society at an earlier date than on the mainland. Nevertheless, similar to what happened on the mainland, Chinese in Hawaii early on formed their own clan, district, fraternal, and labor organizations to provide fellowship, social control, protection, and arbitration. They also maintained close ties to their homeland and culture, establishing their own newspapers, schools, and temples even as they planted roots in Hawaii.

EXCLUSION, 1882–1943

As a direct result of the Chinese Exclusion Act, there was a precipitous drop in the Chinese population, from a high of 105,465 in 1880 to a low of 61,639 in 1920. The Immigration Act of 1924 tightened the noose further by prohibiting the immigration of Chinese wives of U.S. citizens. But as the Chinese found ways to circumvent the Exclusion Acts by being smuggled across the borders or coming posed as sons of U.S. citizens or wives of merchants, the population climbed to 77,504 in 1940, and the male-female ratio decreased from a high of

27 to 1 in 1890 to 2.9 to 1. With the arrival of "paper sons" and merchant wives, family life became possible, and a second generation finally emerged, outnumbering the foreign-born population by 1940.

Throughout the mainland and in Hawaii, the Chinese moved into urban areas where they concentrated in noncompetitive fields of work that required low capital, such as ethnic enterprises in Chinatowns, domestic service, and operating small laundries, restaurants, and grocery stores in out-of-the-way places. Chop suey, chow mein, and fortune cookies became well-known Chinese-American dishes. Other men found seasonal employment in agriculture or canneries, whereas women worked in garment factories and food-processing plants. A number of entrepreneurs had enough capital to enter into large-scale enterprises, including oil wells, mines, automotive plants, canneries, shipping companies, and banks. Although many of these ventures failed due to insufficient capital, managerial inexperience, and racial discrimination, there were some success stories, for example, Joe Shoong's National Dollar Stores (1907), a clothing department store with forty outlets in the West and Hawaii; K. C. Li's Wah Chang Trading Company in New York (1916), which traded in antimony and tungsten from China; and Chun Quon's C. Q. Yee Hop, which started as a Honolulu meat market in 1887 and later expanded to include a cattle ranch, hardwood company, brewery, and real estate. By 1930 the majority of the Chinese in Hawaii had entered the primary labor market, taking on skilled, clerical and sales, proprietory, and professional occupations. One-third of all employed Chinese women were schoolteachers. The same opportunities would not open up for Chinese on the mainland until after World War II.

In contrast to the split-household family in the nineteenth century, the small-producer family dominated among Chinese immigrants from the 1920s to the 1960s. Under this arrangement, the family lived on the business premises (usually a restaurant, laundry, or store), and every family member worked without wages so that overhead would remain low. Family and work life were thus closely integrated and marked by strict discipline, long hours of toil, constant frugality, and collective effort. Marital relationships were interdependent, as immigrant wives worked alongside their husbands to provide for their families and resist cultural onslaughts or racist denigration on the part of the larger society. Not only did women contribute to the family income, but they also bore the responsibility of running the household and passing on cultural traditions to their children.

Out of a strong sense of familial obligation and nationalism, most Chinese immigrants continued to maintain close economic and political ties to their homeland. They were aware that the racial oppression and humiliation they suffered in America was due in part to China's weak international status and inability to protect its citizens abroad; thus, they focused their attention and energies on helping China become a stronger and more modern country, even as they worked to change their unfavorable image and treatment in America. Sizable amounts of money were sent to China to support family and relatives, business enterprises, and educational institutions. On the question of how to liberate China from foreign domination, the overseas Chinese were divided in their support of the Zhigongtang, which favored restoring the Ming emperor; Kang Youwei's Baohuanghui, which advocated a constitutional monarchy; and Dr. Sun Yat-sen's Tongmenghui, which finally succeeded in overthrowing the Qing dynasty and establishing a democratic republic in 1911. They were united, however, in their support of China's War of Resistance against Japan from 1931 to 1945, contributing more than $25 million toward Chinese war bonds and refugee relief.

The exclusion years constituted a period of isolation, economic and political strife, and social transformation in the Chinese-American community. Discrimination remained virulent on the Pacific Coast, and the Chinese were kept out of the professions and trades, segregated in schools and theaters, refused service in public places, and prohibited from buying land, living in white neighborhoods, and sending for their wives from China. Within the community, merchant associations, trade guilds, and tongs fought over control of the distribution and commercial use of limited space and economic resources, while political factions disagreed over the political future of China. In an effort to establish social order, nurture business, and protect family life, merchants and social reformers established new institutions and Western-style organizations, including Chinese schools, churches, hospitals, newspapers, the Chinese Chamber of Commerce, Chinese American Citizens Alliance, and the Chinese YMCA and YWCA. They also worked closely with Protestant missionary workers and law enforcers to eradicate prostitution and opium dens, stop the bloody tong wars, educate women and children, and improve the public image of their community.

Although unwelcomed and targeted by the American labor movement before, Chinese workers participated in boycotts and strikes in the 1920s and 1930s, earning the right to become members of major unions, such as the National Maritime Union and International Ladies' Garment Workers' Union. In New York City laundry workers organized the Chinese Hand Laundry Alliance and were successful in opposing a local ordinance that discriminated against Chinese laundries. Chinese garment workers in San Francisco stayed on strike for 105 days until they won a better union contract from Joe Shoong's National Dollar Stores. The Chinese also continued to take legal action, winning court cases that extended the equal protection clause of the Fourteenth Amendment to noncitizens (*Yick Wo v. Hopkins*); the legal right of Chinese merchants to bring their wives and children into the country (*U.S. v. Gue Lim*); and the right of American-born Chinese women to marry Chinese aliens without losing their U.S. citizenship (amendment to the Cable Act of 1922).

Coming of age in the 1920s and 1930s, many second-generation Chinese Americans experienced cultural conflicts in attempting to follow both Chinese and American values and customs. Despite their ability to speak English, their high educational attainment, and their Western outlook, they found themselves confined to living in segregated quarters, working at low-paying jobs, and being

excluded from participation in mainstream society because of racial discrimination. Although given more opportunities in America than in China, daughters
still experienced an additional layer of sexism, both within and outside their
ethnic communities; thus, their life choices were even more limiting than those
of their male counterparts. Most Chinese Americans accommodated discrimination by creating their own bicultural identity and lifestyle. At home they continued to speak Chinese and observe Chinese customs, but in their social life
outside, they were no different than other Americans in going to the movies,
attending parties and picnics, and participating in sports and club activities,
albeit in a segregated setting. To circumvent job discrimination, they resorted
to working in Chinese-owned businesses or setting up professional practices in
Chinatown communities. Encouraged by their parents and by political developments in China, some opted to go to China for better job opportunities and
where their talents could be put to better use in the service of their ancestral
homeland. Despite the limitations of the exclusion period, a significant number
of Chinese Americans broke racial and gender barriers to make contributions to
their community and to American society in the areas of civil rights, film, literature, art, and military service. For example, Presbyterian minister Ng Poon
Chew was an outspoken advocate of Chinese-American civil rights; cinematog-
rapher James Wong Howe and actress Anna May Wong left lasting impressions
in Hollywood; and Sergeant Sing Kee was awarded the Distinguished Service
Cross for heroic action in World War I.

RESTRICTED IMMIGRATION, 1943–1965

World War II proved to be a major turning point for Chinese Americans,
providing them unprecedented opportunities to improve their socioeconomic and
political status and become full participants in an all-American war effort. Because of China's allied relationship with the United States, American attitudes
toward, and treatment of, the Chinese turned favorable. Touted as loyal sons
and daughters of Uncle Sam by the mass media, over 12,000 Chinese Americans
served in the armed forces, thousands more worked in the shipyards and defense
industries, and Chinese women throughout the country did their part on the
home front—fund-raising, pushing war bonds, and volunteering for Red Cross,
United Service Organizations (USO), and civil defense duties. With the labor
shortage, Chinese Americans were able to find jobs for the first time in private
companies, civil service, and professional fields outside Chinatown. In contrast,
after Japan attacked Pearl Harbor, Japanese Americans were regarded as enemy
aliens, stripped of their civil rights, and herded into concentration camps where
many remained for the duration of the war.

In December 1943, as a goodwill gesture to China and to counter Japanese
propaganda in Asia, Congress repealed the Chinese Exclusion Act and assigned
China a token annual quota of 105. More important, Chinese aliens were granted
the right to naturalization. But it was not until after World War II that additional

legislation was passed that spurred Chinese immigration and changed the complexion of the Chinese-American population. Because of the War Brides Act, allowing the admission of Chinese wives and children of U.S. citizens as non-quota immigrants, 6,000 Chinese women were able to come so that the Chinese male-to-female ratio on the mainland dropped by 1950 to 1.9 to 1 and in Hawaii to 1.1. This, in turn, generated a baby boom and a noticeable infusion of family life in such urban Chinatowns as San Francisco, Los Angeles, New York, and Boston. However, with limited English and job skills, many immigrant women ended up working in garment sweatshops in their attempt to supplement their husbands' meager incomes from restaurant and laundry jobs. This development marked the beginning of a change in the Chinese-American family from small producer to that of dual wage earners and latchkey children. Under this arrangement, both parents had to work outside the home, leaving the children to fend for themselves in the absence of child care services.

After China turned communist in 1949 and the Chinese fought against Americans in the Korean Conflict a year later, U.S.-China relations deteriorated. While the break in diplomatic relations between the two countries and the anticommunist hysteria that followed in the 1950s forced overseas Chinese to sever ties with their homeland, changes in domestic policies encouraged them to set down roots and become a part of America. Anti-Chinese laws, which for decades had denied Chinese Americans fundamental civil rights and legal protection, were revoked one by one, enabling Chinese Americans to intermarry with whites, own land, and find work and housing outside Chinatown boundaries. This development marked the beginning of Chinese integration into mainstream society and a decline of Chinatowns and Chinese cultural institutions.

As the country entered the cold war era, a series of refugee acts were passed that admitted approximately 30,000 professionals, entrepreneurs, intellectuals, and ex-government officials escaping unstable political conditions in China. As a result, by 1960 the Chinese-American population had risen to 237,292. Unlike earlier Cantonese immigrants, many of these newcomers were well educated, cosmopolitan, spoke the Mandarin dialect, and came from central and northern China. Arriving at a time when conditions were turning favorable for Chinese Americans and when their scientific and technical skills were in demand by America's military-industrial complex, they had little trouble finding work in their fields, housing in suburban communities, and social acceptance in middle-class circles.

Representing the beginning of a brain drain from Asian countries, this group of immigrants made immense contributions to America in science, medicine, business, art, and music: In disproving the conservation of parity principle, Nobel Prize winners Chen Ning Yang and Tsung Dao Lee, and physicist Chien-Hsiung Wu, paved the way to other revolutionary discoveries regarding subatomic particles; An Wang helped to develop the desktop calculator, word processor, and minicomputer industries; and architect I. M. Pei was chosen to design the East Building of the National Gallery of Art in Washington, D.C., and the modern addition to the Louvre Museum in Paris.

At the same time that America welcomed political refugees from communist countries, it sought to persecute communist sympathizers at home. In 1955 Everett Drumwright, U.S. consul in Hong Kong, raised the issue of fraudulent entry on the part of Chinese immigrants and with it the implicit accusation of communist infiltration. To avoid tying up the courts with deportation cases, immigration authorities, in cooperation with alarmed leaders in Chinatown, instigated the "confession program," by which "paper sons" could confess and assume their true identities with a guarantee against deportation. Some 14,000 did just that. Although the program presented Chinese Americans with an opportunity to clear their immigration status, it also exerted undue pressure on those who did not want to implicate relatives by their confessions. Federal agents, taking advantage of the program, were known to make periodic sweeps through Chinatown in search of communist sympathizers. Politically Left groups, such as the Chinese American Youth Club, Chinese Workers Mutual Aid Association, and Chinese Hand Laundry Alliance, all fell victims to the "Red Scare," while the Guomindang (Chiang Kai-shek's Nationalist regime in Taiwan) took advantage of the political situation to strengthen its control and influence over Chinatown politics and institutions.

The paranoia and mental anguish suffered by Chinese Americans during this period served to dampen their interest in China politics as well as any involvement in left-wing political activities. But it did not deter them, particularly the American-born generation, from taking advantage of improved opportunities after the war for socioeconomic and political advancement. Chinese-American baby boomers, growing up in the era of the atom bomb, Salk vaccine, suburban living, drive-in movies and television, pop art, and rock 'n' roll, experienced cultural conflicts and identity crises as they tried to become all-American. They were encouraged by the mass media to give up their ethnic identity and conform to white middle-class standards. But in so doing, they encountered communication and cultural problems at home, alienation from within the Chinese community, and continuing racial rejection by mainstream society. Women also found that being Chinese and female were still liabilities in the working world, especially if one had been socialized at home to be obedient, reserved, and collective-minded rather than independent, assertive, and outgoing.

Although 1960 U.S. census data show that a larger proportion of Chinese Americans, as compared to their white counterparts, graduated from college and that they had moved up the occupational ladder from manual labor, domestic service, and clerical work to technical, sales, and professional fields, statistics also show that Chinese Americans did not have the same earning power as white men and women with comparable backgrounds. In other words, their earning power was not commensurate with their level of education. Owing to racial discrimination, cultural barriers, media stereotypes, and the lack of role models and career counseling, Chinese Americans were segregated into the lower-paying, nonmanagerial sectors of the primary labor market. More Chinese Americans were accountants, health technicians, and secretaries than were lawyers, physicians, and business executives. However, some were able to distinguish themselves in new fields of endeavor, notably watercolorist Dong Kingman, sociologist Rose Hum Lee, and March Fong Eu, who was elected to the California State Assembly in 1966 and went on to become California's secretary of state in 1974 and President Bill Clinton's ambassador to Micronesia.

Meanwhile, the Chinese in Hawaii were still assimilating faster than their counterparts on the mainland. In 1960, 74 percent of the Chinese working population were concentrated in white-collar jobs, and Chinese Americans had the highest median income of all ethnic groups in the islands. By 1970, their average family annual income in the Honolulu metropolitan area was 40 percent higher than the comparable average for Chinese on the mainland, and the Chinese outmarriage rate in Hawaii was 30 percent as compared to 13 percent on the mainland. Chinese business tycoons, including Chinn Ho, Hiram Fong, and Hung Wo Ching, helped to diversify the Hawaiian economy and stimulate commerce and travel between the mainland and the islands. After statehood in 1959, Hiram Fong became the only Chinese American thus far elected to the U.S. Senate (1959–1977).

EQUAL IMMIGRATION, 1965–PRESENT

As a direct result of the civil rights movement, sweeping changes in immigration and domestic policies irrevocably changed the composition and lives of Chinese Americans for the rest of the twentieth century. Inspired by Dr. Martin Luther King, Jr., thousands upon thousands of black Americans and supporters took to the streets demanding an end to racial discrimination. Their unrelenting campaign of mass protests and civil disobedience succeeded in pressuring Congress to pass the Civil Rights Act of 1964, which prohibited discrimination in education, employment, electoral politics, and public facilities on the basis of race or sex. Following on the heels of the Civil Rights Act, the Immigration and Naturalization Act of 1965 ended the discriminatory quota system of selecting immigrants by national origin. China was finally placed on an equal basis with other countries and given an annual ceiling of 20,000 immigrants (revised upward in 1990 for all independent foreign states to 25,620). In 1986 and 1990, new immigration legislation set separate ceilings for Taiwan and Hong Kong, respectively.

Intended to promote family reunification, attract educated and skilled workers, and welcome refugees escaping from communist countries, the Immigration Act of 1965 made a major impact on the Chinese American population in terms of numbers and diversity. The population jumped from 431,583 in 1970 to 806,040 in 1980, and 1,645,472 in 1990. Between 1990 and 1995, another 382,300 Chinese immigrated to the United States. Initially, most of the immigrants embarked from Hong Kong or Taiwan. But political upheavals in Cuba, Peru, Central America, Korea, Burma, the Philippines, and Southeast Asia and U.S. normalization of diplomatic relations with the communist government in China in 1979 soon brought thousands more from these areas, as well. In 1990 the foreign-born made up 69.3 percent of the Chinese population in the United States, and the male/female sex ratio finally reached parity.

Because immediate family members of U.S. citizens were counted as "non-quota" immigrants (exempt from preferences), actual Chinese immigration went well beyond its annual quota of 20,000. Many of these new immigrants, joining their spouses and families after many years of separation, came from the rural areas of Guangdong Province. Primarily non-English-speaking and lacking marketable job skills, they settled in urban Chinatowns, particularly San Francisco, New York, and Los Angeles, where they eked out a living in the ethnic economy, mainly in food stores, restaurants, and garment sweatshops. Their arrival injected new life into the Chinatown communities, creating new demands for Chinese food, goods, services, and entertainment. However, their large influx also compounded already existing ghetto conditions of overcrowded and substandard housing, unemployment and underemployment, and inadequate health care, recreational space, and child care services. Under these living and working conditions, the dual-wage-earner families fell apart. The absence of both parents away at work and the pressures of adjusting to American life led to intergenerational conflicts within the home and increased gang-related crimes and violence in the community.

Fortunately for new immigrants at this time, they were arriving at a propitious moment, for President Lyndon B. Johnson's War on Poverty program was getting into full gear. In response to the demands of the civil rights movement, federal funds had been allocated to provide social services to minority communities suffering poverty conditions. A new generation of Chinese-American liberals, going against the judgment and wishes of the Guomindang-controlled Chinatown establishment, marched in demonstrations and filed class action lawsuits to ensure that the Chinese community receive its share of public funding, relevant services, and protection against racial discrimination. As a result, community-based organizations, such as the Chinese American Planning Council and Chinatown Youth Council in New York and the Economic Opportunity Council and Chinese Newcomers Service Center in San Francisco, were formed and staffed by bilingual personnel to help Chinese immigrants learn English, acquire job skills, and cope with their new lives in America. The civil rights movement also inspired the founding of national organizations, including Chinese for Affirmative Action and the Organization of Chinese Americans, to fight for civil rights and affirmative action. Through the efforts of the Neighborhood Legal Assistance office in San Francisco Chinatown, such landmark cases as *Lau v. Nichols* and *Hampton v. Wong*, which established bilingual education and opened federal jobs to resident aliens, respectively, benefited not only Chinese immigrants but also other minority groups. After the United States normalized relations with China in 1979, the Chinese-American community, which had been sorely divided on the two-China issue for thirty years, was finally able to break away from Guomindang control and redirect its energies and financial resources toward American politics and the welfare of the community.

The end of the Vietnam War in 1975 opened the floodgates to over 1 million Vietnamese, Laotian, and Cambodian refugees who found their way to the United States. Approximately 35 percent of those from Vietnam were ethnic Chinese ''boat people,'' who had escaped in overloaded and unseaworthy vessels after being forced out by the new communist government because of their prominent role in the country's former capitalist economy as well as the heightened tensions between Vietnam and China. Many of these Chinese Vietnamese refugees spoke Cantonese, but there were also those who spoke the Chaozhou, Hakka, Minnan, or Hainan dialects. Sharing a common Chinese cultural background, they gravitated toward Chinatowns for employment, grocery shopping, and social services. But as newcomers from Vietnam and arriving at a time of economic recession and anti-Asian backlash, they were not always welcomed by the Chinese community or the larger American society. Once they got back on their feet, however, many went on to establish small businesses adjacent to Chinatowns or in Vietnamese enclaves in California—notably Westminster, Long Beach, San Diego, and San Jose.

Then, beginning in the 1980s, an estimated 100,000 Chinese from Fujian Province, across from Taiwan, were smuggled into the United States by secret societies that were part of a clandestine worldwide network. Most were young farmers and laborers who had paid smugglers $25,000 to $30,000 for a chance at work and wealth in America. Once here, however, they were indentured into low-paying jobs in restaurants, sweatshops, and laundries for as long as five years, while living in squalor in order to pay off their debts. Fears of retribution from smugglers and discovery by immigration officers have forced them into an underground and highly exploitative existence in New York, where most Fujinese have settled. Those caught in transit—as in the case of 286 Chinese passengers packed into the hold of the *Golden Venture* freighter in 1993—were either deported or imprisoned for as long as three years, awaiting hearings on their applications for political asylum.

Nonetheless, not all immigrants arriving after 1965 have faced economic hardships. A good number coming from Taiwan, Hong Kong, and different parts of China under the preference category of professionals, scientists, and artists of exceptional ability have been able to find good-paying jobs in America's expanding technological economy. Many who initially came as foreign students were able to acquire status as permanent residents upon graduation by finding jobs in their professional fields or by marrying U.S. citizens. Because of the Tiananmen Square incident in June 1989, another 48,212 students from China were allowed to become permanent residents between 1992 and 1993. Others who came with capital and entrepreneurial skills have been able to invest profitably in restaurants, supermarkets, shopping centers, hotels and motels, banks, real estate, and computer technology. Their returns have allowed them to realize the American dream of economic inclusion, and their contributions to the prosperity of this country have been immense, judging by the wealth they have generated in Pacific Rim trade, Silicon Valley, and new Chinese communities in San Gabriel Valley and Monterey Park, California; Flushing and Brooklyn, New York; Houston, Bellaire, and Richardson, Texas; and Chamblee, Georgia. This large group of well-educated and bilingual immigrants has also provided the Chinese-American community with a talented pool of social workers and political leaders, such as Lillian Sing, who became a San Francisco municipal court judge in 1981; S. B. Woo, who was elected lieutenant governor of Delaware in 1985; and Elaine Chao, who was appointed deputy secretary of transportation in 1989 and director of the Peace Corps in 1991.

The large influx of Chinese immigrants, combined with improved U.S.-China relations and a renewed commitment to multiculturalism in this country, has led to a proliferation of Chinese cultural institutions and a broader acceptance of Chinese cultural practices in America. Chinese cuisine, fashion, music, drama, martial arts, temples, schools, newspapers, literature, and films have developed at a fast pace to meet the new demands of a growing Chinese immigrant population. At the same time, established family and district organizations in Chinatowns have had to revamp their purposes and services to remain relevant to the needs of a changing population. Chinese restaurants are more popular than ever, and while Cantonese cooking still dominates, there is a growing appreciation of cuisines from other regions of China, including Beijing, Shanghai, Hunan, and Szechwan. In addition, where previously Americans frowned upon Chinese folk religions, medical practices, language, and customs, they now respect and in some cases join Chinese immigrants in seeking solace in Buddhism and Taoism; good health in gung fu, acupuncture, and herbal medicine; and cultural enrichment in celebrating the Chinese New Year and learning about Chinese language, brush painting, classical music, and popular folklore.

Second- and third-generation American-born Chinese have also benefited by the social changes of the civil rights era. They are among the first Chinese Americans to successfully integrate into mainstream society, judging by their middle-class status, suburban residence, social lifestyle, and high rates of outmarriage (37 percent of native-born Chinese were married to non-Chinese in 1980; 54 percent in 1990). Compared to most Chinese immigrant families, their marital relationships tend to be more egalitarian and their parent-child relationships more permissive. Even so, many have held on to their strong sense of ethnic, gender, and gay pride derived from the influences of the civil rights, anti–Vietnam War, Asian-American, women's liberation, and gay movements. Involved in the social movements of the 1960s and 1970s, this group spoke out against discrimination and social injustices, advocated for workers' rights, community services, and ethnic studies, and lay claim to their history and ethnic identity as Asian Americans. They also led the way in challenging racist and sexist stereotypes of Chinese Americans in the mass media, such as Fu Manchu,

Charlie Chan, Madame Butterfly, and Suzie Wong, and in creating more realistic images of Chinese Americans in literature, film, and television. Because of their social activism, Chinese Americans can now claim a place at the multicultural table on their own terms.

Banking on affirmative action programs, the elimination of institutional racism, and expanding Pacific Rim trade in a restructured global economy, Chinese Americans have been able to expand their horizons and participate in many new areas previously closed to them—broadcast media, law and law enforcement, high finance, literature, the arts, athletics, education, astronautics, and politics. Such well-known personages as news anchor Connie Chung, authors Maxine Hong Kingston and Amy Tan, filmmakers Wayne Wang and Ang Lee, cellist Yo-Yo Ma, architect Maya Ying Lin, tennis champion Michael Chang, former University of California chancellor Chang-lin Tien, and Washington state governor Gary Locke are now a part of the Who's Who among successful Americans.

However, for every such success story, there are thousands of other Chinese Americans still struggling to survive or who are striving for upward mobility. According to the 1990 U.S. census, one-third of all Chinese workers are concentrated in managerial and professional occupations; one-third in technical, sales, and administrative support; and one-third in service and unskilled jobs. Although 41 percent of the Chinese population have college degrees, compared to the national average of 20 percent, and a greater proportion of Chinese than whites have white-collar jobs, the average per capita income of Chinese Americans ($14,876) is only a little more than that of the average American ($14,143). In fact, 14 percent of the Chinese-American population live below poverty level, compared to 13 percent of the general American population. The bipolarization in the economic status of Chinese Americans, caused by a rising middle class at one end and an increasing number of struggling immigrants at the other, strongly suggests that not all Chinese Americans are model minorities who have made it in America. The pattern remains that employers will not hesitate to pay Chinese workers less than others for doing the same work or pass them up for promotion despite merit because of race, gender, and cultural differences. As it is, Chinese Americans tend to be stratified into occupations that command less pay, prestige, and power; and they often must work twice as hard to prove themselves equal. Adding to these problems for Chinese-American women are the double burdens they bear as wage earners and homemakers and the rising incidents of domestic violence at home and sexual harassment at work.

Although overall conditions have improved for Chinese Americans since the 1960s, class and racial conflicts broke out anew in the last two decades because of downturns in the American economy due to the global restructuring of capitalism and competition from abroad. Instead of finding ways to protect local manufacturing jobs, revitalize the urban infrastructure, and train American workers for a high-tech, service-oriented economy, the government chose to protect the interests of multinational corporations and retreat from civil rights and a welfare state. In the face of plant closures, rising unemployment, and urban decay, the country once again blamed Chinese and other Asian Americans for its economic problems, especially in light of U.S. trade deficits with Japan and China. In 1982, in one of the most highly publicized cases of anti-Asian violence, Chinese-American Vincent Chin was brutally murdered by two white autoworkers in Detroit, Michigan, who mistook him for a Japanese and blamed him for unemployment in the auto industry. Moreover, despite their long presence in the United States and their many contributions to this country in terms of their labor, taxes, inventive minds, artistic talents, and fulfillment of civic duties, Chinese Americans are still regarded as undesirable foreigners, evidenced by the continuation of ethnic slurs and stereotyping in the mass media, the rash of anti-immigrant legislation that has passed in recent years (e.g., California's Proposition 187; the Welfare Reform Law of 1996; and the Immigration Reform Act of 1996), China bashing and the scapegoating of Chinese and other Asian Americans in the 1996 campaign finance scandal, and the rise in hate crimes symptomatic of the anti-Chinese movement in the nineteenth century.

The difference between 1882 and now is that Chinese Americans have become a political force in their own right. They exercise their right to vote, campaign for political office, agitate for social justice, and form coalitions with other groups to work on common issues of concern. Contrary to the model minority image, they are not afraid to rock the boat and speak up for their rights. Yet their diversity in terms of geographic origin, generation, class, and political perspectives often makes community organizing and collective action difficult on such controversial issues as acculturation and assimilation, partisan politics, U.S.-China foreign policy, affirmative action, and immigration and welfare reform. Chinese-American voters in California, for example, were divided on both Propositions 209, aimed at ending affirmative action programs, and 187, designed to limit public services to illegal immigrants. However, one thing is sure: The lessons of their past have taught Chinese Americans that the road from exclusion to inclusion is not unidirectional; constant vigilance and political action are necessary to ensure a multicultural democracy for all.

BIBLIOGRAPHIC REFERENCES

Important depositories of primary materials on Chinese Americans include the Asian American Studies Library and Bancroft Library at the University of California, Berkeley; California Room of the San Francisco Public Library; National Archives in San Bruno, California, and Washington, D.C.; California State Archives, Sacramento; and the Chinese Historical Society of America in San Francisco. Basic reference books are William L. Tung, *The Chinese in America, 1820–1973: A Chronology and Fact Book* (Dobbs Ferry, NY: Oceana Publications, 1974); Thomas Chinn, ed., *A History of the Chinese in California: A Syllabus* (San Francisco: Chinese Historical Society of America, 1975); and Him Mark Lai, *A History Reclaimed: An Annotated Bibliography of Chinese Language Materials on the Chinese of America* (Los Angeles: Asian American Studies Center, University of California, 1986). Classic studies include Mary Roberts Coolidge, *Chinese Immigration* (New York: Arno Press, 1969 [1909]); Rose Hum Lee, *The Chinese in the United States of America* (Hong Kong: Hong Kong University Press, 1960); and Stanford Lyman, *Chinese Americans* (New York: Random House, 1974). General histories are Diane Mei, Lin Mark, and Ginger Chih, *A Place Called Chinese America* (Dubuque: Kendall/Hunt, 1985); Shih-shan Henry Tsai, *The Chinese Experience in America* (Bloomington: Indiana University Press, 1986); and Judy Yung, *Chinese Women of America: A Pictorial History* (Seattle: University of Washington Press, 1986).

Major studies on the anti-Chinese movement and Chinese exclusion are Sucheng Chan, *Entry Denied: Exclusion and the Chinese Community in America, 1882–1943* (Philadelphia: Temple University Press, 1991); Him Mark Lai, Genny Lim, and Judy Yung, *Island: Poetry and History of Chinese Immigrants on Angel Island, 1910–1940* (Seattle: University of Washington Press, 1991); Charles J. McClain, *In Search of Equality: The Chinese Struggle against Discrimination in Nineteenth-Century America* (Berkeley: University of California Press, 1994); Stuart Miller, *The Unwelcome Immigrant: The American Image of the Chinese, 1785–1882* (Berkeley: University of California Press, 1969); and Alexander Saxton, *The Indispensable Enemy: Labor and the Anti-Chinese Movement in California* (Berkeley: University of California Press, 1971).

Immigration studies include Lucie Cheng and Edna Bonacich, eds., *Labor Immigration under Capitalism: Asian Workers in the United States before World War II* (Berkeley: University of California Press, 1984); Bill Ong Hing, *Making and Remaking Asian America through Immigration Policy, 1850–1990* (Stanford: Stanford University Press, 1993); Paul Ong, Edna Bonacich, and Lucie Cheng, *The New Asian Immigration in Los Angeles and Global Restructuring* (Philadelphia: Temple University Press, 1994); Lynn Pan, *Sons of the Yellow Emperor: A History of the Chinese Diaspora* (Boston: Little, Brown, 1990); and Lucy E. Salyer, *Laws Harsh as Tigers: Chinese Immigrants and the Shaping of Modern Immigration Law* (Chapel Hill: University of North Carolina Press, 1995). Books on Chinese labor include Sucheng Chan, *This Bittersweet Soil: The Chinese in California Agriculture, 1860–1910* (Berkeley and Los Angeles: University of California Press, 1986); Ping Chiu, *Chinese Labor in California, 1850–1880: An Economic Study* (Madison: State Historical Society of Wisconsin, 1967); Sandy Lydon, *Chinese Gold: The Chinese in the Monterey Bay Region* (Capitola, CA: Capitola Book Company, 1985); and Paul Siu, *The Chinese Laundryman: A Study of Social Isolation* (New York: New York University Press, 1987).

Regional studies include Tin-Yuke Char, ed.,*The Sandalwood Mountains: Readings and Stories of the Early Chinese in Hawaii* (Honolulu: University Press of Hawaii, 1975); Clarence Glick, *Sojourners and Settlers: Chinese Migrants in Hawaii* (Honolulu: University Press of Hawaii, 1980); Victor and Brett De Bary Nee, *Longtime Californ': A Documentary Study of an American Chinatown* (New York: Pantheon Books, 1973); Judy Yung, *Unbound Feet: A Social History of Chinese Women in San Francisco* (Berkeley: University of California Press, 1995); Timothy P. Fong, *The First Suburban Chinatown: The Remaking of Monterey Park, California* (Philadelphia: Temple University Press, 1994); James W. Loewen, *The Mississippi Chinese: Between Black and White* (Prospect Heights, IL: Waveland Press, 1988); and Peter Kwong, *Chinatown, New York: Labor and Politics, 1930–1950* (New York: Monthly Review Press, 1979), and *The New*

Chinatown (New York: Hill & Wang, 1987). Biographical works include Pardee Lowe, *Father and Glorious Descendant* (Boston: Little, Brown, 1943); Ruthanne Lum McCunn, *Chinese American Portraits* (San Francisco: Chronicle Books, 1988); and Jade Snow Wong, *Fifth Chinese Daughter* (New York: Harper & Row, 1950).

CUBANS

Guillermo J. Grenier and Lisandro Pérez

> We Cuban people have made Miami. We're making a new Miami. Thanks to the freedoms here in America, we're combining our Cuban natural energies with American knowledge, American know-how, to create a new, more passionate American. We immigrants, these new Americans, are going to be key players in reconstructing the new Cuba once Fidel leaves. We're going to make Cuba the next Japan.
>
> —A Miami Cuban businessman

The sentiments of this Cuban businessman accurately capture the dual identity of the Cuban-American community in the United States. As immigrants to this country, they have proven eager to incorporate themselves into American institutions, adapt American ways of life, and establish a rootedness in an American city as if it were their hometown. At the same time, Cuban Americans remain strongly nationalistic and, regardless of their achievements in the United States, continue to consider Cuba their home—the place where most hope to ultimately make their major contribution. They have taught their children that their cultural roots are Cuban and that they should include the island in their future, as a place to travel and help rebuild.

This essay presents the economic, political, and social characteristics of the Cuban-American community in the United States. In the process, we will clarify, and sometimes debunk, some of the essential characteristics of the Cuban success story. Have Cubans established themselves as the ideal Latino immigrants to these shores? If so, what are the reasons that allowed this to happen? And what have been the repercussions of Cuban immigration for the United States?

CUBAN IMMIGRATION: LIKE WAVES FROM
THE CARIBBEAN

The rise of Cuban Miami as the largest concentration of Cubans in the United States—and the third largest Latino community in this country—effectively starts following the first wave of 1959 with the massive exodus from the island after the rebel movement headed by Fidel Castro overthrew the government of Fulgencio Batista. Before this time, Miami, largely because of its youth and weak economic structure, was never the principal destination of Cuban immigrants to the United States. In the nineteenth century, sizable Cuban communities thrived in New York, Key West, New Orleans, and Ybor City, in the outskirts of Tampa. New York, which contained one of the earliest Cuban-American communities, was still the premier destination for the occasional migrants from the island in the period between World War II and the rise of the Castro government. This pattern of migration changed with the creation of rail and highway links between Miami and Key West and their extensions to Havana by way of regular ferry service. Air service between Miami, Key West, and Havana dates back to the 1920s and represents a pioneering effort in the history of passenger aviation. Those transportation links served to make Miami the principal staging area for the increasingly close relationship developing between Cuba and the Florida peninsula. In the year 1948, for example, Cuba led all countries in the world in the volume of passengers exchanged with the United States.

Including those who were born in the United States, the total number of Cubans in the United States as of 1990 was approximately 1,042,400, of which 73 percent were immigrants. While some Cubans arrived and remained in the United States after the 1898 war of independence (notably in Tampa and New York City), the large majority of Cubans in the United States are a result of four major waves of immigration initiated after the triumph of the Cuban Revolution in 1959.

The pattern of Cuban emigration since 1959 reflects primarily the availability of the means to leave Cuba. From 1959 to 1962, when the Missile Crisis of October 1962 eliminated regular commercial air traffic between the United States and Cuba, some 200,000 persons left Cuba. This first wave, composed of upper-and upper-middle-class Cubans, began immediately after the triumph of the Revolution in 1959. Most of these immigrants were not tied to the Batista government but were bound to a political and economic structure completely dependent on American capital. As Amaro and Portes wrote in 1972:

These executives and owners of firms, big merchants, sugar mill owners, manufacturers, representatives of foreign companies and established professionals were those most acquainted with the United States' political and economic guardianship of Cuba, under which they had created or maintained their position and thus were the least given to believe that the American government would permit the consolidation of a socialist regime in the island.

These Cubans were not the typical immigrants coming to the United States because of the "pull" of economic opportunities. They were motivated by the "push" factors of political upheavals they perceived as threatening their way of life. In fact, the second wave of Cuban immigrants was also motivated by the political changes occurring on the island.

The October Missile Crisis ended all contact between the two countries, slowing down considerably the pace of Cuban immigration in 1964 and 1965. Persons leaving Cuba during those years were doing so clandestinely, often in small boats or through third countries, usually Spain or Mexico. In the fall of 1965, in a move that responded to internal pressures for emigration and that was to be repeated fifteen years later, the Cuban government opened a port and allowed persons from the United States to go to Cuba to pick up relatives that wanted to leave the country. Some 5,000 Cubans left from the port of Camarioca before the United States and Cuba halted the boatlift and agreed to an orderly airlift.

In response to Lyndon Johnson's "open door" policy that welcomed refugees from communism, the Cuban and U.S. governments administered an orderly air bridge known as the *Vuelos de la Libertad*, or Freedom Flights. The airlift started in December 1965 and lasted until 1974. The twice-daily flights brought 260,500 persons during those years. As Table 3 shows, 41 percent of Cubans who immigrated to the United States after the Revolution (and were present in 1990) came over on the Freedom Flights, 1965–1974. Most of these were working class and petite bourgeoisie—employees, independent craftsmen, small merchants, skilled and semiskilled workers. When the first wave began in early 1960, 31 percent of the Cubans who arrived in the United States were professionals or managers. By 1970, near the middle of the second wave, only 12 percent were professionals or managers. By that time, more than half of the arrivals, 57 percent, were blue-collar, service, or agricultural workers.

The termination of the airlift brought on another period, during the mid-to late 1970s, of relatively low migration from Cuba: All was quiet on the Caribbean front. By 1980, however, the pressures for emigration once again caused the Cuban government to open a port for unrestricted emigration. The port was Mariel, giving the name to the boatlift that lasted for six months and that brought over, in a manner uncontrolled by the United States, more than 125,000 Cubans. This third wave of Cuban immigrants to the United States are called *Marielitos*. Few expected the massive flotilla exodus that occurred in 1980, for, suddenly, in April of 1980, a group of Cubans crashed the gates of the Peruvian embassy in Havana and asked for political asylum. Within days, tens of thousands of Cubans crowded the embassy compound. Seizing the opportunity to get rid of some dissident voices within the island, the Cuban government opened the port of Mariel to allow the official, if chaotic, exit of all those who had a means to leave. From Miami, thousands of boats manned by relatives sped across the Florida Straits to gather family and all others who could fit in the boats. When

Table 3
Number of Cubans in the United States by Year of Immigration, 1990

Year of Immigration	Number of Cubans	Percent	Immigrated from 1960 to1990(%)
Born in the U.S.	285,244	27.4	--
1987-1990	33,837	3.3	4.9
1985-1986	16,963	1.6	2.4
1982-1984	23,163	2.2	3.4
1980-1981	125,313	12.0	18.2
1975-1979	33,256	3.2	4.8
1970-1974	109,731	10.5	15.9
1965-1969	173,287	16.6	25.1
1960-1964	174,275	16.7	25.3
1950-1959	50,956	4.9	--
Before 1950	16,406	1.6	--
Total	1,042,431	100.0	100.0
			(689,825)

Source: U.S. Bureau of the Census, *U.S. Census of Population and Housing, 1990: Public Use Microdata Samples* (Washington, D.C.: Bureau of the Census, 1992). *Public Use Microdata Sample*, 5 percent, weighted.

it was all over, 125,000 more Cubans had come to the United States, approximately 18 percent of all Cuban immigrants now in the country.

Once in the United States, the *Marielitos* were front-page news. The media concentrated inordinately on the criminal elements included in the exodus. According to the Immigration and Naturalization Service (INS), of the 125,000 Mariel refugees, around 19 percent admitted that they had been in jail in Cuba. Of those who had been in prison, 5,486 (30 percent) were political prisoners, and the remaining 70 percent had been jailed for minor crimes or for acts, such as vagrancy or black market participation, that were crimes in Cuba but not in the United States. Yet the *Marielitos* were, indeed, different from other Cubans in the United States, but not only because of the deviant element. While earlier waves could be characterized as being composed of white, middle-aged male professionals and middle-class émigrés, discontented with the political and economic reshuffling of the society (and their families), the typical *Marielito* was a young mulatto or black working-class individual who was raised with the Revolution and who probably supported the political and economic reshuffling until some personal encounter with Cuban authorities promoted disaffection (see Table 4). These sort of differences helped create an aloofness between the *Ma-*

Table 4
Number of Cubans in the United States, by Race and by Year of Immigration, 1990

Year of Immigration	Race				Total	
	White	Black	Asian	Other	N	Percent
1987-1990	84.0	2.6	0.4	13.0	33,837	100.0
1985-1986	85.8	3.3	--	10.9	16,963	100.0
1982-1984	76.8	5.6	0.6	17.0	23,163	100.0
1980-1981	77.3	6.0	0.4	16.3	125,313	100.0
1975-1979	74.8	5.6	1.1	18.5	33,256	100.0
1970-1974	84.1	1.7	0.3	13.9	109,731	100.0
1965-1969	82.4	1.5	0.5	15.6	173,287	100.0
1960-1964	90.7	1.9	0.1	7.3	174,275	100.0
Total, 1960-1990	83.5	2.9	0.3	13.3	689,825	100.0

Source: U.S. Bureau of the Census, *U.S. Census of Population and Housing, 1990: Public Use Microdata Samples*, (Washington, D.C.: Bureau of the Census, 1992). 5 percent, weighted.

rielitos and more established Cubans. A black Cuban army officer who arrived in Miami from Mariel spoke of the distance that separated him from the earlier exiles: "I can now see that they feel no ill will toward me and may even want to help me, but they can't help me come to grips with the twenty years I've spent in Cuba. They don't understand how I feel."

The end of the boatlift and the onset of restrictions on Cuban immigration brought about a lull in the exodus during the 1980s. In the mid-1980s, in an attempt to prevent another Mariel, the implementation of an immigration agreement between the United States and Cuba in November 1987 provided for the admission into the United States of about 20,000 persons from Cuba each year. Priority was to be given to those who would qualify for political asylum. Most of the persons who arrived after that date had been former political prisoners and their families, but in reality, only about 2,000 visas were given per year under that accord.

As the economic situation worsened on the island, the desire to leave far outstripped the availability of resources to do so legally. The result was the initiation of a fourth wave of immigration, this time through illegal and highly dangerous means. *Balseros*, or raft people, had begun to drift on to Florida's coast on a regular basis in the mid-1980s. According to the U.S. Coast Guard, 5,791 *balseros* managed to reach safety in the United States from 1985 to 1992. The numbers rose dramatically as the economic situation of the island worsened following the collapse of the communist bloc. While in 1989 less than 500 *balseros* arrived in the United States, by 1991 the number had risen to over 2,000 and by 1993 to 3,656. The numbers reached fantastic levels during the crisis of August and September 1994, when more than 37,000 Cubans were rescued at sea.

The history of U.S.-Cuban relations can be seen as a string of crises, and each one has had an impact on the Cuban community in the United States. August 1994 marked another such crisis. At that time, the Cuban government ceased to patrol its coastal waters, giving a green light to anyone courageous enough to build a raft and set off across the Florida Straits. From August 12 to August 23, the U.S. Coast Guard intercepted 9,000 Cubans attempting the dangerous crossing in homemade rafts. Fearing another Mariel, the U.S. government implemented unprecedented measures. The Clinton administration announced that the United States would no longer automatically accept rafters or other illegal immigrants from Cuba. Any rafter intercepted in the Florida Straits would be sent to makeshift refugee camps established at Guantánamo Naval Base, on the southeastern tip of the island of Cuba, or to Panama. This decision did not discourage those intent on leaving the island. From August 13 to September 13, when the Cuban government resumed patrolling its borders, approximately 37,000 Cubans fled the island. Over 28,000 of them ended up temporarily at Guantánamo or Panama. In April 1995 the U.S. government agreed to accept them into the United States.

The two governments reopened discussions on the issue of immigration on August 23, resulting in a new immigration agreement, signed on September 9. The resulting agreement established as a minimum quota what used to be the maximum (20,000), and this did not include cases where Cubans on the island wanted to be reunited with immediate relatives living in the United States who had acquired American citizenship. Both governments agreed to expedite requests to ensure a regular and regulated flow. The Cuban government agreed to reestablish strong border controls, while the U.S. government agreed to suspend its automatic admission of illegal immigrants. In this fashion, the Clinton administration became the first Democratic administration to restrict the entry of Cuban immigrants into the United States.

SETTLEMENT PATTERNS

Now, it is axiomatic to view the final destination of Cubans, either coming from Cuba or resettling from other points of the Diaspora, as Miami. But this process of concentration was preceded by an intentional dispersion throughout the United States engineered by the Cuban Refugee Resettlement Program. The program was established in February 1961 as a federal effort to provide assistance in handling the large influx from Cuba. One of the stated purposes of the federal authorities in establishing the Cuban Refugee Program was to ease the demographic and economic pressures that the influx was exerting on south Florida. A resettlement program was established through which families arriving from Cuba were given assistance if they immediately relocated away from Miami. The assistance included transportation costs to the new destination, help in finding housing and employment, and financial assistance until such time as employment was secured. The incentives worked. According to a Cuban Refugee Program Fact Sheet of the Department of Health, Education, and Welfare, 300,232 persons were resettled away from Miami between February 1961 and August 1978. This figure represents 64 percent of all Cubans arriving in the United States and registering with the Cuban Refugee Program during that period. It is also equivalent to 37 percent of all persons of Cuban origin enumerated in the United States in 1980.

The bulk of the resettled Cubans went to New York, New Jersey, California, and Illinois. In 1965, 42 percent of the Cuban population in the United States lived in Dade County. Five years later, the 1970 census found that 40 percent of all persons of Cuban origin in the United States lived in the county. The resettlement process reached its peak precisely in the late 1960s. By 1980, the U.S. census found slightly more than 52 percent of U.S. Cubans living in Greater Miami. The concentration of Cubans in south Florida increased during the 1980s as the majority of Mariel entrants settled in Miami, where they could find employment within a familiar cultural environment and use their native language. This trend continued during the 1990s. Thus, contrary to the experience of most immigrant groups for whom concentration in a city or region formed part of the process of adjustment to the United States, the Cubans underwent, early in their recent history of immigration, a process of intentional dispersion. But one that proved to be particularly successful.

The process of concentration in Miami will persist into the next decade. The principal factor in sustaining that trend has been the entry into the retirement ages of the large middle-aged cohort in the Cuban-origin population, many of whom were the young heads of households who were resettled away from Miami in the 1960s. It is likely that many of those who have not yet returned to Miami will do so when they retire in the years ahead. On the other hand, the second-generation Cuban Americans are proving to be extremely loyal to the south Florida area. When this generation moves from the Dade County area, they tend to remain in the adjacent counties. Still, another factor that will sustain the trend toward an increasing concentration in south Florida is the renewal of migration from Cuba as a result of the September 9, 1994, agreement between the U.S. and Cuban governments. No doubt the bulk of those arrivals will settle in Miami, where their adjustment to life in the United States will be facilitated by the large Cuban community there. Aside from the cultural and linguistic advantages that the established community offers to the new arrivals, there is also the importance of ethnic and familial networks that ease incorporation into the labor force.

Despite the emphasis here on the Miami enclave, it is important to note that there are significant numbers of Cubans outside the premier Cuban-American community. Overall, the distribution of those non–Miami Cubans is predominantly metropolitan. The New York City–New Jersey metropolitan area, Los Angeles, and Chicago contain the largest concentrations. Although in the last couple of decades those cities, as well as others throughout the United States, have lost many of their Cuban residents to the process of concentration in Miami, they have nevertheless retained very visible and dynamic Cuban-American communities. Generally, the data show that Cuban Americans living outside of Miami have a slightly higher socioeconomic status than do their compatriots in south Florida. The most likely explanation for that phenomenon is that their economic position enabled them to resist the magnetism that Miami seems to have for Cuban Americans. While there are little data on this point, it is probably the case that there has been a degree of socioeconomic selectivity in the flow of resettled Cubans returning to Miami: Those with better jobs stayed where they were relocated. Also, better jobs may have enticed some to leave Miami, independently of the resettlement program.

The only exceptions to the generalization that non-Miami Cubans are better off than Miami Cubans are those residing in the New York City–New Jersey metropolitan area. The main concentrations of Cubans in that region are on the New Jersey side of the Hudson River, especially in West New York, Union City, and Jersey City, communities on an industrial corridor with a predominance of blue-collar jobs. In comparison with their compatriots who work in Miami's service-oriented labor market, a greater proportion of New York City–New Jersey Cubans are members of the working class.

THE CREATION OF CUBAN MIAMI

While Miami did not have the employment opportunities required by the Cuban immigrants during the first half of the twentieth century, Miami did receive those seeking refuge from the shifting fortunes of the island's turbulent political history. Two deposed Cuban presidents—Gerardo Machado and Carlos Prío Socarrás made their home in Miami. A prominent Cuban politician of the 1940s built Miami's baseball stadium. Even Fidel Castro spent time in Miami in the 1950s, and as leader of the 1959 Revolution, he initiated a process of revolutionary change that, in its rapidity and pervasiveness, alienated large sectors of the Cuban population and contributed to the creation of Cuban Miami.

Before the 1960s, Miami's population consisted largely of black and white southern in-migrants and their descendants, transplanted northerners (including many Jews), and Bahamian and other Caribbean blacks and their descendants. Cubans fleeing Castro's Cuba began arriving in significant numbers in the 1960s, following the failure of the 1961 Bay of Pigs invasion. The flow has been largely one way. Once Cubans come to Miami, few return. The U.S. government encouraged and aided the flow by providing special immigration status and federal aid. While significant numbers of Cubans settled in New York and New Jersey, Miami was the preferred destination of the vast majority, making Cubans Miami's most visible minority.

Miami had always had a service-centered economy, but after the arrival of the Cubans, the focus of those services shifted from tourists and sojourners toward providing Latin America with financial services. During the 1960s, Miami displaced New Orleans as the country's principal trade outlet with Latin America. In 1980, 100 multinational corporations had their Latin American headquarters in Miami, and two years later Miami stood second only to New York as an international banking center. By the mid-1980s, Miami International Airport was the ninth busiest airport in the world in passengers and the sixth largest in air cargo tonnage. About 160,000 workers, one-fifth of Miami's labor force, were directly or indirectly employed in airport and aviation activities. By the late 1980s, Miami's industrial profile was similar to other newer American cities in which the economy was led by services, wholesale trade, finance, insurance, and real estate.

Today, persons born in Cuba or of Cuban descent represent Miami's largest ethnic group. Cubans account for 56 percent of Greater Miami's foreign-born population, and persons of Cuban origin constitute the bulk—nearly 70 percent—of all Latinos in the area. About 30 percent of Dade County's population is of Cuban birth or descent. The demographic importance of the Cuban presence in Miami is evident in a myriad of ways. The "Cubanness" of the area is manifested not only in demonstrable terms, such as economic activities and cultural events, but also in a more intangible manner, namely, "ambience." David Rieff, a New Yorker who has written on Miami, has noted that Cubans have largely taken control of the "atmosphere" of the city. Cubans have a sense of "rootedness" there. In many ways, Miami is the capital and mecca of U.S. Cubans. As Rieff expressed it, "Cubans are probably the only people who really do feel comfortable in Dade County these days. . . . Miami is their town now."

Since Cubans represent nearly 70 percent of the Latino population of Greater Miami, they can be found throughout most of the greater metropolitan area. Generally, the heaviest concentrations of Latinos within the county are found along a belt running west from downtown (which is located east on Biscayne Bay) all the way to the western edges of the metropolitan area. This belt includes the southern half of the city of Miami as well as the incorporated areas of West Miami and Sweetwater, the northern part of the city of Coral Gables, and unincorporated portions of the county in the west. Since the 1960s the settlement of Cubans along this belt has proceeded from east to west, emanating largely from the area known as Little Havana, which is located within the city of Miami, stretching west along Calle Ocho (S. W. 8th Street) for about fifteen city blocks.

But middle-income Cubans, and especially professionals, are now hard to find in Little Havana. Their upward mobility has taken them to more suburban areas to the west. The current residents of Little Havana are likely to be blue-collar and service workers, the elderly, the poor, and the recent immigrants, including non-Cuban Latinos. As one moves north or south of the "Hispanic belt" the proportion of Latinos declines, with the exception of the city of Hialeah, located in the northwestern portion of Greater Miami. About two-thirds of its population are now Latino. Hialeah contains many of the region's manufacturing plants, and during the late 1960s and the 1970s, its predominantly white, non-Latino, blue-collar population rapidly gave way to Cuban blue-collar families. However, while Cubans can be found throughout most of Greater Miami—and, therefore, Latino-Anglo segregation is not as high as one would expect—that is not the case for Latino-black segregation. The two populations exhibit considerable spatial distance, and blacks tend to live in fairly confined areas, segregated from both Latinos and Anglos.

THE CUBAN ENCLAVE

The existence of the Cuban enclave played a pivotal role in the economic success of the Cuban-American community and the transformation of Miami's economic profile. Cubans frequently headed the import and export companies, the banks that financed the transactions, and the smaller transportation and service companies that allowed goods and services to be shipped. There were over 45,000 Latino businesses in Dade County as of 1995, and although the vast majority are small businesses that have been described as the true engines of Miami's economic growth, many of the most powerful economic corporations are Latino owned and operated. Miami has only 5 percent of the U.S. Latino population, but it has close to half of the forty largest Latino-owned industrial and commercial firms in the country and the highest per capita number of Latino-owned businesses. For example, by the mid-1980s, 40 percent of Miami's banks were owned by Latinos. There were Latino insurance companies, shipping firms, and innumerable import and export establishments. Some of the most important developers were Latinos, one having become in the late 1980s the first Latino head of the Greater Miami Chamber of Commerce.

Miami's Cuban community is regarded as the foremost example in the United States of a true ethnic enclave. The community's entrepreneurial base was established largely by those Cuban immigrants (especially those who arrived in the first wave in the early 1960s) who possessed the complex of skills and attitudes that eventually made possible their entry into a wide range of self-employment. They represent one of the most successful transplantations of an entrepreneurial class from their homeland to a new land during the first waves of migration.

The strong and diversified entrepreneurial activity that developed is responsible for the enclave's most important overall feature: institutional completeness. Cubans in Miami can, if they wish, literally live out their lives within the ethnic community. The wide range of sales and services, including professional services, available within the community makes possible its completeness. Three factors promoting Miami Cuban economic and political activity are the human capital Cubans brought with them and their concentration in Miami; the role of the U.S. federal government in providing aid to the arriving Cuban refugees (nearly $1 billion from 1965 to 1976 as well as 47 percent of all small business loans in Dade County from 1968 to 1980); and the creation of a collective Cuban-American identity arising from the interplay of the U.S. government–sponsored and Cuban exile counterrevolutionary organizations (including possibly 12,000 Miami Cubans on the Central Intelligence Agency [CIA] payroll in the early 1960s). The CIA supported what was described as the third largest navy in the world and over fifty front businesses: CIA boat shops, CIA gun shops, CIA travel agencies, CIA detective agencies, and CIA real estate agencies. This investment served far more to economically boost the Cubans in Miami than it did to destabilize the Castro regime.

The first wave of Cubans has been labeled the "Golden Exiles," the top of Cuban society who were most immediately threatened by a socialist revolution. Many had already established a footing in the United States, and when the Revolution came, they simply abandoned one of their residences for another across the straits of Florida. A Cuban shoe manufacturer, for example, before the Revolution produced footwear for a major U.S. retail chain. He had obtained his working capital from New York financial houses. After the Revolution, the only change was that the manufacturing was done in Miami rather than Havana. The Cuban Revolution "made him" and many others exiles in a way that has not occurred for upper-class Mexicans or Puerto Ricans. The Revolution thus upwardly biased the socioeconomic profile of Miami's Cuban population. Even if they could not transfer their investments, their human capital (i.e., their knowledge and experience) came with them.

The favorable reception by the U.S. government translated itself into not only millions of dollars of resettlement assistance but also the establishment of a "direct line" of Cuban exile leaders to the centers of political power in Washington. Unlike the situation of other immigrant and ethnic minorities, who have had to struggle painfully for years or even generations to gain "access" to the corridors of power, this was available to Cuban leaders almost from the start. This window of opportunity greatly boosted the Cubans in the 1960s and the Miami economy in general. Waves of Cuban immigrants stimulated demand and received substantial subsidies from the federal government. With a high rate of labor force participation, especially among women, the Cubans also contributed significantly to productivity growth. Even the 1973–1974 recession had an indirect benefit for Cubans, for in the subsequent recovery of the late 1970s, many Americans fled and a de facto segmentation of the industry emerged: Latinos became the leaders in home construction, and American resident whites maintained dominance in large-scale commercial construction. This division reflected an even more important development within the community, the emergence of the Cuban enclave or institutionally complete community.

Despite the many commercial successes, it is obvious that not all Miami Cubans are rich and powerful businessmen. Even the fact of business ownership is somewhat misleading. Of the 77,300 Latino-owned and-operated businesses in 1992, only 13.6 percent had paid employees, and all together they generated a total of only 72,000 paid jobs, a number only slightly higher than the total number of Latinos in Dade County who belonged to unions. Moreover, most of the Latino employment growth during the 1970s was directly attributable to population growth. Latinos (as well as blacks) were underrepresented in Miami's fastest growing industries, especially financial services, which were dominated by white Americans. The non-Latino white abandonment of Dade County that began in the 1970s was class selective. Non-Latino white laborers and production workers left in great numbers, whereas higher-class workers, notably executives and managers, remained or moved into Dade County. Thus, although Latinos (and blacks) expanded their representation in the higher occupations, non-Latino whites still outnumbered them.

CONSEQUENCES OF THE ENCLAVE

To understand Cubans in the United States, it is important to trace the implications of the structural organization of the enclave. Foremost among them is the well-studied influence on the process of economic adjustment, but the enclave also affects such important areas as acculturation, interethnic relations, and political participation.

Economic Adjustment

First, the enclave somewhat insulates the immigrant against the usual processes of the segmented labor market. In contrast to Mexican immigrants, who must join the open labor market in peripheral sectors of the economy throughout the country, many recent Cuban immigrants enter the U.S. labor market primarily through Miami businesses that are owned or operated by members of their own group who had arrived earlier. While compensation may not be higher in the enclave, ethnic bonds provide for informal networks of support that facilitate the learning of new skills and the overall process of economic adjustment.

Acculturation

Second, the existence of the enclave also has evident implications for the process of acculturation. The completeness of the enclave has the effect of slowing down that process, for it tends to insulate the immigrant from the "dominant" society and culture, allowing for the retention of the culture of origin. Using language as one indicator of the degree of acculturation, one study found that most Cubans used only Spanish at home and in many of their daily activities. For example, in 1980, 43 percent of the residents of Dade County spoke a language other than English at home. Of those who spoke a foreign language at home, one-third indicated they spoke English "not well or not at all." However, the institutional completeness of the enclave has made Spanish a public language in Miami, one that is not confined to the intimacy of the family or the peer group. It is the lingua franca for conducting a wide range of business and personal matters beyond one's primary groups, and that is why language is the frequent battleground for interethnic conflicts. It is not a coincidence that the "English-only" movement was born in Miami.

The retention of the language and cultural patterns of the country of origin is also attributable to the fairly recent arrival of most Cubans to this country. The overwhelming majority of Cubans in Miami are immigrants, with an over-representation of the middle-aged and elderly. The bulk of the population has arrived in this country only within the past four decades. It is a fairly recent immigrant group. Another factor that retards the process of acculturation among Cubans in Miami, especially important in the early stages of the exodus, is the perception many U.S. Cubans have of themselves as reluctant migrants, compelled to leave their country but with the expectation of returning and consequently with little desire or motivation to assimilate into this society. Compounding these sentiments, it is also important to remember, have been the periodic waves of massive arrivals from Cuba, fresh from the culture of origin and renewing and reinforcing that culture within the immigrant community.

Interethnic Relations

A third major consequence of the enclave is in the arena of interethnic relations in Miami. The insulation of the immigrant within the enclave, while it may have positive implications for the initial process of economic adjustment, poorly serves interethnic communications and understanding, making it even less likely that Latinos and blacks will create the basis for a better understanding and a common agenda. Compared to American blacks, Cubans in Miami have a far greater likelihood of being able to work with coethnics, shop in stores owned and operated by coethnics, and obtain professional services from coethnics. While recent evidence indicates that during the 1960s and early 1970s black Miami viewed Cubans as possible allies in the battles for minority empowerment in Dade County, by the 1980s this view was replaced by one of clear antagonism.

Political Culture

Fourth, during the 1980s Cubans in Miami established pivotal local power, exercised through the increasing number of elected officials and such organizations as the Cuban American National Foundation, the Latin Builders Association and the Hispanic Builders Association, and the Latin Chamber of Commerce.

Although participation in the political system of the United States, at all levels, has traditionally taken a backseat to the politics of the homeland, the 1980s saw the rapid and massive entry of Miami's Cubans into the realm of electoral politics in the United States. That entry, however, was not entirely unrelated to, nor did it signal a departure from, traditional exile politics. One factor that encouraged Cubans in Miami to become citizens and register to vote was the candidacy of Ronald Reagan. The ideology of the Republican candidate on foreign policy was appealing to many Cubans, and it served to join exile politics with registering and voting in the United States. Participation in the U.S. political system, therefore, is not necessarily an abandonment of the concern with the political status of the homeland but may actually be an extension of those exile concerns.

The size of the Cuban community in Greater Miami and its fairly high turnout rates during elections have produced a boom in the number of Cubans in elected positions at all levels of government. Cubans have been mayors of the incorporated areas of Miami, Hialeah, Sweetwater, West Miami, and Hialeah Gardens, all within Greater Miami. Cubans comprise a majority in the commissions or councils of those cities. In the City of Miami, the city manager and the county manager were Cubans, and Cubans controlled the City Commission and constituted more than one-third of the Dade delegation to the state legislature. So great is the political involvement of Cubans in Miami that the Cuban voting block has to be considered by any candidate seeking county-wide office. The 1990 county-wide elections for Metropolitan Dade County's Commission emphasized the strength of a unified Cuban voting bloc. During these elections, for example, two of the non-Cuban victors owed their success to the support garnered among the Cuban electorate.

When the 1990s started, there were already ten Cubans in the Florida legislature, seven in the House and three in the Senate, and that number remained steady into the 1997 elections. In 1989, a Cuban reached an elective office at the federal level, when Ileana Ros-Lehtinen was elected to the U.S. Congress, succeeding longtime congressman Claude Pepper, who had died. Lincoln Diaz-Balart, a Cuban-born politician first elected to the state legislature in the mid-1980s, was elected to Congress in 1992. Nowhere else in America, nor even in American history (with the possible exception of the Irish), have first-generation immigrants so quickly, or so thoroughly, appropriated political power.

Perhaps for this reason, no aspect of the Cuban Miami attracts more national and international attention than does its politics. Even after thirty years, it remains a community of exiles, largely preoccupied with the political status of the homeland. At the same time, however, it has demonstrated, at a relatively early point in its development, a strong participation in the U.S. political system at the local and state levels. The political culture of Miami's Cubans is therefore a fundamental and complex topic.

The Persistence of the Exile Ideology

The "exile" ideology among Cubans in Miami has four principal and interrelated characteristics.

1. *Issues and concerns that deal with the political status of the homeland are of primary importance.* Although the 1990s have witnessed a rise of concerns that can perhaps be regarded as "immigrant" issues, that is, issues regarding adjustment to life in the United States and local political questions, the principal focus of political discourse and mobilization in the Cuban-American community remains Cuba. Such issues as T. V. Marti, U.S. policy toward Cuba, and the internal situation in the island continue to predominate and are causes for the mobilization of resources. In contrast, a certain apathy reigns over more domestic issues, such as the adoption of English as the official language of Florida.

2. *The principal element of the exile ideology is an uncompromising struggle and hostility against the current Cuban government.* The goal of the Cuban exile is the overthrow of Fidel Castro and the establishment in Cuba of a democratic government. This is to be accomplished through hostility and isolation, not rapprochement.

3. *The exile ideology is largely not debatable within the community.* The Cuban-American community has been formed by a particular set of political circumstances. Cuban-Americans—as with exiles everywhere—are therefore not likely to be objective about the situation that has so intrinsically altered their lives and compelled them to live outside their native country. Presently there is the obvious intolerance of views that do not conform to the predominant exile ideology of an uncompromising hostility toward the Castro regime. Those inside or outside the community who voice views that are "soft" or conciliatory with respect to Castro, or who take a less-than-militant stance in opposition to Cuba's regime, are usually subjected to criticism and scorn, their position belittled and their motivations questioned. Until recently, any dissent within the community was especially difficult, since greater pressures could be brought to bear on the individual or group than would be the case for entities outside the community. On the other hand, surveys conducted in 1991, 1993, and 1995 reported emerging pluralistic tendencies in views toward political solutions to the Cuban problem. Forty-two percent of a representative 1995 sample of Cuban Americans in Dade County favored a dialogue with the Cuban government for the purpose of changing the current situation. This reflected a real change in community priorities and attitudes, but it is uncertain how this change will affect the overall structure of the Cuban community. After the February 1996 *Crisis de las Avionetas* (Crisis of the Small Planes), initiated by the downing of two Cuban-American Cessnas over the Strait of Florida by Cuban Air Force pilots, the majority of Miami Cubans did not hesitate in calling for a U.S. invasion of the island. Events such as this strengthen the hand of the right-wing hard liners, in Miami as well as in Cuba.

4. *The exile ideology has resulted in overwhelming support for the Republican Party among Cubans in Miami.* Registered Republicans far outnumber registered Democrats among Cubans in Miami. Loyalty to the Republicans demonstrates the importance of international issues in the political agenda of

Cubans. Were Cuban Americans to view themselves as immigrants in this country, rather than as political exiles, and made judgments about political parties based upon their needs and aspirations as immigrants in the United States, they would be Democrats in overwhelming numbers. That is the case with other immigrants in the United States and especially with other Latinos. This would be true not only because of the general social agenda of the Democrats but also specifically because of the experience of Cuban migration: The measures that have greatly facilitated Cuban immigration and the adjustment of Cuban Americans in the United States have all been enacted by Democratic administrations—the Cuban Refugee Emergency Program and its resettlement efforts, the assistance given to the Cuban elderly and the dependent, the Airlift or Freedom Flights, and the permission given for the Mariel boatlift to take place, among others.

The fact that Cubans are overwhelmingly Republicans is therefore a testimony to the predominance of the exile ideology. Yet the Cuban delegation in the Florida state legislature in Tallahassee has shown an ambivalence about supporting the party to which most of their constituency belongs. Strongly influenced by the Cuban labor leadership, this group is viewed as a liberal force within the Republican Party and often enters into coalition with Democrats to impede the domination of the state legislature by conservative Republicans or Democrats.

Intergenerational Shifts and Social Change

Although, as noted previously, the enclave tends to favor the retention of the culture of the homeland, delaying the process of acculturation, it is unlikely that the Cuban community in the United States will be an exception to the usual intergenerational shift toward greater acculturation and assimilation. English is the principal language among Cubans who have lived all or most of their lives in the United States. Indeed, sharp intergenerational differences have been revealed among Cubans in Miami in the level of acculturation, with early adolescents demonstrating the highest scores of all age groups in measures of behavioral acculturation. Furthermore, males evidence greater acculturation than females. An exaggerated acculturational gap is a major source of intergenerational conflicts generating alienation between parents and children.

An important focus of intergenerational tensions are the conflicting value orientations with respect to dependence and independence. Cuban culture stresses the continued dependence of children on their parents, even in the teenage years and beyond. Children, however, are more likely to have internalized the norms of independence commonly found in U.S. society. One adaptation that reduces intergenerational tension is "biculturality," by which each generation adjusts to the other generation's cultural preferences: "Parents learn how to remain loyal to their ethnic background while becoming skilled in interacting with their youngsters' Americanized values and behaviors, and vice versa."

Intergenerational shifts will also be evident in the very structure of the enclave, for coming up rapidly behind that large cohort of first-generation entrepreneurs are those Cuban Americans born in the United States or who arrived as children from the island. Largely educated in this country, the influentials in this group are less likely than the older generation to be entrepreneurs and more likely to be professionals. These younger professionals have the credentials to break out from the ethnic enclave and obtain employment in the larger firms and institutions outside the ethnic community. If this is the case, then it is obvious that a rapid change will take place in the years ahead in the very economic basis of the Cuban community, from a community dominated by first-generation entrepreneurs to one of second-generation professionals. Such a shift will also alter the Cuban community's relationship with the rest of the city.

This shift is already evident in the participation of Cubans within the traditional "Anglo" institutions that hold true economic power in Miami (the banks, law firms, insurance companies, real estate, advertising, professional services, and the public bureaucracies). At the upper levels, there are few Cuban faces in those institutions, especially in the private sector, but at the lower- and middle-management levels there is a critical mass of young Cuban professionals. Furthermore, "Anglo flight" from Dade County has removed the Cubans' Anglo contemporaries from the competition for those jobs. Distanced somewhat from their Cuban origins, the new generation of Miami Cubans will think more like immigrants than as exiles, will have a new agenda, and will easily find common ground and solidarity with other ethnic groups in the community, especially the growing number of non-Cuban Latinos.

CONCLUSION: THE CUBAN-AMERICAN COMMUNITY AT FIN-DE-SIÈCLE

During the 1990s, the Cuban-American community in Miami and elsewhere reached a crossroads. This decade has seen the restructuring of its ethnic social profile as it has advanced from a refugee community, whose agenda is looking back to the father land, to an immigrant community, with a more local agenda interested in promoting bread-and-butter issues. A portion of that community has also begun to view itself as a minority group, with the need to establish alliances with other minority groups.

As we enter a new millennium, both Cuba and Cuban Miami will see fundamental changes. If we soon see the reestablishment of normal transportation, communications, and commercial links between Miami and Cuba, the basic conditions that created and shaped Miami's exile community will finally be meaningfully altered after four decades. Moreover, in 1990, that large cohort of exiles was already between the ages of fifty and sixty-nine, and by the year 2000, their economic and political (and ideological) influence will begin to wane, rapidly making way for the new generation. On the one hand, if white flight continues as the wave of largely poor immigrants continues to arrive,

Miami's success might have seen its last days; cities abandoned to minority populations, no matter how successful a portion of that minority is, do not fare well. On the other hand, if the emerging political and social structures in the city become representative of its multicultural core, then Miami promises to be one of America's great cities, and Cuban Americans can then be proud of their contribution.

BIBLIOGRAPHIC REFERENCES

The literature on Cubans in the United States has traditionally been dominated by analyses of their successful economic adjustment in the United States. The following focus on that issue: Alejandro Portes and Robert L. Bach, *Latin Journey: Cuban and Mexican Immigrants in the United States* (Berkeley: University of California Press, 1985); Silvia Pedraza-Bailey, *Political and Economic Migrants in America: Cubans and Mexicans* (Austin: University of Texas Press, 1985); and Lisandro Pérez, "Immigrant Economic Adjustment and Family Organization: The Cuban Success Story Reexamined," *International Migration Review* 20 (1985): 4–20. General overviews of Cuban Americans can be found in: Thomas D. Boswell and James R. Curtis, *The Cuban-American Experience: Culture Images and Perspectives* (Totowa, NJ: Rowman and Allanheld, 1983); Thomas D. Boswell, *A Demographic Profile of Cuban Americans* (Miami: Cuban American National Council, 1994); and Lisandro Pérez, "Cubans in the United States," *Annals of the American Academy of Political and Social Science* 487 (1986): 1265–1370.

Much of the literature on Cuban Americans during the past decade has focused on the community in Miami, in some cases as part of broader analyses of the social reality of south Florida: Alejandro Portes and Alex Stepick, *City on the Edge: The Transformation of Miami* (Berkeley: University of California Press, 1993); Guillermo Grenier and Alex Stepick, eds., *Miami Now! Immigration, Ethnicity, and Social Change* (Gainesville: University of Florida Press, 1992); Maria Cristina Garcia, *Havana USA: Cuban Exiles and Cuban Americans in South Florida, 1959–1994* (Berkeley: University of California Press, 1996); and Raymond A. Mohl, "An Ethnic 'Boiling Pot': Cubans and Haitians in Miami," *Journal of Ethnic Studies* 13.2 (Summer 1985): 51–74.

Other useful works include: Holly Ackerman and Juan M. Clark, *The Cuban Balseros: Voyage of Uncertainty* (Miami: Cuban American National Council, 1995); Felix Masud-Piloto, *With Open Arms: Cuban Migration to the United States* (Totowa, NJ: Rowman and Littlefield, 1988); Richard R. Fagen, Richard A. Brody, and Thomas J. O'Leary, *Cubans in Exile: Disaffection and the Revolution* (Stanford: Stanford University Press, 1968); José Szapocznik and Roberto Hernandez, "The Cuban American Family," in *Ethnic Families in America*, 3rd ed., edited by Charles H. Mindel, Robert W. Habenstein, and Roosevelt Wright, Jr. (New York: Elsevier, 1988), pp. 160–172; David Reiff, *Going to Miami: Exiles, Tourists and Refugees in the New America* (Boston: Little, Brown, 1987); and Nelson Amaro and Alejandro Portes, "Una sociologia del exilio: Situacion de los grupos Cubanos en los Estados Unidos," *Aportes* 23 (1972): 6–24.

DUTCH

Suzanne M. Sinke

NEW NETHERLAND

The Dutch were entering their "Golden Century" when the relationship with North America developed in the 1600s. Commerce, not to mention art and literature, flourished in Dutch trading centers where goods poured in from all over the world, and merchants and bankers largely controlled foreign policy. The United Provinces, commonly known as the Dutch Republic, had not yet won official independence from Hapsburg rule (a status granted with the Treaty of Münster in 1648) when the Dutch East India Company sent Henry Hudson on a voyage to find a northwest passage to the Orient. Hudson, with his mixed Dutch and English crew, made a voyage up the lower reaches of a river soon to bear his name on the *Halve Maen* in 1609, doing some trading with natives along the way. This journey, and others undertaken later under the auspices of the company, served as the basis for Dutch claims to New Netherland, a territory stretching between the Delaware and Connecticut Rivers. The claims conflicted with those of the British, but the British did not press the case immediately.

The Dutch West India Company, which gained jurisdiction over New Netherland, ignored the colony for the most part, focusing more on other areas of the Americas. Yet it did seek to hold off French and English challenges, which led to the first settlement attempts. Thirty Belgian-Walloon families arrived in the territory in 1624, and they dispersed among four settlements: one at the mouth of each of the major rivers (Delaware, Connecticut, and Hudson) and one further up the Hudson, just south of present-day Albany. Additional settlers within a year created a population of roughly 300 people, many of whom returned to Holland in just a few years, where a number would sue the company for personal losses.

Keeping settlers in the colony remained a problem. Both economic and cultural issues were at stake. For example, although the "Provisional Orders" of the company for settlers were relatively liberal, French-speaking Walloons did not appreciate the stipulation of obligatory church services in Dutch. The Dutch Reformed Church enjoyed special status, both in the colony and in the homeland. Still, the company was more interested in profits than supporting a religious monopoly and, hence, did not enforce the rules and allowed (relative to European standards) significant religious toleration. The interests of the Dutch Reformed Church and the company collided frequently over economic support for the denomination, proselytism of natives, the role of clergy in governing the colony, and the degree and manner of maintaining orthodoxy.

Just as New Netherland was an outpost of Dutch trade and settlement, so, too, was it a settlement area and trading region for the natives of the region, who were involved in their own economic shifts related to the fur trade. In particular, the Algonkian tribes of the lower Hudson and Delaware, with the introduction of firearms, wiped out local fur-bearing animals, resulting in increased competition and then warfare for territory. Attempts by the West India Company to gain more control of the fur trade brought them into the midst of native hostilities. At the mouth of the Hudson, the Dutch support of the Mahicans in their war with the Mohawks threatened to cut the transatlantic fur trade, but it also made possible the purchase of Manhattan in 1626. Geographically, the Dutch settlement of New Amsterdam (later New York City) grew from Manhattan Island outwards and brought the settlers into closer contact with native peoples. In much of New Netherland, the Dutch were simply too small a presence to consider challenging the natives militarily, particularly the Iroquois of the upper Hudson. Indian wars around the Delaware in the 1640s and then again in the 1650s and 1660s weakened the colony's military and financial position. Disputes with natives about territory remained an important part of Dutch colonial experience beyond Dutch rule.

After trying unsuccessfully to monopolize the fur trade, the Dutch West India Company turned in 1629 to agricultural settlement, instituting large estates called *patroonships*. These feudal-style propietorships brought in a number of wealthy individuals but did not lend themselves to recruiting immigrants. Coerced migration from Dutch poorhouses and orphanages, along with state- or company-sponsored migration of economically vulnerable families of day laborers and agricultural tenants, provided a major component of the Dutch population in the colony. Added to this were groups of religious dissenters (French Huguenots, Italian Waldensians), who sought the Dutch policy of some religious tolerance. A group of settlers from the failed Dutch colony in Brazil added to the mix, including numerous Jews and some African slaves. The result was a heterogeneous population, particularly in New Amsterdam, including many different nationalities, languages, and races.

The patroonship experiment failed to attract enough interest and was abandoned within about a decade through most of the colony, replaced with a policy of free settlement. The continuation of the patroon system in Rensselaerswyck (up the Hudson) meant family migration did not occur there prior to 1644. After that time both families and African slaves came into the town, although owners frequently sold the slaves to planters in Maryland and Virginia. Labor would come primarily from the natural increase of the European population and some migration from Europe. In other areas family settlement began earlier, and colonists came from various Dutch provinces, notably Holland, Utrecht, Gelderland, and Friesland.

In the countryside, on the other hand, Dutch settlements were more homogeneous and somewhat more isolated. Especially in these areas, the Dutch settlers were families who relied upon their familial ties in many ways. Settlers who mixed fur trading with farming, transport, brewing, milling, or small-scale manufacturing were often the most successful. Women's work in these family economies was crucial. Dutch civil law as well as custom allowed women significant economic independence, and husbands often allowed wives much leeway to earn money. Women generally used this to better family fortunes, which were passed on to both daughters and sons, part of an overall pattern of bilateral family connections. The emphasis on family ties also meant somewhat less interest in public roles and more on family, church, and home. This would be a hallmark of Dutch immigration for the coming three centuries.

By the 1650s the West India Company was bankrupt, but the colony was thriving through private trade, including smuggling. Beverwijk (later Albany) was founded in 1652. Meanwhile, ongoing disputes over territory made Dutch rule more tenuous. In their conflict with the Swedes, to their south, the Dutch were successful, capturing New Sweden in 1655. After a series of Anglo-Dutch wars, the English finally convinced Governor Peter Stuyvesant to surrender control of the colony to the British in 1664. New Netherland at that point had a population of less than 10,000 people, roughly two-thirds of whom were Dutch immigrants or their descendants. After 1664 the territory was nominally English but retained Dutch characteristics. These helped make the British colonies of the late seventeenth century incredibly diverse, more so than they would be 100 years later when the United States came into existence.

ENTRY INTO BRITISH AMERICA

After the English took control of New Netherland, Dutch life retained many of its characteristics, but immigration from the Netherlands diminished significantly. Aside from a few religious groups, most immigrants to British North America from the Netherlands thereafter were isolated individuals. The Dutch stamp on the region of New Netherland, however, was impossible to erase completely. Not only were there majority-Dutch communities that did not want to change; there were also parts of the culture too well established to readily eliminate. Dutch influence on architecture was notable, as it was in names (such as Harlem, Brooklyn, and Flushing). The British set out to expunge certain aspects of Dutch life, but the efforts were neither systematic nor widespread. The loss of special status for the Dutch Reformed Church was perhaps the most significant blow to Dutch hegemony. But its continued existence, and that of many other religious groups in the colony, would add pressure for religious tolerance under the new regime.

The shift to English rule affected the political situation more than most others, although the Dutch population adjusted at differing rates. Name changes exemplified the turnover, as major hubs like New Amsterdam and Beverwijk switched to English versions (New York and Albany), whereas smaller places retained their Dutch designations. Once the English took over, cultural misunderstandings of political power were common, some based on the English ideal of military governor or lord, which included many more powers than those of their Dutch counterparts. As a whole, the Dutch (and their legal system) were more tied to urban, commercial life and to fostering connections to the trade networks, while the English sought out borders and political control. The conflict of this situation with English law meant that the English sought to put many more limits on trade, although the Dutch continued their contacts among the Iroquois and French on up to Montreal through smuggling. In addition, Dutch law also allowed women more rights than their English counterparts possessed, most importantly the right to engage in commercial culture.

The Dutch gradually adjusted to the introduction of English political dominance. Leisler's Rebellion of 1689–1690, an extension of the English "Glorious Revolution," exemplified this division. German-born Jacob Leisler took the position of de facto governor of Albany with the support of many defenders of the older Dutch style of government. Both Schenectady and Albany Dutch divided on whether to support his efforts. Recent arrivals, the poor, and many Dutch of moderate circumstances supported him. He met opposition from the English, who wanted to centralize control, and from some of the more affluent and professional Dutch colonists, notably wealthy merchants, as well as some of the clergy in the Dutch Reformed Church. Despite the failure of the rebellion and Leisler's execution, elements of Dutch political practice remained in place. Class antagonisms related to and reflected in these political events led some Dutch farmers and artisans, many of them Leislerians, out of the Dutch Reformed Church and into pietist groups.

New York City was a heterogeneous place from the outset of British control. Ethnicity remained a crucial factor in determining one's contacts and institutions for most residents up through 1700, and not until the mid-1700s was it really lost for older European groups. In commerce and trade the shift to English control was rapid. Within a generation, most Dutch merchants were supplanted by English ones. On the other hand, when the English took over, Dutch culture was the majority culture, and most other people had adopted or adapted to it, including the African slaves who used Dutch Pentecost celebrations as a way to build a sense of black community. Many newcomers to New York City after the conquest were also Dutch from elsewhere in the colony. Marital strategies, language retention, charitable bequests, and craft transmission through kinship, in addition to membership in the Dutch Reformed Church, meant that up to

1700 Dutch-descended New Yorkers tended to identify themselves in ethnic terms. This declined somewhat in the following years, partially because a series of epidemics in 1702 broke family lines for many. Additional British migration up to 1730 still did not displace the Dutch as the primary community leaders in certain fields. However, loss of Dutch control was rapid thereafter, largely due to the declining usage of the Dutch language. This came about as much through the undermining of church-related schools as in any other way. Without this, fewer individuals joined the Dutch Reformed Church. Some, particularly the well-to-do, joined the Anglicans, notably in the 1740s, and the loss of this religious tie tended to be related to a loss of ethnicity. New York City managed a form of pluralism, at least at first. Thus, even there, the most polyglot Dutch settlement, it was a two- or three-generation process of contact before angliciization really began, and even thereafter many Dutch patterns remained.

This was true in Albany, too, where a significant majority of the population remained Dutch up to 1710. English and Dutch mingled some but did not merge significantly until the Seven Year's War. Prior to that time, Albany was ruled by a conjuncture of religious and political elites, including a significant contingent of Dutch. After the American Revolution, Albany lost most of its continuing Dutch character due to demographic factors, for between 1779 and 1799 it lost two-thirds of its residents. This occurred simultaneously with a major in-migration (quadrupling the city's population between 1790 and 1820), so that by 1820 the Dutch constituted only 5 percent of the population.

The same pattern applied to Schenectady. When it came into English hands, the governmental and legal structure, at least on an official level, anglicized fairly quickly, but until the 1750s and 1760s those migrating to Schenectady had to adjust to its "Dutchness," for this was the ethnic and linguistic majority. Few English went to this area, leaving the Dutch to do largely as they liked. The isolation also had its disadvantages. The town was devastated by the 1690 massacre. Recovery came slowly, but Dutch-descended people continued to settle in the Mohawk Valley. By 1724, with the group's material success growing, family farms had stretched out fifty miles beyond its confines. A major shift came with the French and Indian War (1754–1763). After that, the local population became more tied to the wider English world and the growing conflict with Britain. The Dutch language receded into the home. Still, naming practices for children continued to illustrate Dutch bilineal patterns, and godparentage remained largely familial, both in contrast to English customs. Further, the Dutch Reformed Church persisted as the center of ethnic consciousness. This kind of slow adjustment to changing circumstances was true in various parts of former New Netherland. In rural areas especially, isolation assisted in the retaining of Dutch patterns. The Flatbush settlement, for example, managed to have little contact with any provincial authorities, either Dutch or English, for a number of generations.

Others in rural areas followed a strategy of close family ties and continuity on a particular farm and surrounding area, even when economics might have suggested moving, a pattern that would remain effective through the nineteenth century. In Tappan, to name but one, west of the Hudson River, Dutch families retained their familial holdings for five generations through a pattern of inheritance that kept children geographically close but also assured them economic security. It did adapt to English inheritance practices after 1700, and members of the Haring family, who dominated the community, often sat in the New York Assembly. To outsiders, however, Tappan still looked liked a Dutch village in 1783.

Nonetheless, by the late colonial period, some rural Dutch were abandoning the lines of continuity in southeastern New York, for farmland had become so scarce and expensive in the early European settlement areas, already 150 years old, that passing it on to another generation became almost impossible. Pursuing family and community relocation to another area was one strategy to maintain cultural integrity. By the late 1700s some Dutch descendants were living in western New York State. Another generation later, some went to Kentucky and to areas around the Great Lakes. Like other groups, they were following the farming frontier, seeking to pass their agricultural vocation on to the next generation. Thomas Archdeacon has estimated that in the first U.S. census (that of 1790) 2.6 percent of Americans were of Dutch ancestry (about 102, 200).

Overall, there were few places in former New Netherland where being Dutch did not matter both in public and private for several generations beyond transfer of power. In cosmopolitan urban areas, ethnic identification faded somewhat faster than in more isolated rural locations. While many scholars see the Seven Year's War as the turning point in Dutch cultural continuity, others see the 1830s as more central to this process. In this latter view, cultural adaptation of the Dutch throughout the Middle Colonies was perhaps less "anglicization"— apart from public acts—and more adaptation of old ways to new conditions and new settings. The new evangelism of the 1830s also led people out of the Dutch Reformed Church, the bastion of Dutch ethnicity. And yet, for some, the connection to a Dutch colonial past remained significant aside from its religious base, and the societies that celebrated these bloodlines would provide many persons in subsequent centuries with contacts to business, political, and social elites.

On the one hand, ethnic continuity proved possible for many Dutch in America. On the other, one of the important factors in Dutch life in America was also the ability of the Dutch to lose their ethnic identity and blend with the English. It was not an option that many chose, at least in the early generations, but it was always there. Cultural affinity based on skin color, economic interests, and Protestantism meant relatively few barriers to success in most fields. From the time of British control onward, and more notably after the American Revolution, many persons of Dutch descent were part of the American dominant class. Others were at least close enough culturally to avoid persecution. The biggest area of conflict was over Dutch-language schools, which the English eventually sought to displace.

Another major advantage enjoyed by the Dutch was the continued presence of the Netherlands as an important international power. Although the Dutch suffered several military defeats in the eighteenth century, the loss of international standing was gradual. It retained important overseas posts in the East Indies and in South Africa, not to mention smaller holdings in the Americas. The relationship of North America with the Netherlands revived in importance after the American Revolution, when the Dutch quickly forged ties with the United States. Despite the upheaval of the Napoleonic period, economic connections between the two nations grew in the early nineteenth century. Dutch banks financed the Louisiana Purchase and the building of many railroads in the nineteenth century.

Just as Dutch identity was largely disappearing from the hinterlands of the mid-Atlantic in the 1830s, a new wave of Dutch immigrants began arriving. This not only reinvigorated the sense of "Dutchness" but also changed the face of Dutch America significantly. It is striking that the new group found a few persons in New York who could still speak the colonial "Low Dutch" dialect in the mid-nineteenth century, 180 years after the territory officially went under English control.

THE SECOND WAVE

Compared to the earlier period, the migration of Dutch in the nineteenth and early twentieth centuries was much larger, though probably less important to U.S. culture as a whole. It benefited in many ways from the presence of earlier arrivals of the same nationality. Although there had been a trickle of migration from the Netherlands in the early nineteenth century, particularly Dutch Jews to New York, they had no contacts with later Dutch Protestant arrivals and did not spark many followers. Then, beginning in the 1840s, a major exodus took place. It followed the same general patterns of other migrations from northwestern Europe. The potato blight that devastated Ireland also hit the Netherlands, as did a rye rust in the mid-1840s. These crop failures led some Dutch to look more closely at the example of migrants from the German states, who sometimes came up the Rhine River, passing through Dutch borders. Still, the migration from the Netherlands had some specifically Dutch characteristics. Roughly 250,000 Netherlanders would arrive in the United States in the subsequent years up until the imposition of strict immigration quotas in the 1920s. At that time, they ranked nineteenth among foreign-born groups.

Most of the heads of household in this wave of immigrants were primarily interested in economic betterment. They came with their families and generally followed patterns of chain migration from their municipality or region. Robert Swierenga painstakingly traced 86,000 of the immigrants from emigration records in the Netherlands, using ships passenger lists and U.S. census documents, which allowed for a much fuller quantitative picture of this group than of many others. The high rates of familial migration, 15 to 30 percent above that of

German or Scandinavian migration, meant relatively balanced sex ratios and less chance of outmarriage. Family migration also ensured low rates of return migration. Up to the turn of the century, the immigrants came primarily from rural areas or small towns. This contrasted with the colonial migrants, of whom at least a significant proportion came from the urbanized western provinces of Holland. These second wave rural dwellers had sometimes been farmers but often were farm laborers or (even less well off) day laborers in rural areas. Village craftspeople added some to the number. Few had been involved in industry prior to migration (which would have necessitated some previous migration). Instead, they tended to emigrate directly from their places of birth or neighboring municipality to the United States.

Like the earlier group, this second wave included a number of religious dissenters, though in this case most of them were Dutch. The levels of migration were less in the Netherlands than in most European nations, but the specificity of the movement meant it had a profound demographic impact on certain municipalities. The earliest groups came from the sandy-soil provinces of Drenthe, Gelderland, and Overijsel, where the economy was stagnant. Later, the largest concentrations of emigrants came from clay-soil farming regions, areas where technological advances in farming meant less need for farm labor and where late in the century international competition made commercial farming and cattle breeding less profitable. Most of the emigrants came from those regions in the provinces of Groningen, Friesland, and Zeeland. Others came in significant numbers from the Achterhoek region of Gelderland and three (Catholic) municipalities in Noord-Brabant.

Much of the migration had a conservative character, with many motivated by the goal of maintaining their economic status in the face of deteriorating conditions in rural areas. The Dutch went disproportionately to rural areas of the United States, where land was comparatively much more available than in the Netherlands. Across the Midwest and Plains the Dutch tended to form isolated communities and colonies. As in the earlier wave, the relative isolation of these rural settlements meant that newcomers could retain their Dutch identity for several generations. Also similar to earlier migrants, many of these immigrants had sponsors, only this time it was generally other family members who provided the capital. Only in a relatively few cases did Dutch municipalities put together the funds to get rid of their indigent. The Dutch also had the advantage of a well-established education system, meaning most migrants were literate and, consequently, could evaluate information coming to the Netherlands about the United States. It also implied that extensive correspondence would cross the Atlantic for years to come, informing neighbors in the "Old World"—which literally had lost some of its young population—about conditions in the "New."

While there was no company sponsoring the movement, there were many territories, railroads, and other businesses that provided free or inexpensive transportation from New York and/or cheap land. In addition, the United States offered relative religious freedom (of particular importance to many of the early group), few military requirements for men, and easy citizenship for white persons. By late in the century steamships regularly plied the waters from Rotterdam to New York, sparing the Dutch of any need to go through additional countries. Compared to many other ethnic groups, the Dutch of this migration had tremendous advantages. Added to this was the assistance of the earlier arrivals. Although the two groups had had little contact prior to migration, the older Dutch Reformed soon recognized the advantages of adding to their numbers in the United States and put money as well as advice behind efforts to help the newcomers. Though the colonial group had officially made English the language of the denomination in 1794, and the last Dutch-language church services ended in the 1840s, there was still a sense of Dutch background for this denomination of 33,000, most of whom were in the New York area.

The initial settlement wave of the 1840s consisted of groups who came en masse to the United States. Among them were congregations of (orthodox Calvinist) Seceders from the quasi-state Dutch Reformed Church. The Seceders (*Afgescheidenen*) were followers of the pietistic revival sweeping Europe. They faced harassment and sometime official persecution in the Netherlands up through the 1830s and a social stigma thereafter. Rev. Albertus C. van Raalte led about 1,000 religious followers to southwestern Michigan, founding the community of Holland and forming the *kolonie* there. Rev. Hendrik P. Scholte led a congregation of 900 to Iowa, where they established Pella. Other ministers and their congregations followed a similar pattern, naming their communities after the provinces or towns of origin. The leaders of these early settlements designed their communities to promote ethnic cohesion and isolation from others. They wanted to maintain the religion they considered true. Seceders were notably overrepresented in the nineteenth-century migration as a whole, and their early arrival meant they had an impact far greater than their numbers would otherwise have allowed. Most later migrants would be adherents to the Reformed Church. Only a smattering of Jews or freethinkers arrived, although among them was Samuel Gompers, a critical figure in the early years of the American Federation of Labor. Catholics also migrated in low numbers relative to their share of the population in the Netherlands. Father Theodorus J. Vanden Broek brought his congregation of 350 Catholic Dutch to the Fox River Valley of Wisconsin in 1848. This settlement, based around Little Chute, eventually grew to 40,000. Like the Protestants, this group remained set apart to some degree by geographic isolation. Religious separatism, however, played less of a role in this instance, and intermixing with other Catholics took place over the generations.

The degree of clustering established by the migrants of the 1840s continued over time. In 1870 nearly 60 percent of the Dutch in the United States lived in twenty-two counties and, within them, primarily in certain townships or wards. Few immigrant groups of comparable size have had this level of clustering. The main settlements were around southern Lake Michigan, including the Holland and Grand Rapids area on the east, Chicago on the south, and Sheboygan and Green Bay on the west. The area around Pella continued to draw immigrants, as did Dutch communities in southeastern Minnesota, western New York, and Paterson and Passaic in northern New Jersey. Subsequently, the immigrants founded "daughter colonies" elsewhere, as in northwestern Iowa. Some of the rural communities that sprang from this movement, such as Friesland, South Dakota, eventually succumbed to agricultural failure. Others, like Amsterdam, Montana, managed to hold on to the present. But the clustering function continued throughout the late nineteenth and early twentieth century. After 1900 more of the immigrants came from urban areas in the Netherlands and went directly to cities where Dutch Americans were already established. This reflected the economic state of farming on both sides of the Atlantic and the growing industrialization of the Netherlands. Other Dutch immigrants, still interested in agriculture, headed for Canada.

Overall, only about 10 percent of the total Dutch Protestant migration of this second wave did not migrate into a Dutch-American cluster. Moreover, these clusters were even identifiable in terms of the settlers' regional or municipal origin. For example, the population of Grand Rapids was 40 percent first- or second-generation Dutch in 1900, and they were divided among twelve neighborhoods known by provincial or town origin. For most, this regional identification would end within a generation or two, though dialectologists from the Netherlands still found some evidence of it among Dutch speakers in Dutch-American communities in the 1960s. Of the regional identifications, Frisian remained the most important, owing to the separate language, as opposed to dialect, of this group.

Religious debates that meant little to those outside of Dutch-American circles raged periodically among Dutch Protestants almost from the outset of the migration. Some of these debates were rooted in the Netherlands, whereas others were related to adaptation to American life. And there was much more than theological orthodoxy at stake, for families' entire social lives, not to mention safety net in times of need, tended to revolve around the church. Because a man changing churches often meant his wife and children had to do so as well, and because leaving one church often meant shunning all who belonged to the old one, these debates could mean rifts in families as well as between neighborhoods and friends. Paradoxically, such schisms kept divided Dutch-American communities separate from others, seeing as only the insiders could understand or care about the differences.

The first major split came after Albertus van Raalte, leader of the Holland (Michigan) settlement, sought to affiliate with the Dutch Reformed Church (later Reformed Church in America), the denomination of the colonial Dutch. Van Raalte and others considered the American denomination free of the taint of declining orthodoxy, which had plagued its counterpart in the Netherlands. Further, members of the old Dutch denomination had assisted the newcomers from the outset. The new groups joined officially in 1850. Others felt the older Dutch Reformed, with their Sunday schools and revivals, were too Americanized. They also wanted to retain their status as Seceders from the Reformed Church, and hence they separated from the coalition and formed what became the Christian Reformed Church.

A second major division took place later in the century, and it had both Dutch and American sources. On the American side, members of the Western divisions of the Dutch Reformed Church (the new Dutch immigration) sought to ban Freemasons from their church. Because many of the colonial Dutch Reformed in the East belonged to this group, they blocked the move. This debate came just as another spurt of migration was taking place. In the Netherlands, religious authorities in many churches warned migrants not to join with the Dutch Reformed. This dispute combined with other developments in the Netherlands. A second secession from the Netherlands Reformed Church was also going on there. As with the *Afscheiding*, this secession, called the *Doleantie*, sparked emigration, and migrants were disproportionately tied to the group. Led by Abraham Kuyper, the *Doleantie* sought not only a shift in theology but also the opportunity to have their religious views enshrined in public practice. They established schools, a university, a political party, newspapers, labor unions, and other religiously based institutions. Kuyper was elected prime minister of the Netherlands in 1892, and his vision of separate institutions sponsored by the state pushed the Netherlands toward a system of religious separatism (*verzuiling*) that would remain in place until the 1950s.

Adherents to the neo-Calvinism of the *Doleantie* in the United States followed this example and generally joined the Christian Reformed Church. It remained wedded to a form of religious separatism in America that has continued to the present. It developed a system of schools, a university, newspapers, homes for the mentally ill and elderly, even cemeteries. While the ties to the Netherlands broke down over time, particularly during World War I, the cultural isolation of the group and its almost exclusive connection to Dutch immigrants meant an ongoing sense of Dutch ethnicity.

Both the newcomers in the Dutch Reformed Church and Christian Reformed Church adapted to U.S. conditions over time, though generally at different rates. The Dutch Reformed were the primary objects of Home Missions from their older counterparts. They received money to pay their pastors and build churches and parsonages. They also received boxes of clothing and food and magazines and other reading material designed to help them learn English. In turn, they tried to become self-supporting and then to become involved in missions themselves. In this, they took the example of the eastern churches, even participating in national women's mission boards. Women had a larger role in the eastern churches, and their theology was more "feminized." This challenged the newer Dutch immigrants, where ministers held tremendous power not only in their churches but also in the communities and where men were solidly in charge of all church functions. Some individuals, such as Christine van Raalte Gilmore, daughter of the Holland founder, sought to increase women's organized participation in Dutch immigrant congregations, but the lack of a Dutch precedent and resistance to any shift in gender roles meant the process was gradual. This was even more true in the Christian Reformed denomination, where women were less likely to have access to separate women's groups. Denominational debates about the grounds for divorce, which raged around the turn of the century, also illustrated this pattern.

Much of the process of adaptation followed this pattern whereby the largest obstacles came from within the group. There was always the option for individuals simply to leave and become "American." However, given the all-encompassing nature of these communities and their isolation from others, this was in many ways a much larger step than migration itself. In some spheres, such as temperance, groups of Dutch adopted the American pattern, although some rejected this as against their ethnic background. For many other cultural ideals, Dutch patterns coalesced with American ones. In one other respect, though, the shift was more clear-cut.

Because the Dutch came to stay in America, and because they wanted to control their local communities as well as gain public money for local projects, most applied for citizenship quickly. By controlling local politics, they could set policies in their schools and communities, policies such as mandating Dutch-language instruction and hiring persons from within the group to teach. The earliest arrivals joined the Democratic Party, largely in response to Whig nativism and Know-Nothingism. For the most part, the group shifted to the Republican Party in the mid-1850s and has remained there ever since. Dutch-language newspapers, including nationally distributed *De Volksvriend* and *De Grondwet*, carried information on national issues of interest to the group as well as news from the Netherlands. Most local Dutch-language papers voiced Republican opinions.

A few Dutch immigrants on the Plains shifted to Populism later in the nineteenth century, but some of them nevertheless supported Republican President William McKinley due to his neutrality regarding the Boer War (1899–1902), during which the Dutch supported their compatriots in South Africa. Pella has also remained an exception among Calvinist communities, generally voting Democratic. Dutch Catholics also have been tied to the Democratic Party. But, overall, Dutch Protestants have swelled Republican ranks. In areas of concentrated settlement, Dutch-descended individuals whose political views correspond to the group have a good chance of election to state and local office. National political power, on the other hand, has not been a concern until recently.

English-language acquisition illustrated a slightly different kind of adaptation. Those who lived in areas where they regularly did business with "Yankees" learned enough to operate successfully. Likewise, most Dutch immigrants wanted their children to learn the language so they could succeed economically and not have difficulties with Americans. The children also learned Dutch, at home and in church, and sometimes in the Christian day schools. This was one of the few areas of significant conflict with American authorities. Laws against foreign-language instruction in Iowa and Wisconsin hit the Dutch as well as others. More important, during World War I, when hysteria against all things

German was at its peak, many could not distinguish "Dutch" from "Deutsch." Nativists torched a Dutch church and school near Pella; others faced burning books or yellow paint. After the war, more community leaders pushed to switch church services into English, and the Dutch-language press largely disappeared in the years leading up to World War II. It was partly a matter of outside pressure but also one of generational change, as many of the communities already contained third-and fourth-generation Dutch Americans. Churches made the shift gradually over two or three decades, starting with one of two major Sunday services in English and moving to two, with only one Sunday a month having Dutch-language services.

The earliest arrivals often had the greatest economic success. Most of those who came as farm laborers, day laborers, or jobless in the 1840s were farmers within twenty years (almost half within ten years). The rates decreased over time, as farmland in the Dutch-American colonies became scarcer. Rural settlement, however, remained the preferred venue. Families tended to work the holdings as a group, and the participation of women and children frequently made the difference in keeping subsistence farming going in addition to a cash crop. Dutch immigrant women (like Norwegian and German immigrant women) tended to take on farming tasks considered inappropriate by Anglo-Americans, but it meant less need for hired hands and greater self-sufficiency. Both the high value placed on landownership and the strength of rural communities meant that some, though by no means all, of these rural settlers managed to continue in farming despite various economic and natural barriers.

In and around urban areas the situation was somewhat different. Some of the Dutch, such as those from South Holland (near Chicago) or Kalamazoo, engaged in vegetable gardening, using their knowledge of draining swamps to good advantage. In other urban areas, the Dutch clustered both in their own neighborhoods, with small shops serving a Dutch clientele, and in certain industries, such as refuse hauling in Chicago. Those who could tried to remain independent in the years around the turn of the century. There was also a Dutch presence in larger companies, as in the furniture factories of Grand Rapids, the Pullman Palace Car Company of Roseland, and the textile mills of Paterson, where Dutch men used ethnic connections to gain jobs for friends and relatives and then to rise in the ranks. The negative views that orthodox Calvinists held toward labor unions made the men particularly attractive to employers. In contrast, while Dutch women were less likely to be involved in wage work, young women might serve as domestics or briefly in factories, contributing to the family economy and earning toward a dowry. Otherwise, home activities to save expenditures and home production to barter or sell were more common.

After 1900, the rates of migration to urban areas rose, and the percentage of immigrants coming from urban regions rose as well. As in rural areas, these immigrants sought home ownership, a value coinciding with American ideals. Individual economic success, however, did not generally lead to significant differences of social stratification. Indeed, in the same way that many of the early arrivals in the 1840s had had their passage and their initial landholding paid by one or two wealthy individuals, later Dutch Americans expected those with money to help those without, particularly by providing jobs as well as by donating substantially to the church, church institutions, and civic projects. Ethnic cohesiveness did not eliminate poverty, but it could ameliorate it.

One other important sphere involved education, for, from the beginning, the Dutch expected all children to have a basic education. They also quickly supported separate institutions of higher education to train ministers and then teachers. In the third and later generations, more children have gone on to higher education, making the move into the professions and civil service. Others used this to further their business interests. As always, the Dutch could choose to use this background to leave the ethnic group entirely and move into the American mainstream. Edward Bok, Dutch immigrant and longtime publisher of the *Ladies' Home Journal*, demonstrated how Dutch individuals could gain widespread acceptance in American culture. Bok, however, had less impact among Dutch Americans. This was the pattern of the second migration. A few would assimilate into American life without much of any trace of their ethnic background, whereas many would remain within the ethnic community.

The second wave of migration basically ended with the imposition of national origin quota laws in the 1920s. There were still migrants from the Netherlands, but the economy had changed in the homeland as well, making more opportunities for workers. The Great Depression cut off nearly all migration, and the upheaval of World War II kept contacts low for years. By the time the two countries had normal relations once again, the second wave had already aged another generation with little or no contact with the Netherlands. Many had lost their Dutch-language skills, and those who retained a sense of Dutch ethnicity generally saw it tied closely to their religious identity.

THE THIRD WAVE

After World War II the number of Dutch immigrants rose dramatically due to several shifts in government policy on both sides of the Atlantic. The Dutch government, assuming it faced overpopulation at a level that would swamp its labor market, openly promoted emigration, including providing free transportation. In the United States the national origins quotas allowed a limited number of Dutch to enter, but under pressure these were supplemented by the Refugee Relief Act of 1953 and two other bills later that decade. These allowed roughly 78,000 Netherlanders, many of them Dutch repatriates from Indonesia (which had just won its independence), to migrate to the United States. By the mid-1960s the Dutch economy had improved significantly, making the Netherlands itself a land of growing immigration. Migration of Netherlanders to the United States then remained at low levels in the latter part of the twentieth century. Through the 1980s and 1990s, close to half of all Dutch migrants (averaging somewhat over 1,000 per year) were spouses or other close relatives of U.S.

citizens. Aside from clusters of Dutch dairy farmers in southern California and (recently) north Texas, these individuals tended to blend into the broader American society rapidly. As in the past, their background generally assured them a reasonable reception, for the Dutch are still considered "good" immigrants.

DUTCH ETHNICITY TODAY

The descendants of the colonial Dutch and their legacies were simply "American" by the mid-nineteenth century, as new waves of immigrants, particularly the Irish, put a new face (and religion) on American ethnicity. In certain regions Dutch colonial descent counted, but just as important, it was not "foreign" to others. Words adopted from Dutch, including *cookie* and *boss*, were integral to American English. The Knickerbocker stories of Washington Irving helped make Dutch folklife a part of much of the population's background, as did the Victorian adaptation of Sinter Klaas (now known as Santa Claus). Dutch names appeared regularly in the lists of political figures of the mid-Atlantic states. Martin Van Buren became the first U.S. president of Dutch background in the 1830s. The Roosevelt family figured prominently in New York State politics, not to mention producing several leading national figures: Presidents Theodore Roosevelt and Franklin Delano Roosevelt and reformer Eleanor Roosevelt (niece of Theodore and wife/cousin of Franklin). The intervening generations and the presence of the Dutch in the United States from its inception meant that the legacies of the colonial Dutch and their descendants do not seem Dutch at all. Many of them cultivated this American image at times while using their Dutch ancestry in other settings. Like most descendants of the Dutch, ethnicity could be a choice for them, one of many identities.

The nineteenth-century migration, not surprisingly, has a more evident ethnic imprint today. It is partly due to the continuation of the clustered settlements, particularly in the rural Midwest, and more importantly to the ongoing role of Dutch-American Protestant churches. Although the language and many of the Dutch customs have disappeared, for many persons originating in this migration religion and ethnicity are too closely linked to lose the "Dutch." The *kolonie* in Michigan is still readily evident in the region around Holland and Grand Rapids, although some of the original farming communities have disappeared. Likewise, the Iowa settlements, particularly Pella and Orange City, make their ethnic roots clear in businesses, colleges, and churches. The same is true for many of the isolated rural settlements, although these face difficult economic conditions in the late twentieth century. For those in southern California the problem is different, as Dutch dairy farmers have been overtaken by suburban sprawl. In urban areas, nineteenth-century Dutch concentrations also remain, though they have generally moved from their original locations to the suburbs.

The most evident Dutch presence is religious. In the small region from Grand Rapids, Michigan, to Chicago, Illinois, lie three religious colleges associated with the group: Calvin, Hope, and Wheaton. Grand Rapids houses three influential religious publishing houses: Eerdmans, Zondervan, and Baker Book House. The Christian Reformed Church, with 300,000 members in North America in the late 1980s, remains almost exclusively of Dutch heritage. That denomination operates a network of Christian schools throughout the United States and Canada, wherever their congregants have settled in any numbers. And both major Reformed denominations support various institutions, such as Holland Home, the largest nonprofit provider of care for the elderly in Michigan and the model for several other institutions of the same name in other states. Such separate, religiously-based institutions mean Americans of Dutch descent in the fourth or fifth generation can still choose to limit their contacts with non-Reformed (and that generally means non-Dutch). As always, maintaining an ethnoreligious identity is a choice in part, and in this instance, it has remained a quite viable one.

In addition (and perhaps in part as much an expression of symbolic ethnicity as can also be seen among other long-resident populations), Dutch ethnicity is vigorously and lucratively celebrated at Tulip Time festivals in several Dutch-American Protestant communities and in the Dutch Catholic *Schut*. Street scrubbing exemplifies the continuing stereotype of the Dutch as particularly clean, or at least willing to work hard at it, enshrined generations earlier with Dutch cleanser. Tulip time is also one of the few occasions when Dutch women and girls are at the center of public attention, for another Dutch legacy is a general conservatism in terms of gender roles. Family relations tend to remain strictly patriarchal, although women may handle family finances and have a say in certain major decisions. Gender role conservatism is also evident in the debates about women's ordination in the Christian Reformed Church in the 1980s and 1990s. The lengthy intellectual and theological debates surrounding that issue, and the threats of schism among the orthodox tied to it, are not exclusively Dutch by any means, but they are typical of Dutch-American history. While Holland bulb-growers directly profit from Dutch traditions, other businesses from the local grocer up to home-marketing leader Amway (founded by two Dutch Americans) retain a legacy of the Dutch migration in their antiunion yet paternalistic policies. Dutch influence is found in U.S. political circles in the latter part of the twentieth century adhering to a Republican philosophy that combines fiscal conservatism with a commitment that government help its citizens.

The identification as "Dutch," however, has been fading, particularly since World War II. Wartime service broke community insularity for many young men, and the impact of national media has made inroads in otherwise isolated social circles. Subsequent migration and the ethnic revival of the 1960s and 1970s sparked some renewed interest, but for as long as it persists, it has been primarily the ethnoreligious tie and geographic or social isolation that have kept Dutch ethnicity alive for so many generations. Nonetheless, although the 1990 census reported only 96,198 foreign-born Dutch persons (0.5 percent of all foreign-born), 6.23 million persons did indicate a first or second Dutch ancestry, and over three fifths of them listed it as their first (or primary) one. This makes Dutch ancestry the tenth largest in the United States—and the seventh largest European one (following the Germans, Irish, English, Italians, French, and Poles). Consistent with their history, over one-third of those reporting a Dutch ancestry reside in the Midwest.

BIBLIOGRAPHIC REFERENCES

Works in English on the Dutch are numerous, with scholarship on religion, economics, and local settlement patterns predominating. While Gerald F. De Jong's *The Dutch in America, 1609–1974* (Boston: Twayne, 1975) and Henry S. Lucas's *Netherlanders in America: Dutch Immigration to the United States and Canada, 1789–1950* (Grand Rapids: Eerdmans, 1989 [1955]) remain the primary overviews, a spate of scholarship in the 1980s and 1990s has added significant insights to their interpretations. Most works relate to either the colonial period or the nineteenth- and early twentieth-century migrations, not both. With the exception of William Petersen's *Some Factors Influencing Postwar Emigration from the Netherlands* (The Hague: M. Nijhoff, 1952) and B. F. Hofstede's *Thwarted exodus: Postwar overseas migration from the Netherlands* (The Hague: 1964), few works exist on Dutch immigration since World War II.

In *Holland on the Hudson: An Economic and Social History of Dutch New York* (Ithaca: Cornell University Press, 1986), Oliver A. Rink overturns the interpretation of New Netherland as a colonial failure by examining the economic success of Amsterdam merchants in the venture. The strength of Dutch influence beyond official Dutch control of the region is evident in Joyce D. Goodfriend's *Beyond the Melting Pot: Society and Culture in Colonial New York City, 1664–1730* (Princeton, NJ: Princeton University Press, 1992), Anita Tien's " 'To Enjoy Their Customs': The Cultural Adaptation of Dutch and German Families in the Middle Colonies, 1660–1832'' (Ph.D. dissertation, University of California, Berkeley, 1990), and Donna Merwick's *Possessing Albany, 1630–1710: The Dutch and English Experiences* (New York: Cambridge University Press, 1990), as well as a variety of studies appearing in *De Halve Maen*. New York State Library's New Netherland Project, which has undertaken transcriptions and translations of many seventeenth-century documents, has also spawned much scholarship. This is partially summarized in Eric Nooter and Patricia U. Bonomi, eds., *Colonial Dutch Studies: An Interdisciplinary Approach* (New York: New York University Press, 1988). Quite a number of primary sources exist in published form. For a selection of these, see Charles T. Gehring, ed., *A Guide to Dutch Manuscripts Relating to New Netherland in United States Repositories* (Albany: State University of New York Press, 1978). Census data were taken from Thomas J. Archdeacon, *Becoming American: An Ethnic History* (New York: The Free Press, 1983).

The most detailed summary of the nineteenth- and early twentieth-century migration remains Jacob Van Hinte's *Netherlanders in America*, originally published in Dutch in 1928 and later reissued in English translation (Grand Rapids: Baker Book House, 1985). A variety of excellent primary sources are available on this group, including Henry S. Lucas, arr., *Dutch Immigrant Memoirs and Related Writings*, rev. ed. (Grand Rapids: Eerdmans, 1997), and Herbert J. Brinks, *Dutch American Voices: Letters from the United States, 1850–1930* (Ithaca: Cornell University Press, 1995). Of particular note to genealogists are Robert P. Swierenga's *Dutch Immigrants in U.S. Passenger Manifests, 1820–*

1880, 2 vols., and *Dutch Emigrants to the United States, South Africa, South America and Southeast Asia, 1835–1880* (both by Wilmington: Scholarly Resources, 1983). Works of the 1980s, and the beginnings of several monographs of the 1990s, appear in brief form in Robert P. Swierenga, ed., *The Dutch in America* (New Brunswick: Rutgers University Press, 1985), or in Rob Kroes and Henk-Otto Neuschaefer, *The Dutch in North-America* (Amsterdam: Free University Press, 1991). Of particular interest are Annemieke Galema's *Frisians to America, 1880–1914* (Groningen: Regio-Projekt, 1996), the only overview of this Dutch regional-linguistic minority; Yda Schreuder's *Dutch Catholic Immigrant Settlement in Wisconsin, 1850–1905* (New York: Garland, 1989), the best work on Dutch Catholic immigrants; and Robert P. Swierenga's *The Forerunners: Dutch Jewry in the North American Diaspora* (Detroit: Wayne State University, 1994), the only overview of Dutch Jews in the United States. The publications of the Association for the Advancement of Dutch-American Studies and the journal *Origins*, produced by Heritage Hall at Calvin College, also contain many works on the nineteenth- and early twentieth-century migration.

Works on religion among the Dutch are numerous, particularly for the later migration. For the colonial period, see Randall Balmer's *A Perfect Babel of Confusion: Dutch Religion and English Culture in the Middle Colonies* (New York: Oxford University Press, 1989). For the later period James D. Bratt's *Dutch Calvinism in Modern America* (Grand Rapids: Eerdmans, 1984) provides an overview of the theological stances, and Elton J. Bruins's *The Americanization of a Congregation*, 2nd ed. (Grand Rapids: Eerdmans, 1995) illustrates the shift from Dutch to American in one Reformed church congregation.

EAST EUROPEANS

Thaddeus C. Radzilowski and John Radzilowski

At the beginning of the nineteenth century, east and east-central Europe were the most economically backward regions of the continent. The peasant majority in these lands lived in a state of serfdom or virtual serfdom. Politically, eastern Europe was under the domination of four empires: Russian, Prussian, Austrian, and Ottoman. The region experienced relatively little large-scale migration, and emigration was actively discouraged, save for the politically troublesome elements of the gentry or intelligentsia who were sent into foreign or internal exile. Yet, by the end of the century, eastern and east-central Europe were a cauldron of migration, both internal and external.

By the middle of the nineteenth century three major changes were under way. The first was peasant emancipation, beginning in Prussia (from 1807), then in Austria (1848), and finally in Russia (1863). In independent Romania, peasants were freed in 1864. The gradual emancipation of peasant populations in the Balkans was completed by 1878 as Ottoman control receded. Although this brought little immediate benefit to the peasants, the conversion of labor obligations into cash rents and the creation of a class of smallholders in some areas facilitated the penetration of a cash-based market economy, even into very remote areas. This provided peasants with the option of working for cash wages outside their villages and presented the possibility that they could earn enough money to improve their standard of living. The expansion of the markets into the countryside brought with it railroads and improvement of overland and water transport that provided for the first time effective means for large-scale migration.

The second important change was an increase in population brought about by a cessation of major wars after 1815, better nutrition due to new crops (particularly the potato), and improved health and sanitary conditions. That population increase led to greater pressure on land and resources and produced an economically redundant population and the fragmentation of landholdings. In Serbia and Carnolia, for example, a majority of farms were under 12.5 acres, whereas in Dalmatia almost 90 percent of peasant farms were that small or smaller. In Hungary more than 50 percent of all farms were less than 7 acres, and landlessness was common. A similar situation existed in Austrian Galicia. The third change, which developed throughout the nineteenth century—beginning first among the intelligentsia and filtering down to the peasantry—was a sense of nationalism. This led to a gradually increasing politicization of the peasantry so that by the turn of the twentieth century myriad new and old power groupings were competing for the peasants' hearts and minds. This gave peasants identities and interests that took them beyond local and regional ties and created linguistic and political grievances that added to and recontextualized older economic, religious, and social differences.

In the second half of the nineteenth century, the peasantry of the region responded to these changes with a series of new strategies, the most important of which was migration. At first, migration often occurred regionally as peasant laborers traveled to work on nearby estates or followed the seasonal harvests. As the horizon of possible labor markets expanded, and better transportation made them more accessible, peasants began moving to new industrial centers in Europe and the Americas. Although this migration was meant to be temporary, and indeed many peasants returned home after making enough money to meet their economic goals, large groups of migrants became permanent immigrants and gradually established themselves in new lands. This usually entailed the creation of discrete ethnic enclaves in the towns and cities where they settled. Another, smaller group of migrants left home permanently with the goal of finding land to establish family farms, especially in North and South America. This latter option was exercised more frequently at the beginning of the migration period and by those who could amass sufficient capital to buy farms in the new land of settlement. It was, for example, more common among the earlier-arriving Czechs than among such later arrivals as Bulgarians and Serbs. The intentions behind the migration also affected the age and gender composition of the migrant stream. Thus, a larger portion of the Czech migration was made up of family groups, whereas Balkan migration was composed primarily of young men. The gender composition and the strategy it implied (e.g., families versus unattached men) led to heavier return migration rates among some groups than others. For example, less than 16 percent of Czechs returned as compared to 85 percent of Bulgarians and Serbs.

Migration from east-central, eastern, and southeastern Europe tended to be highly regional. In the Kingdom of Hungary in the period 1899–1913, to cite one case, of seventy-one counties, a cluster of five initiated overseas migration; fourteen surrounding counties caught the ''fever'' next; eleven more in the rest of the kingdom did so later. Out of the seventy-one counties, only thirty experienced significant overseas emigration. Migration patterns were also highly sensitive to ethnic difference. The urge to migrate was often transmitted across ethnic lines so that ethnically homogeneous areas experienced lower rates of migration than did ethnically heterogeneous areas. In multiethnic areas the daily rub of ethnic groups often resulted in cross-ethnic transmission of information about migration possibilities and destination, as well as in a more acute sense of grievance and a greater and sharper ethnic awareness that helped fuel out-migration.

It is difficult to say with any certainty just how many people left eastern Europe during the late nineteenth and early twentieth centuries, let alone how many ended up in specific destinations. Few of the ethnic groups discussed below possessed independent nations of their own and were thus often grouped into categories that tell us little about who they were. Furthermore, their ethnic self-definitions often overlapped or conflicted. Scholars have a much better idea of how many eastern Europeans left their homelands as a result of the upheavals during and after World War II. Despite many common features, the migratory patterns of each major group are particular enough to merit individual treatment.

This essay will cover the following East European peoples (alphabetical-ly): Albanians, Belarusins, Bosnians, Bulgarians, Carpatho-Rusins, Croatians, Czechs, Estonians, Latvians, Lithuanians, Macedonians, Magyars, Romanians, Russians, Serbs and Montenegrin Serbs, Slovaks, Slovenes, Sorbs, and Ukrain-ians (see Table 5).

ALBANIANS

Albanians trace their ancestry to the ancient Illyrians. They speak a distinct Indo-European language that is divided into two mutually intelligible dialects, Geg and Tosk. Tosks live south of the Shkumbini River, which divides the country in half, and the Gegs live north of the river. Albanian-speaking popu-lations can also be found in northern Greece, Macedonia, and in Kosovo, Serbia, and Montenegro, in the former Yugoslavia. Albania's population was estimated in the early 1960s to be 70 to 73 percent Muslim, 17 to 20 percent Eastern Orthodox, and 10 percent Roman Catholic, with the Muslims split evenly be-tween Orthodox Sunnis and the more liberal Bektashi sect. As a result of a policy of official atheism, the communist government brutally suppressed all religious observance after 1967. Since the fall of communism in 1990, religious practice has resumed, but it is hard to determine how many believers have returned to various faiths.

The traditional areas of Albanian migration were to Greece, southern Italy, and Sicily, where a distinct Italo-Albanian Catholic rite can be found. In more recent times, Albanian immigrants have moved in significant numbers to Can-ada, Germany, Australia, and the United States. The first Albanian immigrants to the United States were young males, who came as labor migrants at the end of the nineteenth century. Most of the early immigrants were Orthodox Chris-tians from rural areas of the south, and apparently, the majority returned to their homeland after World War I. A second wave, most of whom stayed in the United States, came after the war. This new group, also largely Christian Tosks,

Table 5
East European Ancestry Groups in America, by Rank Order, 1990

Group	Number
Polish	9,366,106
East European Jewish	6,000,000(est.)
Russian*	2,952,987
Slovak	1,882,897
Hungarian	1,582,302
Czech	1,296,411
Lithuanian	811,865
Ukrainian	740,803
Croatian	544,270
Romanian	365,544
Czechoslovakian	315,285
Yugoslavian	257,994
Slovene	124,437
Serbian	116,795
Latvian	100,331
Slavic	76,931
Albanian	47,710
Bulgarian	29,595
Estonian	26,762
Macedonian	20,365
Soviet Union*	7,729
Carpatho-Rusyn	7,602
Belarusin	4,277
Moravian	3,781
Ruthenian	3,776
Wendish (Sorbian)	3,189
TOTAL	**20,689,744**

*The categories ''Russian'' and ''Soviet Union'' contain a significant proportion of Jewish Americans with roots in Russia and the former USSR. More recent Russian-Jewish émigrés show a greater tendency to identify with Russian culture. The ''Russian'' category also contains many Carpatho-Rusyns who have come to identify themselves as Russian. The actual number of ethnic Great Russians in the U.S. is unknown.

Source: Adapted from Bureau of the Census, *1990 Census of Population, Supplementary Reports: Detailed Ancestry Groups for States*, CP–5–1–2 (Washington, D.C.: Government Printing Office, 1992), Table 2.

included large numbers of families and thus a more balanced gender ratio. The earliest migrants, who were either Ottoman citizens or citizens of newly independent Albania, did not yet have a strong sense of national identity and were not always listed as Albanians when they arrived in the United States. Therefore, it is difficult to get a clear picture of the extent of Albanian migration in the first decades of the century. After World War II, a new wave of Albanian immigrants arrived as political refugees in the wake of the establishment of communist governments in Albania and Yugoslavia. This group included significant numbers of Muslims, Roman Catholics, and Gegs. By 1970, there were an estimated 70,000 people of Albanian ancestry in the United States, of whom about 17,400 spoke the language.

As unskilled rural immigrants, the Albanian newcomers sought work in the industrial areas of the northeast and north-central areas of the United States. The heaviest concentrations developed in Boston and neighboring areas. Other centers developed in the Bronx, Jamestown, Rochester, New York, Detroit, Pittsburgh, Philadelphia, Chicago, and Cleveland. Subsequent waves of immigration settled in the same areas, and Boston has remained the most important center of Albanian ethnicity in the United States. A new influx of wage-seeking Albanians began arriving after 1970 from the Albanian areas of Yugoslavia. Finally, after the fall of the communist regime in Albania in 1990, a stream of immigrants commenced from Albania proper, the first significant migration from the country in almost half a century. Immigration from Albania proper between 1990 and 1995 totaled about 7,000. There are, however, no figures for Albanians immigrating from outside of Albania. The new population does include a significant number of well-educated professionals. According to the 1990 U.S. census, 47,710 persons identify as Albanian, but the number appears to be an undercount of Albanians and Albanian Americans.

BELARUSINS

An East Slavic people, the Belarusins have been among the slowest of all European groups to adopt a strong national identity. This makes studying them in Diaspora particularly difficult. Early immigrants from Belarusin lands tended to be ethnic Poles or at least identified themselves as such. Although individuals came to North America earlier in the nineteenth century, significant numbers of Belarusins probably did not begin to arrive until the 1890s or 1900s. As many as 100,000 peasants may have settled in the United States before World War I, but precise figures are impossible. Most of these immigrants settled in industrial or mining areas of the Northeast or Midwest, while some settled on truck farms in New Jersey and Long Island, New York. After World War II, a new wave of Belarusins arrived in America as refugees and displaced persons (DPs), fleeing political turmoil in their homeland. This most recent migration was markedly smaller than the pre–World War I migration; however, most of these postwar arrivals were educated, professional people.

Prior to World War II, Belarusins in America did not have their own church but joined Russian Orthodox or Polish Catholic parishes. In addition, most Belarusin secular organizations were small and local in character. The Belaruski Kamitet (Belarusin Committee), founded in the 1920s, and the Belarussian National Council, formed in 1941, were the first attempts to create national organizations. After World War II, the arrival of educated, nationally conscious Belarusins sparked the creation of several new organizations and about a dozen

serial publications. Another important postwar development was the reestablishment of the Belarussian Autocephalic Orthodox Church. Destroyed in Europe
during the war, the church hierarchy came to America and established its seat
in Cleveland. Belarusin-American cultural life centers around parishes, choirs,
and a small number of schools and periodicals.

In the 1990s there were about 4,277 self-identified Belarusins in America,
although many of the older generation of Belarusin immigrants and their descendants have only a vague sense of their ethnic origins, and many were doubt-
less listed as Russians. Between 1992 and 1995, 17,145 residents of Belarus
were admitted to the United States, not all of whom are ethnic Belarusins.

BOSNIANS

Bosnians in the United States are a South Slavic people, Muslim by religion,
who speak Serbo-Croatian. Bosnia was a medieval state that included Catholics
and Orthodox believers as well as members of an independent Bosnian Christian
church. After the Turkish conquest in the fifteenth century, the area experienced
significant conversions to Islam. Bosnia remained a distinct area throughout the
Turkish period and was joined to Herzegovina, a mountainous Serbian-speaking
area, in the fourteenth century. In the nineteenth century, under the influence of
neighboring regions, Bosnian Catholics began to identify as Croatians, and Bosnian Orthodox became Serbs, leaving the name *Bosnian* to the Muslims by
default. Bosnia-Herzegovina was a theater of bitter warfare between Serbs and
Croatians during World War II, with Muslims often forced to choose sides. The
Bosnian Republic of postwar Yugoslavia was 40 percent Muslim and had about
85 percent of the Muslim population of the country, with small numbers residing
in Serbia and Montenegro. The post-1991 civil war, born out of the disintegration of communist Yugoslavia, led to ethnic cleansing that displaced most of
Muslims from neighboring republics as well as the areas of Bosnia bordering
Serbia and Croatia.

The first Bosnian Muslim immigrants to the United States were part of the
migration of young male laborers at the beginning of the twentieth century from
eastern Serb areas and Macedonia. Most came from Herzegovina. They settled
primarily in the Chicago area, with smaller communities developing in Gary
and Milwaukee. They also followed Orthodox Serbs to western mining areas,
in particular to Butte, Montana. There was no significant migration after World
War I, but a second wave of migration, drawn primarily from political refugees,
entered the United States after World War II. These refugees were drawn from
all parts of Bosnia and included urban dwellers and members of the landowning
class. A third group of Bosnians was admitted in the 1970s, after the United
States ended its quota system and Yugoslavia began to allow emigration. The
latest immigration of Bosnian immigrants represents an influx of refugees fleeing
the horrors of civil war and ethnic cleansing. They began to arrive after 1992.
The three waves of post–World War II immigration followed the earliest settlers

to the Chicago-Gary-Milwaukee area and to secondary settlements in Detroit, Cleveland, and New York.

The earliest fraternal organization founded by the first immigrants has died out, replaced in the mid-1950s by the Chicago-based Bosnian American Cultural Center. The first exclusively Bosnian mosque in Chicago dates from the same period. In 1976, reflecting the movement of Bosnian immigrants and their children to the suburbs, a new mosque and Islamic Center were opened in the northern Chicago suburb of Northbrook. Prior to World War II, the small Bosnian community had used mosques established by Turkish immigrants.

As Bosnian ethnic identification was a recent development in Europe, its emergence in the United States also came later than ethnic identification among other South Slavs. Many of the better-educated postwar emigrants identified as Muslim Croatians or, to a lesser extent, as Muslim Serbs, reflecting wartime allegiances. The creation of a Bosnian nationality in Tito's Yugoslavia accelerated the process of differentiation in Europe and in the United States. For American Bosnians the postcommunist civil war in Bosnia emphatically underlined that identity, and among the most recent immigrants, *Bosnian* has become a primary ethnic identity.

It is difficult to estimate the number of Bosnians in the United States because they have been lumped into the South Slavic totals and because the federal government does not collect data on religious groups. (Bosnian is regarded as synonymous with Muslim.) It is estimated that the number of Bosnian Muslims in the United States was about 18,000 prior to the new influx of refugees after 1992. The most recent arrivals number several thousand.

BULGARIANS

Bulgarians are speakers of a South Slavic language who take their name from Turkic tribes that migrated to the western shores of the Black Sea in the seventh century. They were the first Slavs to accept Christianity, and their language was the basis for the creation of Old Church Slavonic. Bulgaria fell under Turkish rule in the late fourteenth century and remained part of the Ottoman empire until the end of the nineteenth century. The Bulgarian state that emerged after the Congress of Berlin in 1878 had strong irredentist claims to Macedonia, which guided its foreign policy and dictated its involvement on the side of the Central Powers in World War I and the Axis in World War II. Bulgaria was ruled by a communist government from 1945 until the early 1990s.

The first migration of Bulgarians began in the early twentieth century from poor rural areas of central Bulgaria that had historically supplied long-term and seasonal labor migrants to other parts of the Ottoman empire and from Macedonia (see Macedonians). The immigrants from Macedonia were drawn into the immigrant stream as a result of their contacts with neighboring Serb and Greek areas. The migration to the United States was overwhelmingly male (about 90 percent) and was dominated by single men. Most of the immigrants intended to return home with sufficient earnings to improve their life chances as farmers or entrepreneurs. More than 85 percent of the first wave of approximately 50,000 migrants from Bulgarian lands returned home, many to fight for their country in the Balkan Wars or World War I. Only a small number of Bulgarians came between 1924 and 1964, when the U.S. national origins quotas were in effect. Some of these migrants were well educated, urban political refugees who fled Bulgaria in the wake of the establishment of a communist regime. Between 1990 and 1995, 5,900 Bulgarians immigrated to America.

The largest concentration of Bulgarian immigrants and their children is in the Detroit area, where they initially found work in the auto industry. Additional concentrations are in the other older industrial areas that had also offered work at manufacturing jobs. These include Lorain, Youngstown, Cleveland, and Akron, Ohio, and Gary and Fort Wayne, Indiana. Bulgarian communities are also found in Los Angeles, Indianapolis, and New York City. Most Bulgarians remained closely attached to the Orthodox Church, although there are a small number of Bulgarian Catholics in Michigan, descended from Bulgarians who had migrated earlier to Austria-Hungary. Bulgarians established over thirty parishes in the United States, but the Bulgarian church has been split over international political issues into two groups. One is part of the Orthodox Church in America; a second faction is in communion with the Bulgarian hierarchy; and there are two independent parishes.

The political and cultural life of the Bulgarian community in the United States has also been fragmented by local as well as international politics. A significant number of Bulgarian immigrants were attracted to radical politics and were found in the ranks of the Industrial Workers of the World (IWW), the American Socialist Party, the Socialist Labor Party, and the Communist Party. Post–World War II politics saw splits between new left- and right-wing anticommunist groups. Although Bulgarian groups have estimated that there are between 75,000 and 100,000 Bulgarian Americans, the 1990 census reported that only 29,595 Americans claimed Bulgarian ancestry. Certainly, some of those claimed by the Bulgarian community probably chose another self-identification, such as Macedonian.

CARPATHO-RUSINS

Carpatho-Rusins (also known as Rusins, Rusyns, or Ruthenians) come from a trio of Slavic peoples indigenous to the Carpathian Mountains of Slovakia, Poland, and Ukraine. They come from three main groups: Hutsuls, Lemkos, and Bojkos. Carpatho-Rusins in Europe are Eastern-rite Catholics, although some converted to Russian Orthodoxy in the New World. Like their east European neighbors, Carpatho-Rusins began coming to the New World in significant numbers in the 1880s. Although an exact count of total Carpatho-Rusin arrivals in America is impossible, an estimated 225,000 arrived up through 1914; 20,000 came in the interwar years; and another 10,000 were admitted after World War

II. Carpatho-Rusins settled in industrial areas of the United States. In 1920, over half lived in Pennsylvania, whereas another 25 percent lived in New York or New Jersey. In 1990, 11,378 Americans claimed Carpatho-Rusin or Ruthenian ancestry, although this reflects only a part of the total Rusin presence in the United States. Another 76,931 claimed "Slavic" ancestry, and many of these respondents are probably Carpatho-Rusin as well.

Part of the problem with estimating the total number of Carpatho-Rusins in America is that on arrival they also lacked a strong national identity. Some immigrants came to regard themselves as Ukrainians, others as Russians, Slovaks, or even Poles, or in rare cases Slovenians. How many came to consider themselves Carpatho-Rusins is unclear, but the fact that in 1910 the Little Russian National Union split between Ukrainians and those with Rusin tendencies shows how intense the division could be. Carpatho-Rusins with different national tendencies shared many organizations and institutions during the early years of community formation in America, but after 1900 each group began going its own way. Carpatho-Rusins also developed their own organizations, such as the Greek Catholic Union, and newspapers, for example, *Amerikansky Russky Viestnik* (American-Rusin Bulletin).

CROATIANS

Croatians are a South Slavic people who share a nearly common language with Serbs, but one that they write in the Latin alphabet. In 1990 they constituted about 22 percent of Yugoslavia's population. Croatians are by tradition Roman Catholic, and except for an early existence as an independent state in the tenth and eleventh centuries, they were in union with the Kingdom of Hungary for over 800 years, until the collapse of the Austro-Hungarian empire in 1918. During most of the twentieth century they were incorporated into royal and later communist Yugoslavia, with a brief interlude as an independent pro-Axis state in World War II. Following the disintegration of Yugoslavia, a new, independent Croatian Republic emerged.

Croatia produced the earliest South Slavic immigrants to the United States, with occasional sojourners from Dalmatia coming as early as the seventeenth century to the Gulf Coast region. By 1861, 3,000 to 4,000 Croatians from Dalmatia lived in the South, and a new migration was beginning to California, where they engaged in fishing, mining, truck farming, and ranching. By the 1880s more than 20,000 Croatians were settled in the United States, most of them spread out over the far west.

Between 1880 and 1914, a new peasant migration, largely male and unskilled, began from Croatia and adjacent inland regions. The new migrants settled in the industrial Northeast and were attracted to coal, iron, and copper mines and heavy industry, in particular, steelmaking. The greatest concentration of Croatians from this new wave was in Pittsburgh and the coal mining areas of Pennsylvania. Other centers developed in Gary, Indiana, Cleveland, Ohio, northern

New Jersey, and New York City and in mining centers in Michigan's Upper Peninsula, Minnesota's Iron Range, and Butte, Montana. This wave of immigrants is estimated at 350,000 to 400,000. The return rate for Croatians prior to 1924 was about 36 percent, considerably lower than their Slavic neighbors to the east. After World War II, about 40,000 political émigrés and refugees came to the United States, followed after 1970 by a steady trickle of new, primarily economic emigrants from Yugoslavia, which added another 50,000 immigrants to the Croatian-American community. Since the collapse of Yugoslavia a few additional Croatians have come as refugees from Bosnia and Slavonia. The postwar emigrations have included many educated, professional people.

Homeland politics have occupied the Croatian community since the late nineteenth century. These have alternatively been about independence and the establishment of a South Slavic state before World War I, anti-Serb and anti-Yugoslav policies in the interwar period, and anticommunism after World War II. As a consequence, Croatian Catholics were much slower than other groups who came from eastern and southern Europe to establish their own parishes, being content to use parishes founded by other groups. The first Croatian parish was founded in Allegheny, Pennsylvania, in 1901. Subsequently, thirty-two others were founded. Byzantine-rite Croatians also have two parishes in Cleveland. Various Croatian sources estimate that there are between 500,000 and 1 million Croatian immigrants and their descendants in the United States. The 1990 census indicates that 544,270 Americans identified themselves as having Croatian ancestry.

CZECHS

Czechs were among the earliest of the East European groups to arrive in America in significant numbers. Individual Czechs had arrived in the New World by the mid-seventeenth century. In 1735 a group of Moravian Brethren immigrated to America, eventually settling in Bethlehem, Pennsylvania. Large-scale Czech immigration dates from the 1850s. Czech immigration patterns mirror most closely those of southern and eastern Germans. Czechs were more likely to arrive in family units, more likely be to better off financially, and more likely to settle on farms in the United States than nearly all other east European groups. Almost half of first-generation Czech immigrants were engaged in agriculture, as compared with about 10 percent of Poles (the next-most rural of east European ethnic groups). Such cities as New York, Cleveland, and especially Chicago attracted large numbers of Czechs as well. Between 1850 and 1950 nearly 400,000 Czechs came to America (which includes about 30,000 in the interwar period and 25,000 postwar arrivals). Some 10,000 more arrived as refugees following the Soviet invasion of Czechoslovakia in 1968. In 1990, Czech was listed as the twenty-seventh largest ancestry group by the U.S. Census Bureau: 1,296,411 Americans claimed Czech ancestry; another 315,285 claimed Czechoslovakian ancestry; and 3,781 claimed Moravian ancestry.

Czech immigrants created a wide array of fraternal organizations, and the reach of those groups even extended into many of the smaller Czech farming communities. Czech fraternals tended to be dominated either by freethinkers or Catholics—the two rival camps that dominated the political scene in the Czech immigrant community. The earliest freethinker association was Ceskoslovanská podporující spolecnost (Czech-Slavonic Benevolent Society, or CSPS), although two other groups split off in 1897 in Texas and the Midwest over the question of admitting women and formed their own societies. Czech women, excluded from full membership in CSPS, had formed Jednota ceskych dám (Union of Czech Women) in 1870. Czech Catholics formed ten major fraternals whose combined total membership exceeded that of the freethinker societies. Catholics, freethinkers, and socialists also formed gymnastic societies (Sokols), and by 1927, there were 125 Sokols of various persuasions across the country.

In addition to a lively but fractious organizational life, Czech immigrants also created a rich cultural life in America that included theaters, newspapers, and book publishing. Perhaps the most notable aspect of Czech-American cultural life was in the field of music. Even the smallest Czech communities had bands. Perhaps the highlight of Czech contributions to the American music scene was made by Antonin Dvorák, who spent three years in New York and in the small Czech farming village of Spillville, Iowa, where he worked on his *New World Symphony*.

In political terms, Czech Americans have often made common cause with their Slovak neighbors. Together, the two groups raised $675,000 to aid the cause of Czechoslovakian independence and lobbied the Wilson administration to support an independent Czech and Slovak state, a goal they achieved in 1918. It was a moment when most Czech Americans were able to put aside their political and philosophical differences to work for a common goal.

In the post–World War II era, Czech Americans moved into the American middle class. New waves of immigrants arriving after the war found varying degrees of acceptance among the older generations of immigrants. Those who arrived in 1948 were relatively well received; those coming after 1968 less so. In the 1970s, there was a modest revival of Czech ethnicity, most significantly in large cities but also in small communities. Many Czech heritage groups appeared throughout the country, signaling the desire of third- and fourth-generation Czech Americans to find new ways to maintain a distinct tradition in the New World. Although this revival did not fulfill the hopes of many Czech Americans, the fall of communism has encouraged an increase in visits to their ancestral homeland. In 1994 a Czech and Slovak museum and research center was created by fraternals in Cedar Rapids, Iowa, to preserve their ethnic heritage.

ESTONIANS

Estonians are a Baltic people related to the Finns. Although the first Estonian immigrants arrived in America before 1700, like most immigrants from the

Russian Empire, they did not form significant communities in America until the 1890s. Prior to World War I, an estimated 200,000 Estonians came to America. Since 1920, another 20,000 have arrived. The largest Estonian communities are found on the East Coast, with New York, Philadelphia, and Boston being among the most significant places of settlement. Smaller Estonian communities can be found in the cities of the Great Lakes states and on farms in Wisconsin, the Dakotas, Montana, Colorado, Washington, and Oregon.

The Estonian Lutheran Church, under the aegis of the Missouri Synod, helped organize some of the first Estonian social and cultural groups. Estonian Baptists, however, provided the community with some of its most energetic organizations. To these were added secular organizations, such as Amerika Eesti Heategew Selts (Estonian-American Beneficial Society), an ethnic fraternal. Estonian immigrants were also very active in founding socialist workers' groups. The larger workers' societies sponsored a range of cultural activities—including choruses, theaters, newspapers, and reading rooms—and were also active as mutual aid groups. The radical movement split following the events in Estonia that culminated in Estonia's independence in 1918, which in turn stimulated the growth of Estonian-American nationalist groups. The nationalist element then grew in strength following the Soviet takeover of Estonia in 1940 and the arrival of Estonian refugees after 1945. Small numbers of Estonians continued to leave their homeland during the cold war, but the Scandinavian countries have been a more common destination for recent political and economic immigrants.

LATVIANS

Unlike their Estonian and Lithuanian neighbors, relatively few Latvians came to America in the years before World War I. Instead, many preferred migration eastward to other parts of the Russian empire. Nevertheless, Latvian immigration to America dates from the seventeenth century, and there were an identifiable number of Latvian Americans by 1850. Although the exact number entering in America before 1920 is unknown, it was probably 10,000 to 15,000. Another 5,000 arrived in America before World War II. The largest influx occurred after World War II, when over 40,000 Latvian refugees were admitted into the United States. Major Latvian settlements can be found in New York, Boston, Philadelphia, Cleveland, Chicago, and Grand Rapids and Kalamazoo, Michigan.

The high proportion of educated people in the Latvian immigrant community gave birth to a rich cultural life. Most early Latvian immigrants formed Lutheran or Baptist congregations, and these naturally became a focus of social and cultural activity. Choirs and theatrical groups have played an important role in Latvian-American life, and national and regional song festivals have regularly attracted large crowds. The Latvian press in America began in the 1890s with the publication of *Amerikas Vestnesis* (American Herald), to which were added several other serial titles, including a number of short-lived socialist or communist newspapers. Following the arrival of the postwar refugees, a regular

Latvian publishing house, Gramatu Draugs (Friend of Books), was established in New York City. In 1990, 100,331 Americans claimed Latvian ancestry. They were joined by 2,630 more immigrants between 1990 and 1995.

LITHUANIANS

During the period of the greatest immigration to the United States, some 300,000 Lithuanians arrived on American shores, making them the most significant of the three Baltic groups in America. Lithuanians began migrating in large numbers after 1870, with some moving to other areas of the Russian empire as well as the New World. Immigration to America peaked in the 1890s and 1900s. Early Lithuanian immigrants came to the coal fields of Pennsylvania, where they took work alongside Poles and other Slavic groups. The largest Lithuanian communities formed in Chicago, Cleveland, Pittsburgh, and New York, but other communities could be found in most of the industrial and mining centers of the Midwest and Northeast. Another 30,000 Lithuanians arrived after World War II.

Many early Lithuanian immigrants assimilated into local Polish communities, a process facilitated by the fact that many Lithuanians spoke Polish and were also Roman Catholic. Under the leadership of a few political émigrés and nationally conscious priests, however, Lithuanian immigrants began to gradually forge a new ethnic identity in America. Among the organizations these ethnic leaders formed was the Susivienijimas Lietuviu Amerikoje (Lithuanian Alliance of America), a fraternal insurance organization that encouraged a Lithuanian-American identity. It published its own newspaper and promoted the idea of an independent Lithuanian state. By the turn of the century, a dense network of organizations—local, national, political, educational, and religious—was being formed along with Lithuanian newspapers and presses. The arrival of another wave of Lithuanian immigrants after 1945 brought new blood to many Lithuanian organizations, but they also formed new groups as well, especially those dedicated to the professions and education. In 1990, 811,865 Americans reported Lithuanian ancestry. Between 1990 and 1995, 2,500 Lithuanians immigrated to the United States.

MACEDONIANS

Macedonians speak a South Slavic language once regarded as a dialect of Bulgarian but now widely assayed as a separate tongue. Slavic Macedonia was once part of the first Bulgarian empire and in the tenth century the site of a western Bulgarian state. The site of this early Slavic Macedonian state subsequently passed under the control of the Byzantine Empire, the second Bulgarian kingdom, and briefly Serbia, before it was overrun in the fourteenth century by the Ottomans. It remained part of the Ottoman Empire until the First Balkan

War in 1912, when it was partitioned between Bulgaria, Serbia (after 1919, Yugoslavia), and Greece. A separate Macedonian Republic was set up in communist Yugoslavia, which contained the bulk of the area inhabited by Macedonians. This supported the idea of a distinct Macedonian identity, which had begun to develop in the early twentieth century. It was further buttressed by the establishment of an independent Macedonian Orthodox Church in 1958. After initial support for the idea, the Bulgarian government turned against it, claiming all Macedonians as Bulgarians. The Greek government has always refused recognition of Macedonians as a separate ethnic or national group and, since the end of the Yugoslavian Federation, has been actively hostile to the establishment of a state claiming to be Macedonian.

The earliest Macedonian immigration to the United States began in 1903, spurred by rural poverty and the brutal Turkish repression of a Macedonian uprising. Most of these immigrants had a Bulgarian orientation and are claimed by the Bulgarian as well as the Macedonian community in America. These were largely single males from extreme southwestern Macedonia who came to earn money to improve their situation at home. This first wave of migrants is usually estimated at 50,000 to 55,000, and about two-thirds of them returned.

A second wave of immigrants with different places of origin came in the interwar period. These immigrants came from Bulgaria proper and from Greece, or Greece via Bulgaria. They were drawn heavily from the Slavic Macedonians, who had been expelled from Greece (whom the Greeks refer to as Greek slavophones). This migration, which began in the early 1920s, doubled the population of Macedonians in the United States. Another wave of Greek Macedonian immigrants came after a second expulsion between 1944 and 1949. They were joined by a few thousand political refugees from Yugoslavia in the immediate postwar period. Finally, a last wave of Macedonians estimated at 20,000 to 25,000, almost entirely from Yugoslavia, have migrated to the United States since Yugoslavia loosened emigration policies and the United States ended its national origin quotas in 1965.

The earliest Macedonian communities settled in the industrial areas of the Northeast and Midwest, with the heaviest concentration in Detroit, and also in the Chicago-Gary area, in the industrial centers of Ohio (such as Cleveland, Lorain, Akron, and Canton), and in western New York, notably Buffalo, Rochester, and Lackawanna. There are, in addition, Macedonian settlements in New York City and northern New Jersey, California, Washington, Wisconsin, and Missouri. These centers, especially in the Midwest, had been set up by the earliest immigrants yet continued to draw subsequent waves of newcomers.

The early Macedonian immigrants, who dominated the pre–World War I Bulgarian migration, were instrumental in creating many of the key institutions of the Bulgarian/Macedonian diaspora, including the first Bulgarian Orthodox churches in America. The more recent immigration from Yugoslav Macedonia led to the establishment of the first specifically Macedonian Orthodox churches under the Holy Synod of the Macedonian Orthodox Church in Skopje. Between 1962 and 1982 eleven Macedonian Orthodox Churches in communion with the Holy Synod in Skopje were created.

The chief organization of the Bulgarian Macedonians is the Macedonian Patriotic Organization, founded in Fort Wayne, Indiana, in 1922. Although it defines Macedonians as Bulgarians, its focus is almost exclusively on Macedonian affairs and pays little heed to Bulgaria proper. The newer Macedonian orientation is supported by local Macedonian groups and the Macedonian Cultural Center Illindin, founded in Detroit in 1976. Greek Macedonians are represented by the Pan-Macedonian Association, established in New York City in 1947. Their official language is Greek, but Macedonian remains the language of choice at home. All the groups share the same basic culture, foods, and dances.

The 1990 U.S. census recorded 20,365 persons who identified as Macedonians. Nevertheless, given the complexity of the Macedonian situation and the tendency of many Macedonians to have more than one identity, or to shift their identity or allegiance from one group to another in response to specific situations in the United States or in Macedonia, it is clear that the census figures undercount the number of Macedonian immigrants and their descendants in the United States.

MAGYARS

Prior to 1918, the Kingdom of Hungary was a multiethnic component of the Austro-Hungarian empire. Although immigrants from this land were of many different ethnic backgrounds, immigration officials often recorded them as Hungarians or Magyars without distinction. This makes it particularly difficult to gauge the exact number of Magyars who came to America. Following World War II there were about 250,000 Magyar Americans who were soon joined by another 60,000 refugees fleeing political unrest in Hungary, about half of whom came after the failure of the Hungarian Revolution in 1956. In 1990, 1,582,302 Americans claimed Magyar or Hungarian ancestry. Between 1990 and 1995, 7,364 Magyars were admitted into America. Like most other immigrants from eastern Europe, Magyar immigrants came first to the northeastern and midwestern states. Many settled in the Pennsylvania coal fields. Chicago, Pittsburgh, Cleveland, and New York have significant Magyar populations.

Unlike some immigrant groups, Magyars in America tended to form mutual benefit societies before they formed ethnic parishes. Indeed, in many cases societies helped to form churches. In the 1890s, Magyar Protestants began forming the first Hungarian ethnic parishes, followed more slowly by Catholics. As ethnic parishes began to organize community life for Magyar immigrants, new national organizations and an ethnic press developed that helped foster a growing sense of Hungarian nationalism. The Magyar-American press reached its high-water mark in the 1920s, when over sixty Hungarian periodicals were being published throughout the United States. Unlike most other east European ethnic groups in America, the Magyars benefited from a sympathetic homeland government that took an active role in developing Hungarian life abroad. Although the acquisition of stable blue-collar jobs allowed Magyar immigrants and their children to move into the American mainstream, they maintained ties and interests in their ancestral homeland.

ROMANIANS

Only a handful of Romanians came to the United States prior to 1870, but between 1870 and 1920 immigration increased so much that by 1920 there were about 85,000 Romanians in America. Among the areas of large-scale out-migration were many regions outside of Romania proper: Transylvania, Macedonia, and Albania. After World War II another 10,000 Romanians entered the United States under the Displaced Persons Act. In 1990, the U.S. Census Bureau listed Romanians as the fifty-third largest ancestry group, with 365,544 individuals claiming Romanian heritage. Between 1990 and 1995, 33,159 more Romanians entered the United States. The majority of Romanian immigrants settled in the industrial regions of the Great Lakes and mid-Atlantic states. The largest concentrations included Cleveland, Detroit, Pittsburgh, Chicago, New York, the mining towns of Pennsylvania, and the smaller factory towns of northern Ohio.

Romanian social and cultural life in America developed apace with the growing size of the immigrant population. This development was hindered, however, by a lack of trained priests and educated laypeople. Early Romanian immigrants often joined local Byzantine-rite Catholic or Serbian, Russian, or Greek Orthodox parishes. The Byzantine-rite Catholics in the Romanian community always remained a minority. Most had emigrated from Transylvania. The lack of established Romanian Orthodox hierarchy led to schisms, which became particularly acute after 1945, when conflicting loyalties to a homeland under Soviet domination sharpened religious differences. The establishment of mutual benefit societies followed a smoother course. The first local Romanian society appeared in 1902 in Homestead, Pennsylvania, and many others were formed in the following decade. By 1911, a central organization of forty-four societies had emerged—the Union of Romanian Beneficial and Cultural Societies. A second organization, the Liga de Ajutor, was founded in 1912, and the two groups remained in sharp competition and conflict with each other until they merged in 1928 in the Union and League of Romanian Societies in America. Since World War II, the sons and daughters of the Romanian immigrants have gradually moved into the mainstream, and although the ethnic revival of the 1970s had a limited impact among Romanian Americans, attempts to preserve ethnic heritage have met with some success. The most notable effort was the establishment of a Romanian cultural/religious center in Grass Lake, Michigan, near Jackson, in the late 1970s. The center is still functioning under the auspices of the Orthodox Church, with the fall of communism enabling it to establish new ties to homeland scholars and institutions.

RUSSIANS

The number of ethnic Russians in America has always been relatively small. This excludes Carpatho-Rusins and Belarusins, who were Russianized in the United States, and East European Jews, who, in the current methodology of the U.S. census, are often counted as "Russian." In recent decades, the majority of those emigrating from the former USSR were of Jewish origin. Those who settled in the United States were often aided by American Jewish organizations that sought to bring these refugees, who had been largely secularized, into the Jewish-American community. Although this effort has been partly successful, some of these immigrants still retain a Russian identity.

Russian ethnic migration to the United States was minimal during the nineteenth and early twentieth centuries because Russian peasants were either drawn to Russia's new industrial cities or attracted to new farmlands and opportunities opening up in Siberia or the maritime provinces of the Russian Far East. In addition, the Tsarist government actively discouraged Russian immigration. As a result, Russian ethnic migration to North America was drawn largely from religious dissenters, such as the various Old Believers sects who had split from the Russian Orthodox Church in the seventeenth century and adherents of evangelical and Pentecostal churches. The other large-scale immigration from Tsarist Russia to the United States, in addition to the Jewish, Polish, Belarusin, and Carpatho-Rusin immigration, was the movement of Russian Germans who had settled in Russia in the eighteenth century.

Despite the small numbers, the history of ethnic Russian immigration is a long and interesting one. The first Russians in America, almost all of them men, came not to the East Coast but to the West, as part of Russia's Alaskan colonial adventure. Beginning in the late eighteenth century, they established a number of small settlements and trading posts and intermarried with the local native population, passing on their religion and some cultural elements as well. In the 1860s, there were about 800 Russians in Alaska. Then, in 1867, the colony was sold to the United States, making these people Americans by default. The California coast was also a destination for small groups of Russian religious dissenters. Although most of Russia's peasant migration was taken up with a migration eastward into Siberia, some did come to America during the several decades before World War I. In the 1920s, some 30,000 Russians fleeing the communist takeover of their homeland came to America. Between 1946 and 1989, approximately 300,000 Soviet citizens were admitted to the United States as immigrants, refugees, and asylum seekers. Only a small minority of these were ethnic Russians, the majority being Jews or Armenians. Since 1989, immigration from the former USSR has increased considerably, totaling 302,603 people between 1990 and 1995. Approximately 50,000 of these new arrivals are believed to be ethnic Russians, two thirds of whom are religious dissidents who have sought homes in the western states, particularly California, Oregon, and Washington.

SERBS AND MONTENEGRIN SERBS

Serbs were the largest group of South Slavic speakers in the former state of Yugoslavia. They took Christianity from Byzantium and formed the westernmost outpost of Orthodoxy. The first Serbian state dates to the tenth century, and the Serbs represented an independent and growing power in the Balkans until their defeat in 1389 by the Ottomans. Serbia remained under Ottoman rule until the nineteenth century, when a long war for liberation resulted in an independent Serbia in 1882. Many Serbian-inhabited territories, however, remained outside of the state, resulting in irredentist claims that helped spark World War I. After 1918 Serbia became the nucleus of the new state of Yugoslavia and, in 1945, a republic in the communist People's Republic of Yugoslavia. Forty-seven years later, it then became the center of a rump Yugoslav state after the disintegration of communist rule there. Montenegro, a Serbian-speaking area in the mountainous southeast that had always remained free of Ottoman rule and whose people have a reputation for fierce independence, was part of both royal and communist Yugoslav and united with Serbia in the new, smaller Yugoslav state in 1992.

The distinguishing feature of Serbian migration to the United States is the disproportionate number who came from areas peripheral to Serbia proper. The overwhelming majority came from Croatia and Voyvodina, north and west of Serbia, or from Montenegro and Herzegovina, in the southeast. The prosperous small farmers of Serbia proper had less reason to migrate than did Serbs from the poor mountain regions of Montenegro and Herzegovina or the members of the Serb minority in Dalmatia and Slavonia. Some regions, such as Montenegro, sent as much as a tenth of their populations to the United States before 1914. The Serbian migration led to settlements in all the industrial cities of the southern Great Lakes, from Buffalo to Milwaukee as well as in the greater New York–northern New Jersey area. Serbs also found work in the mining industry in eastern and western Pennsylvania and in the Minnesota Iron Range. Additional communities developed in Kansas City, Kansas; St. Paul, Minnesota; Butte, Montana; Galveston, Texas; and various locations in California and Arizona. The return rate for Serbian and Montenegrin immigrants in the years before World War I, however, was a very high 87 percent.

A new migration in the wake of World War II brought refugees and DPs, many of them from Serbia proper. This group numbered about 30,000 to 35,000 people and included many well-educated urbanites. Settling in major cities, such as New York, Chicago, and Detroit, they brought high cultural standards and achievements along with intense homeland rivalries. As a result of their influence, the language of the Serbian press and electronic media changed from the dialect of the outlying regions to standard Serbian, and the community adopted the customs, music, and traditions of Serbia in preference to the ones their ancestors had brought from Croatia or Voyvodina.

The first Serbian church in the United States was founded in 1893 in Jackson,

California. It and subsequent parishes were part of the Russian Orthodox Church until 1921, when the patriarch of Belgrade created a Serbian Orthodox diocese for North America. In 1963, the Serbian Orthodox Church in America broke away over allegiance to the patriarch in communist Yugoslavia. The majority stayed with the canonical church, but a significant faction, comprising 40 percent of the parishes, formed an autonomous church. The split continues to plague the Serbian community in America. Serbian immigrants also founded a number of local and regional fraternal benevolent societies, which by 1963 had merged into the Serb National Federation. Although the federation is the only national Serbian organization in the United States, in most major Serbian centers women have established Serbian Sisters Circles for social and charitable work. These are usually associated with the church. Estimates of Serbian immigrants and their descendants in the United States are in the range of 200,000–250,000. The number of persons who identified as Serbian in the 1990 census is given at 116,795.

SLOVAKS

The Slovaks are a West Slavic people who live south of the Carpathian Mountains. After a brief period in the ninth century as part of Great Moravia, when they took Christianity from the Byzantine missionaries Cyril and Methodius, they fell under the rule of the invading Magyars in 906. They remained under Hungarian rule until the twentieth century, when they combined with the Czechs to create the new state of Czechoslovakia in 1918. During World War II Slovakia became a Nazi protectorate. Czechoslovakia was recreated after the war but shifted to communist rule in 1948. In 1969, Slovakia became a separate republic in a new Czech-Slovak federation. In the wake of the collapse of communism, the Slovaks voted to cede from the federation and formed an independent state in 1993.

Hungarian rule had a profound effect on Slovak history. The conversion of the Magyars to Christianity in 1000 led to the replacement of the Slovak Byzantine liturgy with the Latin one. The spread of the Reformation into Hungarian lands introduced both Lutheran and Calvinist forms of Protestantism into Slovakia. Although the majority of Slovaks are Roman Catholic, there is a significant minority of Slovak Lutherans—about 15 percent of the population. Other Protestants and Byzantine-rite Catholics comprise about 5 percent. During the nineteenth century, with the rise of Hungarian nationalism, the Slovaks were subjected to intense Magyarization.

Slovak emigrants arrived in the United States for the first time in substantial numbers in the 1870s, seeking work in coal mines and on the railroads. The 4,000 to 6,000 migrants of the 1870s were followed by tens of thousands annually after 1880. By 1914, over half a million Slovaks had come to the United States. The earliest migrants were from the poor and overpopulated eastern counties, but by the twentieth century, migrants were also coming from the more fertile and prosperous western areas of Slovakia. The majority who came during the same period, as in the case of other Slavic groups, were young single men in search of high wages. Between 1899 and 1924, 36.5 percent of the Slovak migrants returned home with their earnings.

The Slovak migration took most of the newcomers to the booming industrial cities and mining areas of the Midwest and Northeast. The relatively high wages in coal mining and steelmaking led almost half of Slovak immigrants to Pennsylvania. Outside of the Great Lakes and eastern industrial areas Slovaks also moved to mining areas of the West, such as Belt, Montana, and Gallup, New Mexico, and steelmaking towns, notably Pueblo, Colorado. Minneapolis, with its flour mills, also saw the development of a sizable Slovak community before World War I, which, because of chain migration, was disproportionately Lutheran.

Slovak community life was built around parishes and fraternal organizations. About 300 Slovak parishes were created by the immigrants: 241 Catholic, 48 Lutheran, 9 Calvinist, and 4 Byzantine-rite Catholic. By the beginning of the 1890s, local insurance and social societies began to consolidate into regional and national organizations, with twelve major national groups emerging by the twentieth century. The largest were the National Slovak Society, a secular group open to Slovaks of all religions, the Jednota for Catholics, and the Slovak Evangelical Union for Lutherans. In addition, following the Czech example, Slovaks in the United States created a militantly nationalistic Sokol, or Falcons Gymnastic Union, in 1896. In the early twentieth century it split into separate Catholic and secular Sokols. In 1990, Slovaks were the third largest of the East European ancestry groups after Poles and East European Jews (not counting Russians), with approximately 1,882,900 claiming Slovak heritage.

SLOVENES

The Slovenes are the northern and western most of the South Slavic peoples. They inhabit a territory between the Adriatic and the southern border of Austria that makes them neighbors of Italians, Germans, Hungarians, and Croatians. Before 1991 Slovenia had never been an independent state. Under Germanic domination from the ninth century, the area passed to Habsburg rule in the fifteenth century. The Slovenes were located largely in the Austrian part of the Austro-Hungarian empire until 1918, when they became part of the new Yugoslav state. Slovenia remained a part of both royal and communist Yugoslavia until the disintegration of that state after the collapse of communism in eastern Europe.

Even though the vast majority of Slovenes are Roman Catholic, about 5 percent profess other faiths, the largest group being Lutherans. Lutheran Slovenes are a very distinct group found primarily in the Prekmurje region, which had historically been under Hungarian rather than Austrian rule. The people of the Prekmurje region are distinguished not only by religion but also by a very distinct dialect and the use of Hungarian orthography. They prefer to be known as Windish. The Slovene Catholic population of Prekmurje share the Windish identity with their Lutheran brethren. They have continued to maintain that identity in the United States. The largest settlement of Windish Slovenes in the United States is in the Philadelphia area, with the Bethlehem, Pennsylvania, community being the largest.

A distinctive feature of early Slovene migration to the United States was the presence of a large number of Catholic priests who came to minister to the Indians of the Great Lakes and northern prairies. The best known was the Fr. Frederick Baraga (1797–1868). Knowledge of the opportunities available in the New World reached Slovenia as a result of the work of these missionaries. The first wave of peasant immigrants in the 1880s came to the copper and iron ore mines of Michigan's Upper Peninsula and northern Minnesota, settling in Calumet, Michigan, Hibbing, Virginia, and Ely, Minnesota. Later mining jobs would take them to western states, such as Montana.

In the 1890s the destination of the Slovene immigration shifted to the industrial cities of the Great Lakes. Cleveland became—and remains—the center of the greatest concentration of Slovenes in the United States. Other centers grew up in the coal mining areas of western Pennsylvania, the Chicago-Joliet region, and the West Allis–Milwaukee area. As with other Slavic groups, the earliest waves of immigrants were almost entirely made up of single men, and many returned home after a few years of earning money. The return rate for Slovene immigrants was 36.3 percent in the 1899–1924 period. Slovene immigrants came from all areas of the country, but the poorer rural districts of southeast Carniola sent a disproportionate number.

For most Slovenes the parish was the center of social as well as religious life. A significant number of Slovene immigrants, however, came to the United States with a decidedly secular, anticlerical outlook or developed it in contact with anticlerical circles after immigrating. This markedly influenced the evolution of Slovene organizational life in the United States. Thus, the first fraternal group, the Carniolan Slovene Catholic Union (now American Slovene Catholic Union), was founded in 1894, but a decade later, the Slovene National Benefit Society, which appealed to the secularists, was established and soon outstripped its clerical rival. The division and animosity between the two fraternal unions has remained a key feature of Slovene communal life during most of the twentieth century. Both groups have headquarters in the Chicago suburbs. A smaller group, the American Fraternal Union, in Ely, Minnesota, served the northern mining communities. Slovene women also founded their own insurance group, the Slovene Women's Union. Slovene-American sources estimate the total Slovene immigration to the United States at about 300,000. However, the 1990 census reported only 124,437 persons who identified as Slovenes.

SORBS (WENDS)

Sorbs (also called Wends or Lusatians) are a small Slavic group from south-eastern Germany, near the Czech and Polish borders. They are the remnant of a series of Slavic tribes in what is today eastern Germany who were Germanized or destroyed during the Middle Ages. Like the Germans among whom they lived, the Sorbs began to migrate in the 1850s in small numbers. Most of the earliest immigrants were religious dissenters from Saxony, led by Rev. Jan Kilian, who objected to government attempts to force them to worship in the state church. They moved to the Lee County, Texas, area and established a small Sorbian enclave. These pioneers were followed by other Sorbians who came for cheap farmland rather than religion. By 1900, about 1,200 Sorbians (Wends) had settled in Texas. Although they established a few of their own language schools, their equal fluency in German allowed them access to the German-American press and nearby German schools as well. Gradually, German, and later English, came to predominate as the language of the community. In 1990 the U.S. Census Bureau found 3,189 Americans who claimed Wendish or Sorbian ancestry.

UKRAINIANS

The Ukrainians are an East Slavic people. The ancestors of the majority of Ukrainian Americans came from the western areas of Ukraine, especially the foothills of the Carpathian Mountains, near the ethnolinguistic boundaries with Slovaks and Poles. The vast majority were citizens of Austria-Hungary. How many people came to America from this region is especially complicated, since in the United States they developed a variety of ancestries: Ukrainian, Carpatho-Rusin, Russian, or even Slovak or Polish. One current estimate puts the total Ukrainian/Rusin migration to North America prior to World War I at 250,000. Like other East European immigrants, Ukrainians settled primarily in the major industrial areas of the East and Midwest. Newark, New York City, Chicago, Detroit, and coal mining regions of Pennsylvania all have large Ukrainian populations. Some Ukrainian Americans did settle on farms, but the bulk of Ukrainian rural settlement in North America took place on the prairies of western Canada. Between 1947 and 1980 another 90,000 came to America, the majority fleeing Soviet rule in their homeland in the immediate postwar period. In 1990, 740,803 Americans claimed Ukrainian ancestry, but just between 1992 (when the Immigration and Naturalization Service [INS] began a separate enumeration) and 1995, 70,000 residents of Ukraine entered the United States.

Ukrainian social and cultural life in America has often been dominated by a quest for identity. Although originally most Ukrainian/Rusin immigrants who came to America before 1914 had no strong sense of national identity, by the turn of the century they had gradually begun to develop one. Various factions sought to influence the immigrants to one allegiance or another. This was further

complicated by religious differences. Some Roman Catholic bishops, such as St.
Paul's John Ireland, refused to recognize Ukrainian-rite priests and tried to incorporate Ukrainian/Rusin immigrants into existing Polish or Slovak parishes.
Disillusionment with the Catholic hierarchy's attitude and active proselytizing
by "Russophiles" led many immigrants and their priests into the Orthodox
Church, where they often took on a "Russian" identity. By 1916 one source
estimated that 163 Eastern-rite Catholic parishes in America had converted to
Orthodoxy. The appointment of an Eastern-rite Catholic bishop in 1907 and the
work of "Ukrainianizers" kept many immigrants in the Catholic fold, even
though Ukrainian Catholic leaders continued to feel that they were being treated
as second-class citizens.

The church controversy helped spur Ukrainianization, as did the creation of
such organizations as the Ruthenian National Association, which, significantly,
was renamed the Ukrainian National Association (UNA) in 1914. (It remains
the oldest extant Ukrainian organization in the world.) Another important
achievement was the establishment of a Ukrainian-language press in America.
Svoboda (Freedom), the UNA organ, was founded in 1894 and is the oldest
continuously published Ukrainian newspaper in the world. Ukrainian organizational life developed rapidly after World War I and the inability to realize an
independent Ukraine. Organizations spanned the political spectrum and were
both local and national in scope. Although Ukrainian-American organizations
were united in their desire for a free Ukraine, they differed sharply on what
shape it should take. The postwar generation of immigrants from Ukraine
brought new blood to Ukrainian-American institutions, but they also found
themselves in conflict with the older generation of immigrants. Yet the postwar
era saw left-wing elements in the community eclipsed, with most Ukrainian
Americans, as part of the Assembly of Captive Nations and other groups, becoming active supporters of U.S. cold war policies. For many Ukrainian Americans, the creation in 1992 of a free Ukraine for the first time in modern history
was the realization of long years of struggle.

CONCLUSION

Although sharp differences exist between the numerous East European groups
who have come to America, there are also important similarities. Most groups
arriving in the pre-1920 period were poor vis-à-vis the existing U.S. population
and thus took jobs that were the least desirable, the dirtiest, and the most dangerous, such as in coal mines, packing houses, and other areas of heavy industry.
According to U.S. government estimates, 50 percent of workers in heavy industry were Slavs. They were discriminated against, more often than not, on the
basis of either their poverty or their "foreignness." Indistinguishable to most
Anglo-Americans, they were often lumped (along with Poles) under the catchall
pejorative "Hunkies."

In the face of these conditions, the immigrants formed ethnic enclaves, usually centered on an ethnic parish and containing other important institutions, including fraternal halls, parochial schools, newspapers, and saloons. (Creating a network of such institutions was, of course, much harder for the smaller East European groups than for larger ones.) On one hand, these communities had a closed, protective nature that helped shield immigrants from discrimination and potential hardships, whereas, on the other, they developed hybrid cultures using elements taken from the old country combined with forms adopted from American society. Besides the community, the family was a key factor in immigrant life, providing the newcomers with both a protective mechanism and a means to realize common economic and social goals through shared sacrifice, even if that sacrifice at times bred tensions between family members and between generations.

In general, East European ethnic communities proved highly receptive to unionization, especially in the 1930s. The labor movement's successes, and their mass involvement in World War II, provided East European Americans with the chance to move into the lower middle class. The price, however, was a slow erosion of language and culture under the onslaught of Americanization. This process was furthered both by returning veterans—who had seen the world beyond the ethnic enclave—as well as by the groups being cut off from distant homelands due to the Cold War. This long struggle for social acceptance and economic security was not well understood by the post–World War II immigrants, who were often better educated and more likely to take up the banner of entrepreneurship than to work in factories. It took many years for old and new immigrants to find common ground, and the process continues.

Although many observers in the 1950s and 1960s predicted the total and irreversible assimilation of East European Americans, the ethnic revival of the 1970s and its aftereffects showed that ethnic identity had not so much disappeared as changed form. Although significant numbers of them had moved out of the old ethnic enclaves by 1990, for many—if not most—ethnicity remained important, be it in public displays or in private and even spiritual ways.

BIBLIOGRAPHIC REFERENCES

In the nearly two decades since the publication of the *Harvard Encyclopedia of American Ethnic Groups*, there has been relatively little sustained scholarship on many of the ethnic groups discussed in this essay. Unfortunately, despite frequent lip service given to multiculturalism, the general level of knowledge in America about east and east-central European Americans has not advanced very far beyond the "Dictionary of Races and Peoples" created by the Dillingham Commission some ninety years ago.

One of the most important sources for tracking these groups is the ancestry question on the U.S. Census Bureau's long form, which (although imperfect and based on a sample) provides a count of the self-identified members of each ethnic group. The 1980 count was the basis for James Paul Allen and Eugene James Turner's *We the People: An Atlas of America's Ethnic Diversity* (New York: Macmillan, 1988), which provided a more current geographical distribution even for small groups.

Perhaps the most important recent work has come from Europe and from European immigrant scholars in America, especially in the area of migratory patterns on the regional level: Julianna Puskás and Jószef Gellén on Magyars, of Matjaž Klemenčič on Slovenians, of Ladislav Tatják and Frantisek Bielik on Slovaks, of Jirí Koralka on Czechs, and Ewa Morawska on several east-central European groups. See, for example, Julianna Puskás, ed., *Overseas Migration from East-Central and Southeastern Europe, 1880–1940* (Budapest: Hungarian Academy of Sciences, 1990); Rudolph J. Vecoli and Suzanne Sinke, eds., *A Century of European Migrations, 1830–1930* (Urbana: Illinois University Press, 1991); Ewa Morawska, *For Bread with Butter: The Life Worlds of East-Central Europeans in Johnstown, Pennsylvania, 1880–1940* (Cambridge: Cambridge University Press, 1985); and her chapter, "East Europeans on the Move," in *The Cambridge Survey of World Migration*, edited by Robin Cohen (Cambridge: Cambridge University Press, (1996). Important work on the phenomenon of return migration, so vital to understanding the East European migratory experience, has also been undertaken on both sides of the Atlantic. See Mark Wyman, *Round Trip to America: The Immigrants Return to Europe, 1880–1930* (Ithaca: Cornell University Press, 1993).

There have been a few recent attempts at comprehensive studies of individual ethnic groups. Myron B. Kuropas has produced two works on Ukrainian Americans: *The Ukrainian Americans: Roots and Aspirations, 1884–1954* (Toronto: University of Toronto Press, 1991) and *Ukrainian-American Citadel: The First One Hundred Years of the Ukrainian National Association* (Boulder, CO: East European Monographs, 1997). Rusins have received a more popular treatment in Paul Robert Magosci's *Our People: Carpatho-Rusyns and Their Descendants in North America*, 3rd rev. ed. (Toronto: Multicultural History Society of Ontario, 1994). Recent works on Lithuanians include David Fainhauz's *Lithuanians in the U.S.A.: Aspects of Ethnic Identity* (Chicago: Lithuanian Library Press, 1991); and William Wolkovich-Valkavicus's encyclopedic *Lithuanian Religious Life in America: A Compendium of 150 Roman Catholic Parishes and Institutions* (Norwood, MA: n.p., 1991). Vituat Kipel's *Belarusy u ZshA* (Minsk: n.a., 1993) is the only major attempt at comprehensive study of Belarusins in the United States. Robert J. Donia and John V. A. Fine, Jr.'s *Bosnia and Hercegovina: A Tradition Betrayed* (New York: Columbia University Press, 1994) provides an explanation of Bosnian identity for a group that is understudied on both sides of the Atlantic.

Several older works on East European Americans have withstood well the test of time. These include Josef J. Barton, *Peasants and Strangers: Italians, Rumanians, and Slovaks in an American City, 1890–1950* (Cambridge, MA: Harvard University Press, 1975); Emily Balch Greene, *Our Slavic Fellow Citizens* (New York: Armor Press, 1969 [1910]); Victor R. Greene, *For God and Country: The Rise of Polish and Lithuanian Ethnic Consciousness in America, 1860–1910* (Madison: State Historical Society of Wisconsin, 1975); Greene, *The Slavic Community on Strike: Immigrant Labor in Pennsylvania Anthracite* (Notre Dame: Notre Dame University Press, 1968); M. Mark Stolarik, *Immigration and Urbanization: The Slovak Experience, 1870–1918* (Minneapolis: AMS Press, 1974).

Aside from some scattered articles and book chapters and local efforts, Czech Americans await an up-to-date, comprehensive study. See Frederick C. Luebke, *Ethnicity on the Great Plains* (Lincoln: University of Nebraska Press, 1981). Recently, however, a notable translation of Jan Habenicht's 1910 *History of Czechs in America* has appeared (St. Paul: Geck and Slovak Genealogical Society of Minnesota, 1996). Works on South Slavic groups include Nicolay Altankov's *The Bulgarian Americans* (San Carlos, CA:

n.a., 1979); Branko M. Colakovic's *Yugoslav Migrations to America* (San Francisco: R & E Research Associates, 1973); *The South Slavic Immigration in America* (Boston: 1978); and George J. Pipic's *The Croatian Immigrants in America* (New York: Philosophical Library, 1971). Comprehensive works on smaller groups like Albanians and Sorbians remain to be written.

FILIPINOS

Jon Cruz

Filipinos have been a significant part of the American mosaic since the beginning of the twentieth century. The earliest immigrants entered the United States shortly after the turn of the century when the Philippines became an American colonial possession in 1898. It remained a colony until 1934. While formal immigration from the Philippines began after American annexation, a much smaller and earlier Filipino settlement had earlier developed along the southern coast of the state of Louisiana. This settlement, which was already multigenerational by the late nineteenth century, grew from the descendants of Filipino seamen who escaped as early as 1765 from their forced servitude upon the Spanish galleons that linked Spain's colonial port of Manila with trade ports throughout North and South American continents. The Louisiana enclave marks the first settlement of people whom we today refer to as Asian and Pacific Americans.

Over the last century the Filipino-American population has taken shape through four distinct waves of immigration: *students, agricultural workers, U.S. military personnel,* and *professionals.* This introduction will provide an overview. Students and agricultural workers came as early as 1903 and continued to come in large numbers until the mid-1930s. By 1930 more than 121,700 had entered Hawaii to work in the sugar cane plantations, and another 45,000 were on the mainland. As U.S. "nationals," Filipinos were able to migrate freely until 1934. At that time formal immigration was drastically curtailed following the U.S. Congress's passage of the Tydings-McDuffie Act, which allowed for only 50 Filipinos to enter the United States per year. The number was increased to 100 in 1946, the year the Philippines gained its independence, and these formal immigration policies of virtual exclusion remained in effect until 1965, when the immigration laws were greatly liberalized. A small number of Filipinos also entered the United States prior to 1940 by serving in the navy and merchant marines. Indeed, 6,000 had served in the navy by World War I. But it was with the outbreak of World War II that Filipino enlistments in the U.S. military accounted for the resumption of immigration. Between 1945 and 1965 the route to American citizenship was not through formal immigration channels but through routes that were shaped by unprecedented opportunities for Filipinos to serve in the U.S. armed forces, particularly the navy. Prior to legislation in 1946 extending the right of naturalization to Filipinos, it was only through military service during wartime that Filipinos were eligible to acquire U.S. citizenship. In addition, Filipino spouses of U.S. citizens were able to immigrate, and this represented the first substantial opportunity for Filipino immigrants to maintain intact families.

Still, without formal immigration privileges, the Filipino-American population did not grow as rapidly as it would after the passage of the Immigration Act of 1965. Under the new immigration laws the Philippines was extended for the first time the same uniform immigration privileges enjoyed by all other nations. As a result, the Filipino-American population not only grew rapidly; it was transformed demographically and socially. In 1960 the Filipino population was slightly over 100,000. Five years after the liberalization of immigration, their numbers escalated to almost 300,000 in 1970, nearly 800,000 in 1980, and 1,407,000 in 1990. Unlike the early laborers or high school–educated military personnel, 80 percent of the immigrants who entered after 1965 were highly educated and technically skilled. In contrast to the predominantly male population that characterized the first wave, women now constitute at least 60 percent of the recent immigrants. The new immigration laws also allowed for family reunification, with immediate family members of kin who were already American citizens residing in the United States the ones most readily able to be reunited. Over the last thirty years, Filipinos have emerged as one of the fastest growing groups in America. Today, with more than 1.5 million, Filipino Americans constitute the largest Asian American group, and with approximately 70 percent being foreign-born, they represent a perpetually new segment of the American population. By the early twenty-first century their numbers will reach nearly 2 million.

COLONIAL LEGACIES

To understand the origins of the Filipino-American population and how immigration patterns have changed over the century, it is useful to note the impact of the colonial legacy upon the Philippines and its integration within changing global economies. Spain began colonization of the archipelago during the second half of the sixteenth century and held the Philippines for three and a half centuries. Spain's control ended with the Spanish-American War of 1898. However, by the end of the nineteenth century, the Philippines had been incorporated into a global system of agricultural trade based on the production of cash crops, such as sugar, tobacco, and hemp. The development of these cash crops coincided with a massive strategy of land dispossession that involved the uprooting of traditional communities and livelihoods. The agricultural export sector developed most intensely in the provinces of Northern Luzon, particularly in Ilocos Norte and Ilocos Sur. There, sugar cane cultivation had already transformed small landholders and the indigenous population into a subsistence-level peasantry. These factors helped prepare the conditions for the first large wave of immigration.

During the last decade of the nineteenth century, Filipino independence movements against Spain took shape increasingly in the form of armed conflict. When the U.S. Navy demolished the Spanish naval presence in Manila in 1898, Filipinos were in the process of declaring their national independence and establishing their own government. Meanwhile, having been defeated militarily, Spain ceded the Philippines to the United States for $20 million. Viewing the archipelago as a newly acquired colony, the United States refused to accept Filipino claims for independence and mounted a military campaign to resubjugate the population. Filipinos rejected American rule and responded with armed resistance. The result was the Philippine-American war that lasted until 1904, with significant skirmishes continuing until 1910. Estimations vary widely with regard to the number of Filipinos who died in the war, from 300,000 to nearly 1 million.

Under American rule, the United States marshaled teachers and missionaries to the new territory, much as they had done for the ex-slave population some thirty years earlier at the end of the American Civil War. Re-Christianized with a predominantly Protestant mission, educated with American materials, and immersed in the values, popular culture, and imagery of the United States, many Filipinos internalized in an idealized manner the cultural, economic, and political virtues of American society. U.S. annexation, however, did not alter the land-based oligarchic class structure rooted in the quasi-feudal mode of agricultural production; the land-based haciendas controlled by elite families (the legacy of the older Spanish *encomienda* system) were kept intact, and the importance of cash crops for export was intensified. As a result, the Filipinos from the Ilocos region became even more destitute during the first two decades of the twentieth century. When the American labor recruiters came from Hawaii in the early 1900s, they found a population that was not only already displaced but also a labor pool of young males that could be easily enticed to leave. The Ilocos region supplied more than two-thirds of the first wave of laborers to Hawaii and the mainland.

The Philippine economy was, and remains, largely dependent upon huge private landholdings and has a population that was, and continues to be, largely landless. Only a very fragile middle class has been able to develop throughout the twentieth century, and the deeper implications that stem from the colonial legacy continue to be felt in the contemporary dynamics of immigration. The presence of American-influenced educational institutions has facilitated the continued exodus of the nation's most educated, making the Philippines an exporter of both agricultural products and its most professional and skilled human capital, as well.

As residents of an American colony, Filipinos had the peculiar political identity of being "American nationals" or "wards." This distinction applied to Filipinos in the United States. Being a "national" entailed all the obligations but few of the rights of American citizenship. Filipino nationals could not vote, work in government, or own businesses or property in the United States. The Philippines remained a colonial possession of the United States until 1934 and was reclassified as a "Commonwealth" with the promise of independence after a ten-year period. Independence was granted in 1946, after the conflicts of World War II had subsided.

IMMIGRATION WAVES IN THE TWENTIETH CENTURY

Students

The earliest group of Filipinos to enter the United States were students who represented two distinct social classes: *pensionados* and *self-supported students*. *Pensionados*—government-supported students who were selected from wealthy and elite families—began coming in 1903. Their purpose was to obtain education and training and to return to the Philippines where they were to occupy leadership positions within civil, economic, and governmental institutions that were supervised by an American-installed colonial polity. They attended nearly every type of college and university across the United States. *Pensionados* were students at Columbia, Stanford, Northwestern, Purdue, Harvard, Princeton, Yale, University of Chicago, University of Minnesota, University of Oregon, University of California at Berkeley, and University of Washington. They also attended technical schools and four-year liberal arts institutions. In 1923, the New York–based student newsletter, the *Filipino Student Bulletin*, which functioned as a clearinghouse for Filipino students studying in America, estimated that there were at least 2,000 such students in the United States (at least that many were on the *Bulletin*'s mailing list). Toward the end of the 1920s the process of educating *pensionados* was largely complete.

As the wave of *pensionados* drew to an end, another type of Filipino student had begun to enter the colleges and universities in the United States. These students did not have the backing of political power, wealth, or family standing. They came from less-privileged and often poor families and were largely self-supporting. While some came as early as 1910, most entered the United States between 1920 and 1934. During the period between 1910 and 1938, approximately 14,000 such students came. To these students education represented a chance to lift their families from the poverty of landlessness and debt peonage. Most of these students, however, entered on the eve of the Great Depression of the 1930s and were caught in the cultural tide of an anti-Filipino sentiment that culminated in violence and exclusion by 1934. Like the *pensionados*, the self-supporting students also published newsletters. In 1934, one such student-run publication, *The Filipino Student*, addressed the concerns of self-supporting students and observed that "students were beset with more difficulties than before" and "the burden of the hardships are piling on them the more." Many of these students faced a sense of abandonment and failure. As victims of an economic crisis and as objects of intense anti-Filipino animosity, most were forced to abandon their dreams of obtaining an education; their hopes for success in the United States were shattered. As "American nationals" they had come freely to improve their chances of escaping the limited opportunities that had trapped their families at home in the Philippines. Not only did they fall again into poverty; it was clear that, by being reclassified as "aliens," they were no longer even wanted on American soil. Deeply marginalized and with intense shame, they had nothing to bring back to their homelands, and there was also little for them to return to. Although some did return to the Philippines, most stayed. And those who stayed were subjected to the increasingly negative political, economic, and cultural norms that surrounded the larger number of laborers. For the most part, the once aspiring students also became trapped in the low-paid migratory work that was available to the majority of Filipinos on the mainland.

Laborers

Laborers represented by far the largest influx of Filipinos to enter the United States between the opening years of the century and 1934. Their experiences were initially shaped by the labor demands that emanated from the sugar industry in the Hawaiian Islands. Shortly after the turn of the century, Hawaii had emerged as a major region for sugar production. Large-scale agricultural production also began to expand in the arable lands within the western states on the mainland. Recruited to work in both regions, Filipinos began coming first to Hawaii as early as 1906. By the early 1920s they were working in the fields of California, Oregon, Idaho, Montana, and Washington and the fish canneries in Alaska.

At the turn of the century Hawaii's labor force was already a multiethnic mixture of workers from China, Portugal, Germany, Norway, Korea, and Japan. Asians—Chinese, Japanese, and Koreans—constituted the bulk of the labor force that carried out the most harsh and backbreaking work. A powerful organization, the Hawaii Sugar Planters' Association (HSPA), had emerged to represent the growers. In regulating all labor policies and practices, the HSPA had already developed a model of labor diversification as a managerial strategy. Japanese workers had been brought in during the last decade of the nineteenth century to dilute the predominance of Chinese workers. However, by 1900 Japanese plantation workers had organized and begun carrying out strikes for better working conditions. Within a few years the HSPA began recruiting workers from the recently acquired Philippines. In 1906 the first fifteen recruited laborers from the Philippines disembarked from the SS *Doric* in Honolulu, marking the introduction of Filipinos as new laborers on the plantations and their incorporation into a plantation workforce that was rent with cross-ethnic tensions. The experiment with Filipino laborers soon became an increasingly institutionalized procedure, as Japanese workers continued to mobilize against the planters, and the source of Japanese labor from Japan began to dry up. With the passage of the Gentlemen's Agreement in 1907–1908 the Japanese government stopped issuing passports for laborers. Filipinos were still less than 1 percent of the labor force. However, in 1909 Japanese workers launched a strike massive enough to threaten the entire system of sugar production. It was in this context that the HSPA turned to a more intensive labor recruitment strategy in the Ilocos provinces of the Philippines to ensure an influx of workers numerous enough to destabilize Japanese workers. By 1919 Filipinos made up 30 percent of the plantation labor force. When Japanese immigration to Hawaii was formally terminated in 1924, the HSPA turned fully to the importation of Filipino labor, and their numbers soared. Between 1924 and 1930 an additional 44,000 Filipinos were brought to Hawaii, and by 1932 they constituted an overwhelming 70 percent of the labor force.

Many of the Filipino laborers were brought to Hawaii as contract laborers; they were to return to the Philippines after the completion of their contracts. However, the majority of these contract workers were actually inadvertent immigrants in the making. Of the 112,800 workers who entered Hawaii between 1909 and 1931, only 38,900, or 36 percent, returned to the Philippines. Most of them stayed in Hawaii, and—as free "American nationals"—18,600 went on to seek a better fate on the U.S. mainland. As nationals, Filipinos could enter the mainland with no restrictions, and their labor helped augment the expanding agricultural economies of the western states, particularly California's. Of the more than 45,000 Filipinos on the mainland in 1930, 30,500 resided in California. Unlike Hawaii, with its highly institutionalized, plantation-based, single-crop economy, the range and type of jobs and the location of work on the mainland fostered community instability and forced mobility. Filipinos worked in the vast agricultural regions throughout the western United States. They filled jobs that were cyclical and seasonal and followed migratory routes that stretched from San Diego, California, to Yakima, Washington, planting, cultivating, picking, and packing every crop grown. During the summer months, approximately 1 out of 10 Filipinos on the mainland worked in the fish canneries of Alaska. By the late 1920s nearly 4,000 Filipino "Alaskeros" passed annually through the canneries. While most held jobs that were of a migratory nature, a quarter of the Filipinos also held domestic and service jobs, such as hotel workers, cooks, dishwashers, waiters, busboys, and houseboys.

The majority of Filipinos in this first wave were young males, and the relative absence of Filipinas created skewed sex ratios that had long-lasting effects on the first generation of immigrants. Between 1906 and 1919 the sex ratio in

Hawaii averaged 8 Filipinos to every 1 Filipina (8:1), and it worsened as time went on. In 1920–1929 it was around 12:1, and in 1930–1934, it was 22:1. The paucity of Filipinas was similar on the mainland, where in 1920 it reached a staggering rate of 33:1 in Washington State. During the 1930s the sex ratio averaged 14:1 on the mainland. Women were not recruited for a variety of reasons. There were cultural prohibitions against women traveling without male accompaniment. Moreover, labor recruitment policies were designed for a short-term contract labor force rather than for family units. As a result, workers in the recruitment system were presumably not planning to be permanent immigrants. On the mainland the inescapable structure of forced mobility that came with migratory labor discouraged familial units.

Filipino families (including Filipina wives) did exist but were exceptions to the norms that eventually transformed many of these young men into aging bachelor societies. Nonetheless, Filipino men did seek out wives among available women. They married other Asian, Native American, black, Mexican, and white women. However, marriages with white women were fraught with difficulty since many states had cultural prohibitions against whites marrying non-whites, and some states, notably California, had antimiscegenation laws that ruled such marriages between whites and "Negroes, mulattos, or Mongolians" illegal. Classified as "Malays," Filipinos did not fit any of these racial categories. Then, in 1933, and on the eve of Filipino exclusion, the California state legislature amended the antimiscegenation laws to include the "Malay race" under marriage restrictions. Some states, such as Washington, had no such laws, and Filipinos married legally, although such marriages were frequently burdened with tremendous social ostracization. A large number of the workers never married, and after having spent their youthful bodies in the circuits of menial labor, they congregated where they could find lodging in large low-income hotels in such cities as Seattle, Stockton, San Francisco, and San Diego. The fortunate few among them managed to receive the meager Social Security funds for which they were eligible.

Dependent upon whatever jobs were available, Filipino workers were always vulnerable. In Hawaii they were given the worst living conditions and the lowest wages among the plantation system's multiethnic labor force, and the planters used them to undermine the unionization efforts of other workers. The inequality of labor, lodging, and wages were meant to divide Hawaii's workers, and to an extent, the planters were successful. However, in 1920, along with the smaller numbers of Chinese, Portuguese, and Spanish workers, the Filipino and Japanese workers overcame the older patterns of ethnically and racially segregated "blood unions," forged the first multiethnic strike in the history of Hawaii, and gave birth to the Hawaii Laborer's Association. Unionization efforts continued throughout the 1930s, and by 1950 Hawaii's plantation laborers were some of the best-paid agricultural workers in the United States.

Workers on the mainland confronted tremendous odds. Young, homesick, and lonely, they were easy prey for organized prostitution rings. "Taxi-dances"—

events at which workers could buy a string of tickets and then use each ticket to buy a minute-long embrace on the dance floor with a woman—were forms of leisure that quickly stripped the workers of their wages. They were also preyed upon by unscrupulous Japanese, Chinese, and Filipino labor contractors, who helped them land jobs but sometimes absconded with their pay. Destitution, moreover, bred contempt. Much more significant was the mounting resentment that the larger host communities began to feel toward Filipinos. By the late 1920s, the white population on the West Coast began to take direct action against the Filipino laborers. Filipinos had taken jobs that no other group wanted during the 1920s. However, as their numbers grew and as employers came to rely upon them as a cheap and politically powerless labor pool, white workers began to see the Filipinos as threats to their own economic security. Filipinos were viewed as "taking jobs" away from white workers and lowering the wage standards. This, in turn, was seen as ultimately detrimental to white labor.

This anti-Filipino sentiment grew in stages and had cultural as well as economic roots. As early as 1920 and continuing through 1927, Filipinos were frequently viewed as a "social menace." Opinion makers echoed the well-voiced litany of flaws possessed by racially marginalized and undesirable outsiders. Filipinos were "unwilling to assimilate" to American life; or, if they so desired, they were "incapable of assimilating" because they had the wrong values. Combined with these cultural faults was the presumed interplay of biological, hygienic, and sexual pathologies—Filipinos were "disease ridden" and sexually threatening to white women. By 1927 the negative frameworks took on an increasingly economic dimension. Filipinos were thus doubly despised because they were labeled a social menace and because they were accused of being "willing to work for the lowest wages."

Indeed, by 1927 the antagonism was maturing into collective violence. In Yakima, Washington, mobs and vigilante groups attacked Filipinos wherever they were encountered. Some were even assaulted in their homes, while others were forcibly rounded up and escorted to the outskirts of the town. The Filipinos in the Yakima area were somewhat unique in that they had actually developed and invested in small truck farms. Even in the face of such violence, they refused to leave. The anti-Filipino agitation that soon erupted in California was even more violent and had greater national ramifications. In the summer of 1930 several acts of mob violence took place in the area of Watsonville and Monterey. Over several days, white mobs numbering between 400 and 500 harassed a taxi-dance hall frequented by Filipinos. They attacked a Filipino community club and a farmworkers' bunkhouse, and two Filipinos were killed during the assaults.

By the time that the depression began to be felt in the early 1930s, there was an arsenal of negative attributes that fueled the resurgent anti-Asian xenophobia. Wages shrunk and many jobs evaporated. Racism became increasingly entwined with job opportunities. Filipinos, by virtue of their race and the jobs they held, became targets of virulent anti-Asian sentiments. The jobs that whites had long shunned, and that were held by Filipinos, Mexicans, and other minorities during the early 1920s, became increasingly coveted during the 1930s. As the depression took its toll across American society, the populist pressure to eject the Filipinos mounted. They had become victims of the new "yellow peril" that had been experienced by the Chinese and the Japanese immigrants before them.

By 1933 the Filipinos had been deeply marginalized and demonized. As colonials, they had been educated with American ideals and, as "nationals," they had assumed that the United States would help them shake loose the shackles of an older colonialism and pull them into democratic modernization. As immigrants in America, what they imaged and what they experienced were quite different. They had become a "social problem" that took on national significance, and their status and identity as nationals had become an issue. Being a national had always implied a partial inclusion, but the entire cultural context of the depression years had shifted toward a solution of total rejection. Meanwhile, Filipinos in the Philippines were intensifying their insistence on independence. In the end, the colonial legacy had resulted in the incorporation of Filipinos only as a cheap labor source for various agricultural interests in Hawaii and the western United States.

The Tydings-McDuffie Act of 1934 was, in part, a response to the animosity that the economic depression amplified toward Filipinos. With the new legislation, both the clamor for independence abroad and the growing xenophobia and social unrest at home were answered. The Philippines was transformed into a Commonwealth, and in ten years it was to be granted independence. Filipinos in Hawaii and in the United States were politically demoted, losing their status as nationals and being reclassified as "aliens." Immigration was also all but terminated, with an admission ceiling capped at merely 50 per year. In Hawaii the HSPA was able to negotiate a continuation of labor from the Philippines to ensure sugar production, but the Islands' Filipinos were no longer free to leave the plantations and relocate to the mainland. In addition to exclusion, a "repatriation" program was soon launched to remove Filipinos from American soil. While there were over 45,000 Filipinos residing in the United States, only 2,190 chose to be repatriated. The 50-per-year restriction on Filipino immigration remained in effect until 1946, when it was raised to 100 per year.

As they had done in Hawaii, Filipinos resisted the pressures of exploitation and exclusion. In Yakima, they had developed a unique farming enclave that enabled them to survive during the most ravaging years of the depression. And as the national depression deepened and jobs disappeared, even more Filipinos came to the shelter that the Yakima Filipino farmers provided. The lack of options, the total dependence on farming, and the desire to stay—even in the face of intense hostilities—forced the Yakima Filipinos to organize. By 1935, they had successfully pooled their resources to create the Filipino Marketing Cooperative. However, with the passage of the Tydings-McDuffie Act, Filipinos had become aliens. Under pressure from local growers, Washington's 1921 Alien Land Law, which had been designed to target Japanese immigrants, was amended in 1937 to apply to Filipinos. The result made it illegal for Filipinos to own, lease, or rent land; the amended law even prevented sharecropping. Thus, their newly found cooperative was deemed invalid, and twenty-one Filipino farmers were jailed.

Blocked from pursuing their only option for a livelihood, Filipinos responded by forming the Filipino Community of Yakima, Inc. As part of their struggle, Filipinos undertook an intensive letter-writing campaign in 1938 to President Franklin D. Roosevelt, other administration officials, the resident commissioner of the Philippines, and President Manuel Quezon of the Philippines Commonwealth. With the support of the (Native American) Yakima Tribal Council, Filipinos vigorously protested the state's amended Alien Land Act, publicized their local plight, obtained broader support from Philippine Commonwealth representatives, and called for investigations by additional state and federal agencies. Securing such attention helped stiffen their resistance to state laws aimed at dislodging members of the Filipino community from their economic base in farming. The Filipino community's appeal to the Yakima Indian Tribal Council was accepted favorably, and land leases were granted in 1941. The onset of World War II, however, transformed the situation. As the Philippines became a wartime ally of the United States, local anti-Filipino animosities lessened, and Filipinos were able to continue farming without restrictions.

Throughout California, Oregon, and Washington, Filipino farmworkers also began to unionize. These efforts were most significant in the state of California. In 1930 Filipino and Mexican workers in California went on strike to reject cuts in wages. Along with white workers, they formed the Agricultural Workers Industrial League. Although the League was destroyed by government intervention, Filipinos continued to be involved in progressive labor union activities and union reforms. From 1933 through 1936, at the height of exclusionary agitation, the Filipino Labor Union was at the forefront of organizing lettuce workers in the central California areas of Salinas and Watsonville. In 1936 Filipinos joined with Mexican workers and formed the Field Worker's Union; in 1940 the powerful American Federation of Labor supported and chartered the Filipino-based Federated Agricultural Laborers Association.

Although surrounded by intense animosity and corralled by the twin factors of economic depression and the curtailment of immigration, Filipinos did not see themselves as aliens but as belonging to their new home. In fighting for what they believed were the ideals for workers within a democracy, they pressed on with the fight for their right to organize and participate in government-sanctioned collective bargaining. The hard struggles to organize during the 1930s paved the way for the formation of the Agricultural Workers' Organizing Committee, which was joined in 1965 by the National Farm Workers' Association led by César Chávez in another multiethnic strike against grape growers in the San Joaquin Valley. The important United Farm Workers' union was formed out of this struggle. Filipinos had always formed organizations, but in addition to unions, new community-wide umbrella organizations emerged and reached out to Filipinos who belonged to different language groups and who came from different regions in the Philippines. These organizations were designed to mobilize them against the escalating hatred and marked a turning point among the first wave of immigrant workers.

In Hawaii and on the mainland, Filipino workers were central to the emergence of progressive changes within the attempts to organize agricultural labor, changes that helped transform the movement into a more inclusive and multiethnic institution, but they did not anticipate the animosity that would be leveled against them. Despite tremendous odds, they fought for their inclusion within a social and political ideal they felt was implied in their understanding of America.

Military Personnel

On the eve of World War II, the first large wave of Filipinos who sought to make their new homes in America had been met with social ostracization, violence, and political exclusion. Then a new wave began to come through war-induced changes. Although the Tydings-McDuffie Act curtailed formal immigration, Filipinos continued to enter through other avenues that were made possible by the outbreak of war. Immediately after the United States joined the war in December 1941, thousands of Filipinos attempted to enlist in the U.S. military. They were immediately rejected, because no formal provisions as yet existed that would have enabled these "nationals" to serve in the armed forces, for they were neither U.S. citizens nor resident aliens. In addition, the legacy of Filipino exclusion was still strong within the popular as well as political culture. However, two months after the United States entered the war, Manila fell to the Japanese. The war quickly altered the older exclusionary norms, and the United States resumed the role of protector of the Philippines. In the new climate of war, Filipinos gained a peculiar readmission into the American society. By the end of 1942, two all-Filipino infantry regiments of the U.S. Army had been formed, utilizing over 7,000 Filipinos. During 1944, 1,000 Filipino Americans were selected to infiltrate the Philippines, contact anti-Japanese underground groups, and gather intelligence for General Douglas MacArthur, who had established headquarters in Australia.

The military relations established during the war continued and were expanded after all hostilities subsided. In 1947 the Military Bases Agreement between the United States and the Philippines enabled the United States to lease twenty-three sites for military use, including the naval station at Subic Bay. The following year, the U.S. Information and Educational Exchange Act allowed Philippine nationals to enter the United States temporarily as students or college teachers. Through the act's program, Filipinos who returned to the Philippines for two years became eligible to apply for U.S. residency.

Most Filipinos who served in the military enlisted in the navy, and between 1944 and 1973, over 22,000 Filipinos donned navy uniforms. In order to qualify, they had to have a high school education and to be proficient in English. On the average, only 2 percent of those who applied were actually accepted. Once enlisted, most found themselves restricted to the rank of steward, with responsibilities that included dishwashing, table cleaning, mess hall duty, and attending as personal servants to officers. Although the navy had no formal policy with regard to the classification of Filipino enlistees, the segregation of Filipinos as stewards appeared as a routine and traditional practice. By 1970, 80 percent of the nearly 17,000 Filipino navy personnel were serving as stewards. In the wake of the U.S. civil rights movement, and after having received negative press coverage over segregation practices in the military, the navy began to reform this pattern of racial segregation. However, all of these military developments that stemmed from the "special relations" between the United States and the Philippines enabled Filipino enlistees to bypass the formal immigration restrictions that had been put into place by the Tydings-McDuffie Act of 1934. The Philippines was the only nation from which the U.S. military systematically recruited large numbers of noncitizens into the armed forces.

The relationship between the U.S. military and Filipino servicemen significantly transformed the Filipino-American population. Prior to the influx of Filipinos through the military, the Filipino-American population was largely poorly educated, predominantly male, and tied to menial and migratory labor. With the second wave, of military-related immigrants, the Filipino-American population took on new characteristics. Military personnel were at least high school educated, and their dependents were recognized as family members. Thus, in addition to citizenship opportunities, military service facilitated the presence of nuclear and even extended families on U.S. soil. Since the mid-1970s, as a result of navy enlistment, Filipino-American communities have taken hold in cities with naval stations, including San Diego, California; Bremerton, Washington; Jacksonville, Florida; and Charleston, South Carolina.

Yet as this century comes to a close, many Filipino-American military veterans ironically find themselves petitioning the U.S. government to fulfill promises made to them more than fifty years ago. In 1941, enlistees were initially promised full military benefits as well as U.S. citizenship. Congress reneged on that pledge in 1946 when the Philippines was granted independence, leaving veterans feeling betrayed. With the 1990 immigration law, Congress restored to Filipino-American veterans the opportunity to acquire citizenship rights, and 16,870 took advantage of that between 1991 and 1995. However, Congress did not deal with the promises of benefits, and in June 1997, aging Filipino-American war veterans chained themselves together and launched a protest in MacArthur Park, Los Angeles, demanding those benefits.

Professional and Skilled Immigrants

The Immigration Act of 1965 represents a watershed event for the Filipino-American population. More than any other event, the lifting of restrictions upon Philippine immigration altered the size and profile of the Filipino community in

America. Under the new provisions a uniform immigration ceiling of 20,000 for independent nations was applied to the Philippines, including the same preferences that applied to all other nations. Thus, immediate relatives of U.S. citizens (e.g., parents, spouse, minor children) were classified as special immigrants and admitted "nonquota" (over and above the 20,000), whereas others (e.g., older children and siblings) could qualify for one of three family reunification preferences, and immediate family members of legal residents could apply under a separate preference. Since 1965, Filipinos seeking to emigrate have often exercised these options. Throughout the 1970s, the actual number of immigrants who annually came to the United States was approximately 30,000; since 1986 the number has exceeded 50,000 per year—well over 60,000 annually between 1990 and 1993.

The new immigration policies also gave specific preference to "professional, technical, and kindred workers"—in essence the most educated within a nation. As a result, concerns over the problem of "brain drain" have arisen during the last few decades as the Philippines continues to lose a significant proportion of its most educated individuals. The United States, however, clearly benefited from the influx of the Philippine's best trained. In the late 1960s, approximately 70 percent of Filipino immigrants fell in the categories of teacher, accountant, engineer, nurse, or physician. Five years after the immigration laws were changed, immigrant professionals from just the Philippines and India came to outnumber those from all European nations combined. Since the mid-1970s, the Philippines has been a major supplier of professionals to the United States, and among these have been those with advanced medical or medically related training. The influx of medical professionals was in response to demands that stemmed from the expansion of the Medicare and Medicaid programs in the United States and the corresponding shortage of skilled workers to service these programs. But political conditions in the Philippines also added significantly to the exodus of middle-class intellectuals. In 1971 Philippine President Ferdinand Marcos used the pretext of communist insurgency to suspend the electoral process and to install his leadership in perpetuity. Under martial law, Philippine society grew increasingly repressive, and political alliances rather than intellectual, educational, or technical skills played the greater role in shaping the fate of Filipinos. Between 1965 (when Marcos was elected) and 1986 (when he was deposed), 300,000 Filipinos left the country for the United States.

Politics aside, the preponderance of medically trained individuals was phenomenal. By 1970, an estimated 13,500 nurses had immigrated to the United States, and throughout the 1970s, one-fifth of all the nurses trained in the Philippines left for the United States. The pattern has continued. By the early 1980s, professionals deepened their abandonment of a political economy that could not absorb and utilize them. Twenty-five percent of the physicians and surgeons, 38 percent of the dieticians, and over 40 percent of the pharmacists and dentists who immigrated to the United States came from the Philippines. In the early 1980s exiled Philippine Senator Raul Manglaupus argued that the Philippines had sent around 15,000 medical doctors to the United States. According to Manglaupus, it took on average $150,000 to train a physician in the United States, and multiplying this figure by 15,000 immigrant physicians, Manglaupus argued that the Philippines was in effect contributing $2.25 billion to the United States. Regardless of the logic or accuracy, the problem illustrates the significance of the human capital that the Philippines has provided by way of recent immigration. Beyond all doubts, the influx of skilled medical workers from the Philippines has contributed greatly to medical services in the United States.

Professional immigrants have fared much better economically than the earlier waves. However, their high educational background has not always automatically translated into employment levels comparable to their training. For decades Filipina nurses have complained of being denied promotions and given less challenging jobs. In some cases, physicians have been stymied by state licensing requirements and have had to take low-paying jobs unrelated to their fields in order to survive while preparing to gain entry into their professions. Complicating the employment options of professionals is the perception that their training is substandard to that provided in the United States. Speaking English with an accent has also been a factor in the downward mobility of Filipino professionals. Still, since 1965 the third wave of professionals and highly skilled immigrants has settled across the United States, with medical workers being particularly recruited to large urban areas in midwest and northeastern states and many major urban hospitals absorbing the thousands of nurses, lab technicians, and physicians.

However, the Philippine government has recently acknowledged that since the late 1980s Filipinos residing in the United States, Australia, and other countries have sent on the average more than $683 million per year in remittances back to the Philippines. Massive underemployment in the Philippines has therefore been partially mitigated by the export of its most skilled workers, who, in turn, funnel U.S. dollars (or other currency) back into the Philippines. Equally revealing of this pattern is that more than 80 percent of Filipino migrants have at least completed high school, a stark contrast to the general population's high school completion rate of only 6 percent.

FILIPINOS IN CONTEMPORARY AMERICA

The combination of navy and professional immigrants continuing to exercise their options for family reunification has resulted in significant population growth beyond Hawaii and California. The Filipino population in Chicago, which had a substantial Filipino presence in the 1930s, doubled between 1960 and 1970. In that decade, the number of Filipinos in Newark and Jersey City, Pittsburgh, Cleveland, Norfolk, Charleston, and Jacksonville quadrupled. While Filipinos are now dispersed throughout the United States, the overall population reflects a strong preference for California and Hawaii. In 1990 California had 731,685 Filipinos, making it the state with the largest number of Filipinos, followed by Hawaii (168,682), Illinois (64,224), New York (62,259), and New Jersey (53,146). Filipinos also constitute the largest Asian/Pacific American group in California, Illinois, Washington, Virginia, and Florida, and their national population will relatively soon exceed 2 million.

Like most other immigrant groups, Filipino Americans have a long history of forming voluntary community organizations. These organizations run the gamut from social clubs and organizations serving immigrants from a particular hometown, geographic region, or language group to masonry organizations and labor unions. Professional and educational associations have proliferated more recently. In each case, organizations have provided and continue to provide members with an important sense of group solidarity and a sense of place. Yet, in comparison to other Asian-American groups, Filipino Americans have not generated organizations effective in speaking to and representing them as an ethnic group within the larger American context. The result is that Filipino Americans continue to be somewhat invisible in proportion to their growing numbers. The preference for more intimate and local organizations reflects the absence of nationwide coordination, the legacy of social, political, and economic fractures that developed under the long epoch of colonialism and the correspondingly weak Philippine polity vulnerable to other transnational currents. Similarly, the lack of visible economic entrepreneurialism among Filipino Americans is related to the lack of such opportunities among immigrants who come from a political economy steeped in land-based oligarchic rule, the absence of such an established economic class with networking ties within the American context, and the preferences within U.S. immigration laws for professional and skilled human capital. Nonetheless, voluntary associations provide Filipino Americans with indispensable strategies of identity maintenance, and a possible foreshadowing of change was the conference of 1,000 in Washington, D.C., in August 1997 that agreed to establish the National Federation of Filipino Associations (NFFA), with its principal office in the nation's capital.

In 1906 the first few Filipinos stepped onto Hawaiian land to work in the sugar cane plantations. In 1996 Hawaii elected its first Filipino-American governor, Ben Cayetano. Reflecting on the hatred, persecution, and violence aimed at Filipinos on the West Coast during the 1930s, Filipino-American writer Carlos Bulosan wrote that "it was a crime to be a Filipino." Today, the literature of such Filipino Americans as Bulosan, N.V.M. Gonzalez, Bienvenido N. Santos, and Jessica Hagedorn and the writings of literary theorist E. San Juan, Jr., are treated as serious contributions to the intellectual offerings of ethnic and American studies across the United States. A mere thirty years ago few Filipino-American students appeared in the colleges and universities, the result of earlier norms of segregation and exclusion. Today, in states where they are more populous, Filipino-American students represent one of the fastest-growing segments attending colleges and universities. According to 1995 census data, approximately one third of the new immigrants have obtained a bachelor's degree or a graduate or professional degree. It is common, wherever Filipino-American communities have been established, to find one or several local newspapers launched by, and designed to serve, Filipino Americans, such as the *Kapitbahan*, in Ventura, California, and the *Philippine Times*, which serves the greater San Francisco area. These organs of cultural communication are vibrant indexes of the profile and activities of such communities. Although Filipinos have not established the kind of ethnic and entrepreneurial enclaves that are associated with the Chinatown and, more recently, the Korea towns that can be found on both the East and West Coasts, the beginnings of small independent businesses are increasingly evident in areas that have had a steady influx of immigrants, such as Daly City, south of San Francisco. As one of the fastest-growing groups in the United States, Filipinos are rapidly becoming an increasingly salient group within American society.

Over the twentieth century the forces and events that have shaped the lives of Filipinos who have made the decision to leave their homelands to become permanently part of American society have been multiple and complex. In the Philippines, the enduring entrenchment of a feudalistic and oligarchic social structure that lies beneath the veneer of democracy continues to propel its people, poor as well as professional, to leave. The intimate ties between the United States and the Philippines, ties that run deep politically, economically, and culturally, have shaped as well the burgeoning segment of Filipinos within the American mosaic. As a group that has continued to be nearly 70 percent foreign-born, Filipino Americans live with an intractable sense of globalism in which developments that affect the Philippines continue to reverberate in their communities in the United States as they remake their lives as Americans.

BIBLIOGRAPHIC REFERENCES

The significance of the colonial legacy and its impact on both the rise of the agricultural export economy in the Philippines and the early Filipino diaspora is treated in Miriam Sharma's two essays, "The Philippines: A Case of Migration to Hawaii, 1906–1946" and "Labor Migration and Class Formation among the Filipinos in Hawaii, 1906–1946." Both can be found in *Labor Immigration under Capitalism: Asian Workers in the United States Before World War II*, edited by Lucie Cheng and Edna Bonacich (Berkeley: University of California Press, 1984), pp. 337–58, and 579–611, respectively. Useful, too, is John Larkin, "Philippine History Reconsidered: A Socioeconomic Perspective," *American Historical Review* 87.3 (June 1982): 595–628. The Philippine-American War is insightfully discussed in Walter L. Williams, "United States Indian Policy and the Debate over Philippine Annexation: Implications for the Origins of American Imperialism," *Journal of American History* 66.4 (March 1980): 810–831; and Luzviminda Francisco, "The First Vietnam—The Philippine-American War 1899–1902," in *Letters in Exile: An Introductory Reader on the History of Filipinos in America*, edited by UCLA Asian American Studies Center (Los Angeles: UCLA, 1976), pp. 1–22. The early Filipino settlement in Louisiana has been surveyed by Maria E. Espina, *Filipinos in Louisiana* (New Orleans: A. F. Laborde & Sons, 1988).

Assessments of the first Filipinos in Hawaii can be found in Roman R. Cariaga, *The Filipinos in Hawaii: Economic and Social Conditions 1906–1936* (San Francisco: R & E Research Associates, 1974); Sister Mary Dorita, *Filipino Immigration to Hawaii* (San Francisco: R & E Research Associates, 1975 [1954]); Luis V. Teodoro, Jr., ed., *Out of This Struggle: The Filipinos in Hawaii* (Honolulu: University Press of Hawaii, 1981); Marcelino A. Foronda, Jr., "America Is in the Heart: Ilokano Immigration to the United States, 1906–1930," *Bulletin of the American Historical Collection* 4.4 (October 1976): 46–73; and Ronald Takaki, *Pau Hana: Plantation Life and Labor in Hawaii* (Honolulu: University of Hawaii Press, 1983). Edward D. Beechert's *Working in Hawaii: A Labor History* (Honolulu: University of Hawaii Press, 1983) provides an excellent historical context for Filipinos within a broader history of labor in Hawaii.

The plight of Filipino laborers on the mainland is presented in a number of Emory S. Bogardus's essays, including "American Attitudes towards Filipinos," *Sociology and Social Research* 14.1 (September–October 1929): 59–69; "The Filipino Press in the United States," *Sociology and Social Research* 18.6 (July–August 1934): 581–585; and "Filipino Repatriation," *Sociology and Social Research*, 21.1 (September–October 1936): 67–71; and H. Brett Melendy, "California's Discrimination against Filipinos, 1927–1935," in *The Filipino Exclusion Movement—1927–1935*, Occasional Papers No. 1, edited by J. M. Saniel, (Quezon City: Institute of Asian Studies, University of the Philippines, 1967), pp. 1–10. Howard A. DeWitt's studies of labor antagonisms in California can be found in "The Filipino Labor Union: The Salinas Lettuce Strike of 1934," *Amerasia* 5.2 (1978): 1–21, and "The Watsonville Anti-Filipino Riot of 1930: A Case Study of the Great Depression and Ethnic Conflict in California," *Southern California Historical Quarterly* 61.3 (Fall 1979): 291–302. For an analysis of the context in which antimiscegenation laws were applied to Filipinos, see Nellie Foster, "Legal Status of Filipino Intermarriages in California," *Sociology and Social Research* 16.5 (May–June 1932): 441–454.

Recent immigration and its relationship to "brain drain" are studied in Peter C. Smith, "The Social Demography of Filipino Migrations Abroad," *International Migration Review* 10.3 (Fall 1976): 307–353; Ernesto M. Pernia, "The Question of the Brain Drain from the Philippines," *International Migration Review* 10.1 (Spring 1976): 63–72; Charles B. Keely, "Philippine Migration: Internal Movements and Emigration to the United States," *International Migration Review* 7.2 (Summer 1973): 177–187; and Josefina Jayme Card, "The Aftermath of Migration to the U.S. versus Return Home: Data from the 1970 Cohort of Filipino Graduate Students in the U.S," *Philippine Sociological Review* 30 (1982): 63–77. An important study on nurses is presented in Richard Joyce and Chester Hunt, "Philippine Nurses and the Brain Drain," *Social Science and Medicine* 16.12 (1982): 1223–1233. See also the *Asian and Pacific Migration Journal* 2.3 (1993) for a special issue devoted to the Philippine Islands and the emigration of professionals.

Bruno Lasker's *Filipino Immigration to Continental United States and to Hawaii* (Chicago: University of Chicago Press, 1931) remains a historically specific classic. Important general overviews are found in John H. Burma, *Spanish-Speaking Groups in the United States* (Durham: Duke University Press, 1954), chap. 5; and H. Brett H. Melendy, "Filipinos in the United States," *Pacific Historical Review* 43.4 (1974): 520–547. Comparative histories of Asian Americans in general with insightful assessments of Filipino Americans can be found in Sucheng Chan, *Asian Americans: An Interpretive History*

(Boston: Twayne Publishers, 1991), and Ronald Takaki, *Strangers from a Different Shore: A History of Asian Americans* (New York: Penguin, 1989). An excellent introductory essay on Filipinos along with an extensive bibliography is available in Yen Le Espiritu, *Filipino American Lives* (Philadelphia: Temple University Press, 1995).

FRENCH, FRENCH CANADIANS, AND CAJUNS

Bruno Ramirez and François Weil

According to the 1990 census of population, over 10.3 million Americans claimed a French ancestry, another 2.2 million reported a French-Canadian ancestry, and some 668,000 a Cajun (or Acadian) one. In all, over 13 million Americans considered themselves members of either French, French-Canadian, or Cajun ancestry groups—over 5 percent of the country's total population. By no means do these groups constitute a unified or unifying entity—a "French America" of some sort. Their personal and collective history, their experiences of migration and adjustment, differ considerably. So does their historiography: Whereas French Canadians and Cajuns have been studied and analyzed in depth in the last three decades, historians are only beginning to describe the French experience. This diversity of personal experience and historiographical fate suggests that, as will be shown below, there was not one but many "French Americas."

SOCIOGRAPHY OF MIGRATION

The French, French Canadians, and Cajuns experienced very different patterns of migration to the United States. At the beginning of the nineteenth century, a French presence in the United States was largely linked to three historically distinct movements of population. First, French Huguenots, victims of Louis XIV's religious intolerance, immigrated to British North America in the 1680s and the 1690s, settling mostly in the colonies of Massachusetts, New York, and South Carolina. Second, in the late seventeenth century and the first half of the eighteenth century, French Catholic immigrants immigrated to then French Louisiana and settled along the Mississippi River. Last, during the French Revolution numerous French émigrés decided to cross the Atlantic to safety. France's earlier defeat in the Seven Years' War (1763), however, followed now by the Louisiana Purchase (1803), symbolized the end of that era of French presence in North America, despite the fact that its colonial developments help explain later traits of settlement, in Louisiana, for instance.

French people had a long tradition of European intracontinental migration since the Middle Ages. Thus, what changed after 1820 was not that French people decided to migrate but rather that they, like many other Europeans, decided to migrate to Latin and North America and particularly to the United States. Between the 1820s and the 1920s, several hundred thousand French men and women migrated to the United States, mostly to the states of New York, California, Louisiana, and Illinois. Their emigration was not a nationwide phenomenon, and probably not even a regional one; a better unit of analysis seems to be the canton (county), since migrants came from some very specific villages and towns and not others. Most of those centers of out-migration were located in Alsace and Lorraine, the Massif Central, the Pyrenees, and the Alps—all regions on France's national periphery.

It is easier to explain why so few French men and women emigrated by comparison with other European countries than to account for the reasons of departure of those who did migrate. In the eighteenth and nineteenth centuries France experienced both an early decline in birthrates and a fall of mortality rates, which together led to a reduced growth in population. This evolution, or demographic transition, led to reduced population pressures. It also helped maintain France's tradition of small farm property and rural industries. As elsewhere in Europe, many rural French men and women were able to work on the farm and be employed part-time in rural factories, thus remaining on the land rather than leaving the countryside. Indeed, those who left usually came from places where that demographic transition took place at a lesser degree or at a later date. Some of these places fed the major internal migrations to French cities; from other areas, however, usually frontier regions that were culturally and politically less integrated in the nation-state under construction, migrants left for the Americas, particularly the United States and, to a lesser extent, Argentina. Yet others left for America from the cities, particularly Paris, in what was often a secondary migration following a first move from the countryside to the national capital. Until World War I, the ports of Le Havre and Bordeaux, more than Marseilles and Bayonne, channeled the movement toward New York, New Orleans, and San Francisco. Thus, French migrants seemingly belonged to two main social groups: in the one, farmers, farm laborers, or younger sons from farming background; in the other, artisans, small businessmen, and members of the professions—groups that apparently were overrepresented in French communities throughout the United States. Yet still others were industrial workers, headed for the mining districts and steel mills of Pennsylvania.

The French-Canadian case was different. Before their migration to the United States took on the character of a mass exodus, French Canadians were present in a variety of regions. It was a presence largely linked to the fur trade, an activity for which the skills of French Canadians had long been in demand. Not surprisingly, this presence was most visible in the numerous trading posts that dotted the Great Lakes region as well as the Mississippi Valley. By the middle of the nineteenth century, many of these enclaves had developed into communities playing an important role in attracting new immigrants from French Canada. The familiarity with the fluvial system of transportation, easier access to farmland, and the growing development of the forestry and mining industries made the Midwest—and in particular, Michigan, Illinois, and Wisconsin—the main region of destination for French-Canadian immigrants. After the Civil War and up to the 1920s, the Midwest continued to be an important region of destination but was now surpassed by New England.

To be sure, these early migrations were part of a wider westward movement occurring on a continental scale. However, two related developments in particular turned Quebec into a leading region of exodus. One was a long and severe agricultural crisis that placed a heavy toll on commercial farming, forcing a majority of medium-and small-size farmers to survive on a subsistence economy. It began to manifest itself in the 1830s and resulted from the relative scarcity of arable land, from a series of natural disasters, and more important, from the growing competition of western farming (Ontario and the American Midwest). The other development was the rapid population growth due to an exceptional fertility rate. As the old seigneuries and parishes along the St. Lawrence River became overcrowded, many landless Quebecers sought a solution in the back-country—a solution encouraged by the elites and that resulted in an important settlement movement (colonization) in various parts of Quebec. The majority, however, sought a solution in the growing labor markets developing south of the border. Mostly, they were small farmers and farm laborers. Some moved temporarily as single men, but increasingly their migration would become a permanent one and involve the entire family unit.

The linkage of Montreal and other Quebec centers with the U.S. northeastern railway network and the growing importance of manufacturing production were crucial factors that channeled the exodus toward the New England region. Soon after the Civil War, industrial New England became by far the leading destination, maintaining this position until the movement came to an end in the late 1920s. By 1900, French Canadians had become one of the leading ethnocultural communities in New England, as they constituted approximately 10 percent of the region's population. Their presence in the various New England states was, of course, unequal. It was strongest in New Hampshire, where they constituted 18.5 percent of the state's population, and lowest in Connecticut (4.3 percent). But the state that by far attracted the largest number was Massachusetts. It took a lead during the 1860s as the preferred destination and held it throughout the duration of the immigration movement. By 1900, nearly half the entire French-Canadian population of New England resided in Massachusetts, a proportion that grew significantly during the twentieth century.

As for Cajuns, they had originally emigrated from France to Acadia (today's New Brunswick) in the seventeenth century. Their frontier colonial experience and geographic isolation led to the development of a specific Acadian identity, as distinct from the Laurentian French-Canadian or the Anglo-American experience. Following decades of struggle between England and France and numerous transfers of sovereignty of Acadia between the two countries, Acadians' sense of independence and resistance to British attempts to assimilate them led, in the mid-1750s, to Britain's decision to expel the Acadian settlers. During what came to be known as the Grand Dérangement, deported Acadians, preferring cultural transplantation rather than assimilation, settled and resettled in various parts of the North Atlantic regions. Some went to France, others to the French West Indies or to the British colonies of Maryland and Pennsylvania—neither group being welcomed but instead feared and reviled. By the 1760s a number of Acadians were attracted to Louisiana, then under Spanish rule, where land was reportedly available, political rule lax, and a French influence visible. In all, from 2,000 to 3,000 Acadians established themselves in Louisiana during the 1760s, and another 1,600 immigrants arrived in the mid-1780s. Despite the present generalizations about "Cajun Country," original patterns of settlement are now well known. Acadians established themselves in two regions. First in the 1760s and then in the 1780s, some of them settled in the eastern part of Louisiana along the Mississippi River and northern Bayou Lafourche. Others went west, crossing the Atchafalaya River and establishing insular settlements in the fertile yet then undeveloped prairies of the Attapakas, Opelousas, and Vermilion River valley areas.

PATTERNS OF ADJUSTMENT

Acadians transplanted in late eighteenth-century Louisiana exhibited a remarkable degree of pragmatism and flexibility while preserving the core of Acadian culture. Within a few years of their arrival in the lower Mississippi Valley, they had adapted their economic pursuits, culinary skills and tastes, traditional wardrobe, and housing styles to their new subtropical environment. At the same time Louisiana Acadians maintained such traditional values as frugality, independence, and reliance on family structures. Indeed, it is the strength and solidarity of familial ties and cooperative networks, free from outside interference, that ensured community cohesiveness. By the 1800s, however, and throughout the first half of the nineteenth century, Louisiana Acadians were confronted with numerous economic, political, and sociocultural tensions that resulted in social stratification and differentiation within the formerly homogeneous communities. In the postbellum period, the co-optation of the small Acadian upper and middle class by the dominant Anglo-American elite resulted in the retention of Acadian identity only by the majority of impoverished Acadians, or Cajuns. As a consequence, Cajun identity was associated with social and cultural inferiority until the ethnic revival of the 1970s.

Depending on their own personal background, French immigrants went through very different experiences in the United States. Artisans, businessmen, and professionals were confronted with the realities of an urban society quite different from the one they knew in France. Rural French migrants had to adjust not only to America but also to a new urban and industrial life setting. All French migrants, however, shared in the discovery of, and necessary adaptation to, an alien social and cultural universe. Some attempted to blend into their new country. Others decided to create in the United States social and cultural institutions that would help them maintain their premigratory traditions. Of these, most were regional or local cultural and linguistic traditions—from Alsace, Aveyron, the Basque country or Béarn; others were, in a more traditional sense, French. Both "regional" and "national" cultural institutions thus developed in such American cities as New York, San Francisco, New Orleans, or Chicago. Their growth resulted in the emergence of a dual French institutional network in these urban centers, which in turn eased the ethnicization of many migrants from France: From peasants they became Frenchmen—in America's cities. This institutional network was articulated around Catholic churches and parochial schools, French national and regional societies, and French newspapers. For reasons that remain unexplained up to now—perhaps because French immigrants were not very numerous or because they had confidence enough in their social position or their ethnic culture so as not to feel threatened by a competing process of cultural integration—French ethnic institutions were usually not enclaves of cultural traditionalism, or at least not for long. Rather, these institutions constituted collective vehicles to facilitate immigrant adjustment in the host society.

Not unlike French immigrants, the majority of French-Canadian immigrants had to undergo a rapid transition from a rural-agrarian to an urban-industrial society, although a minority of them had known urban work and life in cities, notably Montreal, Sorel, or Quebec. Whether migrating to Houghton (Michigan) or Lowell (Massachusetts), their access to the means of sustenance entailed confronting new work experiences, a different language, an alien religious universe, and a civic culture that demanded total allegiance to the values of the American Republic.

French Canadians proved more capable of adjusting to the new work context than to the cultural and institutional environment in which they lived. To be sure, whether in forestry, mining, or manufacturing, their labor was more often than not in great demand. Still, French Canadians were quite willing to submit themselves to harsh working conditions even when this entailed—as in textile manufacturing—long hours, serious health hazards, and low wages. More difficult was their interaction with a social and cultural environment they often perceived as hostile and threatening to a way of life that they wished to preserve. To accomplish that, they sought as much as possible to re-create in the heart of urban-industrial America the institutions, associations, and forms of social interaction that would allow them to transplant and keep alive their language and their cultural traditions. This process of institution building was uneven and influenced by local circumstances. It was more limited and short-lived in the Midwest, where greater residential dispersion and more varied occupational opportunities, coupled with the smaller number of the French-Canadian population, favored a more rapid integration into local institutions. In the region of greater concentration, New England, French Canadians created a richer and more lasting institutional network that included Catholic parish schools, hospitals, orphanages, and mutual aid societies, such as the Société Saint-Jean-Baptiste de Bienfaisance, founded in 1872, and the Association Canado-Américaine. Newspapers were a leading part of this institutional network, and some of them, such as *Le Travailleur, L'Opinion publique, L'Indépendant*, and *L'Avenir National*, exerted an influence throughout the New England region.

Within this institutional network, articulate leaders preached untiringly the moral duty of surviving as islands of French Canadianness. It was a communal strategy that often resulted in conflictual relations with the Irish-dominated Catholic hierarchy, with the labor reform movements, and with a public opinion that looked down on ethnic isolation. Community leaders, for instance, had to constantly put pressure on the local dioceses to obtain national parishes headed by French-Canadian priests. And when an 1881 Massachusetts government report called French Canadians "the Chinese of the East," they were appalled by this "official" manifestation of nativism and rallied the community so as to present to the host society the more realistic image of an honest and hardworking population that had become an integral part of the New England universe.

The French-Canadian Catholic national parish was the center of the institutional network. That the creation of such parishes was a leading priority is shown by their rapidly growing number. Between 1867 and 1891, 86 of them had been founded in the various dioceses of New England. Their number multiplied considerably during the following two decades, and by 1909, 202 national parishes (along with 101 missions) served the religious needs of the New England French-Canadian population. It was here that the torch of language, faith, and traditions was kindled by priests who had mostly been educated in Quebec. In this, they were aided by the numerous newspapers that sprang up in virtually all major areas of settlement and by a variety of mutual aid societies and cultural associations. To ensure that their children would not succumb to alien influences, French-Canadian leaders invested much effort in the creation of private schools whose curricula were designed to preserve the French language and inculcate ancestral traditions. It was a strategy that bore its fruits, judging from the vitality displayed by many "Little Canadas."

But as the population grew more diversified occupationally, and as the U.S.-born generations made up the overwhelming majority, French Canadians saw the benefits of integration while preserving the basic features of an ethnic identity. This awareness was dictated by the important demographic shift in the French-Canadian population of New England that occurred during the first decade of the twentieth century, when the portion of the U.S.-born population (mostly second and third generations) surpassed for the first time the number of those born in Canada. This transition resulted from the steady decline in the volume of immigration that had begun during the 1890s and from the natural growth of the population already residing in the United States. The massive resurgence in immigration that occurred in the 1920s did little to reverse that trend, and by 1930, nearly two out of three individuals of French-Canadian stock were born in the United States.

ECONOMIC INTEGRATION

Acadians brought with them from Nova Scotia various agricultural and ranching skills, which they quickly adapted to their new surroundings. Prairie Acadians took advantage of the region's excellent grasslands and engaged primarily in ranching. As early as the 1770s, Acadian livestock production was large enough to allow their owners to drive surplus herds of cattle to the New Orleans market and slaughterhouse. At the same time, prairie Acadians also engaged in subsistence agriculture, growing corn, cotton, and vegetables for home consumption. River Acadians, on the other hand, neglected ranching but specialized in agriculture, slowly and painfully clearing small sections of waterfront land, adapting to the subtropical climate, fighting flooding, and learning to grow maize, cotton, beans, and rice. The emergence of a small Acadian slaveholding planter elite in the early nineteenth century, and the widening gap between them and the majority of Acadian small, agricultural surplus producers or ranchers, testified to the group's growing socioeconomic stratification and diversification— one that included planters, farmers, ranchers, artisans, professionals, and laborers. Throughout the antebellum period, economic prosperity generally accompanied Acadians' acceptance of material values. The Civil War, however, had major socioeconomic consequences for the Acadians. It led to the extinction of the planter elite and to the pauperization of many farmers into landless laborers. Antebellum economic diversity gave way to a two-tiered economic structure of a small elite of wealthy farmers and professionals and large masses of impoverished small farmers and day laborers—a situation that lasted well into the twentieth century and the economic rebirth of Louisiana after World War II.

Unlike Acadians, a majority of French immigrants congregated in large urban centers, but unlike French Canadians they did not concentrate primarily in industrial occupations. A few were professionals; some were businessmen, merchants, and clerks; the majority were artisans, skilled workers, or domestics. According to the 1870 federal census of population, out of every 100 French-born immigrants to the United States, about one-third were artisans or industrial workers, about one-fourth worked in the service sector, one-seventh in business, and the remaining one-fourth in agriculture. New Orleans's French butchers, San Francisco's French laundry cleaners, New York's French cabinetmakers— and all over the country French music and dance teachers, hotel and restaurant managers, clerks, waiters, and cooks—were visible French ethnic features of urban America. By the last decades of the nineteenth century, French Americans' concentration in service sectors facilitated their entry into the white-collar middle class.

A minority of French-Canadian immigrants brought to the United States economic skills they had acquired in craft production, in forestry work, or in petty trade. For the majority, however, farmwork had been their only occupational experience. As such, they became part of the army of unskilled labor needed by U.S. industry in its unprecedented expansion from the antebellum era to the onset of the Great Depression. This type of occupational background, coupled with such factors as geographical distance, the nature of specific labor markets, and increasingly the role of chain migration and kinship networks, had the effect of channeling the majority of French Canadians toward industrial New England. Once in this work environment, French Canadians found in textile manufacturing the major sector permitting a rapid integration into the U.S. economy. By 1900, French Canadians represented more than one-quarter of the population of the leading mill towns. In such places as Woonsocket (Rhode Island), Southbridge (Massachusetts), and Suncook (New Hampshire), their number had grown to more than half the total population. Beside its easy access and relative stability, textile manufacturing allowed French Canadians to maximize their labor potential, as it offered work to all members of the family, including children, until child labor laws became strictly enforced.

French Canadians entered textile manufacturing as unskilled labor, yet by the early 1900s they had moved to the middle levels of the occupational structure and in many cases to supervisory positions. Although for many of them their work experience became bound up with the vicissitudes of the textile industry, a growing number (particularly among the second and third generation) embraced a wider diversity of occupations. By the early 1900s they were present in virtually all sectors of the economy, mostly as blue-collar workers, with their entry into labor markets less and less determined by their ethnic status. Moreover, education and the growth of urban economies opened up opportunities in the service sectors, making it possible for them to enter white-collar employment and in some cases to pursue professional careers. By the 1920s, French Canadians working in textile mills had become a minority—a process resulting from the decline of textile manufacturing in the New England region, the new job opportunities that education afforded to second-and third-generation French Canadians, and the unprecedented diversification of the blue-and white-collar labor markets in the U.S. economy. An important dimension of this process of upward mobility was the formation of a middle class, which by the turn of the century was a social reality in most "Little Canadas." It was from this stratum that there emerged a leadership—most often made of businessmen, professionals, journalists, and parish priests—who became the spokesmen of the aspirations of their constituencies, acting as mediators in the complex and often conflict-ridden process of integration into American civil society.

POLITICAL INTEGRATION

Like most immigrants who decided to settle in the United States, French Canadians, French, and Acadians could not escape the reality of their relation with civic institutions and ultimately their political choices as citizens. Their view and practice of American politics were, however, quite different. French immigrants usually did not play any major role at the federal or state level, the only significant exception being in antebellum New Orleans, Louisiana. In local politics, ethnic leaders sometimes attempted to build an ethnic vote, mobilizing immigrants through ethnic political organizations and encouraging them to become American citizens. But French immigrants, at least in the nineteenth century, seemed more interested in their homeland's politics rather than those of their new country.

French Canadians' strong emphasis on "survivance" tended at first to downplay political involvement. Yet most of them found the way to reconcile the maintenance of a strong ethnic identity with their civic and political duties. The process was not a simple one due to some demographic and cultural traits of the French-Canadian population. For instance, the low proficiency in English, the equally low literacy level, and the tendency among some French Canadians to see their stay in the United States as a temporary one resulted in one of the slowest rates of naturalization. Overcoming this required special efforts on the part of community leaders, who launched naturalization campaigns and set up programs to facilitate access to citizenship. The relative success of these efforts, coupled with the growing demographic weight of the American-born, led to a gradual participation in electoral politics. It was a participation shaped less by ideological considerations and more by local circumstances, such as the degree of concentration or dispersion within a given local population, the past relations with the local party leadership, the willingness of the two parties to court the French-Canadian ethnic vote, and the ability of French-Canadian leaders to mobilize their constituencies.

By the turn of the century, French Canadians sat in the municipal councils of a number of New England cities—particularly those in which the French-Canadian presence was numerically strongest. From 1910 to 1914, for instance, Fall River, Holyoke, and New Bedford had more than fourteen such representatives in each council. In Manchester (New Hampshire), French Canadians sent thirty of their own representatives to the city council between 1901 and 1911, and in 1917 the newly elected mayor, Moise Verrette, was of French-Canadian descent. Depending on local circumstances, their election had occurred on either a Republican or a Democratic Party ticket. Despite its importance in the local political landscape, the French-Canadian "ethnic vote" failed to emerge as a component of state and national politics. This did not prevent some individuals from attaining political prominence, such as Hugo Dubuque, elected in 1888 to the Massachusetts State House and subsequently to the state's supreme court, or Aram Pothier, former mayor of Woonsocket, who in 1897 conquered the governorship of his State of Rhode Island, a position he held intermittently until the 1920s.

After several decades of indifference or rejection, Louisiana Acadians generally entered American politics in the 1820s and 1830s. Antebellum Acadian politicians and voters divided along ideological lines. Many Prairie Acadians regrouped behind Andrew Jackson, whereas others preferred the Whig camp. A few Acadians reached regional political prominence, particularly Alexandre Mouton. A Lafayette Parish planter and Jacksonian Democrat, he served as a U.S. senator from 1837 to 1842 and then as governor of Louisiana before leaving elective politics until the secession crisis. During the Civil War, most Acadian River planters chose the Confederate side, unlike many Prairie yeomen farmers, who openly disagreed with conscription and did not hesitate to desert. During the immediate antebellum period and then with the war and military defeat, followed by the Reconstruction and post-Reconstruction eras, socioeconomic changes and the racialization of politics all led to vigilantism and violence. Many Louisiana Acadians joined the Knights of the White Camellia and later linked their fortunes to the Democrats' efforts to eradicate Republicans. The early twentieth-century Acadian political landscape was thus quite different from what it had been fifty years earlier: Whereas the majority of Cajuns were either disfranchised or poorly or not at all represented in state politics, the Americanized Acadian elite had worked its way through New South's racialized Democratic politics to reemerge as political leaders.

CULTURAL INTEGRATION

French-Canadian, French, and Acadian immigrants' acculturation into American society was a long and highly differentiated process and one of the aspects that most marked the three groups' history. In the French case, the importance of professionals, businessmen, and service workers in the French communities seems to have eased the group's integration into mainstream American culture. To be sure, there were at first isolationist temptations within the ethnic enclaves. But these attempts were not based on any ideology, and they did not last long.

Like most immigrant groups, French Canadians sought to preserve their cultural traditions, and in this they were aided by the close proximity to Quebec and by the continuous arrival of new contingents. But more than most other immigrant groups, they were subjected by their community leaders to an ideology of cultural survival centered on the preservation of their language, religion, and folk past. This ideology proved successful, particularly in the early stages of the settlement process, primarily because it pervaded their entire institutional network. But the cultural isolation could not last forever, especially in an urban-industrial environment where almost daily contact with mainstream values and institutions was virtually unavoidable and where the proportion of the U.S.-born within the ethnic group had become a majority. Die-hard cultural isolationists, though increasingly a minority, persisted in promoting the ideology of "survivance," often clashing with proponents of acculturation. This conflict came to a head in what has become known as "the Sentinelliste affair." It began in Woonsocket (Rhode Island) in 1927, when survivance militants grouped around the newspaper *La Sentinelle* in denouncing the local bishop for raising funds among French-Canadian parishes for the purpose of building the

Mont-Saint-Charles school, to be opened to Catholic students of various ethnocultural affiliations. The issue was brought to ecclesiastical and civil courts and ended with the traditionalist forces losing and becoming more isolated and an increasingly marginal voice in a community well on the way to acculturation.

The workplace, public education, and a variety of civic institutions became the main vehicles through which mainstream cultural influences penetrated the universe of most "Little Canadas," transforming attitudes and outlooks on both sides of the ethnic boundary. Moreover, despite the resistance put forth by the more traditionalist community leaders, popular culture exerted a considerable pull, especially on younger generations. The new mass media, such as radio and cinema, fascinated French-Canadian migrants and their children. It did not take long before some of them made their own contribution to the popular culture, particularly in sports where such athletes as Louis Cyr and Napoleon Lajoie attained national fame in the United States. Years later, French-Canadian contributions to the artistic and literary life of the nation would best be represented by one of the leading American writers of his generation, the Lowell-born Jack Kerouac, whose novels discussed the cultural transformations at work in French-Canadian immigrant enclaves.

World War II and the postwar era of prosperity accelerated considerably the acculturation of the group. French-Canadian communities sent their youth to fight in what most of them saw as "their war," producing a strong identification with the ideals for which the country struggled. In the ensuing years, unprecedented prosperity, mass culture (in particular TV), and the "cold war" climate converged to create a strong redefinition of Americanism to which few French Canadians managed not to succumb. Of the three major components that had nourished an ethnic culture—language, religion, and a "spiritual" proximity to Quebec—only religion continued to persist as a feature of the group identity. Even so, religion turned out to be an important vehicle of acculturation, too. From the minority status it had had and the divisive role it had played in earlier years, Roman Catholicism emerged in the 1940s and 1950s as a fully legitimate component of American life, often playing an aggressive role in the definition of Americanism. Consequently, the Roman Catholicism of French Canadians rapidly lost most of its "ethnic" connotations—a process also resulting from the growing ethnic exogamy and the virtual elimination of French from religious functions.

Another important development was the rapid decline in the use of French, as the old French-Canadian parish schools adopted English and relegated French to just one subject among others. Equally rapid was the decline of the French-Canadian press. The handful of newspapers that still survived after World War II closed down as their editors died or as their readership shrank to insignificance. Whatever "ethnic" signs survived (e.g., community buildings, associations, and clubs), efforts were made to maintain them more as "traces" of a past than as activators of ethnic practices and group mobilization. These changes, coinciding in part with the rapid modernization experienced by Quebec society in the postwar era (e.g., secularization and separatist sentiment), under-mined Quebec's previous role as cultural referent and increased the sentiment of "Americanness" of the group.

In the case of the Acadians, cultural integration was a complicated process closely linked to socioeconomic change. Transplanted Acadians brought with them from Nova Scotia cultural characteristics that were redefined and modified in Louisiana. Nineteenth-century socioeconomic change led to cultural differ-entiation and to a double transformation. First, Acadian elites were co-opted into the region's now-dominant Anglo-American mainstream culture. By the 1840s, in a larger regional context of growing francophobia, they had become largely English speaking. Second, despite the fact that they were at the same time absorbing poor Creoles and recent French immigrants of modest means, pau-perized Acadians became Cajuns through a complex process of ethnicization, racialization, and primitivization. By the 1870s, the image of the Cajuns as a poor and primitive people was in place. It lasted for almost a century until the ethnic revival of the 1960s and 1970s.

ETHNIC GROUPS IN CONTEMPORARY SOCIETY

In the United States, the 1970s were a period of ethnic revival. Of the three groups under study, this phenomenon affected only the French Canadians and the Cajuns.[1] The locus of the French-Canadian ethnic revival was primarily New England, where a generation of Franco-American intellectuals attempted to re-formulate the meaning and value of their cultural heritage. Partly influenced by the phenomenon of ethnic pride sweeping the United States, but also by the mounting nationalist sentiment among Quebec French Canadians, these intellec-tuals saw the potential of reviving the cultural traditions they had inherited from one century of immigration and community life. At a historic meeting held in Bedford in 1976, intellectuals—including Claire Quintal, Marcel Bellemare, Yvon Labbé, Raymond Lacasse, and Richard Santerre, among others—assessed the state of their brand of *Franco-Américanie* and explored ways to encourage a renewed ethnic identity in the new North American context. The many initia-tives that followed stressed the importance of education, with emphasis on the teaching of French as well as the history and traditions of Franco Americans. The epicenter of this movement was in Worcester (Massachusetts), where the French Institute at Assumption College, under the direction of Claire Quintal, began annual conferences that attracted scholars from various North American universities as well as from France, then made the results of the new research available to a wider public through the publication *Vie française*. Another no-table initiative was the creation of the Franco American Resource and Oppor-tunity Group (FAROG) at the University of Maine (Orono). Small publishing houses were also created in New Hampshire and in Maine to encourage Franco-American writers and to reprint hard-to-find literary works. By the late 1980s, this cultural movement had attracted the interest of Quebec intellectuals, artists, and politicians, who saw the importance of uncovering for the Quebec public at large an experience that had largely been neglected, if not forgotten.

The ethnic revival of the 1970s and 1980s also touched southern Louisiana. There, it was first spearheaded by a movement for the revitalization of the French language, led by an elite of mixed francophone background. As such, Cajun culture and tradition were not the primary concerns. This movement received the support of the state and resulted in the creation of the Council for the Development of French in Louisiana (CODOFIL). Its most important victories were laws instituting the teaching of French in the school system, the use of French in official publications, and the designation of more than twenty parishes as "Acadiana," with an official flag for the region. The University of Southwestern Louisiana in Lafayette developed a research center dedicated to the study of Acadian culture and history and promoted educational and research programs. CODOFIL leaders, especially James Domangeaux, aimed at transforming Acadiana into a bilingual region and creating cultural and commercial links with francophone countries. They emphasized international French and recruited teachers from various francophone countries. Their elitist approach drew initial suspicion and even hostility on the part of the Cajun population. However, Cajuns were gradually brought into the movement through festivals and public events celebrating the Acadian heritage, often featuring Cajun music and crafts.

NOTE

1. Recent immigration from France has not been voluminous, with only 69,221 admitted into the United States during the three decades following the change in immigration laws, 1966 to 1995. Canadian immigration has not been broken down by French Canadians and others for quite some time, but in the 1990 census, 2,167,127 persons gave French Canadian as their ancestry, with 78 percent citing it as their first one. In contrast, 668,271 indicated a Cajun/Acadian one, with 89 percent listing it as their first one. Finally, 10,320,935 identified with a French ancestry, but with only 60 percent giving it as their first.

BIBLIOGRAPHIC REFERENCES

As noted in the introduction, historians have only just begun to study French migrants. For a summary of the question up to 1980, see Patrice Higonnet, "French," in *Harvard Encyclopedia of American Ethnic Groups*, edited by Stephan Thernstrom (Cambridge, MA: Harvard University Press, 1980), pp. 379–388. Traditional starting points are Abel Chatelain, "Recherches et enquàtes démographiques: Les migrations françaises vers le Nouveau Monde au xixe siècle," *Annales E.S.C.* 2 (1947): 53–70; Louis Chevalier, "L'èmigration française au xixe siècle," *Etudes d'histoire moderne et contemporaine*, vol. 1 (1947): 127–171; and Claude Fohlen, "Perspectives historiques sur l'immigration française aux Etats-Unis," *Revue européenne des migrations internationales* 6 (1990): 29–41. A recent attempt to offer a reinterpretation of French emigration and link its history to larger historiographical trends is François Weil, "French Migration to the Americas in the Nineteenth and Twentieth Centuries as a Historical Problem," *Study Emigrazione* 33.123 (1996): 443–460. On French communities in American cities, see Carl A. Brasseaux, *The "Foreign French": Nineteenth-Century French Immigration into Louisiana*, 3 vols. (Lafayette: University of Southwestern Louisiana, 1990); and Arnold R. Hirsch and Joseph Logsdon, eds., *Creole New Orleans: Race and Americanization* (Baton Rouge: Louisiana State University Press, 1992).

Works dealing with the experience of French Canadians in the United States have focused almost entirely on the New England region. An early synthesis on the subject is Elliott R. Barkan, "French Canadians," in *Harvard Encyclopedia of American Ethnic Groups*, edited by Stephan Thernstrom (Cambridge, MA: Harvard University Press, 1980), pp. 388–401. For a broad synthesis dealing primarily with institutional developments, see Gerard J. Brault, *The French-Canadian Heritage in New England* (Hanover: University Press of New England, 1986). Studies of economic conditions in, and out-migration from, Quebec include Robert Armstrong, *Structure and Change: An Economic History of Quebec* (Toronto: Gage Publishing Co., 1984); and Bruno Ramirez, *On the Move: French-Canadian and Italian Migrants in the North Atlantic Economy, 1860–1914* (Toronto: McClelland and Stewart, 1991). The most thorough historical works dealing with the French-Canadian experience in New England are in French: Yves Roby, *Les Franco Américains de la Nouvelle-Angleterre, 1776–1930* (Sillery Quebec: Editions du Septentrion, 1990), adopts a large chronological frame and traces the different stages of migration and settlement. François Weil, *Les Franco-Américains* (Paris: Belin, 1989), develops the narrative to the 1980s in an analytical perspective. Also in French is the most thorough work attempting to measure the volumes of immigration: Yolande Lavoie, *L'émigration des Canadiens aux Etats-Unis avant 1930. Mesure du phénomène* (Montreal: Pum, 1972). For studies of French-Canadian textile workers, see Tamara Hareven's *Family Time and Industrial Time* (Cambridge: Cambridge University Press, 1982) and Bruno Ramirez, "French Canadian Immigrants in the New England Cotton Industry," *Labour/Le Travailleur* 11 (Spring 1983): 125–142. The major study of French Canadians in the labor movement is Gary Gerstle, *Working-Class Americanism: The Politics of Labor in a Textile City, 1914–1960* (Cambridge: Cambridge University Press, 1989).

On French-Canadian community life, see Claire Quintal, ed., *The Little Canadas of New England* (Worcester: French Institute/Assumption College, 1983). For a study of French Canadians in politics, see, for example, Ronald D. Petrin, "Ethnicity and Urban Politics: French Canadians in Worcester, 1895–1915," *Historical Journal of Massachusetts* 15 (June 1987): 141–153. On the church life of French Canadians, see Mason Wade, "The French Parish and Survivance in Nineteenth-Century New England," *Catholic Historical Review* 36 (July 1950): 163–189; and Richard S. Sorrell, "The Sentinelle Affair (1924–1929): Religion and Militant Survivance in Woonsocket, R. I.," *Rhode Island History* 36.3 (August 1977): 67–80. Among the rare works on French Canadians in the Midwest are Clyde Richard Ford, "The French Canadians in Michigan," *Michigan History Magazine* 27 (1943): 243–257; and Aidan D. McQuillan, "French-Canadian Communities in the American Upper Midwest during the 19th Century," *Cahiers de Géographie du Quebec* 23.58 (April 1979): 53–72.

On Acadians, for a summary up to the 1970s, see Marietta M. LeBreton, "Acadians," in *Harvard Encyclopedia of American Ethnic Groups*, edited by Stephan Thernstrom (Cambridge, MA: Harvard University Press, 1980), pp. 1–3. The most thorough historical works on the settlement of Acadians in Louisiana and their subsequent development as an ethnic community are by Carl A. Brasseaux: *The Founding of New Acadia: The Beginnings of Acadian Life in Louisiana, 1765–1803* (Baton Rouge: Louisiana State University Press, 1987) and *Acadian to Cajun: Transformation of a People, 1803–1877* (Jackson: University Press of Mississippi, 1992). For a historical overview that emphasizes the process of ethnicization of Cajuns up to the early 1980s, see James H. Dormon, *The People Called Cajuns* (Lafayette: University of Southwestern Louisiana, 1983). A collection of studies on a variety of aspects of Cajun history and life is contained in Glenn R. Conrad, ed., *The Cajuns: Essays on Their History and Culture* (Lafayette: University of Southwestern Louisiana, 1978).

GERMANS AND GERMAN-SPEAKING IMMIGRANTS

James M. Bergquist

THE FLOW AND EBB OF MIGRATION

The migration of German-speaking peoples from Europe has been a continuing influence on American life for most of the past three centuries. By the time of U.S. independence, Germans were the largest non-English-speaking European people in the thirteen colonies. The interaction between German and English colonists in the colonial era provided Americans with their first experiences in forming a community based on a diversity of cultures.

Although some Germans had found their way to North American port towns, such as New Amsterdam, during the seventeenth century, the migration of Germans into the colonies in considerable numbers is conventionally dated from 1683, when groups of Germans began to settle in the newly established English colony of Pennsylvania. The early migrants came in response to the invitation from Pennsylvania's proprietor, William Penn, and they founded Germantown a few miles northwest of Philadelphia. Over the next century, the German population spread further north and west into rural areas of Pennsylvania and eventually into the western areas of Maryland, Virginia, and the Carolinas. Between 1700 and the outbreak of the American Revolution, about 85,000 German-speaking people migrated to the Anglo-American colonies. By the time of the Revolution, extensive portions of the interior of Pennsylvania were firmly established as the heartland of the Pennsylvania Germans (sometimes inaccurately called "Pennsylvania Dutch").

The great majority of German-speaking immigrants in colonial times came from the southwestern states of Germany and from Switzerland and were of peasant origins. During the late sixteenth and seventeenth centuries, these areas of origin had seen the effects of disruption from warfare and the increasing pressure of a growing population upon the available land. From Austria, a pioneering group of about 500 German-speaking Protestants from Salzburg, fleeing religious persecution, found their way to Georgia in 1734, shortly after the founding of that English colony. Some colonial settlers had belonged to various pietist groups in Germany; while their cultural and religious practices remained most visible two centuries later, greater numbers of the Pennsylvania Germans were of Lutheran, Reformed, or (less frequently) Catholic persuasions and had been more quickly absorbed into the general culture.

The years following the American Revolution saw a lull in new migration of German-speaking peoples, mostly because Europe was afflicted between 1793 and 1815 by the series of wars of the French Revolution and the Napoleonic empire. After the end of these wars in Europe and of the War of 1812 in America, an expanding society in the United States began to draw new streams of immigrants from the German states. The Germans and the Irish provided the largest number of immigrants between 1815 and the American Civil War, and Americans' perceptions of immigration were formed primarily out of their experiences with these two groups. The factors now creating pressures to emigrate from Europe included a rising population, limitation on land available for those who would cultivate it, and displacement of artisans and the working class by the effects of the Industrial Revolution. These influences were being felt particularly in the western states of Germany during the early nineteenth century.

Migration of Germans to America fluctuated with the movement of the business cycles in the United States; thus, there were slower periods during the depressions following the Panics of 1819 and 1837 and greater waves during the booming years of the early 1830s and around 1850. The peak year of German immigration in the pre–Civil War period was 1854, when about 215,000 arrived from the German states. Although mostly in the western states of Germany, the origins of these migrants were also in Switzerland and in Austria. These immigrants, like their predecessors, were diversified in religion, divided among Lutherans, Reformed, and Catholic Christians, with a significant minority of Jews (most of whom considered themselves thoroughly German as well as Jewish in their culture), and a growing element of "freethinking" Germans. By mid-century, German populations had become important and visible components of eastern seaboard cities, such as New York, Philadelphia, and Baltimore. As settlement spread through the Midwest, Germans found rural land available in the states north of the Ohio River. By the end of the 1830s, Cincinnati and St. Louis were becoming heavily German communities, and over the next two decades Chicago, Milwaukee, and cities along the upper Mississippi River would become centers for German newcomers.

From 1855 to 1865 several factors combined to discourage German migration to America: recession and nativism in the United States, tighter policies on emigration in some German states, and the American Civil War. The principal sources of migrants in the German-speaking areas then shifted after the Civil War from the western regions to eastern Germany and Austria, where changes in land tenure and the forces of industrialism were now beginning to be felt more strongly. The number of German-speaking Swiss arriving between 1865 and 1921 may be roughly estimated at about 150,000. Many ethnic Germans also emigrated from Russia. Known as "Russian Germans," they came from communities established by eighteenth-century German migrants who had gone into Russia at the invitation of the Russian government. Encouraged by propagandists from the American railroads building westward after the Civil War, Germans from Russia began to settle on the Great Plains in the 1870s. The flow of them from Russia increased in the 1880s, when czarist policies became more prejudiced against non-Russian ethnic groups. Thus, after the Civil War the tide of migration rose again, receded during the depression of the mid-1870s, and then reached a new peak in 1882 at about a quarter of a million. This would be the highest point of all German immigration, and in the following years, Germans would increasingly be outnumbered by the "new" immigration from eastern and southern Europe.

Although newcomers from Germany and Austria continued to arrive at a rate averaging 30,000 annually until 1914, the numbers then dropped drastically. The upheavals of World War I were followed by the imposition of immigration restriction (the quota system) in the United States and then by the economic distress of the Great Depression and World War II.

During the Great Depression and World War II, immigration from Germany and Austria shrank to new lows, even below what the new quota laws allowed. But the 130,000 immigrants who did come from Germany and Austria during the years 1931–1945 were largely of a character different from previous German and Austrian immigrations: mostly Jewish refugees fleeing the anti-Semitic policies of the National Socialist regime. While the administration of Franklin D. Roosevelt expressed sympathy for the plight of Jews under Nazism, the numbers of refugees who actually were admitted might have been much larger had it not been for the resistance of the State Department, which was unwilling to pursue more liberal policies, and the reluctance of Congress to enact laws specifically facilitating the admission of refugees. The migration of German and Austrian Jews provided the United States with many prominent intellectual and scientific figures, among them the physicist Albert Einstein, the composer Arnold Schoenberg, and the economist Ludwig von Mises.

Migration from Germany renewed after 1945, reaching an average rate of 50,000 annually during the 1950s. About 40,000 German-speaking people also migrated from Austria to the United States during the period 1945–1960. Now, after the Holocaust and in the wake of the collapse of Nazi Germany, new refugee laws did provide somewhat more opportunity for Jews leaving Germany and for other ethnic Germans displaced from places in eastern Europe. However, after the postwar migrations, German and Austrian migration ceased to be a major flow in comparison with other sources; it tended to be obscured by the rising tide of migration from non-European sources after 1965. Of the total number of legal immigrants between 1966 and 1993 (about 17.4 million), only 1.3 percent (about 227,400) were from Germany. The numbers from other German-speaking areas were also small. One of the principal elements of immigration from Germany after 1945 consisted of the brides of American servicemen who were stationed in Germany during the occupation and cold war years.

ADJUSTMENT TO AMERICAN LIFE

At the end of the twentieth century, one had to search hard in the United States to find much evidence of a separate German ethnic culture, despite the fact that more Americans identify German in their ancestry than that of any other single ethnic group. This would offer some support for the fact that the Germans, in the long run, proved to be quite assimilable into the general American society and have also played a role in shaping its culture.

Nevertheless, at various stages of their development in America the Germans have encountered fear and resistance from native-born persons; they have been among the principal targets during most of the recurring waves of nativism. In the pre–Civil War years, some fear of them arose out of competition for jobs and land, but probably more resistance came when Americans faced the question of whether other nationalities could be readily incorporated into a society and polity thought to be derived from Anglo-Saxon Protestant values. Thus, the proposals of nativists in the 1850s stressed such safeguards as delaying naturalization or restricting the voting rights of the foreign-born after naturalization. During the Civil War, around 200,000 German-born soldiers served the Union cause. Germans, therefore, could represent themselves as defenders of freedom and the Republic, a fact that helped both to lessen the fears of many in the North and to establish in Americans' minds that Germans were solid citizens who, as hard workers, productive farmers, and (often) members of the middle class, had accepted mainstream American values.

When nativism revived in the 1880s and 1890s, German migration was drawing more heavily upon working-class elements in Europe who then became industrial wage laborers in America. That these new Germans included some radical elements sparked a fear among nativists that the labor upheavals of Europe might now infect America. The Haymarket Riot of 1886 in Chicago, after which anarchists from Germany and Austria were convicted of throwing a bomb at police, provided fuel for the fires of nativism, and many other Germans sought to distance themselves from all radicalism and to emphasize their affinity to American values.

The rise of the temperance-prohibition movement in the last three decades of the nineteenth century underscored a cultural chasm separating the Germans (and most other immigrants) from many Americans, especially those bent upon social reform. For many Germans, American insistence on the restriction of alcohol, along with the enforcement of Sunday laws, comprised just another form of nativist prejudice. The drinking of beer and public celebration with music and dancing on Sundays were intrinsic to their social and organizational life. In the early years of the twentieth century, they campaigned fervently against the mounting political pressures for Prohibition; indeed, the strongest nationwide organization the Germans ever had, the National German-American Alliance, was an umbrella organization drawing many diverse organizations together primarily in opposition to Prohibition.

The last great impulse of anti-German feeling arose when America moved toward entering World War I against the German and Austro-Hungarian empires. When the war in 1914 seemed to be just a European matter, many German Americans felt free to espouse the German cause against Great Britain, whose imperial power and ambitions they regarded as much more threatening to the world at large. Interest in the war was much more widespread among recently immigrated Germans, who had come from the newly united Germany and felt some pride in it. Older immigrants, and those of the second and third generations, often had much weaker sentiments about the German and Austrian causes. Nevertheless, in the face of what they considered overwhelming British propaganda influence on the American English-language press, some leaders of the National German-American Alliance and many German-language newspaper editors undertook to give the "German side" of the war. Thus, many "pro-German" statements by German-American spokesmen were on record when Congress declared war on Germany in April 1917. Despite the fact that the overwhelming majority of Germans and their newspapers immediately pledged their loyalty to the United States, those earlier records and statements would now be used to heighten the public's sentiments against the German-speaking people in their midst. In the course of the war, there were riots directed against Germans, restrictions placed upon their newspapers, and even, in some states, efforts to suppress the public use of the German language.

Whether the World War I experiences of German Americans and Austrian Americans deterred or hastened the assimilation process is a question still debated. Certainly, the number of their ethnic organizations and newspapers was greatly reduced by the war's end, and many German Americans consciously abandoned their German identity. Yet there appears to have been some restoration of the German-American community structure after the war. While World War I remains as a major disruptive event in the history of German America, it cannot be regarded as solely responsible for its decline. The steady decline of institutional structures within German America had begun at least as early as 1893 and reflected the greatly reduced number of new arrivals from Europe as well as the movement of second-and third-generation descendants into the institutions of mainstream American society.

ROLES AND OCCUPATIONS IN AMERICAN SOCIETY

Germans who came to America consistently represented a wide spectrum of occupations, classes, and skills. In colonial days they were already known as among the most efficient and intensive farmers, but they also contributed skilled craftsmen and artisans to such colonial cities as Philadelphia and Baltimore.

These traditions continued in the early nineteenth century as German, Austrian, and Swiss artisans with skills in carpentry, furniture making, watch making and clockmaking, and masonry proved of use to a growing America. These skills, sometimes displaced in Germany by the increasing mass-production methods of the Industrial Revolution there, would still be in demand in the newer cities of the West. In 1850 in Milwaukee, for example, 51 percent of the German males in the workforce could be classified as skilled labor, whereas only 22 percent were unskilled (the distribution of Irish in the workforce was almost exactly reversed). The same pattern of class and occupational distribution was reflected in other northern cities. The increasing agricultural productivity of the Midwest also attracted German farmers to those regions; it likewise involved Germans in the new food-processing and canning industries (symbolized by the pork-packing plants of Cincinnati and by the H. J. Heinz Company in Pittsburgh).

Perhaps the industry most identified in the public mind with Germans was the brewery. In the decade before the Civil War, the lager beer introduced by German immigrants took over the market from the ales that stemmed from English origins. The vast and still-decentralized brewing industry that developed in the late nineteenth century was almost entirely dominated by Germans and their descendants. These gradually combined in the twentieth century into a few nationwide brewing companies, with names that continue to show their German origins.

In the late nineteenth century, a growing number of German immigrants came with previous industrial experience in the old country and entered the workforce as factory laborers in the United States. They were found in textile mills in New England and the Middle Atlantic states, in farm implement factories in the Midwest, in the great meatpacking houses of Chicago, and in machine shops across the country. The baking industry continued to involve many Germans, as it was slowly transformed from small bakeshops into large baking-factory enterprises. Printing and typesetting were other activities in which Germans were strongly represented. The German-born Ottmar Mergenthaler invented the linotype machine (patented 1884), which revolutionized the printing and newspaper business. The rising tide of German industrial workers also brought German involvement in labor activism and radicalism. Many unions in such fields as printing, baking, and brewing also functioned as German-speaking ethnic organizations.

Before the Civil War, the refugee migration from the revolutions of 1848 in Germany and Austria included a small but significant element of professionals, lawyers, journalists, and university-based scholars and scientists. They often played an important role in the leadership of German-America but also contributed to the development of new professions in America. In the late nineteenth century, Germany emerged as a world leader in scientific development. Chemical and pharmaceutical manufacturing in the United States derived in many instances from offshoots of German industries, and German professionals played major roles in the management of these industries. German-trained pharmacists framed the standards for that emerging profession in America. German-trained scientists pioneered the training of American scientists in the new American universities, whose doctoral programs were often modeled on those of the German universities. German- and Austrian-trained medical doctors were also a strong influence in the development of American medical schools and the training of their physicians. Germans like John A. Roebling, the designer of the Brooklyn Bridge and other important suspension bridges, also contributed significantly to the profession of engineering in America.

German-language journalists made the German-language press the largest foreign-language press in the United States; they also developed it into a remarkable communication center for German ethnic life. Some leading German-American journalists transferred their talents to the English-language press. Joseph Pulitzer, an immigrant from the Austrian empire, began a journalistic career with the St. Louis *Westliche Post* but later led the *St. Louis Post-Dispatch* and the New York *World* in the introduction of the mass-circulation journalistic techniques that transformed the newspaper business at the end of the nineteenth century. The Ridder family, which took over the largest German-language newspaper in the country, the *New Yorker Staats-Zeitung*, in the late 1890s, eventually sold the paper in the 1920s and took over the New York *Journal of Commerce* and thereafter went on to establish their own chain of English-language newspapers.

In nineteenth-century German America, traditional values brought from Germany about the role of women still prevailed: Their sphere was properly confined to *kirche, küche und kinder*—church, kitchen, and children. But the elaborate organizational structure developing within German America provided new outlets for women, as there developed a growing necessity in modern urban society to support traditional home and family values with organized social welfare institutions. Such areas of German-American life came to be dominated by women. Among German Catholics, women founded religious orders and congregations that devoted themselves to educational and welfare activities. Other German-American women, often working through church-related organizations, established hospitals, orphanages, and refuges for the elderly and handicapped. Women who controlled some wealth frequently devoted it to the philanthropic support of welfare agencies.

The most successful German-American businesswoman of the nineteenth century was Anna Ottendorfer, who, with her husband Oswald, was copublisher of the *New Yorker Staats-Zeitung*. Anna left to her husband political activity and the editorial policies of the newspaper; meanwhile, she ran the paper's business affairs with a strong hand and devoted both her wealth and her organizational skills to founding schools, orphanages, hospitals, and homes for the poor and elderly. As women began to emerge in the professions in the twentieth century, German-American women were notably to be found in such fields as medicine, social work, psychology, and education—outgrowths of their previous involvement with the social welfare of German America.

POLITICAL INFLUENCES

The German-speaking immigrant groups were seen by many of their contemporaries (and by some later historians) as the immigrant group with the most potential for political power, considering their numbers and their concentration in many politically strategic states. Politicians and parties in the nineteenth century frequently adjusted platforms and slates of candidates with a view to attracting the "German vote." Yet the Germans were seldom able to mobilize their political power and instead were often divided between parties. The great diversity among them could not be overcome by political leaders eager to unify them. When the Germans did become unified in a particular election, it was usually on a temporary basis and in response to some perceived threat against the Germans in general.

Perhaps the one period when the Germans were most unified politically was the era of Jacksonian Democracy, from the mid-1820s to the mid-1850s. The politicians who formed the Jacksonian coalition during the 1820s appealed to immigrant groups, especially in the urban areas, and welcomed their votes in a period of widening suffrage. Andrew Jackson's opponents (who later came together in the Whig Party) criticized the Democratic exploitation of the immigrant vote, and many Whigs were perceived by the Germans as nativists attempting to restrict the rights of the foreign-born. The identification of the Whigs as nativists kept most of the Germans fervently in the ranks of the Jacksonians. The Democratic Party sought to cement their relationship with judicious patronage.

This political unanimity among the Germans disappeared with the breakdown of political parties in the 1850s, and no party would ever again claim as large a share of the German vote. The passage of the Kansas-Nebraska Act in 1854 was disruptive of the Democratic Party in many ways, one of which was the disaffection of many Germans. They felt that the act represented Southern slavery interests, which were perceived as inimical to the interests of Germans and other free laborers of the North. Thus, many Germans began to identify with the emerging "Free-Soil" movement, which by 1856 was beginning to take shape as the new Republican Party. During the decade, a new element arose among the political leadership of the Germans: the well-educated and politically idealistic "forty-eighters," who had fled the German states and Austria after the failed revolutions of 1848. The majority of them identified themselves with the new Republican Party as it developed during the 1850s. The most famous of these was Carl Schurz, who settled in Wisconsin, played a strong role in the new Republican Party there, and tried strenuously in the election of 1860 to win the German vote for Abraham Lincoln. Other important leaders who took the Republican side included Gustave Koerner of Illinois, formerly a Democrat and onetime lieutenant governor of the state; Francis Hoffmann, also a former Democrat of Illinois, who was, during the Civil War, that state's Republican lieutenant governor; and Iowa's Nicholas Rusch, who also served as his state's lieutenant governor. German Republican leaders of greater influence emerged in the midwestern states, whereas eastern Republican state organizations were more often under the influence of strong nativist elements hostile toward immigrants.

Nonetheless, efforts during the 1850s to influence the Germans to become Republican met with some resistance from Germans unwilling to abandon their long-standing relationship with German leaders who remained within the Democratic Party, as well as from Catholics and Lutherans who both feared the nativists they saw within the Republican Party and disliked the radicals among the forty-eighters. Consequently, in the crucial election of 1860, the German vote remained considerably divided, and the hopes of Schurz and other leaders that the Germans would make the critical difference in the election of Lincoln were not fulfilled.

During the Civil War, many Germans served in the Union army, which helped to cement their allegiance to the Republican Party in the decades that followed. Yet, there were others, particularly in the rural areas of the Midwest, who were not so supportive and who particularly opposed the imposition of the draft by the Republican Congress in 1863. During the Reconstruction years some Germans became disaffected with the Radical Republican Congress and the scandals of the Grant administration and drifted back toward the Democratic Party. Schurz and some other German leaders joined the "Liberal Republican" movement against Grant in 1872 but after 1876 remained as a reform element within the Republican Party. In the 1870s and 1880s, the temperance cause was taken up by the Republican organizations in some states, causing other Germans to abandon the party. In the late 1880s, the Germans saw a new attack in the form of efforts to ban the use of foreign languages for instruction in the schools. This was particularly reflected in laws passed with Republican support in Illinois and Wisconsin. The Germans were brought together in an anti-Republican reaction, which may have affected the congressional elections of 1890, as a result of which the Democrats took control of the U.S. House of Representatives.

The 1890s have been seen by political historians as transitional years in party politics, with many voters switching allegiances. This probably included some shift of Germans toward the Republicans, particularly in the cities of the East. The "free-silver" doctrines espoused by the Democrats in the election of 1896 alienated some Germans from the Democratic Party. During the Progressive era of American politics, German activism was reflected in the election of socialist municipal administrations in a few cities, including Milwaukee, Wisconsin, and Reading, Pennsylvania. However, the most compelling issue for many who clung to their German-American identity in the first two decades of the century was the growing movement for liquor prohibition. It was this issue to which the National German–American Alliance gave most attention after its founding in 1900. The most prominent German-American politician of the turn of the century was Richard Bartholdt of Missouri, who began his career in German-language journalism but was a Republican congressman from 1893 to 1915. Very active in the Alliance, he based his appeals to the German voters primarily on such cultural issues as Prohibition.

At the outbreak of World War I, the Alliance and many German-American political leaders sought to maintain neutrality and keep America from involvement in the war. Their support of the Republican Charles Evans Hughes in the 1916 election failed to unite German Americans, who remained then—as before—divided between parties. In the 1920 election, the general reaction against Woodrow Wilson led to a significant shift of German Americans away from the Democratic Party.

In the period between the two world wars, overt German-American political activism dwindled considerably. This was attributable in part to the experiences of German Americans who were under attack during the war for alleged disloyalty, but it also reflects simply the decline in numbers of German-American voters as new immigration fell off. Some scholars have identified German-American ethnicity as a significant factor supporting isolationism in foreign policy in the 1920s and 1930s, particularly in the Midwest. However, when the National Socialists came to power in Germany in the 1930s, their efforts to cultivate support among German Americans received a very weak response.

German Americans as a distinct "interest group" in American politics had very largely disappeared by the time of America's entry into World War II, and animosities against Germans during that war were minor when compared to their experiences in World War I. After 1945, the dwindling number of German-American political leaders concerned themselves with such issues as the American occupation of western Germany and the reunification of Germany, but the politically active constituency of German Americans was fast disappearing.

INFLUENCES UPON AMERICAN CULTURE

Over their long history, German-speaking immigrants have generally been more literate and more highly educated than their immigrant contemporaries. Their numbers and their relatively higher income status also allowed them to organize and participate in a wide variety of social and cultural activities. This institutional network developed rapidly during the middle of the 1800s and reached its peak about 1890. While these institutions were originally aimed at preserving German culture within the immigrant community, they eventually had their impact upon the general cultural life of America as well.

Over a period of 250 years, German-American presses produced more than 3,500 different newspapers and periodicals, some directed to very specific special interests. The same audience who read these also bought many German-language books specially produced for an American audience, giving rise to a separate genre of "German-American literature," which flourished during the late nineteenth century. There was also an active German theater, in some cities commanding a larger audience than English-language theaters. The ubiquitous

Turner societies established by Germans after 1848 introduced to America the regimens of gymnastics and the ideals of physical culture as developed by the German nationalist Friedrich Jahn. These gymnastic practices were the principal influence that made gymnastics the most widely practiced sport in the late nineteenth century, as well as the physical educational activity most frequently taught in American schools.

Perhaps the most significant contribution of Germans to organized culture in America was in music. Church choirs and singing societies were always important activities in Germans' community life and helped to carry musical culture into the broader American society. In the colonial period, Germans, especially the Moravians in Pennsylvania and North Carolina, were introducing Americans to concerts of works by the great German composers. Most of the American symphony orchestras founded in the late nineteenth and early twentieth centuries were organized and conducted by Germans, with players who were overwhelmingly German. Conductors included Theodore Thomas in Cincinnati and Chicago and Leopold Damrosch in New York, who worked tirelessly to elevate the musical culture of those cities. In the late nineteenth century, the music teachers available in many American cities and towns would predictably be either German or Italian.

The American educational system has also been influenced by Germans. The schools founded by German Americans in the early nineteenth century introduced to the United States the educational theories of the Swiss reformer Johann Pestalozzi, who stressed education directed at the individuality of each child. These principles ultimately were adopted throughout American public school systems. The kindergarten as the initial environment for adapting young children to school learning was also introduced to America by Germans and later would spread through American public schools. The first kindergarten in the United States was opened by Margaretta Schurz, the wife of Carl Schurz, at Watertown, Wisconsin, in 1856. Higher education in America particularly felt the German influence, as modern universities emerged in the last quarter of the nineteenth century. These new universities, with great stress upon graduate and professional programs and research training, were often modeled upon the German universities of the time, and the methods of instruction in seminars and laboratories were imitative of the German and Austrian models. Moreover, many universities drew upon German-born and German-trained scholars for their professors, especially in the natural and social sciences.

Religious life in America was profoundly affected by the greatly diverse nature of German religious affiliations. German immigrants were divided into larger religious groups of Lutheran, Reformed, and Catholic, with smaller numbers adhering to Methodist, Presbyterian, Evangelical, and Pietist traditions. The majority of Jewish immigrants in America before the 1880s had come from Germany and Austria and established in American Judaism the Reform tradition that prevailed before the advent of East European Jewish migration. German Americans also included, for most of their history, a significant number of freethinking and agnostic Germans, who added their own voices to the religious conflict that was frequently a part of German-American life. The many religious institutions founded by Germans were to remain as important elements of American life long after their ethnic origins had faded away. The great majority of Lutheran churches in America stem from German origins, followed distantly by Scandinavian Lutheran churches. The Reformed Germans comprised a large element of the American churches in the Calvinist tradition. However, the German Catholics, while numerous, could never overcome the dominance of the Irish in the general administration of the American Catholic Church. Nevertheless, they fostered many German-speaking Catholic parishes, comprising the largest group of "national churches" within American Catholicism. Germans controlled a number of important dioceses in German-settled regions and left their mark on church music, liturgy, and theological study. Many schools, social welfare organizations, orphanages, homes for the aged, and hospitals were established under German religious auspices and remained after their German roots were forgotten.

German influences upon mass culture and the American way of life were equally powerful, if more subtle. It was the presence of German-speaking immigrants in American communities that gave many native-born Americans their first experience at confronting diversity within the society. German leaders and spokesmen before the Civil War began to advocate tolerance of diversity within American society, arguing that one did not need to conform to Anglo-Saxon cultural standards to be a responsible citizen of the Republic. The Germans' repeated struggles against temperance reformers and against restrictive "Sunday laws" were, in many ways, campaigns to broaden American cultural standards to include the practices of diverse European peoples. The "Puritan Sunday" of contemplation and restraint still prevailed in the early 1800s, but by the end of the century, the European Sunday, with celebrations, sports, and festivities, had taken over, at least in the great cities of America. Moreover, Germans had played the major role in creating the modern American Christmas holiday. What had been a strictly religious observance among English colonists in the eighteenth century developed in the nineteenth century under largely German influences into a period of celebration, music, festivities, and gift-giving, including, of course, the Christmas tree and the mythic image of Santa Claus created by the German-American illustrator Thomas Nast.

In their communal activities in the middle of the century, the Germans began processes of change that would be followed by other immigrant groups later in the century. The transformation of Sundays and holidays reflected the broader contribution of German Americans to American civic life. They led the way in transforming the general civic culture into a more celebratory and mass-oriented one, well attuned to the democracy that was emerging in the urbanized American society at the beginning of the twentieth century.

RECENT TRENDS IN THE GERMAN-SPEAKING POPULATION

During the year 1995, according to records of the Immigration and Naturalization Service (INS), about 7,000 people immigrated to the United States from German-speaking countries. They represented about 1 percent of the total legal immigrants that year. An average rate of about 7,000 yearly had been maintained over the previous twenty years. The yearly influx represents a tiny fraction (about 0.001) of the 7 million immigrants who have been recorded since 1820 as arriving from the German-speaking areas of Europe. In 1990, about 1.5 million people in the United States reported that German was the principal language spoken at home, but the number of German speakers had been decreasing steadily throughout the twentieth century.

A U.S. Bureau of the Census survey in 1996 of the foreign-born revealed a German-born immigrant component of 523,000 individuals (excluding ethnic Germans from other countries). Among the features of this group reported, three stood out: That specific population was aging, in relatively comfortable circumstances, and disproportionately female. Over four-fifths (81 percent—424,000) of them had entered the country before 1970; a comparable proportion were over the age of forty-five (82 percent—430,000); and some 71 percent had become naturalized citizens. About 42 percent of the German-born were still employed, but many others had already retired. Over 20 percent held college or university degrees, and about 17 percent reported income above $35,000. While a remarkable 78 percent lived in homes that they or their families owned, only 9 percent were reported as being below the poverty level, and only 1 percent were receiving public assistance. Finally, 69 percent of this foreign-born population were females, reflecting in part an important feature of post–World War II German immigration: the many German-born wives of American servicemen stationed in western Germany during the half a century since 1945.

The 1996 survey also indicated that about 53,000 Germans had arrived in the United States since 1990, continuing their average rate of 7,000 to 8,000 yearly. While that slow pace of recent immigration and the high proportion of elderly German Americans indicated that the German-born would continue to diminish as a significant element of the American population, census statistics revealed another story about the overall persistence of the German presence in American society. The 1990 census had reported that over 60 million Americans—about one quarter of the total population—claimed ancestry in one of the German-speaking countries. Germans constituted the most frequent ancestry claimed by Americans—the Irish being second and the English third. Although the German-born are not a very visible element in the current population picture, after three centuries of German migration, their influence has become deeply embedded in American society and culture.

On the one hand, the few remaining annual "Steuben Day" and other ethnic demonstrations are a pale reflection of German public ethnicity a century ago. Three weekly newspapers struggled in the 1990s to keep alive the once-flourishing tradition of German-language journalism. The old German neighborhoods of the northern cities contain mostly a few ethnic restaurants to attract the tourist trade; the descendants of the Germans who once settled there have long since moved to the suburbs. The economic and educational factors that frequently helped German immigrants become upwardly mobile in American society moved them and their descendants away from ethnic associationalism as well.

On the other hand, the cultural and social influences these immigrants have brought to America can be sought within the society at large, rather than within today's distinct ethnic group. Yet those influences are sometimes harder to distinguish because many of the cultural habits and values prevalent among the Germans simply reinforced mainstream American middle-class values: a work ethic, a high degree of literacy, a stress upon education, a desire for upward mobility, strong family ties, and the need for social order and community. The German presence has also strengthened organized religion in America, formed the character of various learned professions, contributed to the culture of science and technology, and enriched the broader cultural life of American cities. The German-speaking peoples provide the principal example of how one common culture may be profoundly changed by others.

BIBLIOGRAPHIC REFERENCES

The primary sources for the history of German immigration are the census records and the reports of new arrivals found on "shiplists" during the nineteenth century and in reports of immigration authorities since then. The most voluminous sources on German-American life are the vast files of German-language newspapers; see Carl J. R. Arndt and May E. Olson, *German-American Newspapers and Periodicals, 1732–1955: History and Bibliography* (Heidelberg: Quelle and Meyer, 1961). Two bibliographies provide an introduction to German-American materials: Henry A. Pochman and Arthur R. Schultz, eds., *Bibliography of German Culture in America to 1940* (Madison: University of Wisconsin Press, 1953), and Arthur R. Schultz, *German-American Relations and German Culture in America: A Subject Bibliography, 1941–1980* (Millwood, NJ: Kraus International, 1984). General treatments of German Americans include La Vern J. Rippley, *The German-Americans* (Boston: Twayne, 1976), and Robert H. Billigmeier, *Americans from Germany: A Study in Cultural Diversity* (Belmont, CA: Wadsworth, 1974). Colonial migrations can be studied in Aaron Fogleman, *Hopeful Journeys: German Immigration, Settlement, and Political Culture in Colonial America, 1717–1775* (Philadelphia: University of Pennsylvania Press, 1996), and A. G. Roeber, *Palatines, Liberty and Property: German Lutherans in Colonial America* (Baltimore: Johns Hopkins University Press, 1993). For nineteenth-century emigration from Germany, see Mack Walker, *Germany and the Emigration, 1816–1885* (Cambridge, MA: Harvard University Press, 1964).

The nineteenth-century development of German-American life is best seen in studies of specific communities, for example: Kathleen N. Conzen, *Immigrant Milwaukee, 1836–1860* (Cambridge, MA: Harvard University Press, 1976); Stanley Nadel, *Little Germany: Ethnicity, Religion, and Class in New York City, 1845–80* (Urbana: University of Illinois Press, 1990); David Gerber, *The Making of an American Pluralism: Buffalo, New York, 1825–60* (Urbana: University of Illinois Press, 1989); and John F. Nau, *The German People of New Orleans, 1850–1900* (Leiden: E. J. Brill, 1958). Studies of rural Germans include Walter Kamphoefner, *The Westfalians: from Germany to Missouri* (Princeton, NJ: Princeton University Press, 1987); and Terry G. Jordan, *German Seed in Texas Soil* (Austin: University of Texas Press, 1966). For the German industrial working class, see Hartmut Keil and John B. Jentz, eds., *German Workers in Industrial Chicago, 1850–1910: A Comparative Perspective* (DeKalb: Northern Illinois University Press, 1983), and Dorothee Schneider, *Trade Unions and Community: The German Working Class in New York City, 1870–1900* (Urbana: University of Illinois Press, 1994). Insights from the letters of immigrants are contained in Walter D. Kamphoefner et al., eds., *News from the Land of Freedom: German Immigrants Write Home* (Ithaca, NY: Cornell University Press, 1991).

Examples of the numerous studies of German-American churches are Colman J. Barry, *The Catholic Church and German Americans* (Milwaukee: Bruce, 1953); Jay Dolan, *The Immigrant Church: New York's Irish and German Catholics* (Baltimore: Johns Hopkins University Press, 1975); and Carl E. Schneider, *The German Church on the American Frontier* (St. Louis: Eden, 1939). On the German-language press, see Carl Wittke, *The German Language Press in America* (Lexington: University of Kentucky Press, 1957), and James M. Bergquist, "The German-American Press," in *The Ethnic Press in the United States*, edited by Sally M. Miller (Westport, CT: Greenwood Press, 1987), pp. 131–159. Important topics in German-American political history are dealt with in Frederick C. Luebke, ed., *Ethnic Voters and the Election of Lincoln* (Lincoln: University of Nebraska Press, 1971); Frederick C. Luebke, *Immigrants and Politics: The Germans of Nebraska, 1880–1900* (Lincoln: University of Nebraska Press, 1969); Philip Gleason, *The Conservative Reformers: German American Catholics and the Social Order* (Notre Dame: University of Notre Dame Press, 1968); and Sander Diamond, *The Nazi Movement in the United States, 1924–1941* (Ithaca, NY: Cornell University Press, 1974). For the role of the "forty-eighters," see Alfred E. Zucker, ed., *The Forty-Eighters: Political Refugees of the German Revolutions of 1848* (New York: Columbia University Press, 1959), and Carl F. Wittke, *Refugees of Revolution: The German Forty-Eighters in America* (Philadelphia: University of Pennsylvania Press, 1952). The World War I experience of German Americans is dealt with most fully in Frederick C. Luebke, *Bonds of Loyalty: German-Americans during World War I* (DeKalb: Northern Illinois University Press, 1974). Interactions between American and German-American cultures is dealt with in several collections of essays: Randall M. Miller, ed., *Germans in America: Retrospect and Prospect* (Philadelphia: German Society of Pennsylvania, 1984); Frank Trommler and Joseph McVeigh, eds., *America and the Germans: An Assessment of a Three-Hundred-Year History*, 2 vols. (Philadelphia: University of Pennsylvania Press, 1985); and Frederick C. Luebke, *Germans in the New World: Essays in the History of Immigration* (Urbana: University of Illinois Press, 1990).

GREEKS

George A. Kourvetaris

The Greek-American experience must be understood within the broader socio-historical, political, and economic contexts of European immigration. This experience can be understood both as part of the Hellenic diaspora and as an ethnic experience in the United States. Moreover, the Greek-American experience cannot be understood if severed from its roots in modern Greek culture. The Greek pioneer immigrants to the United States, along with other southern, eastern, and central Europeans, represent the "new" immigrants vis-à-vis the "old" immigrants from northwestern Europe. Most of those new European immigrants came to the United States after the 1880s, particularly during the first quarter of the twentieth century. Moreover, every new generation of immigrants has frequently experienced social and economic hardships and discrimination at the hands of the groups that preceded it; and, indeed, the Greeks and other southern and eastern European immigrants faced social discrimination from earlier generations of northwestern European immigrants and their progenies.

The early ethnic groups who came to the United States, primarily from such countries of northwestern Europe as England, Scotland, Ireland, Germany, the Netherlands, and the Scandinavian countries, established the basic institutions of government and shaped the nature and character of present American social structures. While subsequent European and other new ethnic, racial, and cultural groups from different parts of the world accommodated to those cultural and institutional characteristics, they also maintained (for varying lengths of time) some of their in-group ethnic, religious, and cultural ties and identities, particularly those pertaining to family and kinship relationships, religion, and the "Dionysian" aspects of their ethnic subcultures (those pertaining to food, dance, and other external material aspects of their subcultures). Still, beyond the third and subsequent generations, most descendants of European ethnic groups have given up many of their ethnic traditions, such as language, literature, and music, in exchange for social mobility and integration into the larger and dominant Anglo-American culture.

The majority of later European immigrants to the United States and their children strove for equality with the dominant northwestern European groups by adopting their values. However, in contrast to the assimilationist and cultural pluralist perspectives concerning this process, the power-conflict, one views each succeeding ethnic group in an embattled position, fighting for its survival as a culturally distinct group. In this struggle, an ethnic group is subject to a perpetual conflict between the bonds with its own ethnic subculture (and its resistance to absorption into the dominant culture) and the strong attraction of that dominant culture and social milieu. Greek Americans, like other southern European and non-European ethnic groups, have been caught between these assimilationist and power-conflict scenarios, creating real dilemmas for them. They want to be part of the larger society and the political economy of the United States, yet at the same time they strive to maintain their ethnic and religious identities. The resulting pluralistic tendencies are not without their tensions.

Greek Americans today, like other Euro-Americans, share American cultural values and experiences, just as their forebears did when they came to the United States. At the same time, Greek Americans share a broader view of Greek cultural and ethnoreligious identity. They perceive themselves as an ethnic group but at the same time feel very much American, adopting, in effect, a dual, hyphenated identity. More and more, however, their Greek ethnic identity is defined by the Eastern Orthodox Church, thus fostering a Christian, ethnoreligious, pluralistic, and denominational model, for Eastern Orthodoxy is the third branch of Christianity, the other two principal ones being Roman Catholicism and Protestantism. And yet, in many respects, the younger generations are moving farther from that hyphenated identity.

GREEK IMMIGRATION TO THE UNITED STATES

Greek immigration to the United States is by and large a twentieth-century phenomenon. Only a few Greeks arrived prior to the American Civil War, and these were sponsored by American Protestant missionaries during and after the Greek Revolution against the Turks in the 1820s.[1] As late as 1880, there were only about 500 Greek immigrants in the United States. By the 1890s their number had reached 18,000, and it then increased tenfold, to approximately 167,000, in the first decade of the twentieth century. It would total approximately half a million by 1940. This phase of Greek immigration, including their second generation, represents the "early" Greek mass immigration to the United States as opposed to the "late" (post–World War II) Greek immigrants to the United States.

During the era of large-scale immigration from southern and eastern Europe, the earlier European immigrants and their descendants often expressed intense racism and xenophobia toward them, depicting the newcomers as undesirable. These antiforeign sentiments, coupled with the impact of World War I and the postwar economic changes, contributed to the passage of restrictive immigration legislation starting in 1917. In 1921 Congress first passed legislation based on nationality quotas. This discriminatory legislation culminated in the Johnson-Reed Act of 1924, in which the quota of entering immigrants from southeastern European countries was based on 2 percent of the nationality distribution in the 1890 U.S. census. The clear purpose of the 1924 Immigration Act was to restrict immigration that came from southern and eastern Europe. The Greek quota was set at only 100 immigrants per year. In 1921, the last year of open immigration, 28,000 Greeks had come to the United States. In 1929, under the National Origins formula, the annual Greek quota was set at 307, and there it remained for most of the next three decades. Nonquota immigrants, however, averaged about 2,000 yearly between 1924 and 1930, mostly members of immediate families already in the United States.

Overall, during the first two decades of the twentieth century, about 370,000 Greeks left for overseas, about 352,000 (95 percent) of whom migrated to the United States. However, a large number of them returned to Greece during the same period primarily because they had not planned to remain in America but also at times due to problems of social adjustment, lack of jobs, discrimination, and nostalgia for the old country. Between the 1920s and 1950s Greek transatlantic emigration subsided. Beginning in the mid-1950s, particularly following the Greek Civil War (1946–1949), a mass exodus from the countryside of Greece took place. Large numbers of people moved to the cities, such as Athens, Thessaloniki, and Patrae. Over a million left for the United States, Canada, Australia, and Western Germany. Since the mid-1970s, external migration from Greece has declined dramatically. Indeed, since 1984, more Greeks have repatriated than left the country, reversing the long-standing pattern of emigration. After the 1973 oil embargo and the international economic crisis of Western capitalism, there was massive unemployment in the United States and western Europe. West Germany, for example, paid migrants to return to their countries, and thousands of Greeks did return to Greece from Germany and other western European countries.

Today, the largest Greek presence outside Greece proper is found in North America (United States and Canada) and Australia. Although Greek transatlantic external migration to these continents is more than 100 years old, we sometimes refer to these Greek emigrants as though they arrived yesterday. The continued Greek emigration after World War II gave the larger Greek-American community a graduated scale of ethnicity and continual doses of "Greek cultural transfusion." Charles Moskos has calculated the generational distribution of Greek Americans in the early 1990s as follows:

First generation   350,000
Second generation   450,000

Third generation	350,000
Fourth generation	100,000
Total	1,250,000

Moskos argues that this number is consistent with the 1990 U.S. census, the 1975 Gallup of American religious preference, and the number of dues-paying family units of the Greek Orthodox Archdiocese.

Yet recently released census data show that Greek Americans are "disappearing." According to the census report, between 1980 and 1990, in more than one out of three states in the United States, Greek Americans ceased to exist on the list of the top twenty-five American ancestry groups. The 1990 U.S. census reported about 1,100,000 persons of Greek ancestry (over four-fifths of whom listed Greek as their primary ancestry). Of course, this does not necessarily mean that Greek Americans will disappear altogether. It does suggest that other groups are multiplying faster, a fact borne out by immigration data: While close to 129,000 Greek-born persons had entered the United States between 1966 and 1975, only 77,350 did so over the next twenty-one years (1976–1996).

From the beginning, the early Greek male immigrant was ambivalent about his permanent settlement in the New World. His original intention was to amass his fortune and return to his place of birth. Because of indecisiveness, the scarcity of Greek women, job insecurity, the problems of social adjustment, and discrimination in the host society, the Greek male was reluctant to commit himself to settling in America and marrying and raising a family. While he was physically in America, sentimentally and emotionally he remained in his land of birth. (This was also somewhat true of the late Greek immigrants). Nevertheless, although a substantial number of early Greek immigrants returned to Greece, the vast majority remained in the United States. Only when the Greek male felt reasonably secure in his job or business did he decide to remain, get married, and have a family. Then he found it difficult to return to his native home in Greece. In fact, for many immigrants, marriage and family were the turning point that not only provided them with a feeling of permanence in America but also made it more difficult, if not unthinkable, for them to return to Greece.

Although we find considerable differences between the early and late Greek immigrants and between generations, a number of students of Greek culture and society maintain that family and religion seem to be the two social institutions largely responsible for preserving the traditions, values, and ideals of modern Greek culture among the Greeks of the diaspora and Greece proper. Ideally, every Greek ethnic community in the United States was also a spiritual community. A Greek church signified the existence of an ethnic colony, and every Greek was potentially a member of his or her church. The admonition of Athenogoras, archbishop of the Greek Orthodox Church in the Americas during the 1950s, who later became the patriarch of Constantinople, was clear. He urged the Greeks of the United States to unite around the Church. Furthermore, while Greek communities and Greek Orthodox parishes were established early in the twentieth century, 1922 marked the beginning of the organized ecclesiastical life of the Greek Orthodox Archdiocese of the Americas (which includes the United States, Canada, and South America). The new archbishop of the Greek Orthodox Church, His Holiness Spyridon, succeeded Archbishop Iakovos in 1996. Certain of Spyridon's administrative changes have stirred controversy, and the 1997 visit of the Greek Orthodox patriarch Vartholomaios to the United States was prompted, some believe, by his effort to reaffirm his authority over the archdiocese. While it is too early to know just what modifications the new archbishop may make, a number of conflicts have emerged throughout Greek American communities. For example, a number of Greek Americans known as Orthodox Christian Laity (OCL), a Greek-American professional organization of over 2,000 members, are demanding a greater role for the laity in the economic and administrative aspects of the archdiocese.[2]

EARLY AND LATE GREEK IMMIGRANTS AND GENERATIONAL PERSPECTIVES

Early Greek immigrants came to the United States during the second phase of U.S. immigration and industrial capitalism (1865–1920), especially at the end of the nineteenth and beginning of the twentieth centuries (1890s to 1910s). Late Greek immigrants came to the United States at the mid-twentieth century, especially between the 1950s and the mid-1970s.

Most early Greek immigrants came from Peloponnese, the southern region of Greece (especially Arcadia and Laconia provinces in southern and central Peloponnese, respectively). Some also came from other parts of Greece and from the islands. A number of Greeks came from Asia Minor, especially following the 1922 Asia Minor war in which over a million Greeks were expelled from their ancestral home of a thousand years. Immigration to the United States was looked upon as a vehicle of social and economic mobility, particularly for the farming and working classes of the Greek countryside. It has been reported that early Greek immigrants, as a rule, were poor, had limited education and skills, came primarily from agricultural communities, and consisted of young males. Included in this group was a small number of Greek schoolteachers, priests, journalists, and other professionals and semiprofessionals, who became the apostles of the ideals and values of Greek society and culture. Like most southern European immigrants, particularly Italians, early Greek immigrants did not come as families because they did not expect to stay in the United States. They intended to better their finances and return to their homeland. Despite their working-class and rural origins, however, the early Greek immigrants had a lower-middle-class work ethic. They were industrious, independent, and thrifty. They had what is commonly known as the "Protestant work ethic," along with a sense of determination, cultural pride, ethnic consciousness, and a sense of community.

Both the early and late Greek immigrants settled in such major cities as Chicago, New York (including Astoria, Queens), Detroit, San Francisco, Philadelphia, Boston, St. Paul (Minnesota), Tarpon Springs (Florida), and generally in those states where jobs were available. Very few settled in southern states and even fewer in farming or small towns. However, during the past two decades this pattern has changed, with new Greek immigrants leaving the larger cities for the suburbs and small towns in metropolitan areas, especially those engaged in the restaurant business. In greater metropolitan Chicago, for example, many late first-generation Greeks are operating restaurants.

The late Greek immigrants were somewhat more educated and did not come exclusively from small agricultural communities. Many came as families, sponsored by friends and relatives who had come earlier. Included in this group were a substantial number of students and professionals who came to the United States either to practice their profession or to pursue higher education in American institutions. By and large, however, late Greek immigrants followed the same occupational patterns as those of the early Greek immigrants. They pursued service-oriented and "middleman" occupations by becoming restaurant owners, tavern operators, grocers, ice cream and candy store operators, realtors, and rentiers. Early and late Greeks were overrepresented in the service industry. As a rule, to cite one major case, Greek restaurants are a phenomenon of first-generation (both early and late) Greek immigrants. Since the proportion of immigration of Europeans to the United States, including Greeks, has declined substantially since 1965 (1941–1965—50 percent; 1966–1975—28 percent), it is only natural that the passing of late first-generation Greek immigrants will likely end the tradition of Greek restaurant ownership. In most instances, the successors to the Greek restaurateurs will not be the children of Green immigrants (the second generation) but those of other ethnic groups, such as the Mexicans, Middle Easterners, Asians, and other newer immigrants.

Both early and late Greek immigrants brought with them a lifestyle that was folk oriented, ethnocentric, familistic, and traditional. Their provincial and traditional ways of life were a carryover from the village subculture in Greece. That subculture was maintained in the United States in the early years of immigrant life. Even today one finds a proliferation of small ethnic village fraternal societies in urban America that reflect the values and traditions of agricultural communities and regions of the country that the Greek immigrants came from. The purpose of these gemeinschaft-type societies was, and continues to be, the maintenance of ethnic identity. They serve as benevolent subsocieties and subcultures to maintain the group's ethnic identity and help their respective communities in the homeland. These village subcultures were transplanted to the New World, and those subcultures have enabled the immigrants to keep in touch with their home communities, find solace and relief from urban life, and facilitate their transition and adjustment to the larger American society. They also reflected the regional diversity, localism, and individualism of the Greeks in Greece proper, which was maintained in the United States even beyond the immigrant generation. Similar urban village subcultures are found in the big cities in Greece as a result of internal, country-to-city migration.

A number of commentators and students of Greek Americans have argued that there was a friction between the early and late Greek immigrants. The former accused the latter of being ungrateful and atheists, whereas the late immigrants stereotyped their earlier counterparts as old-fashioned, ignorant, and backward persons who had remained frozen in their knowledge and understanding of Greece since arriving in the United States. There is, in fact, exaggeration and stereotyping on both sides. In the final analysis, both groups derive from the same origins, and there are not many differences between them.

With the oncoming of the second generation, the Greek ethnic outlook was challenged. Culture conflict between parents and children was inevitable. Out of this generational conflict two major types of Greeks emerged, namely, the "traditionalists" and the "environmentalists." The traditionalists attempted to rear their Greek-American-born offspring as those children were raised in Greece. In most instances, the parental group proved unyielding. These traditionalists usually were found in cities with large Greek immigrant communities. They insisted upon preserving their ethnic institutions, particularly those pertaining to religion, language, endogamous marriage, and family. In many ways, they tried to socialize their children in the traditional Greek folkways and traditions.

On the other hand, the environmentalists, known also as the "assimilationists," believed that their children should be raised as Americans but wanted them to retain membership in the Greek Orthodox Church, keep their Greek names, and be able to communicate in the Greek language. Those who subscribed to the assimilationist model argued that assimilation could not be prevented but only temporarily delayed. The environmentalists were more realistic, and they experienced less conflict with their offspring. They were more cognizant of the fact that powerful social and cultural forces operate in American society that have exerted an unprecedented influence upon their offspring and compelled them toward an Anglo-American conformity.

Following this analysis of second-generation Greek Americans by Theodore Saloutos, Charles Moskos advanced the "embourgeoisement" thesis as the dominant characteristic of the Greek-American experience. The embourgeoisement model is at best assimilationist and accounts for the mobility of Greek Americans into middle-class mass American culture. Against the Moskos embourgeoisement thesis, however, Dan Georgakas has proposed a left-wing, working-class model among Greek Americans. He argues that, prior to World War II, most Greeks were working class and that we do not really know the extent of their embourgeoisement. He believes most of the history of the Greek working class has been lost. Trying to resolve the Moskos-Georgakas debate,

Alexandros Kitroeff concludes that "there is still too little qualitative and quantitative evidence to resolve the question of the relative importance of working class and left wing political activity of the Greek American experience."

It seems that both perspectives actually characterize the Greek-American experience. As we move from the immigrant first generation to the second and subsequent ones, a process of embourgeoisement has been taking place among Greek Americans. It is precisely this class mobility among subsequent generations of Greek Americans that functions as a depressant of Greek-American ethnicity. In general, first-generation Greeks, both early and late, particularly the traditionalists, were faced with major difficulties in carrying out their intent to socialize their children (the second generation) in the Greek ways of life. These difficulties, along with their fear of losing control over their children, were intensified when the children came into contact with the larger American society, particularly when their children attained school age, began working, and became of marital age. In other words, the issue of Greek-American ethnicity is not so much a phenomenon of the first generation. Rather, it begins with the second and subsequent generations, especially among those who believe and act as members of their ethnic groups.

GREEK-AMERICAN ETHNIC INSTITUTIONS
AND ORGANIZATIONS

The most important Greek-American ethnic institution is the Greek Orthodox Church. Most Greek Orthodox Churches are bilingual, and as a rule, they are run by small businessmen and some professionals or the more culturally conservative Greeks. As first-generation immigrants die out, the Greek church becomes more and more Americanized. This means that the Greek language is replaced by English, and the Greek Orthodox traditions become less and less stringent. The Greek Orthodox church is, in fact, a homegrown American religious institution alongside the other two principal branches of Christianity. The American-born Greeks are more interested in maintaining their Orthodox Christian identity than their ethnic Greekness (defined mostly by language and culture). In the mid-1990s, there were about 500 Greek Orthodox Churches in the United States, according to the 1997 *Yearbook of the Greek Archdiocese*. There are also a number of other Greek Orthodox religious institutions under the administrative structure of the archdiocese, which is located in New York.[3] When the Greek Orthodox Church was formally organized in 1922, a group of early Greek immigrants met in Atlanta, Georgia (1922), and established the American Hellenic Educational Progressive Association (AHEPA). Its original purpose was to combat ethnic prejudice and discrimination and the activities of the Ku Klux Klan aimed against the Greeks and other ethnic groups. Later, its scope was broadened to include educational, social, political, cultural, and benevolent activities. AHEPA endorsed a policy of "Americanization" and urged all its members to become American citizens. Although AHEPA is a secular organization, it maintained over the years some ties with the Greek Orthodox Church in America and has become the formal linkage between the Greek and the larger American communities.

Despite its many contributions to Hellenism, AHEPA has had its critics and detractors over the years. There were many who thought AHEPA was an instrument of de-Hellenization for urging its members to become American citizens and replace Greek with English as its official language. In 1923, the Greek American Progressive Association (GAPA) was founded. It adopted Greek as its official language, espoused an anti-assimilationist policy, and established closer ties with the Greek Orthodox Church. GAPA was more oriented toward maintaining as much as possible Greek ethnic identity and traditions, whereas AHEPA was more Greek American. But GAPA no longer exists, and AHEPA still thrives as the largest Greek-American association. In addition to AHEPA and GAPA, a proliferation of other Greek-American federations and ethnic associations continues (over 163 in the United States, and this does not include the much greater number of village fraternal societies).

One important institution that played such an important social and psychological role was the coffeehouse (*kaffeneion*). It was a male institution par excellence that helped both the early and late Greek male immigrant to ease the pains and problems of immigrant life. The coffeehouses served as a center of social life, political discourse, leisure, and meeting place of the male immigrants. It was there that they played cards, sipped Greek coffee, talked, and learned the news from the old country. During both the early and late immigrations Greeks opened Greek restaurants and taverns that served Greek dishes, with many of the restaurants providing entertainment with Greek musicians and dancers. As the first generation died out, so, too, has the coffeehouse declined in importance.

Another national Greek-American association is the United Hellenic American Congress (UHAC), with its headquarters in Chicago. Its purpose is to showcase individuals and causes that are of interest to Greek Americans. It sponsors many programs, including the Hellenic Cultural Center and Museum in Chicago. It maintains good relations with the leadership of the Greek Orthodox Church and serves as a political action committee (PAC) in Congress. Other Greek-American organizations include the American Hellenic Institute and Public Affairs Committee and "KRIKOS" (which means link with Greece). The former two are Washington-based, Greek-American PAC groups founded by Eugene Rossides (a former assistant secretary of commerce in the Nixon administration). For the last twelve years since its inception, the Committee's main objective has been to monitor legislation in the U.S. Congress and the activities in the executive branch concerning foreign policy issues affecting Greece and Cyprus. KRIKOS was founded in 1974 in New York City, and it is primarily an immigrant-based Greek-American professional organization with professional and cultural links with Greece. Its main purpose is to mobilize professional and cultural resources to assist Greece in any way possible for its social, economic, and scientific development. At the same time, KRIKOS organizes a number of lectures and panel discussions on issues concerning Greeks and Greek Americans.

By far the most important academic professional association is the Modern Greek Studies Association (MGSA), established by a group of academic professionals in 1968. Its membership varies and includes mainly professionals in the social sciences and humanities. It publishes a professional journal and holds a conference every two years. Its main purpose is to promote modern Greek studies at the university level; to advance modern Greek culture, the humanities, and social sciences; and to disseminate modern Greek studies through its publications. Other centers of neo-Hellenic studies, chairs, journals, and publishers include the Onasis Center of New York University, the Spyros Vryonis Center for the Study of Hellenism at the University of California in Los Angeles, and the Center of Greek Studies at the University of Minnesota, which publishes a yearbook of modern Greek culture and other Greek publications. Similar centers of modern Greek studies are found at the Ohio State University, Kent State University, Hellenic College, and Princeton. Chairs of modern Greek culture have been established at Harvard, New York University, the University of Florida, San Francisco University, and the Ohio State University.

Greeks of the diaspora established other ethnic institutions, federations, schools, professional societies, and ethnic mass media. The *Yearbook of the Greek Orthodox Archdiocese* (1997) mentions over 140 ethnic radio and TV stations, about 18 religious radio programs (both in the United States and Canada), and newspapers and magazines (both religious and secular). At the present time there are about a dozen religious newspapers and magazines, two dailies (*National Herald* [Greek] and *Proïni* [English]), three weeklies, four biweeklies, thirteen monthlies, and sixteen correspondents. While over the years a proliferation of Greek and Greek-American newspapers has been published, by far the two largest Greek dailies published in New York City were the *National Herald* (*Ethnikos Kyrikos*) and *Atlantis*. The former (which is more liberal) continues to be published, whereas the latter (which was more loyalist) ceased publication in the 1960s.

There is also a Greek Orthodox parochial school system of about twenty-five Greek-American daily elementary and high schools. In addition, there are a substantial number of afternoon Greek school classes attached to Greek parishes that conduct Greek-language instruction primarily for Greek-American children, the second generation of new immigrants. There are also a number of private Greek-language schools and Greek classes offered by Greek teachers. With the exception of lawyers, we find a large number of doctors, academics, engineers, accountants, and other professionals among the first-generation Greek immigrants who came to the United States as students and subsequently remained in the country.

GREEK-AMERICAN ENTREPRENEURS AND PROFESSIONALS

Historically, it has been reported that a number of Greek orphans of the Greek Revolution of 1821 were brought to the United States by American missionaries and sponsored by either American philhellenes or the missionaries themselves. These orphans became the proto–Greek-American professionals in the United States. Some of the orphans maintained their ethnic identity and returned to Greece after their studies and became the first unofficial ambassadors of the United States to Greece. However, the majority became assimilated by changing their faith (from Orthodox Christian to Protestant) and their names. Exact figures for the number of Greek orphans brought to the United States, those who came by other means, and those who studied in institutions of higher learning are not known. It has been estimated by Bobby Malafouris that about forty Greek male youngsters were brought to the United States by American missionaries and American philhellenes following the Greek Revolution of 1821.

First-generation Greek entrepreneurs have followed the same occupational patterns for most of the twentieth century. They are heavily concentrated in service-type entrepreneurial activities. The majority of Greek restaurant owners/ managers are first-generation Greek immigrants. A large number of new Greek immigrants also went into real estate. The 1989, 1990, and 1994–1995 *Hellenic Who's Who in Professions and Businesses* reflect a range of occupations. Greek Americans are lawyers, doctors, academics, educators, engineers, accountants, and the like. However, the large majority, who are small-business people, are not usually contained in the *Hellenic Who's Who*. As individual entrepreneurs, Greek immigrants follow what has been called family capitalism, which was the dominant form of capitalism in the nineteenth and early twentieth centuries. While there has been a decline of family capitalism in American society, the new immigrants—whether Greek, Korean, Mexican, Thai, or Chinese—tend to enter this kind of business. This individualistic and family capitalist orientation reflects the character and nature of the farming classes of rural Greece. The first-generation Greeks brought these rural patterns to America, but they did not have the skills or money to go into managerial forms of capitalism, and the more entrepreneurial among them therefore pursued small business enterprises. With some few exceptions, such as Alexander Pantages and the Skouras Brothers, Greeks have not succeeded in moving into other forms of more organized capitalism, managerial and institutional corporate capitalism.

Despite their rural background, a disproportionate number of first-generation Greeks initiated (or took over) small enterprises, especially in the service sector, including restaurants, groceries, taverns, fruit stores, and candy stores. Why did so many pursue self-employment? Greeks have a long tradition of entrepreneurial activities both in Greece proper and among Greeks of the diaspora. Even before the transatlantic migration commenced, the Greeks of Asia Minor, Egypt, Romania, Pontus (Turkey), and southern Russia were engaged in entrepreneurial activities in those areas. In fact, Greece was a nation of entrepreneurs and migrants even before western Europeans entered the Middle East and Eastern Mediterranean. The Greeks' entrepreneurial spirit is concomitant with their sense of independence and individualism. Even as small farmers in their homeland, Greeks have had their own small farms and learned early on the art of business and exchange. Thus, their work ethic and their sense of ownership, competition, and kinship solidarity were conducive to this entrepreneurial orientation.

The first-generation Greeks established an economic base that later was used as a point of departure by the second and subsequent generations of Greek Americans to move beyond the small restaurant business to chain restaurants and the professions. The absence of managerial-type capitalism in the first generation hindered the ascent of the second generation into the managerial, and indeed the corporate, capitalism of the United States. Of course, the concentration of the first generation in small entrepreneurial activities, especially service-oriented occupations, is not unique among Greeks. Similar patterns were/are followed by many new immigrants as they have entered American society. Italians, Jews, Greeks, and now the new immigrants (Koreans, Thais, Chinese, Vietnamese, Indians, Iranians, Arabs, Mexicans, Cubans, and other Latino Americans) are engaged in small restaurant businesses.

The extent to which second and subsequent generations of Greeks have penetrated the institutional and corporate world is not known for sure. One thing that is certain, however, is that not many Greek Americans are found in the top positions of corporate America. In 1988, *Fortune* magazine listed only one Greek American as a multimillionaire. In Thomas Dye's book *Who Is Running America* (1997), no Greek American is found in any of the twelve elite sectors of American society. In my analysis of the *Hellenic Who's Who in Professions and Businesses*, I did find, not unexpectedly, that the second generation pursues more executive positions in the corporate world than has the first generation. But the type of executive positions pursued and the ranking of the corporations have not been among the leading ones in the United States (with a few exceptions).

Thus, in big cities and small towns across the United States, Greeks have become proprietors and managers of small restaurant businesses, or what one can call facilitators of food preparation and service but not producers of food. They are the middlemen between producers and consumers. The pattern of business ownership followed pretty much the same course across America: Fruit or vegetable peddlers became owners of groceries; flower vendors moved on to florist shops; bootblacks moved into their own shoe repair, hat blocking, or dry cleaning establishments; and confection and sweet shops became a Greek monopoly. Other Greeks went into business in a variety of retail, wholesale, and manufacturing enterprises. Many became wealthy in real estate and stock market speculation. Another area of business that early Greeks followed was movie theaters. The Pantages theater chain controlled about 80 movie houses in the 1920s. The three Skouras brothers brought even greater Greek-American prominence to the movie and entertainment industry. By 1926, the Skouras brothers controlled 37 theaters in St. Louis alone. During the 1930s, the brothers had a chain of over 400 theaters. They became major figures in the motion picture industry in Hollywood itself. Eventually, Spyros Skouras became president of 20th Century Fox.

Alex Rassogianis examined the various businesses of Chicago Greeks during the 1900–1930 period. One of the most important ones discussed was shoeshine parlors, which were the most popular and profitable. Most of these shoeshine parlor owners operated in the best downtown Chicago locations. They were extremely successful, and many Greeks operated chains of shoeshine parlors throughout the city. The Greek shoeshine parlor owners and the boys working in these establishments supplanted the Italians and African Americans. Later, after World War I, the shoeshine business began to decline. In order to remedy this, Greek owners introduced shoe repairing, cleaning and pressing of clothes and hats, and the sale of items found in drugstores, such as tobacco. The majority of the Greek boys working in these parlors were recruited through the notorious padrone system. The "labor boss" wrote to friends and relatives in Greece targeting poor boys from the rural mountain villages of the Peloponnese. These shrewd and ambitious padrone "godfather figures" promised these kids "the world" but in reality lured them into an exploitative system. The earnings of those who worked in the Chicago parlors ranged from $80 to $250 a year, with the average being between $100 and $200. Their counterparts in smaller, less populated cities averaged about $100 a year. In almost all of the shops, money made by the Greek boys from tips was turned over to the owner immediately after a shine or at the end of the day. The owner used the tips to cover the wages and daily expenses of the workers. By the 1920s, the padrone system began to decline along with the shoeshine business.

The next line of business was the confectionery. Confectioners started as peddlers of candy and gradually opened candy and ice cream shops. By 1925, thousands of ice cream parlors and candy shops existed in most metropolitan areas of the country. One of the largest and most popular of the confectionery chains in Chicago was DeMets Candy Stores. The Greeks established candy-manufacturing businesses, which supplied stores. By the early 1920s the Greeks of Chicago dominated all phases of the candy business, a pattern that is no longer the case. Then came restaurants and chains of restaurants. The first restaurants were those serving Greek cuisine. In the early years, many Greeks also operated movable lunch wagons, selling hot dogs, sandwiches, and tamales to factory workers. The traveling lunch wagons later became permanently sited businesses. By 1923, there were 1,035 Greek-owned restaurants in Chicago alone. One of the leading enterprises was John Raklio's chain of restaurants. Raklio went on to establish his own company. Another field in which Greeks were successful was the fruit business. By 1921, for example, the Greeks of Chicago owned 90 retail fruit stores, 26 fruit and vegetable stores, and 80 whole-sale fruit businesses. By 1925, the number of retail fruit stores had risen to 388, backed by 18 wholesale fruit stores. The floral business also sustained some Greeks; in 1923, there were about 13 Greek-owned flower shops in Chicago and 175 in New York.

Many post–World War II Greek immigrants followed the path of their predecessors, going into the food service business. Greek restaurant establishments increased dramatically with the arrival of the new Greek immigrants in the 1950s and 1960s. In 1990, Moskos estimated that there were about 23,000 Greek-owned restaurants and lunchrooms in the United States. Lawrence Lovell-Troy's study of Greeks in Connecticut in the pizza business has shown an ethnic pattern of economic enterprise different from that followed by Italians in the same business. The Greeks tend to establish their pizza businesses in those towns without Greek populations, whereas Italians tend to establish theirs in towns with Italian populations. Given that Greek immigration has dropped dramatically since the mid-1970s, and because Greek restaurants are by and large a first-generation phenomenon, it is reasonable to suggest that the traditional Greek pattern of restaurant entrepreneurship will rapidly decline, too. The extent to which second-generation children of the late Greek immigrants have followed the patterns of their fathers is not known. If we accept the proposition that the children of early Greek immigrants as a rule did not follow their fathers' entrepreneurial activities, it can be argued that the same will happen with the children of the late Greek immigrants. Indeed, there are indications that the second generation of late Greek immigrants are by and large college-bound. Nevertheless, in 1990, Greek immigrants did have the second highest percentage of self-employed men and women among the foreign-born, 17.3 percent and 9.3 percent, respectively (only Koreans had more, 21.3 percent and 14.6 percent). The overall figures for foreign-born were 7.6 percent and 5.7 percent. In addition, over 21 percent of the Greek men were managers/proprietors versus 10.6 percent of all foreign-born persons.

In terms of professionals, we have the same phenomenon. There are several thousand Greek-American professionals (doctors, lawyers, engineers, accountants, teachers, businessmen, salesmen, computer specialists, and the like) but only a few Greek Americans in elite universities, foundations, research institutes, top hospitals, prestigious law firms, or top positions in the communications, media, and movie industries. We have no major Grammy and National Book Award winners. There are no major Greek-American symphony orchestra or music directors. There are no Greek-American Pulitzer Prize winners in journalism or letters (fiction, drama, history, biography or autobiography, poetry, etc.). In 1990, 23.3 percent of Greek immigrant men and 13.4 percent of the women had completed two or more years of college, compared with 29.9 percent and 22.9 percent, respectively, among all immigrants. Furthermore, nearly 11 percent of Greek men and women were professionals as opposed to 11.7 percent and 13 percent among all foreign-born men and women.

Thalia Tsironis Sel, a Greek-American professor at an eastern college, communicated to me that very few Greeks went into the arts due to the fact that

Greeks chose a small number of occupations and professions that offered more financial security. Alice Scourby briefly discusses two dozen first-and second-generation painters and artists whom she characterizes as ''outside the main-stream.'' In addition, Alexander Karanikas covers two dozen or so first-and second-generation Greek prose writers. Furthermore, with the exception of a dozen or so elected and appointed Greek Americans in high positions, there is no real political power among Greek Americans. Most of these appointments were made by the Democratic Party, a few by Republicans. At present we have two Greek-American senators (one in the Republican and one in the Democratic Party) and a few congressmen.[4] There is a tendency to exaggerate the so-called Greek lobby, which became even more noticeable during the Cyprus crisis.

THE FUTURE OF GREEK-AMERICAN ETHNICITY

One of the most important issues concerning Greek ethnicity in particular is the teaching of the Greek language to the children of immigrants. Language is one of the best indices of ethnicity. The issue of bilingualism was very popular in the 1960s and 1970s, encouraged by the resurgence of ethnicity. In terms of ethnic identity, learning the language of the first generation enhances the individual's ethnic image, identity, and understanding of his or her cultural heritage. The first generation (both early and late Greek immigrants) has been more likely to stress bilingual education in Greek and English, whereas the second generation has more commonly stressed English over Greek. By the third generation, the Greek language is rarely spoken by American-born Greek children.

As measured by language, Greek customs, reading Greek newspapers, listening to Greek radio, or speaking Greek, second-generation Greeks in the United States have lost most of their Greek identity. They maintain their Greek names, their Orthodox membership, and their membership in Greek-American organizations primarily for business and professional reasons. (It must also be said that a substantial number of Greeks changed their names by shortening them or adopting another form of Christian faith, following either some Protestant denomination or Roman Catholicism. This was especially the case among early Greeks who experienced more intense social discrimination.) While forty years ago the Greek language was used widely in churches, organizations, and newspapers, by the late 1990s English had replaced Greek in most Greek Orthodox Churches, professional Greek-American organizations, other ethnic organizations, and the ethnic press. This is the case especially in those ethnic organizations composed of second and third generations and mixed membership. While Greek is still used in many Greek Orthodox Churches, particularly those with large Greek congregations, the trend is toward the use of more and more English, owing to the demographic change among Greek Americans, marking their shift from immigrant churches to American-born Greek Orthodox Churches. Dan Georgakas, a Greek-American social historian, believes that Greek ethnic identity and Hellenism in general will be maintained only through an Americanized form of "Greek" who is comfortable with being American but also Greek. The reverse, according to him, does not work, as it leaves the individual in limbo.

CONCLUSION

As one's analysis moves from first to second, third, and subsequent generations, one observes the gradual realignment of Greek ethnicity. From an inner-directed ethnic Greek identity, most strongly represented by the immigrant generation, emerges an identity in the second, third, and subsequent generations of Greeks in diaspora. Concomitant to this transformation are changes in the correlates of Greek ethnic identity: a decline of the Greek traditions; attenuation of family/kinship relations; the decline of Greek language. The first generation was simply Greeks living in America with few identity problems. They had the equivalent of a Protestant work ethic and an entrepreneurial orientation. The fact that they took the initiative to cross the Atlantic made them gutsy, daring argonauts, searching always for the golden fleece. Many of them found it, but a large number of them never managed to come near it. By the second generation, there begins a gradual softening of ethnic identity, and thus it can be argued that the ethnic identity crisis has primarily been a second-generation phenomenon.

As we move across the generations, the institutional/organizational dimension of ethnicity is changing. For the first generation, and to a large extent the second generation, "nationality" and "religion" were the most important aspects of Greek ethnicity. Both the Greek school and Greek church were the most important ethnic institutions, with second-generation identity also manifested through such organizations as AHEPA and the United Hellenic American Congress. However, as we move away from these two generations, Greek customs, Greek traditions, Greek endogamous marriages, and Greek benevolent societies, organized by village or regional societies, more rapidly decline or change. The Greek language gives way to English, the Greek-language schools are far less important, and ethnicity based on nationality gives way to Orthodox Christian religious affiliation. The Orthodox Church as an institution is also changing: from an immigrant church to a homegrown Greek-American Orthodox or mixed church. In every generation intermarriages have also increased. Leadership in most Greek-American ethnic organizations and in the Greek Orthodox Church is also changing. As the old generation of priests is dying out, and few or no Greek priests are coming to the United States, the majority of new Greek parish priests are American-born of second, third, and mixed generations.

Although their numerical significance in most locales has diminished, the economic significance and economic mobility of the Greeks remain impressive. More and more names of Greek Americans appear among the wealthiest of Americans. The number of Greek Americans who support the Greek Orthodox Church with a commitment of over $100,000 per year has reached to about 300. While this socioeconomic mobility of Greek Americans is admirable, it operates as a deterrent of ethnic identity and accelerates the assimilative process of Greek Americans.

NOTES

1. E. P. Panagopoulos, *New Smyrna: An Eighteenth Century Greek Odyssey* (Gainesville: University of Florida Press, 1996), provides one of the few scholarly accounts of the first Greek settlers in the New World in the eighteenth century. According to him, Dr. Andrew Turnbull, a Scottish doctor married to the daughter of a Greek merchant from Smyrna (Asia Minor, now Turkey), was granted lands in east Florida by the king of England and decided to establish a colony there. Turnbull recruited between 400 and 500 Greeks from the region of southern Peloponnese (Mani area). On June 26, 1768, the first ship arrived at St. Augustine, and others followed. The colonists journeyed southward to New Smyrna. Most died of disease. At present, the Greek archdiocese maintains a Greek Orthodox Chapel of St. Photios in St. Augustine in memory of those early settlers.

2. The archbishop is elected by the patriarch, who is, in turn, chosen by the bishops. The patriarch and his bishops reside in Istanbul. The current controversies bring to mind those earlier in the century between supporters of Elephtherios Venizelos (the liberals) and those behind King Constantine of Greece (the royalists) during World War I. They created a schism in the church and communities over entry into the war, with the Venizelists favoring participation alongside the allies and the royalists demanding neutrality. The schism persisted for some time after the war, both in Greece and the United States, and took years to heal.

3. The Greek Orthodox archdiocese is administered by an archbishop who is the primate of the Greek Orthodox Archdiocese of America. The archbishop and five bishops represent the holy synod of bishops who are responsible for the administration of the archdiocese. In addition, there are three more bishops—one is the chief secretary and the other two are auxiliary bishops. There is also a chancellor of the archdiocese who is concerned with the lives of the clergy and their ongoing assignments. The archdiocese consists of a number of departments including, for example, Communications and Public Affairs, Ecumenical Relations, Education and Culture, Finance, Hellenic Cultural Center, Ionian Village, Outreach Ministry, Religious Education, and Youth and Young Adult Ministries.

4. At present, we can identify two Greek-American senators, Olympia Snowe (Rep.–Maine) and Paul Sarbanes (Dem.–Maryland). There are three congressman (two Republicans and one Democrat). Among those serving in high-level positions in the Clinton administration are Ambassador to Luxembourg Clay Constantinou, Assistant Secretary of Housing Nicholas Retsinas, and CIA (Central Intelligence Agency) Director George Tenet. Also noteworthy are former Massachusetts governor Michael Dukakis, the Democratic nominee for president in 1988; Spiro Agnew Anagnostopoulos, vice president under Richard Nixon; Paul Tsongas, the late senator from Massachusetts who sought the Democratic nomination for president in 1992; and George Stephanopoulos, former senior adviser to President Clinton.

BIBLIOGRAPHIC REFERENCES

In preparing this chapter a number of works written by a small group of authors, both Greek American and non-Greek, were useful as sources. George A. Kourvetaris and Betty

A. Dobratz, *A Profile of Modern Greece* (New York: Oxford University Press, 1987), provide an analysis of social institutions of modern Greece based on empirical studies, and Kourvetaris *Studies on Greek Americans* (East European Monographs, 1997) examines a number of different topics on the Greek-American experience. William H. McNeill's *The Metamorphosis of Greece since WWII* (Chicago: University of Chicago Press, 1978) is a short qualitative analysis of social change in postwar Greece. *The Greeks in the United States*, by Theodore Saloutos (Cambridge: Harvard University Press, 1964), continues to be a valuable overview of Greek Americans. Also by the same author is *They Remember America: The Story of Repatriated Greek Americans* (Berkeley: University of California Press, 1952), a study about early Greek immigrants who returned to Greece during the 1910s and 1920s. Other books on early Greek immigrants and their children include Henry Fairchild, *Greek Immigration to the United States* (New Haven, CT: Yale University Press, 1911); Thomas Burgess, *Greeks in America* (Chicago: Sherman, French and Co., 1913); J. P. Xenides, *The Greeks in America* (Reprinted, San Francisco: R & E Research Associates, 1972 [1922]); Michael Dendias, *Greek Colonies around the World* (Athens: privately printed, 1919); and Seraphim Canoutas, *Hellenism in America* (New York: Cosmos Press, 1918 [in Greek]).

Among other useful books on the latter half of the twentieth century is Bobby Malafouris's *Greeks in America 1528–1948* (New York: privately printed, 1948). A special issue on the "Greek American Experience," edited by Dan Georgakas and Charles C. Moskos and published by the *Journal of the Hellenic Diaspora*, 16.1–4 (1989): 1–83, contains a collection of papers on a number of Greek topics. Alice Scourby, *The Greek Americans* (Boston: Twayne Publishers, 1984), examines both early and late Greek immigrants, with emphasis on the early Greek immigrants, Greek American ethnicity, and the Greek-American family. Andrew T. Kopan's *Education and Greek Immigrants, 1892–1973: A Study in Ethnic Survival* (New York: Garland Publishing, Inc., 1990) explores the Greek parochial school system of the Greek archdiocese. Alexander Karanikas's *Hellenes and Hellions* (Champaign-Urbana: University of Illinois Press, 1984) studies various Greek-American and American fiction writers with Greek themes and provides many insights into the Greek-American experience. Charles Moskos, *Greek Americans: Struggle and Success*, 2nd ed. (New Brunswick, NJ: Transaction Publishers, 1990), presents a survey of published writings on the Greeks. Dan Georgakas discusses "Greek American Radicalism: The Twentieth Century" in *The Immigrant Left in the U.S.*, edited by Paul Buhle and Dan Georgakas (Albany: State University of New York Press, 1996), pp. 207–232.

A number of other worthwhile studies are Andreas I. Psomas, "The Nation, the State, and the International System: The Case of Greece" (Ph.D. dissertation, Princeton University, 1974); *Yearbook of Greek Archdiocese, 1997* (New York Archdiocese), a useful source of information on various ethnic and church organizations; Alex Rassogianis, "The Growth of Greek Business in Chicago: 1900–1930" (M.A. thesis, University of Wisconsin at Milwaukee, 1982); Lawrence Lovell-Troy, *The Social Basis of Ethnic Enterprise: Greeks in the Pizza Business* (New York: Garland Publishing, 1990); the *Hellenic Who's Who*, edited by Eugene Rossides (Washington, D.C.: American Hellenic Institute, 1989, 1990, 1994); and, finally, the exchange between Charles Moskos and Dan Georgakas on "Greek Americans" in *Journal of the Hellenic Diaspora* 14.1–2 (Spring and Summer 1987) and Alexandros Kitreoff's "Greek Americans: A Response," ibid. 14.2:55–61.

HAWAIIANS

Pauline Nawahineokala'i King

Hawaiians as Americans are primarily identified with a place: their Island state, the only one in the nation. Moreover, they have always been part of a plural, multicultural society from their entrance as Americans to the present. In 1898 about 29,799 Hawaiians and 9,857 Part-Hawaiians became American citizens by congressional action. The occasion was the annexation of the Republic of Hawai'i by the United States.

Annexation was the result of internal developments in the Kingdom of Hawai'i in the 1890s as a final culmination of the history of the Islands from the 1790s to 1898. In that short period Hawai'i passed from a chiefly society based on a *kapu* system and a subsistence economy to a constitutional monarchy, a Westernized Hawaiian culture, and a commercial economy. The major influence in this transformation was American. First, traders from the eastern United States began to use Hawai'i as a way station in the trans-Pacific trade from Canton, China, to the Pacific Northwest. In time, resident merchants established themselves ashore. The majority of these were American, with some British, French, and German additions.

Following the commercial connection to the outside world, American Calvinist missionaries of the American Board of Commissioners for Foreign Missions landed in the Islands in April of 1820 to bring Christianity to the Hawaiians. By diligent work through the king and chiefs they were successful in converting Hawaiians to Christianity. Although French Catholic missionaries arrived seven years later, the primary influence in the changing Hawai'i was American, both commercial and social. It was also the American missionaries who formed the verbal Hawaiian language into a Western alphabet and began printing and distributing material in the Hawaiian language. They advised the Hawaiian leaders on Western political ideas, and some individual missionaries joined the Hawaiian monarch as advisers and translators. This began the tradition during the monarchy of allowing foreigners to become voting citizens, or denizens. As a result, political Hawai'i was one in which Hawaiians and Caucasians participated together in the life of the kingdom.

WESTERNIZING INFLUENCES

Drastic changes occurred from these external Western influences. The great chief Kamehameha I had united all eight islands into one kingdom by his use of Western military equipment as well as his traditional Hawaiian weaponry. After his death in 1819 his son and a closely related group of chiefs and chiefesses were so influenced by contact with Western goods and ideas for a period of over thirty years that they broke the *kapu* system, ending the state religion. Kamehameha III changed the traditional land system from one of control by the king and chiefs for distribution to one of private property for sale on the open market. In 1850 the legislature, composed of both Hawaiian and Caucasian members, voted to allow foreigners to acquire land. Both of these actions occurred as the kingdom sought to develop commercial agriculture as an export industry. The sugar cane industry began and continued to grow throughout the century. In fact, the kingdom's connection to the United States became overwhelming, for the market for Hawaiian exports, especially sugar, was in the United States. At the same time, the gold rush in California attracted Hawaiians, while others migrated to the new American areas in the Pacific Northwest to work. Hawai'i began to be regarded as part of the western frontier of America, even part of its military perimeter. Residents, mostly citizens of foreign birth or origin from the United States, began to talk of annexation.

In 1893 these same resident Americans plotted a revolution, placing themselves in control of the Hawaiian kingdom. Forming a provisional government, the revolutionists sought annexation to the United States. Refused by the Grover Cleveland administration in 1893, the revolutionists accomplished their objective in 1898, when President William McKinley and the U.S. Congress accepted Hawai'i as part of the nation. Formal transfer of sovereignty took place on August 12, 1898. The initial reaction of Hawaiians at being absorbed into the American nation was one of bitterness and resentment. Hawaiians gloried in the integrity of the Kingdom of Hawai'i and were devoted to the monarchy. When the last monarch, Queen Lili'uokalani, was deposed by the revolutionists, Hawaiians saw it as the triumph of businessmen, mostly American by birth or origin. Thus, there was a sharp division along racial and national lines within the local population.

Moreover, the details of the revolution, investigated by the U.S. Congress, revealed that the revolution was aided and abetted by the U.S. diplomat in Honolulu, John L. Stevens, and the landing of U.S.Marines and sailors from the USS *Boston*, a warship in port. The queen did not yield her throne to the revolutionists but rather to the "superior forces of the United States." She then appealed to the U.S. government to restore her to the throne. President Grover Cleveland made two statements. First, he avoided the question of the restoration of the monarchy by referring the problem to Congress. Second, he confirmed the monarchists' interpretation of the revolution in a long message to Congress on December 18, 1893. He said, in effect, that the American diplomat and naval representatives had assured the success of the local revolution, which would never have succeeded purely as an internal local revolt. He gave this as his reason for rejecting the annexation of the Islands to the United States. Congress replied to Cleveland's message by refusing to interfere in what they considered a purely internal problem of a foreign nation.

RELUCTANT AMERICANS

Faced with this disappointment to their ambitions, the revolutionists formed a republic that would exist until they could ask McKinley for annexation. As a result, Hawaiians entered the American world wary of a society that gave credence to their charges of 1893 yet refused to undo its own wrong. They viewed America with suspicion and resentment and their future with trepidation. Moreover, Hawaiians were at the weakest point in their history. From the date when Captain James Cook placed the Islands on a world map, the population of the Hawaiians had declined rapidly. The major cause of depopulation was the introduction of diseases to which the Hawaiians had no immunity.[1] By 1890, Hawaiians, including a group of mixed ethnic background identified as Part-Hawaiian in statistical records, were outnumbered by the total number of those of foreign origin or birth.

As of 1900 the ethnic distribution of people in the Islands was as follows: Hawaiian, 29,799; Part-Hawaiian, 9,857; Caucasian, 26,819; Chinese, 25,767; Japanese, 61,111; Negro, 233; and Other Groups, 415. The Caucasian population was divided into 18,272 Portuguese and 8,547 "Other Caucasians." The latter term meant all those whose origins were American, British, French, German, and Scandinavian.

Hawaiians had also been eliminated from the labor force in the major industry, sugar cane production. As late as 1887 Hawaiians made up about 17 percent of that labor. By 1899 they had been reduced to about 3 percent, overwhelmed by the expansion of an industry requiring larger numbers of workers and by the government of the Islands, which, under the leadership of the monarchy (beginning with Kamehameha V), had pursued an immigration policy of importing large numbers of contract labor to work on plantations, especially from China and Japan as well as from the Portuguese Islands and Europe.[2] Indeed, the multiracial complexion of the Island population was a result of the government's direction of immigration policy. Nonetheless, Hawaiians did participate in the changing economic world as supervisors on plantations, in lower-level management positions, and in some executive positions in corporations. Those who had kept their landholdings often leased them to large companies or developed their own cattle ranches and farms. Hawaiians were small businessmen, cowboys, artisans, salesmen, and farmers. Nevertheless, they were now aware that they held a minority position in the basic economic life of their land.

Hawaiian culture also had evolved into a Westernized form. The kingdom was still rich in traditional culture. Etiquette and manners, social values, and customs led by the monarchy, which had adopted and adapted European protocol, were still the leading pattern for society, and the Hawaiian language continued to be the language of the kingdom. But English was also being used in trade and politics, and Western musical instruments and melodic forms were being added to Hawaiian chants, producing a different but discernible Hawaiian music accompanied by dance innovations. During the kingdom, national groups had remained isolated from each other, and class distinctions within and between groups had kept the kingdom compartmentalized. The Territory of Hawai'i entered the American orbit with the same divisions among its population. Consequently, it was a plural, multicultural society from its beginnings as an American territory but one that was loosely united as a community possessing a common culture in which all participated.

Politically, Hawaiians were strongest. By 1898 they had had seventy-five years of experience with democratic institutions. Hawaiians had served in the legislature and in the administration of the monarchy; they had served as judges and magistrates; and Hawaiian men had voted, with the law sometimes restricting the vote to those with property and other times allowing universal manhood suffrage. Notwithstanding the overthrow of the monarchy, the political situation of Hawaiians continued and was even strengthened by annexation. In 1900 the U.S. Congress passed an Organic Act to serve as the governing structure of the territory, and by its provisions, all citizens of the Republic of Hawaii, as of August 12, 1898, automatically became citizens of the United States. Thus, Hawaiians and Part-Hawaiians as well as Caucasians immediately became American citizens. Present records do not identify any Chinese or Japanese who fit into this category. Moreover, all aliens of Asian or Malaysian origins could not become citizens because of American naturalization laws.

Given that, Hawaiians dominated the citizen population and registered over 50 percent of the voting population until the 1920s, continuing as a significant percentage of the voting population into the 1960s. This situation made the difference in the assimilation process of Hawaiians into American society, for Congress, with testimony from Hawai'i, established a government for the Territory that gave Hawaiians some recognition in their own land. The Organic Act established several important principles. First, the local government was structured so that the appointment of the executive and the judiciary was made by the president of the United States, with confirmation by the U.S. Senate. The local legislature and a delegate to Congress were elected by popular vote in the Islands. Consequently, the governors of Hawai'i were all, with one exception, Caucasian (or *haole*) men whose appointments came about because of their political connections to the national patronage complex. Local judgeships were also dominated by Caucasian appointments.

A second aspect of the Organic Act was that it established Hawai'i as an incorporated Territory wherein the Constitution applied: All persons born in Hawai'i after 1898 automatically became citizens with the right to vote. Congress had no distrust of Hawaiians, whom they considered a tractable, amiable people. Nor, with a Territorial government controlled from Washington, did Congress fear the growing Asian citizen population. Throughout the Territorial period, appointments from Washington reflected the American belief in white supremacy. On the other hand, Hawaiian leadership had the votes to impose their will on the new local government. At the same time, the Caucasian (or *haole*) leadership had control over the economy of the Territory through its ownership of the corporations that produced sugar and pineapples and through interlocking directorates that dominated the basic industries of transportation, utilities, and financial institutions. Thus, the two groups that were in contention in the new Territory were exactly the same groups that had been in contention over the existence of the monarchy and the annexation to the United States.

At first, Hawaiians proved not to be so tractable. They formed a political party, called the Home Rule Party, to prepare for the first election of a congressional delegate and the territorial legislature. The Home Rule Party won a majority in the legislature and elected Robert Wilcox, a Part-Hawaiian political leader, as a delegate to Congress. That majority prepared to undermine the administration of the new territory. Sanford B. Dole was the appointed governor. He had been president of the Provisional Government and the Republic, was the symbol of the hated revolutionists, and was disliked personally. Dole felt as much contempt for the Home Rulers as they felt for him and his supporters. Both groups spent the first legislature of the Territory of Hawaii harassing each other.

However, many leaders of the Hawaiians believed that a better way for themselves and their people to proceed was to take part in American society on national as well as local terms. They therefore joined the national parties and prepared to participate in national conventions as Republicans and Democrats. Two such Hawaiians were nephews of Lili'uokalani. David Kawananakoa signed up with the Democratic Party. His brother, Jonah Kuhio Kalanianaole, became a Republican and was elected delegate in 1902 and reelected ten more times, serving twenty years in Congress. This move by Hawaiian leadership was instrumental in stabilizing the internal society as American in structure and Hawaiian in sensitiveness. The local legislature showed its agreement with this situation by voting unanimously for a request to Congress for statehood in 1903—at a time when thirty of the forty-five members of that legislature were Hawaiian and Part-Hawaiian. Thus began the political union, sometimes tenuous, of Hawaiians (or *kanaka*) and Caucasians in what the local pidgin English called the "Kaznak" leadership of the territory. Through this process the Territory had become by World War II an English-speaking society with a public school system teaching in every school on every island the democratic principles of equality and freedom and such American values as individualism, hard work, and progress.

Several crises proved that the cooperation of the Kaznaks was anything but perfect. At one point, Kuhio accused Governor Walter Frear of misusing the public lands. Kuhio demanded and obtained an investigation by the federal Interior Department. Frear was absolved of all wrongful acts. Later, the usual business supporters of Kuhio launched an effort to defeat him in his reelection for delegate to Congress, but Kuhio was reelected.

CULTURAL LOSS

Notwithstanding the political situation, the process of Americanization for Hawaiians did not occur without further loss of identity as a people. In fact, the largest category of Hawaiians had become the Part-Hawaiian. Marrying out of their own group, Hawaiians were now most often a mixture of Caucasian, Asian, and Malaysian origins. The Part-Hawaiians accepted the adoption of standard English as the language of the Territory and joined in the effort to stifle the use of the Hawaiian language. They began to write the words of their songs in English or in a combination of English and Hawaiian. They accepted the idea of the superiority of the Caucasian and used for themselves identifications of Hawaiian Caucasian and Hawaiian Chinese, the latter as a term indicating a form of inferiority. They felt that the Caucasians born in Hawai'i had become Hawaiianized. While Islanders still emphasized the uniqueness of Hawaiian culture, the carriers of that culture were often either Caucasians or Caucasians in union with Hawaiians. This occurred when outrigger canoe racing and surfing were emphasized; when painters used Hawaiian subject matter for their art; when architects developed a style reminiscent of Polynesian structures; and when festivals were started that centered the celebration around Hawaiian historical events and subjects. At the same time, individual Hawaiians began migrating to the mainland states, where they worked and often succeeded in business, politics, the military, entertainment, and the arts. These Hawaiians often minimized or lost their Hawaiianness.

Despite the comfortableness of their place in the territory, Hawaiians continued to be displaced as the major workforce of the sugar industry and the newly developed pineapple industry. Large-scale immigration from Japan and then the Philippines continued until 1934. Hawaiian leaders believed that many Hawaiians were being further pressed into a marginalized position in terms of job competition and standard of living. Hawaiian political leadership took up the cause of the poor and undermined, especially those of full Hawaiian blood. Finally, the local legislature and Delegate Kuhio memorialized Congress to establish a special program under territorial control that would provide public land for Hawaiians of 50 percent or more blood quantum so that they could acquire, through a long-term lease at minimum rent, agricultural or residential lots. While hearings in Congress did refer to federal policy toward American Indians, the Hawaiian Homes Commission Act of 1920 did not follow the structure of reservations and Indian laws. Through this program the pressure for improvement of the conditions of Hawaiians was alleviated for a time. Moreover, it was expected that "pure" Hawaiians, and even those of 50 percent blood quantum, would die out and what would be left was a growing population of only Part-Hawaiians.

The dynamic for a multicultural society had been set by the Organic Act. Gradually, the population profile changed as born-in-Hawai'i children added to the citizen category. Optimistic Islanders, including Hawaiians, believed that they demonstrated a perfect example of the ability of American ideals to merge together a racially mixed population. By the 1920s, it had become a common statement that Hawai'i had little or no racism in its society. And if the melting pot was the ideal for American society and hopefully the norm for all American communities, then Kaznak society had succeeded remarkably.

However, two court cases concerning the accusation of gang rape followed by a murder exposed a Hawai'i that was instead a society still divided by class, race, and nationality. The year 1931 was the beginning of the Ala Moana and the Massie cases, involving a wife of a naval officer as the victim, five local men of mixed Hawaiian, Caucasian, Chinese, and Japanese ethnicity as the perpetrators of the crime, and Mrs. Massie's husband and her mother, Mrs. Grace Fortescue, as the murderers of a Hawaiian man who was one of the accused. The rape case ended in a hung jury. The murder case ended in a guilty verdict of Lt. Massie, Mrs. Fortescue, and the sailors who were involved. Mainland newspapers and speeches in Congress reflected the general opinion there that Hawai'i was a community of savage barbarians incapable of a civilized society. As a result, the territorial government was threatened by congressional amendments of its Organic Act to strip the Islands of what self-government it had. In Hawai'i, the governor of the territory decided that he would commute the sentence of the four criminals to one hour served in his office. The people of Hawai'i, on the whole, were bitterly critical of a structure that allowed such an obvious misuse of the judicial system.

In Washington it was decided that a commission from the Justice Department be sent to investigate the quality of the judicial and police systems in the Islands. The Territory survived both the threats and the investigation. But the two cases had revealed that Island society was permeated with prejudices against races and classes that did not seem to fit the American ideal of a comfortable middle-class society assimilated to white, Anglo-Saxon, Protestant norms. Concerted efforts were made in the community to rectify the bitter divisions revealed by the two cases. Community programs of sports and civic associations were intensified to unite Hawai'i's races and nationalities. The movement for statehood was pushed in Congress and in a massive educational program within the Islands.

By the early 1940s Hawai'i had a fully participating citizen population of all its ethnic groups. It seemed that Hawai'i had achieved the ultimate place as an American community deserving of statehood. The ideal, of course, was not reflected in society. Racial feelings did exist, but they were neither institutionalized by public policy (such as with restrictive covenants) nor tolerated in overt verbalizations. Moreover, the record of Hawai'i's people during World War II as a fully mobilized society, and particularly the record of the Japanese Americans serving in the military, had reflected a society whose people were fully assimilated as Americans. In post–World War II Hawai'i vast changes occurred as they did throughout the United States. Sugar and pineapple production began to decline as the economic base of the Islands. Tourism was gradually growing as the major industry. Statehood in 1959 brought the Islands voting representation in Congress. But there was a feeling of disappointment.

On the one hand, the melting pot ideal emphasized assimilation, unity, and homogeneity as the only cultural goal; any deviation from the core pattern was considered an insignificant survival of a dying culture. On the other hand, many Hawaiians either did not want to assimilate or could not adapt to a modern society so alien to their ancient past. For them, the "*haole*fied" Hawaiian culture seemed to have grown stale and far removed from the distinguishing ethos of this people. In time, then, if Hawaiians knew and could foresee that their majority position would change, they could also see that no one ethnic group had reached a majority of the population. Chinese had attained a high of 25 percent of the population in 1884; the Japanese, 43 percent in 1920; and the Filipinos, 17 percent in 1930. Hawaiians were the merging factor that helped make all races cooperate in a unified society. The intermarriage factor helped in ameliorating tensions among groups. But Hawaiians still felt threatened by the changing population profile. The group that Hawaiians most feared was the growing number of citizens of Japanese ancestry, even though the Hawaiian and Part-Hawaiian populations were also growing. By 1960, there were 203,455 who were classified as Japanese in the Islands and 102,403 as Hawaiian and part Hawaiian; 32.2 percent of the population was of Japanese ancestry, whereas Hawaiians made up 16.2 percent.

CULTURAL REVIVAL

Several ethnic Hawaiian movements began in the 1970s. In music and dance, hula masters revived old chants and the vigorous dance forms that accompanied them. They did not dismiss modern hula but distinguished between the old (*kahiko*) and the new (*awana*). Hawaiian artists, artisans, and architects began to express themselves in what they felt was a true expression of the Hawaiian spirit. Calls for the use of the Hawaiian language were advanced. Individuals and small groups of Hawaiians began increasing their demands because of what they perceived as their rightful place in Hawai'i and as American citizens. They sought political rights over and above the rest of the state's population precisely because they were Hawaiian.

Hawaiian leaders working through the state's congressmen obtained federal funds for programs specifically for Hawaiians, and many Hawaiian leaders, such as Myron "Pinkie" Thompson, hoped that Congress would designate Hawaiians as Native Americans. In this manner all legislation that favored Indians would automatically include Hawaiians. Their rationale was that Hawaiians were an aboriginal people of American land like the Native Americans. But Congress preferred to distinguish Hawaiians from the rest of the nation's indigenous populations by enacting special legislation for Native Hawaiians. For the present, then, the term *Native Hawaiian* has both cultural and practical meaning for the Islands.

The term *sovereignty* became a slogan as the Hawaiian movement grew. The focus of the attention of the various groups centered on the public lands. At annexation the republic turned over (ceded) all public lands to the United States. Upon granting statehood, the federal government returned most of those lands to the State of Hawai'i as its public lands. Hawaiians now claimed that these lands, originating in the kingdom, are native lands and should be used for Hawaiian purposes and administered by Native Hawaiians. The movement has had many different groups sometimes seeking different aspects of their claims to rights, but they all center on the point that the public, or ceded, lands of the State of Hawai'i should belong to the Hawaiian people.

The movement was primarily a grassroots movement. In the beginning, most Hawaiians were appalled by the activities of sovereignty groups. Assimilated into modern American society in the professions and business, and throughout the spectrum of the economy, they viewed the activists as somehow retreating into a long lost past. Moreover, they viewed it as a past no longer crucial to their Hawaiian American lives. Gradually, the sentiment changed from one of disapproval to reluctant admiration and then to general support. Hawaiian groups continued to pressure for Hawaiian rights. For example, an organization of young people, the Protect Kaho'olawe 'Ohana (PKO), challenged the right of the navy to continue to bomb the uninhabited Island of Kaho'olawe. The navy had the Island under lease from the Territory of Hawai'i and the state. It was supposed to return the Island eventually to the state. The navy pressured to have the lease converted into ownership. It posted the entire Island as off limits to the general public. In the early 1970s, PKO members began to visit the Island illegally but surreptitiously. In 1975 members defied federal law by landing on the Island and making their activities public. Two members were convicted of trespass in federal court and spent a short term in prison. Members of the group continued to pressure for access to the Island and its eventual return to the state. Another group demanded the acceptance of the Hawaiian language in immersion schools in the public school system. As a result, several immersion schools were added to the public school system wherein all subjects were taught in the Hawaiian language. A nonprofit organization, Alu Like, was formed to begin research into the concerns and problems of Native Hawaiians. It organized a census whereby Hawaiians could identify themselves by registering with Alu Like. No blood quantum was part of this new census.

As other emphases on Hawaiian culture have captured the imagination and participation of more and more Hawaiians and, indeed, of many non-Hawaiian Islanders, the sovereignty movement has taken hold on the minds of most Hawaiians. The strength of the feeling of power by Hawaiians led to significant changes in the political atmosphere. In 1978 a state constitutional convention included a provision for an organization to be formed to represent Hawaiians. The movement was led by Adelaide "Frenchy" DeSoto, a Part-Hawaiian activist from a country district heavily populated by Hawaiians, and assisted by several delegates, among them John Waihe'e, later a governor of the state. The result was that the Office of Hawaiian Affairs (OHA) was established as a state organization but administered by a board of trustees elected by Hawaiians only. OHA is also recognized by the federal government and represents Hawaiians in the state and on the mainland. In the years since its establishment it has become the strongest voice of the modern movement. It has received state and federal funds and has programs of research, grants, development, and future planning. Nonetheless, there are still competing units that wish to represent Hawaiians. Unofficial groups continue to proselytize, seeking objectives counter to those of OHA. Some groups say their aim is seeking the reestablishment of the Hawaiian Kingdom, with full international recognition as a sovereign state. Others call for some form of a state within a state, with differing ideas about how much power should be negotiated to the federal and state governments and how much sovereignty should be granted the Hawaiian nation.

Finally, in 1993 a massive daylong program was held to mark the one-hundreth anniversary of the revolution of 1893. Hawaiians turned out en masse as well as many other residents to acknowledge what they agreed was a wrong committed by the United States against the Hawaiian Kingdom. U.S. Senator Daniel Akaka introduced, and the Congress passed, a resolution of apology to the Hawaiian people for the actions of the American diplomatic and military representatives on the days of January 14–17, 1893. On November 23, 1993, President Bill Clinton signed the apology.

Thus, Hawaiians have reached a state today of reawakening themselves as a distinct and powerful people. They have succeeded in forcing the navy to return the Island of Kaho'olawe to the State of Hawai'i. They have seen the establishment of immersion schools where Hawaiian is the language of learning. Nevertheless, many issues remain unresolved by modern Hawaiians. Not all Hawaiian groups agree on what they mean by, or want out of, sovereignty. The Hawaiian Homes program still exists only for Hawaiians with a blood quantum of 50 percent or more. OHA's census includes Hawaiians by self-identification, and many of their programs include all Hawaiians so identified without a blood quantum requirement. On the whole, Hawaiians are no longer divided among themselves by color or ethnic mixture designations. In 1990 the U.S. Bureau of the Census reported 138,742 Hawaiians out of a state population of 1,108,229. OHA estimates that Hawaiians make up about 14 percent of the population.[3]

In the 1970s, more Hawaiians began to migrate to the mainland states than had been previously common. Hawaiians were motivated by economic opportunities available on the mainland and less and less open to them in the Islands. Many preferred the environment in mainland states. Many retirees found Hawai'i becoming too expensive to provide them with the kind of comfortable life that they had imagined retired life would bring them. With their Hawai'i retirement benefits, they believed they could find such a life in places on the mainland. In 1996, at least 73,000 Hawaiians lived in the continental states, residing in twelve or more states. Fifty-nine percent of them were located in the Pacific Coast states, about 35,000 of them in California. There were at least 25 in Vermont. Unlike the Hawaiians who lived outside the Islands before World War II, these Hawaiians identify themselves as such and register with OHA. Wherever they are located, they often group together to perpetuate their cultural roots and practice their spiritual connections to the past. Dance groups travel to the Islands to compete in the various hula festivals that occur. And they are cognizant of the contemporary Hawaiian issues in the state and in many instances are beneficiaries of Hawaiian programs.

What, then, has been the experience of Hawaiians as Americans? Because of their primary identity with a place, their growth has been identified with the development of the Islands. Often displaced for the most part from the major economic bases of Hawai'i, Hawaiians have felt like strangers in their own land. Throughout the last 200 years of Island history, as immigrant groups have succeeded in business and mainstream society, many of them have convinced Hawaiians that they are indeed strangers in their own land.

Since Hawaiians have been told they are alienated Americans, why have they adjusted to American society and become ardent and loyal Americans? Part of the answer lies in the character of the Hawaiian population. Today, as part of the need to assist needy Hawaiians in education, welfare, and health, studies have emphasized the negative characteristics among Hawaiians. We are told that Hawaiians make up the highest population in local prisons and that Hawaiians are in jeopardy, leading all other ethnic groups in the high incidence of school dropouts, welfare recipients, and such disorders as diabetes as well as the lowest levels of income.

Throughout Island history, however, Hawaiians have also remained among the social and economic elite. Many retained their traditional lands inherited from the 1800s. Today, some of the most profitable private estates have Hawaiian beneficiaries. Hawaiians also have retained their respect for the descendants of the chiefly classes of old. Many of these modern Hawaiians continue the paternalistic practice of assisting the needy members of families that had associations with their families in the past. A major, and difficult, problem for Hawaiians is the classification of who they are. Many Hawaiians believe that they are prejudged as a people. In census statistics gathered by government bureaus of the federal and state governments, and by private associations that analyze society by numbers, Hawaiians are placed in the most negative categories. Yet Hawaiians are such a mixture of racial and ethnic origins that modern Hawaiians challenge the conclusions of such statements as that written in 1974: "It was clear . . . that, statistically speaking at least, contemporary Hawaiian-Americans had become another 'deprived' American minority group." Hawaiians believe that, in the attempt to solve social problems, researchers have simply developed a profile of Hawaiians on the basis of a minority that they have determined to be at risk. They are understandably skeptical of these statistically based studies. They are also struggling with the concepts of identity and culture and what declarations or pronouncements might be made that would reflect their own beliefs.

Today's movement to secure rights specifically for Hawaiians is also part of the American experience. The techniques used to accomplish the objectives as Native Hawaiians are based in the American tradition of protest as seen from Thoreau through the civil rights movement of the 1960s and 1970s. Nonetheless, as a people of color, and at the same time as a people with equal rights in their Island home, Hawaiians have existed as an example of racial equality to the American nation. It is naive to assume that this equality was granted to Hawaiians by all others in a spirit of love and aloha. On the contrary, simply by the nature of Hawai'i's history as an independent nation, annexed by the United States and granted citizenship automatically by Congress, Hawaiians achieved their place as Americans as a right.

The current movement to achieve more rights as Native Hawaiians is certainly consistent with contemporary movements throughout the United States that continue to seek social justice and equal rights for all groups.

NOTES

1. A major controversy exists today on what the total population of the Islands was at the time of Cook in 1778. Anthropologists, population experts, and scholars posit figures anywhere from 250,000 through 500,000 to 800,000. Whatever the basic population was, figures kept after 1778 show the dramatic decline of the population.

2. The government of the Kingdom of Hawaii created a Bureau of Immigration in 1865 so that the government might have some control over population changes. It set the standard contract for laborers and monitored the system by periodic investigations of plantations. Both the government and private companies recruited immigrants in compliance with the general policies of the kingdom. The republic continued the system.

3. As of 1994, OHA estimates Hawaiians to number about 150,000. The figures stated are a mean among OHA, State of Hawaii Health Survey, and Bureau of Census figures as calculated by OHA, which also estimates the present percentage of Hawaiians of the state population as from 14 to 17 percent.

BIBLIOGRAPHIC REFERENCES

For a thorough look at the revolution of 1893 and the process of achieving annexation to the United States, the two works by William A. Russ, Jr., are most helpful. They are *The Hawaiian Revolution (1893–94)* and *The Hawaiian Republic (1894–98): And Its Struggle to Win Annexation*. Both were republications in 1992 by the Associated University Presses, London and Toronto, of the 1961 works by Russ that were first published by Susquehanna University Press. For the Territorial period, the best short form of discussion can be found in the work by Ralph S. Kuykendall and A. Grove Day, *Hawaii:*

A History: From Polynesian Kingdom to American Statehood (Englewood Cliffs, NJ: Prentice-Hall, 1961). The role of Hawaiians as the unifying cultural group in the Territory can be found in the work of Romanzo Adams, *Interracial Marriage in Hawaii* (New York: Macmillan, 1937). For present information on Hawaiians, the publication of the Office of Hawaiian Affairs, "Data Book" (Honolulu, 1994), is the best. OHA keeps its data current and periodically prints its results for distribution to public repositories.

Material on population statistics of Hawaiians from 1778 on can be found in Robert C. Schmitt, *Demographic Statistics of Hawaii, 1778–1965* (Honolulu: University of Hawaii Press, 1968); and Schmitt, *Historical Statistics of Hawaii* (Honolulu: University of Hawaii Press, 1977). Discussion of the controversy over the size of the population before Western contact can be found in O. A. Bushnell, *The Gifts of Civilization: Germs and Genocide in Hawai'i* (Honolulu: University of Hawaii Press, 1993); and David E. Stannard, *Before the Horror* (Honolulu: Social Science Research Institute, 1989).

Articles and studies that have considered the results of contact between Hawaiians and Westerners include Pauline N. King, "Structural Changes in Hawaiian History: Changes in the Mental Health of a People," in *Contemporary Issues in Mental Health Research in the Pacific Islands* edited by Albert B. Robillard and Anthony J. Marsella. (Honolulu: Social Science Research Institute, 1987), pp. 32–44; Michael K. Dudley, *Man, Gods, and Nature* (Honolulu: Na Kane O Ka Malo Press, 1990); Robert H. Mast and Anne B. Mast, *Autobiography of Protest in Hawai'i* (Honolulu: University of Hawaii Press, 1996), which includes an article on sovereignty with writings by Kekuni Blaisdell, Lynette Cruz, Mililani Trask, Davianna McGregor, Hayden Burgess, and Ku'umeaaloha Gomes; and George Hu'eu Kanahele, *Ku Kanaka Stand Tall: A Search for Hawaiian Values* (Honolulu: University of Hawaii Press and Waiaha Foundation, 1986).

Modern protest writings include the work of Haunani K. Trask, *From a Native Daughter* (Monroe, ME: Common Courage Press, 1993); and Michael K. Dudley and Keoni K. Agard, *A Call for Hawaiian Sovereignty* (Honolulu: Na Kane O Ka Malo Press, 1990).

Recently, individuals and publishers have begun to print historical material written in the Hawaiian language in order to indicate how Hawaiians viewed their own lives in the past. Committed individuals and small publishing houses insist on the expensive process of printing the original Hawaiian on one page and the modern translation on the facing page. One of the best of these authors, translators, publishers is Malcolm Naea Chun. For example, he translated and edited a work by Hawaiians, *Must We Wait in Despair: The 1867 Report of the 'Ahahui La'au Lapa'au of Wailuku, Maui on Native Hawaiian Health* (Honolulu: First People's Productions, 1994). The association ('Ahahui) had been formed by those concerned with the present and future health of their people and in an effort to have a positive influence on the problem over and above the work of the then Board of Health of the Kingdom of Hawai'i.

IRISH

Timothy J. Meagher

It is an old saw among Irish Americans that it was an Irishman, a Galwayman from Ireland's West Coast, who first spied the land of the Americas from Columbus's ship or rowed the "discoverer's" boat to shore or first stepped onto the beach. For diehards among Irish Americans, the Irish link to the Americas is even older. They believe that St. Brendan the Navigator, a monk from Ireland's west Kerry coast, had crossed the Atlantic to American shores only a little over a century after the fall of the Roman empire. The second-generation Irish mayor of Worcester, Massachusetts, John J. Duggan, proclaimed without a touch of irony in 1914 that the descendants of Brendan's monks melted into Native American peoples, and their ancestors could still be found among native peoples from Georgia to the Chesapeake Bay. Proof, he argued, was evident in the amazing linguistic similarities between native American tongues and ancient Gaelic.

AN OVERVIEW OF IRISH MIGRATIONS TO AMERICA

Such assertions tell much more about the persistent insecurity of Irish Americans than about when their people actually arrived in America. Yet if these claims contained more than a little special pleading, they do suggest a truth about the Irish presence in the Americas, or more specifically what became the United States. Irishmen may not have arrived before Columbus or even with him, but they were here soon after. In the seventeenth century, anywhere from 50,000 to 100,000 people left Ireland, or were forced to leave it as convict labor, for the Americas. Many, perhaps most, of these emigrants went, or were compelled to go, to the West Indies. In 1660, perhaps as much as a fifth of Barbados's population was Irish. But substantial numbers of Irish found their way to North America or were brought there as servants. In the 1630s, for example, John Winthrop, governor of Massachusetts Bay Colony, brought an Irish boy with him to "Shawmut," the original name for Boston, to tend his sheep, and in 1643, Isaac Jogues, the Jesuit missionary to French Canada, laying over in New Amsterdam after an ocean crossing, was stopped on the street by an Irish Catholic who wished to confess his sins. By the eighteenth century the number of Irish coming to North America had increased to 250,000 and reached a flood tide just before the Revolution.

What is most striking about Irish migration to America is not how early it began but how it continued to grow through the nineteenth century and never really stopped in the twentieth. The Great Famine migration of the late 1840s and 1850s is best known, a tragic uprooting of 2 million people, three-quarters of whom came to the United States. But annual migration from Ireland to America had already reached mass dimensions, over 50,000 people a year, by the early 1830s, a decade before the Great Famine. After the Famine the Irish would continue to come, their numbers rising and falling with changing economic conditions at home or in America, but the stream of Irish men and women never ceased. From 1856 to 1921, 3 million Irish came to America, and the number of Irish immigrants living in the United States continued to grow until it reached its high point in 1890. The heaviest post-Famine migration came in the 1860s and 1880s, the lightest in the 1870s, when the American economy slipped into depression while Irish agriculture flourished. In the twentieth century the flow of Irish immigration to America slowed, but there were surges in the 1920s and 1950s and a recent torrent of young Irish immigrants, many of them illegals, during the 1980s. By the 1980 census over 40 million Americans claimed some Irish ancestry; only Americans claiming English or German roots were more numerous.

The remarkable continuity of Irish migration to America may obscure the radical changes in the kinds of Irish who came here. One obvious change was in the religious background of the immigrants. Little is known about the seventeenth-century Irish immigrants, but one source suggests that as many as three-quarters of them, largely servants and convicts, may have been Catholic. In the eighteenth century the vast majority were Protestants, largely Presbyterians but including many Quakers and some Methodists, as well. These Protestant Irish suffered from poor harvests, rising rents, economic displacement from a spreading British market, and religious discrimination against them as dissenters by the established Church of Ireland. Many moved on from an Irish frontier, where they lived among an angry, if beaten and dispossessed, native Irish population to an American frontier, where there was no less of a threat from dispossessed natives, but the stock of land to be taken was so much greater. By the late 1820s and 1830s the trend had shifted to Catholic immigrants. Catholics had certainly suffered before this time. Indeed, after the English conquest of Ireland in a century of warfare from the 1580s to the 1690s, they were reduced almost en masse to an impoverished peasantry. Yet locked into the tight communal and familial networks that had helped them endure their defeat and degradation, and fearful of travel to a distant and unknown country, they had remained rooted in Ireland, while the more confident Protestants had moved on to the new land. Only as the spread of the market economy and accompanying English culture began to loosen some of those older communal bonds and the constraints of population pressure forced their flight did they begin to leave in great numbers. Catholics have dominated emigration from Ireland to America ever since.

The shifting regional origins of immigrants from Ireland paralleled these changes in religious backgrounds. The majority of the Protestant migrants in the eighteenth century, for example, came from northern Ireland, the province of Ulster. They stopped coming in great numbers in the nineteenth century as industrialization in the areas in and around Belfast opened up new opportunities for them at home. With Catholic migration picking up in the nineteenth century, the principal centers of migration shifted south to the provinces of Leinster in the southeast, and especially Munster in the southwest, where the impact of the spreading British market had become pervasive. By the end of the nineteenth century a disproportionate number of the migrants were coming from the far west, the province of Connaught and the western coasts of Counties Kerry and Donegal, the last strongholds of Gaelic culture.

Finally, the gender balance of Irish migration shifted over the course of the nineteenth century. Early in the century migrants were largely single males and families. During the worst years of the Famine, there was a notable increase in family migration. After the Famine, Irish immigration became increasingly dom- inated by unmarried persons who left their families for America once they reached their late teens or early twenties. This was not uncommon among most immigrant groups; young adults made up the vast majority of migrants among Italians, Greeks, Poles, and many other groups. What was distinctive about Irish migration in the late nineteenth century was that a large number of these young adults were single women. From 1881 to 1921 over half of young, adult Irish immigrants to America (aged fifteen to twenty-four) were women, and in some decades, such as the 1890s, young women outnumbered young men by as much as three to two. For no other group were the proportions of single women so high.

THE IRISH AND THE AMERICAN ECONOMY: MOVING UP THE LADDER—SLOWLY

Assets and Deficits

Irish immigrants had several advantages over migrants from other countries when they came to America. In particular, most of them spoke English. Before 1750, the overwhelming majority of rural people and even many urban dwellers in Ireland still spoke Irish. A little over a century later, only about a quarter of Ireland's people spoke Irish regularly, and far fewer, only a few hundred thou- sand out of about 8 million people, could speak only Irish. Many Irish immigrants, nonetheless, still struggled with English. In the late 1880s and 1890s, as the sources of Irish immigration shifted to western Ireland, as many as a quarter or a third of immigrants leaving for America could speak English but were born into a Gaelic-speaking culture. These people's knowledge of English and ability to use it effectively, as Kerby Miller has noted, may have been quite limited. Still, most Irish going to America in the nineteenth century were at least familiar with the English language before they left Ireland.

Increasing numbers over the nineteenth century were literate in English, as well. Founded in Ireland in 1831, the National School system helped eradicate the Irish language among its young charges and proved extraordinarily success-ful in providing them with a basic education in English. In 1851 about 50 percent of the Irish over the age of five could not read or write; by 1901 the proportion had fallen to 14 percent, and among people aged twelve to forty years, only 6 percent. By that time the Irish literacy rate was actually higher than in Britain or the United States.

A third advantage many Irish brought with them to America was a familiarity with Anglo-Saxon government and experience in political organization. The Irish knew at least the forms of Anglo-Saxon government—common law, jury trials, parliamentary elections—even if they were excluded from some because of their poverty (or religion until the 1820s) and others were manipulated against them to keep them poor and docile. Moreover, through participation in a series of mass political movements, from Catholic Emancipation in the 1820s to Re-peal in the 1840s and the Land League and the Plan of Campaign in the 1880s, Irish peasants gained experience in political organization and mobilization. In-deed, historian Thomas Brown has claimed that as early as the 1840s and 1850s the Irish were the most politicized peasantry in Europe—and probably the world.

Such advantages, oddly enough, proved only marginally helpful to most Irish immigrants in the United States in the nineteenth and twentieth centuries. It is difficult to determine with certainty, but in the early nineteenth century, when immigration seemed to skim off a disproportionate share of the skilled and the bold even among Catholics in Ireland, Irish newcomers in the United States appeared to achieve a modicum of success in moving into trades and other skilled work. Even then, however, significant numbers of Irish immigrants had become stuck in the floating proletariat of canal and railroad workers near the bottom of America's economic hierarchy.

The Famine immigrants—many of them reluctant émigrés, bewildered and demoralized by the disaster that ripped them out of their homeland, unskilled and unprepared for an American economy—fared even worse than their pre-decessors. In many cities approximately half of the men found no work better than common laborer, and few made any serious upward progress thereafter. In Buffalo, for example, as many as 46 percent of Irish immigrant men in 1855 had no regular place of employment; they drifted from job to job, company to company.

More surprising, perhaps, were the poor economic achievements of Irish immigrants who arrived in America after the Famine, in the late nineteenth and early twentieth centuries. Despite the benefits they reaped from the new National Schools at home and the advantages of migrating after Irish communities were well established in America, many of these immigrants began at the bottom of the American economic ladder and still made only inching progress up it over the course of their lives. In 1900, 25.5 percent of Irish immigrant men in America were day laborers; in the same year, 54.4 percent of Irish immigrant women were domestic servants.

For all their knowledge of the English language and Anglo-Saxon political institutions, the Irish throughout most of the nineteenth and twentieth centuries knew next to nothing about getting ahead in a capitalist, industrial economy. All the changes in Irish life over those two centuries were not as important as what remained the same. While urbanization and industrialization gained momentum throughout virtually the entire Western world of Europe and America in the nineteenth century, Ireland was deurbanizing and deindustrializing. In absolute numbers, the populations of many Irish cities actually fell in the nineteenth century, while others grew only very slowly, and the cottage, textile, and other industries that had once flourished even in the far west of Ireland disappeared. Only in Ulster, in and near the rapidly growing city of Belfast, did industry thrive and urbanization keep pace with other Western countries.

Agricultural Ireland also remained peasant Ireland, a country of small producers. The Famine cleared off most of the smallest tenant farmers and agricultural laborers either by death or forced emigration, but as late as 1911, 70 percent of Ireland's farmers worked less than thirty acres, and 46 percent less than fifteen acres. In short, Ireland remained a rural peasant society until well into the twentieth century, and the people who emigrated from it were poorly equipped to make their way in a modern urban industrial world like America. This was most obviously because they did not have any useful industrial skills or experience. But it was also because, more fundamentally, they did not have the entrepreneurial or individualistic values to help them negotiate America's harshly competitive capitalism. The guiding principle of their culture was communal reciprocity; they depended on friends and relatives, not individual initiative, to survive, if not get ahead. In the end, that communalism allowed them to do precisely that; it helped them endure the hardships and horrors of poverty in industrial America, but it did not help them lift themselves out of that poverty.

Obstacles of Prejudice and Discrimination

Irish immigrants confronted another obstacle in America that only complicated their adjustments to this new industrial culture: prejudice and discrimination. In the colonial era, Irish Protestants encountered some resistance and hostility from representatives of established churches. Still, the differences between Ulster Protestants and other Americans were small compared to the chasm that separated Irish Catholics from an American Protestant mainstream. Catho-

lics enjoyed something of a honeymoon of harmonious relations with their Protestant neighbors in the aftermath of the Revolution, as they won the full rights
of citizenship denied them in the colonial era. Irish Republican heroes William
Sampson and Thomas Emmett, though Protestants, were in the forefront of these
civil rights battles for their Catholic countrymen in the first few decades of the
nineteenth century. The momentum of republicanism unleashed by the Revolution and the fact that Catholics were so few that they seemed to pose little
threat to the new Republic or its citizens encouraged such good relations.

Yet hostility between Catholics and Protestants had never been entirely absent
even in the post–Revolutionary era, and as Irish Catholic migration grew, Protestant antagonism did, too. Scattered local nativist political agitations in the
1830s and the 1840s eventually grew into the Know-Nothing nativist political
crusade of the mid-1850s, which took states like Massachusetts and many cities
by storm. By then, native stock Yankee American opinions of the Irish had
become increasingly pessimistic. In the early nineteenth century, native stock
Americans had found much to criticize in Irish immigrants, but they were, nonetheless, confident that the American environment could remake the Irish. By the
1850s, however, those native stock Americans had become discouraged by apparent Irish intractability and fearful of growing Irish numbers. They began,
then, to speak of the Irish as a separate race, genetically fixed in their ignorance
and moral dissolution. Such ideas began to recede after the Civil War, but later
nativist mass agitations, such as the American Protective Association of the
1890s and even the Ku Klux Klan of the 1920s, continued to target Irish Catholics as religious aliens, if no longer as racial inferiors.

But it was not such periodic crusades so much as the day-to-day grinding,
interethnic hostility and suspicions that most affected Irish Catholics. Although
many would later make much of ''No Irish Need Apply'' signs in shop windows
or newspaper advertisements, the discrimination Irish immigrants and their children faced was usually much more subtle, probably expressed as much in Protestant employers' tacit preferences for people of their own religion—
advertisements for domestic servants seeking American or Swedish girls, for
example—than overt rejections of the Irish or other Catholics. This prejudice
and discrimination also varied widely by region. Irishmen in such cities as San
Francisco or St. Louis, Missouri, often escaped discrimination because elites
were less well established or better disposed to the Irish as potential Democratic
Party allies or because other groups—Asians, blacks, or even German Americans but not the Irish—became the targets of hostility. In Boston and other New
England cities, on the other hand, elites were well entrenched, and few other
groups were present in enough numbers to bear the brunt of community opprobrium; as a result, the Irish suffered more prejudice.

Possessing the wrong values and professing the wrong faith, Irish American
Catholics found it difficult to move up in American society. The children of
Irish Catholic immigrants surpassed the status of their parents, but their success
was limited and qualified. If they moved into white-collar work, they often

slipped back into blue-collar jobs, and most never moved out of the blue-collar ranks.

And yet at some point Irish Catholics began to move up the American occupational ladder much more quickly. It is not entirely clear when this happened, but it may have begun as early as the first few decades of this century and increased substantially during the World War II and post–World War II eras. Today, people of Irish descent, even in such New England states as Massachusetts, are as successful educationally and economically as almost all other ethnic groups. Contemporary national sample surveys, unlike the census, can distinguish among religious groups and have found that Irish Catholics are better educated, hold more prestigious jobs, and earn better income than Irish Protestants. Indeed, according to Andrew Greeley's National Opinion Research Center surveys, only Jews, some older Asian American groups (notably the Japanese and Chinese), and old-line denominational WASPs (white Anglo-Saxon Protestants) like Episcopalians are more successful than Irish Catholics today.

There are any number of reasons for this success, some having to do with the Irish themselves and some having to do with the American environments where they settled. No matter how much discrimination the Irish experienced, for example, they were still white. They never faced the kind of color line that held African Americans rigidly in check and excluded Asians from the United States altogether for many years. Indeed, Irish American upward mobility in the city where they were most successful, San Francisco, was due, at least in part, to the fact that they were perceived as acceptable by other European Americans more concerned about the potential dangers of Asian Americans than threats from one another.

Obviously, the leverage of race was not the only advantage Irishmen enjoyed in their move upward. Irish Protestants surely profited from that advantage, but they eventually lagged behind their Catholic fellow ethnics. The bulk of Irish Catholics also profited from where their ancestors landed in America; Irish Protestants, conversely, suffered from where their ancestors chose to settle. In the judgment of contemporary observers in the 1840s or even 1880s, Irish immigrants huddling in the slums of New York's Five Points or Hell's Kitchen or Boston's Fort Hill or North End could not have found worse places to make their homes in America. Indeed, many Irish Catholics themselves tried to lure their fellow ethnics out of these inner-city slums to rural colonies. At that time, those contemporaries were right; the bewildered former Celtic peasants, trapped in wretched, urban slums, suffered and suffered terribly. However, their settlement in northern metropolitan regions permitted their children, grandchildren, and great-grandchildren to take advantage of opportunities offered by the dynamic centers of the world's most dynamic economy. Meanwhile, many descendants of eighteenth-century Ulster Protestant immigrants remained in the South or, worse, in Appalachia, where sluggish or even backward economies produced far fewer opportunities for economic or social betterment.

What is still not clear is precisely how the Irish Catholics of the North took advantage of those opportunities. One question still in dispute is whether an Irish affinity for public employment helped or hindered their upward climb. Stephen Erie, Daniel Patrick Moynihan, and several others believe public employment did not help the Irish because it offered them only dead-end jobs with small salaries and limited opportunities for improvement. Erie, implicitly, and Moynihan, explicitly, seemed to be comparing the Irish with American Jews, who made rapid progress through the private sector. Suzanne Model's recent studies suggest, however, that the Irish, who lacked the experience in entrepreneurship or a capitalist economy that many Jews had (or at least were hampered by peasant values that Jews did not share) may have successfully used public employment as a platform to help boost themselves out of the lower ranks of the working class in the first half of this century. This debate, as Erie points out, has importance beyond merely a better understanding of Irish American social mobility. As Erie and Model both note, African Americans have recently found government employment a critically important means of moving up into the middle class. While Erie argues that the Irish American experience suggests that that is a poor and risky strategy for social mobility, Model disagrees.

Whoever is right, such debates, if nothing else, suggest the importance of politics to the Irish community—and, conversely, the importance of Irish Americans to American politics generally. Several decades ago, D. W. Brogan called the Irish the "governing class" of America. Brogan did not mean its ruling class, for that would connote Irish American economic or cultural power that did not exist; rather, he was pointing to the corps of Irish party and campaign operatives, bureaucrats, and elected officials who dominated the nation's political organizations, legislative bodies, and government agencies.

Irish Catholic involvement in the upper levels of politics occurred in stages. The first big wave of Irish mayors appeared in the 1880s and 1890s: New York in 1881; Boston in 1885; and Chicago in 1893. By 1894 Irish urban power seemed so menacing that such native stock Americans as John Paul Bocock, writing in the *Forum* magazine, worried about "The Irish Conquest of Our Cities." By the 1910s, Irish Americans, including David I. Walsh, Edward F. Dunne, and Alfred E. Smith, had taken over governorships in Massachusetts, Illinois, and New York, respectively. With Smith's nomination for president in 1928, Irish American Catholics reached a landmark. Even Smith's defeat did not seem to slow Irish rise to the highest levels of political power. The New Deal undercut some old Irish machines, like Tammany Hall in New York, but created others where none had existed before, as in Pittsburgh, or secured still others not yet entrenched in power, such as in Chicago. It also helped Irish-led Democratic parties in Massachusetts, Rhode Island, and several other states move up to become majority parties. Franklin D. Roosevelt brought increasing numbers of Catholics to Washington, too. Only one in twenty-five Republican appointments to the federal bench in the 1920s had been Catholic; during Roosevelt's administration one in every four new federal judges was a Catholic. As early as 1934, Father John A. Ryan, of Catholic University, claimed that ''there are more Catholics in public positions, high and low, in the Federal government today than ever before in the history of the country.'' Harry Truman, who began his career as a protégé of the Irish American boss Tom Pendergast, of Kansas City, was similarly generous to Irish Catholics. In the 1960s Irish Catholic John F. Kennedy was elected president; two Irish Catholics, Kennedy's brother Robert F. Kennedy and Eugene McCarthy, contended seriously for the Democratic nomination for president; and Irish Catholics served both as Speaker of the House (John McCormack of Massachusetts) and majority leader of the Senate (Michael Mansfield).

The Irish have thus been successful in American politics—perhaps more successful than any other American ethnic or racial group—but to what end? Some historians and social scientists have found the Irish to be fixated only on the quest for political power in its own right, not power as a means to implement policy; the Irish knew how to gain office, it has been said, but never thought much about what they should do with it. Political power was, as noted, a means of upward mobility, one of the few means that the Irish possessed. Still, the Irish quest for political power in America sometimes seemed an almost obsessive effort to overcome centuries of poverty and degradation endured in the homeland. As Matthew Stanton, the Irish immigrant protagonist in William Alfred's play *Hogan's Goat*, explains: ''Get Power. Without it there can be no decency, no virtue and no grace.'' If the Irish were obsessed with power, however, it was not just because they were oppressed in Ireland but also because they were oppressed there by a liberal state, the most liberal state in Europe or most of the world. Immigrants from autocracies like Russia might believe in laws, courts, and established rights and rules of procedure; the Irish understood from their experience with the English that it was who made the laws or rules and, more importantly, who administered or enforced them that counted. As George Washington Plunkitt, an Irish American Tammany Hall district boss, said in the early twentieth century: ''What is the Constitution among friends?''

Perhaps as a result of this preoccupation with a pragmatic quest for power, or because of a complex blend of Irish cultural influences and American constraints and opportunities, Irish political ideology has been hard to characterize. In the nineteenth century, many Irish Americans were committed to a working-class republicanism that used the language of the American Revolution to critique an increasingly stratified American economy and society. At the same time, some of the same leaders who pledged to this version of radicalism either tacitly or openly excluded nonwhite people from their definitions of the ''people'' and their vision of an egalitarian commonwealth. At the turn of the century, as a more rigorous Marxist-based socialism began to emerge on the American Left and the older republican radicalism faded away, Irish Americans—a number of noteworthy exceptions notwithstanding—became bitterly antiradical. That did not mean, however, that they became conservatives or reactionaries. Most were still blue-collar workers, and their economic interests and persistent values of communalism made them sympathetic if not to socialist revolution then to state intervention in the economy.

Such Irish American bosses as Charles Murphy in New York and Martin Lomasney in Boston recognized the popularity of these types of reforms and helped push them through state legislatures. As Murphy said, "Give the people what they want." In several states across the Northeast and Midwest in the 1910s, Irish American governors and legislators helped forge a new tradition of "urban liberalism." Through much of the first half of the twentieth century, most Irish Catholics probably continued to hew to that version of liberalism: sympathetic to state regulation and welfare, hostile to cultural changes (particularly those affecting family life), and rigorously opposed to socialism and communism.

THE IRISH AND AMERICAN CULTURE: AMERICAN PATRIOTS AND MILITANT CATHOLICS

The complexity of Irish American political ideas suggests their equally complex relation to American culture. Immigrants, but more often second- and third-generation Irish, helped create a new urban American culture that emerged in the late nineteenth and early twentieth centuries. "King" Kelly, Connie Mack, John McGraw, Charles Comiskey, and a host of other Irish American players, owners, and managers played crucial roles in transforming baseball into an American pastime. Irish Americans were similarly important in the evolution of boxing and other sports into big-time leisure entertainment and in the development of urban theater and vaudeville. It would be more accurate to say that the Irish helped invent modern American popular culture than to suggest that they simply assimilated to it.

Yet Irish Americans also led the efforts of American Catholics to create a separate American Catholic social and cultural world. Irish Americans emerged as leaders of the American Catholic Church as early as the mid-nineteenth century. Over the next 150 years, they jealously guarded that position, fending off challenges to their power by several ethnic groups, the most serious one by the Germans in 1891. The Irish staked their claim to power on the need to create an American church. It was a claim that they could assert more effectively than their fellow Catholic ethnics since they were English speakers. However, if the Irish claimed to create an American church, they were no less convinced that it should be separately and distinctively Catholic even as it was American. Irish American clerics, including Cardinals William O'Connell in Boston and Francis Spellman in New York, thus worked to create a "militant" Catholicism that would encase the people of their dioceses in separate social and cultural worlds.

Of course, the immigrant Irish and other Catholic groups had established their own organizations and institutions from the time of their arrival in America, but the Catholic world that Irish Americans and other Catholics created in the first half of the twentieth century was different in several respects. It was, for example, more institutionally complete, for church leaders drew on the wealth and talents of an expanding middle class to finance a broader and more varied array of institutions and organizations. This new institutional completeness may have segregated the Irish and other Catholics as effectively in the first half of the twentieth century as poverty and a foreign culture had isolated them in the nineteenth century. In Detroit, for example, the building of Catholic high schools in the 1910s and 1920s appeared to abruptly stop a trend toward out-marriage among the archdiocese's Catholics. In several other dioceses the accelerated construction of schools, hospitals, and charitable agencies and the formation of a wide and diverse array of associations also raised and strengthened the fortress walls of the Catholic ghetto.

Pan-Ethnic Catholicism and the Irish Identity

On the other hand, the new Catholic community was increasingly panethnic. Although Irish Catholics were its leaders, many Irish Catholic clerics and laymen encouraged their own and other Catholic ethnics to think of themselves as American Catholics rather than as members of ethnic groups. In the Irish case, this American Catholic identity became widely pervasive as new American-born generations grew to maturity in the twentieth century. In the peripheral city neighborhoods or inner suburbs where the Irish middle class began to settle in the 1920s and 1930s, older ethnic organizations, such as the Ancient Order of Hibernians, struggled to find members, while the organizational embodiment of the new panethnic, militant American Catholicism flourished, namely, the Knights of Columbus, which was overwhelmingly Irish but open to Catholics of all nationalities.

The American Catholic identity also became more widely popular in the 1920s and 1930s because an alternative focus of Irish identity, the nationalist movement, began to decline then. Nationalism, the movement to free Ireland from British rule, had roots in the early nineteenth century but did not become broadly popular in Irish America until after the Fenian movement of the 1860s. In the 1880s and again in the late 1910s, the nationalist movement rallied hundreds of thousands of Irish Americans to Ireland's cause. Then, as Ireland won some national autonomy with the creation of the Irish Free State in the 1920s, and factions of the Irish revolutionaries subsequently began fighting each other in an embarrassing civil war, the Irish American nationalist movement disintegrated. It would not revive again until the 1960s and would never again be as widely popular. For most Irish Americans a more narrow, ethnic Irish identity had lost some of its organizational focus and emotional power.

The new separate panethnic American Catholicism was not just a separate social world. Catholics also began to develop a separate culture, a supraethnic Catholic culture that was more than just an artifact of its many ethnicities. It was fiercely loyal to the pope, "ultramontane," a trend characteristic of American Catholicism since the mid-nineteenth century but one that became more powerfully evident in a virtual cult of the pope by the mid-twentieth century. Religious devotions also emerged during this period, practiced not by a single ethnic group but by a broad and ethnically diverse Catholic people. Among Irish Americans, for example, devotions to St. Patrick and St. Bridget, the cherished saints of the homeland, were joined or even crowded out by new religious heroes of broad appeal, particularly St. Theresa of Lisieux (the "Little Flower"), St. Jude, and even St. Anthony of Padua. At a more fundamental level, this militant, panethnic, American Catholic culture was rooted in the twentieth-century revival of medieval, Thomist philosophy that buttressed the confidence of the Irish and other Catholics in a world of moral certainties. Ironically, as Martin Halsey points out, Irish and other Catholic intellectuals rallied around American "innocence" or Victorianism even as many other disillusioned intellectuals were abandoning it in the early twentieth century.

If the content of Irish Americans' culture and the focus of their identity were largely American Catholic by the middle of the twentieth century, many American Celts still retained a sense of themselves as different from other Catholics. They were different, at least they believed, because they were the models and arbiters of what American Catholics should be, and members of all other groups were expected to assimilate to the values, customs, and standards they had established as appropriate. Moreover, enough of a specifically ethnic culture also persisted among Irish Americans to help them mark themselves as different from other American Catholics. Much of this culture had been invented in the United States and was quite literally Irish American, from St. Patrick's Day parades to songs like "When Irish Eyes Are Smiling," "Galway Bay," and "Mother Machree," to characteristic Irish "types" in the movies or the theater: the streetwise urban priest of Spencer Tracy or Bing Crosby; the urban, street-tough guy of James Cagney; the strongwilled, fiery woman of Maureen O'Hara; and the ubiquitous Irish "cop." This invented Irish American culture, integrated with some persistent traces of old country customs, helped mark a separate Irish American identity that was kept alive by Irish competition with fellow Catholic ethnics in the Church or the Democratic Party, even as Irish Americans' everyday culture came to be best characterized as American and Catholic, not Irish.

Assimilation and the Irish Ethnic Identity

In the 1960s, this American Catholic culture and identity, which had dominated Irish America for most of the twentieth century, collapsed. Several trends combined in that decade to undermine the old cultural consensus. John F. Kennedy's election and subsequent "martyrdom," the civil rights movement, and the Second Vatican Council all helped dissolve the historic enmity between Catholics and Protestants that had sustained Catholic militancy and propped up the Catholic ghetto. Kennedy's election meant that Catholics had scaled one of the last barriers to their full inclusion in American life, and his assassination and enshrinement in the pantheon of American heroes assured it. Meanwhile, in a civil rights era, when all forms of prejudice, discrimination, and intergroup hostility came under attack, the longtime mutual hostility separating Catholic and Protestant Christian whites began to appear especially anachronistic and silly. Finally, while Protestant anti-Catholicism abated, the Vatican Council's emphasis on ecumenism encouraged Catholics to break out of their ghetto and find common ground with other Christians and members of other faiths. The Council also broke the stranglehold of Thomistic philosophy on Catholic thought and education and revolutionized the liturgical and devotional life of the Church. By the late 1960s and early 1970s the vast Catholic institutional network began to crumble: Catholic school populations plummeted; priests and nuns left the religious life in droves; mass attendance among the laity fell off drastically; and intermarriage with non-Catholics began to rise at a rapid rate.

By the 1970s there was no longer any single Irish American identity or culture. Some people held on to the old American Catholic militancy by rallying behind the Catholic hierarchy on issues like abortion and sexual freedom. Others faded into a European American group with no distinctive ethnic or religious culture or sense of ethnic identity; they simply became white Americans. Still others sought to fill out an Irish identity by cultivating an interest in Irish literature, folk music and dance, or other elements of traditional Irish culture. Irish studies programs began to crop up in colleges; Irish bars featuring folk singers or traditional bands multiplied in American cities; Irish step-dancing schools flourished; and in places like Chicago or New York, devotees of Irish culture founded Irish arts or cultural centers. Further complicating the mix, Irish immigration began to pick up again in the 1980s, sending over 100,000 or more Irish born into the old Irish American centers of New York, Boston, Chicago, and San Francisco. Although St. Patrick's Day parades had always been sources of contention in Irish American communities, the battles that erupted in New York and Boston over gay marchers in the parades of the early 1990s aptly symbolized the lack of consensus in Irish American communities about what being Irish American meant.

THE FUTURE

Although some Irish Americans may mourn such a lack of consensus, for many, perhaps, it has been liberating. No longer forced or trapped into a single definition of what their heritage means, they have been free to consider it and draw on it for their own purposes. Charles Fanning notes that after the breakup of the old Catholic American culture among Irish Americans in the 1960s, many Irish American novelists and poets, free at last of the Catholic ghetto, wrote bitterly about its harsh strictures and stifling cultural claustrophobia. More recent writers, he suggests, have been less interested in writing off that past than in exploring it: They have come to see "ethnic otherness not as destructive alienation but as an expansion of possibility." Irish Americans, like Ireland now flush with enthusiasm over its membership in a new Europe, have, it appears, come to a new era in their history when they can fashion a rich identity for themselves without fear or compulsion.

BIBLIOGRAPHIC REFERENCES

The best single book on Irish immigration to America is Kerby Miller's *Emigrants and Exiles: Ireland and the Irish Exodus to North America* (New York: Oxford University Press, 1985). Miller's book is a rich, extraordinarily researched study of the causes of Irish emigration and Irish life in the United States during the nineteenth and early twentieth centuries. Unfortunately, there is no study of equal comprehensiveness of the Irish in twentieth-century America, although Lawrence McCaffrey's book-length essay *The Irish Diaspora in America* (Bloomington: Indiana University Press, 1976) and William Shannon's impressionistic survey *The American Irish* (New York: Collier, 1970 [1963]) both address Irish life in these more recent times.

There are several specialized studies of Irish American life worth mentioning: Steven Erie's provocative survey of Irish American machine politics, *Rainbow's End: Irish Americans and the Dilemmas of Urban Machine Politics, 1840–1985* (Berkeley: University of California Press, 1988), for example, and Hasia Diner's analysis of Irish women, *Erin's Daughters in America: Irish Immigrant Women in the Nineteenth Century* (Baltimore: Johns Hopkins University Press, 1983). There have been no similar overviews of Irish American nationalism or Irish Catholics in the church or in the labor movement. On nationalism, Thomas N. Brown's *Irish American Nationalism: 1870 to 1890* (Philadelphia: Lippincott, 1966) remains a beautifully written and insightful look at one of the high points of the nationalist movement. Episcopal biographies by James M. O'Toole, *Militant and Triumphant: William Henry O'Connell and Catholicism in Boston, 1859–1944* (Notre Dame, In: University of Notre Dame Press, 1992), and R. Emmet Curran, *Michael Augustine Corrigan and the Shaping of Conservative Catholicism in America* (New York: Arno Press, 1978), provide insight into Irish American roles in the church, as does Paula Kane's *Separatism and Subculture: Boston Catholicism, 1900 to 1920* (Chapel Hill: University of North Carolina Press, 1994). Hugh McLeod also has a valuable essay about the reasons for Irish belief: ''Catholicism and the New York Irish,'' in *Disciplines of Faith: Studies in Religion, Politics and Patriarchy*, edited by Jim Olbekevich, Lynda Roper, and Ralph Samuel (New York: Routledge, Keegan and Paul, 1987), pp. 337–350.

Studies of Irish workers and unions, such as Joshua Freeman's fine *In Transit: The Transport Workers Union in New York City, 1933–1966* (New York: Oxford University Press, 1989) and David Brundage's *The Making of Western Labor Radicalism: Denver's Organized Workers* (Urbana: University of Illinois Press, 1994) help explore the critically important Irish role in the American labor movement.

There are several studies of Irish American communities. Oscar Handlin pioneered them with his *Boston's Immigrants, 1790–1865: A Study in Acculturation*, rev. ed. (New York: Atheneum Press, 1972). More recent ones include David Emmons, *The Butte Irish: Class and Ethnicity in an American Mining Town, 1875–1925* (Urbana: University of Illinois Press, 1989); Dennis Clark, *The Irish in Philadelphia: Ten Generations of Urban Experience* (Philadelphia: Temple University Press, 1973); Brian Mitchell, *The Paddy Camps: The Irish of Lowell, 1821–1861* (Urbana: University of Illinois Press, 1988); and

Ronald Bayor and Timothy Meagher, eds., *The New York Irish* (Baltimore: Johns Hopkins University Press, 1996).

Several works specifically used in this essay include Suzanne Model, ''The Ethnic Niche and the Structure of Opportunity: Immigrants and Minorities in New York City,'' in *The Underclass Debate: Views from History*, edited by Michael Katz (Princeton, NJ: Princeton University Press, 1992), pp. 161–193; Denis W. Brogan, *The American Character*, rev. ed. (New York: Time, 1962); William M Halsey, *The Survival of American Innocence: Catholicism in an Era of Disillusionment, 1920–1940* (Notre Dame, IN: University of Notre Dame Press, 1980); and Charles Fanning, ''The Heart's Speech No Longer Stifled: New York Irish Writing Since the 1960s'' in *The New York Irish*, edited by Ronald Bayor and Timothy J. Meagher (Baltimore: Johns Hopkins University Press, 1996), pp. 508–531.

ITALIANS

Paola A. Sensi-Isolani

NEW ARRIVALS

The first Italians to come to the United States did so long before their mass migration began in the late 1800s. These first arrivals were explorers, soldiers, sailors, missionaries, and adventurers who helped the Spanish, French, English, and Portuguese exploration and settlement of North America. Columbus, Amerigo Vespucci (to whom the continent of America owes its name), Verrazano, and Father Eusebio Francesco Chino are among the most famous of these early arrivals.

Between 1820 and 1873, 12,000 Italians arrived in the United States, a very small number when compared to the 1.5 million Germans and the 2 million Irish who arrived in the same period. These arrivals, most of whom intended to settle permanently, were generally from northern Italy. Many of them were educated or skilled workers, among them teachers, actors, musicians, sculptors, stonecutters, and other craftsmen. Some were political refugees, others Italian Protestants fleeing religious persecution. By the end of this period, Italians could be found in every state of the Union, the largest number residing in California (2,805), New York (1,862), and Louisiana (1,134). Despite their low numbers, some of these early Italian settlers, Filippo Mazzei and Giuseppe Vigo among them, played an important role during the American Revolution, with Mazzei's political philosophy, for example, influencing Thomas Jefferson's.

The composition and character of Italian immigrants began to change between 1860 and 1880, when nearly 68,000 arrived. Although most still came from the North, more also began to arrive from southern Italy. Many of these arrivals were peasants and farm laborers who intended to remain only a few months or years before returning to Italy. During this period, Italian colonies in New York, Chicago, New Orleans, San Francisco, and other cities began to take definite shape, developing such institutions as the press and mutual aid societies. Census figures show that by 1880, because of return migration, 40,000 Italians remained in the United States, one-quarter of them in New York.

THE GREAT MIGRATION

The turning point in the history of Italian migration to the United States came after 1880, when the trickle of Italian immigrants turned into a flood. Between 1880 and 1914, not taking into account the many who arrived illegally, more than 3 million Italians officially entered the United States, the overwhelming majority of them—72.3 percent—coming from the South. Because in the period spanning the forty years between 1880 and 1920 more than a quarter of Italy's population left the country, it is said that in its size and its many destinations, this Italian emigration may well be without parallel in history. However, it cannot be seen as confined only to travel to the United States. Preceding and later concurrent with the exodus of Italians to the United States, the overall pattern of Italian migration was that of a diaspora to many regions of the world, including more affluent countries in Europe and South America.

The factors that compelled Italians to leave their homeland are rooted in their history, the conditions of the land, and the social-economic system. Even with unification, which took place in the 1870s, Italians, and most especially Southern Italians, were not conscious of themselves as part of a nation-state. Both in the North and in the South, the infertility of the soil, primitive agricultural methods, and pressures of population on the available land combined with a heavy taxation system, lingering feudalism, and a stratified social system that concentrated national wealth in the hands of a few. These problems increased after 1880, when Italian agricultural exports were curtailed by tariffs and its crops and people decimated by epidemics.

These push factors were combined with the expansion of American industry, which wanted cheap, unskilled labor. The Italian government also saw the advantages of emigration, since it provided a social safety valve that relieved economic pressure on the country by reducing the population most likely to push for social and land reform. Moreover, the financially strapped government became increasingly aware that the immigrants' remittances provided it with badly needed capital, which became important for the economy.

Their journey made easier by faster steamship passage, Italian immigrants during the first decade of this period of mass migration were mostly Southern Italian males who, at the outset, saw their migration at least as exploratory, if not as transient. It was the intention of most of these migrants to stay long enough to save some money in order to buy land or set up a small business in their hometown or village. It is said that Italians were among the first great migrations of a people who went back to their native land from the United States in large numbers [see Chinese and French Canadians—Ed.]. Most of these men returned home within five years of their arrival or traveled seasonally to South America when work was scarce in the United States. For many of these so-called "birds of passage," migration to the United States was a process repeated many times. Despite the arrival of increasing numbers of wives and children and of entire family units in the years after 1900, this phenomenon of return migration did not disappear but rather seemed to fluctuate with the economic situation in the United States. Thus, the number of returnees grew to an incredible 72.6 percent of those entering between 1907 and 1911, a time of severe industrial crisis in the United States.

For Italians, the period of mass migration, which saw the arrival of more than 3 million Italians between 1890 and 1914, ended with World War I. While these immigrants found work on ranches or in mines, fishing, industry, and construction throughout the United States, most settled in the urban industrial centers of the Midwest and mid-Atlantic states. Here, men and women worked at a variety of jobs, in construction, the needle trades, manufacturing, and industry, most of this work requiring unskilled labor and long hours. In the first decade of the 1900s, of the approximately 2.3 million Italians who came to the United States, three-quarters went to the heavily urbanized states of New York (993,113), Pennsylvania (429,200), Massachusetts (154,882), and New Jersey (118,680). Another 111,249 were attracted to Illinois and 58,699 to Ohio. Northern Italians were still drawn across the country to California and particularly to the city of San Francisco, which in 1910 contained 16,918 immigrants. By 1910, there were Italian communities in thirty-five states.

WORLD WAR I AND IMMIGRATION RESTRICTIONS

World War I dramatically changed migration patterns and also the attitude of many Italian immigrants residing in the United States. The dangers of travel across the Atlantic, coupled with the need for military manpower in Europe, served to severely restrict emigration, which once again fell to a trickle. All immigration to the United States declined during this period, and that of Italians was no exception, decreasing from 283,738 arrivals in 1914 to 5,250 in 1918. This war was a critical event that also forced Italian immigrants to consider permanently staying in the United States. By 1917, it was too late to consider returning to Italy. Many of them faced the U.S. draft, and an estimated 300,000 Italian Americans, including 89,662 immigrants, served in the U.S. Army. Thus, the acceptance of permanency during this period was not a function of the length of stay of these Italian immigrants but was triggered by political events outside their control.

Italy emerged from the war poor and divided; unemployment was high, and mass unrest, strikes, and violence spread, prompting more Italians to look once again to emigration as a way out of their predicament. Almost half a million Italians arrived in the United States in the five years following the end of the war (1919–1924). But immigration to the United States did not, however, prove to be as easy as it had been in the period of free migration. In the grips of racism, antiradicalism, and religious bias, the United States passed legislation in 1917, 1921, and finally in 1924 that reversed its traditional policy of free immigration. The Johnson-Reed Immigration Act of 1924 in particular represented racist warnings about a threat to the Anglo-Saxon stock and was aimed at freezing the "country ethnically by sharply restricting the 'new' immigration from southern and eastern Europe." Under this act a maximum yearly quota of 150,000 immigrants (from outside the Americas) were to be admitted to the United States, with Italians eligible for 3,845 of these slots. In 1925, after the Johnson-Reed Act was passed, a total of 6,203 Italian immigrants arrived, as compared to 56,246 the previous year. Many Italian immigrants now opted to become permanent settlers; the immigration of Italian women and of family groups increased; and the number of Italian transmigrants who moved to other communities within the United States, most commonly in a westward direction, likewise rose.

The period between the two world wars was one of turmoil in Italy, as fascism gained a stronger foothold and Italy invaded Ethiopia and became involved in the Spanish Civil War. The fascist government discouraged immigration to the United States and Latin America and tried either to attract its migrants back to Italy or to direct them to the agricultural colonies it tried to set up in North Africa. As a result—and combined with the impact of the depression—during the 1930s Italian migration to the United States decreased even more dramatically than it had done in the immediate post-1924 period, falling to less than 1,000 during World War II.

The final phase of Italian immigration, encompassing the post–World War II period to the present, has seen a change in the composition of Italian immigrants. Immediately after the war there was an increase in the number of women who immigrated to join their GI or Italian immigrant husbands. To this group were added other close family members who left war-ravaged Italy. The postwar period also brought to the United States another new group of Italian migrants, those intellectuals who, because of persecution in Italy, sought refuge in the United States. These men and women, who arrived with specialist visas as part of what one can call an intellectual migration, differed significantly, both in numbers and educational level, from the massive movement of Italian immigrants who had been admitted prior to World War II. Among them were the nuclear scientist Enrico Fermi and the biologist Rita Levi Montalcini.

Since then, the Italian American population has continued to be replenished by a small but steady number of Italian immigrants, many of them professionals. Italians entering the United States as immigrants exceeded 20,000 each year between 1966 and 1973, but their number thereafter dropped steadily, to merely 2,300 in 1994. The 1990 U.S. census reported that almost 15 million persons claimed Italian ancestry, making them the fifth largest ancestry group. At present, Italian Americans represent approximately 6 percent of the national population. More than 830,000 of them were born in Italy, with just over 30 percent of these having arrived after 1960. While Italian Americans are now more geographically dispersed than they once were, they still remain, more than most other ethnic groups, heavily concentrated in the Northeast and in urban areas.

WHO WERE THE ITALIANS?: WORK AND COMMUNITY

Most earlier Italian immigrants arrived as unskilled laborers with little capital; for example, in 1904, the average Italian immigrant arrived with enough money to survive without work for four days. They initially found jobs through *padroni*, or labor contractors, men who arranged for their work and transportation and who often took advantage of their ignorance. Increasingly, however, they were attracted to particular places by fellow villagers or relatives. The establishment of this pattern of chain migration, coupled with the hostility they encountered upon arrival as well as their tendency to seek work in cities, resulted in the formation of Little Italys. In such cities as New York, Boston, New Haven, Philadelphia, Denver, and San Francisco, Italian immigrants congregated in neighborhoods with their *paesani*, creating what became known as urban villages.

Within these communities, Italian immigrants developed a series of organizations and institutions that provided them with cultural, physical, and financial support. Mutual aid societies, many of them initially associated with the village or region of origin, provided the immigrant with a form of insurance in case of sickness and death and with a group beyond the family with which to socialize. Initially, it was the mutual aid society more often than the church that organized processions and housed its patron saint in its meeting rooms. Banks were established, which, while often charging high interest, became a source of community development since they were the only agencies that lent money to Italians. Most communities had their own newspapers, helping them to navigate in their new homeland and keeping immigrants in touch with events in Italy and with other Italian communities in the States. Larger communities, for example in New York, Chicago, and San Francisco, had thriving theater groups that performed both serious plays and the more popular vaudeville.

The Catholic Church, of course, existed for most Italian immigrants before they left their homeland. However, in southern Italy the Church was identified with the interests of the dominant class, and while Southern Italians attended church on special occasions, for the most part their rate of church attendance was low. While they did not lack religious devotion—demonstrated in the processions held in honor of patron saints, the novenas, the statues of saints, and so on—most immigrants did not at first identify with the established American church, an alienation aggravated by the discrimination they suffered at the hands of the Irish Catholic religious hierarchy. The Scalabrianian fathers, who ran the first Italian parishes—by 1875 there were Italian parishes in Philadelphia, New York, Boston, and Hoboken—and the Missionary Sisters of the Sacred Heart, founded by Saint Francesca Cabrini, provided Italian immigrants with hospitals, orphanages, and educational institutions at a time when Italian priests and nuns were unwelcome by the Catholic hierarchy. With time, the religious practices and beliefs of Italian immigrants more closely replicated those of the Irish-dominated Church.

The majority of Italian immigrants who arrived prior to 1925 were between eighteen and forty-five years of age, with the proportion of males three times greater than that of females. Many of these men were already married upon arrival, and most of those who decided to settle called their family to the United States as soon as they had saved enough money. Much has been said about the important role that the Italian family has played in the migration process. In reality, extended family unity and strength in southern Italy was more an ideal than an accomplished fact. Poverty, lack of land, and the strains of life made duty to the immediate nuclear family, rather than to the extended family, the norm. Once married, a couple established its own social and economic unit. Family relationships were hierarchical, with the father holding authority over wife and children. While it is true, given the distrust with which Italians held the state and its authorities, that the family played a more important role than it might for some other immigrant groups, that importance does not seem to have been any greater among others who were suspicious of the government of their land of origin.

Over time, immigration and the move away from abject poverty allowed for the development of extended family ties that were not as evident in Italy. There is no doubt, however, that for those who left as well as for the family members who stayed behind, emigration initially served to disrupt family relationships. Wives and children were indeed often called to the United States by their husbands, but many were also abandoned, becoming *vedove bianche* (''white widows'') in Italy as their husbands set up other families in their new homeland. Many stories document the hardships faced by these families. Consider that of Rosa Cavalieri, who arrived from northern Italy in 1888. Rosa had to abandon her child in Italy in order to rejoin an abusive husband in the United States, ultimately leaving him and marrying another Italian immigrant—and then moving from one ethnic enclave to another in search of work to support her family.

The image of these Little Italys, with their colorful street markets, specialty shops, *feste*, and processions, fill the stereotype of the Italian immigrant experience in the United States. But although it appears that Italian immigrants on the eastern seaboard and in Chicago lived more ''segregated,'' in none of these communities were they entirely separate from other immigrant groups. Moreover, despite the sense of community, living conditions were harsh, and poverty and wretchedness led to crime and a deterioration in the immigrants' health. Authorities made an effort to encourage Italians to settle in rural areas where, it was believed, their adjustment and assimilation would be faster. Various state and private agencies, both Italian and American, supported the establishment of agricultural colonies throughout the country, most especially in the southern states of Texas, Arkansas, Mississippi, Louisiana, and Alabama and in California. Most did not succeed for long; Tontitown, Arkansas, was an exception. Settled by Southern Italians under the leadership of Father Pietro Bandini, by 1912 Tontitown was a flourishing community of 700 inhabitants who owned 4,760 acres of productive farmland. Every family owned its own home and livestock, cultivated vineyards, and grew bumper crops of peaches, onions, peas, and beans. The village itself had a hotel, a church, and a school as well as shops and factories.

Most Italian immigrants who were attracted to farming, however, did so without the benefit of outside help from benevolent societies. Lacking capital and needing immediate returns on their labor, many who lived in or near large cities raised vegetables and poultry in truck farms or market gardens at the outskirts of town. From California to New York State, notwithstanding that many Italian immigrants were seasonal farm laborers who traveled from one job site to the other, many others also established flourishing businesses, supplying urban markets with produce and flowers. By 1919, for example, Italian truck farms in the Bay Area of California produced crops valued at approximately $19 million. Besides truck farming, Italians who settled in the country worked in dairies; developed vine growing and wine making in, among other states, California; and cultivated cotton, sugar cane, and tobacco in such Italian-Sicilian settlements as Bryan, Texas.

Italian immigrants who settled in the countryside were always a small minority, no more than 7 percent of the total in 1910, for example. To this number should be added those Italian immigrants who opted to live in small communities scattered throughout the United States, many of them settling there after having built the railroads that connected these towns with larger cities. They also found work as miners in the Iron Range of Minnesota; in the coalfields of Ohio, Utah, and Wyoming; in the lumber mills of Washington and California; and in the copper mines of Colorado and Arizona. Others worked as barbers, shoemakers, and shopkeepers, and women often took in wash and cooked for boarders in order to support their families. Still, despite the pressures, most chose to live in large cities where prospects for employment and financial gain seemed to them much greater.

FACING DISCRIMINATION

Americans have always had ambivalent feelings toward immigrants, and of those who arrived in the early 1900s, Jews and Italians stood out from the rest because of the frightful stereotypes associated with them. For example, states Richard Alba, "The unfavorable associations were partly physical: Italians were 'swarthy,' . . . and to the eyes of Americans they bore other physical signs of degradation such as low foreheads." Many Americans doubted that Southern Italians were white, and they were viewed as having dangerous criminal tendencies and believed to be prone to crimes of passion and vengeance. This association of dubious racial affiliation and criminal tendencies was most apparent in the South, where Italians were criticized for the color of their skin, for being too friendly to blacks, and for being "dirty, lazy, ignorant and prone to violence." In a twenty-year period starting with the lynching of eleven defenseless Italians in New Orleans in 1890, more than twenty Italian immigrants were lynched in the South.

Italian immigrants faced continuous discrimination throughout the United States. Teachers and social workers who worked with them believed that they could do little about the first generation but could force the assimilation of their children. Still, it was the basic assumption of the teachers that Italian immigrant children were a problem element, the product of "an ill adjusted cultural group whose family mores may be detrimental to the formal educational process. Italian children were seen as more crude . . . [and] were disliked both by teachers and non-Italian pupils." Autobiographical accounts of those years written by Italian Americans confirm the effect that such attitudes had on children: "We soon got the idea that Italian meant something inferior," recalled Leonard Covello, "and a barrier was erected between children of Italian origin and their parents. This was the accepted process of Americanization. We were becoming Americans by learning how to be ashamed of our parents."

The differences between the generations caused confusion and tension within Italian immigrant families as well as an erosion of self-esteem for the American-born children of these immigrants. The patriarchal nature of most Italian immigrant families, the value parents placed on manual labor, their suspicion of an educational system that in the process of Americanization robbed them of their children, and the restrictions they placed on their daughters were some of the conflicts that forced a separation between the older generation of parents born in Italy and their American-born children. Consequently, these children (mostly boys, who were allowed more freedom than their sisters) spent more time with their peer group in the streets, forming the gangs so well described by William Foote Whyte in his *Street Corner Society* (1943). Because they were deprived of opportunities, observed Whyte, and moreover could only succeed if they sloughed off "all characteristics that are regarded as distinctively Italian," these sons and sometimes grandsons of Italian immigrants only saw the possibility of advancement through rackets and petty crime.

The stereotype of Italians as criminals and gangsters has played an important role in determining the American image of this immigrant group. While social scientists document that the role of Italians in crime was no greater, and often less, than that of other immigrant groups, the stereotype of Italian gangsters persists in the media and in popular fiction, often fed by Italian American authors themselves. The involvement of Italians in criminal activity followed the pattern of other immigrant groups, such as the Irish and the Jews, who moved from petty crime and preying on their own immigrant community to gang activity and later to more lucrative forms of crime, such as bootlegging, racketeering, and the drug trade. There is no doubt that some Italians did gain notoriety in crime. Most of these men were sons of Italian immigrants or had arrived in the

United States as young children, such as Charles "Lucky" Luciano, Alphonse Capone, and Vito Genovese. The image of Italian Americans as *mafiosi* captured the popular imagination and penetrated the American consciousness to such an extent that, in the 1970s, President Richard Nixon, "after agreeing with his aides that it would be politically wise to appoint some Italian American to a top-level federal post, asked, 'Yes, but where would we find an honest Italian American?' "

LABOR ACTIVISM AND POLITICAL INVOLVEMENT

As with occupations and education, the first two generations of Italian Americans experienced little success with regard to political or economic power. Initially, their activism was concentrated in the economic sector. As early as 1897, Italian coal strikers in the bituminous fields were reported to be even more tenacious than the old immigrants in demanding their rights. As the conflict between labor and capital increased in the United States, Italian workers, many attracted to socialist and anarchist movements, were at the forefront of union-organizing activity and strikes. Chief among them was the 1912 strike in the Lawrence, Massachusetts, mills, where Italian workers were the largest of twenty-five different nationalities to protest the company's pay cuts. This was followed by the Paterson, New Jersey, strike of 1913, which closed down the town's 300 mills and in which once again the Italians, working with the Industrial Workers of the World (IWW), were instrumental both as strikers and as organizers. Italian immigrant workers were involved in strikes that extended from the East Coast to the Midwest and the West Coast, from the coal fields of Virginia and Ohio to the garment industry of Chicago and New York; the factories and construction sites of the Atlantic seaboard; the cigar factories of Tampa, Florida; the mines of Arizona, Colorado, and Utah; and the migrant farm and lumber camps, canneries, and ports of California, Oregon, and Washington. All this was to change, however, as the United States entered World War I, when striking was considered to be seditious and disloyal and when labor shortages opened areas of employment that had previously been closed to Italians.

For Italian Americans the interwar period was fraught with contradictions. Many, especially the grandchildren of the first arrivals, felt assimilated and accepted, whereas more recent arrivals and their children felt the sting of discrimination and prejudice. Many began working in the automobile plants of Detroit and the steel mills of Pittsburgh and other industries, where wages increased with the cost of living. Others still found themselves performing menial tasks and working for very low wages in an environment where rising prices exceeded wage increases. These conditions led to an increase in labor activism and strikes and made Italian radicals the target of imprisonment and deportation. The government's concern about what were considered subversive activities, defined as anything that smacked of radicalism, led to dramatic repression. The raids of 1919–1920, led by Attorney General A. Mitchell Palmer, were aimed at removing any form of radicalism and affected Italians who were active as labor organizers and those involved in the anarchist movement as well as in the IWW. During this period, many Italians were deported as ''alien radicals.'' That the implementer of these deportations was Anthony Caminetti, the first Italian American to be elected to Congress and appointed by President Wilson as Commissioner of Immigration in 1913, demonstrates the range of the Italian immigrant experience at this time. Caminetti, a Californian whose family had settled in the Gold Country shortly after the Gold Rush, had become fully assimilated and, as Patrick Gallo put it, had succumbed to the instincts of the ''pure'' American nativists.

Although they were not leaders in the radical movement, two Italians came to personify to Americans the dangers of immigration and radicalism during the Red Scare hysteria following World War I, which aided the efforts of restrictionists. Both active in Italian-colony working-class organizations, Nicolo Sacco and Bartholomeo Vanzetti were accused in 1920 of robbing and killing a guard in South Braintree, Massachusetts, as well as of an unsuccessful attempt to rob a payroll truck in Bridgewater. It was believed that the money from the robberies was intended to support anarchist causes. While the men denied involvement in either holdup, they were tried and, in an environment replete with prejudicial statements and hysteria, ultimately found guilty and executed in 1927. As Vanzetti stated in the speech he made in his defense, ''I have suffered because I was an Italian, and indeed I am an Italian.''

The struggle to adapt to America involved most Italian Americans in a variety of pursuits aimed at achieving upward mobility. William Whyte's 1943 study, noted above, focused on Boston's North End, yet remains a useful generalization for all Italian Americans who aspired at that time to upward mobility. Whyte concludes that as they interacted with the dominant culture, those Italian Americans who aspired to upward mobility realized that they had to abandon the ways of their parents and grandparents. They thus internalized the WASP (white Anglo-Saxon Protestant) ethic as their cultural ideal and abandoned the Italian language and outward signs of their identity, while maintaining ethnic cultural markers within the home, including those concerning food preparation and consumption together with the frequency and intensity of extended family interaction. It is in this area of the family that Italian Americans have probably been most resistant to change even with intermarriage and changes in the economy. In the United States, Italian immigrants developed and solidified the extended family ties that were impossible to maintain in the harsh environment of the Italy they had left behind.

However, assimilation is a multigenerational phenomenon, subject to a variety of variables. Thus, Italian immigrants from central and northern Italy who settled in California, and lived in communities scattered throughout the state, tended as a whole to assimilate much faster than Southern Italian immigrants who might have arrived at the same time but who had settled in the large industrial centers of the East Coast and of the Midwest.

WORLD WAR II AND BEYOND

One factor that speeded up the assimilation of Italian immigrants was World War II. Prior to the war's outbreak, many Italian Americans saw fascism and Mussolini as a way to gain recognition and a positive identity; this admiration quickly ended with Italy's alliance with Germany against the United States. When the war broke out, Italian American politicians were in a particularly vulnerable position, especially to unfounded accusation, and numerous Italian American leaders, organizations, some newspapers, and even language classes came under scrutiny. Fearing potential sabotage by Italian and German Americans, their internment, together with that of the Japanese, was seriously considered. In California, Italians and Americans of Italian descent were investigated, labeled dangerous, and compelled to resettle inland; those who were U.S. citizens were moved within California, whereas noncitizens were sent to a relocation camp in Montana, and some were forced to move to the Midwest. These events sent a message to Italian American communities throughout the United States, and as immigrants and their children tried to establish their undisputed allegiance to the United States, many of their organizations slowly disintegrated.

In the 1950s, urban renewal projects and highway construction—much of it opposed by the residents—marked the death of Little Italys throughout the country and pushed second-and third-generation Italian Americans bent on Americanization to move to the suburbs. As Anthony Mansueto observed, "No longer did people gather in the barber shop or at the lodge of the *societa*, or pass their evenings on the front porch over wine." Established political parties and the mass media replaced ethnic associations as the principal political and cultural institutions of the immigrant communities. For immigrant Italian American men, in particular, the experience of service in World War II speeded up the development of an American national identity. In particular, the GI Bill further helped in the assimilation process after 1945, for more Italian Americans now went to college and on to professional careers. Even with this upward mobility and increased income, as late as 1969 Italian Americans over thirty-five years of age were almost two years behind other Americans of the same age in years of schooling. By 1980, two-thirds of those over twenty-five had graduated high school and 12 percent from college. They were therefore underrepresented in professional and other high-level positions requiring education; in New York City in 1970, for example, a smaller proportion of Italians than blacks were in professional occupations.

With the maturation of the third and fourth generations, Italian Americans have shown a distinct shift toward the middle class in their income, occupation, and educational levels. In 1990, native-born Americans of Italian ancestry exceeded the median household income of most major European ancestry groups, except for Scots, Russians, and Greeks. Until recently, the educational attainments of Italian Americans were rising more slowly than many others, and yet, while in 1990 well over a majority of foreign-born Italians still lacked a high school education, over 80 percent of the native born (twenty-five and older) did have it, and more than one fifth held college degrees. In fact, Italian Americans aged twenty-five to thirty-four had surpassed all whites in the percentage with such degrees (30 percent men, 28 percent women). Nonetheless, Italian Americans in the mid-1980s were still more concentrated in the working class than most other major ethnic groups of European descent.

Reflective of the suburbanization and social mobility under way, the more liberal political traditions of Italian immigrants, seen in such politicians as Fiorello La Guardia and Vito Marcantonio, gave way to a more conservative political identity. In fact, since the end of World War II, Italian Americans have moved from the Democratic to the Republican Party. Today, their political sentiments are best represented by the conservative politics of the first Italian American Supreme Court justice, Anthony Scalia, rather than the liberal ideals of the past governor of New York State, Mario Cuomo. As the focus of political life for the group has shifted from individual regional societies to national ones, organizational and political pressures have in part been responsible for quickening the political integration of Italian Americans. The Order of the Sons of Italy in America, UNICO (Unity, Neighborliness, Integrity, Charity, and Organization), NIAF (National Italian American Foundation), and FIERI (''Proud''), to name but a few, have been instrumental in highlighting the political power of Italian Americans. In the last decade, Italian Americans have achieved relative visibility in both government and private corporations. From only four Italian Americans in Congress in the 1930s and only eight during the next decade, the number has reached more than thirty-five at present. They have achieved the greatest political success in elected and appointed positions in local and state government, particularly in areas with large Italian American populations, such as New York, New Jersey, Massachusetts, Connecticut, Rhode Island, and California. Italian Americans are in evidence in city and state government, in the Congress, in the presidential cabinet, and as members of the Supreme Court, including Justice Scalia, Senators Alfonse D'Amato (defeated in 1998) and Robert Torricelli, President Clinton's first-term Chief of Staff, Leon Panetta, and New York City Mayor Rudolph Giuliani.

ITALIAN AMERICANS TODAY: IDENTITY, CULTURE, AND ASSIMILATION

Although there has been much discussion as to whether Italian American ethnic identity is really at the twilight, there is no doubt that Italian Americans are still sensitive to prejudice and discrimination. The Sons of Italy and the

NIAF are involved in antidefamation activities, and such opinion leaders as Mario Cuomo regularly maintain that negative media stereotypes are "inflicted" on Italian Americans by the mass media. Accusations of Mafia connections for such political figures as Geraldine Ferraro and Mayor Alioto of San Francisco underscore the sense of vulnerability that many Italian Americans feel. At the same time, politicians like Ferraro have accused the Italian community of being intimidated by accusations of Mafia connections and of remaining silent. On the other hand, while the majority of Italian Americans take umbrage at being defined as a minority group, the pattern of discrimination against them in certain educational institutions (e.g. City University of New York [CUNY]) have entitled them to affirmative action status.

It has been held that discrimination against Italian Americans may also be apparent in the boardrooms of major corporations, where empirical studies show that Italian Americans remain underrepresented in positions of corporate power. Among the exceptions at the higher levels of corporate management or as chief executive officers (CEOs) are Chrysler's former chairman Lee Iacocca, Carl Pascarella (president and CEO of Visa USA), Roger Enrico (CEO of Pepsi Cola), and Louis Camillers (executive vice president of Philip Morris). As happened in the past with such figures as A. P. Giannini, today most prominent Italian Americans in business have achieved success as individual entrepreneurs rather than as men who climbed the corporate ladder to success.

Outside of business, Italians have also achieved marked success in those areas that rely on individual achievement, among them particularly sports and entertainment. Italian immigrants have made a name for themselves in baseball with the likes of the Di Maggio brothers, Yogi Berra, Phil Rizzuto, and Joe Pepitone. Boxers came especially from those cities where there were long-established Italian communities: Rocky Marciano, Carmen Basilio, Jake Lamotta, and Rocky Graziano. While Italians also starred in football, they became prominent only with the start of professional teams, "and that period soon became the Vince Lombardi era," noted Jerre Mangione. Today, assimilation of Italian Americans into American life is so complete that little attention is paid to the ethnic origin of such players as Joe Montana. More recently, Italian Americans have moved into managerial positions in boxing, baseball, basketball, and football. Italian immigrants have also contributed to every aspect of the arts but have received the most recognition in the world of Hollywood and show business, where they have been prominent as musicians, entertainers, actors, and film directors. In none have they played such a prominent role as in the film industry, with the likes of Frank Capra, Martin Scorsese, Brian de Palma, Francis Ford Coppola, Sylvester Stallone, Quentin Tarantino, and Nancy Savoca.

In spite of a plethora of writers and poets, Italian American literature has yet to match the recognition received by Italian American filmmakers, nor has literature played as important a role in reflecting and influencing American tastes. Until the last two decades, the Italian American novel occupied a special but isolated niche in American culture, yet in spite of this marginality, by the 1930s and 1940s some Italian American authors, including John Fante, Pietro Di Donato, and Joe Pagano, had received recognition for their works of fiction, which depicted in a semiautobiographical manner the struggles of Italian immigrants. Alongside these authors were such second-generation Italian Americans as Bernard de Voto, Hamilton Basso, and Paul Gallico, who had either (Jerre Mangione contends) "consciously or subconsciously avoided the subject matter of Italian Americans, or else had deliberately anglicized their names." While by the 1970s the Italian American novel made a great leap forward in American letters—with such popular novels as Mario Puzo's *The Fortunate Pilgrim* and, a few years later, his less-well-reviewed but widely sold *The Godfather* (and in the mid-1990s, *The Last Don*)—they quickly went out of print and were soon forgotten. However, by then the ranks of Italian American novelists did begin to include women, among them Tina De Rosa, Helen Barolini, Diane Cavallo, Nancy Maniscalco, and Barbara Grizzuti Harrison. In 1985, Helen Barolini published *The Dream Book*, an anthology of writings by fifty-six Italian American women.

Unlike novels written by Italian American authors, most poetry, even when it dealt with personal matters, is not easily identified as exclusively part of the Italian American experience. Likewise, as with Italian American writers, only a few of the many Italian American artists who have contributed to American art are remembered. Those who have made the greatest impact in the wider art world are Joseph Stella and Beniamino Bufano, while an artist whose work has focused almost exclusively on the Italian immigrant experience is Ralph Fasanella. To these three most famous Italian American artists must, however, be added the long list of Italian American artisans and craftsmen who were responsible for the sculpture and design of many of the nation's most famous monuments.

For the descendants of those Italian immigrants who arrived on Ellis Island during the peak wave of immigration between 1880 and 1920, the process of Americanization is in many ways complete. Italian Americans can be found at every level of the economy, political structure, and academe. As historian Rudolph Vecoli states in his essay, "Are Italian Americans Just White Folks?", "Over the past century Italian Americans have comprised a considerable segment of the American population; there is no sphere of life in which our presence has not been manifest. To delete that experience is to omit a big slice of American history." Their presence in the United States has influenced American culture in a variety of ways, from its foodways, to its literature, architecture, arts, sports, and popular culture.

In those previously industrialized areas of the Northeast and Midwest, where manufacturing jobs were often filled by working-class Italian Americans, shifts in the economy have generated a strong sense of insecurity. In these areas, some members of the Italian American community see themselves under siege, impoverished, and shut out of affirmative action programs. Relationships with other ethnic groups are directly related to Italian immigrants' socioeconomic status and are most tense in those working-class areas where new arrivals are seen as a threat to the economic, social, and cultural homogeneity of the Italian American community. Examples of this can be seen in the hostility many East Harlem Italian homeowners displayed toward the newly arrived Puerto Ricans shortly after World War II and the more violent resistance to the presence of outsiders, mainly African Americans, in Bensonhurst, New York, in the late 1980s. While it can be argued that their immigrant experience should have taught Italian Americans the evils of racism and nativism, the Italian community is divided between those who resent new immigrants and the so-called privileges they demand and those who, remembering the discrimination and racism their immigrant ancestors faced, are sympathetic to the needs of both new immigrants and other minority groups.

The theory of symbolic ethnicity, based on the assumption of straight-line, inevitable assimilation, has been put forward for Italian Americans and other European ethnics by such social scientists as Herbert Gans, Richard Alba, and Mary Waters. They claim that, for the third and fourth generations, ethnicity has become muted, voluntary, and private; that Italian American ethnic identity has been relegated to a sort of symbolic ethnicity. While Italian Americans are still eating Italian food and attending religious *feste*, they are, according to this theory, indistinguishable from their suburban, middle-class European American neighbors. But while the context and content of Italian American identity have been altered, for many their Italian American identity persists in significant ways. Moreover, as Little Italys become little more than tourist attractions, group affiliation for Italian Americans no longer necessarily depends on physical proximity.

Many Italian Americans may not identify themselves as belonging to any ethnic association, yet there persist a variety of organizations and publications that, through meetings, conferences, public events, magazines, and the like, promote communication at all levels of the national Italian American community. Demonstrating the vitality of the community and its sense of its own particular history are national organizations—some of them more recent, some of them revitalized—such as NIAF, UNICO, and the Order of the Sons of Italy; publications, including *VIA* and *Italian Americana, Arba Sicula, Differentia, Fra Noi*, and *The Italian American Review*; regional associations, among them Figli di Calabria, Piemontesi nel Mondo, Lucchesi nel Mondo, and Cuore Napoletano; the CUNY Endowed Chair of Italian Studies, held by Professor Philip Cannistraro; such institutions as San Francisco's Museo Italo Americano and CUNY's John Calandra Italian American Institute; courses on Italian Americans taught in many universities; and most importantly, the American Italian Historical Association. To these must be added the resilient Italian American family. Although intermarriage and the economy have caused the introduction of new values and lifestyle changes, which have diminished the authority of the extended family, Italian American families have maintained their ethnic distinctiveness even in a society moving toward homogeneity. Many Italian Americans have merged their individual identity with that of mainstream America, but many others remain concerned that the national push for multiculturalism, which would subsume all European ethnics under one common label, will deprive them of their own particular history.

BIBLIOGRAPHIC REFERENCES

Research on Italian Americans can be divided between the early works, such as Robert Foerster's *The Italian Emigration of Our Times* (Cambridge: Harvard University Press, 1919), works published in mid-century, including John Higham's *Strangers in the Land: Patterns of American Nativism, 1860–1925* (New Brunswick, NJ: Rutgers University Press, 1955), and the more recent works on Italian immigration, notably *La Storia*, Jerre Mangione and Ben Morreale's study of five centuries of the Italian American experience (New York: Harper, 1993), which is representative of Italian Americans using their own voice to write about the immigrant experience. The most important sources of material are the annual publication of the American Italian Historical Association, founded in 1966, and the impressive list of studies published by the Center for Migration Studies, in Staten Island, New York. And then there are the seminal studies, particularly Herbert Gans's *Urban Villagers: Group and Class in the Life of Italian–Americans* (New York: Free Press, 1982) and William F. Whyte's *Street Corner Society* (Chicago: University of Chicago, 1943), which provide an inside look at the old Little Italys. Other, more general works providing an overview, besides *La Storia*, are Patrick Gallo's *Old Bread, New Wine: A Portrait of Italian Americans* (Chicago: Nelson-Hall, 1981) and Humberto Nelli's *From Immigrants to Ethnics: The Italian Americans* (New York: Oxford, 1983). A good general pictorial history of the Italian immigrant experience is Jean Vincenza Scarpaci's *A Portrait of the Italians in America* (New York: Charles Scribner's Sons, 1982), while Larry Di Stasi's *Dream Streets: The Big Book of Italian American Culture* (New York: Harper & Row, 1989) provides a general and readable picture of the Italian contribution to every aspect of American life. A very personal imprint to the immigrant experience is Richard Gambino's *Blood of My Blood* (New York: Anchor Books, 1975). For the West, the best work is still Dino Cinel's *From Italy to San Francisco* (Stanford: Stanford University Press, 1982). Paola Sensi-Isolani's *Struggle and Success: An Anthology of the Italian Immigrant Experience in California* (Staten Island: Center for Migration Studies, 1993) is one of the small number of studies covering various aspects of the immigrants' lives in California. For a social, historical, and comparative approach to the study of labor militancy, the most important contribution to date is Donna Gabaccia's *Militants and Migrants: Rural Sicilians Become American Workers* (New Brunswick, NJ: Rutgers University Press, 1988). Gary Mormino and George Pozzetta's *The Immigrant World of Ybor City: Italians and Their Latino Neighbors in Tampa, 1885–1985* (Champaign: University of Illinois Press, 1987) is an important work that looks at the Italian experience in a kind of multiethnic setting. Carla Bianco's *The Two Rosetos* (Bloomington: Indiana University Press, 1974) is a valuable anthropological study of an Italian sending community and its daughter city in the United States.

Important works that look at specific aspects of the Italian immigrant experience include Robert Orsi's *The Madonna of 115th Street: Faith and Community in Italian Harlem 1880–1950* (New Haven, CT: Yale University Press, 1985), which uses the *feste* as an entry point for describing an Italian community divided generationally within itself;

Anthony Mansueto, "Blessed are the Meek . . . Religion and Socialism in Italian American History," pp. 117–36 in *The Melting Pot and Beyond: Italian Americans in the Year 2000*, edited by Jerome Krase and William Egelman (Staten Island, NY: Center for Migration Studies, 1987); Stephen Fox's *The Unknown Internment: An Oral History of the Relocation of Italian Americans during World War II* (Boston: Twayne, 1990); and Thomas Kessner's *The Golden Door: Italian and Jewish Mobility in New York City, 1900–1915* (New York: Oxford University Press, 1977), which uses a variety of sources to analyze immigrant mobility in New York City between 1880 and 1915. There is only one good definitive work that covers the family: Colleen Johnson's *Growing Up and Growing Old in Italian-American Families* (New Brunswick, NJ: Rutgers University Press, 1985). Richard Alba's *Italian Americans into the Twilight of Ethnicity* (Englewood Cliffs, NJ: Prentice Hall, 1985) has generated significant disagreement among Italian American scholars, but it is without a doubt the most important work on Italian American ethnicity. Such volumes as Anthony Tamburri, Fred Gardaphe and Paul Giordano's *From the Margin: Writings in Italian Americana* (West Lafayette: Purdue University Press, 1991), Helen Barolini's *The Dream Book: An Anthology of Writings by Italian American Women* (New York: Schocken Books, 1985), and Rose Basile Green's *The Italian-American Novel* (Rutherford, NJ: Farleigh Dickinson University Press, 1974) are good anthologies of Italian American writers. Fred Gardaphe's most recent work, *Italian Signs, American Streets: The Evolution of the Italian American Narrative* (Durham: Duke University Press, 1996) provides the best analysis of Italian American narrative to date. One other recent valuable perspective is Rudolph Vecoli's "Are Italian Americans Just White Folks?" in *Through the Looking Glass: Italian and Italian/American Images in the Media*, edited by Mary Jo Bona and Anthony Julian Tamburri (Staten Island, NY: American Italian Historical Association, 1994).

Finally, among the important autobiographical works are Constantine Panunzio's *The Soul of an Immigrant* (New York: Macmillan, 1921), Leonard Covello's *The Heart Is the Teacher* (New York: McGraw-Hill, 1958), M. H. Ets's *Rosa: The Life of an Italian Immigrant* (St. Paul: University of Minnesota Press, 1970), Jerre Mangione's *Monte Allegro* (Boston: Houghton Mifflin, 1943), Angelo Pellegrini's *Immigrants Return* (New York: Macmillan, 1951), and Joseph Napoli's memoir *A Dying Cadence: Memories of a Sicilian Childhood* (West Bethesda, MD: Marna Press, 1986).

JAPANESE

Eileen H. Tamura

IMMIGRATION

The first group of Japanese laborers who ventured overseas were mostly men who sailed from Yokohama in 1868 aboard the *Scioto*. They were called the *Gannenmono*, or first-year people, because this was the first year of Meiji rule in Japan. The 150 *Gannenmono* arrived in Honolulu to work on the sugar cane plantations that dotted the Hawaiian Islands. The growing demand for sugar in the United States had created a booming industry in Hawai'i. With the native Hawaiian population having been decimated from Western diseases, planters searched worldwide for other sources of cheap, obedient workers. In 1852 Chinese laborers became the first to arrive, followed by the Japanese.

Many of the recruits aboard the *Scioto*—among them potters, tailors, printers, and woodcutters—were unaccustomed to agricultural work and unable to cope with the harsh conditions of plantation life. While most remained in the Islands, with some men marrying Hawaiian women, others returned to Japan. Their complaints of mistreatment led the Japanese government to ban further labor emigration, a decision that remained in effect for fifteen years.

With drought and famine adding to a prolonged economic depression brought about by the Meiji government's efforts to modernize Japan, officials lifted the ban on emigration. In 1884, they allowed the Hawaiian government consul Robert Walker Irwin to recruit farmers, mainly from the prefectures of Hiroshima and Yamaguchi. Subsequent laborers also came from these two prefectures, as well as from Kumamoto, Fukuoka, and Okinawa.

The arrival of the *City of Tokio* in Honolulu harbor in 1885 began a forty-year period that saw 180,000 Japanese leaving their country for Hawai'i. From 1885 to 1898, an average of over 3,700 recruits arrived each year, and from 1898 to 1904, the average was over 9,900 per year. Men constituted over 80 percent of these early plantation workers. Many returned to Japan, and others traveled back and forth. Accompanying the mass of laborers were doctors, dentists, bankers, and inspectors—men and their families who formed an upper class in the burgeoning Japanese community. By 1900 the Japanese were the largest ethnic group in the Islands.

Unlike in Hawai'i, where Caucasian political and economic leaders actively recruited Japanese laborers, the movement of Japanese to the U.S. mainland evolved without conscious direction. A few Japanese arrived on the mainland in the mid-nineteenth century, among them shipwrecked seamen, diplomats, students, and a small group of pioneers intending to settle. But early Japanese migrants can be said to have significantly begun arriving in the 1880s, when student laborers ventured to the United States to study and worked to support themselves. Like other immigrants to America, they began as sojourners, intending to learn English, gain some knowledge, and return to Japan to begin their careers. By 1890 there were about 2,500 Japanese on the mainland United States, most of whom were student laborers living in San Francisco.

The student laborers were followed by about 27,500 Japanese, most of them laborers, who arrived between 1891 and 1990. Hostile reaction to this influx led the Japanese government to restrict passports issued to laborers during the next six years so that most of the 42,500 persons allowed to enter the continental United States during the restricted period were classified as nonlaborers. Laborers continued to enter Hawai'i, however, and the Islands became a major source of labor for the mainland after annexation in 1898. For the next ten years, about 40,000 Japanese left Hawai'i for the mainland.

With this added influx, anti-Japanese agitators on the West Coast rallied to exclude the Japanese, pointing to the Chinese Exclusion Act as a precedent. They were aided by Japan's 1905 victory in the Russo-Japanese War. Taken by surprise, Caucasians looked with apprehension at the defeat of a European power by an Asian nation and became suspicious of Japan's foreign policy. With public sentiment increasingly anti-Japanese, Congress in 1907 authorized President Theodore Roosevelt to bar Japanese and Korean laborers from entering the continental United States by way of Hawai'i, Canada, and Mexico. This was followed by the Gentlemen's Agreement of 1907–1908, in which Japan agreed to stop issuing passports to laborers bound for the United States, including Hawai'i. Excepted were former residents, parents, wives, and children of current residents and nonlaborers.

The Gentlemen's Agreement ushered in a new phase of immigration—the arrival of wives and picture brides. Japanese men who had not been able to save enough money to return to Japan as soon as they had originally planned began to think of long-term residence in America. Those who were married sent for their wives, and single men returned to Japan to marry or sent for picture brides. Picture-bride marriages evolved from Japanese practices in which family heads selected marriage mates through go-betweens who provided information on the prospective mate's genealogy, family wealth, education, and health. Men in America who could not afford the expense of traveling back to Japan sent their photographs instead and asked their parents and relatives to help select brides for them. They were married legally once the names of the brides were entered into the husbands' family registers. Anti-Japanese hostility convinced Japan in 1920 to stop issuing passports to picture brides bound for the mainland, but it continued to grant them to brides going to Hawai'i. Wives and families brought about greater stability to the lives of Issei[1] men. Soon, complex communities developed, which included Japanese newspapers, Buddhist temples, Christian churches, and Japanese-language schools.

American exclusionists were dissatisfied with the Gentlemen's Agreement, because it allowed nonlaborers and family members of Japanese immigrants to enter the United States. Exclusionist agitation finally convinced Congress to pass the 1924 Immigration Act, which not only decreased substantially the influx of southern and eastern Europeans but also prohibited the entry of all Asians except Filipinos, who were American nationals. By using the phrase "aliens ineligible to citizenship," Congress avoided naming the Japanese, but their intent was clear, since other Asians, who were also ineligible for citizenship, had been excluded earlier. The exceptions were ministers and professors and their wives and children, and students over fifteen years of age.

In the three decades before the 1924 immigration law excluded the Japanese, about 360,000 left Japan to work in the United States, half disembarking in Hawaii and the other half on the mainland. Of that total, thousands returned to Japan, and others traveled back and forth. By 1920, there were 109,274 Nikkei[2] residing in Hawai'i and 111,010 on the mainland. These figures include the Nisei, who were born in the United States. Most of the mainland Japanese lived on the West Coast, with California having the greatest number (72,000). But while the Japanese quickly became the largest ethnic group in Hawai'i—as much as 42.7 percent of the population in 1920—they constituted only 2 percent of the people in California that year.

The 1924 Immigration Act effectively halted the migration of Japanese to the United States until after World War II. Amendments in 1947 and 1948 to the War Brides Act of 1945 enabled some American GIs stationed in Japan to return to the United States with their children and Japanese wives. But it was not until the McCarran-Walter Act of 1952 that immigration from Japan increased substantially. From 1952 to 1960, more than 45,000 Japanese entered the United States (about 4,000 to 6,000 annually), 86 percent of whom were females, primarily wives of servicemen and other U.S. citizens.

When Congress passed the Immigration Act of 1965, which went into full effect three years later, it abolished discriminatory laws that had excluded Asian immigration for decades. As a result, immigration from Asia skyrocketed. Whereas only 9 percent (23,864) of all immigrants came from Asia in 1960, 25 percent (92,816) came from that region in 1970, 53 percent (313,291) in 1982, and 37 percent (356,955) in 1992 (44 percent omitting Immigration Reform and Control Act [IRCA] legalizations). Revisions to the law in 1976 and 1990 did not adversely affect this flow.

However, Japan was an exception among Asian-sending countries. The lifting of U.S. immigration restrictions came at a time when Japan was becoming increasingly prosperous, and few of its people desired to leave the country. Thus, the numbers from Japan remained at about 4,000 to 6,000 yearly, constituting less than 5 percent of all Asian immigrants in 1970 and only 1 percent in 1982 and in 1991. As a result, the Nikkei population in the United States has become increasingly American-born (68 percent in 1990), unlike the Filipinos (36 percent), the Chinese (31 percent), and the Koreans (27 percent). Moreover, Japanese Americans, who constituted the largest Asian American ethnic group from 1910 to 1970, have fallen behind the Chinese and Filipinos.

Post–World War II immigrants from Japan, called shin-Issei (new Issei), are a diverse group. Their American-born children, the shin-Nisei, experience an acculturation process somewhat similar to the pre–World War II Nisei but without the earlier discrimination that blocked employment opportunities. Apart from the shin-Issei are Japanese businessmen living temporarily in the United States with their families, who retain much of their Japanese lifestyle and socialize among themselves. Their children attend American schools and also Japanese schools with a curriculum modeled after schools in Japan.

In 1990 there were 866,000 Nikkei in the United States, compared with over 1.6 million Chinese and over 1.4 million Filipino. In that year, the Nikkei population constituted 11.7 percent of the Asian Pacific Islander population. Seventy-six percent of all Nikkei live in the western part of the United States, with 37 percent in California (312,989) and 29 percent (247,486) in Hawai'i. Other states having substantial numbers of Nikkei include New York (35,281), Washington (34,366), Illinois (21,831), New Jersey (17,253), Texas (14,795), Oregon (11,796), Colorado (11,402), and Michigan (10,681).

ADVERSITIES, ADJUSTMENTS, AND ACCULTURATION

The Immigration Act of 1924 was one of a number of measures taken against the Japanese. Other discriminatory laws and actions brought further adversities that the Issei and their children sought to overcome. In 1913, California prohibited "aliens ineligible for citizenship" from owning land. The Issei responded by leasing land for three years as allowed and placing their land under the ownership of corporations or their American-born children. A 1920 law further barred Issei from leasing and their corporations from owning agricultural land, and it prohibited the Issei from serving as guardians of minors who had title to agricultural land. A 1923 amendment still further prohibited the Issei from sharecropping—working farmland in exchange for a percentage of the profits. Legislatures in Washington, Oregon, Idaho, Arizona, Texas, and Nebraska followed California's actions. Seeing their options closing in on them, the Issei challenged the laws in court, but in 1923 the U.S. Supreme Court stunned the Japanese by ruling against them. Fortunately for the Japanese, the economic impact of these laws was less than it might have been, since many Caucasian landlords circumvented the laws by making verbal agreements, and officials often turned a blind eye to infractions in areas where the laws ran counter to farming interests.

To help them adapt to their American environment, the Issei established Japanese-language newspapers. In this way, they were like other immigrant groups. In 1920, for example, 1,147 publications in thirty-nine languages circulated in the country. Japanese newspapers kept the Issei informed of events in their home country and helped them adjust to American life by interpreting events around them. The first Japanese-language newspapers appeared in the 1880s. In the next two decades they proliferated. At its peak in the 1920s, the *Nichibei Shimbun*, based in San Francisco, maintained a circulation of 25,000. In Hawai'i in 1920, the *Nippu Jiji* rivaled the two English-language dailies in circulation figures, with 5,970 for the *Nippu Jiji*, 4,933 for the *Honolulu Advertiser*, and 6,981 for the *Honolulu Star-Bulletin*.

Another way in which the Japanese sought to adjust to American life was by organizing language schools. At first, the Issei created these schools so that their children would be able to continue their schooling when the family returned to Japan. But as the years passed and many families gradually saw America as their home, the schools adapted their curriculum to the American setting. Issei parents believed that the language schools would facilitate communication between them and their American-born children and help maintain their language and ethnic identity. In creating these schools, too, the Japanese were responding like other ethnic groups, including the Chinese and Koreans in Hawai'i and the Germans, Polish, and Irish on the mainland. The first schools opened in Hawai'i in the 1890s and on the mainland a decade later. The Nisei attended these schools in addition to their all-day regular schools. By 1910, 7,000 students attended Japanese-language schools in Hawai'i, increasing to 20,000 in 1920. On the mainland in 1918, about 2,440 students attended the schools.

Although some European Americans viewed the schools with suspicion before World War I, it was not until the war began that organized opposition arose, when exaggerated feelings of patriotism swept the nation. As German and other mother-tongue languages became targets of suspicion on the mainland, hostility in Hawai'i and California focused on the Japanese language. In both places, the legislatures passed laws aimed at abolishing the schools.

Reaction in the Japanese community in Hawai'i split between advocates and opponents of litigation. Kinzaburo Makino and his newspaper, the *Hawaii Hochi*, together with attorney Joseph Lightfoot, led the effort through the courts. Opposing litigation and advocating restraint and accommodation instead were the Reverend Takie Okumura and Yasutaro Soga, editor-in-chief of the newspaper *Nippu Jiji*. As their situation worsened, more and more Issei favored litigation, and by the end of August 1923, eighty-four schools, about 62 percent of all Japanese-language schools in Hawai'i, joined the suit. The case eventually reached the Ninth Circuit Court of Appeals, which in 1926 decided that the territorial laws and regulations were unconstitutional. Basing its decision on earlier Supreme Court cases of *Meyer v. Nebraska, Bartels v. Iowa,* and *Pierce v. Society of Sisters*, the court noted that "the protection of the Constitution extends to all, to those who speak other languages, as well as to those born with English on the tongue." In 1927 the Supreme Court upheld this decision unanimously. This ruling, together with the *Meyer, Bartels*, and *Pierce* decisions, voided the Hawai'i and California anti-Japanese-language school laws, as well as twenty-two state laws that discriminated against parochial schools and prohibited schools from teaching non-English languages.

Opponents of Japanese-language schools argued that the schools promoted Japanese nationalism and culture and interfered with the learning of English. Supporters argued that the schools promoted good American citizenship because they taught Japanese moral values, which were compatible with American values, and because learning Japanese improved communication between parents and children, thereby promoting family harmony. Moreover, facility in Japanese expanded job opportunities for the Nisei. Ironically, most Nisei, on whom all this attention was focused, did not take Japanese-language schools seriously, attending them only because their parents wanted them to. As a result, most failed to become fluent in the language. With the onset of World War II, all Japanese-language schools closed. The schools reopened after the war but were unable to regain the influence and enrollment they once had.

As the foregoing suggests, the Nisei were more interested in acquiring American rather than Japanese traits and more motivated in doing well in their regular English-language schools than in Japanese-language schools. But while the Nisei acculturated in terms of language, dress, and ways of thinking, they could not change their physical appearance and, as a result, faced discrimination in employment. This was truer on the West Coast than it was in Hawai'i. On the mainland, because teaching and other professional and government jobs were generally closed to the Nisei, those with a high school and college education were forced to work in businesses run by Nikkei, particularly in wholesale and retail produce. Others worked in agriculture, nurseries, gardening, and laundry and domestic services. While in Hawai'i discrimination existed in Caucasian-owned businesses and high government positions, public schools employed aspiring Nisei teachers and in this way provided the Japanese with an avenue for upward mobility. At the same time, with a large concentration of Nikkei in Hawai'i, Nisei dentists and doctors in the islands could count on having enough patients.

The Issei encouraged their children to do well in school and ascend the economic ladder, but they stressed educational and occupational success for their sons rather than for their daughters. Especially in the first two decades of the twentieth century, most Issei believed that a high school education was unnecessary for females. While most Nisei girls followed the dictates of their parents, some refused to do so, reflecting the influence of the American environment. As time passed and families acculturated and became more secure financially, Nisei school enrollments came to reflect American norms. In Hawai'i, for example, six and a half times as many Nisei boys as girls attended high school in 1918, but slightly more girls than boys did so in 1947.

Among the Sansei (the third) and succeeding generations, educational and occupational accomplishments reflect American middle-class norms. The Immigration Act of 1965 did not significantly affect the Nikkei population in the United States, as it did other Asian American populations. With only 4,000 to 6,000 new immigrants from Japan each year since 1950, the Nikkei population has been characterized as increasingly American-born and distant from Japanese norms. Few of the third, fourth, and fifth generations speak Japanese or understand Japanese culture. But while the Nikkei hold American middle-class values and have assimilated structurally within the larger American society, they have maintained their subcultural identity and have continued to participate in ethnic community activities. Some scholars have used the term *ethnogenesis* to refer to this phenomenon, the evolution and creation of a subculture within the larger American culture.

Nevertheless, it would be a mistake to overlook regional differences within the Nikkei subculture, the most striking of which is that between the mainland and Hawai'i. For over a century, the Nikkei in Hawai'i have constituted a large proportion of the Islands' population, peaking at 42.7 percent in 1920 and decreasing since then to 32 percent in 1960 and 19.7 percent in 1992. Because of this high Nikkei density and because Hawai'i has been more racially tolerant than the mainland, the Nisei who grew up in Hawai'i before World War II faced less discrimination and hostility than did mainland Nisei and, as a consequence, felt more comfortable with their ethnic origins. Later generations of Nikkei growing up in postwar America faced less discrimination both on the mainland and in Hawai'i. Yet differences remain, based largely on the Island lifestyle that has affected both the Nikkei as well as other ethnic groups: the more casual lifestyle and greater group orientation in Hawai'i and the prevalent use of Hawai'i Creole English, popularly known as pidgin. But whether on the mainland or in Hawai'i, the Nikkei have maintained their ethnic identity.

Despite this persistence of ethnic identity, the Nikkei out-marriage rate has increased with each succeeding generation. While 2 to 6 percent of all Nikkei intermarried during the 1920s and 1930s, about 35 percent of them did so in the 1970s, increasing to about 50 percent in 1989. Japanese American women have tended to intermarry more than Japanese American men. Only time will reveal the impact of such increasing intermarriage on the persistence of ethnic identity.

Nikkei acculturation has thus been an ongoing process, but in the decades before World War II, it proved inadequate in pacifying European American animosity. The 1924 Immigration Act, which stopped the influx from Japan, temporarily lessened hostility; however, with Japan's aggressive foreign policy during the 1930s, anti-Japanese sentiment again erupted. When the United States entered World War II, the Nikkei saw their status drop precipitously, culminating in their forced removal from their homes and their incarceration in American concentration camps.

Even before Japanese bombers attacked Pearl Harbor, U.S. government officials had taken steps against potential internal subversives. The Department of Justice had formed an Aliens Division that worked with the Federal Bureau of Investigation (FBI) and the Office of Naval Intelligence in listing aliens who would be interned in the event the United States entered the war. During the week after Pearl Harbor, the Department of Justice interned 3,000 Germans, Italians, and Japanese in camps created for enemy aliens. The 1,500 Japanese internees, mostly male, were ministers, Japanese-language schoolteachers, community leaders, and those known to have had contacts with Japanese consulates. In the month following Pearl Harbor, Attorney General Francis Biddle directed FBI agents to make searches without warrants in hundreds of homes in which Issei lived and to confiscate firearms and radios.

The press and politicians both reflected and incited anti-Japanese sentiment. With public pressure mounting, President Franklin D. Roosevelt signed Executive Order 9066 on February 19, 1942. EO 9066 authorized the military to designate the western parts of Washington, Oregon, and California and the southern part of Arizona as military areas from which civilians could be excluded. Instructions posted in the succeeding weeks gave the Nikkei only days to prepare for removal to an unknown place for an unknown duration. Families were forced to sell at a loss or otherwise dispose of their homes, businesses, and personal property. They were allowed to take only what they could carry, including their bedding and linen.

The rationale used for this mass removal was that it was impossible to determine who was loyal and disloyal. But six days after Roosevelt signed EO 9066, government officials proposed to enlist Japanese Americans in the armed forces. If the government could determine who was loyal and could enlist, they could presumably determine who should remain free and who should be incarcerated. That there was no military necessity for EO 9066 can be seen when looking at what happened in Hawai'i. There, with greater possibility of further attack and with a larger concentration of ethnic Japanese—157,000, constituting 37 percent of the population—only 1,500 people, mostly noncitizens, were incarcerated. Unlike on the mainland, Nikkei labor was essential in the territory.

The army removed the West Coast Nikkei to racetracks and fairgrounds that were hastily converted into Assembly Centers, where many families were forced to live in horse stables. Whitewashing failed to sanitize the stalls, and many fell ill to disease. Food was poor and privacy absent. For example, at the Merced Assembly Center, no partitions separated the toilets, which consisted of a board with holes set a foot apart.

Government officials had planned to resettle the people in states away from the West Coast, but protests from these states led officials to change their minds. Instead, the 120,000 Nikkei, two-thirds of whom were American citizens, were taken to what the government euphemistically called Relocation Centers. There were ten major camps, which were administered by the War Relocation Authority (WRA), a civilian agency specifically established to run the camps.

The camps were situated in barren, desolate areas, subject to extremely harsh temperatures. Families lived in hastily constructed barracks with little privacy and comfort. Communal bathing and toilet areas lacked walls unless installed by the inmates themselves. Schools lacked books, equipment, and competent teachers. Family life broke down, as youngsters spent most of their time with friends, even eating their meals in mess halls away from their families. Dust storms frequently swept through the camps, leaving sand and dust in people's eyes, mouths, hair, and food. But, most importantly, law-abiding citizens and their immigrant parents could not come and go as they wished. Barbed wire surrounded the camps, and armed soldiers guarded the perimeters. The Nikkei were inmates deprived of their freedom because of their ancestry.

Underlying tensions coming from resentment at being confined unjustly led to many incidents that sometimes turned to violence. At Manzanar Relocation Center mass protests escalated into a crisis situation in which military police fired at a crowd, killing two and injuring others. At Tule Lake, constant unrest led to a number of hostile incidents between inmates and their Caucasian administrators, with soldiers shooting at unarmed protestors.

An issue that created turmoil within families and the camp community was the leave clearance program administered beginning in early 1943. First conceived when the army sought to recruit Nisei volunteer soldiers—and extended to include all those incarcerated so that WRA officials could determine whom they would permit to leave the camps—the program exacerbated tensions that grew to crisis proportions. The culprit was a loyalty questionnaire with two key questions that lacked sensitivity to and understanding of those confined. Question 27 asked inmates if they were willing to serve in the U.S. armed forces. Many Nisei men answered conditionally, saying they would serve only if their rights were restored. Question 28 asked inmates if they would swear allegiance to the United States and foreswear allegiance to the Japanese emperor. Issei, who were forbidden to become naturalized American citizens, realized that by saying yes they would become stateless. Some Nisei believed that the question was a trap, that to answer yes implied that they once held allegiance to Japan. Out of resentment, many answered no to both questions, while others refused to respond. As a result of the responses they gave, thousands were unjustly classified as disloyal.

Most, however, answered yes to both questions. As a result, thousands left the camps. In 1943, for example, 17,000, mostly eighteen- to thirty-year-olds, left for such cities as Chicago, Denver, Salt Lake City, and New York to attend college or to work. About the same number left the following year. Most of those left behind were Issei and minors.

In January 1944, tensions reappeared when the government extended the draft to include Japanese American males who were confined in the camps. At the Heart Mountain Relocation Center in Wyoming, 85 men of The Fair Play Com-

mittee refused to register, stating that they were protesting the loss of their
constitutional rights and would comply with the draft only when their families
were freed from the camps. In all, 263 men from all the camps were convicted
for draft resistance. They were a minority, as 3,600 joined the army, either as
volunteers or as draftees.

Bitterness and demoralization over their treatment, coupled with pressure from
Issei parents who did not want to be separated from their children, led 5,589
Nisei to renounce their citizenship between late 1944 and mid-1945. Their renunciation, which had little to do with disloyalty to the United States, should
be seen in the context of the incarceration experience, exacerbated by the WRA
announcement in December 1944 that all the camps would close within a year.
Many Issei feared violence and economic hardship if they tried to resettle outside
the camps. Believing that they would not be forced to leave if they sought
repatriation to Japan, they pressured their children to renounce their U.S. citizenship so that the families could remain together.

Earlier during the war, about 2,000 Japanese, mostly diplomats and Issei, had
sailed on the Swedish liner *Gripsholm* in a prisoner exchange program. After
the war, 1,659 Issei, 1,949 Nisei minors who accompanied their parents, and
1,116 adult Nisei renunciants left the United States for life in Japan. Many of
the Nisei who renounced later regretted their decisions and asked to rescind their
renunciation. Most had never left the United States. Through the unrelenting
efforts of attorney Wayne M. Collins, their cases remained in the courts for
twenty-two years. Of the 5,409 Nisei who sought to regain their citizenship,
4,978 succeeded.

NIKKEI AND AMERICAN MATERIAL CULTURE

Both in Hawai'i and on the mainland, Japanese immigrants made their biggest
economic impact in agriculture. During the late nineteenth and early twentieth
centuries, thousands of Issei laborered in Hawai'i's expanding sugar cane industry. Workers performed backbreaking labor in dust-filled air, under the
scorching sun, and in fields thick with knife-sharp leaves. They often sang *ho-
lehole bushi*, melancholy folksongs that reflected their plight.

"Send us money, send us money!"
Is the usual note from home.
But how can I do it
In this plight?
My husband cuts the cane stalks.
And I strip their leaves.
With sweat and tears we both work
For our means.

Besides having to labor strenuously, workers resented the low wages and ill treatment accorded them. When Hawai'i became a territory in 1898, voluntary labor replaced the system that had bound workers to their contracts. Strikes erupted spontaneously, but they were generally unsuccessful in achieving needed changes. In 1909 workers staged the first organized strike, the territory's longest and largest strike to date. Although management broke the strike, workers soon received higher wages and improved working and living conditions. The next massive strike occurred in 1920, for the first time involving workers of all ethnic groups. Once again, although strike leaders conceded defeat, wages increased and conditions improved.

On the West Coast, most Issei also began working as agricultural laborers. Soon, they began acquiring formerly uncultivated lands and supplemented existing crops with vegetables, fruits, and flowers that were new to the marketplace. By 1919, the Japanese grossed 10 percent of the value of California's produce by using only 1 percent of the state's agricultural land. They were able to accomplish this on small family farms using labor-intensive methods of farming, thus playing an important role in feeding the dramatically growing population in California and the rest of the West Coast. In Los Angeles, Seattle, and other places, the Japanese formed networks of wholesale and retail merchants who sold Japanese-grown crops to local consumers. In states further inland— Idaho, Colorado, and Utah—the Issei were instrumental in establishing the sugar beet industry. In 1913, for example, they produced one-third of the crop in Idaho.

Most of the Issei and many of the older Nisei, both in Hawai'i and on the mainland, had to remain in agriculture or agriculture-related businesses; but, in contrast to the West Coast, in Hawai'i—where Japanese constituted 38 percent of the population in the 1930s—younger Nisei formed a sizable proportion of the available educated workforce, and many were hired as teachers, nurses, and officeworkers. Others, who became doctors and dentists, served the Nikkei community. Since World War II, both on the mainland and in Hawai'i, succeeding generations of Japanese Americans have filled all occupational areas, professional and nonprofessional.

The Nikkei advance into the middle class was like the experience of other immigrant groups who pursued the American dream through hard work and persistence in school. By 1960, the median school years of California Japanese was 12.4 for males and 12.3 for females, compared to the state figures of 11.7 for males and 12.0 for females. The end of the twentieth century saw their level of education continue to exceed other Americans. In 1990, 34.5 percent of all Nikkei completed four or more years of college versus 20.3 percent of all Americans. In employment, the Nikkei have made considerable advances since World War II. In California, Nikkei male professionals in 1940 constituted only 3.8 percent of all employed Nikkei males. In 1950 the percentage remained low at 4.4, but by 1960 it had increased to 15 percent. Nationwide in 1990, 19.6 percent of employed Nikkei men and 19.3 percent of employed Nikkei women had professional jobs.

NIKKEI IN AMERICAN POLITICS

Because of their birth on American soil, the Nisei were American citizens. Their parents, however, were barred from becoming naturalized U.S. citizens until after World War II. The first naturalization law, enacted in 1790, limited naturalization to "free white person[s]." In 1870, after the Civil War, Congress extended this right to aliens of African descent but stopped short of including Asians. When Asians applied for naturalization in the decades that followed, some were granted citizenship, so that by 1910, there were 1,368 Chinese and 420 Japanese naturalized citizens.

The case that determined the citizenship status of Japanese immigrants was *Ozawa v. United States*. Takao Ozawa had lived in the United States for twenty years, first in California and then in Hawai'i. In 1914 he petitioned the U.S. District Court for naturalization. When the judge denied his petition, he appealed to the Ninth Circuit Court and then to the Supreme Court. Ozawa called attention to his family's American lifestyle and to the fact that his children attended an American school and church, spoke no Japanese, and were not registered with the Japanese consulate. But, in 1922, the Supreme Court decided that Japanese aliens were nonwhites and therefore ineligible for citizenship. As a further affront to their status, Nisei women lost their citizenship when they married Issei men. In 1922 Congress passed the Cable Act, which decreed that an American woman who married an alien ineligible to citizenship lost her own citizenship. This act was finally reversed in 1931.

A number of veterans of Japanese descent had become American citizens as a result of a congressional act in 1918 that allowed the naturalization of aliens who had served in the armed services in World War I. Their citizenship was short-lived, however, for in 1925 the U.S. Supreme Court decided in *Toyota v. United States* that even war veterans were ineligible for naturalization. Ten years later, the Nye-Lea Act allowed some 500 Asian veterans of World War I to become naturalized American citizens, but it was not until 1952 that Congress passed the McCarran-Walter Act that allowed all Asian immigrants to become naturalized citizens.

Because the Issei were barred from becoming American citizens before World War II, they lacked voting power during the late nineteenth and early twentieth centuries. It would not be until an increasing number of their children reached adulthood in the 1930s that Japanese Americans began to make inroads in politics and government. In 1934 the Nisei constituted 21.5 percent of all registered voters in Hawai'i. By then a couple of Nisei had been elected to the Territorial House of Representatives. The Nisei population was proportionately smaller in mainland communities, and as a result, its political influence there was less than in Hawai'i.

In the election after Hawai'i attained statehood in 1959, Daniel Inouye, a veteran hero of World War II, became the first Japanese American congressman. After serving two terms, he was elected a U.S. senator. Patsy Takemoto Mink, the first Asian American congresswoman, was elected from Hawai'i in 1964. In 1973 Hawai'i's George Ariyoshi became the first Japanese American governor. In the 1970s three mainland Nikkei were elected to national office: Senator Samuel Hayakawa and Representatives Norman Mineta and Robert Matsui. Since the 1970s, succeeding generations of Japanese American men and women have been elected to political office and have served in local, state, and national government. In 1997, Inouye, Mink, and Matsui remained in office, Mineta having retired from Congress before the 1996 election.

Despite the generational maturity of the Nikkei community, its visibility as a nonwhite group has made it a target of anti-Asian racism that has erupted from time to time. As in earlier decades, international relations with Japan have continued to affect the status of Japanese Americans caught in the middle. During the 1980s and 1990s, the United States saw its economy falter at the same time as Japan's automobile and electronic sales in the United States flourished and the value of the yen increased. Many Americans blamed Japan—a phenomenon referred to as *Japan-bashing*—for the problems in the American economy, and hate crimes increased against Nikkei and other Asian Americans.

But unlike earlier times, the Nikkei have become far more vocal in speaking out against such injustices. Their involvement in political and social issues can be traced back to the 1960s and 1970s, when the Sansei were coming of age amidst the civil rights struggle, Black Power movement, anti-Vietnam War protests, and student and community activism. As with other ethnic groups, the Nikkei student activists explored their history and ethnic identity at the same time that they worked on local and national causes.

One particularly visible group has been the Japanese American Citizens League (JACL), whose collaboration with the U.S. government during the World War II incarceration of the Nikkei made it an object of resentment among most Japanese Americans. It was only in the 1970s, with the emerging leadership of the Sansei within the organization, that the JACL began to change its previously conservative stance. During the 1970s and 1980s the JACL took an active role in the movement for redress, an action that revitalized the organization and redeemed its reputation. Once focusing solely on issues concerning the Nikkei, the JACL has since the late 1980s looked beyond its own ethnic group to support the struggles of other Asian American groups as well as Latinos and African Americans. In Hawai'i, the JACL has supported the struggle for Hawaiian sovereignty.

NIKKEI IN AMERICAN CULTURE

Japanese Americans have contributed to American arts, literature, music, and theater. Recognized internationally as important twentieth-century artists are Isamu Noguchi, best known for his sculptures and gardens; George Nakashima, appreciated for his hand-crafted wooden furniture; Toshiko Takaezu, recognized for her pottery; and George Tsutakawa, distinguished for his designs of water fountains.

Nikkei writers have also enriched American literature. In the 1950s, at a time when the heroism of the 442nd Regimental Combat Team (discussed later) overshadowed other aspects of the Japanese American experience, John Okada's novel *No-No Boy*, published in 1957, met with little notice. Later recognized as a classic in Asian American literature, the novel highlights the tragedy of the Japanese American incarceration through the experiences of a Nisei who refuses to register for the draft and who encounters European American hostility in the postwar period.

Other important Japanese American writers include Hisaye Yamamoto, one of the earliest Nisei short-story writers to receive national attention after World War II; Toshio Mori, perhaps best known for his book *Yokohama, California*; Wakako Yamauchi, well known for her outstanding play *And the Soul Shall Dance*; and Milton Murayama, whose novel *All I Asking for Is My Body* explores early plantation life in Hawai'i. Succeeding generations have produced nationally such recognized writers as Philip Gotanda, Lawson Fusao Inada, Janice Mirikitani, David Mura, and Lois-Ann Yamanaka.

In music, Seiji Ozawa has received worldwide recognition for his accomplishments as conductor and musical director of the symphony orchestras of Toronto, San Francisco, and Boston. Among popular music groups, Hiroshima emerged in the 1970s as a creative force, distinguishing itself by fusing such traditional Japanese instruments as the koto, shakuhachi, and taiko drums with jazz instrumentation and forms.

The post–World War II period has witnessed Japanese American actors in leading roles in film and theater. Among them have been actress and singer Pat Suzuki, who in 1957 held a leading role in Rogers and Hammerstein's *Flower Drum Song*; Goro Suzuki, better known as Jack Soo, and probably best known for his role as Sammy Fong in the stage and screen productions of *Flower Drum Song* and as Nick Yemana in the television series *Barney Miller*; actress Nobu McCarthy; George Takei, best known for his role as Mr. Sulu on *Star Trek*; and James Shigeta, the first Japanese American actor to play romantic leads in Hollywood films. In 1957, two Japanese Americans won Academy Awards: Sessue Hayakawa, one of Hollywood's leading actors of silent film, for his role as Colonel Saito in *The Bridge over the River Kwai*, and Miyoshi Umeki for her role in *Sayonara*.

In the 1960s and 1970s, Asian American theater emerged in the context of national interest in ethnic identity issues. The first Asian American theater, East West Players, was established in 1965 in Los Angeles under the artistic direction of Japanese American Makoto Iwamatsu. In the decades that followed, East West Players became a force in the larger American theater scene. Since the 1960s, other Asian American theaters have emerged in cities such as San Francisco, Seattle, San Diego, Chicago, and New York. Their widening popularity has had an important role in breaking old stereotypes and educating the larger public about Asian Americans. Contributing to this effort is Steven Okazaki, among the country's gifted filmmakers, who won an Oscar in 1991 for his documentary *Days of Waiting*, on the incarceration of Japanese Americans during World War II.

Japanese Americans have also contributed to the American religious scene by establishing Buddhist churches in Hawai'i and on the West Coast. In the late nineteenth and early twentieth centuries, Buddhist priests arrived from Japan to minister to the spiritual needs of the immigrants, most of whom were Buddhists. Soon temples dotted the landscape of Hawai'i and the West Coast, where Nishi Hongwanji became the largest of the Buddhist sects. During the first half of the twentieth century, Buddhist leaders recognized the importance of adapting their religion to the American environment. As a result, they conducted services in English as well as in Japanese, encouraged Nisei to become ministers, installed pews and organs as in Christian churches, composed hymns, initiated Sunday schools, and sponsored Young Men's and Young Women's Buddhist Associations, patterned after the Young Men's and Young Women's Christian Associations.

In 1971, of the 80 percent of Honolulu Nisei who declared having a religion, 60 percent identified themselves as Buddhist, whereas 29 and 5 percent, respectively, declared themselves as Protestants and Catholics. As in Hawai'i, a large percentage of Nisei on the mainland continued to identify themselves as Buddhists. But with smaller concentrations of Japanese Americans living together, which made it more difficult to maintain ethnic institutions, proportionately more of the Japanese on the mainland than in Hawai'i converted to Christianity. Furthermore, among succeeding generations, the percentage of Buddhists has decreased, whereas that of Christians has increased.

NIKKEI LEGACY AND STATUS

World War II proved to be a watershed in the legacy and status of Japanese Americans. Soon after the attack on Pearl Harbor, Japanese Americans serving in the armed forces were discharged or removed from their units and assigned to menial jobs. In addition, the Selective Service classified Japanese Americans of draft age as 4C, enemy aliens ineligible to serve. But the Draft Act's anti-discrimination provision forced the army to keep men already drafted. As a result, 1,432 Nisei in the Hawai'i National Guard remained on duty. In June 1942, after being organized into a separate unit, later called the 100th Infantry Battalion, they were transported to Camp McCoy, Wisconsin, and in January 1943 moved to Camp Shelby, Mississippi. The army kept them for over a year in training because it did not know where to send them. Finally, in August 1943, they were sent to Europe.

In January 1943 President Roosevelt announced that the government would form a special combat unit of Japanese Americans, subsequently called the 442nd Regimental Combat Team. When the military issued a call for volunteers, about 10,000 Japanese American men in Hawai'i responded. On the mainland, the military recruited Nisei who were incarcerated in the camps. Disillusioned and bitter about the treatment they were receiving from the government, fewer than 2,000, of the 20,000 who were eligible volunteered. (After the draft was reinstated for Nikkei men, 2,800 more served.) In May 1944, after months of training at Camp Shelby, the volunteers were sent to Europe, where they joined the 100th Battalion, by then having earned a reputation as a strong fighting unit.

The 100th/442nd suffered enormous casualties in battling the Germans in Italy and France. In October 1944 Germans trapped a Texas unit of American soldiers, the 36th Infantry Division, on a hilltop in southern France. The 100th/442nd soldiers had just returned from liberating the towns of Bruyeres and Biffontaine. Dogged tired, they were nevertheless ordered to free the trapped battalion. They advanced slowly, amidst a barrage of heavy, incessant gunfire. After five days of continuous battle, the 100th/442nd rescued the ''lost battalion.'' The costs were high: 800 soldiers in the 100th/442nd died to save 211 trapped soldiers. After the war ended, the 100th/442nd became known as the most decorated unit of its size. Of 23,000 soldiers, 18,143 received decorations, including one Congressional Medal of Honor, 47 Distinguished Service Crosses, 350 Silver Stars, and more than 3,600 Purple Hearts.

Unlike the men of the 100th/442nd, Nisei in the Military Intelligence Service (MIS) returned home without fanfare. They had been recruited as early as June 1942, at the same time that U.S. government officials were debating the merits of accepting Nisei as soldiers. These MIS recruits were sent to language school at Camp Savage, Minnesota, and at nearby Fort Snelling. Only about 7 percent of all Nisei men were proficient enough in Japanese. Most of them were Kibei, those Nisei born in the United States but educated in Japan. About 5,000 Nisei served in the MIS, participating in all of the major battles in the Pacific. They translated captured documents, monitored communications between Japanese fighter planes, and questioned Japanese prisoners of war. After Japan's surrender, they served as interpreters and translators at the war crimes trials and with the U.S. occupation forces in Japan. Unrecognized for what they did until decades after the war ended, the men in the MIS played a crucial role in the Allies' victory in the Pacific. The heroic efforts of Nisei soldiers during World War II transformed public sentiment toward Japanese Americans from hostility to admiration and their status from pariah to model citizen. Unfortunately, neither extreme does justice to the Nikkei experience.

While the Nikkei soldiers were fighting the war in Europe and the Pacific, another kind of battle was being waged at home. Among the 110,000 Nikkei living along the West Coast in 1942, three young citizens dared to challenge the military curfew and exclusion orders. Minoru Yasui, a lawyer in Portland, Oregon, and Gordon Hirabayashi, a University of Washington senior, each decided on his own to disobey the curfew. Fred Korematsu, a shipyard welder in

San Francisco, was engaged to a Caucasian woman and refused to move out of the excluded area designated by the military. Each was convicted in 1942, and each appealed to the Supreme Court. In each case, the Court upheld the government's wartime actions of depriving citizens of their constitutional rights solely on the basis of their ancestry.

Then, in 1981, lawyer Peter Irons discovered crucial Justice Department papers that showed that government lawyers had withheld evidence and submitted false evidence to the trial court and later to the Supreme Court. In 1983, four decades after their clients' convictions, lawyers for the three men filed legal petitions asking that the convictions be vacated—that is, that they be erased from the judicial record. The lawyers used an obscure legal procedure called a writ of error *coram nobis*, Latin for "error before us," which asks the original trial court that heard the case in 1942 to correct a fundamental error that occurred during the trial. In the cases of the three men, the error was the government's withholding of evidence and submitting false evidence. After five years of litigation, the convictions were vacated. This was an unprecedented victory in American legal history. For the first time, convicted cases that the Supreme Court had decided on were overturned. Note that it was the convictions of the three men that were overturned, not the Supreme Court decisions.

A related case was that of Mitsuye Endo. Unlike the three men, Endo's challenge came after she was ordered to move to an assembly center. Endo was a Methodist, could not read or speak Japanese, and had never visited Japan. Moreover, her brother was serving in the army. Her lawyer filed a habeas corpus petition, asking the San Francisco federal district court to require the War Relocation Authority to show why Endo must continue to be incarcerated. In December 1944 the Supreme Court decided that the government could not incarcerate loyal citizens against their will. But instead of holding the president, the army, and Congress responsible, the Court chose to blame the War Relocation Authority, the civilian-run agency that administered the camps.

These four cases raised important questions about the constitutional rights of citizens in times of war. Unfortunately, they remain as precedents that allow the government to use military necessity as a reason for depriving citizens of liberty and property.

Concurrent with the legal proceedings in the courts during the 1980s, a movement for redress gained momentum. The idea of reparations, however, was not new. As early as 1942, when the government ordered Nikkei from their homes, some Japanese Americans protested and called for redress. In 1948, after the war, Congress provided for some financial compensation, allowing Nikkei the right to file claims for property losses due to the forced removal. The law failed to provide compensation for loss of income or loss of liberty and required proof of property losses. Although some Nikkei were able to file claims, most had lost their documents and were thus unable to prove their losses. During the late 1960s a new generation of Japanese Americans began to organize to correct the wrongs their parents and grandparents had experienced. While some worked to clear the names of Yasui, Hirabayashi, and Korematsu, others sought financial redress from the government. In March 1983, the National Council for Japanese American Redress filed a class action suit in federal court in Washington, D.C., asking the court to award $10,000 for each of twenty-one government violations. The judge dismissed the suit, and the Supreme Court refused to hear it. Meanwhile, Congress in 1980 had created the Commission on Wartime Relocation and Internment of Civilians (CWRIC) to review the incarceration of Nikkei and recommend remedies. The CWRIC analyzed historical documents and held hearings throughout the country. Many of the 750 Nikkei who testified spoke for the first time in public about their experiences. In a highly charged emotional atmosphere, tears of shame, anger, and resentment, suppressed for decades, burst forth. In their December 1982 report, the nine-member commission unanimously agreed that a ''grave injustice'' had occurred and recommended that $20,000 in compensation be paid to each survivor, recognizing that the amount fell far short of the losses suffered. In August 1988 Congress enacted a redress bill that provided this compensation. Six days later President Ronald Reagan signed the bill into law.

The vacated convictions of Yasui, Hirabayashi, and Korematsu, the presidential apology in 1988, and the congressional redress payment serve as deterrents to future wrongful imprisonment of a group of people based solely on their ethnic origins.

NOTES

1. *Issei* refers to the first generation of Japanese immigrants; *Nisei* refers to the second generation, the children of immigrants. *Sansei* is the third generation.

2. *Nikkei* refers to ethnic Japanese.

BIBLIOGRAPHIC REFERENCES

Important basic books on the Japanese American experience are Roger Daniels, *Asian America: Chinese and Japanese in the United States since 1850* (Seattle: University of Washington Press, 1988), and Paul R. Spickard, *Japanese Americans: The Formation and Transformation of an Ethnic Group* (New York: Twayne, 1996). Harry H. L. Kitano, *Generations and Identity: The Japanese American* (Needham Heights, MA: Ginn, 1993), and Brian Niiya, ed., *Japanese American History: An A-to-Z Reference from 1868 to the Present* (New York: Facts on File, 1993), provide a wide range of useful information on the Nikkei. For an examination of immigration, see Alan T. Moriyama, *Japanese Emigration Companies and Hawaii, 1894–1908* (Honolulu: University of Hawaii Press, 1985), and Hilary Conroy, *The Japanese Frontier in Hawaii, 1868–1898* (Berkeley: University of California Press, 1953). A thorough analysis of the first generation on the mainland is in Yuji Ichioka, *The Issei: The World of the First Generation Japanese Immigrants, 1885–1924* (New York: Free Press, 1988). For the Hawaii immigrant experience, see Yukiko Kimura, *Issei: Japanese Immigrants in Hawaii* (Honolulu: University of Hawaii Press, 1988), and Barbara F. Kawakami, *Japanese Immigrant Clothing in*

Hawaii, 1885–1941 (Honolulu: University of Hawaii Press, 1993). Eileen H. Tamura, *Americanization, Acculturation, and Ethnic Identity: The Nisei Generation in Hawaii* (Urbana: University of Illinois Press, 1994), analyzes the experiences of the Nisei growing up in Hawaii before World War II. Evelyn Nakano Glenn, *Issei, Nisei, War Bride: Three Generations of Japanese American Women in Domestic Service* (Philadelphia: Temple University Press, 1986), studies an important aspect of Nikkei economic and social history. Paul Spickard, *Mixed Blood: Intermarriage and Ethnic Identity in Twentieth-Century America* (Madison: University of Wisconsin Press, 1989), compares intermarriage among Japanese Americans, Jews, and African Americans.

Numerous works examine various aspects of the Japanese American incarceration experience during World War II. Two comprehensive accounts of this dark chapter in our nation's history are Michi Weglyn, *Years of Infamy* (New York: William Morrow, 1976), and Roger Daniels, *Concentration Camps: North America* (Malabar, FL: Krieger, 1993). Yuji Ichioka, ed., *Views from Within: The Japanese American Evacuation and Resettlement Study* (Los Angeles: Asian American Study Center, UCLA, 1989), includes fascinating chapters on the researchers who observed the camp inmates. Thomas James, *Exile Within: The Schooling of Japanese Americans, 1942–1945* (Cambridge: Harvard University Press, 1987), provides a much-needed analysis of schooling in the camps. Among available oral histories are the excellent multivolume set by Arthur A. Hansen, ed., *Japanese American World War II Evacuation Oral History Project*, parts 1–5 (New Providence, NJ: K. G. Saur, 1991–1994), and Sue K. Embrey, Arthur A. Hansen, and Betty K. Mitson, eds., *Manzanar Martyr: An Interview with Harry Y. Ueno* (Fullerton, CA: OHP, California State University, 1986), an outstanding interview with a camp resistor. Peter Irons, *Justice at War: The Story of the Japanese American Internment Cases* (Berkeley: University of California Press, 1993 [1983]), focuses on the government's suppression of evidence and the legal challenges of Yasui, Korematsu, and Hirabayashi. Gary Okihiro, *Cane Fires: The Anti-Japanese Movement in Hawaii, 1865–1945* (Philadelphia: Temple University Press, 1991), examines the treatment of the Nikkei in Hawaii. John J. Stephan, *Hawaii under the Rising Sun* (Honolulu: University of Hawaii Press, 1984), analyzes the complexities of Japanese American attitudes during the war. Important among the raft of books on Japanese American soldiers during World War II are Thomas D. Murphy, *Ambassadors in Arms* (Honolulu: University of Hawaii Press, 1954), on Hawaii's 100th Infantry Battalion; Masayo U. Duus, *Unlikely Liberators: the Men of the 100th and 442nd* (Honolulu: University of Hawaii Press, 1987); and Lyn Crost, *Honor by Fire: Japanese Americans at War in Europe and the Pacific* (Novata, CA: Presidio Press, 1994), one of the few books that includes an extensive discussion on the Nisei serving in the Military Intelligence Service.

JEWS

Edward S. Shapiro

Of all the European ethnic groups that immigrated to the United States, the Jews were the most idiosyncratic. Not only were they culturally and socially different from the dominant white Anglo-Saxon Protestant (WASP) native population, but, in contrast, for example, to the Polish, Irish, German, and Italian immigrants, they were also not Christians. Thus, added to the normally difficult acculturative process that all immigrant groups experienced, the Jews had an additional problem of adapting to a culture that was overwhelmingly Christian. The Jewish situation in America was even more problematic because the Jews were not always clear themselves as to what it meant to be a Jew. The question of ''Who is a Jew?'' which has vexed contemporary politics in Israel, was also a question that Jews in Europe and the United States asked of themselves during the nineteenth and twentieth centuries.

If American Jews were an ethnic group, they comprised a most peculiar one. They did not have a common language. Jews from central Europe spoke German; those from eastern Europe spoke Yiddish; and those from North Africa and the Balkans often spoke Ladino, a Spanish form of Hebrew. None of these languages (with the partial exception of Yiddish) were passed on to the second, much less the third, generations. Indeed, the U.S. census noted that Jews, in their quest to adapt to America, gave up using their native languages more rapidly than other immigrant groups.

THE WAVES OF NEWCOMERS

One of the salient features of American Jewry is its cultural heterogeneity. In part, this is due to the different waves of immigration that brought Jews to the United States. This cultural heterogeneity was already evident by the time of the country's independence from Great Britain. In 1776, there were perhaps 3,000 Jews in the thirteen former mainland colonies of England. Some were the descendants of families that had fled Spain in 1492 and settled in Holland and Brazil. The majority, however, were Ashkenazic Jews whose roots went back to central and eastern Europe and who had immigrated to America in the eighteenth century. The most famous of these was Haym Salomon, the financier. America's colonial Jews were mainly merchants and shopkeepers (and their families), and they lived mainly in the port cities of Newport, Rhode Island, New York City, Philadelphia, Savannah, and Charleston, South Carolina. There were also Jews scattered throughout the hinterland engaged in trading of one sort or another. The Jews of the port cities had created an embryonic Jewish institutional life that would thicken and deepen with the larger waves of immigration in the nineteenth and twentieth centuries. By 1800 the centers of Jewish population contained synagogues, kosher butchers, benevolent societies, schools, and cemeteries. The small size of the Jewish population, however, led to intermarriage and rapid assimilation, while the shortage of trained rabbis hampered the development of Judaism. Colonial America, Salomon wrote to a relative in England, had "vinig yiddishkeit" (little Jewishness).

The second wave of Jewish immigration to America commenced in the 1820s and continued to the 1870s. These immigrants came largely from the Germanic-speaking areas of central and eastern Europe, and their most prominent member was Rabbi Isaac Mayer Wise, who was born in what, until recently, was called Czechoslovakia. The immigration increased the Jewish population of the United States to nearly a quarter of a million by the 1870s. Contrary to their predecessors, the "Germans" spread throughout the United States, and, in fact, the percentage of Jews living in the great cities of the East in the 1870s was lower than that of the general population. Wise, for example, settled in Cincinnati, whereas the grandfather of Barry Goldwater opened his first store in Prescott, Arizona.

Most of the German Jews became merchants. Many began as peddlers and, after accumulating sufficient capital, opened modest stores. There was hardly a fair-sized town in America in the late nineteenth century without a German Jewish commercial presence. The more successful of these merchants became department store magnates. They included Alan Gimbel, Isidore Straus, William Filene, and Simon Lazarus. Some German Jews moved from the wholesale and retail clothing trade into clothing manufacturing. In Chicago a family of Jews from Bavaria established Hart, Schaffner, and Marx, which by 1900 had become the largest manufacturer of men's clothing in the world. By that date German Jews dominated the garment industry of Chicago and New York. The most prominent of America's German Jews, however, were "our crowd," an interlocking group of Jewish families in New York involved in banking. They included the Loeb, Lehman, Seligman, Salomon, and Goldman families, the founders of several of America's most important investment banking houses.

As German Jews moved up the social and economic ladder, they rapidly dropped many Jewish rituals whose purpose was to isolate Jews from the general population. Distinctive Jewish dietary restrictions and Jewish dress, the German

Jews believed, were incompatible with the social and economic demands of American life and with the social status to which they aspired. They wished for a distinctive form of Judaism that would not detract from these goals. This demand gave rise to a number of Jewish reformers who, in the late nineteenth century, developed what came to be known as Reform Judaism. Its major institution was Isaac Mayer Wise's Hebrew Union College in Cincinnati. Reform Judaism emphasized the ethical teachings of Judaism rather than its ritualistic demands. In the Pittsburgh Platform of 1885, a group of Reform rabbis rejected messianism and Zionism and stated that "we consider ourselves no longer a nation, but a religious community." Judaism, they declared, was a "progressive religion." Some of the more extreme reformers even argued that Jews should celebrate the Sabbath on Sunday rather than Saturday since Sunday was the American day of rest. Such thinking created an inevitable backlash. In 1886, a group of traditional rabbis created the Jewish Theological Seminary (JTS) in New York City as an alternative to Hebrew Union College. The JTS would limp along until 1901, when it received an infusion of funds from several German Jewish bankers that enabled it to entice the eminent scholar Solomon Schechter from Cambridge University to become its president.

The American Jewish community of today is a product of the great wave of immigration to America from eastern Europe during the late nineteenth and early twentieth centuries. Later waves of immigration from eastern Europe (particularly Russia), Israel, Iran, and the Arab lands during the five decades after World War II did not significantly change the character of American Jewry. Between 1880 and 1924, approximately 2 million Jews from Poland, Russia, Romania, and other parts of eastern Europe immigrated to the United States. Generally impoverished and bedraggled, the "Russians," as they came to be known, were both an embarrassment and a challenge to the quarter of a million Jews who were already residing in the United States.

The latter were primarily immigrants from Central Europe and their second-generation children. Probably less than half of these were originally from Germany, although they came to be known collectively as Germans. They looked down upon their eastern European "coreligionists," a term they used in order to draw a sharp distinction between themselves and those Jews they considered socially and culturally backward. The Germans presumed that the only thing the two groups had in common was religion. Eastern European Jews were not welcome in the clubs and organizations of the German Jews, and they were certainly not viewed as suitable marriage partners. The unofficial motto of the Harmonie Club of New York City, a bastion of the city's German Jewish elite, was "more polish and less Polish."

Even among Jewish immigrants from eastern Europe, there were rivalries and tensions. For example, the Litvaks, Jews from Lithuania, were contemptuous of other Jews, particularly those from Galicia in Poland. They viewed the Galitzianers, as well as Hungarian Jews, as country bumpkins and ignoramuses. These inter-Jewish tensions partially explain the proliferation of synagogues and mutual aid societies in Jewish immigrant neighborhoods in the early twentieth century, particularly on New York City's Lower East Side. These organizations and synagogues catered to Jews who had come from various parts of eastern Europe, such as the different synagogues frequented by Romanian, Hungarian, and Polish Jews. At this time one rabbi on the Lower East Side supposedly affixed to his door the words "Chief Russian Rabbi of New York." When asked who had made him the Chief Russian Rabbi of New York, he replied, "the sign painter."

RELIGION OR ETHNICITY?

If the question of "Who Is a Jew?" could not be answered in terms of national origin, it also could not be answered in religious terms. Most of the immigrants from eastern Europe had already been infected by secularism and modernism prior to leaving Europe. Religious apathy and even opposition to religion in general and Judaism in particular were widespread. Most of these Jews were drawn to the synagogue, the historian Michael A. Meyer claimed, out of a "desire for ethnic identification, or in the language of social psychology, to sacralize their identity." Jewish political radicals saw traditional Judaism in Marxian terms. Its major role was to strengthen the hated capitalistic system by keeping the Jewish masses in poverty and ignorance. Zionists, for their part, saw religious orthodoxy as part and parcel of the ghetto mentality of eastern Europe, which thankfully would disappear once the Jews had their own homeland. The attenuated hold of religion among Jewish immigrants was indicated by the large majority of Jewish shopkeepers who kept their stores open on the Sabbath and by the scarcity of yeshivot (Talmudic academies) and *mikvot* (ritual baths that religiously observant Jewish women use once a month). There were no more than five Talmudic academies and ritual baths on New York's Lower East Side in 1910, even though approximately half a million Jews lived in the area.

Modern Jewish identity has never revolved solely around religion. An Irishman who became an atheist remained Irish, although he was no longer a good Catholic according to the Church. Nonreligious or even antireligious Jews, by contrast, were considered to be Jews in good standing, and there were no serious efforts made to ostracize them from the Jewish community. Indeed, had such an effort occurred, the Jewish population would have shrunk dramatically. The hospital associated with the medical school of New York City's Yeshiva University, an Orthodox institution, was named after Albert Einstein, who never hid his doubts about the existence of God. The philosopher Sidney Hook wrote for Jewish magazines and consulted for Jewish organizations, despite his well-known opposition to supernaturalism. Indeed, few of the American Jewish intellectuals and writers whom American Jews pointed to with such great pride were believers.

Despite their hostility to Judaism, radical Jews were considered by other Jews to be an important and legitimate element within the Jewish community. This contrasted with the efforts of the Roman Catholic Church to discredit the political radicals within its ranks. Left-wing Jews established Yiddish newspapers and magazines to reach the masses. The most important of these was the *Jewish Daily Forward*, which in its heyday had the largest circulation by far of any American immigrant newspaper. On the *Forward*'s masthead was a quotation from *The Communist Manifesto*, "Workers of the world unite." The *Forward* never made a secret of its opposition to traditional Judaism, and the religiously observant countered by not allowing it into their homes and spitting at the mention of its name. Competing Yiddish newspapers were established to counter the influence of the *Forward* and to present a more affirmative view of Judaism.

European-trained rabbis were horrified by the ease with which Jews in America gave up the trappings of traditional Judaism. They referred to America as *trefa* (impure), where Jews did not observe the religious holidays, the dietary prohibitions, the Sabbath, and the other religious commandments mandated by the Torah. Typical was the comment in 1900 of Rabbi Jacob David Wilowsky of Slutsk, who was then visiting New York. Wilowsky admonished his listeners for having migrated to America, and he told them that, for the sake of their souls, they should immediately return to eastern Europe. Traditional Judaism had no future in America, he declared, and by leaving Europe, Jews had left behind "their Torah, their Talmud, their yeshivot . . . their entire Jewish way of life." Ironically, Wilowsky himself would settle in Chicago three years later. This, however, did not change his pessimism. "The Jews came to the United States, a land blessed with prosperity," he said in 1904. "Here they prospered and are honored among peoples. But the ways and customs of this land militate against the observance of the laws of the Torah and the Jewish way of life." He predicted that "those who have strayed from their faith, estranged themselves from truth, piety and Jewish observance, [and] who enjoy with fullness of heart this country's pleasures—such are mostly to descend to the Gehenna [i.e., hell]." The next year Wilowsky left Chicago for Palestine.

In addition to this widespread indifference and even opposition to Orthodox Judaism, there was a sharp dichotomy between the Reform Judaism of America's German Jews and the Orthodoxy of the eastern European immigrants. The Judaism of Temple Emanu-El, the most important and wealthiest of the Reform congregations in New York City, had little in common with the Orthodox congregations of the Lower East Side. In order to differentiate their religion from that of the eastern European immigrants, the Germans frequently referred to themselves as "Hebrew" while calling the residents of the Lower East Side "Jews." The organization of Reform congregations in America was named the Union of American Hebrew Congregations to indicate that its congregations espoused an Americanized form of Judaism and that its members traced their lineage back not to the Jews of Europe but to the ancient Hebrews. These Reform congregations developed a Judaism that did not impede the economic and social mobility of Jews or discourage increased contact with Gentiles. Cast aside were those elements of Judaism that had isolated Jews from the rest of society and impeded their acculturation, such as the dietary laws and the wearing of skullcaps. (Reformers, it was said, gave up traditional Judaism at the drop of a hat!) Jewish religious services were revised to correspond more closely to the dignified and solemn religious rites of upper-class Protestantism. The Jewish reformers also eliminated references to Zion and the Temple sacrifices in the prayers, since these implied that Jews were not at home in America and hankered to restore the Jewish commonwealth. The use of the word *temple* by Reform congregations was also revealing. They wished to make clear that the temples of America's Jews were not in Jerusalem but in New York, Philadelphia, and Boston. "This synagogue is our temple, this city our Jerusalem, this happy land our Palestine," Rabbi Gustavus Poznanski told the congregants of Beth Elohim synagogue in Charleston, South Carolina, prior to the Civil War.

If the Jews were not simply a religious group, they also were not a nationality group. In contrast to other European immigrant groups, they did not leave any homeland. Although they were often nostalgic about the life they had left behind in Europe, they did not desire to return to a continent where they had suffered so much from anti-Semitism and economic and social deprivation. Moreover, except for a small minority of Zionist dreamers, prior to the 1930s American Jews did not support a Jewish national restoration in Palestine. While the Holocaust convinced American Jews of the need for a Jewish state, their financial and political support for the state of Israel has always been qualified. American Jews were not Zionists to the point where they actually contemplated transplanting themselves to the Jewish state. One cynic described American Zionism as a movement in which one group of Jews gave money to another group of Jews to bring a third group of Jews to the Middle East. After 1948 and the establishment of Israel, the Jewish state's leaders were puzzled and angered by the failure of American Jews, and particularly the leaders of the so-called American Zionist movement, to forsake the fleshpots of America and settle in the Jewish homeland. Abba Eban, the Israeli statesman, noted that, with the establishment of Israel, the American Zionist movement confirmed one of the basic tenets of religion—that there can be life after death.

When Jews migrated to America, they did so with a finality not found among other immigrant groups. The percentage of women among Jewish immigrants was higher than that among any other group with the exception of the Irish, who included many women hoping to find work in the United States as domestics. The percentage of children among the Jews was also larger than that of any other European immigrant group. When Jews left for America, they did so as families, with no intention of returning to Europe except as tourists. Other immigrant groups, by contrast, consisted largely of adult males, who hoped to work for several years in America, save money, and then return to Europe to live lives of relative affluence. In some years the erstwhile immigrants returning to Europe were more numerous than the immigrants coming to America. Such temporary sojourners were called "birds of passage." Not surprisingly, in contrast, the Jewish rate of expatriation was the lowest of any European group, since there was little in Europe for which to return, despite the pleas of such men as Wilowsky. The rapidity with which the Jews learned English and became citizens indicated that they were here to stay. It is no coincidence that the classic story of immigrants attending night school to learn English and American history and government is Leo Rosten's *The Education of H*Y*M*A*N K*A*P*L*A*N*. It concerns a Jew struggling with the English language who is convinced that America's sixteenth president is Abraham Lincohen.

Thus, the question remains: If Jews did not comprise a language or a nationality group, if they did not resemble other American ethnic groups, and if they were not simply a religious group, what were they? What was the quintessential element of Jewishness that bound the group together? How does one account for the hold that Jewishness has had over Jews, a hold far stronger than that found within most other ethnic communities? How does one explain the relatively low rate of exogamy among Jews until recently? America's Jews, the sociologist Nathan Glazer declared in 1950, were "a social group with clearly marked boundaries . . . but the source of the energies that hold [it] separate, and of the ties that bind it together, has become completely mysterious."

It is not surprising, therefore, that Jews, more than any other group, have been concerned with the question of ethnicity and cultural pluralism, or that Jewish entertainers, such as Woody Allen and Jerry Seinfeld, have used ethnic themes in their work, or that the three classic definitions of American identity were written by Jews (Emma Lazarus's sonnet "The New Colossus," Israel Zangwill's play *The Melting Pot*, and Horace Kallen's essay "Democracy versus the Melting Pot"), or that Jewish academicians have been in the forefront of the study of ethnicity. "No group in twentieth century America," the historian Moses Rischin wrote, "has been so consistently and clinically concerned with the problems of human identity, its relation to group morale, psychology, personal fulfillment, inter-group relations, and inevitably to group survival as have America's Jews. . . . Jews have seen their own dilemmas as part of the common plight. They have sought to identify, to define, and to conceptualize perceptions heightened by their own personal and collective autobiographies in universal terms." Abraham J. Karp, another historian of American Jewry, agreed. The Jew, "more than anyone else, has struggled with the challenge of how to live creatively in such a society, how to partake most fully of the political, social and cultural life of America while at the same time fashioning a creative communal, cultural, and religious life of its own. To do so the American Jew had to work out a conception of America and his own identity within it."

EXPLAINING JEWISH SUCCESS

Of all these "dilemmas" none has been more important than the conflict between "making it" in America and the maintenance of Jewish identity and continuity. If America was not the Promised Land, it was certainly the land of promise for Jews. For every Jew who migrated to Palestine between 1880 and 1920, over forty settled in the United States in the hope of achieving social and economic mobility and religious and political freedom. As the sociologist Marshall Sklare noted, America was more than a place merely to make money. It was for Jews "a kind of promised land, a kind of holy land. . . . [It was] a veritable paradise in comparison to the countries from which they had come." The motto on the Great Seal of the United States is *novus ordo seclorum*—a new order of the ages. This new American social order was particularly new for Jews. Here, anti-Semitism was notable for its relative absence. In America there were neither powerful anti-Semitic political parties nor officially sanctioned barriers to the social and economic advancement of Jews. Instead, local and national governments protected their property and lives. As Washington stated in his famous letter of 1790 to the Newport, Rhode Island, synagogue, which echoed the words of a letter sent to him by an American Jew, the policy of the United States was neither to sanction bigotry nor to assist persecution. "The children of the stock of Abraham" as well as Christians will "possess alike liberty of conscience and immunities and citizenship."

In this *goldene medinah* (golden land), a Jew, Emma Lazarus, would proclaim that America was a refuge for the "huddled masses yearning to be free"; another Jew, Mary Antin, a Jewish immigrant in Boston, would entitle her 1912 autobiography *The Promised Land*; and a Jewish immigrant who first settled in the Lower East Side, Irving Berlin, would write "God Bless America." They had good reason for thinking of America as a blessed land for Jews, because American Jewry was already well on its way to becoming the wealthiest and most influential Jewish community in the 2,000-year history of the Jewish Diaspora. No American ethnic group had ever experienced such a rapid economic and social ascent. The black sociologist Thomas Sowell declared that the saga of America's Jews was the greatest collective success story in American history. By the 1960s, the American Jewish community had become an anomaly, for it was the only major American ethnic group without a numerous working class. Within three generations, Jews had moved en masse out of the sweatshops and small retail businesses into the professions, the academy, and corporate and government employment. *Death of a Salesman* was more than a literary creation by the Jewish writer Arthur Miller. It was also a sociological and historical reality. One person quipped that in one generation Jews had moved from membership in the International Ladies' Garment Workers' Union to belonging to the American Psychiatric Society.

The reality of this economic and social mobility is not in doubt. Why it occurred is another question. The most popular explanation points to the fervor of Jews for higher education. Jews began attending college in significant numbers prior to World War II. Harvard, Yale, Princeton, and other elite institutions responded to the Jewish invasion of their hallowed halls by establishing informal quotas limiting the percentage of Jewish undergraduates. But the largest number of Jewish undergraduates were at urban institutions in centers of Jewish population. The preeminent example of this was the City College of New York, which by the 1930s was known as the "Jewish Harvard." The great Jewish entry into the university, however, was a post-1945 phenomenon, and by then the Jewish move up the economic ladder was already well under way. A more likely explanation for Jewish mobility was the entrepreneurial skills of the Jews, honed during centuries of life in Europe and the Arab lands, which encouraged them to enter business. Beginning in fields where there was a large Jewish presence, such as the garment industry, wholesale and retail merchandising, scrap metal, and entertainment, Jews soon branched out into other areas. By the 1980s, Jews had even become prominent in banking, insurance, telecommunication, and automotive manufacturing, industries that had not welcomed Jewish employees prior to World War II.

The success of East European immigrants and their children in business enabled future generations to enter universities en masse and to become professionals. This tendency became prominent after World War I when Harvard President A. Lawrence Lowell complained that too many Jews were being admitted to Harvard College. His counterparts at Yale, Princeton, and Columbia had the same fear and also instituted restrictions to limit Jewish undergraduate enrollment. These restrictions were dropped after World War II as the American academy became more meritocratic. By the 1950s going to college had become de rigeur among young Jews, with nearly 90 percent continuing their education after high school, a rate double that of the general population. And Jews were increasingly going to more elitist and residential institutions rather than to public colleges in the large cities where they lived. A far higher percentage of Jews also continued their schooling after receiving their B.A. They flowed into professional schools to become physicians, lawyers, accountants, and other professionals. Jews, who had never comprised more than 4 percent of the American population, came to comprise well over 10 percent of the nation's lawyers, doctors, and accountants.

A large number of Jews also attended graduate achool and became academicians. Perhaps nothing demonstrated the new status of Jews in America more clearly than their position in the university. Harvard, Yale, Princeton, and Columbia, institutions that had restricted Jewish enrollment prior to World War II, would be headed by Jews (or half-Jews) in the 1980s and 1990s. Indeed, for a period in the 1990s, persons with Jewish backgrounds were simultaneously presidents of five of the eight Ivy League universities. Jews also made up a disproportionate percentage of the faculty at America's more prestigious universities. By the 1970s, Harvard's faculty was at least 25 percent Jewish. It was the business skills of their parents and grandparents that had enabled these Jews to go into less lucrative but higher-status fields of employment.

At the turn of the century, wealthy German Jews, themselves successful businessmen, looked askance at the passion of East European Jews for business. The German Jews, seeking to disprove the anti-Semitic stereotype of the Jew as an economic parasite, founded trade schools and agricultural colonies in New

York and New Jersey. Here East European Jews could become "productive" workers and live in a more wholesome physical and moral environment than that found in the slums of New York City and Philadelphia. In these farm settlements, one person commented, Jews would become sowers of oats rather than sewers of coats. These resettlement efforts were, by and large, unsuccessful. Few Jews moved from the major cities to Sullivan County, New York, or to Woodbine, New Jersey, and those who did so then found their children moving to Philadelphia and New York at the first opportunity to become professionals or businessmen. To expect Jews to become successful farmers when they had little experience in agriculture, and to do so at a time when the American population was moving from the countryside to the cities, was to expect the impossible.

The success of Jewish businessmen was also due to the growth of the American economy and the spread of science and technology during the twentieth century and particularly after World War II. "Plastics," Dustin Hoffman is told in the movie *The Graduate*, would be the industry of the future. A magazine article in the 1960s drew attention to the "egghead millionaires," individuals who had become financially successful in high-tech. A disproportionate percentage of these were Jews, and some of these would even make the annual survey by *Forbes* magazine of America's 400 wealthiest individuals. Jews were overrepresented on the list by a factor of ten, and most of these were the children and grandchildren of poor eastern European immigrants whose entrepreneurial instincts had enabled them to take advantage of the opportunities offered by a burgeoning economy.

JEWS IN URBAN AMERICA: THE CHALLENGE OF ACCULTURATION

Another reason for the success of American Jews was their good fortune in having settled in the urban centers of the Northeast and Great Lakes. Here was the heart of America's economic growth during most of the twentieth century. Yet Jews had not always congregated in the large cities of the Northeast and upper Midwest. In fact, prior to the 1880s a smaller percentage of America's Jews than among Gentiles lived in the Northeast, and Cincinnati, the home of Hebrew Union College, was then the intellectual center of American Jewry. This changed with the mass migration of East European Jews beginning in the 1880s. New York City soon became the unquestioned demographic, religious, cultural, and economic hub of American Jews. By the early twentieth century, approximately half of America's Jews lived in New York City, and for many people, Jew and Gentile alike, the images of the Jew and the New Yorker became interchangeable. In the 1970s, Alfred Kazin, the prominent literary critic, thought it appropriate to title one of the volumes of his autobiography simply *New York Jew*. In fiction, film, or television, the quintessential New Yorker has been a Jew, with Jerry Seinfeld being the latest example. So close has been this identification between Jew and New York that anti-Semites frequently referred to America's largest city as "Jew York."

In 1972, the sociologist Marshall Sklare published an essay entitled "Jews, Ethnics, and the American City." In it, he claimed that of all American groups the Jews had best accommodated to the urban ambiance. Jews, Sklare wrote, "have been among America's most enthusiastic city dwellers, regarding the urban environment not as a problem or a source of pain, but as an opportunity and a place of pleasure. . . . American Jews have constituted the perfect urbanites." Sklare's essay was prompted by a bitter controversy over a proposal to locate a large public housing project in a heavily Jewish middle-class neighborhood in Forest Hills, in the New York borough of Queens. Previously, Jews had fled neighborhoods invaded by poor minorities. In Forest Hills, however, they had dug in their heels. For Sklare, this was "an act of affirmation, signifying a desire to keep faith with the city, its possibilities and potential rewards."

Sklare was a poor prophet. The response of the Jews of Forest Hills was less an act of affirmation than an act of desperation by people who had fled from changing neighborhoods in other parts of the city and had no place else to run. Hundreds of thousands of other "perfect urbanites" had already deserted the city for the suburbs of Long Island, Westchester County, Connecticut, and New Jersey. The Jewish population of New York City had been declining for years prior to 1972, and it continued to decline, *pace* Sklare. Jews today comprise at most only 15 percent of New York City, a far cry from the time when they numbered nearly a third of its residents. And what occurred in New York City has taken place elsewhere as well. Few Jews now live in Newark, Boston, Cleveland, and Detroit, for the most important demographic development among Jews after World War II was their movement out of the metropolis to the suburbs and to the Sunbelt states of Florida, Arizona, and especially California, reflecting again national trends and the national temperament. No romantic attachment to the possibilities and potential rewards of the city could overcome the social and economic forces dispersing Americans, Jews and Gentiles alike. The percentage of Jews living in the major cities of the Northeast is lower today than at any time in this century. There are now more Jews in San Diego than in Pittsburgh and twice as many in the San Francisco Bay Area as in Baltimore, whereas the second and third largest concentrations of American Jews are in Los Angeles and the southeast corner of Florida.

For Jews who have remained in the Northeast, most reside in what the historian Kenneth T. Jackson has called the "crab-grass frontier" of suburbia. Newton, Massachusetts, Sklare's own town, one person jested, chose the nickname "the garden city" because there was a Rosenbloom on every corner. Newton was also the locale for the classic study of Jewish suburbia, Albert Gordon's *Jews in Suburbia*. In suburbia, Jews carved out a lifestyle of ranch houses, barbecue grills, station wagons, and soccer leagues for the children that differed little from that of their Gentile neighbors. Missing were the Jewish bookstores, the kosher delicatessens, and the small synagogues that marked urban Jewish neighborhoods. While the move to suburbia has been good for the Jews, it is arguable whether it has been good for Jewishness and Jewish identity.

In this land of promise, American Jews have confronted a unique challenge of maintaining Jewish identity not in the face of adversity but of prosperity. The buzzwords of Jewish spokesmen are no longer "defense," "anti-Semitism," and "survival." Jews have survived and prospered in America, but have they survived and prospered as Jews? Or has their survival and prosperity been at the expense of their Jewishness? It is these concerns that account for the emphasis of American Jewish leaders on the new buzzwords of "continuity," "identity," and "intermarriage." This fear for Jewish continuity in America was not an invention of the postwar years. As early as the 1790s, Rebecca Samuel of Petersburg, Virginia, described to her parents in Hamburg, Germany, what it was like for a Jew in America. "You cannot know what a wonderful country this is for the common man," she wrote. "One can live here peacefully." But Samuel was skeptical that one could live as a Jew in Petersburg.

I know quite well you will not want me to bring up my children like Gentiles. Here they cannot become anything else. Jewishness is pushed aside here. There are here ten or twelve Jews, and they are not worthy of being called Jews. . . . The way we live is no life at all. We do not know what the Sabbath and holidays are. On the Sabbath all the Jewish shops are open.

Her solution, she told her parents, was to move to Charleston, South Carolina, which contained perhaps sixty Jewish families. One wonders why, if they were so concerned about the Jewish future of their children, Rebecca Samuel and her husband ever moved to the United States in the first place, much less to the rural South.

Prior to the 1970s, the underlying premise of American Jewish life was that there was no conflict between American and Jewish identities, that being a good Jew and a good American were symbiotic. Fearful of anti-Semitism, Jewish communal and religious leaders continually emphasized that American Jews were in no significant respects different from American Christians. In June 1952, for example, *Look* magazine published Rabbi Morris Kertzer's article "What Is a Jew?" Kertzer's answer was that a Jew was like everyone else. Jews and Christians alike, he wrote, "share the same rich heritage of the Old Testament. They both believe in the fatherhood of one God, in the sanctity of the Ten Commandments, the wisdom of the prophets and the brotherhood of man." Left unstated was the obvious question: If Jews were like everyone else, and if being Jewish did not place distinctive demands on its practitioners, then what rationale was there for Jews to continue to identify as Jews?

In 1960 sociologist Erich Rosenthal used the phrase "acculturation without assimilation" to describe how Jews were adapting to American life. While adopting the lifestyle and mind-set of the general population, they had created a separate social world. The result was that Jews associated with Jews, married

Jews, and lived among Jews. But even this limited separation was not maintained after 1960. For Jews, the most troubling conclusion of the comprehensive National Jewish Population Survey of 1990 was the statistic that 52 percent of Jews were marrying non-Jews. This, however, was to be expected, since Jews now live in suburbia, where many of their neighbors are not Jews, and their children attend colleges where they are in a distinct minority. Indeed, Conservative rabbi Robert Gordis argued as early as 1966 in *Judaism in a Christian World* that intermarriage was less a problem for which there was a solution than it was a condition with which Jews would have to live. Intermarriage, Gordis wrote, "is part of the price that modern Jewry must pay for freedom and equality in an open society."

In 1950, the Labor Zionist Hayim Greenberg, anticipating the direction of American Jewry, predicted that American Jews were in "grave danger of becoming merely an ethnic group in the conventional sense of the term . . . but without the consciousness of a specific drama and tension in its life." In his 1959 apologia for Orthodox Judaism, *This Is My God*, the novelist Herman Wouk described a mythical Mr. Abramson, a Jewish amnesiac, "pleasantly vanishing down a broad highway at the wheel of a high-power station wagon, with the golf clubs piled in the back." When his amnesia clears "he will be Mr. Adamson, and his wife and children will join him, and all will be well. But the Jewish question will be over in the United States."

In the halcyon days of the 1950s and 1960s, Jews saw the fears of Greenberg and Wouk as unduly alarmist. These years, after all, were a golden era, when Jews were making unprecedented strides up the social and economic ladder, new and ornate synagogues were being constructed at a rapid rate, and Jewish intellectuals were even saying good things about Judaism. In 1955, theologian Will Herberg published *Protestant-Catholic-Jew: An Essay in American Religious Sociology*, in which he argued, among other things, that Judaism had achieved parity with Protestantism and Catholicism. This was mind-boggling in view of the fact that Jews comprised at most little more than 3 percent of the population. No major public event was now complete without a benediction or invocation by a rabbi, and rabbis had become major "wisdom" figures. Rabbi Joshua Loth Liebman's *Peace of Mind* (1946) and Rabbi Harold S. Kushner's *When Bad Things Happen to Good People* (1981) were pop-psychology bestsellers.

One of the bad things that seemed to have happened to America's Jews was widespread assimilation. A 1988 national survey of American Jews by the *Los Angeles Times* reported that fully 25 percent of born Jews no longer saw themselves as Jews, and another 25 percent neither had any affiliation with any Jewish organization nor contributed funds to any Jewish cause. The largest and fastest growing segment of American Jews during the 1970s and 1980s was not Reform, Conservative, or Orthodox but "none of the above." Such statistics account for the widespread pessimism within Jewish circles regarding the future of American Jewry. Among the pessimists was the sociologist Samuel C. Heilman, who had come to America as a young child with his parents, who had survived the Holocaust. He ended his somber 1995 volume *Portrait of American Jews: The Last Half of the 20th Century* speculating on whether Judaism and Jewishness had any future in America. "If I am to be certain that my children and their children will continue to be actively Jewish," he wrote, "then the boat that brought my family here to America in 1950 may still have another trip to make." This voyage would be to the state of Israel.

The pessimism of the sociologist Charles S. Liebman and the historian Jerrold Auerbach stemmed from something more fundamental than assimilation. Rather, they challenged the widespread assumption that American and Jewish identities were mutually reinforcing. In *The Ambivalent American Jew* (1973), Liebman argued that American Jews were "torn between two sets of values—those of integration and acceptance into American society and those of Jewish group survival." Auerbach agreed. In his *Rabbis and Lawyers: The Journey from Torah to Constitution* (1990), he asserted that American Jews were heirs to two disparate and, at times, contradictory traditions—Jewish and American. Committed American Jews were thus fated to live in competing and discordant worlds. "The synthesis of Judaism and Americanism," he said, was "a historical fiction." On the one hand, there was American culture, which emphasized individual autonomy, freedom, and personal gratification and whose folk heroes included such loners as the cowboy, the mountain man, and Daniel Boone. On the other hand, there were Jewish teachings, which stressed religious obligations and communal commitments. As one famous study of the shtetl put it, *Life Is with People*.

AMERICAN JEWS: A CHOOSING PEOPLE

In this conflict, American culture emerged victorious. Long ago, American Jews ceased to be a chosen people observing God's laws. Rather, they became a choosing people, selecting those aspects of Jewish culture and tradition that comported with their lifestyles. In America, Heilman noted, being Jewish was no longer "simply a matter of birth, or, more precisely, a matter of irrevocable destiny." The religious culture of Judaism had metamorphosed into a religious "persuasion" to be accepted or rejected. To a point, all American Jews are now "Jews by choice," the term generally applied to converts, since it was so easy to cease being Jewish and Jewishness had become whatever one wanted it to be. There was even a group of "Messianic Jews," or "Jews for Jesus," who claimed that being a good Jew necessarily led to a belief in the divinity of Jesus. (They forget Heinrich Heine's comments that Jews did not make good Christians because no Jew could believe in the divinity of another Jew.)

And, for that matter, the slogan of the United Jewish Appeal, "We Are One," was hardly an accurate description of American Jewry. In America, Jews could be any type of Jews they wanted, or cease being Jewish at all. "Never had a Jewish community been to such an extent voluntary and so divided," the historian Robert M. Seltzer stated. The choices that Jews made as Jews were generally those that were the least demanding and that did not challenge their status as modern and affluent Americans. With Jewish identity now a matter of prescription rather than of ascription, what assurance is there that a sufficient number of American Jews will choose the same things? What, in other words, is to be the cement of American Jewish identity? What is to be the lowest common denominator of Jewishness in America?

Certainly, traditional Judaism cannot fill that role. No more than one quarter of American Jews make a stab at observing the dietary laws; about 10 percent keep the Sabbath as a day of rest; and over half do not light Sabbath candles. Despite their lack of religious observance and affiliation, most American Jews claim that being Jewish is very important to them and that they are "very good" Jews. This is part of the feel-good mood of modern America in which self-esteem has become the mark of mental health. "I'm okay, you're okay." But American Jews are unable to describe what is demanded of a "very good" Jew. They believe in a Jewishness without content.

This Jewishness without content was particularly conspicuous among Jews for whom being Jewish was primarily a matter of fighting anti-Semitism. Virtually every survey of public opinion revealed that anti-Semitism had peaked during the 1930s and World War II and then had begun a half-century of decline. Although some Americans continued to harbor anti-Semitic sentiments, there was no significant institutional support for such emotions. By the 1970s, the overwhelming majority of American Jews rarely, if ever, experienced serious anti-Semitism, and it certainly had little, if any, influence on their economic and social situation. Indeed, if anything, American public opinion had become philo-Semitic. Thus, the most popular Broadway show of the 1960s and 1970s concerned a shtetl in Eastern Europe (*Fiddler on the Roof*), whereas the most popular television program in the 1990s, *The Jerry Seinfeld Show*, focused on the angst of a New York Jew and his friends. It was, however, difficult to convince American Jews regarding the good news of anti-Semitism's apparent demise. They continued to believe in its saliency, despite their own experiences and what the scholars were telling them, and they were encouraged in this by organizations, such as the Anti-Defamation League, which had an institutional interest in emphasizing the presence of anti-Semitism.

For Jewish survivalists, the continuing vibrancy of Orthodoxy has been one of the few signs for optimism within American Judaism. Few observers of American Jewry prior to the 1960s, including the spokesmen for Orthodoxy, believed that Orthodoxy had any future in America. Orthodoxy, it was argued, was attractive to immigrants, but their children would inevitably move away as they acculturated and moved up the social and economic ladder.

The Orthodox obituary, however, proved to be premature. A small percentage of Jews, numbering no more than 10 percent of America's Jews, have remained faithful to Orthodoxy. These include not merely residents of crowded neighborhoods in Brooklyn and Queens but also affluent suburban professionals and businessmen. With Orthodoxy no longer the preserve of the poor and uncultured, it has acquired a certain cachet. In addition, because the Orthodox claim, and many American Jews believe, that they, and they alone, are "Torah-true Jews," they have acquired greater power within the American Jewish community than their numbers might warrant. Many American Jews view other forms of Jewish observances not as legitimate alternatives to Orthodoxy but as deviations from the Orthodox norm. It is doubtful, however, that Orthodoxy will ever greatly increase its numbers. Not only does Orthodoxy have a "dropout" problem of its own, but its stringent restrictions on behavior, many of which run counter to the norms of American society, also have only a limited appeal to American Jews. They might admire the Orthodox, but few want to join them.

JEWISH IDENTITY AND LIBERAL POLITICS

At one time it was hoped that the memory of the Holocaust and the existence of Israel could counter the solvents of Jewish identity. But the Holocaust was never a likely instrument to instill Jewish identity. Who, after all, would choose to be Jewish if it meant that the essence of being Jewish is victimhood status? In addition, the deification of the Holocaust experience, popular among the survivors of the Jewish tragedy and their descendants, simply fails to resonate throughout the rest of the population that did not experience the Jewish tragedy, and this is particularly true the further we are from the 1940s.

As the heroic events of the Israeli wars of 1948, 1967, and 1973 faded from memory, Israel has also lost its ability to command an automatic response from American Jewry. In this era of inexpensive jet travel, less than 30 percent of America's Jews have even visited the Jewish state. Many American Jews have also been turned off by the right-wing Israeli governments of the 1980s and 1990s and by the role of the Orthodox political parties in Israel. The successful campaign of Orthodox politicians there to delegitimize Reform and Conservative rabbis, in effect, delegitimized the Judaism of the overwhelming majority of American Jews. Israel has also grown up and is in less need of aid from American Jews. With a gross national product of over $80 billion and a per capita income approximately that of England, Israel is not desperate for American dollars. Any aid American philanthropists can provide Israel is no longer significant in the scheme of things. A half-billion dollars from American Jewish sources meant one thing when Israel's gross national product was $25 billion. Today, it means something else. In recognition of the new economic realities, some Israeli leaders have even broached the hitherto heretical idea that the time has come for Israel to stand on its own feet without the aid of world Jewry.

Some observers have argued that the essence of American Jewish identity is not to be found in the Holocaust, Israel, or Judaism but in the politics of American Jews. As political scientist Daniel Elazar has noted, "Jews who maintain only the most pro forma links with the Jewish religious tradition, who know little or nothing of Jewish culture, increasingly express themselves Jewishly in connection with Jewish political causes or interests." "Today, when the qualities that once differentiated Jews from other Americans have all but vanished," historian Henry F. Feingold wrote, "the distinctive political culture of Jews persists." A survey among Los Angeles Jews in the 1980s revealed that the most important element in their Jewish identity was not the ritual obligations of Judaism or support for the state of Israel but a commitment to equality and social justice. This belief that liberalism was the essence of American Jewish identity was the theme of Leonard Fein's 1988 book *Where Are We? The Inner Life of America's Jews*. Only a concern for economic and social justice, Fein wrote, "can serve as our preeminent motive, the path through which our past is vindicated, our present warranted, and our future affirmed."

Politics is one of the few areas in which Jews have not acculturated to American norms. Indeed, the laws of political sociology seem to have been repealed when it comes to America's Jews. Milton Himmelfarb's famous aphorism that Jews earn money like Episcopalians and vote like Hispanics is as accurate today as when he first expressed it in 1969. For proof, one need only look at the voting record of congressmen who represent heavily Jewish districts, such as Barney Frank of suburban Boston, Jerry Nadler of Manhattan, and Henry Waxman of Los Angeles. Ironically, it has been the least assimilated segment of American Jewry, the right-wing Orthodox of the Boro Park and Crown Heights neighborhoods of Brooklyn, who have most approximated the voting patterns of the general American population. By contrast, the more affluent Jews of Manhattan and suburbia have remained faithful to the liberal gospel despite their elevated social and economic status. "The Jewish businessman and professional, if he were following his self-interest," sociologist Nathan Glazer wrote, "would by now have become a Republican, as his Catholic and Protestant business and professional colleagues have become." But this has not occurred.

One index of the anomalous character of Jewish voting behavior comes from a comparison of it with the voting behavior of Gentile Americans in presidential elections. Over the past three decades, Democratic candidates have had difficulty with the white electorate. In 1972, George McGovern got 31 percent of the white vote but two-thirds of the Jewish vote, and this despite his gaffe of ordering milk with his chopped chicken liver sandwich while campaigning in New York City's garment district. Walter Mondale in 1984, Michael Dukakis in 1988, and Bill Clinton in 1992 secured well under 40 percent of the white vote. Yet they ran up large majorities among Jews, including approximately 80 percent for Clinton in 1996. Jews have also tended to vote for liberals in congressional, state, and local elections. Black mayors in New York, Philadelphia, and Chicago would never have been elected if not for the votes of Jews.

The aberrant Jewish voting patterns have spawned a cottage industry of political scientists, social psychologists, and historians seeking to explain this phenomenon. Some social scientists have argued that Jewish liberalism is a product of the Jews' marginal position in American society. Historians, by contrast, have contended that the loyalty of Jews to the liberal wing of the Democratic Party can be traced back to the political values of the immigrant generation, which contained a large number of socialists, or to the 1930s, when Franklin D. Roosevelt became a veritable saint among Jews because of the New Deal and his opposition to Hitler. Jews, Judge Jonah Goldstein of New York said in 1944, had three *velts* (worlds): *die velt* (this world), *yene velt* (the other world), and Roosevelt. In the 1930s, the Jewish population of Chicago was concentrated in the Greater Lawndale area. Here was located the famous 43rd ward, which provided 36,000 votes for Roosevelt in 1936 and only 900 for his opponent, Alf Landon. Roosevelt called the 43rd ward the "number one ward in the Democratic party." It was in Greater Lawndale that Leo Rosten taught Jewish immigrants English and conceived the idea for *The Education of H*Y*M*A*N K*A*P*L*A*N*. The voting statistics in the 43rd ward and in Jewish wards in other cities reveal the symbiotic relationship between liberal politics and Jewish acculturation.

In contrast to blacks, Jews have supported both of the two major aspects of modern liberalism—social and economic egalitarianism and civil rights and civil liberties. As Jew have left the ranks of the working class, their support for redistributive economic legislation has become less prominent. Their advocacy of civil liberties, however, has not waned. The Jewish stance toward civil liberties springs from a deep distrust of authority. For good reason, Jews have viewed political and religious authority as hostile. When the rabbi in *Fiddler on the Roof* is asked to say a prayer for the Czar, he thinks for a moment and then prays that God should keep the Czar far from Anatevka. This hostile attitude toward authority helps explain why Jews comprise a disproportionate percentage of the nation's civil liberties lawyers, why Jews support feminism and freedom of choice regarding abortions, why Jews have never viewed the police and the military as attractive professions, and why Jews have a knee-jerk cynicism toward politics and authority in general.

The American Irish, by contrast, have had a love affair with American politics and law enforcement. If the Irish have been the force of order, the Jews have been the force of discontent, continually challenging authority. While the Irish have been attracted to the police and fire departments, the Jews have been attracted to academia, where dissent and the unfettered intellectuality are respected. Few Jews have chosen careers in the police or fire departments, the military, the Central Intelligence Agency (CIA), or the Federal Bureau of Investigation (FBI). In 1972 comedian Alan King, while performing before the Republican National Convention in Miami Beach, joked that it was refreshing to be in a city where the police chief was named Rocky Pomerance. The audience realized, as did King, how incongruous it was for a police chief to be Jewish, much less one who had a daughter studying for the rabbinate at the Hebrew Union College in Cincinnati. Seven hundred miles to the north, the city of Charleston would also select a Jewish police chief. This was more understandable, since Reuben Greenberg, although a Jew, was also a black.

In their anthology of Yiddish literature, Irving Howe and Eliezer Greenberg have noted that the great themes of Yiddish literature have been "the virtue of powerlessness, the power of helplessness, the company of the dispossessed, [and] the sanctity of the insulted and the injured." The same is true of Jewish humor. Jewish humor does not revolve around the tall tale, as does American western humor, with its stories of Paul Bunyan and Davy Crockett. Rather, Jewish humor is ironic, self-deprecating, and intellectual. In Jewish humor, bad things happen to good people. Rodney Dangerfield gets no respect; the only clubs that will accept Groucho Marx are those he does not want to join; and Joan Rivers claimed that a peeping tom saw her naked in bed and pulled down the shade. Jewish humor involves *schlemiels* and *schlemazals*. In the classic Jewish joke, the stupid *schlemiel* pours hot soup on someone else. He, however, is not as big a victim as the *schlemazal* on whom the soup is spilled. This sense of powerlessness and beleaguerment, of being a victim rather than a maker of history, has been passed down from one Jewish generation to another. It is the reason why Jews widely exaggerate the extent of American anti-Semitism and why many feel they have more in common with blacks in the inner cities than with their Christian suburban neighbors.

A FUTURE OF UNCERTAINTIES

Whatever the reasons for Jewish liberalism, it is likely that in the future this, too, will eventually fade. Jews constitute an elite social and economic group in America, and it is only a matter of time before they lose their sense of insecurity and estrangement and their fear of authority. At a time when Jews (or half-Jews) are the presidents of Harvard, Princeton, and Yale, when one-tenth of the U.S. Senate are Jews, when six Jews were members of President Clinton's first-term cabinet, when two Jews sit on the Supreme Court, and when a Jew heads the CIA, the image that Jews have of themselves as outsiders is a rather extreme case of cognitive dissonance. But there is no guarantee that this dissonance will disappear soon. Predictions about the imminent decline of Jewish liberalism have been around for a long time. In 1963, for example, historians Lucy S. Dawidowicz and Leon S. Goldstein predicted, "Acculturation and full acceptance by Christians may in time deaden or at least dull Jewish sensitivity and feelings of insecurity. When this happens, class interests will probably affect voting more than Jewish group identity." But, they concluded, "that time is still in the future." It still is.

Both optimists and pessimists were able to point to the women's issue within American Judaism and the American Jewish community to confirm their fears and hopes for the future. The burgeoning feminist movement began to influence American Jewish women in the late 1960s. By the 1980s, the women's issue had become one of the most contentious ones within American Jewry. The grievances of Jewish women were multifaceted. Some criticized the exclusion of women from decision-making positions within Jewish communal and religious institutions. Others complained of their inferior position in the synagogue, including the refusal of the Conservative movement to ordain women rabbis, the difficulty women had in securing religious divorces without their husbands' permission, and the reluctance of Orthodox leaders to provide the same type of Jewish education for women as for men. The Statement of Purpose of the Jewish Feminist Organization, founded in 1974, laid out the goals of the feminist Jews: "We seek nothing less than the full, direct and equal participation of women at all levels of Jewish life—communal, religious, educational and political. We shall be a force for such creative change in the Jewish community."

For optimists, the impassioned debate occasioned by women deeply committed to Jewish survival indicated an untapped source of vitality for American Jewry, and they welcomed the decision by the Conservative movement to ordain female rabbis, the selection of women to head various Jewish federations, and changes in Orthodox institutions concerning religious education for women. Pessimists, in contrast, argued that these changes resulted from the sociological pressures emanating from the general society, which were often incompatible with Jewish continuity. They noted that while Jewish women had capitalized on the opening up of the educational and occupational opportunities since the 1960s, this had resulted in later marriages, fewer births, and less time for Jewish communal involvement. The mothers of working women had viewed voluntary work as a break from the drudgery of housework and child rearing. Their daughters, by contrast, have lacked the time and energy for Jewish communal work after spending eight or more hours in the office. As a result, the major Jewish women's organizations have experienced a shrinking and graying of their membership. One leader of Hadassah described the crisis in voluntarism as "the panty hose syndrome." "If we can find a way to have a meeting when a woman has her panty hose on, she'll go. But the minute she comes home and they're off, that's it."

The migration of Jews from Israel and eastern Europe during the 1970s, 1980s, and 1990s helped counteract the low birthrate of American Jews. Without this immigration, the decline of the Jewish population would have been even more dramatic. Prior to 1988, the flow of Jewish emigration from the Soviet Union was determined by how much the Soviet leadership wished to curry favor with the United States regarding trade policy and other matters. By 1985 a quarter of a million Russian Jews had been allowed to emigrate, with about 40 percent settling in the United States. Massive emigration was then halted by the Soviet Union only to be resumed in 1988. The end of the Cold War and the collapse of the Soviet Union accelerated Jewish emigration from eastern Europe, and it averaged well over 100,000 persons per year in the early 1990s. Although a majority of these persons went to Israel, perhaps a third arrived in the United States. They followed the demographic patterns of their predecessors. They chose to live in large cities, particularly in New York City, which received approximately half of the Russian immigrants to the United States. For nearly two decades the most numerous group of immigrants to that city had been from the Dominican Republic, but by the mid-1990s, the Russian immigration had surpassed it. So many Russian Jews lived in the Brighton Beach area of Brooklyn that it came to be known as "Odessa by the Sea."

Yet these Russians bore little resemblance to the Jews from eastern Europe who had immigrated prior to World War I or in the decade after that war. They did not speak Yiddish, were religiously unobservant, and viewed the Jewish communal structure with suspicion. For them, being Jewish was a national and not a religiocultural condition. American Jews were disappointed that the Russians seemed so apathetic regarding Jewish matters and so consumed with improving their economic condition and enjoying the material pleasures of a consumer culture. The Israelis also disappointed American Jews. Not only had they deserted the Promised Land, but most were also little inclined to involve themselves in American Jewish affairs. They were, by and large, secularists and Israeli nationalists. Nevertheless, sociological studies indicated that the longer the Russians and Israelis were in the country the more they approximated the religious and communal patterns of native-born Jews. In any case, there was little likelihood of future major demographic infusions of American Jewry from Russia or Israel. Changes in American immigration policy had diverted most Russian Jewish emigrants to Israel, while improved economic conditions in Israel removed the major cause of Israeli immigration to the United States.

As the twenty-first century approaches, American Jews remain a troubled people. While not fearing for their physical safety, they are concerned about the future of the American Jewish community. American Jewry has experienced major demographic hemorrhaging since the 1960s due to a low birth rate, exogamy, religious and cultural apathy, and the lure of a secular culture idealizing individual autonomy and personal gratification. History, however, should teach one to be cautious about predicting the future, particularly when it comes to Jews. Who in 1988 would have predicted the demise of the Soviet Union or the two-term election of an obscure governor of Arkansas as President? The last chapter in the history of American Jewry is a long way off. American Jews have created a parochial school system encompassing six hundred all-day schools. Its fund-raising efforts collect over a billion dollars a year. There is now an American Jewish intelligentsia which staffs the country's many rabbinical seminaries and university programs in Jewish studies. More importantly, Jews still feel the need to identify with the Jewish community, although the basis for this identity is often unclear. "Over and over again," the historian Jonathan Sarna wrote, the Jewish community "has confounded those who predicted gloom and doom, and has experienced surprising bursts of new life. There is no guarantee that this will happen again. . . . [but] If history offers us no guarantee of success, it does at least provide us with a warrant for hope." Or, as Lawrence P. (Yogi) Berra, that prominent student of American culture, put it, it is déjà vu all over again.

Jews, historian Simon Rawidowicz once pointed out, have been "an ever-dying people," and this remains also true today in America, where there are doubts that Jewish identity can survive the challenges of freedom and opportunity. As Robert Seltzer has stated, the major question facing American Jewry is whether it will be capable "of generating its own self-perpetuation in yet another era of Jewish history." On May 5, 1964, *Look* magazine published T. B. Morgan's article entitled "The Vanishing American Jew." The American Jew has not vanished, but *Look* soon did. Whether the former editors of *Look* will have the last laugh, however, remains to be seen.

BIBLIOGRAPHIC REFERENCES

The two major archival repositories for the history of American Jewry are Hebrew Union College in Cincinnati and the American Jewish Historical Society in New York City. Guides to secondary sources on American Jewish history include *The Jewish Experience in America: A Historical Bibliography* (Santa Barbara, CA: ABC-CLIO Books, 1983); Jeffrey Gurock, *American Jewish History: A Bibliographical Guide* (New York: Anti-Defamation League, 1983); and Sharad Karkhanis, ed., *Jewish Heritage in America: An Annotated Bibliography* (New York: Garland, 1988). The most comprehensive history of America's Jews is the five-volume *The Jewish People in America* (Baltimore: Johns Hopkins University Press, 1992), edited by Henry L. Feingold. There are also several good one-volume histories of America's Jews, including Oscar Handlin, *Adventures in Freedom: Three Hundred Years of Jewish Life in America* (New York: McGraw-Hill, 1954); Henry L. Feingold, *Zion in America: The Jewish Experience from Colonial Times to the Present* (New York: Hippocrene 1974); Arthur A. Goren, *The American Jews* (Cambridge: Harvard University Press, 1982); Abraham J. Karp, *Haven and Home: A History of the Jews in America* (New York: Schocken Books, 1985); Arthur Hertzberg, *The Jews in America: Four Centuries of an Uneasy Encounter: A History* (New York: Simon and Schuster, 1989); and Howard M. Sachar, *A History of the Jews in America* (New York: Knopf, 1992). The story of the German Jews in America is told in Naomi W. Cohen, *Encounter with Emancipation: The German Jews in the United States* (Philadelphia: Jewish Publication Society of America, 1984). The "Russian" immigration is covered in Moses Rischin, *The Promised City: New York's Jews, 1870–1914* (Cambridge: Harvard University Press, 1962); Irving Howe, *World of Our Fathers* (New York: Harcourt, Brace, Jovanovitch, 1976); and Thomas Kessner, *The Golden Door: Italian and Jewish Immigrant Mobility in New York City, 1880–1915* (New York: Oxford, 1977).

There is also a wealth of material on New York's East European Jews during the 1930s in several unpublished reports produced by the Writers' Project of the Works Progress Administration. For developments in two cities besides New York, see Jonathan D. Sarna and Ellen Smith, eds., *The Jews of Boston* (Boston: Northeastern University Press, 1995), and Irving Cutler, *The Jews of Chicago: From Shtetl to Suburb* (Champaign: University of Illinois Press, 1996). For religious trends, see Nathan Glazer, *American Judaism* (Chicago: University of Chicago Press, 1972); Michael A. Meyer, *Response to Modernity: A History of the Reform Movement in Judaism* (New York: Oxford, 1988); Alan Silverstein, *Alternatives to Assimilation: The Response of Reform Judaism to American Culture, 1840–1930* (Waltham, MA: Brandeis University Press, 1994); Charles S. Liebman, "Orthodoxy in American Jewish Life," *American Jewish Year Book* 66 (1965): 21–97; Lynn Davidman, *Tradition in a Rootless World: Women Turn to Orthodox Ju-*

daism (1991); Marshall Sklare, *Conservative Judaism: An American Religious Movement,* rev. ed. (New York: Schocken Books, 1972); Jack Wertheimer, "Recent Trends in American Judaism," *American Jewish Year Book* 89 (1989): 63–162; and Jonathan D. Sarna's provocative pamphlet, *A Great Awakening: The Transformation That Shaped Twentieth Century American Judaism and Its Implications for Today* (New York: New York Council for Initiatives in Jewish Education, 1995).

Other important aspects of the American Jewish experience are discussed in Jenna W. Joselit's two studies, *Our Gang: Jewish Crime and the New York Jewish Community, 1900–1940* (Bloomington: Indiana University Press, 1983) and *Wonders of America: Reinventing Jewish Culture, 1880–1950* (New York: Hill and Wang, 1994); Sylvia B. Fishman, *A Breath of Life: Feminism in the American Jewish Community* (New York: Free Press, 1993); Melvin I. Urofsky, *American Zionism from Herzl to the Holocaust* (Garden City, N.Y.: Anchor Books, 1975) and *We Are One! American Jewry and Israel* (Garden City, N.Y.: Anchor Books, 1978); Howard Brotz, *The Black Jews of Harlem: Negro Nationalism and the Dilemma of Negro Leadership* (New York: Schocken Books, 1970); Herman D. Stein, "Jewish Social Work in the United States," *American Jewish Year Book* 57 (1956): 3–98; Daniel Elazar, *Community and Polity: The Organizational Dynamics of American Jewry* (Philadelphia: Jewish Publication Society of America, 1976); Marshall Sklare and Joseph Greenblum, *Jewish Identity on the Suburban Frontier* (Chicago: University of Chicago Press, 1979); Steven M. Cohen, *American Modernity and Jewish Identity* (New York: Tavistock, 1983); Allen Guttmann, *The Jewish Writer in America: Assimilation and the Crisis of Identity* (New York: Oxford, 1971); Leonard Dinnerstein, *A History of American Antisemitism* (New York: Oxford, 1994); William B. Helmreich, *Against All Odds: Holocaust Survivors and the Successful Lives They Made in America* (New York: Simon and Schuster, 1992); and David M. Gordis and Yoav Ben-Horin, eds., *Jewish Identity in America* (Los Angeles: Western Institute, 1991).

The following books and articles are mentioned in the text: Thomas Sowell, *Ethnic America, a History* (New York: Basic Books, 1981); Alfred Kazin, *New York Jew* (New York: Alfred A. Knopf, 1978); Marshall Sklare, "Jews, Ethnics, and the American City," *Commentary* 53 (April 1972); 70–77; Kenneth T. Jackson, *Crabgrass Frontier: The Suburbanization of the United States* (New York: Oxford University Press, 1985); Erich Rosenthal, "Acculturation without Assimilation? The Jewish Community of Chicago," *American Journal of Sociology* 66 (November 1960); 275–288; Robert Gordis, *Judaism in a Christian World* (New York: McGraw-Hill, 1966); Herman Wouk, *This Is My God* (Garden City, N.Y.: Doubleday, 1959); Will Herberg, *Protestant-Catholic-Jew: An Essay in American Religious Sociology* (Garden City, NY.: Doubleday, 1955); Joshua Loth Liebman, *Peace of Mind* (New York: Simon and Schuster, 1946); Harold S. Kushner, *When Bad Things Happen to Good People* (New York: Avon, 1981); Charles S. Liebman, *The Ambivalent American Jew: Politics, Religion and Family in American Jewish Life* (Philadelphia: Jewish Publication Society of America, 1973); Jerold S. Auerbach, *Rabbis and Lawyers: The Journey from Torah to Constitution* (Bloomington: Indiana University Press, 1990); Mark Zborowski and Elizabeth Herzog, *Life Is with People: The Culture of the Shtetl* (New York: Schocken Books, 1952); Robert M. Seltzer, introduction in *The Americanization of the Jews,* edited by Robert M. Seltzer and Norman J. Cohen (New York: New York University Press, 1995); Leonard Fein, *Where Are We?: The Inner Life of America's Jews* (New York: Harper & Row, 1988); Milton Himmelfarb, "Is American Jewry in Crisis?" *Commentary* 47 (March 1969): 33–42; Irving Howe and Eliezer Greenberg, *A Treasury of Yiddish Stories* (New York: Schocken Books, 1973); Lucy Dawidowicz and Leon S. Goldstein, *Politics in a Pluralist Democracy* (New York: American Jewish Community, 1963); and Simon Rawidowicz, "Israel: The Ever-Dying People," in *"Israel: The Ever-Dying People" and Other Essays* (Cranbury, NJ: Associated University Press, 1986). The articles by Morris Kertzer and Hayim Greenberg are quoted in Samuel C. Heilman, *Portrait of American Jews: The Last Half of the 20th Century* (Seattle: University of Washington Press, 1995), and Gerald Sorin, *Tradition Transformed: The Jewish Experience in America* (Baltimore: Johns Hopkins University Press, 1997).

KOREANS

Kwang Chung Kim

Koreans came to the United States in two different time periods. At the dawn of the twentieth century, several thousands of Korean immigrants arrived in Hawaii. This first group of Korean immigrants worked hard on Hawaiian sugar cane plantations. The second group of Koreans are those who have been immigrating to the United States since the revision of the U.S. immigration law in 1965. They constitute the great majority of the current population of Korean Americans. Thus, to review Korean immigration to the United States properly, the immigration experience and history of the first group and life conditions of the post-1965 immigrants and their descendants must both be discussed.

THE FIRST WAVE OF KOREAN IMMIGRATION

At the end of the nineteenth century, Korea was in terrible shape: The government was corrupt and repressive; the interferences in Korean affairs by the foreign big powers were relentless; and a series of various kinds of natural disasters and famines occurred. These conditions on the Korean peninsula enormously disturbed the life conditions of its people. This was when Horace Allen, American missionary and diplomat, actively negotiated with the association of Hawaii sugar plantation owners for the immigration of Korean people to Hawaii. Owing to the expanding sugar cane industry, plantation owners badly needed more laborers. Moreover, Japanese plantation workers at the time had staged several strikes, and the plantation owners wanted to use Koreans to counterbalance the striking Japanese and to keep wages low. Thus, the association of sugar plantation owners and Allen reached an agreement to bring Korean workers to Hawaii.

On January 13, 1903, 101 Korean immigrants arrived in Honolulu with the consent of Korea's King Kojong. By 1905, when Korean immigration was halted abruptly, 7,226 Korean immigrants had reached Hawaiian shores by sixty-five different ships, but Japanese laborers still numerically dominated the sugar plantations (65.8 percent) versus Korean (9.7 percent) and Chinese (9.4 percent) laborers. Among the Koreans there was an extremely skewed sex ratio—110 males to 1 female—and 80 percent of Korean laborers were bachelors. Since out-marriage was generally unthinkable, male laborers exchanged pictures with women in Korea, and arranged marriages took place until 1924, when the U.S. national origins quota system came into full effect. Altogether, about 1,100 picture brides arrived in Hawaii.

Unlike Chinese and Japanese laborers, the social backgrounds of Korean workers on the sugar plantations were highly diversified. In Korea, they were farmers, common coolies, former soldiers, household servants, former government officials, Confucian scholars, clergymen, and so on. Regardless of social backgrounds, they all met the same harsh conditions in Hawaii. They lived in segregated quarters on the sugar plantations and worked long hours for low wages. They suffered from loneliness, hardship, and fatigue. Mainly due to harsh working conditions, nearly one-third of Korean male laborers left the plantations when their labor contracts expired and settled elsewhere. During the time period of 1921 to 1926, more than half of the immigrants left the plantations and moved to cities in Hawaii and on the mainland. They generally engaged in manual work, but a large proportion of them eventually managed to open small businesses, such as grocery and vegetable stores, laundry shops, and barbershops. Some became farmers and owners of trucking businesses. Although most of them came originally as sojourners, they ended up settling permanently in the United States.

Churches were the Koreans' most important ethnic organization, and the early immigrants were very active in churches. They also vigorously supported the movement for Korean independence from Japan. By the end of World War II in 1945, these immigrants were very old, and their children increasingly married out. During the period between 1960 and 1968, when the second wave of Korean immigration began, 80 percent of Korean brides and grooms in Hawaii married out. Because of the original small number of Korean immigrants and the high rate of out-marriage of their children and grandchildren, the descendants of the early Korean immigrants are scattered around the United States, racially mixed and invisible as Korean Americans. The current Korean immigrants in the United States, then, have developed their own settlement pattern independent of the early immigrants and their descendants. In this sense, their settlement pattern is similar to that of the current Asian Indians and Vietnamese and considerably dissimilar from Chinese immigrants who settle in the Chinatowns of major American cities.

THE CURRENT WAVE OF KOREAN IMMIGRATION

From the outbreak of the Korean War in 1950 to 1964, about 15,000 Koreans came to the United States as immigrants. More than 40 percent of them were Korean women married to American servicemen stationed in Korea. The rest were children adopted by American families as well as professional or skilled immigrants and their family members. The second wave of Korean immigration actually began with the liberalization of the U.S. immigration law in 1965. Table 6 shows that the number of Korean immigrants began to rise gradually in the second half of the 1960s. According to the 1970 census, close to 70,000 Koreans were in the United States. Immigration further accelerated in the 1970s. By 1973, the annual number of Korean immigrants reached the 20,000 level, and three years later, it jumped to 30,000. The 1980 census shows that a total of 350,000 Koreans resided in the United States, and immigration continued to increase throughout the 1980s. The peak was the late 1980s, during which the number of immigrants from Korea annually exceeded 34,000. Only Mexico and the Philippines sent more immigrants than Korea during this period of time. The decline in immigration began imperceptibly, in 1988. Since 1991, the annual number has decreased significantly. The current annual number of Korean immigrants is less than half that observed during the peak periods.

At the same time, the number of Korean immigrants who return to Korea (the returned migrants) has also increased. According to an August 1995 *New York Times* article, the number of Korean reverse migrants was very small in the past (e.g., 800 in 1980), but in the first half of the 1990s, the number of those who permanently returned to Korea ranged between 5,000 and 6,500. What these numbers indicate is that, in 1994, for example, 1 immigrant returned to Korea for every 3 new ones from Korea. In addition, Table 6 shows that in recent years the number of visa adjusters (i.e., those already in the United States when they change visa status to immigrants) has gradually increased. These findings— the trend in the annual number of immigrants, the number of return migrants, and the proportion of adjusters—reveal that the first phase of the post-1965 Korean immigration to the United States was virtually over by the end of the 1980s. In other words, the post-1990 Korean immigration represents a smaller number of Koreans with different social backgrounds and orientations than was the case with the first phase of the post-1965 immigrants.

Why did Koreans immigrate to the United States in large numbers? Until the end of the 1980s, Korean immigration was pushed by multiple factors, political and military as well as economic. Ivan Light and Edna Bonacich succinctly analyzed these factors in terms of the following events that seriously affected the relationship between South Korea and the United States: (1) the division of the country, (2) support of the military dictatorship, and (3) economic development. The division of Korea and the military threat from the North made living in South Korea potentially dangerous, and the military dictatorships became oppressive, arbitrary, and corrupt. The subsequent economic development exacerbated structural disturbances and brought about overcrowdedness and congested living conditions to the whole Korean society.

In sharp contrast, the United States appeared to be a country with political freedom and a safe and clean environment. Korean immigrants desired to live in such a society where they would be free from the threat of war and power

Table 6
Koreans admitted to the United States as permanent residents, 1950–1995

	Status at Entry		
Year of entry	New Arrivals	Adjustments*	Total
1950-54	538	n.a.	538
1955-59	4,990	n.a.	4,990
1960-65	11,686	1,583	13,269
1966	2,492	598	3,090
1967	3,956	1,424	5,380
1968	3,811	1,098	4,909
1969	6,045	1,820	7,865
1970	9,314	2,079	11,393
1971	14,297	4,049	18,346
1972	18,876	5,513	24,389
1973	22,930	4,961	27,891
1974	28,028	4,658	32,686
1975	28,362	2,364	30,726
1976	30,803	1,881	32,684
1977	28,437	2,480	30,917
1978	25,830	3,458	29,288
1979	26,646	2,502	29,248
1980	29,387	2,933	32,320
1981	28,819	3,844	32,663
1982	27,861	3,863	31,724
1983	29,019	4,320	33,339
1984	28,828	4,214	33,042
1985	30,532	4,721	35,253
1986	30,745	5,031	35,776
1987	32,135	3,714	35,849
1988	31,071	3,632	34,703
1989	28,248	5,974	34,222
1990	25,966	6,335	32,301
1991	18,351	8,167	26,518
1992	14,062	5,297	19,359
1993	12,375	5,651	18,026
1994	10,661	5,350	16,011
1995	9,397	6,650	16,047

*Adjustments apply to persons who had previously entered the United States with a nonimmigrant status (e.g., student, visitor, or businessperson) and who changed their status to that of permanent resident.

Sources: *Annual Report of the INS*, years 1966–1978 (Washington, D.C.: Government Printing Office); U.S. Bureau of the Census, *Statistical Yearbook of the Immigration and Naturalization Service*, 1979–1995 (Washington, D.C.: Government Printing Office, 1980–1996).

abuse and could provide good educational opportunities for their children. Their life goals or aspirations were thus to pursue good-quality family life, including a good education for their children—the middle-class dream. They were convinced that the United States was a land of opportunity where hard work would pay off. With such a strong belief in the United States, they were willing to work hard and to endure hardship to achieve that dream.

The specific mechanism to bring this immigrant labor force to the United States is the current U.S. immigration law. In each decade of the 1970s and the 1980s, about 42,000 Korean wives of U.S. servicemen came to the United States. In the same two decades, more than 3,000 Korean children were also adopted annually by American families. In the early part of the 1970s, however, Korean immigration to the United States was numerically dominated by Korean professional or skilled workers and their family members. Eventually, those who were invited by their kin for family reunification numerically dominated Korean immigration. This pattern of immigration shows that although adopted children and Korean wives of U.S. servicemen comprised important parts of Korean immigration, the kinship-based chain migration played the most important role in the recent phase of Korean immigration to the United States.

Why, then, has the immigration trend reversed since the early 1990s? Principally, the influences of the factors that had originally pushed Koreans to emigrate from their native country have been considerably weakened or eliminated. The recent social changes and economic development in Korea have made life there increasingly attractive. Economic development in Korea has also significantly improved the living standard in Korea, for today per capita income in Korean exceeds $10,000. In fact, Korea has become a relatively high-wage country, attracting foreign workers. As a result, the gap in the living standard between Korea and the United States has been considerably narrowed, and this narrowing gap has reduced the desire of Koreans to immigrate to the United States. Moreover, although the situation remains tense, the worldwide collapse of communist countries has reduced the cold war tension in the Korean peninsula, lessening the fear of renewal of war. Also, the oppressive political regimes are gone; democratization in Korea has advanced considerably with widely enjoyed political freedom.

At the same time, as shockingly exposed by the 1992 Los Angeles racial unrest, people in Korea are now keenly aware of the difficult life and marginalized position of Koreans as a minority group in the United States. Such a life experience of Korean immigrants renders immigration to the United States quite unattractive to people in Korea. It is not surprising, then, that the number of Korean immigrants continues to decrease. As a result, Korea has become the first country that shows such a trend among the Asian countries that have been sending large numbers of people to the United States since 1965.

The 1990 U.S. census showed that about 800,000 Koreans were in the United States. Approximately half of them resided in the Los Angeles and Orange counties area of southern California (250,000) and in the New York–New Jersey metropolitan region (150,000). The Chicago metropolitan area was the distant third, with slightly more than 40,000 Koreans. The distribution of Korean immigrants is similar to those of other current Asian Americans, with a heavy geographical concentration in major American cities. Currently, the total number of Koreans in the United States is estimated to slightly exceed 1 million. The majority of these 1 million Koreans live in suburban areas of major cities. As length of residence in the United States extends, the number of suburban dwellers has been found to increase. This suburbanization is an important feature of their settlement in the United States. Furthermore, most of the suburban Koreans are also found to be home owners.

The experiences of the post-1965 wave of immigrants will be reviewed along two aspects: the political-economic and sociocultural dimensions. More specifically, this essay will review the following aspects of their life experiences: occupations, political consciousness, family and kinship relations, church participation, and other sociocultural life features. The economic and political aspects of their lives concern their position in the highly stratified United States. Analysis of their family and kinship relations, church experience, and other aspects of their sociocultural life examines the relative influence among the various factors brought from their native country and those of the United States, as well as the subsequent development of their own ethnicity.

POLITICAL-ECONOMIC LIFE OF KOREAN AMERICANS

Occupational Experiences

The middle-class background of Korean immigrants has been demonstrated by their pre-immigration education and occupation. Like other recent Asian immigrants, a high proportion of Korean adult immigrants had already completed their college education prior to emigration from their native country. Some of these college graduates were further educated in the United States—the American college graduates. Most of those with occupational experience in Korea held managerial/administrative or professional/technical occupations in Seoul and other major cities in Korea. The social backgrounds of Korean immigrants indicate that many of them have had considerable access to human capital resources. In the United States, however, they could not actively utilize these resources, owing to their limited English and cultural understanding and the discrimination they encountered. Under this adverse condition, most husbands in Korean immigrant families have tended to be underemployed, and many have experienced substantial downward mobility through immigration. This situation has forced a high proportion of wives to seek employment for family support, usually as full-time workers. According to the Chicago study by Won Moo Hurh and Kwang Chung Kim, which randomly interviewed 621 Korean immigrant adults in 1986, most of the male respondents (285, 85.3 percent) and two-thirds of the female respondents (198, 68.8 percent) were employed. Most of the female respondents were married, and the married female respondents (163, 74.8 percent) showed a higher rate of employment than the nonmarried female respondents (32, 51. 4 percent). This is noteworthy because married women are expected to stay home as full-time homemakers in Korea. In spite of such a cultural background, a great majority of Korean wives have been employed from the beginning of their American life. Moreover, most of the employed wives work full-time and remain employed regardless of length of residence in the United States.

The current pattern of employment shows that Korean immigrants in the United States are distributed into four types of occupations: professional/technical occupations, office or clerical work, self-employed small businesses, and service/manual jobs. The proportion of Korean immigrants distributed into the four occupational categories varies by city. On the whole, though, the proportion of professional/technical workers ranges between 20 and 25 percent whereas that of self-employed small-business owners ranges between 30 and 45 percent. The proportion of officeworkers and other clerical workers is relatively small (10 percent and 20 percent), but a higher proportion of Korean immigrants are today in service/manual workers (25 percent and 30 percent).

This pattern of Korean immigrants' employment does not support the assimilation/mobility model. The model suggests that immigrants are initially employed at the bottom of the occupational hierarchy and then gradually move up through the occupational ladder as they become more assimilated and accumulate their human capital resources. In contrast to this model, Korean immigrants initially entered various strata of the occupational hierarchy, demonstrating multiple modes of incorporation into the American labor market. Furthermore, each occupational group exists independently of other groups rather than as part of a linked mobility pattern. The only such pattern observed is the mobility of those who started their lives in the United States as manual/service workers and later became small-business owners. But such a shift is not part of the promotional mobility but a jump between the two unrelated occupational groups following the accumulation of financial and nonfinancial capital in the United States.

In spite of the occupational diversity, the employed Korean immigrants generally share one common trait: They tend to be employed in occupations that do not require direct competition with native-born Americans, especially white workers. For example, current Korean and other foreign-educated physicians were accepted in the past owing to a short supply of physicians, and they did not compete with native-born American physicians. A limited supply of nurses also explains why Korean and other foreign-born nurses are continuously employed in the United States. Today, Korean small-business owners predominantly deal with Korean and other minority customers that white merchants tend to avoid. Korean manual/service workers are also heavily employed in jobs with a concentration of immigrant or minority workers. Their earnings are generally lower than those of other Korean immigrants who work with white workers.

Henry Jay Becker made a distinction between two types of employment segmentation: (1) the disproportional concentration of minority workers in certain
occupational categories and (2) segregation of whites and minority workers in
the same occupation across different places of employment. We call the former
the *occupational segmentation* and the latter *workplace segmentation*. An analysis of Korean workers exhibits both types. For example, the concentration of
Korean immigrants in small business demonstrates occupational segmentation.
Working conditions (such as wages, promotional opportunities, ethnicity of co-
workers, etc.) of other Korean immigrant workers indicates workplace segmentation. The two types demonstrate that Korean immigrants are generally
employed in less-favored segments of the American labor market as minority
workers.

Self-Employment of Korean Immigrants

Since an unusually high proportion of Korean immigrants are in self-
employed small businesses and their entrepreneurial activities are highly visible
in major American cities, their business experience warrants further discussion.
In the late 1980s, when Korean employees of Korean-owned small businesses
were added in, the majority of Korean immigrants were found to be employed
in small business. Compared to the business experiences of other recent immigrant groups, the small-business experience of Korean immigrants is thus distinguished in two ways. First, proportionally more Korean immigrants are
engaged in self-employed small businesses than any other current immigrant
groups regardless of the level of education received. Second, markets for Korean
small-business entrepreneurs are more diversified than those of other entrepre-
neurially active immigrant groups. Immigrant entrepreneurs usually control the
market for coethnic customers, but that market is a highly limited one. To expand entrepreneurship beyond the boundary of coethnic markets, several immigrant groups have specialized in certain types of businesses. For example,
Korean entrepreneurs are active in the laundry and dry cleaning business, fruit
and vegetable markets, and grocery and/or liquor stores. Likewise, Chinese entrepreneurs are actively engaged in the Chinese restaurant business, whereas
Asian Indians are active in the operation of donut shops, motels, and the newspaper vending business. Vietnamese entrepreneurs tend to be specialized in the
manicure (nail) business.

In addition to the two types of markets (coethnic and specialized markets),
Korean immigrant entrepreneurs are also found to be active in inner-city, low-
income minority communities. Currently, Korean entrepreneurs are one of the
few non-African-American groups active in such urban minority communities.
In this respect, markets for Korean entrepreneurs are clearly distinct from those
for other immigrant groups. The question often is asked regarding the reason
for Koreans' business entry into inner-city, low-income African-American communities. It reflects an unusual coincidence of three major historical events. First,

in the early 1970s, when Koreans started to immigrate to the United States in large numbers, South Korea actively exported a variety of consumer goods manufactured with cheap labor. Second, around the same time period, white merchants, big corporations, and chain stores that had commercially dominated inner-city African-American communities withdrew from these markets after the urban riots in the 1960s. Their withdrawal created an enormous business vacuum that offered valuable entrepreneurial windows of opportunity to the newly arrived Korean immigrants in the 1970s. Third, under these combined circumstances, they managed to develop an ethnic-based global market network, importing a variety of consumer goods manufactured in South Korea and other Third World countries and distributing the goods in inner-city African-American communities.

In the inner-city minority markets, Korean small-business owners emerge as vulnerable middleman entrepreneurs. As the middleman entrepreneurs, they are an easy target for local minority residents' anger and frustration. Korean store owners' conflict with African-American residents in major American cities demonstrates the precarious position of Korean entrepreneurs in inner-city minority communities. Their vulnerable position and related incidents of group conflict between Korean entrepreneurs and inner-city minority residents are currently the leading research topic regarding Korean immigrants and have generated a number of publications and provocative ideas in recent years.

Korean and African-American conflict usually takes three forms: interpersonal dispute at the store level, boycott, and mass violence. All three forms are observed in major American cities, such as New York City, Los Angeles, and Chicago. But a boycott was launched most systematically in New York City by Brooklyn African-American residents for one and a half years in 1990 and 1991. Mass violence, which involved looting and/or burning Korean stores, took place most conspicuously in Los Angeles in 1992. About half of the stores destroyed by the violence were Korean-owned ones located in South Central Los Angeles and Koreatown. As a whole, 2,300 Korean-owned stores were destroyed, and their total economic loss reached $350 million. The Los Angeles event clearly demonstrated that Korean and African-American conflict was not a biracial conflict between Koreans and African Americans alone but a multirace-ethnic event involving whites, African, and Hispanic residents and Korean Americans.

Political Consciousness

In the past, Korean Americans were keenly interested in the political situation in Korea, not in the politics of the United States. This situation of indifference to American domestic politics has been dealt a drastic jolt by the Los Angeles racial unrest. As already noted, serious conflict developed between Korean store owners and African-American residents. The Los Angeles racial conflict and conflicts in other cities between Korean and African Americans heightened Koreans' political consciousness. Through the agonizing experience of the disturbances, many Korean Americans came to believe that their powerlessness was a major source of their experience of victimization during the mass violence. On September 18, 1990, 7,000 Koreans participated in the protest rally against New York City mayor David Dinkins, who had hesitated to end African-American boycotts of Korean stores. On May 2, 1992, one day after the Los Angeles disturbance ended, 30,000 Koreans from all over the Los Angeles area marched and called for peace, justice for Rodney King, and rebuilding Koreatown and the destroyed Korean stores.

Korean Americans' political consciousness was further heightened by two major legislative events: reform of the immigration law and welfare reform in recent years. Through the reforms, Korean elderly and their family members feared that the elderly's welfare benefits would be cut as long as the elderly remained permanent residents and did not become citizens. A high proportion of Korean elderly rushed to become naturalized. In the process of their preparation for naturalization, they went through numerous painful experiences. In sum, the racial conflicts in major American cities and the 1996 reform bills made Korean Americans keenly aware of their minority position in the multirace-ethnic American society.

The Los Angeles racial disturbance and other Korean and African-American conflicts also stimulated the younger generation of Korean Americans as they watched their helpless parents being victimized. This experience heightened their own political consciousness and their sense of identity as Korean Americans. The racial disturbances thus offered young Korean Americans an opportunity to become actively involved in the American political process and in Korean community events. As a result, many were actually involved in the process of helping the victims of the Los Angeles disturbance and of protecting the victims' political rights.

As Min observes, however, there is a serious difference in the way that Korean immigrants and their children view the racial conflict. Korean immigrant parents see hostile behaviors of African-American residents as the major source of the disturbance. Thus, many immigrant merchants take a negative or hostile attitude toward the inner-city African-American residents. Young Korean Americans, on the other hand, regard both Korean and African Americans as the victims of the white dominant group's exploitation. Thus, young Korean Americans want to organize the resources of both groups against their common adversary, the white dominant group. One can argue that Korean parents take a realistic view of the racial disturbance, whereas their children take an idealistic position as members of a minority group.

In 1992, Jay Kim, the first Korean American congressman, was elected from a congressional district in southern California. His election and reelection since then were possible because of white voters' support in his district and enormous support from Korean Americans. Besides him, three Korean Americans were elected as members of state legislatures in Washington, Oregon, and Hawaii. Their elections were actively supported by the Republican Party and also by Korean Americans. (Kim was defeated in 1998.)

In spite of these political developments, three serious problems are evident regarding Korean Americans' participation in American politics. First, the number of Korean Americans is too small to develop an effective voting block. Their voting power is further weakened by the suburbanization of Korean Americans in major cities. This situation raises the strategic issue of who represents the political interests of Korean Americans. For example, since Congressman Jay Kim represented white voters in his district, he voted as a Republican congressman on the issues of immigration and welfare policies that went against the position taken by the majority of Korean Americans. Second, as already discussed, the first generation of Korean immigrants and their children tend to see the nature of Korean and African-American conflict differently. This tendency suggests the split between the two generations concerning their political views and related activities. Such a split weakens the political position of Korean Americans in the United States. Third, as political crises gradually subside, Korean Americans tend to regress to a state of indifference or powerlessness. This regression makes them further powerless. A big challenge that Korean Americans face today is how to renew their political consciousness.

In sum, an analysis of Korean immigrants' political-economic life reveals that they are minority workers in the American labor market, enduring occupational and workplace segmentations; that their massive involvement in small businesses in inner-city, low-income African-American neighborhoods causes them to become vulnerable targets for the residents' anger and frustration; and that they remain a genuinely weak voice in American politics.

SOCIOCULTURAL LIFE OF KOREAN AMERICANS

Like many other immigrant groups, Korean immigrants closely associate with their own people socioculturally. Unlike some immigrant groups, however, they are not geographically concentrated and have no geographically based ethnic enclave. Koreatowns in major American cities are commercial rather than residential areas. In fact, a late 1980s study found more non-Korean residents living in Koreatowns than Koreans. As noted before, Korean immigrants are rather widely dispersed in suburban areas of major American cities. An analysis of their associational networks reveals several distinctive features of Korean Americans' sociocultural life. Their experience can be analyzed in terms of their kinship and family relations, affiliation with an immigrant church, and association with their friends and other acquaintances.

Family and Kinship Relations

A prominent feature of Korean immigrants' family life is the prevalence of the independent nuclear family. It is particularly noteworthy because they came to the United States with strong extended family ties. The emergence of the nuclear family among Korean immigrant families is considered a product of their absorption into the highly industrialized U.S. economy. As members of the independent nuclear family are employed with their personal resources in the current American labor market, the controlling power of the head of the traditional extended family is considerably limited. Currently, their nuclear family system in the United States thus stands between the family systems in Korea and the United States. For example, the average family size of Korean Americans is smaller than that in Korea but bigger than that in the United States. The divorce rate of Korean Americans is lower than that of Americans but higher than that of Koreans in Korea.

As most wives in Korean immigrant families are employed and make a substantial contribution to family income, the wives' power now gradually increases in their marital relations. As a result, their family life increasingly is centered on the husband and wife relationship, with the husband and wife now needing to discuss and consult with one another on most family affairs. Nonetheless, it is the wives who still perform most household tasks, such as grocery shopping, cooking, dishwashing, and laundry, regardless of their outside employment. In other words, most Korean wives experience the burden of double roles—employment and family. And yet, the wives themselves adhere to the traditional gender role orientation. Why?

Korean wives' employment is for family support and is not an expression of careerism. They continue to believe that traditional housework is their primary responsibility and take their employment as a temporary and transitory task, even though their employment lasts for a long time. When they are employed with the traditional gender role orientation, they still feel that they have to perform most of the housework. As long as they feel a sense of duty, they carry it out with little attempt to negotiate with husbands or children. However, the current situation of wives' gain of marital power along with their performance of housework is a fertile ground for generating marital tensions and conflict.

Furthermore, since married couples decide their family life, Korean immigrant families exhibit considerable variation in the couples' lifestyles and their relationships with children. In some families, they treat their children like an American middle-class family would. But in many others, parents treat children more authoritatively. Regardless of their approaches, parents are highly interested in the achievement of their children. Their high aspiration for the children's achievement is an expression of the Confucian-Korean culture and has been reinforced by the parents' experience of blocked mobility in American society.

Another aspect of family life concerns kin. Owing to the history of kinship-based chain migration, most Korean immigrants have kin in the area. When kin invite other kin to migrate and then help with the newly arrived individuals' initial settlement, their kinship ties are naturally strengthened. But once the newly arrived settle in, they are expected to support and manage their own nuclear family. Thus, their kinship ties become somewhat limited and vary with the dynamics of couple-centered nuclear families, although the kinship-based help system continues to exist.

Finally, the couple-centered nuclear family also changes the traditional norm of filial piety, which has obligated married sons, particularly the oldest son, and their wives to take care of the husbands' parents. Even today, most Korean immigrants continue to believe they have an obligation to take care of their elderly parents. But they now think that, along with married sons, married daughters should have an obligation to support their elderly parents. The other side of this change is their expectation to support the parents of both the husband and wife. This attitude of Korean immigrants signifies a considerable change from the traditional norm of filial obligation. Such a change in immigrants' attitudes suggests that the traditional kinship relationships and related filial norms have been modified to accommodate the emergence of the independent nuclear family.

Korean Immigrant Church

Immigrants tend to be more religious in the United States than in their native country. This point is clearly manifested in the religious behavior of Korean immigrants. A good proportion of Korean immigrants were Christians in Korea. Virtually all of these premigration Christians are currently affiliated with Korean immigrant churches. In addition, about half of those who were not Christians in Korea are also currently affiliated with ethnic churches. It is not surprising, therefore, that about 70 percent of Korean immigrants are currently found to be affiliated with immigrant churches. Furthermore, most of these persons regularly attend Sunday worship service.

The intensive church life of Korean immigrants can be explained by multiple roles that immigrant churches perform in response to the stresses experienced by church members. Immigration involves a painful process of uprooting from the familiar environment and of rerooting in a strange place. Under such an uncertain and stressful situation, immigrants seek a firm guideline for a meaningful immigrant life and the support of comforting hands. As a racially and culturally distinct immigrant group, Koreans are segregated from other race/ethnic groups in the United States. Their social life is, thus, limited to a small circle of their family members, relatives, and Korean friends. The ethnic church is the only social institution widely available to them to broaden the range of their social activities and thereby to satisfy their primary group needs (meeting new friends) and secondary group needs (holding some church position—status enhancement). When immigrant churches attempt to handle these needs of members, the churches emerge as good ethnoreligious organizations and become solidly institutionalized in Korean American communities.

As Korean immigrant churches perform multiple roles, the churches attract not just those with a firm belief in God (the believers) but also those who are mainly interested in the satisfaction of their social or personal needs (the participants). As many individual members try to satisfy their personal needs, Korean ethnic churches are often troubled by internal conflict and schism. Obviously, church conflict and schism are not unique to Korean ethnic churches. But their frustrated life experiences in America intensify such conflicts. Status concern and the qualifications of ministers are the two major sources of conflict and schism for Korean ethnic churches, and as church conflicts and schisms deepen, some Korean immigrants would like to change their church affiliation. But even those who change their church usually move to other Korean immigrant churches or create a new immigrant church, rather than switching to American churches. It again implies that immigrant churches perform essential functions for their immigrants' life in the United States.

Friendships and Ethnic Identity

Along with their family and kinship relations and regular attendance of immigrant churches, Koreans' social life is extended to their participation in organizations, such as alumni associations and various types of voluntary associations. But these organizations are not generally active and meet only a few times a year. As a result, their meaningful activity is found to be in association with their personal friends. Some of these Koreans' current friends were already friends when they were in Korea, but many new ones are made in America, including those whom they meet at churches. An interesting point of their friendship is that association with Korean friends does not necessarily reduce the chance of having non-Korean friends or jeopardize association with them. Today, Korean immigrants continuously associate with other Koreans as their personal friends regardless of length of residence in the United States, but as time goes by, the proportion of those who report having non-Korean friends also increases.

For many European immigrant groups, religious revival has provided a structural base for developing ethnicity in the United States. Not so for Korean immigrants. Their identity is based on their common nationality and shared history and culture. Korea is a small country with a homogeneous culture and racial composition. Their historical experience of being surrounded by big powers has further strengthened their common identity. When Korean immigrants closely associate with other Korean immigrants as family/kinship members, members of the same church, and friends, they develop their own ethnicity, with a shared identity and distinct lifestyle, that is different from that of people in Korea and others in the United States. Consequently, one can say that what they do in their sociocultural life is to create their own ethnic life and identity.

FUTURE PROSPECTS

Korean immigrants' life experiences in the United States are a product of the joint influences of the two sets of factors, the sociocultural factors that they brought from their native country and the sociocultural conditions that they encounter in the United States. As reviewed, most of the current Korean immigrants came in the 1970s and 1980s with middle-class backgrounds. They are currently placed in various occupations. As a whole, though, the occupational opportunities available to them are the ones that do not require direct competition with the native-born white workers, placing them into unfavorable segments of the American labor market. In addition to the small number of Korean immigrants in the United States, their immigrant status and current occupational positions contribute to their political powerlessness.

Proportionally more family members in Korean immigrant families are employed than in American families. A high proportion of Korean immigrants are also currently employed in professional/technical occupations or self-employed in small businesses. These factors contribute to their higher-than-average family income, but that higher-than-average family income does not justify the stereotyped success image of Asian Americans. Their individual (per capita) earnings are less than whites' when their education, hours of work, and other input factors are simultaneously considered.

Korean middleman entrepreneurs are considered to be economically active but politically weak. This has been the case for Korean small-business owners in inner-city African-American and Hispanic communities. Moreover, today this paradoxical position seems to extend to the whole population of Korean immigrants in the United States. Their occupations are generally conspicuous even in the segmented secondary labor markets, but their political influence in the United States is at the minimum, if it exists at all.

With such a delicate minority position in the stratified American society, Korean immigrants maintain their own ethnic way of life through independent nuclear families. With couple-centered family life, they maintain delicate relationships with other family members and kin. They attend immigrant churches regularly and intensely and closely associate with their fellow friends. Their family and kinship ties, church life, and association with Korean friends provide the structural conditions of their ethnic life in the United States. Their ethnic life then gives a strange disjunction between their social and cultural ethnicity, for while their ethnic consciousness extends to the whole Korean population in the United States, their daily ethnic life is limited to their family and kinship ties, church relations, and friendships.

In the 1970s and 1980s, Korean American communities consisted of the immigrants and their young children. Now the children are growing up and comprise a significant portion of the Korean American population. Some of them have already completed their formal education and have started their own adult life with full-time employment and their own family life. Many more children are current students or will soon become students at various universities and colleges. This means that Korean ethnic communities in the major cities are now undergoing a great deal of change. The younger generation of Korean Americans is familiar with the Korean way of life through their parents and the parents' ethnic institutions, such as churches and Korean-language schools. At the same time, they have been exposed to the American system from the early stage of their life. Such life experiences of the young generation suggest that the content of their ethnic life could be quite different from that of their parents, although both generations would keep a Korean American identity.

A high proportion of young Korean Americans are expected to complete college education and be employed accordingly. Thus, we can expect highly diverse occupations, with fewer of the younger generation engaged in self-employed small businesses, particularly in the types of businesses their parents currently operate. A high proportion of them are also likely to get married to non-Koreans. Their out-marriage would complicate their lifestyle and ethnic experiences. Their churches will be different from that of their parents. While their parents worship with their fellow Koreans in their native language, more and more of the children will worship God in English and in many non-Korean congregations.

Unlike past immigrants, contemporary Korean immigrants and their children live in the age of globalization. As a result of the export-oriented nature of the Korean economy and the development of mass media, there is frequent contact between Korean Americans and Koreans in Korea. Most Korean immigrants read the Korean newspapers daily, edited in Korea but printed and distributed in the United States. They listen to Korean radio and watch Korean TV and videos. As tourists or businessmen, many Koreans visit the United States, and their number annually exceeds 1 million. Many Korean Americans also visit Korea. Some children of Korean immigrants go to Korea and stay there for lengthy periods of time to teach English in Korea and/or to study Korean language and culture. Such close contact suggests that Korean immigrants and their children will continue to retain Korean social and cultural ties in their ethnic life in the United States, even when they are highly Americanized. The specific contents of this hybrid ethnic way of life are difficult to predict. Nonetheless, it will surely be different from the one expected by the assimilation model.

BIBLIOGRAPHIC REFERENCES

With respect to the history of Korean immigration to the United States, three works are most useful: Wayne Patterson, *The Korean Frontier in America: Immigration to Hawaii, 1896–1910* (Honolulu: University of Hawaii, 1988), analyzes the early Korean immigration to Hawaii, which took place at the turn of the twentieth century, and describes the vital role of American missionary/consul general Horace Allen, as a result of which about 7,000 Korean laborers eventually came to Hawaii and worked on the sugar plantations. Bong-Youn Choy, *Koreans in America* (Chicago: Nelson-Hall, 1979), provides a detailed and scholarly work on Korean Americans' socioeconomic, cultural, and political activities in America from 1882 to 1976. Insook Park, James T. Fawcett, Fred Arnold, and Robert W. Gardner, *Korean Immigrants and U.S. Immigration Policy: A Predeparture Perspective* (Honolulu: East-West Center, 1990), examine social backgrounds and expectations of the post-1965 immigrants, based on interviews with 10 percent of new immigrant visa holders in 1986 as well as with 549 status adjusters. The immigrants came from urban backgrounds, had a higher socioeconomic status than the general Korean population, and expected to do well in the long term in the United States. This opportunity expectation drew many to America.

In terms of Koreans' occupational adjustment, see Ivan Light and Edna Bonacich, *Immigrant Entrepreneurs: Koreans in Los Angeles, 1965–1982* (Berkeley: University of California, 1988). This is a comprehensive study of Korean immigrants' small businesses in the Los Angeles area. It examines the international context and roots of emigration of Koreans from their native country. It then focuses on Koreans' settlement in the Los Angeles area, class and ethnic resources of their businesses, and the locations of those businesses. The authors also deal with the sources of Korean entrepreneurship, the hostile reactions of African-American customers to Korean store owners, and the owners' ensuing solidarity. A particular set of issues was discussed by Henry Jay Becker in "Racial Segregation among Places of Employment," presented at the American Sociological Association, San Francisco, September 1978. Pyong Gap Min, *Caught in the Middle: Korean Communities in New York and Los Angeles* (Berkeley: University of California, 1996), provides an overview of Korean small businesses and documents—from Korean American perspectives—conflict events in two major cities, New York and Los Angeles, between Koreans and African Americans. However, another aspect that held true for quite some time can be seen in Pam Belluck, "Healthy Korean Economy Draws Immigrants Home," *New York Times*, August 22, 1995.

Two studies in particular cover family and kinship relations: Pyong Gap Min, *Changes and Conflicts: Korean Immigrant Families in New York* (Boston: Allyn and Bacon, 1998), is based on his numerous ethnographic studies and interviews. Min examines the following aspects of Korean immigrants' family and kinship relations in New York: marital relations, parent and child relationships, the elderly's adjustment, and transnational family ties. The key issues in Korean immigrants' martial relations are the employed wives' double burden of family and work roles and their husbands' perception that the wives challenge or threaten their traditional male privileges. Despite this, Min documents both changes and conflicts in family and kinship relations. Kwang Chung Kim and Won Moo Hurh, "The Burden of Double Roles: As Wives in the U.S.A.," *Ethnic and Racial Studies* 11 (1988): 151–167, based on 1979 Los Angeles data, also analyzes the double burden of the employed Korean wives, noting that the wives' problem comes not just from their double roles but also from their belief that it is their duty to perform most of the housework. The authors compare such a persistence of traditional gender roles with the experiences of employed white and black wives.

A major place in Koreans' adjustment to life in America is taken by their church experiences. Won Moo Hurh and Kwang Chung Kim, "Religious Participation of Korean Immigrants in the U.S.," *Journal for the Scientific Study of Religion* 29 (1990): 19–34, use their 1986 Chicago data on Korean immigrants to test four theoretical propositions regarding the role of religion for Korean immigrants and found that the Koreans' intensive participation provided a meaningful way of life for them without having any particular negative effect on the immigrants' experience of mobility or assimilation. Pyong Gap Min, "The Structure and Social Functions of Korean Immigrant Churches in the United States," *International Migration Review* 26 (1992): 1370–1394, provides descriptive information on the structure of Korean immigrant churches in the United States and, more importantly, analyzes the social functions of those churches. With respect to the larger pattern of cultural adjustment, see Kwang Chung Kim and Won Mo Hurh, "Beyond Assimilation and Pluralism: Syncretic Sociocultural Adaptation of Korean Immigrants in the U.S.,'' *Ethnic and Racial Studies* 16 (1993): 696–713. Critical of a common assumption that immigrants' Americanization and their retention of native ways of life are mutually exclusive, the authors present a model of sociocultural adaptation of immigrants and test it with data collected from 622 Korean immigrant adults in the Chicago area in 1986. The authors detail the additive adaptation that Koreans exhibit in certain dimensions of their lives: continuous retention of Korean sociocultural ties while gradually Americanizing—and without weakening their sociocultural ties.

MEXICANS

David G. Gutiérrez

In 1997, an estimated 17 million persons of Mexican descent lived within the boundaries of the United States. Although ethnic Mexicans (that is, the combined population of American citizens of Mexican descent and Mexican immigrants living in the United States) can be found in significant numbers in every state of the union, more than 84 percent continue to reside in the southwestern region (California, Arizona, New Mexico, Colorado, and Texas), where Spanish-speaking people have maintained an unbroken presence for nearly 400 years. When the ethnic Mexican population of Illinois is added, fully 88 percent of the total population is concentrated in just six states. The history of those four centuries is complex and difficult to periodize. However, for the purposes of developing a general overview, it is useful to think of this group's history as unfolding in four overlapping stages: the colonial era (roughly 1598–1821); the era of conquest, annexation, and incorporation (1821–1900); the first era of twentieth-century Mexican migration (1900–1964); and the current period of Mexican migration (1965–present).

THE COLONIAL ERA: 1598–1821

The first permanent settlement of Spanish-speaking people from Mexico dates from 1598, when a lower-level Spanish aristocrat, Juan De Oñate, led a group of approximately 200 settlers and soldiers up the Rio Grande Valley from Mexico on an expedition to colonize New Mexico. After occupying several temporary sites, Oñate's group established the site for Santa Fe, New Mexico, in 1609. From this first outpost on the upper Rio Grande, the Spanish colonial presence in what is now the southwestern United States expanded slowly over the next two centuries. In 1687, a group of Spanish-speaking settlers moved into a small cluster of settlements in Pimería Alta (present-day southern Arizona and northern Sonora). By 1691, colonists began entering into what is presently southern and eastern Texas. And with the establishment of the Catholic mission at San Diego in 1769 (the first of what would become a chain of twenty-one missions stretching from San Diego to Sonoma), Spaniards began the gradual settlement of upper California.

The colonies' distance from central Mexico and from one another guaranteed that the northern provinces would remain underpopulated hinterlands on the far edges of the Spanish empire well into the early nineteenth century. The development of society in the northern provinces reflected this isolation. Although the colonists of each of these regions had moved north hoping to replicate as much as possible the culture and institutions they had left behind in Mexico City and other centers of Spanish colonial society, the presence of hostile Indian groups and the harsh physiography of the region severely constrained the growth of the northern frontier settlements. New Mexico's non-Indian population would grow to approximately 30,000 by the time Mexico won its independence from Spain in 1821, but the populations of California, Texas, and Arizona had only grown to 3,500, 3,000, and 1,000, respectively, by that time.

Given these conditions, it is not at all surprising that Spanish-speaking inhabitants of the north were compelled to make dramatic social and cultural adjustments and adaptations to their environment. One of the most fundamental transformations in the northern provinces involved changes in the structure of the family. Since social status in Mexico (as elsewhere in colonial Latin America) was based on a combination of a family's bloodlines and accumulated wealth, a premium was placed on "marrying well" by choosing a partner of equal or better material wealth and with the requisite family pedigree. However, given the chronic gender imbalance in the colonies, sexual liaisons between Spaniards and Indians soon began to produce a growing mestizo population (the mixed-blood offspring of Spanish and Indian parentage). This demographic trend proved crucial to the subsequent development of colonial society. Despite the premium placed on "racial purity" in the New World, the mixing of peoples inevitably contributed to the emergence of an exceedingly complicated demographic structure. Under the caste system that emerged, European-born Spaniards occupied the highest position, followed, in descending order, by American-born creoles of Spanish parentage, a rapidly growing number of mestizos, Indians, blacks, and the various combinations of people that gradually developed as society matured and became more variegated. However, as the process of intermixture continued, it became increasingly difficult to maintain clear lines between the various castes.

On the northern frontier, gender imbalances were even more pronounced, and thus the process of *mestizaje* (i.e., the mixing of peoples) appears to have been even more widespread. To be sure, status distinctions based on caste and property ownership structured society even on the frontier, but the most important social difference was the line that divided Spanish-speaking Catholics, who considered themselves *gente de razón* (i.e., "civilized" people of reason), from non-Christianized Indians. Based on these broad status categories, frontier society developed into a social hierarchy in which a small group of landowners, military officers, and Catholic clergy constituted the elite; a larger group of mestizo small farmers, ranchers, and artisans made up the middle sectors; Christianized Indians comprised the lower stratum; and non-Christianized Indians were considered apart from, or outside of, organized society.

Economic life during the colonial era was largely ordered by the rhythms of subsistence ranching, farming, and artisanal manufacturing, although trade with Mexico and local indigenous peoples was also important. Hard currency was in chronic short supply, and most exchanges were based on barter for goods in kind. Thanks to the widespread use of coerced Indian labor, some Catholic missions produced small surpluses of foodstuffs, wine, and cattle hides (especially in California), but in general, the provincial economy of the early Mexican Republic remained sluggish and underdeveloped throughout the colonial period.

Religious life in the north also reflected the rustic conditions of the frontier. Although propagation of the Catholic faith had been one of the major impetuses of Spanish colonial expansion into the New World, the northern provinces were always short of ordained clergy. Lacking a strong institutional foundation as a result, Spanish-speaking inhabitants of the northern provinces were forced to improvise in their religious practices. Most inhabitants understood and tried to follow the basic tenets of the Catholic faith, but, over time, they interpreted their religion in ways that seemed best to meet their daily needs. Consequently, the norteños gradually developed distinctive regional folk variants of orthodox Roman Catholicism. Distinctive religious customs, including the special veneration of the Virgin Mary and a panoply of saints, the assembly of home altars, and the perpetuation of such lay confraternities as New Mexico's penitente brotherhood, are all modern vestiges of these early practices.

THE ERA OF CONQUEST, ANNEXATION, AND INCORPORATION: 1821–1900

The tenor of everyday life was to change very quickly in the first decades of the nineteenth century after Mexico won its independence from Spain and once travelers from the United States and elsewhere began to come into contact with the Spanish-speaking inhabitants of northern Mexico. Up to this point, Americans had had very little contact with the inhabitants of New Spain. But as American clipper ships began to ply the seas in the 1790s, and trappers, traders, and adventurers began to venture into Indian lands in western North America in the early 1820s, Americans soon became more familiar with the Spanish-speaking communities to the west. Local people in the north generally welcomed the communication and opportunities for trade that contact with American and European travelers brought them. Indeed, years of pent-up demand in the northern provinces soon helped to create a vibrant market for imported goods. In fact, by the early 1830s, the volume of trade flowing east and west between the

United States and northern Mexico now exceeded the north-south flows between the provinces and central Mexico.

In the age of Manifest Destiny, it was only a matter of time before Americans began to eye Mexico's northern provinces for themselves. Earlier in the century, U.S. envoys had made several attempts to purchase large expanses of territory from Mexico, but in each instance these overtures were rebuffed. Attempting to blunt the effects of expansionist pressures from the east, the Mexican government struck on the novel idea of using American settlers in Texas as a buffer against future encroachments from the United States. Mexican officials implemented the colonization scheme in 1824, offering American settlers grants of land in Texas, provided that they agree to become Mexican citizens, learn Spanish, convert to Catholicism, and otherwise attempt to become assimilated into the mainstream of Mexican life.

By 1835, more than 30,000 Americans had taken advantage of the Mexican offer, but, not surprisingly, few seemed to have actually tried to follow the letter of the colonization law. On the contrary, by the mid-1830s tensions between Texans and Mexican authorities had deepened to the extent that many Anglo Texans (and some "Mexican Texans" as well) called for the creation of an independent Texas. In 1835, these tensions erupted into war, and after a series of bloody battles (including the infamous massacres at the Alamo and Goliad), Texas won its independence the following year.

However, tensions continued to fester between Mexico and the Texas Republic, and, in response, Texans petitioned the United States for admission into the Union. Growing concern over the expansion of slavery into new territories stymied these efforts for a time, but when expansionist James K. Polk was elected president in 1844, the balance tipped in favor of annexation. After repeated diplomatic failures to convince Mexico to drop its claims on Texas and to sell California and New Mexico to the United States, Texas was annexed in March 1845, which in turn led to war between the United States and the Republic of Mexico. After a protracted struggle in which more than 63,000 were left dead on both sides, Mexico was forced to capitulate to General Winfield Scott in Mexico City in the autumn of 1847. On February 2, 1848, representatives of both governments signed the Treaty of Guadalupe Hidalgo. In addition to ending hostilities, the treaty formally ceded the northern third of Mexico to the United States for $15 million, recognized the annexation of Texas, and "extended all the rights of [U.S.] citizens" to the Mexican population (estimated at the time to be between 75,000 and 100,000) who chose to remain in annexed territory after the change in sovereignty.

Mexican officials had hoped that the citizenship guarantees they had negotiated would protect the rights and property of their former compatriots. Yet as thousands of American immigrants began to pour into the region after gold was discovered in California in January 1848, it soon became clear that most of the newcomers seemed to care little about the rights of the Mexicans they encountered in the annexed territory. And even if Americans had agreed to respect the rights of this first generation of Mexican Americans, the inundation of California by immigrants during the gold rush and the slow but steady growth of the immigrant population in Texas later in the century inevitably undermined the social, political, and economic position of the ethnic Mexican minority—and hastened them down the path toward a subordinate status in their own homelands.

Although the pace of change varied from place to place (depending largely on the ratio of American immigrants to Mexican inhabitants in local areas), ethnic Mexican landowners did begin a slow yet inexorable downward slide. Outmaneuvered in the courts, outnumbered at the polls, and increasingly unable to pay taxes and compete effectively in an economy that was rapidly shifting from a foundation based on ranching and subsistence agriculture to a more complex capitalist system, ethnic Mexican landowners were forced to sell off parcels to pay taxes and meet mounting legal costs. While landowning Mexican Americans in New Mexico were able to maintain a modicum of both economic and political influence because of their greater numbers there (Hispanic New Mexicans would continue to constitute a majority of the population until the early 1940s), by the 1870s and 1880s Mexican Americans in the rest of the region had lost a huge proportion of their formerly vast landholdings.

For members of the Mexican-American working class, the conquest of the Mexican north had similarly dire consequences. Ethnic Mexican workers had a shorter relative distance to fall in the emerging regional labor market, but they, too, experienced downward mobility because of deep-seated Anglo prejudices and the changing nature of the economy. As the structure of the economy changed from one based on family farming and ranching to one based on trade, mining, construction, transportation, and large-scale commercial agriculture, many Mexican-American workers found that their old livelihoods had been rendered obsolete. Even though they technically had rights equal to other American citizens, they discovered that Anglo-Americans were intent on maintaining a stranglehold on skilled and better-paying occupations.

As a consequence, in the half-century following the Mexican War, displaced Mexican-American workers, whose jobs had once been rather evenly distributed between skilled and semiskilled occupations, were steadily pressured into the lowest levels of an increasingly ethnically segmented labor market. By 1900, a starkly defined ethnic division of labor had emerged in the region, one in which whites dominated skilled occupations and managerial positions and ethnic Mexicans were overwhelmingly employed in unskilled or semiskilled occupations. In addition, a dual wage system emerged in which white non-Hispanic workers earned as much as twice the pay Mexicans made for the same jobs. This ethnic division of labor and discriminatory wage system would characterize the regional economy well into the twentieth century. Many immigration scholars have argued that the historical association of Mexican workers with low-paying, low-status occupations continues to influence American attitudes about ethnic Mexicans in contemporary American society.

THE INITIAL ERA OF TWENTIETH-CENTURY MEXICAN IMMIGRATION: 1900–1964

It is interesting to speculate about what might have occurred to the ethnic Mexican minority had the population remained at the comparatively low levels of the nineteenth century. Given their long cultural tradition of *mestizaje* and social adaptation, it is conceivable that they might have gradually "melted" into the mainstream of regional life. Nevertheless, continuing patterns of discrimination in employment, education, and housing, combined with a sudden increase in the number of Mexican immigrants moving into the United States between 1900 and 1929, helped to create a situation that intensified misunderstanding and conflict between ethnic Mexicans and other residents of the Southwest.

Several interlocking sets of circumstances served as catalysts for a dramatic increase in migration from Mexico at this time. The first of these involved the explosive economic development between the 1870s and the 1920s of both the western United States and northern Mexico. The extension of the American national railway system into the West after the Civil War and the expansion northward of the Mexican railroads under the regime of Mexican President Porfirio Díaz (who ruled Mexico between 1876 and 1910) together provided the transportation revolution that allowed capitalists to begin to develop rich resources on both sides of the border.

On the American side, the only limitation on such plans was the region's chronic shortage of labor. After experimenting with Chinese laborers between the 1850s and 1880s, and then with Japanese workers beginning in the 1890s, regional employers increasingly looked to Mexico to satisfy a growing demand for labor. Although the general trend in American law between the late 1880s and the 1930s was to restrict the flow of immigrants into the United States, these requirements were consistently ignored or relaxed for Mexican workers throughout this period. As a consequence, employers began recruiting workers in Mexico to do arduous, low-paying, and often dangerous work on regional railroads, in the fields, in construction, and in the mines. Soon recognizing that this labor force might also be effectively utilized elsewhere, by the late 1910s and early 1920s American employers had also begun to hire significant numbers of Mexican workers in agricultural pursuits in the upper Midwest, in the automobile, steel, and packing-house industries of the Great Lakes region, and in canneries as far away as Hawaii and Alaska. Thus began the process of population dispersal away from the border region that continues to the present.

On the Mexican side of the equation, the rapid modernization of the national economy under Díaz, while providing some Mexicans with work in railroad construction and mining, had the larger effect of displacing peasant workers from the land—and from their means of subsistence—and thus contributing to the attraction of potential employment in the United States. As the rail systems expanded, connections between the two nations provided a natural conduit for the northward movement of Mexican labor. In addition, consumer price inflation caused by the rapid shift in this period from a largely agrarian/pastoral system to an export-based economy made it even more difficult for workers to make a living. And, of course, once revolution erupted in Mexico in 1910, growing numbers of Mexicans looked for political and economic respite in the North.

The combination of events in Mexico and the formal recruitment and informal word-of-mouth communication between Mexican workers in the United States and their friends and family at home soon helped to turn a trickle of Mexican workers into a steady stream. Although only about 78,000 foreign-born Mexicans were counted in the 1890 census, this population grew to 100,000 in 1900, 222,000 in 1910, 478,000 in 1920, and about 639,000 in 1930. Estimates vary, but most demographic historians agree that high rates of migration and natural increase raised the combined foreign-born and U.S.-born ethnic Mexican population of the United States to between 1 and 1.5 million by 1930.

The Great Depression put an abrupt halt to these developments. Whereas Mexican workers had been recruited by employers for more than thirty years, once American citizens began losing jobs, authorities at the federal, state, and local levels began to pressure Mexicans—and their U.S.-born children—to leave the country. It is impossible to determine exactly how many ethnic Mexicans were pressured to depart, but most scholars agree that at least 500,000 and perhaps as many as 600,000 were repatriated during the depression years.

The initial cycle of migration from Mexico may have been broken during the Great Depression, but this proved to be but a brief lull. When labor demands skyrocketed after the United States entered World War II in December 1941, American employers once again looked to Mexico. Arguing that the national emergency dictated that they be allowed once again to recruit foreign laborers on a massive scale, American employers (particularly in California, Arizona, Texas, and the Pacific Northwest) convinced the federal government to establish a bilateral labor agreement with Mexico. After the repatriation campaigns of the 1930s, the Mexican government was understandably wary of allowing Mexicans to participate in such a program (and actually prohibited the recruitment of its citizens in Texas because of the hostile racial environment there) and insisted that Mexican workers be provided certain guarantees as to wages, working conditions, housing, and protection against discrimination. Only then did Mexican leaders agree to approve the Emergency Farm Labor Program in August 1942.

Dubbed the ''Bracero Program'' (after the Spanish word for day laborer), the labor agreement quickly helped to reestablish the transnational migratory circuits that had been laid earlier in the century. Even though much of this new migratory flow was formally regulated and controlled under the terms of the binational agreement, the program had the unanticipated effect of encouraging undocumented migrants to try their luck in the United States. Of course, employers welcomed such a development because the presence of large numbers of un-documented workers kept wages low and helped to undermine the efforts of American farmworkers (many of whom were Mexican Americans) to organize into unions. By the late 1950s, when up to 500,000 Mexican braceros were working under contract in the United States each year, at least as many undoc-umented workers were circulating in and out of the American labor market. By 1954, public outcry against the presence of undocumented Mexican workers stimulated the Immigration and Naturalization Service (INS) to begin ''Opera-tion Wetback''—the second major apprehension and repatriation campaign of the century. Between June 1954 and the end of 1955, the INS reported that the campaign had netted more than 1.25 million illegal aliens—the vast majority of them Mexican nationals.

Despite these efforts, the reestablishment of Mexican labor recruitment and employment patterns greatly complicated the social and political landscape of the Southwest (and to a lesser extent other areas as well). Although the number of foreign-born Mexicans enumerated in the census had dropped from 639,000 in 1930 to 377,400 in 1940, the reopening of the border during the war stim-ulated a steady expansion of the ethnic Mexican population. Legal, documented Mexican immigration totaled 54,000 in the 1940s, 293,000 in the 1950s (about 12 percent of all immigrants during this period), and 431,000 in the 1960s (about 14 percent of the total). Changing enumeration techniques and the presence of large numbers of undocumented migrants make it difficult to know exactly how much the total ethnic Mexican population grew during this period, but most demographers agree that the combined citizen and noncitizen population climbed from at least 1.4 million in 1940, to 1.7 million in 1950, 3.5 million in 1960, and to at least 4.5 million in 1970. Although the trend was for greater population dispersal throughout this period, in 1970 more than 87 percent of all ethnic Mexicans continued to be concentrated in the five southwestern states.

Since so many of the immigrants coming from Mexico were young, working class, and poorly educated, the sustained flow of immigrants inevitably created economic, social, and political strains in the daily lives of ethnic Mexicans in the United States. On the most fundamental level, the population's sociode-mographic characteristics placed ethnic Mexicans at a competitive disadvantage in American society. Until World War II, ethnic Mexicans had lagged behind almost every identifiable ethnic group in virtually all categories of socioeco-nomic status. In 1930, for example, the median education level for ethnic Mex-icans was less than seven years, and fewer than 20 percent would finish high school. Of course, lower educational opportunities also helped determine their job opportunities. In 1930, about one-third of all ethnic Mexican male workers nationwide were unskilled or semiskilled agricultural laborers; another third were unskilled or semiskilled industrial workers; only 15 percent were skilled craftsmen or operatives; and well below 1 percent were employed in such pro-fessions as law, medicine, and education.

After World War II, ethnic Mexicans began to register significant gains in

English-language proficiency, education levels, job opportunities, and income, yet, as a group, they continued to lag behind other Americans in these areas. For example, although median education levels for U.S.-born male and female Mexican Americans (who had access to more schooling than foreign-born Mexicans) increased from 5.4 years in 1950, to 7.1 years in 1960, and to 9.2 years in 1970, in 1970 Mexican Americans on average still completed 3 fewer years of education than did non-Hispanic white Americans. Similarly, although the percentage of ethnic Mexican male workers in semiskilled or skilled craftsmen or operative occupations increased from 15 percent to about 31 percent in 1950, and nearly 48 percent in 1970—and the number of those engaged in professional occupations increased from 1.7 percent to 5.1 percent in the same period—in 1970, these figures remained to lag well behind those of the "white" population. Data for ethnic Mexican women showed similar, though more modest, trends. Between 1950 and 1970, as ethnic Mexican women (especially native-born Mexican Americans) gained more years of education, the general trend was for female workers to move out of operative and farm labor jobs (about 49 percent of the total in 1950) to clerical and service occupations (about 45 percent of the total in 1970).

As the ethnic Mexican population became more demographically complex and class stratified over time, traditional Mexican cultural forms and practices changed apace. As would be expected, during the period of the first mass migration from Mexico, the influx of large numbers of working-class immigrants and temporary sojourners helped simultaneously to revitalize ethnic Mexican communities and to slow the processes of acculturation—especially in the border region. Usually settling in, or adjacent to, existing Mexican-American enclaves (which tended to be in the most run-down and, therefore, cheapest parts of American towns and cities), Mexican nationals helped such communities by intermarrying and establishing families with Mexican Americans, buying homes and property, and establishing a growing network of small businesses that catered almost exclusively to an ethnic Mexican clientele. Perhaps just as important, the steady influx of Mexicans into the United States helped to reinforce the use of the Spanish language and guaranteed that Mexican cultural and religious practices would continue to flourish. In addition, the sending of remittances to relatives (estimated to be in excess of $10 million between 1917 and 1929 alone), combined with the constant flow of migrants back and forth across the U.S.-Mexico border, helped to forge lasting linkages between communities in the United States and towns and villages deep in the interior of Mexico.

Despite the constant interaction between immigrants and natives, by the 1940s and 1950s enough ethnic Mexicans had come of age in the United States that clear social and cultural differences began to emerge within the population. Perhaps the most important example of this was the gradual shift from Spanish to the English language by second-and third-generation Mexican Americans. Whereas at least two-thirds of the population was either monolingual in Spanish or Spanish-dominant in 1930, by the mid-1940s the clear trend among both the

U.S.-born children of Mexican immigrants and Mexican-American natives (that is, at least third generation) was the steady acquisition of English. Historical statistics are sketchy, but most scholars agree that by the third generation an overwhelming majority of ethnic Mexicans had become English proficient. In urban areas where ethnic Mexicans constituted only small enclaves (such as Chicago, Gary, Detroit, and Kansas City), English-language acquisition apparently occurred even more quickly.

As more Mexican Americans moved from rural to urban areas, learned English, gained more years of education, and began to be hired in more highly paid occupations, the process of acculturation accelerated, and increasing numbers of Mexican Americans inevitably aspired to move more toward the "mainstream" of middle-class American life, which in turn led to a rise in class- and culturally-based tensions. These trends manifested themselves in many ways. Among the most prominent were the increasing tensions between U.S.-born Mexican-American youths and their immigrant parents over issues ranging from language usage, clothing styles, musical tastes, to relationships between young men and women. Related frictions arose out of rapidly changing gender roles in ethnic Mexican families. As more Mexican-American women became educated and entered the workforce, traditional systems that held women inferior and subservient to Mexican men rapidly eroded. Of course, all these tensions were exacerbated by the powerful socializing effects of the public schools and perhaps the even more powerful influence of American consumer culture generally. Still, it is important to recognize that for those who remained insulated in working-class urban neighborhoods (notably those in East Los Angeles, Albuquerque, El Paso, or San Antonio), or in remote rural areas (such as southern Arizona, northern New Mexico, or south Texas), traditional cultural tastes and customs changed more slowly, a tendency that was often the result of a conscious choice made by individuals intent on resisting assimilation into the "mainstream" of American life.

Such internal differences also manifested themselves in politics. For example, in 1929, a group of mainly middle-class Mexican Americans met in Corpus Christi, Texas, to establish the League of United Latin American Citizens, or LULAC. Based on the fundamental notion that Mexican Americans were American citizens, LULAC broke new ground by stressing the importance to permanent ethnic Mexican residents of acquiring citizenship, English-language ability, education, and knowledge of American political traditions and practices. The organization also advocated immigration restriction as a key component of its strategy to encourage the integration of ethnic Mexicans into the mainstream of American society.

As important as the emergence of such organizations was, however, it is important to note that such groups as LULAC represented but one strain of political thought and action in the ethnic Mexican community. In fact, dating from the mid-nineteenth century, ethnic Mexicans had engaged in a wide variety of alternative political activities. For example, in the 1850s, Los Angeles newspaper publisher Francisco Ramirez used the pages of his weekly, *El Clamor Público* (The Public Outcry), to protest against the discrimination and violence experienced by his people in California. In 1859 and 1860, Brownsville, Texas, rancher Juan Cortina mounted an armed insurrection against what he considered to be the injustice of Anglo domination over Mexicans in the border region. And in New Mexico between the 1870s and the 1890s, Hispano vigilante groups, such as La Mano Negra (the "Black Hand") and Las Gorras Blancas (the "White Caps"), cut fences, wrecked machinery, and destroyed rail and telegraph lines in protest over Anglo encroachments into their lands.

In general, however, ethnic Mexicans employed other means to articulate their grievances. The most common was through the formation of mutual aid associations, or *mutualistas*. Although usually established in the late nineteenth and early twentieth centuries to provide mutual death and burial insurance benefits to members, these community-based groups often served as organizational springboards from which ethnic Mexicans formed labor unions and launched strikes. This tradition of activism was carried forward into the 1930s and 1940s by progressive coalition organizations, in particular the Congress of Spanish-Speaking Peoples. Established by labor and community organizers Luisa Moreno, Josefina Fierro de Bright, Eduardo Quevedo, and Bert Corona, the Congress advocated a political platform that included calls for greatly liberalized naturalization and voter registration procedures, equal rights for immigrant and women workers, and bilingual and bicultural education in communities with significant ethnic Mexican populations.

To a certain extent, Mexican-American politics since the late 1920s has continued to revolve around the two poles represented by LULAC and the Congress of Spanish-Speaking Peoples. Indeed, much of the radical rhetoric and anti-assimilationist political positioning of Chicano movement activists during the 1960s and 1970s, especially by New Mexico's Reies López Tijerina, Colorado's Rodolfo "Corky" Gonzales, and Texas's José Angel Gutiérrez, drew on a long tradition of militant politics among ethnic Mexicans. Still, the mainstream of Mexican-American political opinion was probably represented more by groups that included the American G.I. Forum (established in Texas in 1947), the Community Service Organization (established in California two years later), and the Mexican American Political Association (founded in California in 1959)—organizations that followed integrationist strategies and a commitment to civil rights–oriented politics similar to LULAC's. Although it is important not to overgeneralize, prominent community activists—among them labor organizers Ernesto Galarza and César Chávez (who got his start as an organizer with the Community Service Organization); journalist Rubén Salazar; educators George I. Sánchez and Carlos Castañeda; elected officials stretching from New Mexico Senator Dionisio "Dennis" Chávez (who served in Congress from 1931 until his death in 1962) to Texas Congressman Henry B. González (1961 to the present) and California Congressman Edward R. Roybal (1962 to 1992); and such prominent politicans as former cabinet member Henry Cisneros and current

Los Angeles County Supervisor Gloria Molina—can be said to have drawn from the same integrationist political tradition.

CURRENT PERIOD OF MIGRATION: 1965–PRESENT

Since many of the major features that have characterized Mexican-American history since World War II continue to the present day, it is reasonable to expect that many of the same challenges faced by previous generations will persist into the foreseeable future. As always, many of these challenges have their roots in population demographics. Spurred by a resurgence of both legal and undocumented immigration and high birthrates (which are nearly twice as high among ethnic Mexicans than in the non-Hispanic white population), the ethnic Mexican population has grown dramatically since 1970. From a population of about 4.5 million in 1970, the population grew 93 percent to 8.7 million in 1980. By 1997, the population nearly doubled again to nearly 17 million people. According to Census Bureau calculations, of this total, 6.63 million, or nearly 40 percent, are foreign-born. As a percentage of all foreign-born in the United States, Mexicans have grown steadily from about 6 percent in 1960 to 8 percent in 1970, 15.6 percent in 1980, nearly 22 percent in 1990, and 27.2 percent in 1996. (For the years 1966–1995, 21.1 percent of all immigrants admitted were Mexicans.) The population has become more dispersed (in 1990, the states with highest concentrations of ethnic Mexicans were, in descending order, California, Texas, Arizona, Illinois, New Mexico, Colorado, Florida, Washington, Michigan, and Oregon), but more than 83 percent continue to live in the border states, with 80 percent of this number in the states of California and Texas alone.

Given the volatility of the current demographic situation, the socioeconomic, political, and cultural prognosis for the nation's ethnic Mexican population is decidedly difficult to predict. On the one hand, it is clear that a slowly growing percentage of third-, fourth-, and fifth-generation U.S-born Mexican Americans have made measurable progress in terms of educational achievement, socioeconomic mobility, and rates of political participation in mainstream American electoral politics. For example, whereas in 1970 the median education level of native-born Mexican Americans was nine years, by 1980 the median had risen to ten years and to a bit more than twelve years in 1990. Similarly, although Mexican Americans continue to be severely underrepresented in four-year colleges and universities and in graduate and professional programs, recent research has indicated that as much as 21 percent of the native-born population of Mexican descent has achieved occupational and income levels sufficient to be considered part of the middle class. In 1990, 8.3 percent of the total ethnic Mexican population held professional or managerial positions, and another 21.2 percent were employed in skilled precision production or craft occupations.

Moreover, despite the recent outcry about the "Latinization" of certain parts of the United States, virtually all reputable research on language retention and acquisition indicates that ethnic Mexicans historically have acquired English only a little less quickly than was true of previous immigrants from European countries. Although recent immigrants clearly continue to use Spanish as their primary language, school-age foreign-born children and the overwhelming majority of the U.S.-born children of immigrants show dramatic shifts toward English dominance. For example, a study of ethnic Mexican schoolchildren conducted between 1991 and 1995 found that rates of English proficiency and preference rose from 53 percent to 79 percent among the U.S.-born group and from 32 percent to 61 percent among the Mexican-born group. These findings are consistent with those of most scholarly studies on language acquisition published since the 1970s. Thus, most researchers have concluded that the apparent high levels of language loyalty among ethnic Mexicans is largely an effect of continuing high levels of immigration from Mexico.

In the area of popular culture, the explosive growth of the ethnic Mexican population has helped to transform "American" cultural tastes in food, architecture, literature, music, dance, film, and other areas. For example, growing awareness of Mexican cultural forms has led to the "crossover" successes of popular Mexican-American entertainers, such as Los Lobos, Linda Ronstadt, and the late *tejana* singer Selena; actors and filmmakers, including Edward James Olmos, Luis Valdez, Richard "Cheech" Marin, and Gregory Nava; sports stars, for example, Nancy Lopez, Fernando Valenzuela, and Oscar de la Hoya; and such writers as Sandra Cisneros, Ana Castillo, Rodolfo Anaya, Victor Villaseñor, Rubén Martínez, and the controversial Richard Rodríguez.

In terms of politics, there are equally clear signs that ethnic Mexicans are becoming increasingly influential. Largely as the result of efforts to register new voters by organizations, in particular the Southwest Voter Registration Project and the Mexican American Legal Defense and Education Fund (MALDEF), ethnic Mexican participation in electoral politics has increased dramatically over the past twenty years. During the past decade, the number of Mexican-American and other Latino elected and appointed officials has more than doubled nationwide, including Cruz Bustamante, chosen Speaker of the California Assembly in 1996. If recent rates continue, experts predict, the population of registered Mexican-American voters will grow from the estimated 4.3 million registered in 1996 to at least 5.5 million in 2000.

Still, it is important to recognize that in some ways the increasing political, social, and cultural visibility of ethnic Mexicans in American society is an outgrowth of a resurgence in *anti*-Mexican sentiment in the United States. As the result of the combination of massive economic restructuring, the erosion of tax-supported public health, education, and social services, and the rapid growth of the Spanish-speaking population, many Americans are insisting not only that immigration be severely restricted but that the government also implement harsh measures designed to make living in the United States less attractive to immigrants and their children. At the federal level, such concerns served as catalysts for the passage of the Immigration Reform and Control Act (IRCA) of 1986, which, while granting "amnesty" to nearly 2 million undocumented residents in 1990 and 1991 (of the estimated 3.032 million applicants for legalization under IRCA, 2.267 million were Mexican nationals) also imposed civil and criminal sanctions against American employers who knowingly hired undocumented workers. Ten years later, Congress passed welfare reform legislation that led to drastic cuts in social welfare benefits previously available to immigrants. At the state level, in 1994, California voters passed Proposition 187, which if upheld by the courts, would deny undocumented aliens (including children) access to most public education, welfare, and health services. In addition, as of 1995, twenty-two states had passed legislation making English their "official language," marking a growing concern with the proliferation of "foreign" languages and cultures on American soil.

If what is intended by such measures is to speed the process of immigrant integration and assimilation, the irony is that they may have exactly the opposite effect. On the one hand, it is clear that these measures have induced unprecedented numbers of Mexican nationals to apply for U.S. citizenship: Between 1995 and 1996 naturalization applications nationwide rose from nearly 446,000 per year to 1.2 million. (Already from fiscal years 1994 to 1995, the number of newly naturalized Mexicans had jumped 56 percent.) On the other hand, however, if one accepts the premise that political integration and social assimilation are not possible unless immigrants are afforded real opportunity for upward socioeconomic mobility, the future may be bleak. Although many more established Mexican Americans and Mexican immigrants have prospered in American society, evidence is emerging that raises some troubling questions about the socioeconomic, educational, and political trajectory of a growing number of working-class ethnic Mexicans.

The reasons for this are complex. Clearly, the steady influx of legally sanctioned and (especially) unsanctioned immigrants from Mexico has exerted some downward pressure on social and economic indicators in the resident population, particularly in those states with high immigrant populations. Even though immigrants tend to have higher levels of literacy and education than Mexicans who do not emigrate, immigrants enter the labor market with much lower skill levels and an average of four fewer years of education than their citizen counterparts (in 1990, only 24 percent of resident Mexican immigrants had completed high school, and only 3.5 percent had completed college). As a consequence, Mexican workers begin with very low starting wages relative to natives. But disparities in the human capital that immigrants bring with them tell only part of the story. Although differences in job skills, education levels, and language proficiency all contribute to the socioeconomic position ethnic Mexicans occupy in American society, research has demonstrated that persistent patterns of discrimination and the ongoing restructuring of the economy play perhaps even greater roles in determining their possibilities for economic success.

For Mexican immigrants, these "contexts of reception" have worsened considerably over the past three decades. Entering a labor market that continues to undergo radical restructuring, immigrants face very different prospects than was true earlier this century. Of course, specific trends vary from region to region, but in general, in recent years the job market has become severely bifurcated between the high-wage, high-skilled, high-status jobs dominated by an educated white middle class and low-wage, low-skilled, low-status jobs held by working-class immigrants. Of course, this situation has been exacerbated by the erosion of the American public education system. Recent data indicate that, despite making steady gains in education levels between 1945 and 1965, ethnic Mexicans' educational profile began to erode thereafter. Indeed, one of the most troubling trends in the ethnic Mexican population over the past thirty years has been the simultaneous rise in high school dropout rates combined with declines in the rates of growth of college enrollment. As of 1991, while 78.4 percent of the American population age twenty-five and older had completed high school and 21.4 percent had college degrees, only 43.4 percent of ethnic Mexicans had finished high school and only 6.2 percent had earned a college diploma. Obviously, inferior educational opportunities and egregiously high dropout rates have helped to produce and reproduce conditions of inequality among working-class ethnic Mexicans. Moreover, negative experiences in K–12 education, combined with the knowledge among ethnic Mexican children that the job market offers little hope for meaningful upward mobility in the future, have reinforced one another in a vicious circle that, in the view of one researcher, has encouraged these children "to learn not to learn." Other researchers have reinforced this disturbing finding, noting that student performance among ethnic Mexicans actually seems to *decline* the longer the students' families are in the United States.

The pernicious effects of these developments on Mexican immigrants and Mexican Americans can be seen in virtually all current gauges of socioeconomic status. Although, as noted previously, the average earnings of Mexican immigrants have slowly risen over time, the gap between their earnings relative to natives has not closed appreciably over the past thirty years. In fact, recent research indicates that this gap may be growing: Whereas in 1970 Mexican immigrant workers earned approximately 66 percent of what native workers earned, in 1989 the average earnings of Mexican immigrants had dropped to 39 percent of natives' earnings. Overall, the median income in 1990 for the total ethnic Mexican population ($22,477) was only about 57 percent that of non-Hispanic whites.

More ominously, recent data suggest that even native-born American citizens of Mexican descent appear to be losing ground relative to other Americans. For example, a recent study of third-generation Mexican Americans in California notes that while median education levels have slowly risen, the level of Mexican-American educational attainment relative to non-Hispanic whites has remained the same *since 1950*. Studies examining income trends in the period between 1959 and 1989 reinforce these findings, indicating that working-class Mexican-American citizens in southern California had not only not closed the earnings gap separating them from white workers but that they have also experienced significant slippage relative to whites. Whereas Mexican Americans earned about 81 percent of the median income of non-Hispanic white men in 1959, the figure had dropped to 74 percent in 1982 and to 61 percent by 1989. A recent study of the Los Angeles metropolitan area, where nearly 4 million people of Mexican descent now live, confirmed these findings. In the study, sociologist Vilma Ortiz notes that ''[native-born Mexican Americans] and blacks remain substantially behind whites in earnings, and more so . . . than in previous years. The recent changes in the region's labor market appear to have increased the racial bonus enjoyed by whites, reinforcing the preexisting barriers to [Mexican-American] progress.'' Other socioeconomic indicators tell a similar story. Between 1979 and 1987, poverty rates among ethnic Mexicans increased from about 20 percent to more than 25 percent and have held there since. Understandably, poverty rates for Mexican immigrants are even worse: In 1989, nearly 30 percent of all Mexican immigrants—and 40 percent of immigrant children—were living below the poverty line.

The combination of the continued influx of working-class Mexican immigrants, the erosion of educational opportunities, and the decline in stable, full-time high-paying jobs available to immigrants and their U.S.-born children raises some deeply troubling questions about the potential for the successful social, cultural, and political integration of a huge proportion of the ethnic Mexican population. Whereas previous generations of Mexican immigrants and their U.S.-born children were able gradually to improve their education levels and move from impoverished entry-level jobs to higher-paying, higher-status occupations, current trends indicate that this may not be as feasible in the future. Given the profound uncertainty of the socioeconomic outlook for ethnic Mexicans, it is not surprising that their political and cultural future in the United States appears ambiguous as well.

Although it is true that such developments as the passage of California's Proposition 187 and Proposition 209 (the latter, upheld by the U.S. Supreme Court, disallows most ''affirmative action'' programs in the state) have spurred record numbers of ethnic Mexicans to apply for naturalization and to register to vote, large numbers remain reluctant to become American citizens—and thus remain outside the formal civic culture of the United States. Indeed, a recently published study on identity formation seems to confirm this in other ways. Comparing ethnic Mexican high school students to their Cuban counterparts in Miami, researchers found that increasing numbers of Mexican immigrant and U.S.-born Mexican-American students continue to consider themselves ''Mexican'' (rather than ''Mexican American''), a development the authors have interpreted as yet another sign of growing alienation among ethnic Mexican youth. The recent move in Mexico to explore the possibility of granting dual citizenship to the vast expatriate community may eventually encourage more Mexicans to apply for U.S. citizenship, but for many this sense of alienation—together with the ease of movement between the two countries, strong family and community ties, and a fierce sense of nationalistic pride in Mexico—may lead a great many others to continue to live in the uneasy political and cultural spaces that exist between the formal national systems of the United States and Mexico.

With the current population of Mexico at 94 million and expected to double within thirty years, and the ethnic Mexican population of the United States conservatively estimated by the Census Bureau to grow to at least 29 million people in 2020 and to perhaps as many as 48 million in 2050, it is clear that the status of the Mexican-origin population will continue to remain a crucial issue in the United States for the foreseeable future. What that future holds will depend to a great degree on the ability of Americans to recognize the permanence of these demographic shifts and to devise methods to ensure that these new Americans are afforded every opportunity to become integrated into society as citizens and as fully vested members of their communities.

BIBLIOGRAPHIC REFERENCES

For general overviews of Mexican-American history, Carey McWilliams's classic *North from Mexico: The Spanish Speaking People of the United States*, rev. ed. (Westport, CT: Greenwood Press, 1990) remains a basic source. For a more recent and contentious political interpretation see Rodolfo Acuña's own classic, *Occupied America: A History of Chicanos*, 3rd ed. (New York: Harper and Row, 1988). Good overviews of Mexican immigration history are also presented in Lawrence A. Cardoso, *Mexican Emigration to the United States, 1897–1931* (Tucson: University of Arizona Press, 1980), and David G. Gutiérrez, ed., *Between Two Worlds: Mexican Immigrants in the United States* (Wilmington: Scholarly Resources Publishers, 1996).

Good contemporary treatments include Alejandro Portes and Robert L. Bach, *Latin Journey: Cuban and Mexican Immigrants in the United States* (Berkeley: University of California Press, 1985); Douglas Massey et al., *Return to Aztlán: The Social Process of International Migration from Western Mexico* (Berkeley: University of California Press, 1987); and Pierrette Hondagneu-Sotelo, *Gendered Transitions: Mexican Experiences of Immigration* (Berkeley: University of California Press, 1994). Basic historical and contemporary demographic data on ethnic Mexicans and immigration patterns can be found in Leo Grebler, Joan W. Moore, and Ralph C. Guzmán, *The Mexican American People: The Nation's Second Largest Minority* (New York: Free Press, 1970); A. J. Jaffe, Ruth M. Cullen, and Thomas D. Boswell, *The Changing Demography of Spanish Americans* (New York: Academic Press, 1980); Frank D. Bean and Marta Tienda, *The Hispanic Population of the United States* (New York: Russell Sage Foundation, 1987); and Alfred N. Garwood, ed., *Hispanic Americans: A Statistical Sourcebook*, 1993 ed. (Boulder, CO: Numbers and Concepts, 1993).

The scholarly literature in Mexican-American history has exploded over the past thirty years. For some of the best studies on the social and political history of Spanish and ethnic Mexican men and women in colonial northern New Spain and the early Mexican Republic, see Ramón A. Gutiérrez, *When Jesus Came, the Corn Mothers Went Away: Marriage, Sexuality and Power in Colonial New Mexico* (Stanford: Stanford University Press, 1991); David J. Weber, *The Mexican Frontier, 1821–1846: The American Southwest under Mexico* (Albuquerque: University of New Mexico Press, 1982); Douglas

Monroy, *Thrown Among Strangers: The Making of Mexican Culture in Frontier California* (Berkeley: University of California Press, 1990); and Lisbeth Haas, *Conquests and Historical Identities in California, 1769–1936* (Berkeley: University of California Press, 1995).

Some of the important works on the nineteenth and twentieth centuries include Tomás Almaguer, *Racial Fault Lines: The Historical Origins of White Supremacy in California* (Berkeley: University of California Press, 1994); Mario Barrera, *Race and Class in the Southwest: A Theory of Racial Inequality* (Notre Dame, IN: University of Notre Dame Press, 1979); Albert M. Camarillo, *Chicanos in a Changing Society: From Mexican Pueblos to American Barrios in Santa Barbara and Southern California* (Cambridge: Harvard University Press, 1979); Arnoldo De León, *The Tejano Community, 1836–1900* (Albuquerque: University of New Mexico Press, 1982); Mario T. Garcia, *Desert Immigrants: The Mexicans of El Paso, 1880–1920* (New Haven: Yale University Press, 1981); Richard Griswold del Castillo, *The Los Angeles Barrio, 1850–1890, a Social History* (Berkeley: University of California Press, 1979); David G. Gutierrez, *Walls and Mirrors: Mexican Americans, Mexican Immigrants, and the Politics of Ethnicity* (Berkeley: University of California Press, 1995); David Montejano, *Anglos and Mexicans in the Making of Texas, 1836–1986* (Austin: University of Texas Press, 1987); Leonard Pitt, *Decline of the Californios: A Social History of Spanish-Speaking Californians, 1846–1890* (Berkeley: University of California Press, 1966); Vicki L. Ruiz, *Cannery Women, Cannery Lives: Mexican Women, Unionization and the California Food Processing Industry, 1930–1950* (Albuquerque: University of New Mexico Press, 1987) and *From Out of the Shadows: A History of Mexican Women in the United States* (New York: Oxford, in press); George J. Sanchez, *Becoming Mexican American: Ethnicity, Culture, and Identity in Chicano Los Angeles, 1900–1945* (New York: Oxford, 1993); Carlos G. Vélez-Ibáñez, *Border Visions: Mexican Cultures in the Southwest United States* (Tucson: University of Arizona Press, 1996); and Vilma Ortiz, ''The Mexican–Origin Population: Permanent Working Class or Emerging Middle Class?'' in *Ethnic Los Angeles*, edited by Roger Waldinger and Mehdi Bozorgmehr (New York: Russell Sage Foundation, 1996), pp. 247–278.

For studies of communities outside the Southwest, see Erasmo Gamboa, *Mexican Labor and World War II: Braceros in the Pacific Northwest, 1942–1947* (Austin: University of Texas Press, 1990); Dennis Nodín Valdés, *Al Norte: Agricultural Workers in the Great Lakes Region, 1917–1970* (Austin: University of Texas Press, 1991); and Zaragoza Vargas, *Proletarians of the North: A History of Mexican Industrial Workers in Detroit and the Midwest, 1917–1933* (Berkeley: University of California Press, 1993).

The history of various campaigns of Mexican repatriation is recounted in Abraham Hoffman, *Unwanted Mexican Americans in the Great Depression: Repatriation Campaigns, 1929–1939* (Tucson: University of Arizona Press, 1974); Camille Guerin-González, *Mexican Workers and American Dreams: Immigration, Repatriation and California Farm Labor 1900–1939* (New Brunswick: Rutgers University Press, 1994); and Francisco Balderrama and Raymond Rodríguez, *Decade of Betrayal: Mexican Repatriation in the 1930s* (Albuquerque: University of New Mexico Press, 1995).

The definitive history of the Chicano movement has yet to be written, but for good initial efforts, see Mario Barrera, *Beyond Aztlán: Ethnic Autonomy in Comparative Perspective* (Notre Dame: University of Notre Dame Press, 1990); Richard Griswold del Castillo and Richard A. García, *César Chávez: A Triumphant Spirit* (Norman: University of Oklahoma Press, 1995); Carlos Muñoz, Jr., *Youth, Identity and Power: The Chicano*

Movement (London: Verso, 1980); Juan Gómez-Quiñones, *Chicano Politics: Reality and Promise, 1940–1990* (Albuquerque: University of New Mexico Press, 1990); and Francisco A. Rosales, *Chicano!: A History of the Mexican American Civil Rights Movement* (Houston: Arte Publico Press, 1996).

MIDDLE EASTERNERS AND NORTH AFRICANS

Linda S. Walbridge

The Middle East and North Africa are occupied by various ethnic groups, the most numerous being Arabs, Turks, Iranians, and Jews, with Arabs constituting the majority. Each of these groups, along with numerous other smaller ones, has its own language, the principal ones being Arabic, Turkish, Persian, and Hebrew. Outside of Israel, the dominant religion in the Middle East is Islam, particularly Sunni Islam. In Iran, Twelver Shi'i Islam is the dominant sect, although approximately half of the Iraqi population is Shi'i, with large minorities of Shi'a residing in Lebanon, Kuwait, and Bahrain. In Yemen, Zaidi Islam—a branch of Shi'i Islam—is the major sect. In Syria, President Assad is a member of the minority Alawi sect, an esoteric and syncretistic Islamic sect. Besides other minor Islamic sects, there are also a variety of old, Eastern-Rite Christian groups scattered throughout the region.

Christians predated Muslims in arriving in the United States, and their descendants constitute the majority of immigrants from this part of the world. Only since 1967, and even more so since 1975, have Muslims begun coming to America's shores in large numbers. For Muslims, the idea of coming to the world of the Christians was a frightening thought. But the pervasive instability of the Middle East region—the Arab-Israeli conflict, the Lebanese civil war, the Iranian revolution, the Persian Gulf War—have forced people to leave their homelands to seek safety and hope.

The diversity of peoples from the region could hardly be greater, so it should not be surprising that they lack a sense of solidarity. In a sense, writing about Middle Eastern immigrants is like writing about "European Christian immigrants." For example, Iranians, who constitute the largest number of immigrants to the United States from the Middle East, are Muslim, but the vast majority are not Arabic speakers nor are they ethnically Arab. Level of education, types of occupations, their views on the importance of sustaining religion and the type of religion to be sustained, and the desire to be accepted by the larger society

Table 7
Peoples from the Middle East and North Africa—Their Places of Origin

Lebanon/Syria	Iran
Christians	Shi'i Muslims
Maronites	Baha'is
Melkites	Jews
Greek Orthodox	Zoroastrians
Armenians	Kurds
Muslims	Armenians
Sunni	Assyrians
Shi'a (Shi'ites)	**Iraq**
Palestine (Israel)	Shi'i Muslims
Palestinians	Chaldean Christians
Yemen	Kurds
Zaidi Muslims	Assyrians
Shafi'i Sunni Muslims	**Turkey**
Egypt	Turks
Sunni Muslims	Kurds
Coptic Christians	

are only some of the issues that divide peoples coming from this region. Table 7, which lists Middle Eastern and North African groups, exemplifies the diversity but is not exhaustive.

It should also be noted that among the Muslim immigrants to the United States there are large numbers of non–Middle Easterners from such places as Pakistan, India, Indonesia, Malaysia, Central Asia, and Africa. In certain locales, immigrants from these countries may have an enormous impact on the development of Muslim communal life, and some of these communities are also joined by an increasing number of African-American Muslims.

Immigrants from the Middle East live under certain disadvantages in the United States, for the Middle East and the West have been in an adversarial position since Crusader times. Recent events have prompted reactions that have frequently resulted in media depictions of Middle Easterners as terrorists and a threat to democracy and world peace. Painfully aware of the negative portrayals and images of Islam as alien and dangerous, Middle Easterners are keenly sensitive about being "the other." Events fanning the flames of hostility for these immigrants have included the Iranian revolution of 1979; the bombing of the U.S. Army barracks in Beirut in 1982; animosities between the United States and Libya that resulted in the bombing of Libya in 1986; the Persian Gulf War of 1991; and the ever-present dispute between Arabs and Israelis.

Information about the various groups is often uneven and sketchy. Many are recent arrivals and frequently are reluctant to divulge information to social scientists and census takers, whereas those groups that are more concentrated and have formed organizations have tended to attract more scholarly attention. Also, because of the diversity, the focus of attention here will be more on some issues than on others. For example, the Yemenis tend to work in occupations with little security and with health risks. Iranians, on the other hand, who are far more likely to be employed in white-collar occupations, do not face these risks. Some issues cut across ethnic/religious lines. Religion—and whether or not to practice it and, if so, in what form it should be practiced—is a consideration in all of these groups. This does not mean that they all had been practicing their religion, only that religion and religious differences loom large in the Middle East. All groups likewise face generational problems, but not all face the same sorts of problems. For example, the majority of Yemenis coming to the United States have traditionally been devoutly religious and intent on preserving religious devotion in their children, whereas Iranians in the United States are predominantly secular and, in some cases, actually hostile toward religion; some actually fear their children becoming pious Muslims. In both cases, there is concern about a breach in communication between parents and children.

The two largest communities to be discussed are Arabs of Lebanese background, the group that has also been in the United States the longest, and Iranians. However, as we will see, even these two groups need to be subdivided. The essay is divided according to region or country.

THE LEVANT

The Levant refers to the eastern shore of the Mediterranean Sea, and the groups covered here who derive from that region are (leaving aside Israelis) primarily the Lebanese/Syrians, Palestinians, and Druze. Most of the earliest immigrants from the Middle East were what could be termed Lebanese, or Syrian, Christians. Under the Ottomans, Christians of the empire maintained some autonomy. Through silkworm production, a staple of the nineteenth-century Lebanese economy, they prospered, but their condition seriously deteriorated when this industry was ruined by periodic droughts, famine, and insect blights. In addition, there was severe overpopulation and communal violence. While these conditions were driving Lebanese Christians from their homeland, the promise of economic opportunity was attracting them to the United States. Between 1900 and 1910 about 5,000 people a year came to the United States, with the peak period being 1913–1914, when 9,000 arrived. They and their descendants constitute the largest group of people of Middle East descent in this country. They are divided into several sects, the largest being the Maronites, followers of St. Maron, a monk who lived in northern Syria at the end of the fourth century. In the twelfth century the Roman Catholic Church accepted the

Maronites into its fold, although they were permitted to retain their distinctive rituals and practices, which they continue to do in this country.

Other groups of Lebanese/Syrian Christians include various branches of the Eastern Orthodox churches as well as Melkites. The latter group had been Orthodox but became affiliated with the Roman Catholic Church, although they, too, retained their distinctive practices. Armenian Christians also came to the United States from Lebanon. However, most were latecomers to Lebanon, and their history is such that they are classified separately from other Lebanese Christian groups. Today there are, according to 1990 ancestry census data, 308,096 people of Armenian descent in the United States, but they have not all come from Lebanon, as they have long been dispersed throughout the Middle East.

Among this first wave of newcomers, pack peddling was adopted as the major, though hardly the sole, means of earning a living, while those who did not become peddlers often found themselves in the role of suppliers of goods for them. Women also joined in this occupation, along with their children. The entrepreneurial spirit for which the Lebanese are famous served this community well. A large proportion rapidly moved into the middle class. Not uncommonly, in a single generation members of this group became professionals, owners of their own businesses, and involved in other occupations requiring specialized skills. By the 1940s, as they took on the values of middle-class American culture, their prosperity gave them wider contact with American society. Moving to more prosperous suburbs, they dropped the outward symbols of their ethnicity and gave the appearance of being totally assimilated into the American melting pot. Having Anglicized their names and abandoned any distinctive clothing, they are quite indistinguishable from other Americans.

Meanwhile, during the nineteenth century, poverty and famine had affected Muslims as well as Christians in their Middle East homelands, but fear of a hostile reception in predominantly Christian America had discouraged most Muslims from seeking refuge in this country. However, around the beginning of the twentieth century, a small group of Muslims began to test the waters and traveled to America. Yet not until they were faced with mass starvation in the wake of World War I did they begin to migrate in significant numbers. Lebanese Muslims are divided into Sunni Muslims, the majority Muslim sect in the world, and Shi'i Muslims, who outnumber the Sunnis in Lebanon. The Shi'a, while in large numbers, where the lowest ranking of all religious groups in Lebanon, for the Sunnis had the advantage of sharing the same religious affiliation as their Ottoman Turkish overlords, giving them a relatively privileged position in society. The Shi'a, on the other hand, had no advantageous connections at all and were, consequently, in an inferior political and economic condition.

Early Lebanese/Syrian Muslim immigrants were mostly men and were frequently illiterate or poorly educated. They were more likely than Christians to gravitate to industrial cities, including Detroit, Pittsburgh, and Michigan City,

Indiana. While there were Islamic centers and standing buildings converted into mosques in most of these cities, Cedar Rapids has the distinction of being the first community to build from scratch a mosque with a minaret and dome, which it did in 1935. In the 1990s, Cedar Rapids has approximately 200 Muslims of Arab background, many of them Lebanese.

In the first half of this century, Lebanese Muslims, whether Shi'i or Sunni, joined up with other ethnic Muslims in urban areas, such as Palestinians and South Asians, to hold religious services together and even jointly to purchase buildings for Islamic centers or mosques. The fact that they were Muslims living as a minority among Christians was sufficient to bring them together, yet the Shi'a always maintained some sense of their distinctiveness, and it became far more pronounced after the mid-1970s as a consequence of the civil war in that country and the Iranian revolution. Also, in the 1980s Israel's control of a "safe zone" in the south of Lebanon had a major effect on immigration, for the population of that region is largely Shi'a. Because the Israelis wanted to reduce the population of the area, the United States cooperated in giving green cards to residents there, setting in motion a chain migration. According to 1990 census data, there were 394,180 people of Lebanese origin residing in the United States, 91,037 of them foreign-born. Lebanese Muslims and their descendants do now constitute the largest group of nonindigenous Muslims in the United States.

Prior to 1975 and the onset of the Lebanese civil war, the ethos in the United States among the Lebanese Muslims was to assimilate into American society. There is now far more emphasis on maintaining the Arabic language and Islamic codes of behavior and dress and preserving as much of the Lebanese culture as possible. Thus, up through much of the 1970s women did not cover their hair, but today women commonly cover their hair whenever they are out of doors. And the use of mosques has also changed. Until the mid-to late 1970s, parties and weddings were regularly held there in the United States, something unheard of in the Middle East. Today, such activities are either forbidden or frowned upon.

Although not highly educated, this later wave of immigrants, arriving often as families, has been relatively successful economically, their entrepreneurial skills serving them very well. The strength of the kinship network has allowed for the pooling of resources, enabling family members to purchase businesses and real estate and to employ family members to run enterprises. Some family members do attain professional-level positions. In fact, 451 immigrants admitted to this country in 1994 were listed as having a professional or technical specialty. The next largest occupational category for the Lebanese was "executive, administrative, and managerial," with 241 immigrants. This may represent a trend toward more highly educated Lebanese entering the United States.

In regions of the United States where Lebanese and other Shi'ites are in a minority, the Shi'ites generally follow Sunni customs. Their doctrine of *taqiyya* (dissimulation) allows them to hide the disputes that divide these two sects, and Shi'ites even frequent Sunni mosques. However, there are Shi'ite centers, the most prominent one being the Al-Khoei Foundation of Jamaica, Queens (New York), and Sunnis residing closeby will go there for Friday (*jum'a*) prayers and for holidays shared by Sunni and Shi'a alike, a satisfactory arrangement as long as the universal aspects of Islam are stressed during these religious services.

Where the Lebanese Shi'ites are found in large numbers, they tend to be active in establishing Islamic centers. This has been the case in such cities as Dearborn, Michigan (where the largest Arabic-speaking Muslim community in the United States resides), Toledo, Ohio, and Los Angeles, California. The tendency has been for the Iran- and Iraqi-trained clerics to expect increasing conformity with Islamic law and to emphasize those aspects of the religion peculiar to Shi'ism, although the community consists of people who are as religiously observant as ultra-Orthodox Jews and as lax in attention to law as Reform Jews. These differences have tended to produce tensions between immigrant cohorts. On the other hand, although there are glaring exceptions to the rule (as compared with Shi'ite Lebanese), the Sunni Lebanese—since their religious beliefs are those of the majority of Arabs—have generally had less difficulty in sharing their mosques with other national groups. For example, one may very well find Lebanese Sunnis with people of Palestinian origins.

Indeed, Lebanese Shi'ites in the United States have faced particular problems in terms of their relations with other immigrant Arab-Muslim groups as well as with the larger American society. For example, a mosque in the Los Angeles area, referred to as the "Lebanese mosque" by locals, is divided among those who are followers of Khomeini, those who follow Muhammad Fadlallah of Lebanon, and those who do not wish to have the mosque identified with any religious/political figure. Tensions can run high over many issues.

In particular, both the Iran–Iraq war and the 1991 Gulf War posed dilemmas for the Lebanese Shi'ites. Sympathy for Iraq came naturally for other Arab Muslims during the Iran–Iraq war, since Iraq is an Arabic country and Iran is not. Furthermore, the United States tended to support Iraq. However, the Lebanese Shi'a, though Arab, in reality share their specific religious beliefs with Iranians. And there is a large population of Shi'a in southern Iraq who have experienced extreme persecution at the hands of the Iraqi government. Therefore, during Desert Storm, although there was a general expression of disapproval that the United States would involve itself in a war against Arab peoples, there was also hope that the situation for the Shi'a in Iraq might be alleviated and that the Shi'i religion could be strengthened in the region. Regardless, though, of their personal political persuasions, the Lebanese Shi'a, like other Arabs in the United States, faced sporadic harassment during all of these Middle East crises.

The case of the Palestinians in the United States is a particularly interesting one. Although many have come to the United States from Lebanon, and although they may have spent their entire lives in that country, they do not consider themselves Lebanese. The 1990 census reported that there were 44,651 persons of Palestinian origin in the United States, 25,399 of them foreign-born. Like other early immigrants from Greater Syria, most of the early wave of Palestinians were Christian, but this changed after 1948, when the state of Israel was recognized and many Palestinians—both Christian and Muslim—found themselves homeless. By now, the children of the refugees from the 1948 war and those who had come before them to the United States have essentially assimilated into American society, for they rarely learned Arabic, generally had Americanized names, and were not raised with a strong sense of Palestinian nationalism. Although generally poor when they arrived here, they worked their way up the socioeconomic ladder and are now considered middle and upper middle class. For example, census data for 1990 indicate that 33.3 percent of Palestinians in the United States reported managerial and professional occupations, whereas 40.3 percent were in technical, sales, and administrative positions. Yet the Palestinian assimilation into American life, their economic condition, and their political attitudes have been affected by multiple forces.

After the 1967 Arab–Israeli war and the onset of the Lebanese civil war in 1975, the number of Palestinian immigrants increased substantially. The majority of this new wave of immigrants were Sunni Muslims. Of the more than 44,600 Palestinians in the United States in 1990, 11,487 had migrated between 1980 and 1990. These later immigrants constitute a separate group, not part of a chain migration linking them to earlier immigrants, for their migration was a result of the confiscation of their lands by the Israelis. Coming from traditional peasant backgrounds, these Palestinians sought an escape from political and economic hardships that have intensified since the 1967 war. Among them are those who had first migrated to Jordan and/or Lebanon. In 1970 many fled Jordan when war broke out between the Palestine Liberation Army and the Jordanian government. Most of these went to Lebanon, only to face the Lebanese civil war, triggering their migration to the United States. This latest wave of Palestinians has tended to settle as families in urban neighborhoods, attempting to preserve as much of their Palestinian culture as possible. They retain an ardent desire to return, should an independent Palestinian state be created.

Recent immigrants of both Lebanese and Palestinian Muslim background are rarely involved in local American politics, although they do understand that such involvement is important. Aside from their demanding work schedules, they are reluctant to involve themselves in a society that they consider to be hostile to Muslims. This has not, however, necessarily brought together Palestinians and Lebanese, for they became bitter enemies during the civil war, and the friction between the two has sometimes been carried over into community life in the United States.

In fact, the Palestinians themselves are a fragmented community. They are divided on the basis of the city or village of origin, religion, political orientation, and so on. Organizations, such as the American Ramallah Federation, consist of immigrants from particular villages and their offspring—in this case, the city of Ramallah—and they have been founded to perpetuate a sense of identity with a specific place of origin. Broader organizations have also been established, for example, the Palestine Congress of North America, which was quite active in the early 1980s but then suffered a setback after the Israeli expulsion of the Palestine Liberation Organization (PLO) from Beirut in 1982.

This community is also divided along lines of social class. Although Palestinians value education and, as the statistics above indicate, have established businesses and gone into the professions, there are still many who work in low-paying jobs or who are unemployed. Organizations have not brought together these various social classes. Those from the professional classes, such as academics, distance themselves from the activities of the average Palestinian in the United States. The educated classes with left-wing tendencies, interested in maintaining their Arab/Palestinian identity and downplaying Christian/Muslim differences, formed such organizations as the Arab-American University Graduates (AAUG) in the 1970s, the most prominent member being Professor Edward Said of Columbia University. For religiously oriented Muslim and/or working-class Palestinians, however, this organization lacks appeal.

The vast majority of Lebanese and Palestinian Muslims do share at least one concern: how to pass on their traditional cultural and religious values to their children in this society. While the majority of the latest wave of immigrants do not (at this time) show signs of becoming assimilated into American society, their children are strongly affected by American culture and tend to see themselves as Arab Americans. Families with daughters face severe problems in trying to maintain their family honor, which is tied to the girl's virginity. Tensions over the issues of dating can reach unbearable and even disastrous levels. For example, in Missouri recently, a Palestinian man had a teenage daughter who had an American boyfriend, a fact that led to bitter altercations between the daughter and her family. While her teachers and the school officials tried to persuade her family that she was a normal teenager, the father was being criticized by family members for being unable to control his daughter, who was seen as bringing disgrace on the family. In 1989, the father killed her and was given the death penalty but died in prison of natural causes. While the vast majority of Arabs in the United States distanced themselves from this case, they still placed a very high value on controlling a girl's sexuality.

Another group from the Levant that deserves mention is the Druze. Originating from Lebanon and Syria, they began immigrating to the United States to avoid conscription into the Ottoman army, the first immigrant having arrived in 1881. An offshoot of Ismaili Shi'ism, the Druze are a syncretistic sect in which some Islamic concepts and practices have survived, whereas others, which are completely anathema to mainstream Islam, have flourished.

The Druze religion has been difficult to keep alive in the United States for a variety of reasons. For example, in the early days of immigration, the elders forbade the women to leave the Middle East. Although there were restrictions on interfaith marriages, it was not uncommon for men to find Christian wives in America. The children of these marriages often attended Bible or church schools so that, at best, only the "tradition" of being Druze could be passed down. Even after women could come to the United States and establish Druze families, there was the problem of being able to transmit knowledge of the religion from generation to generation, since the traditional doctrines of the Druze religion are secret, with the sacred texts restricted to the initiates. In addition, they do not have formal structures for holding religious services, but there is an effort under way for reform so that the faith can be taught openly and made accessible. A cultural center established to meet the social, religious, and ritual needs of the community was opened in 1990 in Los Angeles, where the largest concentration of Druze can be found. In Seattle there is a Druze community of about 200 people. The first Druze organization was founded in that city, but it was not until the Lebanese civil war that more Druze began to migrate to Seattle.

Linked as this religion is to the Middle East, particularly to the mountains of Lebanon, it has been a particularly difficult tradition to sustain, and many Druze have simply converted to American Christian denominations. Again, though, events in the Middle East have had their effect on those residing in America, for the Lebanese civil war aroused a sense of loyalty, and the Druze in America were inspired to speak out against the Israeli invasion of Lebanon in 1982 and the events that followed. They have been increasingly active in such organizations as the Arab-American Anti-Discrimination Committee, the National Association of Arab Americans, and the Arab-American University Graduates. In the 1980s the Druze formed the American Druze Public Affairs Committee (ADPAC). It was ADPAC's aim to convince the U.S. government to listen to their perspective and to that of other Arabs. Casey Kasem, a popular television and radio personality of Druze background, is a prominent member of ADPAC and has been actively involved in the campaign to help Arab Americans gain respect and recognition in this country.

OUTSIDE THE LEVANT

This section covers a number of peoples originating in North Africa and in the region to the east of the Levant, including Yemenis, Egyptians, Iraqi, and Chaldeans.

While Muslims from the Levant had enough trouble envisioning life in a Christian country, they had had significantly more exposure to the West than had Arabs from outside the region, owing to the colonial presence of the French and the British in Lebanon and Palestine and the fact that American Christian missionaries were active in establishing educational institutions in the region. But for the peoples of the Arabian Peninsula, Europeans and Americans would have seemed very unfamiliar and alien indeed.

Thus, it is not surprising that Yemeni migration to the United States did not begin until later or that the number of immigrants from Yemen to the United States has been smaller than those from the Levant. There are accounts of a few stowaways who made their way on to ships after the opening of the Suez Canal in 1869. And there is evidence that Yemeni men dribbled into the United States through the 1920s. It was not, though, until 1965, that we begin to see any significant numbers in the United States. Most were from the central region of Yemen, which, before reunification, was known as North Yemen, although some also came from South Yemen. Yemenis from North Yemen are predominantly Zaidi Muslims, members of a branch of Shi'ism. In the south, the people belong to the Shafi'i legal school of Sunni Islam. The number of Yemenis arriving in the United States increased sharply during the mid-1970s, when political and economic conditions in their homeland deteriorated. Immigration and Naturalization Service (INS) data show, for example, that in the twenty-year period between 1976 and 1995, 17,057 were admitted into the United States, with a peak of 2,056 in 1992.

Most of the Yemenis who have come to the United States have been men of peasant background. They are generally seen as sojourners. Their intent has been to save money so that they can return home either to be reunited with their wives and children or to start a family and live on land purchased with the money they made on their jobs as farmworkers in California, factory workers in Detroit or Buffalo, or restaurant employees or owners in New York City. Wherever Yemenis live, or whatever type of labor they perform, they tend to remain very isolated from mainstream America, living in poor housing, often with several men sharing a small room or apartment. It is not unusual for men with different work schedules to use the same bed. Their poor living and difficult work conditions, such as carrying heavy loads and working long hours in the sun, leave them vulnerable to illness and injuries. They generally socialize only with other Yemenis. Of course, not all Yemenis remain so isolated or refrain from partaking of vices while residing in the United States, a fact that causes within-group tensions. The most flagrant violation of the code of correct behavior, though, is to refuse to send remittances back home to one's family.

But when the hope of being able to return to the homeland began to diminish, Yemenis increasingly found themselves remaining in this country and started bringing their wives and children with them or sending for them. At that point, one of their responses to life in the United States has been to increase their religious commitment, for settling in the United States has placed the additional burden on the men of trying to maintain their traditional family life in a secular, materialistic society. This they have attempted to do by secluding the women in their homes as much as possible. In Dearborn, Yemeni women are far less visible in public places than are Lebanese women. In southeast Dearborn, where there is a large Yemeni population—recognizable by the girls' colorful dresses and, often, men's traditional robes—coffeehouses, restaurants, and grocery stores are largely the domain of men. In the northeast part of Dearborn, dominated by Lebanese Shi'ites, there are no coffeehouses, only restaurants, where one finds both men and women. However, the grocery stores and other shops in that part of town are as much female as male spaces. In addition, notably with respect to the uses of the mosques, tensions between Yemenis and other

Arab Americans are not uncommon. The more assimilated Arab Americans view the Yemenis as backward and inferior, a view expressed even by very traditional Lebanese Shi'ites. However, there are occasions when Arab solidarity will come into play in this community, too, such as when there are demonstrations in support of Palestine.

As for Arabs from North Africa, it is only Egyptians who are in the United States in significant numbers. The 1990 census shows that there were 73,097 persons of Egyptian ancestry in the United States, with 69.2 percent of these being foreign-born. Nearly 46 percent of employed persons of Egyptian ancestry are in managerial and professional occupations, and 28.5 percent held technical, sales, and administrative positions. Unfortunately, it is not possible to differentiate Muslims from Christians in these census figures.

There is a large concentration of Egyptian Muslims in the part of Jersey City referred to as "Little Egypt," which centers on the as-Salam Mosque that gained notoriety after the February 26, 1993, bombing of the World Trade Center. The imam of the mosque was Sheikh 'Umar 'Abd al Rahman, who was charged with complicity in the assassination of President Sadat and who is now in prison in the United States for terrorist activity in this country. Egyptians are also relatively numerous in Manhattan. Meeting at area hotels for Friday prayers, an Egyptian group known as "The Islamic Society of Mid Manhattan's Uthman bin Affan Mosque" has reportedly solicited donations from the Muslim World League and foreign governments, as well as private individuals, in order to purchase a structure.

Algerians, Tunisians, and Moroccans are far more likely to migrate to Europe, particularly France, their former colonizer. Only Moroccans are listed in the U.S. census data. In 1990 there were 15,541 foreign-born Moroccans in the United States. A community of Moroccans resides in New York City, where the influence of dedicated, activist Moroccan Muslim leaders is still felt. They were largely responsible for building the second mosque in the city, the Islamic Mission of America for the Propagation of Islam and Defense of the Faith and the Faithful.

The latest group of Arabs to enter the United States in any significant numbers are the Iraqi refugees from the Gulf War. Between 1991, the year of the war, and 1994, 15,000 Iraqis came to the United States, with 13,009 classified as refugees. The 1990 census shows that there were 44,916 Iraqis in this country. Prior to the Gulf War, the Iraqi immigrants would have been from a variety of ethnic and religious groups. However, the newcomers are Shi'i Muslims from southern Iraq who came to this country via refugee camps in Saudi Arabia. Their towns and villages had been decimated by the Iraqi army following a revolt encouraged by the U.S. government but then abandoned by it. As Shi'ites, they were unwelcome by the Saudis, members of the puritanical Wahhabi Sunni sect founded in the eighteenth century.

The situation of the Iraqis is by far the most deplorable of all the groups. Many come from rural backgrounds and do not bring with them entrepreneurial or other skills that would make adjustment easier. Nor do they have the tradition of emigration that the Yemenis have. The majority speak only Arabic and, prior to their arrival in the United States, had lacked significant contact with the outside world. This group is largely dependent on government and other assistance and is isolated from other Arabic immigrant groups and from other Iraqi Shi'a. These other Iraqi Shi'a also live in exile from their homeland because of the policies of the Iraqi regime and the severe persecution they and their families have experienced, but they tend to be from the religious elite classes or closely associated with those classes. The relationship between these two groups of Iraqi émigrés is complex. In Iraq there would have only been formal (usually religious) contact between the two. In the United States, the religious leaders (*ulama*)—some more than others, of course—have reached out to what they refer to as "refugees," thereby making a clear distinction between themselves and their poorer countrymen.

But even the best-intentioned, most determined *ulama* express frustration at being unable to assist the refugees and are bewildered by the fact that the Lebanese Shi'ites have faired quite well in the United States, while these Iraqis show no sign of being able to be self-supporting, let alone prosperous. They also are frustrated over the social problems that the Iraqis have had in their new surroundings, not realizing that the traditional and rather rigid social structure that had shaped their lives is completely lacking in the United States. However, while the problems of the Iraqis may be more intense in this regard, the Arabic Community Center for Economic and Social Services (ACCESS) in Dearborn faces similar problems with all the Arabic immigrant groups. In fact, 34 percent of all visits to the center, according to a 1996 study published, are related to family crises having to do with, for example, financial problems, discipline of children, and desertion of a wife by a husband who has used the marriage to obtain a green card.

Iraqi parents share another problem with other Arabic immigrant groups: controlling the sexual behavior of daughters. In the fall of 1996 there was a well-publicized case in Lincoln, Nebraska, of an Iraqi refugee father of two girls in their early teens who married both daughters to Iraqi men in their late twenties. One of the girls ran away, was reported missing to the police, and was found with her boyfriend. The girl told the police that she did not wish to be married, and the police proceeded to arrest the father and the two men, with the husbands being charged with statutory rape because the girls were underage. The father was baffled by the reaction of the legal system and the public. Other Arab immigrants have legally married off their daughters as young as thirteen years of age by going to a state that has lower age limits.

The Iraqi refugees, brought here by the U.S. government, have been gravitating to urban areas with large Arab populations, such as the Detroit area, where the large concentration of Arabs means that they are at least in an environment where their native language is spoken and where some familiar cultural features can be found. However, there are cultural differences between the Lebanese

Shi'ites and the Iraqis that produce tensions. Although there are several mosques that Lebanese attend, it was deemed necessary to open a new Islamic center on the Detroit/Dearborn border to cater to the needs of the Iraqi refugees. To intensify the problems, the Iraqis fear that Saddam Hussein has planted infiltrators among them. Groups of Iraqi refugees are also found in other cities, such as Washington, D.C., San Diego, and Los Angeles, where they find themselves amidst a variety of other Muslim immigrants and refugees, many of them non-Arab, such as Afghan refugees. Some of these pray at the Shi'i mosque, while others join their Sunni brethren.

There are relatively few Sunni Iraqis in the United States. These are mainly people who came to this country for education or employment and do not form specific communities. However, among the Sunni immigrants from Iraq are Kurds. There is a fairly large concentration of Kurds—about 1,000—in San Diego. Even though they are fragmented along political lines, reportedly there is a plan to establish a Kurdistan Islamic Center to be funded by the Saudi Arabian embassy.

One other Iraqi group that has formed a distinctive nucleus is the Chaldeans, a Christian minority from northern Iraq that began migrating to this country in the early part of this century and has continued to do so ever since. As with the Lebanese, their strong extended kinship network has benefited them, so that they have tended to prosper through retail business. A large community of Chaldeans resides in Southfield, a suburb of Detroit. Their ancestral language is not Arabic but Aramaic, although those raised in Iraq needed to learn Arabic to carry out their daily activities. They share the Aramaic language with two other Middle Eastern Christian communities: the Nestorians, who have a community in Chicago, and Protestant immigrants of Assyrian background, such as those living in Turlock, California. Americans, unfamiliar with distinctions among Middle Eastern groups, associate Chaldeans with Arabs, leaving Chaldeans open to the same sorts of discrimination that other Middle Eastern groups experience, especially during times of crisis.

Even in communities where there are large numbers of Muslims from non-Arab countries, such as Indonesia, Pakistan, India, Bangladesh, and Afghanistan, Arabs are still likely to be very visible. Because of the increased number of Arab students in the United States, there has been a steady "Arabization" of the Muslim Students Association, which was founded in 1963 but reformulated in 1975 to address the changing priorities of Muslims residing in the United States. The focus shifted to a more assertive approach to spreading Islam and more effort in establishing institutions. And yet Shi'ite Arabs broke away from the Muslim Student Association in the 1980s and formed their own organization, the Muslim Group. Although the Islamic Society of North America (ISNA)—an organization that grew out of the Muslim Student Association—prides itself on its inclusivity and appeal to mainstream Muslims in America, it is very much dominated by immigrant Arab Muslims and particularly Sunnis.

In mosques founded by other immigrant groups, Arabs can become the preponderant group. For example, they make up half of the congregants at the Masjid Fatima, a mosque founded by Pakistani taxi drivers and mechanics in 1987 in Queens. Moreover, Arab regimes often finance mosques. It was largely Persian Gulf, and particularly Kuwaiti, money that paid for Manhattan's huge mosque, the Islamic Cultural Center at Third Avenue and 96th Street, which officially opened with 'Id al-Fitr services on April 15, 1991. As mentioned regarding the planned Kurdistan Islamic Center, Saudi Arabian foundations and individuals also contribute money to Islamic organizations in the United States.

In general, the later waves of Arab Muslim immigrants are more religiously observant than earlier immigrants. This can be attributed to a few factors. First, earlier immigrants from rural areas lived according to their cultural traditions and were not religiously sophisticated. They knew only the essentials of their religion, so that avoiding pork and praying occasionally constituted for them the practice of religion. In the 1960s there had been a surge in the number of students coming to study in the United States, and they had been influenced by a number of ideologies that were not compatible with strict religious observance. It has only been since the 1970s that large numbers of Middle East and North African Muslim immigrants have seen Islam as being the principal source of inspiration and guidance for their private and communal lives.

In this respect, it should be noted that "religiously observant" does not necessarily mean politically radical. The majority of Arab Muslims in the United States are outspoken about the fact that they do not wish to involve politics in their religious lives. Whatever the ethnic or sectarian group, these immigrant Muslims are all concerned that their religion be transmitted to their children. A key element in sustaining this religion is the Arabic language, particularly the classical form of the language, since the holy book, the Qur'an, is written in this language. Along with mosques, there has been a proliferation of Islamic schools—either for full-time or after-school study—where Arabic is taught. Of course, as with any other group, the spoken form of the language is important in simply keeping alive the sense of peoplehood and the traditions of the group. Census data show that in 1990 Arabic was spoken in the home by 355,150 persons.

IRAN

Iranians, the majority of whom speak Persian, are ethnically and culturally distinct from Arabs. According to INS records, about 35,000 immigrants came to the United States from Iran between 1950 and 1977. During this time, Iran was sending its young people here to study with the expectation that they would return to Iran to help in the country's development. Yet many of these students were dismayed that political freedom was not matching the economic advances being achieved in their country. The late 1970s saw increasing protests by Iranian students. In the years immediately before the Iranian revolution of 1979, the numbers of Iranians seeking admission to the United States had already begun to rise dramatically, many of them students present in the United States.

Following the overthrow of the shah in 1979, a dramatic change in immigration patterns occurred. With the closure of the American embassy in Tehran in 1980 in the wake of the hostage crisis, U.S. relations with Iran deteriorated. While travel between the two countries came to a virtual standstill, Iranians continued to gain admission to the United States, primarily as refugees or as immediate relatives of Iranians who were already U.S. citizens. Between 1981 and 1990, 154,000 Iranians entered the country. And, indicative of recent patterns, of the 68,266 admitted between 1991 and 1995, 44 percent had been living in third countries. Iranians today constitute the largest number of Middle East immigrants and continue to come in significant numbers. Thus, in 1994–1995, 20,623 Iranians entered the United States, whereas the next largest group, the Lebanese, accounted for only 8,203.

Many of those who fled the new regime were among the Iranian elite occupational classes and mostly from secular middle- and upper-middle-class families—and some were extremely prosperous. On the other hand, while the majority of destitute Iranians went to border countries, such as Pakistan and Turkey, there are Iranians who also came to the United States with close to no resources. For those once accustomed to wealth, adjustment to the United States can be difficult. For example, women who left behind a life of affluence in Iran often lack household skills, accustomed as they were to cooks and servants.

Ninety-eight percent of Iranians are Shi'ite, yet, as in so many other instances, it is the minority groups who are generally in need of refuge when civil war or revolution breaks out. Therefore, although the majority of the Iranian immigrants who left Iran during the time of the revolution are Shi'i Muslims—at least nominally—significant numbers of Jews, Zoroastrians, Baha'is, Armenian and Assyrian Christians, and, to a lesser extent, Kurds likewise migrated to the United States. The largest concentration of Iranians is in the Los Angeles area, but sizable numbers also reside in the greater New York area, San Diego, Washington, D.C., Chicago, Houston, Texas, and other urban centers.

In 1990, behind only the Asian Indians and Taiwanese, foreign-born Iranians were the most well-educated immigrant group in the United States, even though there is considerable variation among the diverse ethnic/religious groups that came out of Iran. Overall, the percentage of such Iranians holding a bachelor's or an advanced degree was over 50 percent. In terms of occupation, Iranians of all groups are active in the construction business and are often self-employed. Indeed, in 1990 only Koreans and Greeks had higher percentages of foreign-born men and women who were self-employed. However, among the Iranians, the Jews and Armenians are the most entrepreneurial, while Baha'is are often employed in health and legal services.

In the United States, one of the features that distinguishes the Muslim Iranian population from other groups of Muslim immigrants discussed thus far is the secular character of their communal life. The Iranians are eager to preserve their language, arts, and customs but, bitter over the takeover of Iran by clergy, reject Islam, at least as practiced in Iran today. They are likely to have lavish Naw Ruz celebrations (the ancient Persian New Year, which falls on the first day of spring) and events centering on Persian music and food, while completely ignoring strictly Islamic holidays. In Los Angeles, nightclubs and parties with alcohol and dancing constitute a conspicuous part of Iranian social life, cutting a sharp contrast with the minority of Shi'i Iranians who are actively religious and, in some cases, pro-Islamic Republic. Tensions between the secularists and the prorevolution communities can become virulent at times. The secularist, anti-Khomeini Iranians appear determined not to let the pro-Khomeinists have the upper hand in the United States and, for instance, control the active Iranian media in this country.

Nevertheless, the majority of Iranian immigrants are deeply concerned with sustaining their Iranian (as opposed to their Muslim) identity in a society that strongly encourages assimilation. Organizations, such as the Society for the Promotion of Iranian Culture, bring together a cross section of Iranians in terms of ethnic/religious identity. One of their main issues is preserving the Persian language, for census data in 1990 suggested that the Persian language was "usually" spoken in the home by 201,900 people. In addition, while those who were raised with some traditional religious values are eager, as a result of the revolution, to distance themselves from the symbols of strict Shi'i Islam, they still have a desire for at least a quasi-religious element to the major rites of passage: weddings and funerals. For such occasions it is common to have a prominent member of the community—preferably one with knowledge of religion, though not a member of the *ulama*— to preside at such functions.

Some Iranians of Shi'i background, nonetheless, want more than simply traditional weddings. They wish to have a richer religious life, but one devoid of stern religious injunctions. And they are especially concerned with instilling spiritual values in their children. In Los Angeles, a society called IMAN (Iranian Muslim Association of North America), consisting of 300 to 400 people, has been meeting, and it has initiated the building of the Iranian Muslim Community Center in West Los Angeles, a building for prayer as well as for seminars, lectures, classes, and national and religious celebrations. To some extent, these activities have been initiated in response to parents' concerns that their children have not been raised with any religious or spiritual dimension to their lives and are facing their own challenges in establishing an identity.

The IMAN activities differ markedly from those of Shi'i Iranians who adhere to a stricter model of Shi'ism. Because of their relatively smaller numbers, those Iranians who are actively observant of religious laws often have to rely on other ethnic Shi'i, such as Arabs and Pakistanis, to establish mosques and to lead religious observances. In Los Angeles, for example, two mosques that have been opened to cater to the needs of observant Shi'i, including Iranians, were founded by *ulama* from Iraq. The majority of Iranians who attend these mosques, though, are not necessarily supporters of the Islamic Republic of Iran. In fact, actively pro–Islamic Republic Iranians have tended to be the most isolated of all categories of Iranians in the United States.

The experiences of Iranian Baha'is in the United States have been, in some respects, notably different from those of Shi'i Iranians. While the Baha'i Faith grew out of Shi'ism, the Baha'is in Iran became a very distinct and separate religious community of about 300,000. A persecuted minority, they formed a close-knit community with an active administration and an array of social and educational activities. In coming to the United States, they found some continuity with their past, since the Baha'i Faith had grown substantially among Americans in the late 1960s and early 1970s. Hence, there was an established community in existence here. A committee of the National Spiritual Assembly of the Baha'is of the United States was formed to assist these refugees and to help ease the Iranian Baha'is into life in the United States. While those who chose to live in large metropolitan areas, particularly Los Angeles, still interact mostly with other Iranian Baha'is, those who live in smaller towns and cities socialize with the usual spectrum of Baha'is found in the United States. The Iranian Baha'is, though, like their less religious countrymen, are very attached to the cultural traditions of their homeland and are also likely to be active in secular Iranian activities as well as specifically Baha'i ones.

Zoroastrianism, the ancient Persian religion, now has only about 30,000 adherents in Iran. Although they did not face the active persecution that the Baha'is have suffered, the Islamic government in Iran attempted to suppress their holidays and festivals. These Iranian Zoroastrians joined the Parsis (Indian Zoroastrians) in the Los Angeles area. Since the Iranians are far more liberal than the orthodox Parsis and since they are also divided culturally from them, disputes between the two groups can become heated, especially over issues regarding certain traditional religious practices. Unlike Islam and the Baha'i Faith, Zoroastrianism is not a missionary religion, and there is a dispute in the community over whether a person who has not been born into Zoroastrianism can ever be a Zoroastrian. Thus, this is a religious community that ultimately faces the possibility of extinction in the United States.

Thousands of Armenian Christian Iranians, a prosperous minority that fared well under the Pahlavi regime, decided to immigrate to the United States after the revolution. Armenians have been economically successful, tending to cluster in affluent Los Angeles suburbs. Assyrians comprise another group that transcends national boundaries, being found principally in Iran and Iraq. In the United States their largest concentration is in Chicago. The 1990 ancestry census data indicated that there were 51,765 Assyrians in this country. They have been noted as being very eager to assimilate into American society, partially because they had a strong network already based in the United States from an earlier immigration period and partially because their form of Christianity is so similar to other Christian traditions found in this country.

Finally, Iranian Kurds are ethnically, culturally, and linguistically distinct from other Iranians. Those from Iran have suffered under both the Pahlavi regime and the Islamic Republic. They are predominantly Sunnis, though Shi'i Muslims as well as Jews are among their numbers. Although Kurds have their own language, the dialects that divide Iraqi, Turkish, Iranian, and Syrian Kurds have forced them to adopt English when socializing in the United States. They also tend to be factionalized by the political loyalties that divided them in their homelands.

TURKEY

Turks are far fewer in number than Arabs and Iranians, with only 23,164 having entered the country between 1985 and 1995. They have settled in various urban areas in the United States, such as Rochester, New York, and Detroit. About 200 to 300 Turkish families immigrated in the late 1960s to work in the Rochester men's clothing industry. Initially, they worshiped with other Muslims—Iranians, Palestinians, Egyptians, African Americans, and Pakistanis—in a room at the University of Rochester's Interfaith Chapel, but in 1980 they established their own mosque. There, the imam is Turkish, and administrative and social meetings are conducted in Turkish, for many of the older members of the Turkish community do not speak English. Religious taxes (*zakat*) are collected for support of projects in Turkey. The Turks in Rochester have been more exclusive than other Muslims, and they also tend not to speak out on political and social issues, as do the Arabs in the community.

The Detroit/Dearborn Turks present a different picture. In Detroit there had been a small community of Turks—mostly single men—but their numbers increased after World War II when men came from Turkey to study engineering or medicine. Frequently, they did not return to their homeland but remained here and established families. These better-educated immigrants were hardly aware of the older Turkish community and did not celebrate holidays with them at the South Dearborn Turkish Crescent coffeehouse, which closed in 1968. While this later wave of immigrants has not been uniform in terms of social class, they do tend to reflect the more secular, nationalistic atmosphere that took hold of Turkey after World War I and that has only been seriously challenged in recent years.

SUMMARY

Immigrants to the United States from the Middle East are extremely diverse in their religious, ethnic, and linguistic backgrounds. While the majority of Middle Easterners, outside of the State of Israel, are Sunni Muslims, the Shi'i Muslims and non-Muslims are overrepresented in the U.S. population. However, Eastern-Rite Christians, many of whom have become assimilated into American life, predated Muslims in arriving in the United States. Their descendants constitute the majority of immigrants from this part of the world, many of whom have become highly successful in all arenas of life. Such persons as James

Abourezk, U.S. senator from South Dakota in the 1970s, Health and Human Services Secretary Donna Shalala, and Michigan Senator Spencer Abraham are among those who have advanced in the political arena.

While Muslims began to migrate to the United States in the early part of this century, they have only come in substantial numbers since 1967 and even more so since 1975. Immigration patterns reflect the degree and specific location of warfare and instability in the Middle East, and tensions do exist between pre-1967 immigrants and later ones. Earlier immigrants tended to assimilate into American society, to be less religiously observant, and to avoid public involvement in politics. Later immigrants have been far more open about both their religious convictions and their political allegiances. They are also more desirous of maintaining the Arabic language and other markers of their cultural identity.

Of all Middle Eastern countries, Iran has sent the most immigrants and refugees to this country. Culturally and linguistically distinct from Arabs and other Middle Eastern ethnic groups, they rarely, if ever, socialize or join organizations with those of non-Iranian background. Because the majority of Iranians came to the United States as a result of persecution by the new regime or their dislike of it, they have eschewed religious life, especially as reflected in the new government initiated by Ayatollah Khomeini. Hence, the major division in this community is between the majority who are secularists and the pro-Khomeini minority.

Owing to the multiple sources of identity—region of the world, ethnicity, language, religion, nationality, and political/religious ideology—it is extremely difficult to find a common denominator that could unite immigrants from the Middle East. A brief expression of common cause may arise when they are discriminated against as a group, but this has never been sufficient to maintain any solidarity. In the final analysis, the divisions are also accentuated by the fact that the states from which these immigrants hail have a history of being at war (or on poor relations) with each other, and those animosities were not left in the homelands.

BIBLIOGRAPHIC REFERENCES

Good sources for the early Arab immigrants to the United States are Alixa Naff's *Becoming American: The Early Arab American Experience* (Carbondale: Southern Illinois University Press, 1985) and Gregory Orfalea's *Before the Flames: A Quest for the History of Arab Americans* (Austin: University of Texas Press, 1988). The focus in these books is largely on the assimilation process of Christian Arabs.

Abdo Elkholy's *The Arab Muslims in the United States* (New Haven, CT: College and University Press, 1966) broke new ground by focusing specifically on the development of Muslim Arab communities. Yvonne Yazbeck Haddad and Jane Idleman Smith have edited a very useful volume entitled *Muslim Communities in North America* (Albany: SUNY Press, 1994). The diversity of Muslims in North America is well reflected in its many articles. Rather than focus on a particular ethnic or sectarian group, most describe the Islamic activities in particular American cities. Haddad and Idleman have also written a book (*Mission to America* [Gainesville: Florida University Press, 1993]) about several nonmainstream Islamic communities that either have originated in the United States or have been transplanted here. Information on the Druze community comes from this source.

A recently published volume of articles addressing a wide range of issues facing Muslims of Middle East background in the United States is entitled *Family and Gender among American Muslims*, edited by Barbara C. Aswad and Barbara Bilge (Philadelphia: Temple University Press, 1996). Information about social and economic problems facing Arab immigrants can be found in this volume. Another collection of articles dealing with challenges facing Arab Muslims and Christians in the United States is *The Development of Arab-American Identity*, edited by Ernest McCarus (Ann Arbor: University of Michigan Press, 1994). Particularly useful in this volume are discussions about Palestinian women, Arab stereotypes in the American media, and violence toward Arabs in the United States. Issues that Muslim families face in adapting their religious life to American and Canadian societies are discussed in Earle H. Waugh et al., eds, *Muslim Families in North America* (Edmonton: University of Alberta Press, 1991).

An older collection of articles on Arab Americans, but one that is still useful, is *Arabic Speaking Communities in American Cities*, edited by Barbara C. Aswad (New York: Center for Migration Studies of New York, Inc., 1980 [1974]), where, among other things, information about Chaldeans can be found. Somewhat more updated information about the Detroit Arab communities can be found in *Arabs in the New World*, edited by Sameer Y. Abraham and Nabeel Abraham (Detroit: Wayne State University Press, 1983). A book devoted to the full range of the Arabic language in this country, including the way in which it is changing under the influence of English, how it is being maintained in homes and mosques, and the methods used for teaching Arabic, and so on, is *The Arabic Language in America*, edited by Aleya Rouchdy (Detroit: Wayne State University Press, 1992).

An excellent compilation of articles about Yemeni migration, entitled *Sojourners and Settlers: The Yemeni Immigrant Experience*, edited by Jonathan Friedlander (Berkeley: University of California, 1988), includes material about the Yemeni experience in California and New York. The photography in this book is especially compelling. This book covers a wide spectrum of issues relating to the Yemeni experience in America, as well as background information about conditions in Yemen itself. Nabeel Abraham's chapter, "The Yemeni Immigrant Community of Detroit: Background, Emigration, and Community Life," in *Arabs in the New World*, edited by Sameer Y. and Nabeel Abraham (Detroit: Wayne State University Press, 1983), pp. 110–134, is also an important contribution to understanding the Yemenis in this country, as is Shalom Staub's *Yemenis in New York City* (Philadelphia: Balch Institute Press, 1989). *Iranian Refugees and Exiles since Khomeini*, edited by Asghar Fathi (Cost Mesa, CA: Mazda Press, 1991), includes articles specifically related to the lives of Iranians in North America. *Irangeles*, edited by Ron Kelley and coedited by Jonathan Frielander and Anita Colby (Berkeley: University of California Press, 1993), is based on the same style as *The Yemeni Immigrant Experience*. It is an excellent and comprehensive look at the lives of Iranians of various backgrounds in the Los Angeles area and is enhanced by many wonderful photographs. Finally, *Without Forgetting the Imam: Lebanese Shi'ism in an American Community*, by Linda S. Walbridge (Detroit: Wayne State University Press, 1996), is an ethnographic account of the religious life of the Lebanese Shi'i community in Dearborn, Michigan.

MORMONS

Steven Epperson

To denominate the members of a church with an international missionary force of 50,000, operating in 146 nations and territories, with a majority of its population residing outside the United States—and with more than 400 different ethnic/foreign-language congregations within the United States alone—as comprising an American ethnic group may seem more than a little strange. To a large majority of its members, the category would appear foreign to their own self-description. Defining the Mormon community is a well-known conundrum to historians and social scientists. Their various definitions will vex anyone who would sum up this tradition and its adherents primarily in ethnic terms. Sidney Ahlstrom's foray into nomenclature is a prime and honest example. In attempting to define Mormonism, he wrote: "One cannot even be sure if the object of our consideration is a sect, a mystery cult, a new religion, a church, a people, a nation, or an American subculture; indeed, at different times and places it is all of these." Recently, however, descriptions that stress the ethnicity of the Mormon community and that identify Mormons as an authentic American ethnic group have become more common. The inclusion of an essay on Mormons in the 1980 *Harvard Encyclopedia of American Ethnic Groups*, written by Dean May, is a noteworthy example of this trend. Both before and since May's essay, a number of distinguished historians, geographers, and other social scientists have written important studies of Mormonism in which ethnicity served as an illuminating heuristic category. The reasons for this trend may have more to do with an American fin-de-siècle preoccupation with identity politics than with the enduring traits of ethnicity.

The overarching argument of this essay is that while once quite accurate, descriptions of the Mormon community as an American ethnic group will become increasingly ill-fitting. For more than a century after the founding of their religious community, Mormons came to possess many of the attributes of ethnicity. They defined themselves as a covenant people and were perceived by others as a separate, even sinister, population. Mormons shared a territorial homeland, myths of origins and migrations, and particular cultural traits, including identities reinforced by kinship, discourse, theological claims, and liturgical practices. From the 1820s until well into the first decades of the twentieth century, they lived virtually unto themselves. According to Thomas O'Dea, Mormons "came closer to evolving a genuine, locally and independently conceived ethnicity . . . on this continent than did any other comparable group."

However, the very traits once deemed essential for defining the distinctiveness of the Mormon community are undergoing fundamental change. A "gathered" people are dispersing throughout the country; a pariah community is now dubbed the "quintessential embodiment" of "mainstream American culture"; dramatic growth by proselytization outside the United States (421 percent in Latin America from 1980 to 1990, for example) swells a once homogeneous community of largely British and Scandinavian descent with multiethnic converts; and changes in theology are making the public discourse of the faith more congruent with evangelical Christian scruples. In sum, an antebellum millenarian religious sect that became an "emerging nation" now strives to attain respectability as a worldwide church.

And yet Mormon church elites who once pursued the erosion of a number of traditional boundaries separating Mormons from "Gentiles" as a matter of policy from the 1910s to the 1960s have also recently led a program of "retrenchment," which traffics portentously in the emblems of ethnicity. Whether first- and second-generation Mormons who reside outside of the United States will assent to and mold their identities to conform with the traits prescribed by the appeal to etḥnicity embedded in programmatic retrenchment remains to be seen. In the long run, in spite of the extraordinary authority church leaders wield in their relations with church rank and file, the prospects of success for appeals to ethnicity seem doubtful. These new church members and their children share neither an American westward pioneering heritage nor an effusive allegiance to American exceptionalism nor the kinship networks of "birthright" Mormons of British and Scandinavian descent who preside overwhelmingly in the Mormon Church hierarchy and staff its bureaucracies. The universalizing thrust of its missionary efforts, the strong and steady growth of its population base outside of the United States and among people of non-European descent residing in this country, and the authority of the Mormon scriptural canon—which enjoins neither the creation nor maintenance of a narrowly ethnic community—are auguries of a multiethnic church.

MIGRATION, SETTLEMENT, AND THE PROCESS OF ADJUSTMENT

Tens of thousands of individuals forged an emergent Mormon ethnic identity in the nineteenth century by conversion to the beliefs and practices of their "restored" gospel, by their subsequent experience of migration and community building on the American frontier, and by developing new ideals, institutions, and group sentiments, which they then passed on intact from one generation to another in the face of extraordinary opposition.

The ecclesial-theological claims of Joseph Smith may have been ridiculed along with the credulity of his followers, but in the sectarian hurly-burly of antebellum American culture, the new religious movement would have been grudgingly tolerated but for one key doctrine, what Mormons called ''the gathering.'' Mormons in the nineteenth century believed in the imminent Second Coming of Christ and the establishment of a millennial kingdom of righteousness on earth through the joint efforts of divine powers and the labors of the ''Saints.'' Joseph Smith revealed that the true believers in Christ and his gospel must prepare for these events by gathering out from ''Babylon'' and settling as religious communities of anticipation within a prophetically designated, sanctified territory called ''Zion.''

It was the exclusionist, geopolitical practices of the nineteenth-century Mormons that proved intolerable to their neighbors and to local and federal governments. For in their attempts to create a distinctive territorial enclave, Mormons encountered the ''relentless pressures of American imperialism,'' which, as D. W. Meinig observed, denied absolutely ''the creation or formal recognition of any kind of ethnic territorial units'' within the American state. But that was precisely the aim of the Mormon gathering: the creation of economically and socially self-sufficient, self-governing religious communities. To establish their ''Zion'' on the American frontier, Mormon converts hurled themselves into a nearly perpetual state of migration, settlement, and conflict from 1830 to 1900.

Mormon migration and settlement began with the founding of three congregations of about 70 people in New York State who believed in the teachings, prophetic claims, and authority of Joseph Smith. They were kinsfolk, neighbors, and friends and, like most Mormons through the 1840s, of British descent. From these three congregations in 1830, the Mormon community grew rapidly into a thriving sect of over 20,000 by 1841. By that time, Mormon missionaries had preached in every state in America, in many parts of eastern Canada, and in Great Britain. To build Zion, converts flocked to sites designated by Joseph Smith in eastern Ohio and western counties in Missouri and Illinois. Between 1831 and 1837, over 2,000 Mormons settled in Ohio. Before their expulsion from town sites in Missouri in the winter of 1838–1839, Mormons numbered over 8,000; and in western Illinois, by 1846 they had built a thriving Mississippi River city called Nauvoo and outlying farming settlements, with a total population of over 20,000.

Under centralized church authority, they laid out and settled in small urban townships that became characteristic of Mormon settlements throughout the 1800s. Typically, their towns had wide streets oriented in grid fashion to the four cardinal directions, individual family dwellings set back from the street on lots sufficiently large to accommodate kitchen gardens, an orchard, outbuildings, and a small number of livestock. Businesses and workshops were dispersed throughout the town, which was ringed about by a wide green belt for those who farmed. Based roughly on an ideal city plan sketched by Smith in 1834, these settlements offered alternatives to congested American and British urban and industrial centers and the isolation of scattered homesteading. They facilitated the orderly social interaction and ecclesiastical oversight of individual behavior prized by nineteenth-century Mormon leaders.

In contrast to this orderly vision for group life, Mormons encountered disorder and conflict in their relations with neighboring populations through the mid-1840s. "Gentile" citizens objected strenuously to Mormon attempts to control both territory and the character of the society under their jurisdiction. They viewed Mormon sectarian separation as clannish and unrepublican; and Mormon fraternization with Native American tribes was roundly condemned as consorting with the nation's implacable foes. In sum, Mormon ideology and practices appeared so alien that state and local officials resorted to the strategy of forced expulsion (one usually focused on Native Americans). The entire Mormon population of Missouri was uprooted by state decree, and in 1846, more than 20,000 Mormons were forced from homes and farms and sent off on an epic migration to the remote mountain valleys of the Great Basin in what was then Mexican territory.

The effects of persecution and forced migrations had an enormous impact on the development of a distinctive Mormon identity. They fostered a sectarian, binary worldview wherein the "Saints" formed cohesive group solidarities ranged against a demonized outside world. They alienated Mormons from predominant American cultures and institutions for decades. The violence and movement of the 1830s and 1840s helped Mormons to create a powerful mythic history. As a biblically centered, millenarian sect, they read the experiences of settlement, expulsion, and relocation through the narrative template of scripture: a garden lost, a people in exile, a promised homeland, epic migration, kingdom building, and the hope of redemption. The imaginative analogies Mormons drew to biblical Israel embraced not only narrative constructs but also the liturgical and social institutions of temple worship, prophetic and priestly offices, and a mythic anthropology that located Mormon converts among the dispersed remnants of Israel. Indeed, by calling themselves the descendants of "Ephraim" and the indigenous American peoples "Manasseh," Mormons linked the heritage and future of the exiled and marginalized in this country together, connected them with those of the Jewish people, and claimed a central redemptive role for all three "tribes" in the imminent messianic/millennial age when "the first would be last, the last first." Beset from without and constructing identity from within together fostered strong communal ties of rhetoric and kinship and, between 1846 and 1900, enabled Mormons to build a commonwealth and a near ethnicity, aspects of which persist to the present.

Over a span of forty years, an extraordinary variety of people hailing from America's many regions, British metropolitan and imperial domains, Scandinavia, continental Europe, and the Ottoman Middle East congregated in the

Great Basin to create Zion yet again. What they produced, Meinig concluded, was a "homeland . . . with a homogeneity, unity, order, and self-consciousness unequaled in any other American region." Before the centrally orchestrated colonization of this region came to an end, more than 150,000 Mormon settlers had established nearly 700 towns, villages, and way stations stretching from southern Alberta to northern Mexico, and from western Colorado to San Bernardino, California.

More than 80,000 Mormon converts emigrated from Europe to participate in settlement efforts. The vast majority came from Great Britain (43,346 between 1840 and 1887) and Scandinavian countries (30,000 from 1850 to 1900). Most British converts were urban artisans, mechanics, and industrial laborers, who subsequently tended to settle in the growing city centers of northern Utah. By contrast, Scandinavian proselytes were drawn largely from rural and agrarian backgrounds, and they pioneered and farmed the landscapes of central and far northern Utah and southern Idaho. By 1886, more than a third of the population of Utah was foreign-born.

For these people, "the gathering to Zion" began in the ocean ports of Europe, not the trail heads along the Missouri River. Church immigration agents organized and supervised 333 voyages in all. Passenger lists show that church members traveled in family units and even as members of intact congregations with intentions of permanent settlement. Indigent members who could not afford sea, wagon, and/or rail fare were assisted by the Perpetual Emigration Fund, established by church members in 1849. Until the Fund was disbanded in 1887 by hostile federal legislation bent on excluding further Mormon immigration to the United States, 36 percent of all Mormon immigrants were assisted directly from the $12.5 million contributed in cash and kind by church members.

Converts were drawn by the undeniable appeal of Mormon missionary themes of fraternity and economic franchisement. Missionaries promised the faithful that Zion would provide a sanctuary from economic privation and class ostracism and that the Saints would arrive to find sufficient land to cultivate, gainful employment, guaranteed association with fellow believers, and upward mobility. The remaking of Swedes and Scots into Mormons began during the long journeys to Zion and continued through their arrival and placement in Mormon settlements.

Between 1850 and 1890, Mormons came closest to inventing a distinctive ethnicity for themselves. During this period they grew from a sect of 52,000 to an important regional population of over a quarter of a million. Mythic kinship, particular religious beliefs, geographical isolation, political autonomy, economic autarchy, uniform town planning, and outside perceptions of their distinctiveness were the principal factors contributing to the near success of transforming a sectarian religious group into a separate people. Dean May concluded that church members representing extra-Mormon ethnicities assimilated rapidly upon entering Zion because, unlike non–Mormon immigrant settlers, they moved into "tightly structured, hierarchical, closely-knit villages where pressures to conform were great." The result was "considerable uniformity in cultural expression."

It is not clear, however, that Mormon material culture of the nineteenth century confirms the scholarly consensus that this was an era of such "uniformity" and "homogeneity" that one can say that even here—and by this point in time—Mormons had become a separate and distinct American ethnic group. It is true that American graphic artists, such as Thomas Nast, drew Mormons with beards, goat horns, and harems and placed them among Uncle Sam's other troublesome ethnicities. It is also true that Mormons in this period shared distinctive beliefs, institutions, stories, and experiences. But numerous other institutions, folkways, and cultural traits that served to maintain numerous ethnicities within the Mormon community also persisted. For example, church members supported dozens of ethnic congregations and foreign-language newspapers from 1880 to 1915 and yet again in the 1920s and 1930s. These media may have served the purpose of integrating foreign members into a composite American Mormon ethnicity while fostering lingering ethnic ties to native countries, cultures, and languages, as well.

Mormons may have created a landscape imprinted sporadically with towns, public and domestic buildings, farms, and water systems of their own design, which resulted in geographers speaking of a distinctive Mormon "country" and "cultural region." Closer scrutiny, however, reveals that even in the nineteenth century Mormons brought with them a widely eclectic range of architectural styles, construction techniques, and handcrafts. What were considered "typical" Mormon landscapes and material culture in the Intermountain West have, in the twentieth century, been rapidly subsumed into national, not ethnic, styles of building and settling. By the end of this century, there is little that differentiates the way Mormons settle, communicate, vacation, commute, work, and consume from non-Mormons, no matter in what region of the United States Mormons happen to live. They have abandoned village and agrarian life for suburban tract housing, urban apartments, and congested roads. Vast orchards of fruit, planted by pioneers as part of a drive to create a diverse, self-sustaining agrarian-based culture, have been hewn down to make way for strip malls, gated communities, and automobile dealerships. Mormon folk music and dance—even these were derivative from British Isles and Scandinavian styles—have been largely displaced by commercially formatted, mass-produced pop music.

Even if Mormons had consciously set out to create a distinctive "ethnic" identity, fifteen years of conflict, settlement, and migration in the American Midwest and forty years of relative isolation in the Great Basin were periods of insufficient duration in which to create a separate and enduring material, aesthetic, and religious culture. In the mid-1800s, a Mormon theorist like Louis Bertrand, a former French socialist who converted to Mormonism, predicted that the Mormon community would become a "new people" gathered from all the nations and faiths who would then "coordinate" all "good and true principles" from their former cultures into an unprecedented "general symbol." What happened, instead, was that in the 1910s other emigrant Saints, for example, the Norwegian-born John A. Widstoe, advised converts to "assimilate . . . into the American life-stream" and "acquire an American identity." They readily complied.

Between Bertrand's predictions in 1862 and Widstoe's post–World War I counsel, Mormons had undergone what historian Thomas Alexander has described as a "paradigm shift." Due to the impact of intrusive and punitive federal legislation, the death of the militant first generation, insufficient arable land to support a rapidly growing community, and the growing desire to normalize relations with dominant American cultures, Mormons abandoned many of their most distinctive institutions and practices. Polygamous marriages, church-owned cooperative businesses, a religious political party, and the doctrine of the gathering to Zion—all of these and more were discontinued by the Mormon community beginning in the 1890s.

The end of the gathering led directly to the reconfiguration of Mormon population patterns and accelerated the erosion of ethnicity. In search of employment, second-and third-generation Mormons began to move to urban areas in Utah and along the West Coast. In the 1890s, Utah's overwhelmingly Mormon population was about 65 percent rural and 35 percent urban. By 1910, with an urban growth approaching 60 percent, the mix was even.

Meanwhile, church leaders, in a marked departure from the sectarian rhetoric of the nineteenth century, advocated a policy of assimilation. A 1907 official declaration, issued by the church hierarchy and ratified by the lay membership, stepped away from the millenarian and separatist rhetoric of the previous century by urging all church members to "join hands with the civilization of this age" to promote the well-being of the human family through evangelization, education, the sanctification of marriage and family life, and the advocacy of religious liberty. Between 1920 and 1965, migration out of the core area of Mormon settlement continued, with significant numbers of Mormons becoming established in major American metropolitan areas on the West Coast, the Midwest, and Northeast. In 1930, the first Mormon "stake" (diocese) outside of the Great Basin was organized in Los Angeles. Whereas in 1900, 72 percent of all Mormons resided in Utah, out-migration reduced that number to 46 percent by 1950. At the same time, church-wide growth continued at a steady, if unspectacular rate, from a total membership of two-thirds of a million in 1920 to over 2 million in the mid-1960s.

Service in the military and employment in the industries and bureaucracies supporting the American world war and cold war efforts accelerated Mormon geographical diffusion, intermarriage, and professional specialization. Altogether, these forces eroded territorial-, and familial-, based ethnicity. They also introduced compelling alternative allegiances to American Mormons for the first time since the creation of their religious community. Mormons coming of age in this period migrated physically and ideologically from the relatively simple society of parents and grandparents into a diffuse and complex world, where identities were not based on regional, religious, and familial narratives steeped in Mormon myth. As never before, Mormons had to imperfectly balance loyalties and forge identities between the nation-state, workplace colleagues, the institutions of non-Mormon civil society, and their own religious tradition. They ended up exceeding the goal of reducing intercommunal tensions: In the 1950s and 1960s, Mormons viewed social, economic, and political issues through the same lens held by their "middle American" contemporaries. They had, in the words of sociologist Armand Mauss, "spent the first half of the century trying (with considerable success) to live down the deviant image of their earlier history." But they purchased "respectability" at a high price, namely, "the erosion of a sense of unique identity that Mormons . . . have traditionally felt."

Nonetheless, in response to the real concern that Mormonism would elide into cultural Protestantism, the Mormon community devised strategies to tone down the cognitive dissonance of waning sectarian/ethnic identity. Beginning in the late 1950s, they funded an ambitious national construction program to erect multipurpose church buildings according to "standardized plans" drawn up by architects employed by central church administration. Mormon men and women implemented church education, culture, recreation, and welfare programs outlined in correlated instructional material devised and disseminated by the burgeoning church bureaucracy in Salt Lake City. They staffed and ran women's and youth auxiliaries, Sunday schools, Boy Scout troops, and missionary outreach efforts. They attended interminable congregational and diocesan executive planning sessions and church meetings that were spread out through the entire week. They endured pronouncements by church officials intent on both defining fundamental doctrines for a heretofore essentially creedless religion and coercing the rank and file to view contemporary social and political issues through the template of those fundamentals. Cumulatively, these strategies have produced a major American religious denomination that looks and acts far more like a church than a distinct ethnicity.

WOMEN, ECONOMIC AND POLITICAL CULTURES, AND THE PROCESS OF INTEGRATION

American Mormons are deeply embedded within American territory, its markets, politics, and culture. That location has and will continue to entail the ongoing creation of individual and group identities selected from a range of attributes both "Mormon" and American. The reciprocating nature of that active work of construction can be seen in the development of the roles women have taken on from the beginnings of Mormonism to the present, as in the integration of American Mormons to national economic and political cultures. The evolution of those public and private identities argues in favor of the thesis of this essay: Mormons began building a millenarian sect, nearly became a distinct people, and presently more nearly resemble an international church struggling with the temptation of fundamentalism.

Mormon women have fashioned identities through periods of great change in response to a combination of distinctly Mormon insights and needs and external structural forces. From 1830 to 1845, Mormon men and women exercised spiritual gifts in ways that made little distinction by gender, thereby making manifest the fullness of life all the Saints would enjoy in the coming Kingdom of Christ, where "there is neither male nor female." Mormon women stood alongside men in witnessing to the sectarian orientation of their community by healing, prophesying, speaking and interpreting tongues, and discoursing publicly and rationally about the faith and powers shared by both sexes in the church. Finding common cause in building up the church and handling formidable powers of the spirit, Mormon men and women participated jointly in the sphere of religion exactly at that moment in American history when men and women were filing off into "separate spheres" of work and recreation.

Ceding neither exclusive powers over religious life to men nor claiming it as their sole possession, Mormon women petitioned in the spring of 1842 to add administrative powers over significant aspects of communal life to complement their exercise of spiritual and intellectual gifts. In response, Joseph Smith organized a women's "Relief Society" to parallel the male priesthood quorums of the church. Eventually, members of the Relief Society directed their own social welfare and mutual assistance programs, authored instructional curricula, published journals, established their own granaries, hospitals, and nursing programs, and spearheaded political action for women's rights.

Women invested with these powers, both public and private, served the Mormon community well during its pioneering period in the American West. They fashioned a distinctive identity for themselves and contributed to the creation of a near-nation. Migration and settlement required women to step out of narrow spheres of influence and performance. Public attacks against their community and its beliefs were met by women who spoke and published in defense of Mormon ideology and social practices. Indeed, this wide field of action may have constituted a significant part of the allure of Mormonism during the second half of the nineteenth century. Mormon women enjoyed "ungendered spiritual gifts," exercised the political franchise in Utah beginning in 1870, and were encouraged by church leaders to acquire and exercise both the training and skills needed to support domestic and village economies. Many women became de facto heads of households during the frequent and extended absence of menfolk serving as missionaries, emigration agents, and Mormon trail teamsters and as men attended to other households under polygamous marriage arrangements. Many women derived real satisfaction from their religious lives, which provided occasions for the dramatic experience of pentecostal gifts, the exercise of priestly powers in Mormon temples and homes, and charitable works rendered between sisters in the faith.

Finally, the religious ideology of the gathering had enabled tens of thousands of Mormon men and women to recreate many of the conditions of pre–Industrial Revolution societies from which American and European farmers and artisans had been alienated. The prospect of restoring dignity to working men and women—by taking them out from the industrial and urban centers of Europe and America and returning them to village life, artisan labor, and pioneering yeoman agriculture—was profoundly attractive to many women and men searching for viable solutions to the woes of displaced laboring and agrarian workers. Heading into the last decades of the nineteenth century, Mormon women had created an astonishing range of identities for themselves in order to fulfill the needs of pioneering in the West. The distinctive roles they played in shaping Mormon culture in this era contributed to perceptions of Mormons as a people apart. For example, opponents of Mormon geopolitical and social practices were incredulous when articulate Mormon women stepped forward to deliver spirited defenses of their religion *and* the national movement for women's rights.

All of these conditions changed with astonishing speed beginning in the late 1880s. Under extreme pressures from without and within to conform to forces from which they had fled in the pre–Civil War years, Mormons at the end of the century began to opt out of sectarian and ethnic lifestyles and beliefs. Instead, they decided to follow national trends in urbanization, the bureaucratization of work, the separation of men's and women's spheres, the subsumption of regional economies within national markets, and the consumption of mass-produced goods and services. On the far side of their "paradigm shift," accommodation meant the end of the autonomous institutions and the rough parity in the public possession and use of spiritual gifts that Mormon women had enjoyed with their male counterparts.

Church leaders began to redefine the distribution of power between men and women. They also assigned "appropriate" gender roles that would become characteristic of Mormon society throughout the twentieth century. After years of internal debate over the extent and nature of gendered public authority, male church leaders used official publications, beginning in 1903, to deny that Mormon women had ever received designated priestly spiritual powers. By 1913, the Relief Society was retooled as a denominational auxiliary under the administration of the male-only priesthood. Changes toward increasing the subordination of women in Mormon society were justified by appeals to the discourse of contemporary business administration, turn-of-the-century biology, and transcendent archetypes. Mutable constructions of gender, prescribed during the Victorian era as normative for Anglo-Protestant women of the middling classes, acquired an aura of binding and eternal sanction. These changes in official attitudes toward the roles of women in the Mormon Church coincided with national developments—particularly the widespread efforts to diminish the public presence of women—and served to align Mormon beliefs and practices closer to acceptable national norms and away from roles once typified as essentially Mormon.

Throughout the first half of the twentieth century, the behavior of Mormon and white Protestant women in their private and public lives did not differ significantly. The goods they consumed, the neighborhoods in which they lived, the sites of their employment within and outside the home, the public schools their children attended, the language they spoke, and the race they shared all served to erode significant differences between Mormon and non-Mormon communities. These women may have attended different churches, whose theologies offered various prescriptions for salvation, but these religious sites were sustained by emphasizing gender and hierarchical orders. Each religious community created a plethora of programs, service opportunities in religious auxiliaries, and clerical—not administrative—positions to engage the creative skills and energies of women church members. It was a strategy that encouraged modest but sustained growth between the 1920s and 1960 and increased the geographical dispersion and assimilation of the Mormon community. As long as the structural foundations sustaining the authority of male-dominated institutions—like the churches—remained relatively stable, gendered roles and other social practices of Mormon and non-Mormon communities converged.

The cultural and financial shocks from the 1960s to the present altered the assumptions and institutions of the white middle class. Mormons, embedded deeply within them, were not immune to those shocks. Rates of divorce, depression, declining earning power, and the interaction between family members within the Mormon community reflected national trends. Mormon Church leaders responded to the erosion of middle-class living standards and the subsequent entry of women into the workforce with attacks on government growth and feminism and appeals to Mormon women to focus on domestic and family responsibilities. While these appeals may have created, since the early 1970s, an environment in predominantly Mormon Utah favorable to conservative political interests and contributed to gender wage inequities that are among the highest in the nation, they did not stem the tide of women entering the workforce or inoculate Mormon populations from mimicking national consumer trends.

Overall, nevertheless, from sectarian beginnings to nation building and cultural convergence, Mormons traveled from being numbered among the poorest and least powerful members of America's religious communities to enjoying, currently, an average socioeconomic status comparable to members of mainline Protestant denominations. The twentieth-century Mormon quest for rapprochement with dominant American institutions has paid off in terms of augmented public power.

In the nineteenth century, Mormons had focused their economic and political efforts on creating autonomous geopolitical enclaves consistent with their core theological principles of the physical gathering and social equity. Settling in vastly different physical environments entailed that Mormon men and women remain flexible in creating institutions for realizing their lofty communal goals. Decades of privation served to foster a disciplined attitude toward personal consumption, time management, and a willingness to cooperate in efforts organized under centralized administration. Economic and political behaviors based on self-sufficiency, cooperation, and collective management became hallmarks of the nineteenth-century Mormon community. American political, cultural, and business elites objected to all three because they were tied intimately with the Mormon attempt to create an autonomous geopolitical enclave, and they pursued a well-documented strategy throughout the century aimed at dismantling Mormon enclaves and assimilating their populations. Their efforts succeeded beyond expectations. Between 1862 and 1887, in a series of laws similar to those aimed at reducing the autonomy of Native American tribes, Congress passed antipolygamy legislation, disincorporated the church, dissolved the Perpetual Emigration Fund, seized church property in excess of $50,000, abridged basic civil rights, and imprisoned hundreds of church and local leaders.

Threats to the continued viability of the church were perceived as so acute that Mormon leaders capitulated. Beginning in 1890, they discontinued polygamous marriages and the doctrine of the gathering, sold nearly all of the church's economic properties to eastern capitalists, disbanded the church's political party, and preached accommodation to the national political system and the market economy. And most Mormons readily embraced the changes. Housewives and laborers in northern Utah had already largely ignored boycotts called by church leaders against Gentile (non-Mormon) businesses in the 1870s and 1880s. At about the same time, leading Mormon citizens were discovering that their own economic and political interests intersected with those of national elites. In 1922, E. E. Ericksen identified this development: ''The most influential men of the Mormon priesthood are businessmen and as such place high value upon pecuniary ideals and methods.'' During the western colonization period, church revenues were collected and programs administered conscientiously by a small number of church authorities. This priesthood bureaucracy acquired specialized skills and an administrative outlook. They worked full-time in these positions and began drawing salaries derived from income generated by church investments in a broad range of business corporations. Ericksen states, ''Naturally, these church authorities became interested in promoting the businesses from which they received their income. This explains why some of the apostles became active businessmen and adopted the businessmen's point of view.''

Taking up the cause of capital in the 1910s, many church leaders began preaching against organized labor and government-administered social and economic programs aimed at modest efforts to redistribute income to the less affluent. During the depression years, nevertheless, church members ignored the strenuous opposition of the church's First Presidency and voted overwhelmingly for Roosevelt. A number of Mormons, including prominent banker Marriner Eccles and classics professor-turned-politician Elbert Thomas, became stalwart allies of the Roosevelt administration and important spokesmen for New Deal programs.

The deviation did not last. More than seventy-five years after Ericksen's pioneering study, the ''businessmen's point of view'' is even more thoroughly entrenched among Mormon officialdom. In 1997, almost all of the nearly 100 members of the church administrative hierarchy were successful in business or the legal profession. By training and association they are members of an administrative culture. Collectively, they preside over and direct what the *Arizona*

Republic, in 1991, called "the most rapidly growing and powerful economic institutions in the United States, particularly in the West, where much of its wealth is concentrated." A 1997 *Time* magazine article estimated annual church revenues at $5.3 billion in tithes and offerings and $600 million in investment and business income. The church controls over 100 businesses that generate in excess of $4 billion in sales annually and total assets of over $30 billion, but these estimates of revenue and assets are very conservative and underreport the true figures. The Mormon Church is a major source of income for contractors, craftsmen, and vendors in the Intermountain West. It directly employs more than 10,000 men and women to staff and direct an extensive worldwide bureaucracy and an additional 20,000 to work in its universities, colleges, and businesses. Most of the annual revenue is dedicated to promoting its religious and social agenda and has not been abused by the "personal wealth-building" that has plagued some religious organizations.[1]

In response to historical and theological commitments to the needy in their midst, church members have maintained a welfare system that assists participants temporarily with food, clothing, housing, and employment. Church members volunteer countless hours in "service projects" and have warmly supported recent administrative trends toward participation in international relief efforts. The effects of welfare and humanitarian programs, however nobly intended, are not the same as those of a classless, cooperative society envisioned by the nineteenth-century Mormon community. Once advocates of an economic philosophy Ericksen called both "radical and socialistic," most American Mormons have come to embrace, as Nathan Hatch recently pointed out, "the spirit of free enterprise capitalism" and tend to disparage (unlike their fellow Saints in western European nations) the very concept of a "welfare state."

Since the late 1960s, a majority of American Mormons, following broad national trends, have tended to adopt the political and social conservatism of the Republican Party culture. A half century of partisan attacks by conservative political elites and outspoken Mormon Church leaders, such as former Agriculture Secretary Ezra Taft Benson, against "big government," "radical feminism," and the civil rights movement contributed to persuading many rank-and-file Mormons to vote against their own economic and civic interests and to turn away from a history within the church of nuanced moderation with regard to a range of issues from militarism to women's rights. Adopting conservative social and political agendas paid off handsomely during the 1980s, when Mormons, in unprecedented numbers, served in numerous key government positions in the Reagan and Bush administrations.

MORMONS AND CONTEMPORARY AMERICAN SOCIETY AND CULTURE

Generally speaking, Mormons have divested themselves of distinctive practices that readily set them apart as an American ethnic group. Public Mormon statements and practices with regard to gender roles, sexuality, government, welfare, patriotism, prayer in public schools, and "secular humanism" do not constitute a discourse expressive of an enduring, particularistic ethnicity nor even of inherent distinctions between Mormon theology and social ethics and those of Christian fundamentalism. Rather, they disclose how deeply connected the Mormon Church elite and the audience they seek to persuade have become to significant segments of American religious culture. The question that needs to be asked is, Whose interests are served by the application of the term *ethnicity* to the contemporary Mormon community?[2]

Since 1965, the Mormon community has undergone changes as far-reaching as those in the 1840s and 1850s and the 1890s–1910s. Once, Mormon men and women created a people by means of differentiation; then they pursued strategies of convergence with the host society; presently, they are attempting to remake themselves into an international religion. In 1950, the Mormon community numbered 1.2 million people; in the spring of 1997, there were more than 10 million church members, due largely to the efforts of a missionary force approaching 50,000. The rate of membership growth between 1981 and 1991 exceeded 75 percent and shows no signs of abating. As of February 1996, more Mormons lived outside of the United States than within, and most of them are first- and second-generation church members. In 1996, Utah accounted for only 16.5 percent of total church membership. If current regional growth trends continue to 2020, Spanish-speaking Mormons in Mexico and Central and South America will account for 71 percent of the Mormon community; all those residing in the United States, Canada, and Europe will amount to only 11 percent.

What will the realities behind these numbers mean for Mormon identity as the center of gravity of the church community shifts south of the Rio Grande? Two dissimilar tracks seem plausible. In the first, while the Anglo-American Mormon community, particularly in Utah, continues to diminish in size relative to international church membership, it will continue to maintain inordinate control over church administration and policies, privilege its mythic narratives, and pursue a strategy of convergence with the American religious Right. Anglo-American Mormons will continue to pursue practical alliances with other conservative American religious groups who learned in the 1980s to claim government protection for their cultural institutions and practices by resorting to the discourse of ethnicity. Taking the course suggested above would isolate and reconfigure the Anglo-American community, especially the one resident in Utah, into something like a separate ethnicity within a burgeoning international church. This may end up constituting the particular locus around which an ethnicity will endure; but, in that case, ethnographers will have to speak of a "Wasatch Front," or "Utah Mormon" ethnicity, and not "Mormon" ethnicity *tout court*. The alternative track is a prescription for a more cosmopolitan, multiethnic religious community, which, in the long run, corresponds more fittingly to Mormonism's profound twentieth-century ideological and institutional commitment to growth by indiscriminate and international evangelism. It is not yet clear if Mormonism will prove capable of transcending the particularity of its history and succeeding as an enduring world faith. It seems certain, however, that, if it does, Anglo-American Mormons will have learned to value the languages, customs, mythic narratives, rhythms, and arts of their "brothers and sisters" in the gospel as much, if not more, than their own. If that materializes, how can one speak intelligibly of "Mormonism," or its world-faith community, as an ethnicity?

MORMONS AND AMERICAN CULTURE: A POSTSCRIPT

If culture means the production of significant artifacts in the arts and letters that have created styles, "schools," or ideas that have changed society, then the contribution of the Mormon community to American culture has been negligible. While there are many truly accomplished Mormon artists, musicians, dancers, academics, and writers, they have been the disciples, rather than the creators, of momentous new lines of inquiry, narrative, vision, sound, and motion. However, by participating as productive artists and scholars, Mormons have added to the presence and import of cultural arts and letters in American society. Some of them, including prize-winning historians Laurel Thatcher Ulrich and Richard Bushman, literary critic Wayne Booth, and environmental writer Terry Tempest Williams, have made significant and enduring contributions to their disciplines.

If the definition of culture expands to take in the manners and institutions of a particular people or nation, then the assessment of a Mormon contribution to American culture looks quite different. Here Mormons have made two significant additions to the American landscape. First, Mormons have shown that typically "one way of becoming American was to invent oneself out of a sense of opposition." America is a nation composed, in part, of self-proclaimed outsiders. To find a place in this nation, and that includes a place in the religious landscape, communities seeking the center have often camped at the peripheries of American culture. Becoming a "fixture" in the scene is contingent upon asserting difference and then finding the media to express it as persistently as possible. Mormons can be seen as harbingers of the rise of a multiethnic society. Certainly, they demonstrated how ethnic identities can be constructed, refashioned, even transcended on American soil.

Americans, however, have not tended to perceive the Mormon experience as a typical expression of American culture. Which brings up Mormonism's second significant contribution to American culture: that the belief system and social practices of the Mormon community have functioned as a foil to core American cultural norms.[3] That is, non-Mormons have frequently measured the meaning of America by invidious comparison to Mormonism. By turns neither evangelical nor democratic nor nativistic nor capitalistic nor monogamous nor cosmopolitan enough, Mormons have rendered crucial service to the construction of America's cultural amour propre: At least *we* are not as bad as *they* are. Regardless of how Mormons may, in fact, feel about the attributes assigned to some putative Mormon "substance," seemingly they will continue to play an important role in the creation of American social myths. Does that mean they are an American ethnic group, after all?

NOTES

1. The *Arizona Republic* story is discussed in "LDS Financial Empire Puts Church at Fortune 500 Level," *Salt Lake Tribune*, June 30, 1991, pp. A1, A4–A5. See also "The Kingdom Come," *Time* 4 (August 1997): 50–57.

2. It is Armand Mauss who first raised this crucial question in "Mormons as Ethnics: Variable Historical and International Implications of an Appealing Concept," in *The Mormon Presence in Canada*, edited by B. Y. Card et al. (Edmonton, Alberta: University of Alberta Press, 1990), p. 346.

3. Reading Mario Depillis's 1995 address to the Mormon History Association suggested this idea. "The Emergence of Mormon Power since 1945," *Journal of Mormon History* 22 (1996): 1–32.

BIBLIOGRAPHIC REFERENCES

Richard Bushman's *Joseph Smith and the Beginnings of Mormonism* (Urbana: University of Illinois Press, 1984) is the best entry into Mormon origins, early worldviews, and cultural setting. Two excellent, single-volume histories covering the 170-year history of the community are Leonard Arrington and Davis Bitton's *The Mormon Experience: A History of the Latter-day Saints* (New York: Knopf, 1979) and *The Story of the Latter-day Saints*, 2nd rev. ed. (Salt Lake City: Deseret Book Co., 1992), by James Allen and Glen Leonard. The first work provides both a chronological and thematic view of issues and events of particular interest to a general audience; the second offers a chronological, more detailed approach and focuses more on institutions. *The Story of the Latter-day Saints* is particularly valuable for its extensive and learned bibliography.

Mormons are a community convoked by religious beliefs and experiences. Mormon life is influenced by the attention men and women pay to the Bible, the Book of Mormon, The Doctrine and Covenants, and Pearl of Great Price. The Book of Mormon and the Pearl of Great Price, like the Bible, contain myths of origins, narratives of covenant, and prophetic and liturgical writings. The Doctrine and Covenants is a collection of revelations written down by Joseph Smith and a number of his successors. The topics of those revelations range from the wording of liturgical prayers to economic issues. For how those texts situate Mormons theologically the best work is still Sterling McMurrin's *The Theological Foundations of the Mormon Religion* (Salt Lake City: University of Utah Press, 1965). Jan Shipps's *Mormonism: The Story of a New Religious Tradition* (Urbana: University of Illinois Press, 1985) is an important analytic work from a religious studies perspective. For how Mormon men and women "translate" canon, church programs, and modernity on a congregational level, see Susan Buhler Taber's *Mormon Lives: A Year in the Elkton Ward* (Urbana: University of Illinois Press, 1993).

Essential reading for social scientific examinations of Mormonism include *The Angel and the Beehive: The Mormon Struggle with Assimilation* (Urbana: University of Illinois Press, 1994) by Armand L. Mauss; *Contemporary Mormonism: Social Science Perspectives* (Urbana: University of Illinois Press, 1994), edited by Marie Cornwall, Tim B.

Heaton, and Lawrence A. Young; and *Mormon Identities in Transition* (New York: Cassell, 1996), edited by Douglas Davies. To keep up with important articles on Mormon history, thought, and social issues, the following journals are indispensable: *Dialogue: A Journal of Mormon Thought, Sunstone, Brigham Young University Studies*, and the *Journal of Mormon History*.

Works specifically cited in the text include: Sidney Ahlstrom, *A Religious History of the American People* (Garden City, NY: Image Books, 1975); Thomas O'Dea, *The Mormons* (Chicago: University of Chicago Press, 1957); D. W. Meinig, ''The Mormon Nation and the American Empire,'' *Journal of Mormon History* 22.1 (Spring 1996): 44–45; Thomas G. Alexander, *Mormonism in Transition: A History of the Latter Day Saints, 1890–1930* (Urbana: University of Illinois Press, 1986); Armand Mauss, *Angel and the Beehive: The Mormon Struggle with Assimilation* (Urbana: University of Illinois Press, 1994); E. E. Ericksen, *The Psychological and Ethical Aspects of Mormon Group Life* (Chicago: University of Chicago Press, 1922); and Nathan Hatch, ''Mormon and Methodist: Popular Religion in the Crucible of the Free Market,'' *Journal of Mormon History* 42.20 (Spring 1994): 24–44.

POLES

Dominic A. Pacyga

The earliest mention of Poles in North America can be traced back to the Jamestown settlement, when Captain John Smith invited Polish artisans to the English colony. Although present throughout the colonial period in British North America, the Polish population remained small. This was a migration of individual adventurers, fortune seekers, or exiles. During the American Revolution two prominent Poles, Thaddeus Kosciuszko and Casimir Pulaski, joined American forces in their fight for independence. Kosciuszko, a highly trained military engineer, provided valuable service to American forces in various campaigns. Pulaski, often referred to as the "Father of the American Cavalry," gave his life for the American cause at Savannah in 1779. In 1784, after the War of Independence, Kosciuszko returned to Europe, where he led the struggle for Polish liberty against the encroachments of Poland's powerful neighbors, especially Russia. He remained a symbol of freedom in exile until his death in Switzerland in 1817.

By the end of the eighteenth century Poland had disappeared from the political, if not the cultural, map of Europe. It reappeared in a truncated and short-lived form as the Napoleonic Duchy of Warsaw but vanished again after the Congress of Vienna (1815). Poland's political struggles in the late eighteenth and nineteenth centuries provided a major source of immigration to western Europe and, to a lesser extent, the United States. This era of immigration, often referred to as the *Wielka Emigracyja*, or Great Emigration, was fueled by the Polish-Russian War of 1830–1831. Later, the Polish Insurrection of January 1863 also resulted in emigration. Once again, the numbers of immigrants to the United States were small and usually from the upper classes and intelligentsia. These upper-class Polish exiles often came to the United States with the intention of establishing a New Poland, but their plans were unsuccessful, and they either returned to Europe or were quickly assimilated into American society.

The establishment of a large and lasting Polish immigrant community resulted from a protracted emigration that drew its strength not from the nobility and intellectual classes but from the peasantry.

THE ECONOMIC MIGRATION: ZA CHŁEBEM

The Polish peasant in the nineteenth century lived through a period of enormous change. Poland's relationship with Europe and the world shifted quickly as modernization, urbanization, and industrialization transformed first western and then eastern Europe. Poland found itself divided among its three powerful neighbors: Prussia, Russia, and Austria. The political state had disappeared, and the traditional economy was fractured. For some time, however, the Polish lands continued to play the traditional role of agricultural supplier to western Europe. Economic and cultural shifts, however, quickly took place, a result of the expansion of the capitalist industrial market economy across the North American continent and into eastern Europe. By the end of the 1800s Poland no longer served as western Europe's breadbasket. Instead, Poland became the frontier between industrialized Europe and the great expanse of Russia to its east. Polish peasants experienced these changes in several ways, not the least of which was emancipation from the ancient chains of serfdom. Economic competition, land hunger, and the dissolution of traditional peasant cultures followed. Polish peasants acted individually and in groups to try to protect themselves and to better their position in the new economy. The transformation of the Polish economy from a feudal agricultural society supplying farm products to the capitalist centers of Europe to an integral part of industrialized Europe resulted in part in Polish peasant immigration to the United States: Migration became one answer to peasant Poland's problems and opportunities.

Laying the groundwork was the peasants' emancipation, or *uwłaszczenie*, which took place at different times in the three partitions. Prussia abolished serfdom in 1807, during the Napoleonic Wars, whereas Austrian-occupied Galicia eliminated serfdom in 1846, and the Russian partition finally saw emancipation in 1864, one of the results of the Polish Insurrection. Peasants no longer tied to the land now faced modern market forces, providing both challenges and difficulties. Emancipation and other factors, including the division of already small landholdings among peasant generations, resulted in a large and growing population of landless peasants, a rural proletariat. A further economic dislocation took place when North American farms began to replace Polish estates as the source of imported agricultural products in western Europe. The world crisis in grain prices hit Poland severely in the mid-1880s, and during the next decade Russian Poland suffered through a harsh agricultural depression as grain prices dropped 50 to 60 percent. Russian-occupied Poland stopped exporting wheat to the West. Instead, an industrializing Poland became a supplier of textile goods to Russia and cheap labor via emigration throughout the capitalist system.

Wage labor became more common across Poland and all of eastern Europe. Large estates often were sold off, and this provided opportunities for wealthier peasants and others who could accumulate cash to purchase land.

The peasant need for capital to purchase land provided an important impetus for immigration both to European and American industrial centers. Polish peasants worked as seasonal laborers on German farms and, then, as industrial workers in German and French coal mines, Polish factories in such emerging industrial centers as Lodz and Warsaw, Siberian agricultural settlements, Brazilian farms, and in rural and urban locations across North America. This vast Polish peasant emigration has been called *za chlebem*, or "for bread," and it lasted from the 1860s until it was brought to an end by World War I and U.S. immigration restriction in the 1920s. Over 3 million immigrants left the Polish lands between 1850 and 1914. The largest part of this migration went to the United States, but it was only a portion of a larger movement that saw Poles settle across Europe, parts of Asia, and the Western Hemisphere.

Thus, it was after 1850 that Polish immigrants made their way in large numbers to the United States. Those from Silesia formed the first permanent Polish settlement in the United States in Panna Maria, Texas, in 1854. The following year another group of Silesian Poles established a community at Bandera, Texas, about 100 miles from Panna Maria. Both colonies eventually saw the creation of a Polish Catholic parish. In these early years the Rev. Leopold Moczygemba attended to the spiritual needs of both Panna Maria and Bandera. The 1850s also saw several Polish rural communities being established in Texas (St. Hedwig, 1857), Michigan (Parisville, 1857), and Wisconsin (Poland's Corner, or Polonia, 1858). These settlements were the first of various Polish rural settlements that were located primarily throughout Texas, the East, and the Midwest, and especially in Connecticut, Wisconsin, Indiana, and Illinois.

After the Civil War, large urban Polish settlements appeared throughout the nation's industrial belt. While Chicago quickly emerged as the leading Polish settlement, other urban centers grew rapidly. These included Brooklyn, Rochester, Utica, Detroit, Milwaukee, and many cities across New Jersey, Connecticut, Pennsylvania, and Ohio. By 1880 immigrants had formed some 75 Polish Roman Catholic parishes in the United States. Ten years later, the number reached 170 and grew to over 800 by the 1930s. Polish immigration to the United States reached its peak in 1912, when roughly 175,000 immigrants entered the country from all parts of Poland. Perhaps the most reliable estimate has between 1,150,000 and 1,782,000 Poles entering the United States between 1899 and 1932.

As noted, Prussian-occupied Poland (Poznania and Silesia) provided the first major source of Polish immigrants to the United States, but Poles only began to emigrate in large numbers after the Franco-Prussian War (1871) and the creation of the modern German state. The 1880s witnessed the greatest numbers of emigrants from the Prussian partition. This was a result of changes in the economy of Poznania and a deliberate policy set by Chancellor Otto Von Bismarck to replace Polish peasants with German settlers and to strip Poles of their native culture. Bismarck's program of *Kulturkampf*, while also aimed at German Catholics, included an aggressive campaign of Germanizing the Polish sections of the Reich. The forces driving Polish immigration to the United States and to the Western Hemisphere in general spread to Russian-occupied Poland in the 1890s, and between 1890 and 1892 approximately 70,000 Poles left that region. After 1900 Galician emigration gained momentum, and that part of the Polish lands supplied the greatest numbers going to the United States. From 1899 to 1910, some 500,000 Poles left Galicia for America. The greatest single year for Galician emigration was 1910, when over 60,000 persons left the Austrian-held province.

The Galician countryside had particularly suffered from the maldistribution of land. In 1902, 79 percent of the farms in the province contained only 5 hectares (12.5 acres), and these covered a mere 29 percent of the land. Large holdings of between 20 and 100 hectares covered 7 percent of the land. Estates of over 100 hectares covered 40 percent of Galicia. These large estates were held by the Polish nobility, or *szlachta*. The poverty of the peasant class also resulted in a high rate of illiteracy, for in 1900, 67.7 percent of the Galician population could not read. Under these conditions immigration seemed a positive response to the realities of economic life in the Austrian partition. Money sent home from the United States as well as brought back by returning emigrants played an important role in Galicia's economy before World War I.

The primary problem for Poles living outside the German empire was crossing the imperial borders so as to reach the ports of western Europe and eventually the United States. At various times the different imperial authorities either promoted or discouraged emigration. Like other immigrant groups, Poles practiced a form of chain migration. After the initial migration took place a system of information and mutual aid quickly developed. Those who first arrived in the United States sent letters filled with information concerning the trip. Polish immigrants also sent money or prepaid tickets back to their villages in order for family, friends or fiances to join them. After the early waves of emigration in the middle to late nineteenth century from the various partitions, most emigrants knew that they could find *rodacy*, other immigrants from their villages and regions, in the American immigrant centers. The new settlements had vast and intricate ties with the villages and farms of the Polish countryside.

POLONIA: THE COMMUNAL RESPONSE

Once in the United States, Polish peasants, now immigrants, were defined by the dominant American culture as cheap industrial labor. As the nation's economy exploded after the Civil War, Polish workers joined the mass of unskilled and semiskilled laborers filling American factories. They worked in coal mines, slaughterhouses, factories, steel mills, and the garment industry. Later, in the twentieth century, they worked in the steel, auto, and electrical industries, among others. After 1880, most of the large cities of the industrial Northeast and Midwest saw the emergence of a Polish immigrant colony or "Polonia." The term *Polonia* quickly came to mean the institutionally rich community that developed in the original Polish immigrant settlements and that was connected in a web linking Poles throughout the United States both with each other and with the homeland.

The Catholic Church played a central role in both the institutional and communal life of Polonia. Immigrants arriving in either urban or rural areas searched out a Catholic Church in order to maintain the religious legacies that connected them to their identity as Poles. Immigrants from Prussian Poland often settled first near a German Catholic Church. Quickly, however, they organized a separate parish to more completely reflect the traditions and rituals of Polish Catholicism, for, in Poland itself, Catholicism had been closely identified with the Polish cultural and political cause. Two of Poland's occupiers, Bismarckian Germany and Czarist Russia, often pursued anti-Catholic policies, and the Church therefore identified with the Polish people. In the eyes of many patriots and peasants, to be Polish meant to be Catholic. With such a historical legacy it is not surprising that impoverished Polish working-class communities in the United States would construct an intricate and expensive parish system.

Indeed, the creation of a Catholic parish was central to the identity of Polonia. It was also central to what might be termed the *communal response*, a reaction to life in the United States designed to give stability and continuity to the Polish immigrant community. This response was inward looking in nature but necessary for Polonia if it were to eventually integrate into the larger American society. Polish peasants sought to create community institutions that would both serve their immediate needs and protect then from outside forces. Catholic parishes, schools, fraternal groups, hospitals, ethnic stores, funeral parlors, and even cemeteries appeared in most Polonia centers. In the end, the American Polonia appeared to be an almost institutionally complete ethnic community.

The Catholic parish served as a community center in Poland, and it seemed natural that this venerable institution should serve the same purpose in the Polish colonies in the United States. A Catholic organization or society usually preceded and provided the basis for the creation of an actual parish. In Chicago, Poles organized the St. Stanislaus Kostka Benevolent Society in 1864 as the first Polish organization in the city. Three years later, the group agreed on definite plans to form a Polish congregation. It took another three years for Rev. Adolph Bakanowski, a Resurrectionist priest, to come to Chicago to serve as pastor for the quickly growing community. Finally, in 1871 the community completed construction of the original combination church and school building. St. Stanislaus Kostka was the first of over sixty Polish parishes in the Chicago Archdiocese alone. Some of these parishes grew to be very large community organizations. By 1900 Chicago's St. Stanislaus Kostka Parish had 40,000 parishioners. Just a few blocks away neighboring Holy Trinity served 25,000 parishioners. These two parishes were among the largest Catholic parishes in the world at that time.

The establishment and maintenance of a parish, or *parafia*, provided a central focus for the creation of community. Church steeples rising high against the industrial skyline provided a symbol of continuity for Polish immigrants. No longer drifters, they now had a home in the United States. Angelus bells brought back memories of Poland, and the religious practices of the *parafia* replicated those of the Polish countryside. Besides the uniformity of the Latin Mass and the major holy days celebrated by all Catholics, Polish variations of church practices directly connected the immigrants to their cultural heritage. The church calendar closely resembled that of eastern Europe. Festivals still marked the change in seasons for those now separated from the natural cycle of rural life. Customs, such as the *Wigilia* meal on Christmas Eve and the *Swieconka*, or blessing of Easter baskets, remained important family and communal events. Once a community established a parish, the religious celebrations provided a constant reminder of the group's Catholic and Polish identity.

It should not be surprising that the creation and maintenance of a parish often proved to be a very controversial event in the Polish community. Lay leaders, who had led the development of parishes in all of the Polonia centers, quickly saw their control over the institution erode as more and more Polish clerics arrived on the scene. In rural Poland local noblemen maintained the feudal tradition of *ius patronatus*, which gave them the right to name the pastor of the local parish. In the United States, ownership and control of the parish remained in the local bishop's hands. Conflict often arose between the Irish-controlled American Catholic Church and the new Polish parishes. Much of this conflict arose over control of the local parish finances and the appointment of a pastor. On many occasions this dispute became violent, such as in Omaha where a gunfight broke out in 1898 as well as other incidents in Chicago and Detroit. Several separatist movements resulted. In 1904, Father Franciszek Hodur united the Polish independent churches and founded the Polish National Catholic Church. Hodur's movement led to the largest permanent schism in American Catholic history. While most Polish immigrants and their children remained in communion with Rome, the seriousness of the situation eventually led to the consecration of a Polish American bishop, Paul Rhode of Chicago, in 1908. This ordination was seen by many Polish priests and laymen alike as a necessary step for the maintenance of a Polish identity in the United States. The Catholic hierarchy also saw the appointment as a way of preventing further inroads by the Polish National Catholic Church, which by 1916 had some 30,000 communicants.

The desire to preserve a sense of Polishness, or *Polskość*, drove much of the institutional life of Polonia, in the United States, especially the Polish school system. The oldest Polish parochial school opened in Panna Maria, Texas, in 1858. The years after the Civil War, however, saw the growth of a large and intricate Polish American Catholic school system. Parochial schools were run by orders of Polish sisters, such as the Felician Sisters, the Sisters of the Holy Family of Nazareth, and others who, of course, taught in them. In 1894, Josephine Dudzik (Sister Theresa) founded the Franciscan Sisters of Blessed Kunegunda in Chicago to serve Polonia's schools.

Children crowded into the schools, and the sisters often taught classes of 90 to 100 working-class children. In some parish schools Polish was the language of all instruction. In fact, many schools originally used texts adopted from the Galician Catholic school system. Under pressure from the American Catholic hierarchy, this quickly changed to a bilingual curriculum that included English. The sisters taught children four hours a day in Polish. These classes included religion, the Polish language, and Polish history. Other classes were taught in English. Ironically, because of the lack of formal education of many peasant Poles, their children, having attended Polish American parochial schools, often spoke a more grammatically correct Polish than did their parents. Also, of course, they became interpreters of the English-speaking world for their immigrant parents. The impetus behind these schools was not simply ethnic but also practical in nature. It became increasingly obvious that education, and especially the ability to speak English, would be necessary for children in the new industrial milieu.

The Poles' aim to use education to further mobility did not surface immediately. Initially, it was simply a way of preserving the religious and cultural values brought from Europe. Peasants often regarded formal education as a waste of time. In Polonia's early years typical Polish children attended parochial school until they received the sacraments of the Catholic Church. They then transferred to public school or entered the workforce. In the average life cycle of the family, older children left school at a young age in order to help the family accumulate enough money to purchase a home. Younger children frequently stayed in school through at least the eighth grade. In the years before World War I higher education remained out of reach of the vast majority. In 1911, only thirty-eight men and six women of Polish descent studied in the seventy-seven institutions of higher learning in the United States. This number, however, did not take into account those who studied for the priesthood or had entered the various religious brotherhoods and sisterhoods and thereby earned an education.

Eventually, Poles organized not only parochial grammar schools but also high schools, colleges, and seminaries. In 1886, Father Joseph Dąbrowski opened SS. Cyril and Methodius Seminary in Detroit, the precursor to St. Mary's College in Orchard Lake, to train Polish Catholic priests, brothers, and sisters in the United States. A quarter of a century later, in 1912, the Polish National Alliance opened Alliance College in Cambridge Springs, Pennsylvania, as a Polish college.

The Polish Catholic parish provided a sound foundation for the creation of an institutionally rich Polonia. This was true in all of the settlements across industrial America. Other organizations followed soon after the creation of a parish. Chief among these were fraternal organizations, such as the Polish Roman Catholic Union (1873), the Polish National Alliance (1880), and the gymnastic and paramilitary group, the Polish Falcons (in the United States, 1887). Polish women also organized their own ethnic organizations, perhaps the most important of which was the Polish Women's Alliance, founded in 1898 when several women met at the Chicago home of Stefania Chmielinska. Wherever Poles settled in the United States, a great explosion of Polish organizations quickly appeared. Many reflected the regional origins of their members, for example, the Polish Highlanders Alliance of North America, which was founded in Chicago in 1929. Other organizations represented local Polonias while maintaining a national presence, including the Polish National Alliance of Brooklyn, U.S.A., established in 1903. Many of these provided economic aid and life insurance. By World War I some 800,000 American Poles belonged to at least 1 of the approximately 7,000 Polish organizations in the United States.

Other organizations were of a purely cultural and educational nature, such as the Kosciuszko Foundation, started in New York City by Stephen Mizwa in 1925, and the Polish Institute of Arts and Sciences in America (1941), founded by Polish-born intellectuals fleeing Hitler's Europe. Middle-class, second- and third-generation Polish Americans also organized fraternal groups and social clubs, based on the models of their immigrant elders, among them the Polish Arts Club of Chicago (1926), Chopin Fine Arts Club of South Bend (1940), and many others in all of the major Polonia centers. Numerous fraternal organizations that developed on both a local and national scale advocated Polish independence and celebrated Polish national holidays as a means of rallying the community to the Polish national cause. The struggle for Polish independence played an important role in the creation of the ethnic community in the United States, with Poles often referring to the American settlements as the "Fourth Partition." Ethnic leaders hoped to use the American Polonia as a force to help resurrect the Polish state.

From the earliest history of the American Polonia, Polish immigrants have organized to help the cause of Polish independence. In March 1863 Polish émigrés formed a committee in New York City to send aid to Poland during the Polish insurrection against czarist rule. In 1886, the Polish National Alliance formed the Skarb Narodowy i Rząd Centralny (National Treasury and Central Administration) to work toward the resurrection of the Polish state. Polish American organizations responded to various issues and movements in the Polish lands, such as the school strikes in German-occupied Poznania at the beginning of the twentieth century. After the outbreak of World War I, community leaders organized the Polish Central Relief Committee and urged President Woodrow Wilson to declare January 1, 1916, as Polish Relief Day. Once the United States entered the war, Polonia raised a Polish army to fight on the Western Front. But besides the army, Polonia lobbied the Wilson administration to support Polish independence and created propaganda on behalf of the Polish cause. In August

1918, Polonia formed the Congress of Polish Emigration to show unity under the leadership of Polish pianist and patriot Ignace Jan Paderewski and Chicago banker and politician Jan Smulski. The organization eventually raised $5.5 million for the Polish Independence Fund, despite political and ideological divisions reflecting fissures in the independence movement in Poland itself. Besides taking part in purely Polish war efforts, Polish Americans also led the purchase of U.S. Liberty Bonds and volunteered in large numbers for the American armed forces.

After World War I, as Poland regained its political independence, the American Polonia began to turn away from European concerns and focus on its own problems in the United States. The Polish National Alliance led the way in this movement, proclaiming Polonians to be Americans first and of Polish descent second. Polish Americans felt under attack as the Red Scare, the Harding depression, labor strife, anti-immigrant behavior, and finally Prohibition and the closing off of immigration affected Polonia and other recent immigrant communities. A lack of newcomers after the mid-1920s also diminished Polish American identification with the homeland.

While the large fraternal organizations provided insurance benefits and cultural continuity, and the churches maintained both the religious and cultural lives of Polonians, other organizations and businesses appeared in order to cater to Polish Americans. Even small Polish communities developed ethnic business centers, for example, those in such small rural towns as Riverhead, Long Island. In Chicago, the largest of the Polonia centers, at least seven original Polish neighborhoods boasted of large commercial districts. Chicago's Milwaukee Avenue, Archer Avenue, 47th Street, and Commercial Avenue contained shops, professional offices, funeral parlors, and taverns that served Chicago Poles.

Many of these commercial strips had a mixture of Polish Jewish as well as Polish Christian businesses. Polish Jews had interacted with Polish peasants over the centuries, and many came to America and reestablished the relationship. While most Poles considered Jews a separate ethnic group, and Jews often suffered from anti-Semitic behavior, the relationship between the two groups continued to be an intricate one in the United States. Jewish merchants often spoke Polish, and immigrants felt comfortable doing business with them according to centuries-old traditions. In turn, the growing Polish Christian entrepreneurial class both in Europe and America attempted to break the customary ties by stirring up anti-Semitic feelings. Nevertheless, the streets of Chicago, Milwaukee, Detroit, Greenpoint in Brooklyn, and other Polish centers saw many Jewish businesses prosper.

BEYOND POLONIA: THE EXTRA-COMMUNAL RESPONSE

Beyond parishes, schools, fraternal organizations, social clubs, and businesses, the American Polonia also developed a series of charitable organizations, including hospitals, day care centers, orphanages, homes for working women, welfare organizations, immigrant aid, and cemeteries. This institutionally rich

Polonia satisfied Polish immigrant needs from cradle to grave and beyond as Masses and prayers were offered for the repose of the souls of those who had died in the faith. While Polonia became almost institutionally complete, it could never be institutionally independent, especially with regard to its economic life. To deal with larger societal problems, the Poles had to reach out beyond the immigrant community. This response was extracommunal in nature, and it involved building bridges to other groups politically, institutionally, economically, and culturally. The original institutional experience of the immigrant generation, and the solid foundation for community that it provided, proved crucial for this extracommunal response to take place. Still, this would not always be an easy task in an America divided by ethnicity and social class.

The American labor movement provided a major outlet for this reaching out beyond the immigrant ghetto walls. Polish immigrants found themselves on the lower rungs of the American industrial labor ladder. As their numbers in the United States grew, they became involved in various labor struggles. Polish Americans took part in the 1886 Eight Hour Strikes, the Homestead Strike (1892), the Anthracite Strike (1902), the 1904 Packinghouse Strike, the 1919 Steel Strike, and many other confrontations between capital and labor before 1930. During and after the Great Depression, Polish American workers played crucial roles in the Congress of Industrial Organizations' (CIO's) organizational drives. Polish American labor leaders, notably Jan Kikulski, Alex Nielubowski, Mary Janek, Leo Krzycki, Stanley Nowak, and others, helped organize workers across the nation. Later, other second-and third-generation Polish Americans, among them Chicago's Ed Sadlowski, played a vital role in the labor movement.

Polish Americans also reached out to other ethnic groups in their neighborhoods through participation in grassroots organizations. In the 1930s Polish Chicagoans were instrumental in the creation of the Back of the Yards Neighborhood Council and the Russell Square Community Committee, both of which provided models for neighborhood organizing across the nation. Similar developments could be seen in Buffalo, Brooklyn, and other cities. The immigrant parish and fraternal group building experience proved crucial to the development of these neighborhood organizations.

Beyond the shop floor and the neighborhood, Polish Americans quickly found themselves involved in politics, especially on the local level. In Chicago, while never capturing the mayoralty, Polish Americans became involved in local politics as early as 1877, when Piotr Kiolbassa was elected to the Illinois state legislature. In 1891, Chicagoans chose him as city treasurer. Later, voters picked Jan Smulski for city attorney in 1903 and state treasurer in 1906. In South Bend, Indiana, Polish Americans played an important role in local politics but here, too, did not capture the mayor's office. In 1919, Jan Leczka, a Republican from Wisconsin, became the first Pole to be elected to Congress. Eventually, politicians emerged out of the American Polonia to have an impact on national politics, especially Edmund Muskie of Maine, Dan Rostenkowski of Illinois, and Barbara Mikulski of Maryland. Polish-born political scientist Zbigniew Brzezinski played an important role in the Carter administration and among Democratic Party policymakers.

Polish Americans also surfaced as active participants in the popular culture, emerging amidst technological changes in mass communications. Baseball and other organized professional sports provided outlets for Polish American working-class youth who hoped for the fame and fortune that the new American culture promised. Wrestler Stanisław Cyganiewicz, known by his nickname "Zbyszko," after a Polish medieval hero, provided an immigrant role model for Polish Americans in the 1920s. Cyganiewicz, recognized for his physical prowess, actually held a doctorate from the University of Vienna and spoke eleven languages. Milwaukee-born baseball player Al Simmons (Szymanski) played for the great Philadelphia Athletic teams of the 1920s and early 1930s, hitting 307 home runs in his twenty-year career, while Pennsylvania-born Tony Piet (Pietruszka) broke in with the Pirates in 1931. The 1940s saw Stanley Musial begin his incredible twenty-two-year career with the St. Louis Cardinals, hitting 471 home runs and earning a lifetime batting average of .331. Also in the 1940s, the Gary, Indiana, working-class Polonia gave the boxing world Tony Zale, the two-time world champion middleweight boxer, who fought three of the most famous bouts in professional boxing history against Rocky Graziano. Names like Kluzewski, Kubek, Yastremski, Niekro, and Skowron remain a testament to Polish American involvement in professional sports.

In the 1920s Polish immigrant actress Apolonia Chałupiec came to the United States and became the renowned silent film star Pola Negri. She took up where the famous actress and Polish patriot Helena Modjeska (Modrzejewska) had left off. Polish Americans would remain important on the stage and screen, with Charles Bronson (Buchinski), Jack Palance (Palaniuk), and Stephanie Powers (Federkiewicz), among others, making their way into the popular culture.

In 1930, over 3.3 million people in the United States listed Polish as their mother tongue. This was the height of the impact of the Polish immigration on the demography of America. But just as the population of Polonia reached this figure, the nation fell under the impact, first, of the Great Depression and then World War II. These two ordeals had major consequences for Polish Americans. In many ways these were two Americanizing events in the history of the ethnic group. The Great Depression increased the need for extracommunal responses, which in turn led to more participation in institutions outside of the immediate immigrant group. This, combined with the lack of new immigration and the expansion of popular American culture, challenged the American Polonia. While still living in a primarily Polish world whose boundaries were formed by the neighborhood and the local parish, second-generation Polish Americans found themselves involved in labor unions, neighborhood organizations, and such New Deal programs as the Civilian Conservation Corps, Works Progress Administration, and Neighborhood Youth Corps.

POST-WAR POLONIA: ASSIMILATION, REINVIGORATION, SUBURBANIZATION

The events of September 1939 changed the American Polish community forever. As Polonia watched the newly reconstituted Polish Republic fall under the Nazi onslaught, it organized attempts at economic relief in Polish neighborhoods across the nation. This time a Polish army was not raised in the United States, despite an ill-fated attempt known as the Kosciuszko Legion in Canada, because few Polish Americans saw this as a viable response to the Nazi attack. Instead, Polish organizations emphasized relief and aid as well as political lobbying in Washington, D.C. Once the United States entered the fighting, however, Polish Americans rallied behind the American cause and served valiantly on all fronts. And their service in the American armed forces accelerated the changes in Polonia, for Polish Americans returned home more committed to the United States than ever before. As with many others, military service proved to be the ultimate Americanizing experience for second-and third-generation Polish Americans.

Nonetheless, during World War II, Polish Americans once again found themselves concerned with Poland's political independence. The newly formed Polish American Congress (1944) became the principal advocate for the Polish cause in Washington, D.C. The organization not only lobbied for Polish political rights and protested against the Yalta Agreements between the Allied Powers but also put extensive pressure on the U.S. government to permit those uprooted by the war to come into the United States. After extensive negotiations these "displaced" persons were allowed to enter the country.

With these dual developments, the postwar period produced a complex landscape for Polish Americans. On one hand, among the native-born, greater assimilation was more evident. On the other hand, a new immigration of Poles occurred, mostly refugees from the war and from the communist takeover of Poland after liberation from the Nazi occupation. Thus, while the slow breakup and dispersal of the old Polonia neighborhoods began in earnest once Polish American GIs returned from the war, the arrival of large numbers of displaced persons at the same time lessened the full impact of that trend on traditional Polish American neighborhoods and institutions. These two demographic forces brought both opportunities and conflict to the American Polonia.

Newcomers reinvigorated Polonia institutions. Those immigrants who came from peasant and working-class backgrounds in Poland often fit well into the American Polonia. However, Polish Americans often resented newcomers who came from the middle and intellectual classes of Poland. They referred to these immigrants derisively as "D.P.'s" (displaced persons). In turn, new immigrants often chastised Polish Americans for a lack of "Polishness." Many were shocked at the Polish spoken in the United States, with its mixture of poor grammar, English words, and nineteenth-century peasant slang. They had ideas about Poland and ethnic identity very different from the "old" Polonia. Often, these refugees took working-class jobs in order to survive, and this caused more resentment. Polish Americans, who remained heavily working class in the years immediately after the war, also complained about the "airs" that the refugees put on. Many newcomers, on the other hand, felt that, given their position in prewar Poland, they should have been treated with more respect in the United States. To a degree, the old peasant resentments toward the Polish upper classes reemerged in these neighborhoods that were occupied by a mix of old immigrants, their children, grandchildren, and the displaced persons of the war years. This clash was evident even in the large fraternals, where new immigrants tried to find an institutional home. Nonetheless, the differences notwithstanding, the two Polonia groups did share a fierce anticommunism and a devotion to the Catholic Church. Moreover, the post-1945 immigration resurrected an interest in Polish culture in America and laid a groundwork for the continued interaction of Polonia with the homeland.

By 1950 the Polish foreign-stock population (immigrants and their children) had declined to just under 2.8 million individuals, this despite the immigration of large numbers of Poles after the war. The impact of age and the growth of the third generation, which census takers counted as native-born white, changed the statistical abstract of the American Polonia. Still, even with war and depression, Polish Americans tended to live for the most part in the urban Northeast and Midwest. As late as the 1950s the heaviest concentration of Americans of Polish descent remained in the greater New York–New Jersey area, whereas Chicago claimed the title of largest Polish city outside of Poland proper. Large concentrations persisted in Detroit, Buffalo, Rochester, Milwaukee, and other urban centers in the old industrial belt. Foreign-born Poles tended to live in central-city neighborhoods with a long-standing Polish identification, such as Brooklyn's Greenpoint, Milwaukee's South Side, and Chicago's Milwaukee Avenue corridor, South Chicago, and Back of the Yards.

Technological change, a newfound prosperity, and racial change compounded the transformation of the old American Polonia. Prewar immigrants and their children and grandchildren found themselves participating in the postwar boom, symbolized by the automobile, television, and suburbs. They set off a series of changes that altered the landscape of urban America and the demography of traditional urban industrial groups, among them Polish Americans. While still overwhelmingly working class in orientation, Polish Americans began to enter the postwar consumer society with gusto. Many left inner-city neighborhoods for newer housing developments on the outskirts of cities or in the suburbs. Good union jobs fueled much of this mobility, as did the automobile and the emerging highway system.

Moreover, twenty years of depression and war had left their impact on the American city and on Polonia. Inner-city neighborhoods suffering from a lack of investment deteriorated at the same time that the newer suburban developments attracted many inner-city residents. In many cities, African-American and Hispanic communities had developed near the old Polonia centers, and Polish

Americans often clashed with them, as in the Sojourner Truth Homes riot in Detroit in 1943, then temporarily shared their neighborhoods with the new groups, and finally abandoned much of the old Polonia for the suburbs. This process unfolded slowly in part because of the tremendous institutional commitment that Polonia had made in the inner-city and because of the high rate of home ownership that Polish Americans enjoyed. For example, in 1970 in Chicago 62 percent of all Polish Americans owned their own homes, compared to 35 percent for all Chicagoans. This financial commitment, as well as an emotional commitment to their neighborhood, slowed Polish flight to middle-class suburbs. It also intensified Polish American resistance to racial integration.

Urban renewal provided another factor in the decline of Polish inner-city neighborhoods. Urban planners identified many older Polish centers as slums and in need of reconstruction. Often, this took the shape of highway construction and industrial park development as well as new residential construction. In Detroit the destruction of "Poletown" for the building of an auto plant meant the uprooting of a large and stable Polish community. In Brooklyn's Greenpoint neighborhood the expansion of an industrial district led to the demolition of Polish American homes. In Chicago the construction of the Kennedy Expressway resulted in many families being pushed out of St. Stanislaus Kostka parish. New housing in that area ended up being largely occupied by African-American and Puerto Rican families.

By 1968 the *Chicago Sun-Times* claimed that as many as 400,000 Polish Americans had left Chicago for the suburbs. This total may have been exaggerated, but it nevertheless pointed to a conspicuous trend. Even so, as late as 1970 many Polish Americans remained in inner cities. That year, 191,955 Polish Americans, or about 8 percent of the nation's Polish foreign-stock population, called Chicago home. At the same time, the U.S. census counted 108,793 foreign-stock Poles in Chicago's suburbs. A 1975 survey that included all Americans of Polish descent found roughly 250,000 in Chicago, with another 190,000 in the suburbs. The suburbanization trend proved to be a steady one. By 1990, nearly 65 percent of all Polish Americans in the area made their homes in suburban Chicago.

This process of suburbanization did not necessarily represent a change in social class. The demographic profile for Chicago's Polonia showed Polish Americans still firmly entrenched in the working class in 1970. According to census data that year, at 32 percent operators and laborers made up the largest occupational group among Polonians. Sales and clerical workers accounted for another 28 percent of Chicago's Polish American population. Also, it should be noted that much of the Polish American suburban population in 1970 resided in industrial working-class suburbs on the fringes of the city, such as Calumet City, Cicero, Posen, and Chicago Heights. Polish American suburbanites signaled their commitments to the suburbs with home ownership rates of over 85 percent.

Moreover, by the 1970s, large-scale intergenerational mobility could be seen in Polonia. Several researchers have pointed to the increased Polish American participation in higher education after World War II. This was especially true for younger Polish Americans, many of whom had benefited from living in northern urban areas with a good deal of opportunity for attending college and both professional and graduate schools. In 1969 Polish American men and women between the ages of twenty-five and thirty-four had reached a median level of educational achievement of 12.7 years, second only to the Russians' amazing 16+ years (most of whom were Jewish). Polish Americans nationwide surpassed the English, the Germans, and the Irish in this twenty-five- to thirty-four-year-old group—all of whom had a higher median educational level among older members of these respective ethnic groups. A study of Chicago's Polonia in the mid-1970s showed Polish Americans actively participating in area professional schools.

Both the persistence of inner-city Polish neighborhoods into the 1970s and 1980s as well as the continued movement of Polish Americans to the suburbs underscore the historical realities of the long-established Polish immigration to the United States. The presence of Polish Americans in the United States is a multigenerational experience. Various waves entered the United States and overall gave Polonia a rather mixed demographic picture as well as mixed levels of assimilation. In the 1980s and 1990s still another wave of immigration from Poland transformed the American Polonia.

THE SOLIDARITY MIGRATION

The emergence of the Polish Solidarity labor movement in 1980 and the resulting crackdown and imposition of martial law by the Polish communist regime led to another emigration from Poland. As in the nineteenth century, much of this initial political emigration went to western Europe, but now the United States—with its long-established Polonia—also provided a home for the émigrés. During the time period 1980 to 1989 Polish refugees outnumbered legal Polish immigrants to the United States 34,903 to 28,966. At the same time, 374,622 Poles entered the United States as vacationers. How many of these disappeared into Polonia and remained as illegal immigrants is hard to determine, although most Polonia centers witnessed a good deal of unsanctioned immigration. The new refugees fled to the major Polonia centers. Although sometimes they stopped in smaller ones for a short time, such as South Bend, their presence was quickly felt in the large centers, notably Chicago, Brooklyn, and Detroit. In Chicago, for example, Polish immigrants made up the largest group of legal immigrants during the years 1986 to 1996. Most estimates cite the Polish illegal immigrant population as second only to Hispanics in Chicago during this same decade. Once in the United States, Polish immigrants entered established ethnic institutions and reawakened many struggling cultural organizations declining under the strains of age and assimilation.

For the most part, however, these newer immigrants were even more removed from the peasant past of the original Polish Americans than were the postwar refugees. Intellectuals, artists, professionals, and political activists made up much of the "Solidarity" immigration. Many had traveled abroad before and knew or learned English easily. They often quickly entered into American society. The generational and class divisions discernible between post–World War II immigrants and their precursors became even more obvious between the Solidarity immigrants and earlier generations of Polonia. Like most new aliens, Solidarity immigrants at first often focused on events in their homeland. They had grown up in a very different Poland either from the peasant Poland of the nineteenth century or from the capitalist Poland that had emerged between the wars. Solidarity immigrants appreciated the help offered them by both individuals and institutions in Polonia, but many were embarrassed by their American cousins. Their experiences and expectations were different from Polish Americans, and many saw little that was really Polish in Polish America. In turn, while Polish Americans viewed the Solidarity struggle sympathetically and welcomed Poland's liberation in 1989 with great joy, older Polish Americans found interacting with Solidarity immigrants difficult. To an extent, history repeated itself.

By 1990 the total Polish American ancestry population had reached 9.37 million persons.[1] Despite some increases in several states, it remained clustered in the traditional areas of concentration in the midwest, mid-Atlantic, and northeastern states. New York continued to be the state with the largest Polish population, 1.18 million, a slight increase of 0.2 percent over 1980. Illinois saw a 7.9 percent increase in the 1980s, to 962,827. In addition, those indicating a Polish ancestry made up more than 10 percent of Wisconsin's residents. Nonetheless (and despite numerical increases in New York and Wisconsin, for example), the 1990 census also showed a clear movement of Polish Americans to the Sunbelt, where traditionally the Polish American population has been small. Thus, Arizona witnessed a 56.9 percent increase in the Polonia population, with reporting 102,405 there by 1990. In 1980 the Texas Polonia had numbered 167,465, but ten years later it had increased by 41.9 percent, to 237,722 individuals. Showing the largest percentage gain of any state in the nation, North Carolina's Polish American population jumped 86.9 percent, to 59,722 persons. By way of contrast, however, the total foreign-born population, down by 7 percent, masked a significant passing of the first generation, for the pre-1980 population fell by approximately 35 percent during the 1980s and was only partially offset by the 116,575 who noted their arrival between 1980 and 1990.

Polish immigration has been an ongoing phenomenon in American history. It has passed through various phases and therefore remains an extremely complex occurrence. Polish Americans reflect various degrees of assimilation. Descendants of the oldest Polonia are largely assimilated, and incidents of intermarriage, loss of ethnic language skills, social mobility, and ethnic identification are similar to those among other groups. Yet the persistence of an organized Polonia allows the entrance of newer immigrants to maintain the institutional, cultural, and political life of the group. This vitality also allows heirs of the older Polonia to have a choice as to the intensity of their ethnic identity. Polish America has maintained a cultural attachment to Poland and a somewhat tenuous political and economic connection. As a result of these historical realities, and of the legendary struggle of the oldest American Polonia to establish a sound institutional base, Polonia remains an important factor in the ethnic cultural, political, social, and economic life of the United States.

NOTE

1. Those reporting a first or second Polish ancestry, nearly seven-tenths of whom listed it as their first one.

BIBLIOGRAPHIC REFERENCES

Polish immigration to the United States has been widely studied. The academic journal *Polish American Studies* has developed into a first-rate source for those interested in the history of this group. The seminal work of William I. Thomas and Florian Znaniecki established a long tradition in both the sociological and historical literature concerning this important group. Their classic study, one of the founding documents of the Chicago School of Sociology, *The Polish Peasant in Europe and America (1918–1920)* (New York: Knopf, 1927), set the intellectual parameters of the argument concerning Polish immigration since its publication. There are several good historical surveys in English, including Andrzej Brożek, *Polish Americans, 1854–1939* (Warsaw: Interpress, 1985); John J. Bukowczyk, *And My Children Did Not Know Me: A History of the Polish Americans* (Bloomington: Indiana University Press, 1987); and James Pula, *Polish Americans: An Ethnic Community* (New York: Twayne, 1995). An excellent collection of Polish immigrant letters exists in English translation: Witold Kula, Nina Assorodobraj-Kula, and Marcin Kula, *Writing Home: Immigrants in Brazil and the United States, 1890–1891* (Boulder, CO: East European Monographs, 1986), edited and translated by Josephine Wtulich. A more sociological approach, with an interesting discussion of the most recent Polish immigration, is Helena Znaniecka Lopata (with Mary Patrice Erdmans), *Polish Americans*, (New Brunswick, NJ: Transaction Publishers, 1994). Erdman's most recent book, *Opposite Poles: Immigrants and Ethnics in Polish Chicago, 1976–1990* (University Park, PA: Penn State Press, 1998), is an excellent sociological study of the most recent phase of Polish immigration. Early overviews from a more ethnocentric and popular approach include the voluminous work of Joseph Wytrwal, especially his *Behold! The Polish Americans* (Detroit: Endurance Press, 1977). One of the best sources for the discussion of Polania's historiography can be had in the above-mentioned book by John Bukowczyk as well as in his excellent edited collection, *Polish Americans and Their History: Community, Culture and Politics* (Pittsburgh: University of Pittsburgh Press, 1996). Scholars should also look at two somewhat dated overviews: Joseph L. Zurawski, *Polish American History and Culture: A Classified Bibliography* (Chicago: Polish Museum of America, 1975), and the sociological collection by Irwin T. Sanders and Ewa T. Morawska, *Polish American Community Life: A Survey of Research* (New York: Polish Institute of Arts and Sciences in America, 1975).

After a long period of inattention by the academic community, Victor Greene revived scholarly interest in Polonia with his path-breaking study of Slavic miners, *The Slavic Community on Strike: Immigrant Labor in Pennsylvania Anthracite* (Notre Dame: University of Notre Dame Press, 1968). Greene's *For God and Country: The Rise of Polish and Lithuanian Ethnic Consciousness in America, 1860–1910* (Madison: The State Historical Society of Wisconsin, 1975) discusses the Chicago Polonia. A large number of community studies emerged in the 1970s, 1980s, and 1990s. Chicago, the largest Polish American center, is also the most studied. Besides Greene's work, Edward R. Kantowicz, *Polish-American Politics in Chicago, 1888–1940* (Chicago: University of Chicago Press, 1975), Joseph J. Parot, *Polish Catholics in Chicago, 1850–1920* (DeKalb: Northern Illinois University Press, 1981), and Dominic A. Pacyga, *Polish Immigrants and Industrial Chicago: Workers on the South Side, 1880–1922* (Columbus: Ohio State University Press, 1991), have looked at various aspects of the nation's largest Polonia. James Pula and Eugene E. Dziedzic's study of an upstate New York Polonia, *United We Stand: The Role of Polish Workers in the New York Mills Strikes, 1912 and 1916* (Boulder: East European Monographs, 1990), is one of the more interesting local studies. Janusz Mucha's *Everyday Life and Festivity in a Local Ethnic Community: Polish-Americans in South Bend, Indiana* (Boulder:East European Monographs, 1996) is a look at another smaller Polish settlement. Ewa Morawska's *For Bread and Butter: The Lifeworlds of East Central Europeans in Johnstown, Pennsylvania, 1890–1940* (Cambridge: Cambridge University Press, 1985) is a classic local study. The work of Dennis Kolinski on the rural Polonia is an important step in looking at this aspect of the immigration, especially his article "Polish Rural Settlement in America" *Polish American Studies* 50.2 (Autumn 1995):21–55.

Polish scholars, especially Grzegorz Babiński, Dorota Praszałowicz, Adam Walaszak, and others connected with the Polonia Institute, have also written extensively on Polonia. This group of sociologists, historians, and others affiliated with the Jagiellonian University in Kraków are writing, in Polish, some of the most interesting studies on the immigration to the United States. Much of this work should be translated into English.

PUERTO RICANS

Carmen Teresa Whalen

Puerto Ricans migrate to the continental United States as U.S. citizens. The United States acquired Puerto Rico in 1898, at the end of the Spanish-American War, and has retained sovereignty ever since. In 1917, the U.S. Congress passed the Jones Act, making Puerto Ricans citizens of the United States. Governors were appointed by the U.S. president until 1948, when Puerto Ricans elected their governor for the first time. Two years later, Congress passed legislation allowing Puerto Rico to draft a Constitution to be approved by the Congress and the people of Puerto Rico, and in 1952, Puerto Rico became the Estado Libre Asociado, or Commonwealth. Puerto Rico was self-governing on internal matters within the parameters established by federal legislation, whereas the United States retained authority over the military, the federal judiciary, and foreign affairs. Although U.S. citizens, Puerto Ricans living in Puerto Rico could not vote in national elections and had no voting representation in Congress. They were also exempt from federal income taxes but subject to military conscription. This ambiguous status, which remains unchanged, has been debated in Puerto Rico, the continental United States, and the United Nations.

This political status has shaped Puerto Rican migration to the continental United States. U.S. investment and U.S. government policies have affected Puerto Rico's economy, causing unemployment and migration. On the one hand, as U.S. citizens, Puerto Ricans can migrate to the mainland free from immigration barriers. On the other hand, as among immigrants, informal networks of family and friends, or "the family intelligence service," have played an important role in their migration process. That U.S. citizenship has also brought about government-sponsored contract labor programs and private labor recruitment for low-wage jobs on the mainland. Such continuing political and economic ties with the mainland have shaped the formation of Puerto Rican communities and Puerto Rican politics, fostering an adaptation to U.S. society that has been marked by bilingualism and biculturalism as well as by an ongoing concern with the unresolved political status of Puerto Rico. Puerto Rican migration increased when European immigration was restricted in the aftermath of World War I and has coincided with the peak periods of African-American migration from the southern states that followed World Wars I and II.

Puerto Rican migration increased dramatically with the end of World War II and continued during the 1950s and the 1960s; it slowed in the 1970s but increased again in the 1980s. By the 1990 census, more than 2.7 million Puerto Ricans lived in the continental United States. While it has significant parallels to African-American migration, Puerto Rican migration also proved to be an important precursor to increased immigration from Central and South America and the Caribbean after the immigration reforms of 1965.

MIGRATION PATTERNS AND ECONOMIC INTEGRATION

Puerto Rican migration is a labor migration that reflects economic conditions in Puerto Rico and the continental United States. A number of factors caused Puerto Ricans to migrate in search of jobs. U.S. investment patterns and Puerto Rico's policies caused unemployment and underemployment on the island. In addition, Puerto Ricans were actively recruited to low-wage jobs on the mainland by private employers and government contract labor programs. Since the late 1970s, the scholarship in Puerto Rican studies has examined how the colonial relationship and economic development have shaped Puerto Rican migration. This scholarship has challenged earlier views that pointed to "overpopulation" and "backwardness" as causing migration. Instead, as political economist Frank Bonilla has demonstrated, it has been Puerto Rico's model of economic development that has caused unemployment and necessitated emigration. In short, it is not "backwardness" but industrialization and not too many people but too few jobs that have together compelled Puerto Ricans to migrate in search of work. Moreover, although public and scholarly attention has focused on New York City, Puerto Ricans have increasingly settled beyond the barrios of that city.

Although the post–World War II era was the peak period of migration, earlier migrations set important precedents. Labor recruitment began in 1900, when more than 5,000 Puerto Ricans were recruited to work on sugar plantations in Hawaii. In 1926, more than 1,000 Puerto Ricans, including whole families and children, were brought to harvest the cotton crops of Arizona. Conditions were harsh; migrants complained that housing was inadequate, that workdays were ten to sixteen hours, and that they could not live on the wages of less than two cents per pound of cotton picked. These labor recruitment schemes fostered the early settlements of Puerto Ricans in the continental United States and paved the way for later contract labor programs.

Migrants also came without formal labor recruitment and established a community in New York City. During the nineteenth century, migrants were merchants, students, political exiles working for Puerto Rico's independence from

Spain, and skilled and unskilled workers in search of jobs. After World War I, several factors contributed to increased migration. In Puerto Rico, because of large-scale investments by U.S. sugar corporations, landownership became increasingly concentrated, subsistence agriculture and coffee production decreased, and small farm owners and agricultural laborers found themselves landless and jobless. In the states, World War I and the restriction of European immigration created labor shortages for unskilled jobs. Facing unemployment at home, Puerto Ricans—now U.S. citizens—migrated to fill those jobs. By 1940, almost 70,000 Puerto Ricans lived in the continental United States—and most (88 percent) in New York City.

During World War II, Puerto Ricans were recruited by the War Manpower Commission (WMC) for war industry jobs. The WMC was the government agency charged with addressing labor shortages in war industries, and it recruited African Americans from the southern states, foreign workers, prisoners of war, and local women who were not yet in the labor force. Policymakers were reluctant, however, to recruit Puerto Ricans, whose status as U.S. citizens meant that, unlike foreign workers, they could remain when the war was over. The *Washington Post* revealed this concern: "Heretofore, Puerto Ricans have been bypassed in the farm labor importation program because of the fear they might want to remain in this country when the war is over." The benefit of employing Jamaicans, Mexicans, and workers from Newfoundland, the article explained, was that they "could be returned because they are not American citizens." Although not recruited for agricultural work, about 2,000 Puerto Ricans were recruited in 1944 and placed with two canneries in southern New Jersey, the Campbell Soup Company and the Edgar F. Hurff Company, or with the Baltimore and Ohio Railroad. Two hundred workers were sent to the copper mines of Bingham, Utah.

After World War II, migration increased dramatically. This was not only the peak period of migration but also the first airborne migration, as Puerto Ricans boarded the two-engine planes, many of them army surplus planes, for the six-hour trip from San Juan to New York City. Policymakers in Puerto Rico and in the United States promoted contract labor, while unemployment in Puerto Rico sent migrants in search of work. Between 1950 and 1970, more than one-quarter of Puerto Rico's 1950 population migrated to the states. Between 1940 and 1950 the Puerto Rican population on the mainland increased from fewer than 70,000 to 226,000, and by 1970, 810,000 Puerto Rican migrants and another 581,000 mainland-born Puerto Ricans lived in the states. During this time, urban areas in the Northeast and the Midwest provided jobs for migrants in certain sectors of their economies. The era thus witnessed more dispersed settlement, and the percentage of Puerto Ricans living in New York City decreased from 88 to 58 percent between 1940 and 1970.

Puerto Rico's agricultural economies declined rapidly in the postwar era, while the industrialization program, known as Manos a la Obra (or Operation Bootstrap), offered U.S. investors tax exemptions and other incentives, and wages in Puerto Rico were lower than those in the states. However, the industrialization program failed to replace the jobs lost in agriculture. The industries concentrated in the San Juan metropolitan area, and most of the new jobs employed women. Not only did the jobs not replace those lost in agriculture, but the results were declining rates of labor force participation and still more migration by both men and women from the rural areas to Puerto Rico's metropolitan areas and to the mainland. Puerto Rico's policymakers, however, defined the problem as one of overpopulation instead of a lack of jobs and turned to population control and emigration as solutions. The sterilization of Puerto Rican women increased, and by 1965, one-third of the Puerto Rican women between the ages of twenty and forty-nine had been sterilized. In addition, although the officially stated position was to ''neither encourage nor discourage migration,'' the government established the Bureau of Employment and Migration in 1947 and promoted contract labor programs. Policymakers worried that the continuing migration to New York City and the hostile reactions that migrants were encountering there might limit U.S. investment in Puerto Rico and tourism. The Migration Division then issued ''publicity in Puerto Rico announcing the greater supply of jobs in the Midwest'' and promoted the farm labor program as parts of their ''strategy of dispersing migrants outside of the New York City region.'' Puerto Rico promoted two contract labor programs. The first recruited women to the mainland as domestic workers. Hoping to reduce the population and foster dispersed settlement, policymakers established domestic training centers in Puerto Rico. Although some women were sent to the states, the program was short-lived, as women seemed to prefer the garment industry and other jobs that were available in U.S. cities. The policymakers then turned their attention to a contract labor program for men to migrate as seasonal agricultural laborers. The Migration Division oversaw the farm labor program and the supervised labor contracts that were signed by the employer and the worker and approved by Puerto Rico's Commissioner of Labor.

The U.S. government also promoted the farm labor program. The cooperation between employers and government agencies that emerged during World War II continued, as the U.S. Employment Service handled the requests for Puerto Rican workers and facilitated placements. During the cold war, Puerto Ricans' U.S. citizenship was transformed from a liability to an asset. With foreign workers being repatriated and continued labor shortages in agriculture, Puerto Ricans became a preferred source of labor. They, along with southern African Americans, were recruited for the least desirable of jobs. Despite the government-sponsored labor contracts that were supposed to protect Puerto Ricans, working and living conditions were harsh and wages were low for seasonal farmworkers throughout the post–World War II era.

Puerto Ricans migrated with and without labor contracts to work on farms or to find other jobs in the cities. During the 1950s and 1960s, between 10,000 and 17,000 agricultural contract laborers came to the mainland each year. Others came without labor contracts to work on the farms. While many agricultural laborers returned to Puerto Rico, still others stayed, settling in nearby towns and cities and sending for their families. Others migrated directly from Puerto Rico to the cities. Informal networks of family and friends helped the migrants make the move and find jobs and housing. Urban economies provided jobs for Puerto Ricans in the secondary sector. The available jobs were low paying and provided few opportunities for advancement. Although some found manufacturing jobs, many men ended up working in the services sector, particularly in restaurants and hotels. Women found manufacturing work, especially in the garment industry, for in New York City, Puerto Rican women had started working in the garment industry as skilled hand sewers, embroiderers, and seamstresses in the years after 1898. By 1920, according to historian Altagracia Ortiz, Puerto Rican women were an identifiable component of the labor force, and after World War II, they became the largest ethnic group in such trades as dressmaking, skirts, and blouses.

By 1970, as noted, dispersion had increased and Puerto Rican migrants had established communities in several industrial cities of the Northeast and Midwest. Nonetheless, New York City remained the largest community, with more than 817,000 Puerto Rican residents. Chicago had become the second largest, with over 79,000 Puerto Ricans. The farm labor program had its greatest effect in the mid-Atlantic states, with most contract laborers going to New Jersey. Many went to Pennsylvania and New York, as well. The Puerto Rican community of Philadelphia grew rapidly during the 1950s, from fewer than 2,000 to more than 14,000, as farmworkers from New Jersey and Pennsylvania and migrants directly from the island settled in the city. Contract laborers also went to Delaware and Maryland, and during the 1960s increasing numbers went to Connecticut and Massachusetts. In the 1970s, for example, contract laborers contributed to the growth of the Puerto Rican community in Waltham, Massachusetts. Communities of more than 10,000 had emerged in Newark, Jersey City, Paterson and Hoboken, New Jersey, Bridgeport, Connecticut, and Los Angeles.

The 1970s witnessed lower migration rates and increased return migration to Puerto Rico. During the decade, there was an estimated net gain of 157,600 migrants settling in the states. Economic recessions shook the United States, while food coupons were extended to Puerto Rico, enabling some potential migrants to stay. Yet economic conditions during the 1980s again propelled Puerto Ricans to search for work in the states, and migration accelerated once more. The industrialization program increased the island's gross national product but still did not provide enough jobs. Between 1950 and 1980, labor force participation decreased by nearly 20 percent, whereas unemployment increased from 13 to 17 percent. Policymakers promoted capital-intensive industries, such as petrochemical products, which employed fewer workers, albeit at higher wages. The extension of the minimum wage to Puerto Rico and the increased competition wrought by the Caribbean Basin Initiative in 1983 hampered Puerto Rico's ability to attract and keep labor-intensive industries.

Puerto Rico's economy shifted from manufacturing to services, and by the early 1980s an estimated 60 percent of all workers were employed in services. During that decade, more than 301,000 Puerto Ricans migrated to the states in search of work, bringing the total Puerto Rican mainland population to over 2.7 million. And the dispersion continued, for by 1990, only one third of Puerto Ricans lived in New York City, compared with 58 percent in 1970 and 88 percent in 1940. While most Puerto Ricans (68 percent) continued to live in New York, New Jersey, Massachusetts, Pennsylvania, and Connecticut, the Puerto Rican populations in Florida and Texas increased by 10 and 7 percent, respectively.

COMMUNITY, CULTURE, AND POLITICS

As Puerto Ricans settled in the cities of the Northeast and Midwest, they re-created communities to meet their needs in their new environments and to affirm their culture, traditions, and language. Community life centered around extended family networks, emerging ethnic neighborhoods, or "barrios," and religious institutions. Puerto Ricans struggled to counter discrimination and make existing social institutions responsive to their needs. They developed community organizations that evolved over time and reflected changing social and political contexts. Puerto Ricans entered the political realm through community activism, the protest movements of the late 1960s and early 1970s, and traditional electoral politics. In these endeavors, they sought both to adapt to life on the mainland and to affirm Puerto Rican culture. Many saw no contradiction in these two goals and advocated bilingualism and biculturalism as desirable and achievable outcomes.

Those who migrated to New York City in the post–World War II era encountered a well-established Puerto Rican community. Historian Virginia Sánchez Korrol notes that between the world wars Puerto Ricans founded a wide variety of formal community organizations, including mutual aid societies, hometown clubs, fraternal groups that represented Puerto Ricans citywide, and political associations. Yet, for Sánchez Korrol, "community" extended beyond formal community organizations. Puerto Rican neighborhoods were defined by businesses and professional services catering to Puerto Rican residents, by "the persistence of the Spanish language, customs, and habits for the maintenance of a shared identity as Puerto Ricans," and by "life-cycle celebrations and popular culture." In addition, informal networks played important roles in maintaining the community, and Puerto Rican women were central in these networks. Child care arrangements and the taking in of lodgers reinforced and expanded kin and fictive kin networks.

In the post-1945 era, Puerto Ricans in New York City continued prewar community efforts and developed new organizations to meet emerging needs. Incorporated in 1956, El Congreso del Pueblo included eighty hometown clubs. These hometown clubs continued their earlier efforts to provide shelter, jobs, and emergency financial help, while also expanding their activities to include leading mass demonstrations against discrimination and police brutality. Puerto Ricans established several social service–oriented organizations, such as the Hispanic Youth Adult Association, which became the Puerto Rican Association for Community Affairs by 1956; the Puerto Rican Forum, Inc. in 1957; Aspira in 1961; and the Puerto Rican Family Institute in 1963. The Family Institute provided basic necessities, referrals, social service counseling, and tutoring programs as well as working to re-create extended family networks by having more established families serve as *padrinos*, or godparents, for newcomers. Puerto Rican women were founders and active participants in many of these community organizations. In addition to these, Puerto Rico's Migration Division had offices in New York City, and it sought to facilitate the adjustment of Puerto Rican migrants by supporting community organizations, managing public relations (especially with city officials), and providing such services as employment and social service referrals. The impact of the Migration Division on New York City's Puerto Rican community has been debated. Although it ostensibly supported community-based organizations, some scholars have suggested that the existence of a government-funded agency hindered local, grassroots organizing.

Education became a central concern and an arena for community activism, as Puerto Ricans confronted the public school system and established organizations to ensure that Puerto Rican students could succeed. During the late 1930s and early 1940s, one grassroots parents organization, Madres y Padres Pro-Niños Hispanos, challenged the school system's placement of Spanish-speaking children several years behind their grade level or in remedial and special education classes. They provided volunteers to serve as interpreters in the classroom. After World War II, struggles centered around bilingual education, access to postsecondary education, and the development of Puerto Rican studies departments. The hiring of Spanish-speaking teachers as substitute auxiliary teachers (SATs) in 1949 was crucial in the promotion of bilingual education, according to Sánchez Korrol. In addition to their work in the classroom, SATs, most of whom were Puerto Rican women, encouraged parental involvement as hall monitors, crossing guards, playground aids, and chaperones for field trips, even enlisting parents to teach each other English. In 1962, SATs succeeded in shifting their status from "substitutes" to regular bilingual teachers. Aspira, founded in 1961, worked to prepare youth for leadership roles by establishing high school clubs and providing counseling. As an advocacy group, Aspira joined the Puerto Rican Legal Defense and Education Fund in a class action suit against the board of education. In 1974, the Aspira Consent Decree guaranteed bilingual education to all public school students who needed it. Puerto Rican activists also called for increased access to higher education and for the founding of Puerto Rican studies departments. In 1969, the City University of New York instituted open admissions and, within the next couple of years, established Puerto Rican studies departments on several campuses.

In cities where there were no sizable prewar communities, Puerto Ricans encountered similar challenges and responded with an array of organizations.

Migrants were, as sociologist Felix Padilla notes, "forced to develop and staff a parallel set of personal and social services, neighborhood businesses, and communication networks to meet the tastes and needs of a growing Puerto Rican population." In Chicago, according to Padilla, the most important community organization was Los Caballeros de San Juan (The Knights of St. John). Founded in 1954 by the Catholic Church and Puerto Rican laypersons, it served as a fraternal and civic group for men. This exclusion of women contrasts with the prominent roles of women in many other community organizations. From 1956 to 1965, Los Caballeros's largest event was the celebration of El Día de San Juan (St. John's Day), which became La Parada Puertorriqueña (The Puerto Rican Parade) in 1966 in order to include the other organizations that had emerged. In Philadelphia, the Concilio de Organizaciones Hispanas was the main Puerto Rican organization of the era. It started as an umbrella organization for hometown clubs and other groups. Like Los Caballeros in Chicago, the Concilio in Philadelphia was instrumental in initiating the Puerto Rican Parade in that city.

The Puerto Rican Parade became an important cultural and political event throughout the communities of the Puerto Rican diaspora. In New York City, the Puerto Rican Parade first marched in 1958, and it has become an annual event, with tens of thousands marching down Fifth Avenue to the cheers of hundreds of thousands of spectators. The parade mirrors the organizational history of the community. Initially, hometown clubs predominated. In the late 1960s, state-funded social service agencies assumed dominance, and by the mid-1970s, commercial enterprises became more visible. The organization of the parade has become a site for local leadership struggles. The continuing debates over Puerto Rico's political status and the three competing perspectives—commonwealth, statehood, and independence—appear in the politicians invited from Puerto Rico and in protest contingents promoting independence. At the same time, the parade represents a unified expression of cultural pride and a blending of island and mainland influences.

This expression of ethnic pride and the blending of cultural elements extends beyond the parades. As Juan Flores suggests, even third-generation Puerto Ricans have retained the use of Spanish, and there is "a conscious and widespread connection to bilingualism." Examining the linguistic practices of Puerto Ricans living in East Harlem, Flores concluded that most Puerto Ricans "found no conflict between speaking English and being Puerto Rican, or speaking Spanish and being actively involved in American culture" and "readily admit that many speakers mix both languages in discourse and view this positively." These trends are also evident in the extensive body of Puerto Rican literature produced by those living on the mainland. Thematically, this literature reveals the hardships and celebrates the accomplishments of Puerto Ricans in the states.

Puerto Ricans brought these commitments to their political activism, which evolved over time and reflected the larger political contexts in the United States and Puerto Rico. Social service agencies and their staff became recognized as leaders in the Puerto Rican communities, a position that was solidified with antipoverty funding in the mid-1960s. These leaders sought to provide services with sensitivity to Puerto Ricans' needs, increase access to resources, influence public policy, serve as role models, and prepare youth for community leadership. The War on Poverty funded existing organizations, like Aspira, and fostered the creation of new ones. In New York City alone, Community Corporations established by the Office of Economic Opportunity funded over 200 Puerto Rican organizations. These organizations provided a foundation for political leaders and a way to bypass entrenched political machines. Yet dependence on external funding fostered professional bureaucracies and a style of patronage politics that opened these social service agencies to the criticism that they were no longer meeting the community's needs. In Chicago, Los Caballeros began to decline in the mid-1960s, as community members questioned its ideology and tactics. In Philadelphia, the Concilio encountered similar complaints.

By the late 1960s, emerging political movements provided alternative visions and strategies. The Young Lords were one of the most visible groups, with branches in Chicago, New York City, Philadelphia, Newark, Hartford, and elsewhere. While each branch had its own origins and agendas, they shared a commitment to grassroots activism and their advocacy for community control of neighborhood institutions and for the independence of Puerto Rico. They criticized the social service agencies for having an assimilationist approach and for collaborating with public officials—in short, for working within existing social structures instead of challenging "the system." Former gang members in Chicago had started the Young Lords in 1967 to challenge the "urban renewal" that was displacing Puerto Ricans from Lincoln Park, using protests, physical force, and vandalism. They took over the McCormick Theological Seminary in 1969 to publicize the issue and to demand that the Seminary support low-income housing, a children's center, a cultural center, and legal assistance for the community. In New York City, a Young Lords branch was organized in 1969 and mounted its first campaign, the "Garbage Offensive." They initiated neighborhood clean-ups, and when city officials failed to provide brooms or to pick up the collected garbage, they put it in the middle of the street, forcing the city to collect it. In December 1969, they occupied a Methodist church and converted it into a "People's Church," operating clothing drives, breakfast programs, political education classes, a day care center, health programs, and entertainment. In January 1970, police arrested 105 Young Lords, ending the People's Church. Undaunted, the Young Lords took over Lincoln Hospital, demanding community control of health care institutions. In Philadelphia, the Young Lords ran breakfast programs for children, clothing drives, and health care programs, while confronting the problems of drugs, gangs, and police brutality in their neighborhoods. The Young Lords also organized mass demonstrations. In 1972, they opened branches in Puerto Rico to promote independence—a move that contributed to the splintering of the Young Lords in 1973.

In addition to this history of political activism, Puerto Ricans have participated in traditional electoral politics. In 1937, Oscar García Rivera became the first Puerto Rican elected official on the mainland, representing East Harlem in the New York State Assembly. During the 1930s and the 1940s, Puerto Ricans had a vocal advocate in U.S. Congressman Vito Marcantonio, an Italian American who represented East Harlem. Puerto Ricans' participation in electoral politics declined during the 1950s and 1960s, with the low voter turnout in New York City a striking contrast to the high turnouts in Puerto Rico. This suggests, according to political scientist Angelo Falcon, that the low participation in New York City cannot be attributed to cultural apathy or to low socioeconomic status but rather to the impact of differences in the political structures. Puerto Ricans confronted entrenched political machines on the mainland, and until 1964, they were required to pass a literacy test in English in order to register to vote in New York State. By the 1970s, Puerto Ricans were less likely to vote but more likely than other ethnic groups to participate in politics by joining organizations, signing petitions, and attending protests.

Since the 1970s, electoral victories for Puerto Rican candidates have increased, and some Puerto Ricans have formed political alliances with African Americans. In New York, between 1970 and 1978, the number of Puerto Rican state senators increased from one to two, state assembly members from three to five, and city council members from zero to three. In 1970, Herman Badillo became the first Puerto Rican elected to the U.S. Congress, representing a newly created congressional district. He served until 1977, when he accepted a position as deputy mayor for management in Mayor Edward Koch's administration. In the special election to fill his seat, Robert Garcia was elected and remained until 1990, when he resigned after being convicted of extortion—a conviction later overturned. During the 1980s, many Latino/a voters in New York City, most of whom were Puerto Rican, split from the established Puerto Rican leadership to support the candidacy of Jesse Jackson for president in 1984 and in 1988. The Puerto Rican/Latino vote was also instrumental in the election of the city's first African-American mayor, David Dinkins, in 1989. In Philadelphia, Puerto Ricans formed a coalition with African Americans and liberal whites to defeat Democratic mayor Frank Rizzo's efforts to alter the city's charter in 1978 so that he could run for a third term. Electoral victories followed when Angel Ortiz was elected city councilman in 1984 and Ralph Acosta was elected as a state representative in 1985 and was followed by Benjamin Ramos. In Chicago, following court-ordered redistricting, José Berrios was elected the first Puerto Rican to the general assembly in 1982, and Latinos, including Puerto Ricans, contributed to the mayoral campaign of Harold Washington. Nevertheless, despite the gains, Puerto Ricans remain underrepresented in electoral politics, and issues of redistricting persist.

Meanwhile, Puerto Rico has remained a commonwealth, and much of Puerto Ricans' political energies focus on the status issue. The political movements of the late 1960s and 1970s, like the Young Lords and the Puerto Rican Socialist Party, called for independence and linked the status of Puerto Rico to the conditions confronting stateside Puerto Ricans. In Puerto Rico, status has remained a constant political issue. The advocacy of one status or another—commonwealth, statehood, or independence—defines the political parties. In 1989, the leaders of the three parties wrote to the president and Congress demanding that Puerto Ricans be consulted, for the first time, in resolving Puerto Rico's status. The United States remained interested in Puerto Rico for national security reasons and because it was a profitable site for U.S. investors, yet all three status options have been considered problematic. Meanwhile, Puerto Ricans themselves remain deeply divided over the issue of status. Nonetheless, a 1989 opinion poll by the Institute for Puerto Rican Policy found that the majority of stateside Puerto Ricans believed that they should participate in any plebescite and that their status preferences did not differ significantly from those living in Puerto Rico. Not surprisingly, these findings suggest that stateside Puerto Ricans remain concerned with issues affecting Puerto Rico and continue to share perspectives with those in Puerto Rico. After all, the connections between Puerto Rico and Puerto Ricans in the states are constantly reinforced by the continuing political and economic ties between Puerto Rico and the United States, immigration and return migration, and the relative ease of transportation and communication. These ties, in turn, reinforce the biculturalism and bilingualism of stateside Puerto Ricans.

These connections with Puerto Rico have not, however, prevented Puerto Ricans from establishing roots in the continental United States. Instead, recent scholarship on Puerto Ricans' community, culture, and politics challenges earlier assertions that Puerto Ricans have had no mainland community. Social scientists had argued that the lack of community and the lack of organizations distinguished Puerto Ricans from earlier European immigrants and was a defining element of Puerto Ricans' presumed "culture of poverty." Those arguments reflected prevailing views of the era and were based on narrow definitions of both community and politics. As Sánchez Korrol suggests, "community" is more than formal organizations. Narrow definitions rendered much of the Puerto Rican community and its politics invisible, and more recent scholarship is remedying this invisibility.

OBSTACLES AND CONTEMPORARY SOCIETY

Arriving in the post–World War II era and settling in urban areas in the Northeast and the Midwest, Puerto Ricans encountered obstacles that stemmed from U.S. racial attitudes and the changing nature of U.S. cities. As a multiracial group, Puerto Ricans confronted a biracial system of classification that defined people as either black or white. Legalized racial segregation prevailed in the southern states, and antimiscegenation laws and attitudes perpetuated a climate of hostility toward racially mixed peoples. In 1976, the U.S. Commission on Civil Rights observed, "The United States has never before had a large migration of citizens from offshore, distinct in culture and language and also facing the problem of color prejudice.'' Finding discrimination against Puerto Ricans in employment, education, and War on Poverty programs, it concluded, ''Official insensitivity, coupled with private and public acts of discrimination, has assured that Puerto Ricans often are the last in line for the benefits and opportunities made available by the social and civil rights legislation of the last decade.'' Poverty and unemployment were more severe for Puerto Ricans than for other ethnic groups: Some 33 percent lived in poverty, in contrast to 12 percent of the total U.S. population. The commission predicted ''an uncertain future'' for Puerto Ricans in the states.

Puerto Ricans also confronted popular and scholarly assertions that blamed them for their poverty. Social scientists writing in the 1950s and 1960s suggested that Puerto Ricans' poverty was caused by a ''culture of poverty.'' Anthropologist Oscar Lewis considered ''poverty and its associated traits as a culture . . . with its own structure and rationale, as a way of life which is passed down from generation to generation along family lines.'' From this perspective, Puerto Ricans had a ''defective'' culture and family structure. Nathan Glazer and Daniel Patrick Moynihan wrote that, generally, poverty was often mitigated by ''the existence of a network of culture, religion, art, custom . . . [and] a strong family system that again enhances life.'' But, they concluded, ''in both these aspects Puerto Rico was sadly defective,'' and as a result, Puerto Ricans lacked ''the basis for an improvement in life.'' Instead, they were experiencing a ''circle of dependency,'' as ''[t]he culture of public welfare . . . is as relevant for the future of Puerto Ricans in the city as the culture of Puerto Rico.'' Similarly, Joseph Fitzpatrick attributed Puerto Ricans' ''problems'' to what he considered ''traditional features of Puerto Rican culture (machismo, the practice of the mistress, consensual unions, the culture of poverty).''

More recently, scholars have examined the changing nature of urban areas and the impact on Puerto Ricans. As historian Theodore Hershberg suggests in ''A Tale of Three Cities,'' it was a different urban environment than that which had been encountered by earlier immigrants. Puerto Ricans, along with African Americans who migrated in the postwar era, bore the brunt of deindustrialization and residential segregation. After a brief postwar economic boom, industries began leaving urban areas for the suburbs, for lower-wage areas of the United States, and for overseas locations. As whites also left the cities for the suburbs, Puerto Ricans and African Americans were left in the inner cities where unskilled manufacturing jobs were increasingly scarce and where the quality of education was declining with the eroding tax base. The situation was compounded by residential segregation. As sociologist Douglas Massey notes, Puerto Ricans and African Americans are the only urban groups that experienced residential segregation and increased poverty at the same time. While economic change affected individuals, the fact that large numbers of the affected individuals lived in the same neighborhoods meant that economic change could devastate entire communities.

Indeed, Puerto Ricans had settled in industrialized cities that were among those most affected by the economic restructuring of the 1970s. In those cities, Puerto Ricans, especially women, were concentrated in manufacturing jobs, but as the manufacturing industries relocated, those workers were displaced from the labor force. Employment increased in the professional and financial services, but Puerto Ricans were unable to secure jobs in these sectors. In short, Puerto Ricans were concentrated in the declining economic sectors and underrepresented in the growth sectors. Examining the greater poverty of Puerto Ricans than African Americans in New York City, economist Andrés Torres found that African Americans were employed in several sectors of the city's economy, whereas Puerto Ricans remained predominantly in a very few areas. In particular, African Americans' employment in the government sector increased more than Puerto Ricans', and significant differences emerged in the employment patterns of Puerto Rican and African-American women. These economic shifts affected other cities with large Puerto Rican populations, including Chicago and Philadelphia. Instead of encountering expanding opportunities, Puerto Ricans confronted a contracting economy.

Thus, scholars do not debate the existence of Puerto Rican poverty; rather, they disagree over its causes. By 1987, 40 percent of all Puerto Ricans were classified as poor, in contrast to 11 percent of whites and 33 percent of African Americans. Although poverty rates had increased for all ethnic groups between 1978 and 1987, Latino poverty increased more dramatically, and Puerto Ricans had the highest poverty rate of any racial or ethnic group. Puerto Rican poverty, according to Rebecca Morales and Frank Bonilla, reflects the increasing income inequality that characterized the unprecedented economic growth of the 1980s. Compounding the earlier patterns, this economic growth was accompanied by economic restructuring that had begun earlier, which displaced workers, increased job instability, and contributed to lower wages and cuts in social services. While the rich got richer, the middle class stagnated, and the poor fell further behind. Consequently, for Puerto Ricans, who were concentrated in urban areas, the traditional paths for upward mobility were closed due to the continued erosion of stable jobs and the reorganization of the manufacturing that did remain.

Puerto Rican women were particularly hard hit by the economic restructuring because of their concentration in the manufacturing sector. During the 1960s, the labor force participation of Puerto Rican women in the mid-Atlantic states had actually decreased, whereas African-American and white women continued entering the workforce. Women who headed their households were particularly vulnerable, and poverty was most severe for this segment of the Puerto Rican population, leaving these women poorer than other female heads of household. Then, during the 1970s, female-headed families increased from 27 to 40 percent of Puerto Rican families, whereas female-headed families increased from 12 to 16 percent of all families. However, the 1970s also witnessed an increase in Puerto Rican women's labor force participation, as women with more education entered white-collar employment. As sociologist Alice Colón-Warren suggests, cultural explanations based on an assumed lack of a work ethic or prohibitions against women working fail to explain the changes over time or the regional variations in Puerto Rican women's employment. Approaches that include a historical perspective challenge earlier explanations based on "culture of poverty" assumptions.

By 1990, the Puerto Rican population in the states reflected the complexities of economic restructuring and its impact. There were signs of economic progress at the same time that Puerto Ricans continued to have one of the highest poverty levels. Between 1979 and 1989, Puerto Ricans' mean household income rose by 25 percent (adjusted for inflation), which was one of the highest rates of income growth in the United States. More Puerto Ricans were in managerial, professional, technical, sales, and administrative positions, as the proportion of Puerto Ricans in the labor force increased from 40 to 47 percent. Puerto Rican women's labor force participation increased by almost 10 percent. There were also improvements in education, as Puerto Ricans with less than a high school diploma decreased from 58 to 47 percent of all Puerto Ricans who were twenty five years of age or older. The increase of those with a college degree was slight, however, rising from 6 to 10 percent. And the per capita household income of Puerto Ricans was still only 53 percent of that of whites. Income inequalities within the Puerto Rican population were likewise sharp, with 30 percent living in poverty—a decrease from 36 percent in 1980 but still among the highest poverty rates. While lower levels of education may have hindered economic mobility, higher educational levels have not guaranteed economic success. Recent migrants from Puerto Rico to the states—those arriving between 1985 and 1990—have had more education than their counterparts already residing there but have had lower earnings and higher poverty rates. This suggests that issues of language proficiency, adaptation to mainland life, a perception that education in Puerto Rico is inferior to that in the states, and discrimination may still play a role. There are also regional dimensions to the income polarities among Puerto Ricans. Those in the mid-sized urban areas of the Northeast are poorer than those in the emerging communities in the southern and western states. The recession of the early 1990s also seems to have increased the rate of poverty among Puerto Ricans. It is too early to tell how that economic slowdown, followed by the economic recovery of the mid-1990s, may shape Puerto Ricans' future economic status and migration patterns.

To these new challenges Puerto Ricans have responded through grassroots community organizing, national organizations, and electoral politics. As Padilla asserts, "Community-building efforts among Latinos were undertaken at the same time that Chicago experienced a series of major economic changes that left many working-class individuals and families without traditional avenues for earning a living and organizing their lives." While Puerto Ricans moved to a neighborhood of second settlement to secure a better education for their children and better housing, they found, instead, decreasing employment opportunities, rising housing costs, an ineffective public school system, and an increasing drug trade. They continued organizing efforts around education and housing and established citizens' watch groups to confront gangs and drugs in their neighborhood. Studying a Brooklyn neighborhood, Mercer Sullivan concludes, "Despite the emergence of considerable poverty among Puerto Ricans in Sunset Park, including local areas of concentrated poverty, the neighborhood has shown considerable institutional resilience in several sectors along with evident stress in others." Since the late 1960s, a coalition of grassroots Puerto Rican community organizations and white, church-based liberals has expressed the concerns of their community. They founded a local redevelopment organization to build and rehabilitate low-income housing. There were antipoverty programs, church-sponsored youth programs, small Pentecostal congregations that formed mutual support networks, and commercial vitality in the form of small businesses and services. Residents' efforts to get police to respond to gangs and drugs failed initially, but Sullivan suggests that since the mid-1980s special police interventions and community residents have been able to contain crime in this neighborhood.

Beyond the neighborhood level, Aspira International promotes an educational agenda on a national level. Other national associations include the Institute for Puerto Rican Policy, the National Puerto Rican Coalition, and the National Congress for Puerto Rican Rights. In the 1990s, Puerto Ricans José Serrano and Nydia Velasquez, Democrats from New York, and Luis Gutierrez, a Democrat from Illinois, have been elected to the U.S. House of Representatives.

Despite new scholarship, earlier attitudes have proven remarkably resilient. The earlier scholarship is still cited often and uncritically, and many of the attitudes underlying the "culture of poverty" have resurfaced in the "underclass debate." While some scholars and policymakers have focused on concentrated poverty and the impact of economic restructuring, others have focused on "behaviors" and point to welfare dependency, criminal activities, and female-headed households as causing poverty. Those who suggest that "behavior" causes poverty echo the "culture of poverty" hypothesis. For them, the focus has remained on Puerto Ricans' "problems," with little attention to the history of Puerto Rican migration, the larger contexts affecting Puerto Ricans, or Puerto Ricans' continued efforts to improve their lives and their communities. At the same time, Puerto Ricans have remained "an invisible minority" in much of the scholarly and policy-oriented discussions of poverty.

In addition to highlighting the impact of U.S. racial attitudes and the changing nature of urban life, a historical perspective on Puerto Rican migration sheds light as well on the post-1965 immigration from Central and South America and the Caribbean. The parallels are evident: Latino/a immigrants have come from countries where the United States has intervened politically and/or economically and, in many cases, where export processing zones mirror Puerto Rico's industrialization program. Women have been displaced by economic changes and have joined migrant streams as labor migrants. In the United States, Latino/a immigrants encounter an increasingly two-tiered economy, finding jobs either in the better-paid services or in the lowest-paid services and sweatshops. As racially heterogeneous groups, some with histories of significant racial mixing, they too confront a U.S. system of racial classification that grapples with diversity. The building of transnational communities and the promotion of bilingualism and biculturalism exist as possibilities.

In the late 1960s and early 1970s, government agencies began to use the ethnic label "Hispanic" to categorize Puerto Ricans, Mexican Americans, and more recent immigrants from other Spanish-speaking countries. This ethnic label, as Suzanne Oboler suggests, sought to homogenize diverse groups with distinct histories, and it became imbued with negative stereotypes. It did not emerge as a term of self-identification for the groups that found themselves thus classified. Instead, most Puerto Ricans and other Latinos/as continued to identify themselves on the basis of nationality, that is, as Puerto Ricans, Dominicans, and so forth. Nonetheless, in his study of Puerto Ricans and Mexican Americans in Chicago, Padilla found that in some situations more than one nationality group chose to join forces as "Latinos/as" to confront shared obstacles. For Padilla, identification as "Latinos/as" is a political choice that coexists with a specific national identity rather than replacing it. As some settle in Puerto Rican communities, Latino/a immigrants have contributed to the neighborhoods and their diversity and have confronted similar challenges. The potential for cultural borrowing and political coalitions remains an area for future scholarship on comparative migration history and intergroup relations.

BIBLIOGRAPHIC REFERENCES

The scholarship on Puerto Rican migration and on Puerto Ricans in the continental United States has increased dramatically in the past decade. Yet few historians have focused on Puerto Ricans on the mainland. Instead, the scholarship on Puerto Ricans remains interdisciplinary, as scholars from other disciplines include historical perspectives and historians rely on interdisciplinary approaches. On the economic and political causes of migration, see Centro de Estudios Puertorriqueños, *Labor Migration under Capitalism: The Puerto Rican Experience* (New York: Monthly Review Press, 1979); Luis Falcon, "Migration and Development: The Case of Puerto Rico," in *Determinants of Emigration from Mexico, Central America, and the Caribbean*, edited by Sergio Díaz-Briquets and Sidney Weintraub (Boulder: Westview Press, 1991), pp. 145–188; and Edwin Maldonado, "Contract Labor and the Origins of Puerto Rican Communities in the United States," *International Migration Review* 13 (Spring 1979): 103–121. For the post–World War I era, see Virginia Sánchez Korrol, *From Colonia to Community: The History of Puerto Ricans in New York City* (Berkeley: University of California Press, 1994); and Ruth Glasser, *My Music Is My Flag: Puerto Rican Musicians and Their New York Communities, 1917–1940* (Berkeley: University of California Press, 1995).

For the post–World War II era, see Felix Padilla, *Puerto Rican Chicago* (Notre Dame: University of Notre Dame Press, 1987); Clara E. Rodríguez and Virginia Sánchez Korrol, eds., *Historical Perspectives on Puerto Rican Survival in the United States* (Princeton:

Markus Wiener, 1996 [1980]); Michael Lapp, "The Migration Division of Puerto Rico and Puerto Ricans in New York City, 1948–1969," in *Immigration to New York*, edited by William Pencak, Selma Berrol, and Randall M. Miller (Philadelphia: Balch Institute Press, 1991), pp. 198–214; Altagracia Ortiz, ed., *Puerto Rican Women and Work: Bridges in Transnational Labor* (Philadelphia: Temple University Press, 1996); and United States Commission on Civil Rights, *Puerto Ricans in the Continental United States: An Uncertain Future* (Report of the U.S. Commission on Civil Rights, October 1976). For historical perspectives on contemporary issues, see Clara Rodríguez, *Puerto Ricans: Born in the U.S.A.* (Boulder: Westview Press, 1991); and Andrés Torres, *Between Melting Pot and Mosaic: African Americans and Puerto Ricans in the New York Political Economy* (Philadelphia: Temple University Press, 1995). For examples of earlier perspectives on the postwar migration, see Oscar Lewis, *La Vida: A Puerto Rican Family in the Culture of Poverty–San Juan and New York* (New York: Random House, 1965); Nathan Glazer and Daniel Patrick Moynihan, *Beyond the Melting Pot: The Negroes, Puerto Ricans, Jews, Italians, and Irish of New York City* (Cambridge, MA: Massachusetts Institute of Technology Press, 1963); and Joseph P. Fitzpatrick, *Puerto Rican Americans: The Meaning of Migration to the Mainland*, 2nd ed. (Englewood Cliffs, NJ: Prentice-Hall, 1987).

On politics, see James Jennings and Monte Rivera, eds., *Puerto Rican Politics in Urban America* (Westport, CT: Greenwood Press, 1984); Angelo Falcon, "Puerto Rican Political Participation: New York City and Puerto Rico," in *Time for Decision: The United States and Puerto Rico* (Lanham, MD: The North-South Publishing Co., 1983), pp. 27–53; Andres Torres and Jose E. Velazquez, eds., *The Puerto Rican Movement: Voices from the Diaspora* (Philadelphia: Temple University Press, 1998); and Carol Hardy-Fanta, *Latina Politics, Latino Politics: Gender, Culture, and Political Participation in Boston* (Philadelphia: Temple University Press, 1993). On the changing nature of cities and contemporary issues, see Theodore Hershberg, Alan Burstein, Eugene Ericksen, Stephanie Greenberg, and William Yancey, "A Tale of Three Cities: Blacks, Immigrants, and Opportunity in Philadelphia, 1850–1880, 1930, 1970," in *Philadelphia: Work, Space, Family and Group Experience in the Nineteenth Century*, edited by Theodore Hershberg et al. (New York: Oxford University Press, 1981), pp. 461–491; Douglas S. Massey, "American Apartheid: Segregation and the Making of the Underclass," *American Journal of Sociology* 96 (September 1990): 329–357; and Francisco L. Rivera-Batiz and Carlos E. Santiago, *Island Paradox: Puerto Rico in the 1990s* (New York: Russell Sage Foundation, 1996). On culture and identity, there is Juan Flores, *Divided Borders: Essays on Puerto Rican Identity* (Houston: Arte Público Press, 1993); Suzanne Oboler, *Ethnic Labels, Latino Lives: Identity and the Politics of (Re)Presentation in the United States* (Minneapolis: University of Minnesota Press, 1995); Felix Padilla, *Latino Ethnic Consciousness: The Case of Mexican Americans and Puerto Ricans in Chicago* (Notre Dame: University of Notre Dame Press, 1985); and Frances Negrón-Muntaner and Ramón Grosfoguel, eds., *Puerto Rican Jam: Rethinking Colonialism and Nationalism* (Minneapolis: University of Minnesota Press, 1997). For examples of the extensive body of literature, see Roberto Santiago, ed., *Boricuas: Influential Puerto Rican Writings—An Anthology* (New York: Ballantine Books, 1995).

Two anthologies focus on diverse aspects of the Puerto Rican experience: Edwin Melendez and Edgardo Melendez, eds., *Colonial Dilemma: Critical Perspectives on Contemporary Puerto Rico* (Boston: South End Press, 1993), and Carlos Antonio Torre, Hugo Rodriguez Vecchini, and William Burgos, eds., *The Commuter Nation: Perspectives on Puerto Rican Migration* (Rio Piedras: Editorial de la Universidad de Puerto Rico, 1994).

Several anthologies on Latinos/as include important essays on Puerto Ricans and lay the groundwork for comparative analysis. See Joan Moore and Raquel Pinderhughes, eds., *In the Barrios: Latinos and the Underclass Debate* (New York: Russell Sage Foundation, 1993); Rebecca Morales and Frank Bonilla, eds., *Latinos in a Changing U.S. Economy: Comparative Perspectives on Growing Inequality* (Newbury Park, CA: Sage Publications, 1993); and Gabriel Haslip-Viera and Sherrie L. Baver, *Latinos in New York: Communities in Transition* (Notre Dame: University of Notre Dame Press, 1996). Two journals routinely publish new scholarship on Puerto Ricans: the *Bulletin* of the Centro de Estudios Puertorriqueños and the *Latino Studies Journal*.

SCANDINAVIANS

David C. Mauk

HISTORIOGRAPHIC PERSPECTIVES ON THE INTERNATIONAL MIGRATION OF SCANDINAVIANS

Between 1821 and 1930 some 3 million Scandinavians took part in the second great wave of European immigration to the United States. Of these, roughly 20 percent returned to Scandinavia. Between 1951 and 1995, an additional 144,000 immigrated, mostly in the 1950s and 1960s. In 1990, roughly 11 million people (4.5 percent of the general population) claimed a Scandinavian ancestry.

For some of these contemporary Americans, the few Nordic immigrants who arrived much earlier, in the Viking age or during Europe's seventeenth-century occupation of North America, have assumed the status of ethnic forbears, symbolic founders of their modern-day ethnic groups. In 1988 the Swedish royal family joined in elaborate celebrations of the 350th anniversary of New Sweden on the Delaware River, whose population of some 500 in its seventeen years of existence included many Dutch and Finns. About the same time, some Norwegian Americans noted that distant relatives of colonial Norwegian settlers in New Amsterdam were claiming financial compensation for the loss of farmland in lower Manhattan and, having appropriated the entire Viking heritage in North America to themselves, felt pride in their contemporary political clout when President Ronald Reagan officially proclaimed Leif Ericsson Day a national holiday.

These earliest modern emigrations from Scandinavia also remind us that an international labor market had developed even on the outskirts of Europe by the early 1600s. In fact, it developed especially there because the Norwegian, Finnish, and to a degree, the Swedish economies were "colonial" in the sense of supplying raw materials and labor to Germany, England, and the Netherlands. Over 10,000 Norwegian sailors, for example, joined the Dutch merchant fleet for economic gain and to avoid serving in the Danish-Norwegian navy. The background for this tradition of long-distance international migration—and emigration overseas out of Europe—is the age-old practice of labor migrations within each of these countries, between them, and from nearby countries in northwest Europe that, during important periods, supplied commercial, technical, and administrative expertise lacking in Scandinavia.

If one discounts the continuing trickle of concealed migration by ship-jumping seamen over the next two centuries, immigration from Scandinavia did not begin again until 1825, when a small party of Quakers and religious sympathizers arrived in New York from southwestern coastal Norway. In the imagination of the ethnic elites who evolved a Norwegian-American identity during the first decades of this century, that ship, the small sloop *Restauration*, became the Norwegian *Mayflower* in the iconography of the ethnic group's claim to an American birthright.

Because the people of Scandinavia comprised roughly 3 percent of Europe's total population in the nineteenth century, it should not be surprising that emigration from the Nordic countries contributed but one-twentieth of the total overseas migration from the continent between 1820 and 1914. What is worthy of attention is the exceptionally high intensity of emigration from these countries in proportion to their home populations. Norway and Sweden ranked second and third in this respect (after Ireland) throughout the nineteenth century. Iceland ranked third in the 1880s, and Norway continued to be second through the 1920s. Thus, Scandinavians came to comprise one of the largest European immigrant groups arriving in the United States between 1820 and 1890, despite the relatively small size of their homelands' populations.

Among the Nordic countries, only emigration from Norway took place on a large scale in the 1850s, its earliest small waves of departures occurring in the 1830s and 1840s. Most early pioneers of Swedish and Danish emigration did not leave until the 1850s. Thereafter, all three major Scandinavian countries experienced a massive exodus in great waves that largely paralleled those from the rest of Europe: 1866 to 1873, 1880 to 1893, 1900 to 1914, and 1920 to 1929. Emigration from Norway not only began earliest but was also the most intense and remained the strongest in the two twentieth-century peak periods. Explanations for this commonly emphasize the country's exaggerated case of the push factors common to all of the Nordic countries: an even greater population increase caused by superior health conditions; a generally later urbanization and industrialization (with the partial exception of Oslo and Bergen); a consequently starker contrast between rural and urban areas and classes; and an even smaller percentage of arable land in a rural culture that put a premium on landownership for starting a family and maintaining socioeconomic status.

Some scholars claim that another variable was the exceptional success of American Mormon evangelizers in Sweden and Denmark in the 1800s, for it represented one form of the common people's protest against state churches that were arms of upper-class control. In all three countries (Sweden, Denmark and Norway) resistance to state-church Lutheranism produced pietistic awakenings, charismatic low-church and lay preachers, and so-called free forms of the official faith, all of which may have influenced migration decisions.

A century or more after similar events in England and parts of Germany, the nineteenth-century population explosion and nascent urbanization first in Denmark and then in Sweden and Norway led to an enclosure movement, improved farming methods, and more commercial agricultural production. The new wealth, however, was unequally distributed. As the century progressed, the loss of village common lands, the consolidation of farms by large landowners, the subdivision of farms among heirs, or the rule of primogeniture resulted in a ballooning class of landless day laborers and farmworkers whose living standards sank while landowners' rose. Typically, emigrants were rural people threatened by landlessness who either found no satisfactory opportunities in nearby urban centers due to the slowness of industrialization or preferred attempting the reconstitution of their rural culture on the American frontier to migration internally up to the underpopulated Arctic north or internationally to other parts of the world. The emigration did not represent the movement of a rural proletariat, because the very poor usually lacked the resources to emigrate. In this case, the majority departed *before* sinking into poverty.

The general trends in the demographic characteristics of Nordic emigrants show a progression from family and group—rural-to-rural agricultural migration with nearly equal numbers of relatively young married men and women in the mid-nineteenth century—toward an increasingly young, literate, unmarried, urban-to-urban industrial (or service occupation) stream that was still only marginally more male than female in the early twentieth century. The emigration process for specific groups and regions varied, however, according to combinations of those groups' occupational training, religious belief, ethnic background, and the economic opportunities in the United States. Female domestic workers, miners, fishermen, loggers and sawmill workers, engineers and other professionals, and seamen from the Nordic countries moved through distinctive migration processes and settled in equally distinctive ways and locations in the United States. In the far Arctic north, the Saami (Lapps), Kven (Finns who settled in the mining towns of northern Sweden and Norway), and Laestadian religious sect, to name three examples, immigrated to the Upper Michigan Peninsula, central Michigan, northern Minnesota, and the Pacific Coast in ways just now being examined by Einar Niemi.

Compared with other Scandinavians, Danish emigrants more often came from towns and cities, chose destinations other than the United States (where 89 percent settled), and spread their settlements widely across ten or so American states, from New York through the Scandinavian core states of the Upper Midwest to Mormon Utah and California. Eventually, Iowa became the state with the largest and best-known Danish rural communities, which, as Jette Mackintosh's comparative studies of Elk Horn and Kimballton exemplify, show the ethnic group's distinctive configuration of cultural characteristics. Only two miles apart, these communities exhibit Danish Americans' historic religious division into the strictly pietistic Inner Mission Lutheranism of the lower classes and the broadly tolerant Lutheranism (introduced by Danish Bishop F.N.S. Grundtvig) of the middle-class landowners, as well as the later, secularized forms of these differences. These appeared in Danish-American politics as loyalty to either the Republicans or the Democrats and in education as the early acceptance of Americanizing public schools and the English language or long-lasting adherence to Danish language and culture through the philosophy of the Grundtvigian "folk high school" (which had open admissions, no examinations, and combined liberal arts and vocational curricula). In agriculture and economics the dichotomy appeared as cautious expansion and conservative methods versus the rapid introduction of Danish agricultural innovations, especially in cooperative dairy farming and livestock production.

The pronounced strength of emigration from Norway after 1900 resulted from several factors, the most important perhaps being a long tradition of emigration, the uneven geographic spread of industrialization, short-term economic recessions, and the over thirty-year depression in the country's commercial shipping fleet, on which its southern region very largely depended. An important additional cause was Norway's lack of politico-cultural autonomy, due to domination by first Denmark and then Sweden from 1442 to 1905, which may have produced a particularly strong version of the opposition to the upper classes and government officials common among Scandinavian emigrants. In Norway the socio-economic establishment was often of foreign descent, if not foreign-born. In fact, according to the classic work of George Stephenson, Norwegian Americans looked on their mother country very positively, championing the (by western European standards) very late Romantic Nationalism there, which portrayed their rural farming cultures as the true Norway; resolving to preserve that folk culture in America; and agitating from across the Atlantic for the final break with Sweden. Many Swedish and Danish Americans expressed more critical views of their homelands, especially of their oppressive class systems, and more eagerly asserted their preference for American ideals of socioeconomic mobility. Compared with these other Scandinavian Americans' aspirations, Norwegian Americans showed a notably greater interest in maintaining their ethnic identity and institutions in the last years of the twentieth century.

SHIFTING PATTERNS OF SETTLEMENT AND ADJUSTMENTS: PATHFINDERS, STEPPING–STONE COMMUNITIES, AND TRANSPLANTED CULTURAL TRADITIONS

Some 95 percent of Swedish and Norwegian emigrants settled in America. In 1910 nearly half of first- and second-generation Swedish Americans and between seven- and eight-tenths of Norwegian Americans lived in the upper midwestern core region, both groups mostly concentrated in Minnesota, which— with its smaller but noticeable populations of Danish, Icelandic, and Finnish

Americans—had become the New Scandinavia that the visiting Frederika Bremer hoped for in the mid-nineteenth century. But secondary Swedish migration had only changed its core state from Illinois (with its largest urban community in Chicago) to Minnesota in the later nineteenth century, and Norwegian settlement first began in border areas of Illinois, Iowa, and Wisconsin before centering on Minnesota, where Minneapolis became that ethnic group's recognized "capital city" in America. Scandinavian rural settlement (a mixture of the second generation and newcomers seeking land) moved west of Minnesota into the Dakotas and beyond in the 1870s and 1880s and, from 1890 to the 1920s, was most active in Washington and California. Norwegian Americans were the most rural and agriculturally employed of all American ethnic groups in 1910, whereas fewer and fewer farmers were reported among other Scandinavian Americans—the Finns, Swedes, and Danes included, respectively.

A remarkable feature of this later rural-to-rural immigration and remigration was the movement of people along a "stepping-stone" trail of older settlements—first in New York State, Illinois, and Wisconsin and later in states farther west—which served as way stations on the journey to the newest settlement areas. In the early part of the period, groups of families directly from Europe traversed this trail, but increasingly Scandinavian Americans joined them in the search for good land and compatible neighbors. Typically, the migrants chose stepping-stone community transit stops where they had family and cultural ties from localities or regions at home (either in Scandinavia or in more easterly Scandinavian America). Indeed, Jon Gjerde for Norwegians (1985), then Robert Ostegren for Swedes (1988), and most recently Steffen Jørgensen (1991) for Danes have published studies examining patterns of family chain migration over several generations that fused emigration from and maintenance of particular local cultural milieux with integrated religious, socioeconomic, agricultural, and linguistic traditions. Thus evolved a process that helped preserve (and even strengthen) family, religious, and old-country regional cultures from the Great Lakes to the Pacific Northwest, as Scandinavian immigrants and their children exploited the socioeconomic potential and met the trials of geographic mobility on the frontier in the United States.

These pathways across the continent also had strong roots in the Old World class system of the nineteenth century. As in Denmark, the people in Norway and Sweden who faced the harshest socioeconomic reality tended to turn to pietistic forms of Lutheranism that condemned drinking and "loose" entertainments, viewed life as travail, and urged an orderly and self-disciplined existence as a moral and practical necessity. These people often chose to emigrate together, stop in communities of like-minded people, and establish new rural enclaves of the same sort farther west. And those more fortunate in the old country, who had evolved different cultural values from their experiences of religion and class, did the same. While investigating these striking patterns of cultural maintenance and persistence, scholars also note that such distinct cultural groups frequently formed more or less segregated parts of the same community or farming district and that adjusting to life in "mixed" populations of Scandinavian and non-Scandinavian immigrants and old-stock Americans was more common than living in homogeneously Norwegian-, or Danish-, or Swedish-American settlements representative of a provincial old-country culture. Among Swedish and Norwegian immigrants, such ethnic and religious allegiances occasionally became decisive factors in political activity, but they commonly assumed importance only in conjunction with salient local economic and social issues, that is, within the framework of local and state party and election rules and through negotiations in which the size and views of other groups played a role.

Nonetheless, recent research also strengthens the evidence that each of the Scandinavian nationalities worked to dominate a particular rural community when it could, even buying contiguous farmlands in homogeneous subnational, regional enclaves *within* a Swedish-, Danish-, or Norwegian-American area to the exclusion of others. The simplest and perhaps most convincing explanation for this is many immigrants' near-instinctive wish to live among people of similar background who were therefore more likely to understand not only their mother tongue but also their cultural reflexes and attitudes. Hard-line Grundtvigian Danish Americans consciously determined to preserve their language and culture by establishing a string of isolated rural colonies. However, even when (often *especially* when) such hegemony proved possible, internal religio-class schisms weakened Scandinavian Americans' political and cultural influence. An old joke about Norwegian Americans applies nearly as well to their Scandinavian compatriots: You can always recognize one of their settlements instantly, because it is the one with identical white wooden churches on opposite sides of a country road.

Mackintosh, Gjerde, Ostegren, and Jørgensen explore the transplantation of community (including whole sets of related institutions) through this kind of family and cultural chain migration. They then trace how distinct Old World cultures evolve in response to both the American environment and the continuing evolution of society in Scandinavia, charting accommodation and even assimilation but asserting the existence of a documentably Scandinavian form of each. Odd Lovoll has shown convincingly how loyalties to old-country, rural subcultures among Norwegian Americans were revived and strengthened in the latter nineteenth century through the organization of the *bygdelag*, national alliances of people from the same valley or region in Norway. To a degree these organizations were part of the larger American reaction against the transformation of traditional rural community forms and social values by increasing urbanization and industrialization. Yet they also served as a way for immigrants and their children to meet at *lag* reunions to celebrate their common *American* experience as pioneers on the frontier, and they functioned as an early step in the construction of a self-conscious Norwegian-American identity. Similar processes seem to have been occurring among the other Scandinavian groups, too. Swedes founded similar regional or district societies, although they never reached the extent or won the popularity of their Norwegian parallels. It appears that both Danish and Swedish Americans had been less interested in reacting to social change at the time through the medium of their regional or national ethnic backgrounds.

"OLD" IMMIGRANTS IN THE TWENTIETH CENTURY: CITIES, TOWNS, AND SUBURBS

A sign of the international urbanization taking place was that from the late 1880s an ever increasing portion of the Scandinavian immigrant population left a city in the homeland to settle in another city in the United States. At the turn of the century, more than a third—and by the 1920s over half—of those leaving were town or city dwellers. Moreover, an even larger proportion of the incoming stream took up residence in American cities, for even rural people hoping to own their own farms now chose to work for a time in a city in order to purchase the land that had risen in cost as the frontier disappeared. By the 1920s in Scandinavia, the large numbers of newly urbanized people produced a longing for old ways and a wish to preserve rural cultures, which took the form of city social clubs (in Norway called Bondeungdomslaget—The Farmer Youth League) established by young people, where the crafts, music, and dancing of the countryside were practiced. Soon, these same clubs appeared in Brooklyn, Chicago, and Seattle. Scouting and 4-H clubs served as parallel ways of guiding young people away from the perceived dangers of urban life by inculcating rural culture and its traditional values.

Urban settlement among Scandinavians in this period produced a Scandinavian Chicago of over 40,000 people as early as the city's 1884 school census. By 1920, some 58,000 Swedes represented the city's fifth largest foreign-born group, along with a population of 60,000 first- and second-generation Norwegian Americans. Scandinavians also boasted of having large "colonies" in New York City, but at its peak in 1930, the largest group there, the Norwegians, amounted to less than 2 percent of Brooklyn's population. In fact, the only large city where Scandinavian Americans could count on decisive influence when they united behind a cause was Minneapolis, where they accounted for over half the foreign-born in the 1890s and a very large voting bloc even after the influx from southern and eastern Europe. On the other hand, one or more of the Scandinavian groups grew to dominance or great influence in smaller cities across the country by the 1920s: Swedes in Jamestown, New York, and Rockford, Illinois; Swedes and Finns in Worcester, Massachusetts; Danes in Omaha, Nebraska, and Racine, Wisconsin; a mix of all the Scandinavian groups in Seattle-Ballard and Tacoma, Washington, and Portland, Oregon. In addition, there are the small cities and towns, often with a college related to one of these national groups, that have (as Dag Blanck and others have pointed out) functioned as ethnic cultural nerve centers, exerting a strong influence on the evolution and maintenance of a *national* Danish-, Norwegian-, or Swedish-American identity. Among them are

Northfield, Minnesota (St. Olaf College) and Rock Island, Illinois (Augustana College).

In the 1950s and 1960s, a small wave of Scandinavian immigrants arrived, seeking greater opportunities than they could find in homelands trying to rebuild their economies after the war. As might be expected, nearly twice the percentage of the population of Norway (1.3 percent)—the Scandinavian country most devastated by the war—departed for America as left from Sweden and Denmark, although in absolute numbers the more than 26,000 Danes and nearly 50,000 Swedes outnumbered the Norwegians who came. These roughly 100,000 Scandinavian people settled overwhelmingly in cities, assisted a revitalization of ethnic institutions and Old World ties in the 1970s, and, along with the presence of Norway's fleet in New York during the World War II years, helped Greater New York become the home of the largest urban concentration of Norwegian Americans in the United States.

According to Anita R. Olson, Swedish Americans began moving to the suburbs of Chicago as early as the 1880s, a trend that was very pronounced by the 1920s, when many of those earliest outlying areas had been annexed by the city. Odd Lovoll has shown a similar, contemporary movement among Norwegian Americans away from commercializing downtown Chicago and into the suburbs. On the East Coast, Scandinavians joined the general exodus out of southern Manhattan to Harlem and Brooklyn, especially after the Brooklyn Bridge opened in 1883. In Brooklyn, the main Norwegian community migrated south toward the margins of the city from around 1900, according to studies by sociologist Christen Jonassen and historian David Mauk. Jonassen attributes this move to the immigrants' desire to be in countrylike surroundings reminiscent of Norway near the sea. Mauk traces it to the opportunities to join other groups occupying new row houses in less commercial-industrial areas, which were available at reasonable prices because the immigrants themselves were helping to construct them. In any case, as with other immigrant groups in urban areas generally, Scandinavian Americans moved when their main sources of work moved. In Brooklyn, where the largest number of wage earners and small businessmen were in maritime trades, that meant following the southward construction of dock areas farther and farther from the city center. In the 1920s, and to a much greater extent again after World War II, as John Jenswold has shown, Scandinavian Americans participated in the flight to the suburbs of the general white population. Sometimes, this contributed to mixing with other groups and a flagging interest in ethnic origins. But when Swedish and Norwegian Americans eschewed the new subdivisions and instead winterized country cottages in ethnically homogeneous vacation colonies dating from the prewar years, as was frequently the case around New York City, they created a ring of tertiary satellite settlements in the suburbs. There, they sustained group traditions and family ties and returned to the mother colony in the city on religious and patriotic occasions.

THREE DISTINCTIVE PATTERNS OF ACCOMMODATION, ADJUSTMENT, AND ETHNIC PERSISTENCE

The overall similarity of the three Scandinavian nationality groups made the course of their accommodation to and integration in American society comparable in many ways. But popular and even scholarly perceptions have all too often lumped them indiscriminately together as easily assimilated northwest European, white Protestants. However, it is necessary to give visibility, first, to the broad features of each nationality's distinctive experience and, second, to the historic reality of difficulties in adjustment that they perceived as so serious as to require wrenching accommodation and concerted action.

Differences in their old-country societies colored Scandinavians' perceptions of their situation in the United States, and each wave of Scandinavian immigrants came from a changed old country and met a changed America. In general and throughout the period from the 1860s to the 1930s, according to Dorothy Skårdal and Kristian Hvidt, the Danish-American experience of adjustment had been distinctive in that Danes constituted a much smaller and very widely scattered group and, therefore, were most willing to participate in pan-Scandinavian-American institutions. On the other hand, they have showed less interest than Swedes or Norwegians in ethnic organizations in general. They more often both left from and settled in urban areas. Over 48 percent lived in American towns and cities in 1910. Until after World War I, over nine-tenths of them arrived as day laborers, landless farmworkers, or craftspeople but, nonetheless, exhibited the highest levels of literacy and proficiency in English among Scandinavians throughout the classic immigration period. Danes have assimilated faster, for several of these reasons, as well as the fact that they have higher intermarriage rates with non-Scandinavians. Still, their experience in concentrated, rural, mostly agricultural settlements was much closer to—although not identical with—that of other Scandinavian immigrants.

Distinctive Swedish-American traits have been fewer in the sense that the group has had more in common with Norwegian Americans. Although numerically the largest group overall and usually the largest contingent in urban Scandinavian quarters, Swedish Americans have shown less energy in ethnic maintenance than have Norwegian Americans, according to some scholars, because nineteenth-century emigrating Swedes were both more critical of socioeconomic inequality and class injustice at home and more positively oriented to American institutions and values than were Norwegians. Swedish scholar Ulf Beijbom early pointed out that Swedes have long been significantly more urbanized than Norwegians (61 versus 42 percent when the foreign-born generation of both groups was at its peak, in 1910), and he suggests that because of that they have also been more susceptible to Americanization. Norwegian Americans' larger number of relatively isolated, nearly exclusively farming settlements have enhanced their ability to construct and maintain a Norwegian-American ethnicity and have given exceptionally long life to subnational, regional Norwegian-American identities. Beijbom notes that Swedish Americans have been the slowest of the Scandinavians to intermarry but sees assimilation to American life occurring *within* the group.

Christen Jonassen's and Nathan Kantrowitz's studies of Norwegian Americans in the New York and Chicago metropolitan areas showed them to be the least willing to intermarry of European groups and in those cities, as recently as the 1960s, the most socially and economically segregated ''old'' ethnic group. After the work of Swedish-American historian George Stephenson, one repeated explanation for the unusual degree of ethnic maintenance characteristic of Norwegian Americans is that an exceptionally intense ethnic consciousness among Norwegian Americans resulted from the nineteenth-century Norwegian intelligentsia's identification of Norwegian nationalism with the culture of the rural peasantry and the very late climax of Norwegian nationalism around 1905. Against this view, one must weigh the equally common claim that most immigrants from Norway lacked a national identity entirely, seeing themselves instead as members of a provincial culture and constructing a national identity only in response to American conditions and out of indifference to Old World regional cultures. A different perspective (explored by Odd Lovoll and David Mauk, among others) is that the rising tide of pride in agrarian nationalism at home provided a very usable past for an ethnic group that needed both to distinguish itself from neighboring Scandinavian nationalities (that had been sources of oppression in Europe) and to effectively mark its profile in America, where such a small group could so easily be overwhelmed by the presence of much larger immigrant populations.

Language problems constituted a serious barrier to Scandinavians' adjustment until the wave that entered the United States after World War II. Like other immigrants in all periods, until they acquired a working proficiency in English, Scandinavians experienced the loss of Old World socio-economic status. Until then, their self-esteem and education were effectively reduced or rendered useless, and they suffered significantly more unemployment, job discrimination, economic exploitation, and difficulty in general. To a degree, Swedes, but especially Norwegians, faced the additional difficulty of dialect differences that complicated adjustment even within their own enclaves. For first-generation Grundtvigian Danes and for immigrant Swedish and Norwegian Lutherans, religion and culture were but pallid shadows unless experienced through the mother tongue. Important leaders in the first generation, especially churchmen, believed that their children's interest in the group's heritage as well as their keeping of the faith and respect for their elders all depended on language maintenance. That belief (or fear) buttressed the appeal of the folk high school among Danes. Among Norwegian Americans in the Midwest, it also fueled an almost thirty-year controversy in the mid-1800s over the advisability of establishing a separate system of ethnic parochial schools, which pitted business and press leaders (and the majority of ordinary Norwegian Americans) on one side against conservative Norwegian Lutheran church leaders on the other. In 1889 Wisconsin's Scandinavian and German Americans combined forces to form an overwhelming majority for repeal of the state's draconian Bennett Law, which required both private and public schools to teach core subjects solely in English. According to Lowell Soike's persuasive political history, at the first election during World War I after Iowa's Governor Lloyd Harding banned all languages but English in public life (including all schools and churches), he experienced a drop of 39 percent in support from Norwegian- and Danish-American communities, compared with their usual support for Republican candidates.

The heavily agrarian Scandinavian settlement on the prairies and Great Plains required another kind of difficult adjustment: accommodation to dramatically different topography, climate, crops, and farming methods. As Gjerde and Ostegren have documented, they had to learn to break the deep sod, acquire a new sense of seasonal timing, grow corn and wheat, and give up a gender division of labor that earned the opprobrium of Americans as the exploitation of women for dairy and haying work—to name but a few of the necessary changes for agrarian success in America.

Scandinavians' conventions regarding religion also seemed unacceptable to many old-stock American Protestants, because in the 1800s all three nationality groups were accustomed to a state religion, clerics representing the hegemony of the upper classes, and the expectation of near-total religious homogeneity. P. A. Munch and many after him have described the resultant religious apathy of many Scandinavian immigrants. They wanted a church to be there for the necessary business of getting baptized, confirmed, married, and buried but resented ministerial authority and interference in secular affairs; were unused to the voluntary individual religious and financial commitment of American congregation members; and expected the church to eschew comment on their drinking, dancing, and other festive folk traditions. But members of pietistic religious groups that had been officially frowned upon at home were more likely to emigrate, and the mainstream Scandinavian religious organizations adjusted to a more puritanical Protestant consensus in the United States. Both high- and low-church Scandinavian Lutheranism became strengthened but, at the same time, more critical of drinking, dancing, and card playing and more supportive of sabbatarian views in general. Marcus Lee Hansen asserted that this occurred as Scandinavian Americans strove to assimilate religiously by making their religious forms and values acceptable to Protestant America. In addition, anti-Catholicism and anti-Semitism, which had been largely latent in homogeneously Lutheran Scandinavia, became evident when Nordic immigrants came into contact with Catholic Irish and southern German Americans almost everywhere as well as with Italian and other eastern and southern European Catholics and Jews in American cities. Only after World War II did this legacy of once latent Old World attitudes dissipate.

CONTOURS OF THE SCANDINAVIAN–AMERICAN
POLITICAL LANDSCAPE OVER TIME

In the 1990s the popular press has sometimes shown a glib tendency to equate Scandinavian Americans' long-standing allegiance to the Republican Party with conservative stands on social issues that place them at the right of center in that party. They are lumped together with other white ethnics now asking for more policy emphases on family values, welfare reform, and the curtailment or end of affirmative action. How much truth the press reports hold has only begun to be addressed by scholars as they start to evaluate the relevance of the work of Lizabeth Cohen, David Roediger, and others on the conjunction of ethnicity, class, and race in the evolution of an American working-class sensibility. The question remains unanswered not least because there has thus far been no comprehensive investigation of Scandinavian Americans' involvement in unions and because we possess only partial analyses of their views on issues vital to lower-middle or working-class people. And that is the situation despite the well-noted fact that they have provided both leadership and important membership components to unions representing saw- and flour-mill workers, construction workers and carpenters, fishermen, seamen, and dock builders.

Historically speaking, Scandinavian Americans voted largely Democratic until the mid-1860s, because the party of Jefferson and Jackson had the reputation of being the common man's party that (outside the South) championed social equality and defended unhindered immigration, access to citizenship for the foreign-born, and the latter's participation in politics. Starting with the election of 1856, however, and overwhelmingly by the end of the Civil War, Scandinavian immigrants voted Republican. The issues of slave labor and cheap land moved them and many other immigrants to contribute to a massive party realignment. The Homestead Act and the promise to prefer free labor functioned unassailably to keep them in the Republican fold, even though some Scandinavian-American opinion makers had to swallow hard to accept the party's associations with Know-Nothingism.

Still, none of the three nationality groups under discussion here has ever been monolithic in political terms. In general, the roughly 70 percent that were rural in background up to World War I brought a few broad attitudinal tendencies with them, which combined with the agricultural crisis in the wheat belt of the Midwest to play central roles in their political choices in America: an inbred opposition to officialdom and centralized power; a suspicious dislike of urban areas; a perception that the entrepreneurs and middlemen in towns and cities exploited the farm population of the hinterland; a proud sense of their ancient agrarian culture; and a dynamic tension between anticlerical, religiously apathetic elements and pietistic, evangelical institutions and awakenings. Politically, there existed some major, relatively stable groups: the generation that settled before 1860 and had prospered by the time of the postwar wave of arrivals; the town-dwelling merchants, millers, and bankers all through the 1800s; and the more elderly in the southeasterly midwestern settlements. They all voted with the moderate-to-conservative wing of the Republican Party. On the other hand, the one-crop wheat farmers in northwestern Minnesota and the Dakotas, Scandinavians in the closely connected secondary settlements farther west, and the unionized workers in the cities voted with and elected countrymen from the reform-minded, independent Populist or Progressive wing of the party. And, as Odd Lovoll and Lowell Soike tellingly point out, in 1890 over half of Minnesota's Norwegians lived in the northwest region of the state, and there, as in the Dakotas, Scandinavians were the dominant ethnic group—and the backbone of the wheat growers.

So the inescapable conclusion is that the largest part of midwestern Scandinavian Americans between the 1880s and 1944 (when the Farmer-Labor Party was folded into the Democratic Party) were liberal or even radical Republicans. But their contribution to the moderate and conservative wing was sizable. Hans Norman and Harald Runblom, moreover, are right in supporting a tripartite typology for understanding the region's Scandinavian-American politics. The third, much smaller but highly significant element is the radical presence that generated a crucial part of the groups' disproportionate support for the Farmers' Alliance, Populism, Progressivism, the NonPartisan League, the Farmer-Labor Party, and (to a lesser degree) the International Workers of the World and socialist clubs and parties. The size of the independent-to-radical Left group increased with each great wave of newcomers from the homelands, as Scandinavia progressively responded to agrarian and labor movements that advocated elements of socialism and thus sent to the United States immigrants used to roles for the state that were outside the American political mainstream. The rural radicals were always a small but a vocal and (at times) charismatically mobilizing minority. In North Dakota, for example, the radical Nonpartisan League ran on a platform of state-controlled and -operated grain elevators and government wheat marketing and, even during the wartime wave of anti-foreignism in 1918, swept the elections in that "Scandinavian" state. During the 1930s, Swedish-Norwegian-American Floyd B. Olsen three times won election as the governor of Minnesota on the Farmer-Labor ticket.

The political situation and allegiance of the large urban Scandinavian-American communities in the Midwest and on the East and West Coasts have also evolved distinctively. In Minneapolis–St. Paul, Scandinavian workers distinguished themselves by their support for Populists and Farmer-Labor candidates. Across the country, Scandinavian socialist newspapers, clubs, and chapters of larger American socialist organizations won noticeable support among Scandinavian working people and functioned as the staging areas for radical activity from the late 1860s on—but especially between the 1880s and the late 1930s. In the cities, lower-middle-class service and white-collar Scandinavian Americans, especially the religiously active, have often voted (together with German and other Protestant Americans) for independent or moderate Republicans in opposition to coalitions of Democratic, largely Catholic population groups. Generally, the more socioeconomically upwardly mobile the urban entrepreneurial elite becomes, the more conservatively Republican its voting patterns are, particularly among its members who are moving into nonethnic, mainstream affiliations. On the other hand, ever since it incorporated elements of Populism and Progressivism around the turn of the nineteenth century, the Democratic Party has made lasting inroads among Scandinavian Americans on the West Coast and generally in urban and suburban areas. As with many historically Republican groups, however, the key electoral defections or lasting realignment of significant numbers of these ethnic populations came with support for the New Deal. In the Twin Cities (and for the first time, in Minnesota), in Chicago, and in New York, Scandinavian-American majorities helped elect a Democratic president in 1932. Ever since Franklin Delano Roosevelt's victory, the Republican grasp on Scandinavian America has been less total and less sure. But in the late 1990s, it is clear that empirical analyses of these groups' working-class attitudes and voting patterns are needed as one test of their role in the so-called new conservativism and their possible discovery of common ground with the southern and eastern European Americans who are generally considered the main crossover groups among the Reagan Democrats.

THE AMERICAN DREAM REALIZED

Like its political landscape, the socioeconomic and cultural topography of Scandinavian Americans that emerges from the 1990 census and the most current research shows a mixture of tendencies. There are familiar and distinctive contours, strikingly enduring historical patterns, formations suggesting progressively greater integration into the overall American terrain, and yet rising heights of ethnic involvement.

As has been the case since the 1890s, the largest of the three groups is Swedish Americans (43 percent of Scandinavian Americans in 1990), followed by Norwegians (36 percent), Danes (15 percent), and ''Scandinavians'' (6 percent), a group whose sense of having a generalized or mixed Nordic identity suggests the group's well-known historical tendency to marry within their European cultural region. In 1990, however, all three Scandinavian American groups were among those most likely to marry outside the group. Geographically, Scandinavian Americans are still concentrated in the Upper Midwest, which contains 43 percent of Nordic Americans, and in Minnesota in particular, where over a third of the population claims Scandinavian ancestry. North and South Dakota, Montana, Washington, and Utah (respectively) rank after Minnesota in proportion of people with Scandinavian ancestry. The West, including Alaska, contains 35 percent of Scandinavians. The prominence of the West in this respect is not new, because of the ethnic groups' large historically late settlement there, but the region is, in contemporary terms, gaining on the Midwest as the rightful heartland of Scandinavian America.

More surprising is that the South, almost entirely because of expanded settlement in Texas and Florida, has a larger Nordic-American population than the Northeast. As Arizona is now home to a significant percentage of the West's Scandinavian American population, so, too, is Florida for the South. Although the foreign-born in 1990 comprised just over 1 percent of the total Scandinavian population, the elderly immigrants are retiring in large numbers to those two states, adding to the migration of younger people looking for economic opportunity or climate change there. Since the 1950s, the economic expansion of Texas in energy and computer technology has also attracted sizable additions to its Scandinavian ancestry groups, who first settled there in the nineteenth century. That development parallels the striking rise in the proportion of Scandinavians in California, which now is the state with the second largest population of Scandinavian Americans in the country.

The Northeast is home to somewhat over a million members of these ethnic groups (10 percent). The relative recency of these communities' development has kept memories of vibrant urban colonies so fresh in this fourth-ranking region that ethnic festivals (in particular but not only the Norwegian Constitution Day in Brooklyn) bring large numbers of people into the mother colonies from the suburbs and the entire region. Overall, however, the broad lines of Scandinavian Americans' internal migration are one indication of their structural integration in American society as a whole, reflecting the movement of the general population to the West, Southwest, and South.

Each of the nationality groups remains the dominant Scandinavian element in its historic stronghold: Swedish Americans in Texas, California, Illinois, Massachusetts, and the East Coast generally, and Norwegians in New York City, Washington, North and South Dakota, Minnesota, Wisconsin, and Iowa. Danes are predominant only in Utah and its cities, where their historically much greater tendency to convert to Mormonism is still clearly in evidence. In the mountain and plains states, Swedes and Norwegians split dominance from state to state, except in Oregon, where they show matched strength, and in Nebraska, where Swedes and Danes outnumber Norwegians.

On the other hand, the 15 percent of the population in Utah that is Scandinavian American (237,000 people), like other Scandinavian-American communities in thinly populated areas, may gain a visibility denied much larger populations in such places as California, Illinois, Texas, and New York. On the other hand, only in Minnesota, the Dakotas, Washington, and perhaps Wisconsin and Iowa are both the absolute numbers and percentages of the Scandinavian-American population large enough that the group might continue to carry significant political weight. But even here Scandinavian Americans no longer comprise either the largest ethnic population (outnumbering German Americans) or the majority of voters or the decisive swing block that Sten Carlsson and Jon Wefald found so crucial in electing state and federal representatives around the turn of the century. Still, the relatively large size, well-established position, and political tradition of the group in these areas give it today a general influence out of proportion to its contemporary size.

The other demographic and socioeconomic traits of Scandinavian Americans reinforce the portrait of a well-integrated, older ethnic group that, though still distinct, is less so than earlier in part because of its very success. Understandably, the median age of a group that is 99 percent native-born is close to (but somewhat older than) the whole American population. However, the dramatically contrasting median ages of the rather small population of foreign-born are telling: Those who immigrated between 1980 and 1990 are in their late twenties, whereas those who immigrated before 1980 are almost precisely forty years older.

In educational attainment, median family size, per capita income, and general occupational profile, Scandinavian Americans—and foreign-born Scandinavians—show achievements and prosperity above the levels of the general native-born population. The statistics for the three main nationality groups are very similar in all these respects, but in terms of achievement or income, Danish Americans consistently rank highest, Swedish Americans in the middle, and Norwegian Americans lowest. (This is also true of the three foreign-born groups and of women in all these categories.) Proportionally, less than half as many native-born Scandinavian Americans as in the general population (including women) have only an education through the eighth grade or less. Compared in percentage terms to the American population, only two-thirds as many foreign-born Scandinavian men and just about one-ninth as many of these foreign-born women have so little education. In addition, more of both the native- and foreign-born Scandinavian Americans have also had two or more years of college.

Their higher levels of education are one factor in Scandinavian Americans' higher incomes and relatively prestigious employment patterns. The median family income for Scandinavian Americans in 1989 was $39,867, about $4,000 above that of all native-born in the United States, whereas the per capita income in the ethnic group, $17,441, was over $3,000 higher. Foreign-born Scandinavian families surpass both all other foreign families (by $7,000) and the American-born (by $3,000) in their median incomes and per capita median income. Whereas in the early 1900s, farming, forestry, and fishing employed a large majority of all three nationality groups, and today they are still quite evident in these occupations (3.4 percent compared to 2.7 percent of the general population), in occupational terms they have come remarkably close to approximating the national distribution. Thus, in building and construction work, where they had long been overrepresented, they are today merely typical of the general workforce. On the other hand, they (and recent immigrants from Scandinavia in particular) are significantly more likely than other Americans to be self-employed, managers, or professionals.

Overall, in 1990 Scandinavian Americans appeared moderately above average in their socioeconomic success and, generally speaking, structurally integrated into American society. Over a thousand in-depth interviews carried out across the nation in 1995–1996 (as part of Odd Lovoll's contemporary Norwegian-American History project ''The Promise Fulfilled?'') gave strong indications of two tendencies in that ethnic group that appear to characterize Scandinavian Americans as a whole: They increasingly share the attitudes and positions on social issues typical for the socioeconomic class they occupy in American society, and yet they simultaneously exhibit a renewed or strengthened interest in preserving and celebrating their ethnic background.

BIBLIOGRAPHIC REFERENCES

Seminal and central recent work in Scandinavian-American studies include: H. Arnold Barton, "Where Have the Scandinavian-Americanists Been?" *Journal of American Ethnic History* 15.1 (Fall 1995): 46–55; J. R. Christianson, "Scandinavian-Americans," in *Multiculturalism in the United States*, edited by John D. Buenker and Lorman A. Ratner (Westport, CT: Greenwood Press, 1992); Kristian Hvidt, ed., *Emigrationen fra Norden indtil 1. Verdenskrig: Rapporter til det Nordiske Historikermøde i København, 1971* (Copenhagen: Gyldendal, 1971); Steffen Elmer Jørgensen, Lars Scheving, and Niels Peter Stilling, eds., *From Scandinavia to America: Proceedings from a Conference Held at Gl. Holtegaard* (Odense: Odense University Press, 1987); Birgit Flemming Larsen, Henning Bender, and Karen Veien, eds., *On Distant Shores: Proceedings of the Marcus Lee Hansen Immigration Conference, Aalborg, Denmark, 1992* (Aalborg: Danes Worldwide Archives, 1993); Odd S. Lovoll, ed., *Scandinavians and Other Immigrants in Urban America: The Proceedings of a Research Conference* (Northfield, MN: Norwegian-American Historical Association [hereafter NAHA], 1985); Odd S. Lovoll, ed., *Nordics in America: The Future of Their Past* (Northfield, MN: NAHA, 1993); Harald Runblom and Dag Blanck, *Scandinavia Overseas: Patterns of Cultural Transformation in North America and Australia* (Uppsala: Center for Multiethnic Research, Uppsala University, 1986); and Hans Norman and Harald Runblom, *Transatlantic Connections: Nordic Migration to the New World after 1800* (Oslo: Norwegian University Press, 1987). See also "Danes," "Norwegians," and "Swedes" in Stephan Thernstrom et al., eds., *Harvard Encyclopedia of American Ethnic Groups* (Cambridge: Harvard University Press, 1980).

Among other valuable studies specifically concerning Danes, see Birgit F. Larsen and Henning Bender, eds., *Danish Emigration to the U.S.A.* (Aalborg: Danish Worldwide Archives and Danish Society for Emigration History, 1992); Kristian Hvidt, *Flight to America—The Social Background to 300,000 Danish Emigrants* (New York: Academic Press, 1975); Steffen E. Jørgensen, " 'Emigration Fever': The Formation of Early Rural Emigration Tradition on Lolland-Falster and Møn, Three Danish Islands, ca. 1830–1871" (Ph.D. dissertation, European University Institute, Florence, Italy, 1991); and Peter L. Petersen, *The Danes in America* (Minneapolis: Lerner, 1987). Note, too, *The Bridge* (a journal of Danish-American studies)(Danish-American Heritage Society, 19 vols.).

With respect to Norwegians, see Odd S. Lovoll's *The Promise of America: A History of the Norwegian-American People* (Northfield, MA: NAHA, 1983) (second Norwegian-language edition, *Det løfterike landet* [Oslo: Scandinavian University Press, 1997]) and *A Century of Urban Life: The Norwegians in Chicago before 1930* (Northfield, MA: NAHA, 1988); Carl H. Chrislock, *Ethnicity Challenged: The Upper Midwest Norwegian-American Experience in World War I* (Northfield, MA: NAHA, 1981); Jon Gjerde, *From Peasants to Farmers: The Migration from Balestrand, Norway to the Upper Middle West* (Cambridge: Cambridge University Press, 1985); David C. Mauk, *The Colony That Rose from the Sea: Norwegian Maritime Migration and Community in Brooklyn, 1850–1910*

(Northfield, MA: NAHA, 1997); Einar Niemi, "Emigration from Northern Norway: A Frontier Phenomenon? Some Perspectives and Hypotheses," in *Norwegian-American Essays 1996*, edited by Øyvind Gulliksen, Dina Tolfsby, and David Mauk (Oslo: Norwegian Emigrant Museum, 1996); Einar Niemi, "The Finns in Northern Scandinavia and Minority Policy," in *Ethnicity and Nation Building in the Nordic World*, edited by Sven Tägil (London: Hurst and Co., 1995); Lowell J. Soike, *Norwegian Americans and the Politics of Dissent* (Northfield, MA: NAHA, 1991); *Norwegian-American Studies*, 34 vols. (Northfield, MA: NAHA, 1926–1996); *Norwegian-American Essays, 1993* and *1996* and *Essays on Norwegian-American Literature and History, I* (1984), and *II* (1990) (Oslo: Norwegian-American Historical Association, Norway Chapter).

Finally, in terms of Swedes, take note of Harald Runblom and Hans Norman, eds., *From Sweden to America: A History of the Migration* (Minneapolis and Uppsala: University of Minnesota and University of Uppsala, 1976); Philip J. Anderson and Dag Blanck, *Swedish-American Life in Chicago: Cultural and Urban Aspects of an Immigrant People, 1850–1930* (Uppsala: Uppsala University, 1991); Dag Blanck and Harald Runblom, eds., *Swedish Life in American Cities* (Uppsala: Center for Multiethnic Research, 1991); H. Arnold Barton, *A Folk Divided: Homeland Swedes and Swedish Americans, 1840–1940* (Carbondale; Southern Illinois University Press, 1994); Ulf Beijbom, *Swedes in Chicago: A Demographic and Social Study of the 1846–1880 Immigration* (Växjö: The Emigrants' House, 1971); Dag Blanck, "Constructing an Ethnic Identity: The Case of the Swedish Americans," in *The Ethnic Enigma: The Salience of Ethnicity for European-Origin Groups*, edited by Peter Kivisto (Philadelphia: The Balch Institute Press, 1989); Sten Carlsson, "Scandinavian Politicians in Minnesota Around the Turn of the Century," in *Americana Norvegica*, vol. 1 (Olso: University of Oslo, 1971); Robert C. Ostegren, *A Community Transplanted: The Trans-Atlantic Experience of a Swedish Immigrant Settlement in the Upper Middle West, 1835–1915* (Uppsala: Uppsala University, 1988); and *The Swedish-American Historical Quarterly*, 48 vols. (Chicago: Swedish-American Historical Society).

A number of works referred to in the essay include Anita Olson, *Swedish Life in American Cities*, edited by Dag Blanck and Harald Runblom (Uppsala: Center for Multiethnic Research, 1991); Nathan Kantrowitz, *Ethnic and Racial Segregation in the New York Metropolis: Residential Patterns among White Ethnic Groups, Blacks and Puerto Ricans* (New York: Praeger, 1973); Peter A. Munch, *A Study of Cultural Change: Rural–Urban Conflicts in Norway* (Oslo: University of Oslo Press, 1956); Marcus Lee Hansen, *The Immigrant in American History* (Cambridge: Harvard University Press, 1941); Robert Ostegren, *A Community Transplanted: The Transatlantic Experience of a Swedish Immigrant Settlement in the Upper Midwest* (Madison: University of Wisconsin, 1988); Jette Mackintosh, " 'Little Denmark' on the Prairie: A Study of the Towns of Elk Horn and Kimballton in Iowa," *Journal of American Ethnic History* 7.2 (Spring 1988): 46–68; and John R Jenswold, " 'The Hidden Settlement': Norwegian Americans Encounter The City, 1880–1930" (Ph.D. dissertation, Storrs: University of Connecticut, 1990).

SOUTH ASIANS

Bruce La Brack

IMMIGRATION

A South Asian presence (see "Note on Terminology" at end of essay regarding names used and scope of coverage of this essay) in North America can be traced as far back as 1790, when a visiting Indian *lascar* (seaman) is mentioned in a colonial diary along with an Indian man-servant of a New England family. Again, diary entries in 1851 place a half-dozen South Asian sailors in Salem, Massachusetts, where they were observed at Fourth of July celebrations. Sporadic newspaper accounts exist of "Hindus" in the gold fields of California and merchants visiting New York and San Francisco from the mid-nineteenth century onward.

However, significant South Asian immigration to North America did not commence until the first decade of the twentieth century. By that time Canada and America were but two of many destinations in a worldwide diaspora from the 1880s onward that saw South Asians spreading across the globe to East and South Africa, the Caribbean, East and Southeast Asia, western Europe, and the South Pacific. Some went as indentured servants to provide labor in colonial plantation economies, while others followed as independent "passenger migrants" who sought economic opportunity as the British empire extended its influence around the globe. For many, notably Sikhs, service in the British military provided an avenue leading to useful training, travel, and exposure to new people, places, and ideas. The first immigrants to North America were almost exclusively males from Punjab Province in then–British India. Their subsequent half-century experience illustrates how the history of South Asian immigration to the United States both reflects and is a product of major American cultural attitudes, economic conditions, and legal circumstances as well as sociopolitical conditions in the Indian subcontinent.

South Asian immigration can be divided into two general, profoundly contrasting periods. The first period extends from the turn of the century until 1965, characterized by an initial decade of open immigration (1900–1910), followed by (1) legal discrimination in the form of a series of exclusionary acts, (2) social isolation, (3) the illegal immigration of perhaps an additional 3,000 South Asians in the interwar years, and (4) a subsequent precipitous population decline that was reversed only in the post–World War II era. There were individual economic successes in the first period and the fascinating formation in California of "Hindu-Mexican" (a.k.a. "Mexidu") family units. This unusual social component was composed of families headed by South Asian Punjabi Sikh or Muslim males, their Spanish-heritage wives, and their offspring, eventually forming networks statewide. Nevertheless, overall it was a time of encapsulation, struggle, and slow population decline.

The second period (1965–present) is different in every respect. Whereas single, uneducated, poor, male Punjabi sojourners from largely rural backgrounds characterized the first fifty years of immigration, the new immigrants have often been highly educated, financially secure, urban, arriving as families and representing all the ethnic and cultural diversity of South Asia itself. Marked by exponential growth in both the numbers and variety of South Asians immigrating to America, this dramatic reversal of earlier trends was made possible by the Independence of India (1947) and set in motion by sweeping changes in U.S. Immigration and Naturalization laws (1965), which reversed the anti-Oriental bias of previous legislation and created preferences available to skilled Asians. These time periods reflect stark differences in South Asian immigrant experiences. Between the initial influx to North America and today's South Asian population, there lie nearly 100 years of turmoil and change. At mid-century there were 1,500 Indians remaining in the United States. The South Asian American population now totals around 1 million.

EARLY DEMOGRAPHY

Concentrated on the West Coast, there were never more than 6,000 or 7,000 legal South Asians in residence, most (6,100) arriving between 1904 and 1911. Between 1915 and 1929 some 1,650 more came. During the depression years through World War II, only 183 additional South Asian immigrants were recorded. However, in the first two decades, some 6,750 South Asians were either deported or "voluntarily" left, many to support anti-British political activities in India or abroad or for personal reasons. By 1930 the "Hindu" population had declined to 3,130 and by 1940 to 2,405. Even including a further 3,000 illegals who sporadically filtered in via Mexico in the 1920s and 1930s, fewer than a total of 10,000 ever came to the United States in the first half of the twentieth century, and only 15 percent of them remained by mid-century.

The overall loss of nearly 7,000 persons, coupled with a ban on replacement through immigration and the natural aging and demise of the original "pioneers," resulted in the situation in California described by Gerald Hess (1974):

Although the preponderance (sixty percent) of the East Indians in 1940 still lived in California, their numbers had declined by forty-six percent since 1910. . . . The status of the small community had not improved over the years. By 1940 only a handful (four persons) were professionals, nearly half were farm laborers, fifteen percent were farmers or farm managers, and an additional twenty percent were engaged in non-farm labor. . . . [O]f the 1,600 East Indians over age twenty-five, more than a third had not completed even a year of schooling. The median school years completed among East Indians were 3.7. . . . Moreover, the East Indians now constituted an aging community; fifty-six percent were over age forty, thirty-two percent over fifty, and nine percent over sixty.

This portrait of population in decline, while accurate, does not reflect much of significance about the lives, ambitions, or accomplishments of the early South Asian immigrants.

PUNJABI IMMIGRANT EXPERIENCES

The majority of early immigrants were Punjabi male peasants from the northwest of British-controlled India, as high as 85 to 90 percent of whom identified themselves as Sikhs. The rest were also Punjabis, most identifying themselves as Muslims (perhaps 10 percent at various times), whereas Punjabi Hindus were a minor presence in this period. This is a reversal of Sikh-Hindu numbers in modern India, where today 85 percent of the population consider themselves followers of Hinduism and less than 2 percent of the population are Sikhs. Muslims constitute around 13 percent of contemporary India and are the majority in Pakistan and Bangladesh (both Islam-dominated states once part of British India and now independent nations). The early migrants came predominantly from a few relatively small districts of Punjab and often had firsthand experience with agricultural or entrepreneurial enterprises. The majority of the Sikhs were Jats, a caste designation denoting agrarian pursuits and a certain warrior cachet. Jats often were the dominant presence in rural Punjab farming communities. Punjabis generally, and Sikhs in particular, were atypical of the general population in India in a number of other important ways.

Although contemporary South Asian religious communities here and abroad often assert distinctive and exclusive identities, the Punjabis in late nineteenth-century India based their self-image and interactions more on kinship, lineage, and community than sect affiliation. Further, Sikhism and Islam are alike by doctrine, casteless religions, regardless of actual endogamous realities. Immigrant Sikhs and Muslims were therefore theoretically less restricted, if not less devout, in their religious and social practices than were followers of more conservative, Brahmanical traditions. This meant that the rigid, hierarchical relationships that lie at the heart of traditional South Asian social organization were undercut by a more equalitarian and openly competitive ethos that included personal courage, risk taking, maintenance of individual and family honor, defense of the faith and the weak, and a strong spirit of industry wherein manual labor was honored and landownership was a goal. These qualities were to prove crucial to survival in what was for most South Asian immigrants a difficult adjustment in an often hostile American environment.

Unfortunately, South Asians had begun immigration just when general anti-Oriental sentiments were peaking in response to earlier and much larger influxes of Far Eastern peoples to America, particularly California. An unfortunate by-product of this backlash was that the South Asian presence, in spite of tiny numbers, attracted immediate and virulent attention in Washington, Oregon, and California. Their darker skin, distinctive turbans, non-Christian faiths, food preferences, and cultural traditions marked them as strangers and foreigners. Whatever the reality of their situations, they were openly and actively discriminated against and broadly stereotyped by the media. They were widely held to be culturally unassimilable and socially undesirable as citizens.

In the face of these circumstances the immigrants exhibited a "pioneer" ethos that stressed self-reliance as well as cooperation based on kinship and socio-religious commonalities. They shared rural, small landholding, and/or military backgrounds and were largely uneducated. In 1912 an Immigration Commission estimated that between one-half and three-fifths of the South Asian immigrants of that time could neither read nor write. As economic migrants they sought work with the intention to earn enough capital to return home and buy land. Their initial attraction to California was affected by a combination of cultural familiarity with agriculture; opportunities for them in the state's "factories in the fields" (which had by 1900 developed into large-scale operations utilizing successive waves of immigrant labor); and exclusion from other urban job markets due to racism or their lack of education. With the exception of very small numbers of South Asian businessmen or academics who lived in such urban areas as San Francisco, Detroit, Chicago, and New York, there were few professionals among the early immigrants. Some South Asians found work in cities as peddlers, day laborers, restaurant help, or other menial tasks, but the bulk of the early immigrants sought their fortunes outside metropolitan centers.

Within a few years of arriving and despite keeping a low profile, South Asians were subject to persecution and "riots" and were sometimes driven from towns by anti-Asian forces, including labor and nativist organizations. As early as 1910 restrictive housing covenants barring sales to "Hindus" appeared in the Los Angeles area, followed by the passage of California's (and then other states') anti-immigrant Alien Land Law (1913), designed to make it difficult or impossible for noncitizens to own or even lease land. Added shortly thereafter to these city and state restrictions were further restrictions on leasing and landownership (1920), the federal "Barred Zone" provision (1917), and the infamous *Thind* decision by the U.S. Supreme Court (1923).

The federal law cut off immigration from an "Asiatic Barred Zone" that included all India, Burma, and Siam (Thailand), effectively encapsulating South Asians. It removed even the possibility of visiting India and returning to the United States or of having family members join immigrants already here. The

Thind case involved an overtly racist Supreme Court decision that essentially rendered South Asians, as a class, ineligible for citizenship because—although they were Caucasian—they were not "free white persons." Once again, anti-Asian sentiments, which had not been primarily or directly targeting South Asians, focused on them as a by-product of general agitation. The *Thind* case had severe consequences, including not only the loss of the possible right to citizenship but the actual revocation of citizenship from a number of South Asians who had already been granted it. It rendered many South Asians "stateless persons."

Regardless of these social and legal barriers, many South Asians did well on the West Coast. Within a decade of their arrival, many had established themselves in farming ventures, often in partnership with Punjabis or other farmers. They took an active role in securing credit, establishing banking and attorney relationships, learning the local markets and crops, and using their networks to seek employment and opportunity. While they worked at almost anything that came to hand in the early period, including building railroads and bridges, logging, mining, and road construction in Canada and the American Northwest, it was in California agriculture that they found their most promising niche.

Land records show an initial pattern of leasing followed, if possible, by purchase. South Asians were in the central California valley by 1906 and became successfully involved in establishing rice culture in the northern Sacramento Valley (Glenn and Colusa Counties) as well as orchard and vineyard cultivation in Yuba and Sutter Counties. By 1908 they were in the Imperial Valley of southern California, where they helped initiate cotton growing and later vegetable row crops. A 1920 report listed 85,000 acres in the Sacramento and San Joaquin Valleys as under the control of "Hindus" and an additional 30,000 in the Imperial Valley, most of which was leased. The northern California nucleus, which was founded around the ten to thirty-acre peach, prune, almond, or walnut farms in the Yuba City—Marysville area, was to endure through the difficult 1920–1940 period. During that time the South Asian population dwindled and by 1946 stood at around 350 to 400 persons owning less than 1,000 acres. With the slight reopening of immigration from India in the year before its Independence in 1947, including family reunification and the ability to sponsor relatives, Yuba City–Marysville was to become the largest South Asian agricultural community outside India, with some 10,000 Sikhs making their home there today. There remained pockets of Punjabi immigrants in Washington, Oregon, Arizona, and even along the northern Mexican border, but they were minuscule and never became major immigration destinations.

A large role in Punjabi success in agriculture was due not only to traditional occupational skills but also to the assistance, stability, and support of family units and networks that were eventually formed between Sikh and Muslim men and Spanish-speaking women. There were no South Asian women on the West Coast in the first decade of immigration and perhaps no more than 100 ever entered the United States before 1945. From the beginning, it was difficult, and later impossible, either to (1) reunite with a spouse if married (and the majority of the Punjabis were married prior to immigration but came alone) or (2) obtain Indian brides of appropriate social status and background through the traditional Indian arranged-marriage system. The cumulative impact of the restrictions on immigration by 1910 and further curtailments of 1917 and 1924 was to cut these men off from India indefinitely, possibly permanently. Once they decided to stay in America they began to seek women they could legally marry.

This was complicated by California's antimiscegenation laws, generally enforced at the time and not repealed until 1948, which prohibited interracial marriage. By 1916 South Asian men had begun to form unions with Mexican and Mexican-American women in southern California. Eventually, these biethnic families came to number over 300 and became an exotic part of the California cultural mosaic. Seen by outsiders as well as themselves as a separate, culturally hybrid community, the men in these unions totaled from one-fifth to one-third of the entire Indian male immigrant population in America. Therefore, they were not a California Punjabi-Mexican anomaly but represented the fundamental and dominant pattern of South Asian immigrant family life in America in the 1910–1950 period.

Interestingly, for complex reasons, these families developed and maintained a strong sense of connection to India, adopting an identity they referred to as "Hindu," although most of their fathers were Sikhs and their offspring were raised in the Roman Catholic faith. Beginning in the Imperial Valley and spreading northward to the central and northern Sacramento Valleys, these intermarriages, while not without stress and cultural clashes, worked well enough to provide hundreds of South Asian men a relatively normal home life and much desired children. These were not social isolates but formed large networks composed, on the one hand, of Punjabi men who farmed, worshipped, and discussed politics together and, on the other, their wives and Mexican kin who formed their own subset within California rural society.

One sociologist in the 1950s had posited that this process represented a circuitous assimilation model, based on the melting pot ideology, through which the Punjabi men would gradually join mainstream America. As it actually turned out, it was an interlude between immigration waves, the resumption of which would eventually engulf this most interesting and unusual social construction. Much has been recently written about this chapter of South Asian American history in general and in particular about the descendants of this group who retain to this day a sense of specialness and pride in their dual heritage. However, once immigration resumed from both India and Pakistan in the late 1940s and accelerated after 1965, there was a gradual estrangement between Punjabi-Mexican families and the South Asian newcomers as they became the majority. Those recently arrived held more traditional ideas of proper marriage and customs and displayed superior, ambivalent attitudes toward the obviously nontraditional nature of earlier Punjabi-Mexican arrangements.

THE NEW IMMIGRANTS

The South Asian immigrant's world after 1965 changed so quickly both quantitatively and qualitatively that it would be unrecognizable to the early pioneers. In numbers alone the figures are impressive. First, Asians, not Europeans, now constitute a plurality of immigrants to America. Second, the United States has one of the largest foreign-born populations in the world (9.3 percent of the U.S. total in 1996), and the number of "Asian Pacific Islander Americans" is expected to triple within the first twenty-five years of the twenty-first century. In the same period, 4 in 10 Asian Americans will live in California. In terms of overall future immigration, barring any substantial change in immigration preferences and quotas, South Asians will remain a significant proportion of all newcomers. In 1980 the census term "East Indian" was replaced with "Asian Indian," and that census reported 360,000 South Asians. By 1985 that figure had increased to over 525,000, by 1990 to 685,000, and by 1995 was well over 900,000 (with 757,000 Indians alone reported in 1996). In the 1990s Asian Indians moved from the fourth to third largest component within the Asian American category. Although India has provided the largest number of South Asian immigrants, newcomers from Bangladesh, Sri Lanka, and Afghanistan have increased since the mid-1980s as events in those countries have led to outflows that include refugees and political asylum seekers as well as economic migrants. (Immigration from Nepal and Bhutan is negligible at this time.) By 1990 the Bangladeshi population had grown tenfold from their 1980 number, to nearly 12,500. During the same decade Sri Lankans went from less than 200 to about 14,450 giving a Sri Lankan ancestry, whereas Afghanis in 1990 had more than twice that number, about 31,300. By 1995 South Asian immigration was running over 52,000 a year. In 1997 the total South Asian American population was approximately 1 million. The largest numbers of immigrants come, in order of magnitude, from India, Pakistan, Afghanistan, Bangladesh, and Sri Lanka. India and Pakistan together constitute around 90 percent of current South Asian immigration, although in the mid-1990s Pakistani immigration usually amounted to about one-fourth of India's yearly totals.

The immigrants of the first half century constituted a highly unrepresentative sample of South Asian populations, the majority of whom originated almost solely from a single province, spoke primarily one language (Punjabi), were members of a minority religious tradition, and came from rural, landowning backgrounds. There were few urban professionals or educated persons among the early immigrants. Further, they tended to cluster after arrival in three agricultural centers on the West Coast of the United States. The new immigrants represent every country, state, province, territory, and region of South Asia, speak every major language and dialect, and overall include a large percentage of highly trained and educated professionals who practice and support a wide range of cultural and religious traditions. They reflect all castes, classes, and segments found in their natal societies, and many had experienced significant periods of residence in other countries and cultures as well. The South Asian immigrant no longer necessarily comes directly from India or Pakistan but may arrive from Fiji, Surinam, Kuwait, Guyana, Saudi Arabia, England, Australia, Kenya, Uganda, South Africa, the United Arab Emirates, Hong Kong, Trinidad, Singapore, Thailand, and any of the other over fifty countries that have, or had, significant South Asian communities, some dating back a century or more.

The impact of residence, schooling, and exposure of varying lengths of time in one or more nations prior to arrival in America gives a distinctively international flavor to many South Asians, whose tastes and values may reflect more of a global or transnational quality than a stereotypical view would recognize. A new "South Asian" immigrant might be a British-educated Ramgarhiya Sikh—whose family resides in Kenya but whose ancestors originally emigrated from Hindi-speaking north India—or a Vaishnava Fijian mill owner whose ancestors came from Tamil-speaking south India, or a Gujurati-speaking Parsi educated in Germany from a family currently living in New Zealand whose origins are in Bombay, western India. South Asian immigration patterns and immigrant experiences are among the world's most complex, mirroring to different degrees (1) the expansion and subsequent demise of the British colonial world; (2) the inherent diversity of the subcontinent itself; (3) the waxing and waning of Western legal barriers and attitudes toward South Asia and its peoples; (4) the technical and scientific coming-of-age that has been under way in South Asia for the past several decades; and (5) the creation of worldwide marriage networks and global financial interests.

Available data for Asian Indian Americans reveal that their education levels are extraordinary. For all adults over twenty-five years of age in 1990, the rate of attaining a B.A. degree was approaching 70 percent, with 34 percent earning M.A.s, 8 percent professional degrees, and nearly 9 percent doctorates. Just under 50 percent of Asian Indian women had earned their college degrees, over twice the rate of the general population. In high school where the graduation rates of 85 percent for immigrants and 81 percent for the second generation were reported, Asian Indian children had the highest mean grade-point average (3.8) of all Asian Americans as well as the lowest dropout rate. That over 46 percent of Indian males held managerial/professional jobs is likewise not surprising, given their academic credentials.

Although not technically immigrants, Indian students seeking higher education currently comprise the fourth largest group of international students studying in the United States (after Japanese, Koreans, and Chinese), and upon completion of their degrees, many apply to have their student visas converted to resident alien status. This is a steady source of new immigrants, along with refugees and seekers of political asylum (mostly since the 1980s, as political separatists from Kashmir and Punjab in India intensified their struggles and the Sri Lankan and Afghani civil wars dragged on).

LANGUAGE

Although no firm, reliable national statistics are available on the numbers or proportions of South Asian linguistic diversity in America, there are some estimates from regions with high concentrations of immigrants, such as New York and Los Angeles. In 1980 the percentages for New York were given as 34 percent Gujurati, 20 percent Hindi, and 24 percent combined Dravidian languages (Tamil, Kannada, Malayalam, Telegu). Distribution in southern California in the same period was estimated at 20 percent each for Punjabi and Gujurati; Urdu, 18 percent; Hindi, 16 percent; Dravidian languages, 12 percent; and Bengali, 11 percent. It is certain that these have already changed somewhat (Gujurati likely having gained overall) and will continue to do so as the combination of new immigration and internal population shifts rearrange the mix of languages, religions, settlement patterns, and destinations across America.

There is a very active ethnic South Asian press that regularly publishes books, newsletters, tracts, magazines, journals, newspapers, and political commentary on scholarly, religious, artistic, political, and sociocultural topics in at least twenty South Asian languages (in over a dozen scripts) and English. South Asian English-language journalism includes such publications as *India Abroad* (New York, New York), *India-West* (Los Angeles, California), *India Currents* (San Jose, California), *India Tribune* (New York), *India Journal* (Los Angeles), *Pakistan Link* (Los Angeles), among many others. South Asians, mostly in large metropolitan areas, are equally active in programming and supporting a wide range of radio and television programs in English and/or their mother tongues. A few are imported from India and Pakistan but most are locally produced. Examples in Los Angeles include: a Saturday midnight Afghan-hosted TV program that features Persian (*dari*) and Pushtu songs and poetry; an all-Urdu radio station; and music, religious, and news programs in Hindi and Punjabi, with more in the planning stages.

SOUTH ASIANS AND AMERICAN MATERIAL CULTURE

After 1965 the preeminence of California as the center of South Asian American life declined, becoming only one of eight popular destinations. By the 1990s eight major industrial-urban states located in the East (New York, Pennsylvania, New Jersey), Southwest (Texas), Midwest (Michigan, Illinois, Ohio), and West (California) accounted for 70 percent of the U.S. South Asian population. This obviously reflects a distribution of the nation's industrial, university, service, and high-tech sectors of the economy in which engineers, scientists, academics, doctors, and nurses would find employment. Within these states are preferred cities, such as New York, Chicago, San Jose, Los Angeles/Long Beach, Washington, D.C., and Houston. South Asian immigrants, unlike some earlier Asian groups, have not generally tended to cluster in identifiable residential "Little Indias," although there are significant centers of South Asian business in the greater New York area (the Jackson Heights area of Queens, Lexington Avenue in Manhattan, Edison, New Jersey), Chicago (Devon Avenue), Los Angeles (Artesia), and Berkeley (lower University Avenue), among many others. However, the residential distribution patterns appear more dependent on economic and social strata than desire for mere ethnic proximity. Most South Asian populations are "dispersed communities" found scattered throughout a city. However, there is some tendency for sponsored immigrants to live near their patrons and for extended family members to live in proximity to one another, if possible.

Many of America's major educational institutions, health care facilities, or research laboratories have South Asians as part of their staffs. Significant numbers of South Asians are to be found in entrepreneurial endeavors, ranging from small retail operations to venture capital and manufacturing concerns. Many have found market "niches" and been very successful. For example, the rhyme "hotel, motel, Patel" denotes the success of a group originally from Bombay in acquiring U.S. commercial properties. The name *Patel* is very common in Gujarat state. Contemporary Patels have come to dominate the small motel/residential hotel markets in both northern and southern California and are significant players across the United States in that industry. The Patel-dominated Indo-American Hotel Owners Association joined the Asian American Hotel Owners Association in 1994. Now 85 percent of its members are South Asians. Other associations whose names reveal both professional status and South Asian orientations are the Indian Lawyers Association of America, the Pakistan American Chamber of Commerce, and the Urdu Journalists Association of America.

Doctors of South Asian descent are represented in numbers out of all proportion to the size of their population cohort and are emblematic of the high educational level that symbolizes the South Asian professional immigrant of the past thirty years. As early as 1980, of the some 400,000 South Asians in America, 11 percent of the men and 8 percent of the women were physicians and another 7 percent of the women were nurses. Married South Asian couples who are both physicians are quite common. Moreover, 17 percent of the remaining males were either engineers, architects, or surveyors. From the perspective of India and Pakistan, this may raise a different issue in terms of "brain drain," as perhaps one-fourth of the graduates of Indian medical schools and significant percentages of engineering and management graduates come to the United States annually. The overproduction of South Asian graduates in technical fields and their chronic underemployment in their homelands have led to emigration, which has had unanticipated benefits: significant remittances; a large nonresident population with capital to invest in government-sponsored projects; and a small but steady return of experienced persons wishing to set up businesses, apply transfer technology, or retire. On balance, the "drain" has perhaps been an investment with profitable returns to the home countries. By mid-1997 it is estimated that perhaps 4 percent (22,000) of America's entire population of medical doctors are South Asian immigrants from India or of South Asian descent. It has been claimed that many inner-city public hospitals simply could not function if South Asian medical personnel were unavailable, for they can constitute as high as 40 percent of the staff physicians and 50 percent of the nurses. In Ohio, one out of six physicians is South Asian, and several other states approach that ratio.

Although not technically political organizations, the prominence of South

Asian medical associations and their lobbying activities give them high social status and political weight. Their associations include such national groups as the American Association of Physicians from India, the largest ethnic organization of physicians in the United States, the Association of Pakistani Physicians of North America, and many hundreds of local groups, including the Indian American Physicians of South Indian Origin in Florida. There are additional South Asian organizations for Indian pharmacists and Indo-American physicians and dentists. They are all active in the ongoing debates over health maintenance organizations (HMOs), managed care, Medicare, medical training/internships, and qualification/certification issues.

Statistically, the new immigrants appear intellectually, financially, and socially accomplished. A profile of those born in India shows a relatively young, upwardly mobile population. Perhaps most dramatic when compared to the early immigrants, the socioeconomic and educational portraits of India-born U.S. South Asians are a complete reversal of circumstances of their predecessor's first half century. In the 1990 census they were shown to have the highest median household income, family income, per capita income, and annual median income ($40,625) of any foreign-born group. A 1991 survey of five Asian American groups found that they also ranked first in holding stocks and individual retirement accounts (IRAs), in rates of educational achievement, and in the attainment of managerial or professional positions.

However, this favorable overall picture of South Asian American achievement is somewhat misleading. The major gains and benefits have been enjoyed mostly by South Asian immigrants who established themselves *prior* to the 1980s or those trained in medicine or cutting-edge technologies that are in high demand, such as computer engineering and software, lasers, or physics. For those entering after around 1985, the picture is one of declining median income, fewer professional/managerial positions, a much higher unemployment rate, higher rates of business failures, and higher rates of families in poverty. India-born immigrants ranked twelfth in a national survey of individuals and families in poverty in 1993, and a regional Pacific Rim States study in 1995 claimed that California had the highest percentage (14 percent) of Indian American children living in poverty.

Some of this is a result of cyclical U.S. economic recessions, but part is a result of different criteria being used more recently to select visa preferences (favoring family reunification versus skilled workers). The result is likely to be a continuing downward trend in overall socioeconomic indicators for the less educated segment of the South Asian American community and a widening gap between them and the highly skilled, affluent South Asian groups. Nor does this picture include the illegal immigrants who continue to come without papers, sometimes having been smuggled in, and those who simply overstay tourist, student, or artistic visas. The cabdrivers, convenience store clerks, gas station/garage attendants, restaurant workers, newsstand owners, and other entry-level positions, which once may have been a temporary springboard to better jobs, may have become a permanent niche for some. Many recent immigrants work for fellow South Asians in the self-employed sector of ethnic grocery, import, sari, fabric, appliance, jewelry, and clothing stores or attempt to secure employment through relatives. In the 1980s a concerted effort was made to obtain minority group status for South Asians in order to secure low-cost federal small-business loans or other types of advantages reserved for non-Caucasians or groups historically discriminated against. This controversial issue continues to be hotly debated, although the National Association of Americans of Asian Indian Descent (NAAAID) in 1982 requested and was granted recognition of South Asians as a "socially disadvantaged minority" by the Small Business Administration. The present degree of achieved, collective financial success by the South Asian community and the increasingly negative American political climate toward questions of affirmative action and preferences may shortly render all such classifications moot.

AMERICAN POLITICS

The contrast between the nature and amount of political participation practiced by early South Asian immigrants and those who have come in the past thirty years may seem more apparent than real. It was true that the legal barriers on South Asian citizenship were nearly insurmountable until 1946, whereas those concerning immigration were profoundly restrictive until 1965; that the vote was denied to most early South Asian immigrants; that the relative lack of resources and education in the community made for organizational and financial difficulties; and that the legal disabilities were compounded by the complex relationship between Great Britain, America, and the colonial government of the British Raj in India. However relatively disadvantaged the South Asian immigrants of fifty years ago were, they were never passive actors in political debates about freedom, self-determination, self-rule, group and individual rights, and issues of justice and redress. These issues were important to the South Asian immigrant community from the very beginning and became more evident as they suffered further humiliation and discrimination, often linking the "slave" status of India with their own disadvantaged position in America. Vigorous debates took place over local, ethnic, religious, national, and international events that were occurring both *within* America and India, respectively, as well as *between* those two nations and England.

One of the most thoroughly documented early political movements was the Ghadar ("revolution"/"mutiny" in Punjabi) Party, a militant organization dedicated to the overthrow of British rule in India. Founded in 1913 by Lala Har Dayal while teaching at Stanford, the California-based organization evolved into a worldwide network that eventually established cells or links with radical groups in such places as Hong Kong, Thailand, Russia, Ireland, and Germany. Punjabi farmers throughout the American West were its main financial supporters. Its heyday was from 1913 to 1917, when it was headed by urban, often

Hindu, intellectuals. Never particularly effective in implementing its goal, it nevertheless survived British, British-Indian, and American government surveillance and counterintelligence, deportation of some leaders, and the spectacular "Hindu Conspiracy Trial" of 1917–1918 in San Francisco. California Sikhs continued their support and efforts to raise funds and publish Ghadar materials until Indian Independence in 1947. From interviews with many of the South Asians from the Ghadar era, it is clear that, in their minds, the organization was not simply about the achievement of Indian freedom but about the status of Indians outside the subcontinent. They conflated the subservient role of India with their own minority status in America and keenly felt the inequality and inequity of their position in U.S. society. From before the beginning of World War I through the end of World War II, there were organizations that sought to organize and create political pressure for change. Some were sparked by outside influences, whereas others were completely domestic in origin.

Examples of the former would include the All-India Muslim League and Lala Lajpat Rai. Rai visited the United States in 1906 and again between 1913 and 1919, bringing the message and the views of the Indian National Congress before sympathetic Americans and educated Indians, founding the Home Rule League in New York. Although it did not survive long after he returned to India, it did set a pattern of alliances between South Asians concerned about social and political conditions in India and similar U.S. groups, which has lasted to the present. The latter are exemplified by the India League of America, founded by J. J. Singh, the National Committee for India's Friends, the India Welfare League, and other groups of Indian businessmen and intellectuals during World War II who sought to put India's case for independence effectively before liberal American audiences. Most of these were centered on the East Coast and only marginally involved the majority Sikh farmers of California, but these organizations were important sources of information and pride for South Asians in America seeking to sway American public opinion on important Indian issues.

Although South Asian political influence between 1900 and 1970 never approached the magnitude that presently characterizes political activity for contemporary South Asians, there were a series of propaganda efforts, congressional and senate hearings, and court cases in which immigrants consistently sought to represent their views through offering testimony, bringing legal suits, raising money, and supporting lobbying efforts. Given their small numbers and disenfranchised status, it is not surprising that as a group South Asians never achieved much serious political influence in the power structure of that day. One exception was Dilip Singh Saund, a Punjabi immigrant who came for an education, remained as a farmer in the El Centro area, and achieved prominence as the first—and to date only—South Asian to win election to the U.S. Congress (1956), where he served three terms in the House of Representatives. An active and able spokesman for his southern California districts, he wrote a revealing autobiography on his experiences, *Congressman from India*.

Currently, there are dozens of competing and overlapping socio-political

South Asian organizations, but only four major national federations have broad support and national constituencies and act as coordinating bodies: the NAAAID, the Indian American Forum for Political Education (The Forum), the NFIA (National Federation of Indian Associations in America, established circa 1971), and the AIA (Association of Asian Indians in America, established in the mid-1960s). The first two are concerned exclusively with politics, whereas the NFIA and AIA sponsor social and cultural events as well. The NFIA began on the East Coast and over several decades became the umbrella federation for some eighty associations and hundreds of affiliated groups.

These are all very active and often cooperate with one another to achieve common goals, as when the AIA and NFIA coordinated efforts to separately list ''Asian Indian'' as an enumeration category in the 1980 U.S. census. In 1984–1986 the Forum and the NFIA joined to protest against Medicare funding and immigration issues. In 1988 all these groups and many additional Asian American organizations successfully lobbied to keep intact country-of-origin subcategories under the Asian American census heading. The NAAAID is the most purely political group, as its main function is to identify, recruit, and fund candidates for political office. Although it has thus far had only modest success in doing so, there being relatively few elected South Asians at the highest levels of state or national government, there have been more South Asians seeking U.S. political offices in the 1990s than during any previous period in history. Recently, there has emerged a pool of South Asian candidates of Indian or Pakistani background running for Congress, but none won in 1996. On the state level there has been more success, for South Asians have achieved major elective and appointed departmental and association positions, sit on prestigious advisory boards and review committees, act as advisers on technical and medical matters, and frequently occupy highly visible leadership roles in public organizations.

RELIGION AND AMERICAN CULTURE

American consciousness of South Asian religions before 1900 was limited to largely philosophical issues. The impressive appearance of Swami Vivekananda at the World Parliament of Religions in Chicago in 1893 is often noted as a signal event, for it symbolized a South Asian ''holy man'' from the East bringing traditional religious knowledge directly to the West. He founded the Vedanta Society of New York in 1896. Others who came in the early years were Swami Paramahansa Yogananda (Self Realization Fellowship), J. Krishnamurthi (Theosophical Society), and H. I. Khan (Sufi Order), but these remained relatively small, elite sects within an overwhelmingly Christian-denominated society.

Among the most dynamic consequences of recent (post-1970) South Asian immigration is the apparent importance of establishing and supporting religious institutions and/or personages. The growth in numbers of immigrants has not only seemed to intensify as well as diversify the variety of religious expression but also to have made religion an increasingly integral part of immigrant life and an important component of social identity. Whereas in South Asia one's religious behavior was part of a whole range of well-understood signifiers that were a more natural part of the cultural environment, the diaspora has perhaps encouraged a more conscious cultivation, practice, and identification with South Asian religious traditions. From having primarily Punjabi Sikhs and Muslims representing immigrant South Asian faiths for the first fifty years, the contemporary situation finds practitioners of every variety of South Asian Hindu, Muslim, Buddhist, Christian, Sikh, Jain, and Parsi (Zoroastrian) tradition.

South Asians are currently willing and able to carry out their traditional forms of worship and over the past quarter of a century have built an impressive collection of worship centers, including Hindu and Buddhist temples, Sikh *gurdwaras*, Islamic mosques, Parsi fire temples, and distinctive South Asian congregations within larger Christian churches. In addition to these more formal centers, there are ashrams, academies, yoga centers, retreat houses, monasteries, convents, and so on, that may be sectarian, ecumenical, or nonsectarian in their approach but can all trace their origins to South Asian beliefs and practices. Indeed, such architectural features as South Indian *gopurums* (towers) and North Indian temple carvings, once seen only in South Asia, have become almost commonplace features in the American religious landscape from East and West Coast urban centers to the rural Midwest towns. Some of the more impressive are the Sri Venkateswara Temple in Pittsburgh, Pennsylvania, the Ganesh Temple in Flushing, New York, the Meenakshi Temple in Houston, Texas, the Sri Venkateswara in Los Angeles, the Sri Viswananta in Flint, Michigan, the Sri Venkateswara Temple in Chicago, and the Shiva-Vishnu Temple in San Francisco. There are some seventy-five Hindu temples in the United States, and more are planned. The number of Sikh *gurdwaras* in the United States is expanding rapidly and currently approaches seventy, the first having been built in Stockton, California, in 1912.

Distinctive movements have also emerged, such as the followers of groups and individuals as diverse as the International Society for Krishna Consciousness (ISKON), Maharishi Mahesh Yogi (transcendental meditation movement), the Satya Sai Baba movement, Meher Baba, the Aga Khani Ismailis, Sufi orders, Bhagwan Shree Rajneesh, Eckankar, Radhasoami, the Sikh Dharma Brotherhood (3HO) of Harbhajan Singh Puri, Indian Tibetan Buddhists (Lamists), and Black Muslim groups. As these distinctive offshoots or new interpretations of older traditions began to grow, they often incorporated (some being composed mainly of) non–South Asian adherents, adding another complexity to the diaspora religious fabric. Yet even without the complicating factor of new kinds of believers, the actual practice of South Asian religious traditions today exhibits contradictory twin trends: Some groups are beginning to emphasize narrow, esoteric, or regional beliefs in ways that tend to restrict participation, whereas others are making "adjustments" to their new American context and become more encompassing. In the early years, when immigrants were few and from a limited area of origin, the social cohesion, regardless of faith, was stronger, particularly when everyone was suffering under the same colonial rule in India and were subject to the same legal disabilities in the United States. Organizations had a more inclusive, egalitarian ethos to them, and the commonalities they shared seemed to bridge very real religious differences. Respect for religious difference was not theoretical but transactional, and this was to remain so until well into the 1950s in many areas of South Asian American society.

Today, it appears that such easy interaction across a wide range of traditions is not as easy or as salient for the second-generation growing up in a U.S. context. In part, this occurs because the "ethnic," linguistic, and regional distinctions do not have the same meanings for them as they did for their parents and because there is simply so much greater diversity. But being raised biculturally in America also contributes to a distinctively different perspective. Even for first-generation immigrants, the context of their communal worship reflects a process of globalization as much as it does the impact of South Asian religious transplantation to America. For example, in America, Indian Parsis share sacred space in their Zoroastrian fire temples with devotees from Pakistan and Iran, particularly in Los Angeles where Persian worshipers are the majority.

Islam is not only one of the world's fastest growing religions, but it is also one of the largest minority religions in America. Sunni, Shi'a, and Sufi traditions are all practiced by South Asians in America. Collectively, South Asian Muslims constitute a significant portion of *all* Muslims in the United States. Rather than finding themselves isolated, South Asian Muslim immigrants find themselves in proximity both to American black Muslims and to Muslims from around the world, people with very different cultural backgrounds who display a wide range of doctrine and practices. Indian Muslims may worship with Pakistanis, Bangladeshis, and Afghanis as well as coreligionists from the Middle East and Central Asia. At the same time, although most Buddhist enclaves in the United States have historically derived from Chinese and Japanese sects of the Mahayana tradition, Sri Lankan Buddhists of the Theravada tradition have become highly visible in America since the 1960s. Their Los Angeles community of 4,000 to 5,000 has established five temples in that area alone, of which the Dharma Vijaya Buddhist Vihara is the largest facility, encompassing not only South Asian Buddhists but American, European, Thai, and Japanese members.

In thirty years (1960–1990) the full religious complexity of South Asian traditions took root in America and has been flourishing, with sufficient *pundits, maulvis, granthis*, and priests to provide the full array of traditional religious rites and rituals. What synergy will occur in even the near future is impossible to say, but the variety of South Asian religious expressions and interfaith dialogues has never been more diverse or vigorous.

POPULAR CULTURE

South Asian cuisine, fashion, jewelry, music, holistic health practices, and even books and films by South Asian American artists are so ubiquitous in the United States today that, on a superficial level, it seems that South Asian material culture and artistic expression have been well integrated into the multi-cultural mix of the American mainstream—and certainly so if judged by the popularity of South Asian cookbooks, the recent fashion fad of *mehndi* body designs (intricate designs drawn mostly on hands and feet with henna dye), and even Indian music in American film sound tracks (e.g., Nusrat Ali Khan's score for *Dead Man Walking*). The annual Indian Independence Day parades, public religious processions and services, Diwali Festivals, South Asian fashion shows, and Indian sports events (e.g., *kabbadi* teams in northern California) all offer public performances that both assert ethnic pride and culture and invite the general American public to recognize and participate in its presentation.

One positive indication is the establishment or growth in the last twenty years of programs for South Asian cultures and religions at many American universities, including endowed chairs for language (Tamil at University of California at Berkeley; Bengali at Arizona State University, Tempe); a chair of Punjab and India Studies at the University of Wisconsin at Milwaukee; endowed chairs in India Studies at Columbia University, University of Michigan, and the University of California at Santa Cruz; and the inclusion of South Asian American Studies in departments of Asian American and Ethnic Studies programs. Prestigious academic journals and organizations have been founded by South Asians to serve South Asian constituencies as well as other scholars, for example, *South Asia Bulletin*, Committee on South Asian Women (COSAW) and their *Bulletin, South Asian Magazine for Action and Reflection (SAMAR)*, and *South Asia Forum/Quarterly (SAFQ)*.

On more popular levels, access to the rich artistic, musical, and literary legacies of South Asian cultures has expanded out from static museum displays or an occasional *bharatanatyam* dance demonstration to a truly international spectrum of live performances, resident writers and painters, dance and music schools, filmmakers, poets, and international traveling groups offering everything from Pakistani religious, devotional *qawwali* singers to Bollywood (Bombay Hollywood) star extravaganzas. Not only can American audiences see some of the best modern practitioners of Indian classical and popular traditions on a regular basis, but readers can also choose from the literary works of several generations of South Asian men and women authors (Bharati Mukherjee, Bapsi Sidhwa, Agha Shahid Ali, Meena Alexander, Dr. Mantosh Singh Devji, Chitra Divakaruni, Amitav Ghose, Zulfiqar Ghose, Gita Mehta, Ved Meta, A. K. Ramanujan, Raja Rao, and Dr. Abraham Vergnese), who draw themes and inspiration from the issues and tensions of the immigrant experience, producing short stories, fiction, reportage, and autobiography. Significant external recognition came when the *New Yorker* dedicated its 1997 annual Fiction Issue (June 23–30) to the emergence of important and creative "Indian" novelists, all of whom write in English and many of whom live in the United States. Finally, film writers, producers, and directors (Amin Chaudhuri, Krishna Shaw, Ashok Amrit Raj, Mira Nair, Radha Bhardwaj, Deepa Mehta, Jagmohan Mundhara, Ismail Merchant) are also constructing and presenting their unique cinematic perspectives on South Asian culture, South Asian immigrant experiences, and the often contentious, funny, and poignant interactions between the two.

CONTEMPORARY AMERICAN SOCIETY

Beyond sitar, curry, and the *kurta*, the impact of the new South Asian immigration upon American culture outside of technical/professional fields, religion, or popular culture has been primarily in the area of public perceptions. The first arises out of the recent and relatively high visibility of South Asians within American society. This has had many manifestations, both positive (i.e., recognition of high occupational and economic achievement) and negative (e.g., stereotyping Hindus as "clannish," Sikhs as "terrorists," and Muslims as "fundamentalists"). Another positive perspective arises from the recognition of the high level of education attained by South Asians in America, which has contributed to their inclusion, sometimes reluctantly, in the "model minority" category of hardworking, upwardly mobile Asians. However, despite their high socioeconomic profiles, in 1992 Asian Indians ranked rather low in social standing in a national poll comparing thirty-three (and sometimes fifty-eight) ethnic and religious groups. Although Asian Indians ranked first in educational level and fifth in household income, they came out twenty-eighth of thirty-three in social standing. In a field of fifty-eight groups, they ranked only thirty-eighth. This would seem to confirm that some level of prejudice remains against immigrants from India and, probably by extension, all South Asian immigrants. Instead of being congratulated for their achievements after a half century of discrimination and social insolation, it seems that their economic achievements have bred a certain amount of jealousy and their increasing numbers a degree of unease.

One infamous series of anti–South Asian attacks took place in New Jersey in 1987 and involved gangs of white and Hispanic youths. It began with harassment of South Asian women on the streets, targeting them because they wore the cosmetic red *bindi* (mark) on their foreheads. Eventually these self-identified "dot-buster" gangs escalated their attacks until one Indian man was killed and another severely disabled. The incident raised questions about how safe America was for those perceived as different and to what extent the system would respond if they were threatened. Similar issues have arisen among New York taxi drivers, 90 percent of whom are immigrants and a good percentage of that number South Asian. Their work hours and public contact often make them vulnerable to robbery and assault. A similar problem exists for small shop owners, particularly nightshift convenience stores clerks.

Some of the negative images have been generated by political events that occur in South Asia but that spill over into the American and immigrant political arenas. The South Asian separatist movements in Punjab, Kashmir, and Sri Lanka and the worldwide coverage of over a decade of political assassinations, skyjackings, bombings, guerrilla warfare, and frequent atrocities on all sides have caused many Americans to react warily to certain groups, often lumping any "swarthy foreigner" in with potential terrorists. The seemingly ancient, complex, intractable nature of the conflicts and the obvious fragmenting impact they have upon different South Asian groups in the United States are viewed by many Americans as an unwelcome consequence of "foreign involvement" by "domestic immigrants."

The destruction of the Babri Masjid religious structure in India and reactions of celebration by South Asian American supporters of the BJP Hindu Nationalists was seen as just the latest example of an unnecessary and undesirable transplantation of Old World ethnic/religious conflict to inappropriate settings. From their perspectives, many South Asians see little difference between their continued interest in, and support of, sociocultural and political events in their homelands and the ethnic ties to England, Ireland, Sweden, Poland, Korea, Japan, and so on, maintained by Americans of European or Far Eastern descent. Thus, proponents of Khalistan ("Land of the Khalsa/Pure"), among others, will continue to lobby Congress whenever they perceive a way to further their agenda, particularly when it involves foreign aid or human rights issues in India. Continuing immigrant concern with events in their homelands is likely to persist as virtually instant communication informs them about vital issues of faith and community as they arise in South Asia. The extent to which these issues surface in the larger political scene (e.g., become the focus of legal battles in the courts or produce fractures between or within South Asian groups) will probably determine how the general public will react.

The tension between America's official philosophy of pluralism and recurrent anti-immigrant sentiments may remain indefinitely; however, unlike earlier periods, today's immigrants can openly, effectively oppose racism and discrimination and have recourse to the courts. Second- and third-generation descendants of South Asian immigrants are likely to protest negative images and actions as they feel increasingly sure of their rights and roles in America. A second impact is a result of the cultural adjustment and adaptations made by second- and third-generation South Asian Americans who are moving into the mainstream U.S. culture while maintaining, and negotiating, their South Asian identity. While this is a largely internal process, it does come to public attention in school and legal settings as cultural conflicts, misunderstandings, and different ideas of appropriate behavior and rights arise. As all immigrant groups before, South Asians are deeply concerned over how to raise their children, how to transmit their traditions and retain their heritage, while still allowing for adjustments to living in American culture.

As a "bridge" generation, the American-born or -raised South Asian youth are confronted with a long list of difficult, interrelated sociocultural issues concerning virginity, open sexuality, homosexuality, dating, arranged marriage, dowry, and gender roles within the family. For them and their parents, divorce and remarriage may become issues. In addition, there are even broader community issues over degrees of individual responsibility, freedom, and choice;

the authority and care of the elderly; and child and spousal abuse. All of these topics are made more challenging in that some proposed traditional South Asian solutions may be difficult to impossible to enforce or ill-advised in a Western context. For parents of children being raised in America, the fact that some South Asian "family values" (i.e., arranged marriage and prohibition on "dating") are diametrically opposed to the dominant "American" values complicates the situation immeasurably. While the majority of the South Asian American second generation currently accept some form of arranged marriage (perhaps 80 percent minimum for many groups and over 90 percent for some), complete with horoscope consulting, matrimonial ads, and dowry negotiations, this does not mean that there are not significant shifts in their perceptions of gender relations, religious injunctions, women's work, and family roles. They exhibit a keen eye for what they see as hypocrisy, "double standards," and "old-fashioned prejudices" among some of their elders.

Across the entire spectrum of South Asian immigrant groups there are attempts to lessen the tension through sponsoring "youth camps," teen conferences, public dialogues between parents and children, panel discussions, lectures by religious figures on duty and moral behavior, and a near industry on "advice" columns and "question & answer" formats dedicated to smoothing relations between parents and their offspring. The results of all this are unclear for a generation that sometimes sees itself as "neither there nor here." What is certain is that further changes will occur and adjustments will have to be made, but the pace and extent of such adaptations will vary enormously across the spectrum of South Asian cultures, just as degrees of conservatism, orthodoxy, education, immigration flows, and outside pressures and opportunities vary. Whether it is the wearing of the *hijab* (Islamic head covering), the gender separation of Sikh men and women in *gurdwaras*, or South Asians setting up hotlines and shelters for battered women, the American context has changed some of the terms for debates of this sort. These discussions are destined to intensify in the future. A projected continued loss of fluency in South Asian languages in succeeding generations will affect religious instruction; exogamous marriage patterns are likely to rise; and even "family" as a concept will become subject to interpretation. After all, that is what happened before, between 1904 and 1947.

CONCLUSION

The early immigrants were severely restricted for fifty years in their choices of occupation, marriage partners, freedom to travel abroad, landownership, and mainstream political participation, but they reacted with remarkable endeavor and ingenuity. They formed a loosely knit society of bicultural families and Punjabi compatriots. These men exhibited a quiet respect for each other and stoic personal dignity in the face of persistent external pressure. After Indian Independence, many reestablished ties in South Asia that would lead in time to a resurgence in the United States far beyond anything they might have then imagined. The new South Asian immigrants are already an important component of American society and are further recognized abroad as a valuable and successful resource by the governments of their former homelands. This is a complete reversal of the circumstances prevalent in the early phases of South Asians in America.

While part of every South Asian immigrant's ethnic heritage are the examples of those Punjabis who came before, some might look back and judge harshly how far their patterns may have differed from an arbitrary cultural standard. Others will see more deeply into the circumstances they faced and admire their courage, tenacity, and faith. In any event, it is unlikely *South Asian* in America will ever again have a single meaning in any sense except as a geographic or census denotation. Still, the emergence of unique, syncretic South Asian *American* identities should, eventually, be a source of pride and celebration for the future descendants of one of the oldest and most enduring civilizations on earth—and who happen to be living now in the New World.

NOTE ON TERMINOLOGY

Over the past century there have been many terms used to refer to immigrant peoples and cultures from the Indian subcontinent. Today, ongoing debates among new immigrants and their descendants continue over which are the best, most accurate, and most inclusive terms to adopt when referring to groups whose ancestry is Southern Asian. Historically, *Hindu* was the most common referent in North America until the 1960s, although it was wholly inaccurate if used in a religious sense to categorize the early Punjabi Sikhs and Muslims who formed the bulk of the immigration to America until the post-1965 period. In addition, there are historical and contemporary sources that use *Indian, Indian American, East Indian, Asian-Indian, Indo-American, Pakistani-American*, and many other hyphenated and/or geographically oriented labels. For our purposes here, the term *South Asian* will be used to encompass the peoples and cultures who were indigenous to, or whose ancestors derived from, the current nations of India, Pakistan, Bangladesh, Sri Lanka, Nepal, and Afghanistan.

BIBLIOGRAPHIC REFERENCES

Accounts of early South Asian immigration to America are available in Joan M. Jensen, *Passage from India: Asian Indian Immigrants in North America* (New Haven: Yale University Press, 1988), and Bruce La Brack, *The Sikhs of Northern California 1904–1975: A Socio-Historic Study* (New York: AMS Press, 1988). The best and most comprehensive description and analysis of the "Hindu-Mexican" families on the West Coast is presented by Karen Isaksen Leonard in *Making Ethnic Choices: California's Punjabi Mexican Americans* (Philadelphia: Temple University Press, 1992). The autobiography of the only South Asian to date to be elected to Congress is Dalip Singh Saund, *Congressman from India* (New York: E. P. Dutton & Co., 1960).

Sikh movements out of India and to America are discussed in N. Gerald Barrier and Verne A. Dusenbery, eds., *The Sikh Diaspora: Migration and the Experience beyond*

Punjab (Columbia, MO: South Asia Publications, 1989). General information on recent Asian American immigration including South Asian Americans can be obtained in Su-cheng Chan, *Asian Americans: An Interpretive History* (Boston: Twayne, 1991), and Ronald Takaki, *Strangers from a Different Shore: A History of Asian Americans* (Boston: Little, Brown, 1989). Background overviews on the South Asian diaspora can be found in Roger Daniels, *History of Indian Immigration to the United States: An Interpretative Essay* (New York: Asia Society, 1989); Peter Van der Veer, ed., *Nation and Migration: The Politics of Space in the South Asian Diaspora* (Philadelphia: University of Pennsylvania Press, 1995); S. Chandrasekhar, ed., *From India to America: A Brief History of Immigration* (La Jolla, CA: Population Review Publications, 1982); and Carla Petivich, ed., *The Expanding Landscape: South Asians in the Diaspora* (Chicago: American Institute of Indian Studies monograph series, forthcoming).

A recent and comprehensive review of both early and contemporary South Asian life in America is Karen Isaksen Leonards's excellent *South Asian Americans* (Westport, CT: Greenwood Press, 1997). The author gratefully acknowledges Dr. Leonard's generous sharing of her prepublication manuscript; it provided an invaluable source of information. Additional studies specific to America include: Maxine P. Fisher, *The Indians of New York City* (Columbia: South Asia Books, 1980); A. Wesley Helweg and Usha M. Helweg, *An Immigrant Success Story: East Indians in America* (Philadelphia: University of Pennsylvania Press, 1990); Johanna Lessinger, *From the Ganges to the Hudson: Indian Immigrants in New York City* (Boston: Allyn and Bacon, 1995); Sathi S. Dasgupta, *On the Trail of an Uncertain Dream: Indian Immigrant Experience in America* (New York: AMS Press, 1989); Iftikhar Haider Malik, *Pakistanis in Michigan: A Study of Third Culture and Acculturation* (New York: AMS Press, 1989); and Usha R. Jain, *The Gujaratis of San Francisco* (New York: AMS Press, 1989). Bibliographic collections include: Jane Singh et al., eds., *South Asians in North America: An Annotated and Selected Bibliography*, Occasional Paper No. 14 (Berkeley: Center for South and Southeast Asia Studies, 1988), and Darshan Singh Tatla, *Sikhs in North America: Sources for the Study of Sikh Community in North America and an Annotated Bibliography* (New York: Greenwood Press, 1991).

Overviews of South Asian religious traditions in America are available in John Y. Fenton, *Transplanting Religious Traditions: Asian Indians in America* (New York: Praeger, 1988), and his more recent *South Asian Religions in the Americas: An Annotated Bibliography of Immigrant Religious Traditions* (Westport, CT: Greenwood Press, 1995); and Diana Eck, ed., *On Common Ground: World Religions in America* (New York: Columbia University Press, 1997), CD-ROM. Islam in America is covered in J. Gordon Melton and Michael Koszegi, eds., *Islam in North America: A Sourcebook* (New York: Garland Publishing, 1992); Yvonne Haddad and Jane Idleman Smith, eds., *Muslim Communities in North America* (Albany: SUNY Press, 1994); and Yvonne Yazbeck Haddad and T. Lummis Adir, *Islamic Values in the United States: A Comparative Study* (New York: Oxford University Press, 1987). Hindu traditions are discussed by Raymond Brady Williams, ed., in his "Sacred Threads of Several Textures," in *A Sacred Thread: Modern Transmission of Hindu Traditions in India and Abroad* (Chambersburg, PA: Anima Press, 1992), pp. 228–257. A sensitive look at challenges facing Sikhs in America is described by John Stratton Hawley and Gurinder Singh Mann in *Studying the Sikhs: Issues for North America* (Albany, NY: State University of New York Press, 1993).

A comparative look at women and changing family forms and functions is available in Priya Agarwal, *Passage from India: Post 1965 Indian Immigrants and Their Children*

(Palos Verdes, CA: Yuvati Publications, 1991); The Women of South Asian Descent Collective, eds., *Our Feet Walk the Sky: Women of the South Asian Diaspora* (San Francisco: Aunt Lute Books, 1993); Nita Shah, *The Ethnic Strife: A Study of Asian Indian Women in the United States* (New York: Pinkerton and Thomas, 1993); and Deepika Bahri and Mary Vasudeva, eds., *Between the Lines: South Asians and Postcoloniality* (Asian American History and Culture Series) (Philadelphia: Temple University Press, 1997).

Two other works referred to in the essay are Gary R. Hess, ''The Forgotten Asian Americans,'' *Pacific Historical Review* 43 (November 1974): 576–596; and Dilip Singh Saund, *Congressman from India* (New York: E. P. Dutton, 1960).

SOUTHEAST ASIANS

Steven J. Gold

ORIGINS AND NUMBERS

Southeast Asians are a diverse group, hailing from the eastern portion of the peninsula that juts into the South China Sea between India and China. Sometimes referred to as Indochinese, their numbers comprise three nationalities—Vietnamese, Cambodians, and Laotians—and several ethnic subgroups, including the ethnic Chinese and Hmong.

Prior to the mid-1970s, only a handful of Southeast Asians (mostly Vietnamese) lived in the United States. However, by the 1990s, Southeast Asians and their children exceeded 1 million, with about 750,000 more resettled in other western countries, especially France, Australia, and Canada. A majority of Southeast Asians came to the United States as refugees from the Vietnam War, beginning in mid-1975, but others arrived as immigrants or as the spouses of U.S. military personnel. From 1982 through 1994, Southeast Asians entered the United States at a rate of between 40,000 and 80,000 each year. Thus, new arrivals continued to shape the population in both size and culture.

As of 1992, there was a total of 1,223,699 persons (refugees and immigrants) of Southeast Asian origins in the United States, including approximately 845,000 Vietnamese (69 percent of the total); 230,000 Laotians (19 percent); and 148,000 Cambodians (12 percent). Because the U.S. government collects these data by nationality alone, nonofficial estimates are the sole source of information regarding the fractions of ethnic subpopulations, such as the Hmong and Chinese. By 1994, the number of Southeast Asians admitted into the United States as refugees (persons who must flee because of persecution or a well-founded fear of persecution due to their religion, race, family background, ideology, or other factors) had exceeded that of Cubans, making them the largest refugee group to enter the country since World War II.

U.S. involvement in Southeast Asia—which ultimately led to these arrivals—

can be traced to the late 1940s. After China became communist in 1949, the United States and other nations sought to halt "the spread of communism" in Asia. According to the widely accepted domino theory of that era, as one nation became communist, unless proper steps were taken, those around it would also adopt this system of government. Vietnam, Laos, and Cambodia had been French colonies since the nineteenth century, and U.S. officials thought that by shoring up the French presence in the region and rebuilding war-ravaged France, communism could be thwarted. After France's 1954 defeat at the hands of Vietnamese communists at the Battle of Dien Bien Phu, Vietnam was partitioned into two nations, the communist north and the nationalist south. Upon the French withdrawal, the United States extended its involvement in the region, initially by advising and equipping the South Vietnamese and later through extensive deployment of U.S. forces. The war, which spilled over into Cambodia and Laos, resulted in the deaths of nearly 4 million Vietnamese soldiers and civilians, about 10 percent of the nation's entire population.

At the same time, with so many U.S. troops and so much U.S. technology deployed in Southeast Asia, many Southeast Asians were first exposed to the language, culture, and ways of the country they would eventually call their new home. April 30, 1975, the fall of Saigon, marked the end of the U.S. military presence in Southeast Asia and the beginning of the flow of Southeast Asian refugees to the United States.

The stateside resettlement of Southeast Asians, carried out at first very ad hoc, was soon placed within the parameters of refugee resettlement legislation enacted by Congress. The most important law was the Refugee Act of 1980. Refugee services were delivered and administered by a diverse network of government, religious, nonprofit, and profit-making agencies and organizations. Refugee resettlement was carried out under the supervision of fourteen voluntary agencies, or VOLAGS. Most VOLAGS, including the U.S. Catholic Conference, Church World Service, and the Hebrew Immigrant Aid Society, had religious affiliations, and all were funded by the federal government. Services available to refugees included housing, physical and mental health care, cash assistance, job training and placement, and language instruction. In addition to cash benefits and social services, government funds also supported the creation of mutual assistance associations (MAAs) among refugee groups to facilitate community organization and self-help. The nature, availability, and extent of services varied considerably across states and regions. Finally, refugee status also provides its incumbents with legal rights, the most significant being legal resident status, which provided those so designated with the opportunity to be employed and to become a U.S. citizen.

Working in conjunction with the VOLAGS, the U.S. government resettled Southeast Asian refugees throughout the United States. This was done in order to avoid their concentrating in a single location—as had occurred with the Cuban refugees to the United States, of whom well over half currently reside in Miami. However, despite plans to disperse the Southeast Asian refugee population, the group revealed a very high level of geographical mobility, or "secondary migration." Only months after their arrival, thousands left their initial locations of settlement in the South, East, and Midwest for the West Coast, where the climate was more moderate, Asian culture more prevalent, welfare more generous, and the economic downturns of the late 1970s and early 1980s less severely felt. In fiscal 1982 alone, 24,000 Southeast Asian refugees entered California from other states, constituting about 4 percent of all Southeast Asian refugees in the United States at that time. By 1987, 40 percent of all Southeast Asians congregated in California. Except for Texas, where 7.5 percent of Southeast Asians reside, no other state is home to more than 5 percent of the total refugee population.

GROUP DIFFERENCES

Southeast Asian refugees share many commonalities, including their region of origin, the time of their departure (most came to the United States between the mid-1970s and the early 1980s), and their flight from communism. Concurrently, however, the groups are diverse in terms of language, culture, educational level, religious outlook, contact with Western life, and a variety of other factors.

Vietnamese

As the largest and most diverse Southeast Asian population in the United States, Vietnamese have been well studied. Observers have noted that while over 60 percent arrived between 1975 and 1983, the Vietnamese community includes several vintages characterized by distinct patterns of adaptation. Refugees who entered the United States between 1975 and 1977 have made remarkable strides in adapting to the United States. The more recently arrived, however, have encountered greater difficulty in adjusting to America. Although these groups frequently interact, they also retain many differences and have developed fairly distinct patterns of adaptation to the United States.

1975-Era Refugees

The first group of Vietnamese refugees, numbering about 175,000, avoided many of the most traumatic elements of the flight from Vietnam. Reaching the United States between 1975 and 1977, most were U.S. employees and/or members of the South Vietnamese military and government (and their families). As an elite, they feared punishment by the northern communists. Their suspicions proved to be correct. While there was no bloodbath on a par with what later occurred in neighboring Cambodia, many South Vietnamese were incarcerated in reeducation camps for up to fifteen years.

Evacuated by American forces, the first wave of Vietnamese avoided life under the new regime and spent only a short time in refugee camps before being resettled in the United States, with their families intact. Funds for their resettlement were relatively generous: three years of cash assistance. Their links to Western culture are indicated by the fact that almost half were Catholic, even though well over 80 percent of all Vietnamese are Buddhists. Drawing upon their skills, education, competence in English, familiarity with Western culture, and extended families, many adjusted rapidly. By the mid-1980s, the Office of Refugee Resettlement reported that their average income matched that of the larger U.S. population.

Despite their swift economic adjustment, the first cohort of Vietnamese refugees did encounter many difficulties. A major hardship was the rapidity of their exit. Sixty-one percent had less than twenty-four hours to prepare for their departure, and 83 percent had less than one week. While this group had a greater proportion of unified families than later arrivals, many relatives were left behind.

Between April and December of 1975, prior to permanent placement, refugees were housed in four resettlement camps: Camp Pendleton, near San Diego; Fort Chaffee, Arkansas; Eglin Air Force Base, near Pensacola; and Fort Indian Town Gap in Pennsylvania. As noted, the first waves of Vietnamese were resettled throughout the country, sponsored by churches and other non-Vietnamese voluntary organizations. While this provided the Vietnamese with contacts for finding work and opportunities to become familiar with American culture and the English language, both refugees and sponsors experienced a great deal of culture shock as they encountered one another.

The Boat People

The second group of Vietnamese began to enter the United States following the outbreak of the Vietnam-China conflict of 1978. Generally called *boat people*, these refugees were of lower class standing than first-wave refugees and included both Vietnamese and ethnic Chinese persons. (The latter will be discussed separately below.) They had lived for three or more years under communism, sometimes laboring in reeducation camps or remote "new economic zones" before leaving Vietnam. Many refugees who arrived in the United States as post-1978 boat people described making a conscious decision to stay in their homeland despite the communist takeover. They felt loyal to their families and country and thought they had nothing to fear from the communists.

Their exit, involving open sea voyages in leaky, overcrowded boats or long journeys on foot across revolution-torn Cambodia to Thailand, was subject to attacks by pirates and military forces. Reportedly, up to half of these refugees perished in flight. Having crossed the high seas, boat people then languished for several months in the overcrowded refugee camps of Thailand, Malaysia, Indonesia, the Philippines, or Hong Kong before being admitted into the United States (or in much smaller numbers, into other countries, from Canada and Europe to Australia and Israel). In the camps, they received aid from an international bureaucracy of resettlement agencies under the supervision of the UNHCR (United Nations High Committee on Refugees). Many were housed in Pilau Bidong, a giant island-based camp off the coast of Malaysia. The refugees were kept quarantined from the larger society because this Muslim nation feared that the heavily Chinese refugee population would upset the country's delicate ethnic balance between Chinese and Muslim. In refugee camps, various ethnic and nationality groups were housed together, making them a microcosm of the nations that had been involved in the Indochina conflict and often reflecting the ethnic and national antipathies long present in the region.

To ease their adaptation, those refugees selected for eventual resettlement in the United States received three months of training in English and American culture at one of two "RPCs" (Refugee Processing Centers) in Galang, Indonesia, or Bataan, Philippines. Following their stay in the RPC, refugees boarded charter flights for the United States, where they were met by representatives of resettlement agencies or sponsors and were set up with apartments in refugee neighborhoods.

Due to the dangers of escape, far more young men left Vietnam as boat people than did women, children, or the elderly. For example, in 1984 there were approximately 204,000 male Southeast Asian refugees in the United States between the ages of twelve and forty-four but only 156,000 females in the same age group, a 24 percent difference. Accordingly, this group was marked by broken families. In addition, post-1978 entrants experienced financial troubles more severe than those of earlier-arriving Vietnamese. While Vietnamese refugees coming to the United States in 1975 had averaged nine and a half years of education and two-thirds knew some English upon arrival, those arriving between 1980 and 1982 had an average of seven years of education, and half had no competence in English. Disadvantaged by lower levels of both education and English-language ability, and contending with the depressed economy of the early 1980s, boat refugees faced difficulties in finding their first American jobs. Further, while the 1975 cohorts were sponsored by Americans who often provided job referrals, subsequent arrivals were resettled by Vietnamese who generally lacked such connections to employers. Post-1978 arrivals also had to contend with shrinking government benefits (halved to eighteen months). Because of these many disadvantages, the later-arriving Vietnamese had a more difficult time in adapting to the United States than had their earlier-arriving compatriots.

Amerasians and Reeducation Camp Survivors

Since the late 1980s, the U.S. government has established special programs for Amerasians and reeducation camp survivors, two groups of Vietnamese who have been subject to particularly harsh treatment in their home country. Amerasians are youth whose fathers were American servicemen, whereas reeducation camp survivors are recently released political prisoners who generally held high positions in the South Vietnamese military or government. In contemporary Vietnam, both groups are highly marginal and encounter both popular and official discrimination. Because they have an American parent, Amerasians are U.S. citizens, but, due to their plight, they are also eligible for the full package of refugee benefits. As of September 30, 1996, 84,318 Amerasians and accompanying relatives, 158,245 reeducation camp survivors and their relatives, and another 210,393 Vietnamese of various statuses—yielding a grand total of 452,956 persons and constituting over a third of all Southeast Asians in the United States—had entered through the Orderly Departure Program (ODP). Avoiding covert escapes and stays in refugee camps, ODP refugees fly directly from Vietnam to the United States.

Cambodians

Cambodians, who identify themselves as members of the Khmer ethnic group, trace their national culture to the kingdom of Angkor that long ago directed the social and economic life of their country and supervised the building of stone temples, palaces, tombs, roadways, and a network of reservoirs and canals for growing rice. By the thirteenth century, the Ankorean civilization began to decline, and the nation went through periods of occupation by neighboring Thais and Vietnamese. The French occupation of Cambodia (from 1863 to 1954) allowed the country and its royal family to survive intact but prevented economic growth and development. Further, the French colonists relied upon Vietnamese to serve as political and economic administrators, thus precluding the creation of a Westernized Cambodian middle class.

In the 1950s, Cambodia became independent of France and under the leadership of King Norodom Sihanouk. It enjoyed a period of relative peace and prosperity until 1970, when the effects of the conflict in neighboring Vietnam became unavoidable. Incursions of various Vietnamese and allied armies, together with the impact of American influence, eroded social traditions and disrupted the country's agricultural economy. In an attempt to deter the use of Cambodia as a sanctuary by North Vietnamese troops, the United States engaged in extensive bombing. Between 1969 and 1973, as many bombs were dropped on Cambodia (a nation of less than 8 million) as had been hurled at Japan (with a population of over 73 million in 1940) during the entire period of World War II. Bombardment and other wartime action resulted in the death of some 500,000 Cambodians during the first half of the 1970s.

During the later years of the Vietnam War era, the Cambodian communists, known as the Khmer Rouge, grew increasingly powerful. Under the leadership of General Pol Pot, they took over the country on April 17, 1975, two weeks before the fall of South Vietnam. As was the case in Vietnam, an initial wave of Cambodians escaped at the time of the communist takeover. Some 6,000 of these—many of whom were middle-class urbanites with links to the U.S. military or government—were resettled in the United States between 1975 and 1977.

Renaming the country Democratic Kampuchea, the Khmer Rouge sought to purge the nation of Western, capitalist, and traditional influences. Declaring that it was "Year Zero," they set about rebuilding the entire society. They forced citizens out from urban regions, broke families apart, destroyed Buddhiᶜt temples, and killed monks. By the time the Pol Pot regime was finally ousted by the Vietnamese communists in 1978, approximately 1 million of the country's 8 million citizens had been killed or had died of starvation or illness. Unlike other major acts of genocide that took place during this century—particularly those involving European Jews and Armenians—most Cambodian victims were members of the majority population of their own country. Moreover, owing to their nation's poverty, Cambodians were not annihilated by a relatively impersonal and technologically advanced "death machine," as used by the Nazis. Instead, they were slaughtered with rough-hewn agricultural implements because ammunition was considered too valuable for use in mass executions.

Following Cambodia's occupation by Vietnam, thousands sought refuge in neighboring Thailand. Initially, the Thais objected to the presence of so many Cambodians in their country, but they later bowed to international pressure and allowed international agencies to establish refugees camps in Thailand and also to create a "land bridge" so that aid could be delivered to Cambodia. Between 1975 and 1993, just under 150,000 Cambodians were resettled in the United States.

The Cambodian community in the United States includes educated urbanites and rural farmers. Their numbers also contain a significant group of ethnic Chinese, who play a major role in developing ethnic businesses. Forty-six percent of Cambodians in the United States reside in California, with their largest settlement in Long Beach. Other sizable populations are in Massachusetts and in Washington State.

Laotians

Like Vietnam and Cambodia, Laos was colonized first by a neighboring nation (Thailand), followed by France. The United States established a major presence there after the nation's mid-1950s independence. Laos is an ethnically diverse country and includes Thais, Vietnamese (many of whom were brought in during the French colonial period as administrators), and ethnic Chinese. About half of the nation's population, those who self-identify as Lao, speak a language similar to Thai and are concentrated in the lowlands along the Mekong River. Living in the mountains of the northern part of the country are several groups culturally and linguistically distinct from the lowlanders. Although the Hmong people (to be discussed below) are from Laos, they do not consider themselves to be members of the Lao ethnic group.

Following the end of the U.S. presence in Southeast Asia, a Vietnamese-backed communist government took over Laos, precipitating the exit of over 300,000 Laotians. Of these, 230,000 have been resettled in the United States.

Hmong

The Hmong, an ethnic group that lives in mountainous territory throughout China and Southeast Asia, were little known in the United States prior to the late 1970s, when they began to enter as refugees. Hmong are relative newcomers to Laos, having migrated there from China and Vietnam in the early nineteenth century. Living in rugged regions, the Hmong valued their independence and became skillful in developing alliances with various political interests—including the French and the Chinese—in order to maintain autonomy. Beginning in the late 1960s, various groups of Hmong were recruited by the Central Intelligence Agency (CIA) to fight against Laotian and Vietnamese communists, who were seeking to establish control over them. Once communist control over the region was established, the Hmong became victims of brutal treatment intended to impose conformity and punish them for their wartime opposition.

As a result, the Hmong fled, and thousands have been resettled in the United States as well as in France, French Guyana, Canada, Australia, Argentina, China, and Japan. In the United States in 1990, Hmong resided in forty-three states, but 90 percent of their population lived in only three: California (about 47,000), Minnesota (17,000), and Wisconsin (16,000). While California is a common destination for Southeast Asian refugees (and immigrants in general), the concentration of Hmong in the midwestern "Frost Belt" states appears to be a unique pattern.

Because of their way of life in Southeast Asia, the Hmong's cultural outlook and experience are especially distant from that practiced in the United States. Few members of this population could read or write in any language or had a formal education or any experience with urban life prior to their flight. Accordingly, they faced considerable culture shock in the United States and have encountered substantial difficulty in achieving economic self-sufficiency and otherwise adapting to America. Researchers have found that almost half of Hmong refugees experience depression, and because of their lack of resources in the United States, the passing of time has brought little improvement in their mental condition.

Many Hmong continue to reside in public housing or substandard rental units in inner-city neighborhoods. While this pattern is largely due to economic difficulties, it is also the result of Hmong's desire to dwell in a co-ethnic milieu. Resettlement in such contexts sometimes results in conflicts with established residents. On the other hand, the low cost of housing in inner-city settings and the willingness of many Hmong to live together allow them to purchase homes. With time, some groups have been able to move up to more desirable suburban locations. The basic units of social organization among the Hmong are extended families and clans. A fairly large fraction, especially those middle-aged and older, have attempted to retain agricultural occupations in the United States. However, like native-born farmers, many find this economic sector to be incapable of generating adequate income.

On the group level, Hmong suffer from difficulties in adaptation and have very little experience with formal education. Despite these liabilities, the evidence suggests that Hmong youths are achieving in school. Studies in St. Paul, Minnesota, and San Diego show that they are doing well in high school and pursuing postsecondary education at rates comparable to the general population. Moreover, the Hmong spend more time on homework and receive higher grades than their peers, while getting in trouble and dropping out with less frequency.

The Ethnic Chinese

The great majority of the ethnic Chinese arrived in the United States as boat people after 1978. Hailing mostly from Vietnam (prior to 1975, Saigon's Chinatown of Cho Lon [big market] was superseded only by Singapore as the largest Chinese settlement outside of China), the ethnic Chinese also lived in Cambodia and Laos. Constituting an entrepreneurial class, this group has a long history but marginal status in Southeast Asia. Many ethnic Chinese can trace their origins to China's Guandong province, directly north of Vietnam. Their communities were highly organized, usually on the basis of their dialect and region of origin in China. Many Chinese-Vietnamese were self-employed, and occupational specialization often took place among various dialect groups.

Some ethnic Chinese were highly assimilated to Vietnamese, Cambodian, or Lao culture and intermarried with natives. Others retained a strong Chinese identity and were little involved with the language, culture, or politics of their place of residence. Maintenance of Chinese culture was facilitated as larger communities provided an extensive network of social, economic, and cultural institutions, including schools and even hospitals. The 1978 outbreak of hostilities between Vietnam and China was a pivotal event for the ethnic Chinese. As a minority group living in a communist society who were known to be strongly capitalist in orientation and ethnically linked to a hostile nation, their status throughout Southeast Asia (which was by this time under Vietnamese hegemony) was precarious. Consequently, the ethnic Chinese were permitted—for a sizable fee—to exit. Their experience of flight was much the same as that of the boat people.

Relying on past experience and sources of capital and goods from overseas Chinese communities, a number of ethnic Chinese have been able to reestablish their role as entrepreneurs in America, both in existing Chinatowns as well as in new Southeast Asian enclaves, such as Little Saigon in Orange County, California; on Anaheim Street in Long Beach, California; and in Revere Beach, Massachusetts. One of the most successful ethnic Chinese entrepreneurs, Frank Jao, arrived in southern California in 1975. After stints as a door-to-door vacuum cleaner salesman and night watchman in a sugar factory, Jao got involved in real estate. Fifteen years later, he headed Bridgecreek Development Co., a company responsible for the construction of half a million square feet of commercial property in southern California. Established with the cooperation of co-ethnic investors from Malaysia and Taiwan, Bridgecreek owns assets of $150 million and has a record of community organization and philanthropy.

Jao's experience, however, has been far from typical. Lacking a Western-style education and sometimes subject to discrimination from ethnic Vietnamese in the United States, the ethnic Chinese have experienced a slower economic adjustment than that of the ethnic Vietnamese, and that adjustment has been marked by distinct patterns of education, residence, and occupational distribution. The size of the Southeast Asian Chinese population in the United States, itself divided by political and linguistic differences and varying degrees of assimilation to the country of origin, is difficult to determine. U.S. census data offer little help because many Southeast Asian Chinese identify themselves simply as "Chinese" on census forms, regardless of their national origins in Vietnam, Laos, or Cambodia.

CHARACTERISTICS OF SOUTHEAST ASIANS IN THE UNITED STATES

Southeast Asians are a rapidly growing group. Despite their short time in the United States—only a few thousand were here prior to 1975—over 20 percent are native-born, including almost 35 percent of the Hmong. The large percentage of native-born can be attributed to the groups' relative youth and high rates of fertility. Southeast Asian families are large in size. On the average, American women age thirty-five to forty-four have just under 2 children. In contrast, Vietnamese women have 2.5 children; Lao and Cambodians average 3.5; and Hmong women an average of 6.1 children, the highest of all groups in the United States. Further, while less than half of all American households include children under eighteen, as of 1996 two-thirds of Vietnamese, 80 percent of Lao and Cambodian, and 90 percent of Hmong households contain minor children.

Although there is a moderate level of female-headed households among some of these groups (due to war-related male fatalities and selective migration patterns), Southeast Asians generally maintain stable families. Several studies have shown that the structure of these families is a vital source of social, economic, and psychological support for this population. For example, partly because of their positive health practices, Southeast Asians have among the lowest infant mortality rates of any ethnically defined population in the country despite the fact that they rank low in income, educational level, and English ability—indicators commonly associated with elevated rates of infant mortality.

Young Southeast Asians often experience conflicts as they must move between the traditional Asian values and expectation of their parents and ethnic communities, on the one side, and those of the larger society, on the other. Faced with this paradox, it is not uncommon for teenagers to maintain dramatically different identities, depending upon their circumstances, a transition that often entails changing one's clothes, hairstyle, and makeup in addition to language and attitude upon entering or leaving one's home. While young Vietnamese struggle to please both their parents and peers, the older generation is often less flexible. Upon observing their children adopt American social mores and individualistic attitudes, disregard their advice, and become monolingual English speakers, they sometimes feel that their families have disintegrated.

At the same time, however, many refugees have been able to keep families and communities intact and have developed generally positive ways of retaining valued traditions while coping with the opportunities and challenges presented by American society. Notable among these have been increased gender equality and opportunity for women, which, while threatening traditional family patterns, yield economic and child-rearing benefits for entire families. Despite their low incomes and the high cost of housing in many of the regions where they live, according to the 1990 census, a considerable fraction of Southeast Asians own their homes, ranging from 11 percent of Hmong, to a fifth of Cambodians, a quarter of Laotians, and over 40 percent of Vietnamese. Among recent home buyers in Orange County, California, Nguyens (the most common Vietnamese surname) outnumbered Smiths 2:1. Family-based and other collective sources of funding frequently support these purchases.

On the one hand, one of the more positive aspects of the Southeast Asian refugee experience has been this group's ability to do relatively well in school, despite the trauma of being refugees, their cultural and linguistic unfamiliarity with the American context, and the fact that many attend poorly funded urban schools. Research among Southeast Asian students in San Diego found that although two-thirds were limited English proficient, they had higher grade-point averages than the district at large and even exceeded the grades of native-born whites. Such impressive results were maintained even by the Hmong and Cambodians, whose often preliterate background and traumatic refugee experience would seemingly hinder academic achievement. Similar findings have been reported in studies of Southeast Asian students attending underfunded urban schools throughout the United States.

While American-educated youths have made marked progress, the educational attainment of Southeast Asians as a whole remains well below the national average. As of 1990, just under 60 percent of Vietnamese and just over a third of Cambodians and Laotians were high school graduates; 16 percent of Vietnamese and about 5 percent of Cambodians and Laotians in the United States were college graduates. This can be contrasted to a 77 percent high school completion rate and a 20 percent college graduation rate for the whole country.

On the other hand, Southeast Asians (especially the non-Vietnamese) have been characterized by low rates of labor force participation, a sizable proportion of households below the poverty level, and significant reliance on public assistance. First-wave Vietnamese—an elite group whose numbers include professionals and other high-level workers—matched the average earnings of the U.S. population by 1987, and both Vietnamese and ethnic Chinese reveal rates of self-employment near the national average. However, many members of the broader Southeast Asian population continue to rely on public assistance or minimum wage jobs as laborers or operatives or in service industries. According to the 1990 census, of those employed, over a third of all Vietnamese, nearly half of Cambodians and Hmong, and 64 percent of Laotians held blue-collar jobs. Of those Southeast Asians in the United States five years or less in 1994, only 23 percent were self-supporting, whereas 40 percent relied on public assistance as their only source of income. Many refugees reluctantly accept public assistance because taking a job means an end to their eligibility for Medicare and Medicaid, and the minimum-wage positions for which they qualify seldom provide health benefits.

In 1992, 37 percent of Southeast Asian refugees age sixteen and above who had been in the United States five years or less were employed, with an additional 9 percent looking for work. Twenty percent were unemployed versus 5.4 percent for the country at large. However, Vietnamese tend to make better economic adjustment than do other Southeast Asian groups. In 1994, for example, Vietnamese had a lower unemployment rate (4 percent) than the country at large (5 percent), whereas other Southeast Asians revealed a rate of unemployment of 42 percent—ten times the Vietnamese average. Moreover, as of 1990, labor force participation rates (the fraction of those working or looking for work) at 46 percent for Cambodians and 29 percent for Hmong (age sixteen or older) were far below that of the 65 percent rate for the U.S. population. Vietnamese and Laotian rates, at 64 percent and 58 percent, respectively, were considerably higher than those of other Southeast Asian groups. The better economic performance of the Vietnamese can be accounted for by their longer tenure in the United States, their greater familiarity with Western culture, their higher levels of education and English competence, and more possibilities for employment within their growing ethnic economy.

Economic difficulties are not surprising, given that Southeast Asians are characterized by numerous social and economic disadvantages. They have few transferable job skills, know little English, and are often in poor physical and mental condition as a consequence of their lives in, and flight from, Southeast Asia. Even among those with premigration occupational skills, downward mobility is common. According to a U.S. Office of Refugee Resettlement employment survey, "Thirty percent of the employed adults sampled had held white collar jobs in their country of origin; 17.5 percent held similar jobs in the United States in 1988. Conversely, far more Southeast Asian refugees hold blue collar or service jobs in the United States than they did in their countries of origin." As a result of these many factors, family incomes are relatively low, and research indicates that those Southeast Asian households with incomes that exceed the poverty level are able to do so only with many workers per household. Various scholarly and journalistic accounts suggest that in an attempt to compensate for economic hardships, Southeast Asians are also relatively active in the informal economy, supplementing their incomes with "off the books" pay earned in business, swap meet sales, home-based production, and the like. Given that a disproportionate number of Southeast Asians live in California and other West Coast settings associated with a very high cost of living, their economic plight certainly is a difficult one.

THE ETHNIC GROUPS IN CONTEMPORARY
AMERICAN SOCIETY

The presence of Southeast Asian refugees in American society has brought up a variety of themes suggestive of some of the best and worst elements in American society. From the beginning, these people were reminders of what some pundits have labeled "The War Nobody Won"—one of the most divisive periods in American history. However, America's willingness to take responsibility for over a million people adversely affected by the war and its aftermath has certainly been a positive humanitarian gesture. While some Americans treated the refugees with hostility and even violence (in perhaps the ugliest incident, a racist gunman shot thirty-seven mostly Southeast Asian elementary school students in Stockton, California, in 1989), thousands of other Americans helped the new arrivals find jobs, learn English, and join U.S. communities. Like other ethnic groups who run small businesses in inner-city locations, Southeast Asian entrepreneurs suffer from urban violence. Despite the great toll suffered by Korean shop owners in the 1992 Los Angeles urban uprising, Thanh Lam, a twenty-five year-old Chinese-Vietnamese, was the only store owner killed during the riot. His murder has been investigated as a hate crime.

Due to economic problems, difficulties in adjusting to American society, and their resettlement in declining inner-city communities, a fraction of alienated Southeast Asian youth have become involved in gangs and other unlawful activities. Because of the frequency of home invasions and crimes of extortion, a 1989 *Los Angeles Times* survey found that fear of co-ethnic gangs and crime was the greatest concern of Orange County Vietnamese. While fellow refugees are the most common victims of these ethnic gangs, violence has occasionally spread to the larger society. In April 1991, armed members of the "Oriental Boys" gang seized a Sacramento electronics store, taking forty-one hostages. In the resulting melee, three gang members and three hostages died. In 1993, reflecting the community's frustration with the threat of co-ethnic gangs, Vietnam-born, Westminster, California, city councilman Tony Lam (who made controlling crime a cornerstone of his campaign to become one of the first elected Vietnamese Americans, in November 1992) called for the deportation of any noncitizen convicted of a serious offense.

Notwithstanding these difficulties, Southeast Asians have struggled to create communities in the United States. While the nationality and ethnic groups that make up the broader Southeast Asian population share common perspectives resulting from their opposition to communism and experience as refugees, they are also diverse in their political, religious, and ideological outlooks. Each group contains factions disposed toward cultural preservation and home country concerns, on the one hand, and the group's development within an American context, on the other.

The Vietnamese community reveals a melange of contentious factions, vying for community leadership and addressing a variety of issues, interests, and constituencies. Bases of communal activism include veterans' associations, business development groups, resettlement agencies, and religious leaders, many of which publish their own newspapers or magazines. Lao communities have been most absorbed with religious activities, building Buddhist churches in several locations of settlement. The Cambodians, too, reveal a record of Buddhist involvement, although political concerns related to their country of origin catalyze another base of activism. The Hmong have established a number of close communities, many of which offer their members economic assistance. The ethnic Chinese already understand something about providing mutual assistance, having been able to draw upon their premigration experience as an organized ethnic minority in Southeast Asia. Relying upon their involvement in small business and their links with co-ethnics in the United States and overseas, they have made significant progress toward rebuilding organized communities in the new setting.

The host of Southeast Asian refugee associations thus represents the whole diversity of these people and serves myriad functions. Specifically, they include, for example, the Association of Vietnamese Elderly; the Vietnamese Catholic Community (Stockton, California); the Vietnamese Fisherman Association; the Cambodian American Foundation (San Francisco) and the United Khmer Society (Austin, Texas); the Hmong Association (Long Beach, California); and the Lao Family Community (Richmond, California) and the Southern California Lao Soccer League.

Southeast Asian communities have been unified by active media industries producing newspapers, magazines, radio and cable television programs, and frequent festivals. Ethnic business districts offer a variety of services, restaurants, and coffeeshops and all kinds of financial, wholesale, and retail establishments, while an extensive recording industry produces many styles of music (ranging from traditional to Madonna-influenced) on both cassette and compact disk.

Since the 1994 normalization of relations between the United States and Southeast Asian nations, travel and economic exchange with these countries have become much more accessible, allowing refugees to reestablish ties with their countries of origin. This opportunity is especially controversial within the Vietnamese community, which includes both seasoned entrepreneurs ready to profit from relations with their home country as well as anti-communists who fear that infusions of Vietnamese-American capital and know-how will prop up the Hanoi regime.

Regardless of their involvement in more formalized organizations, or their positions regarding relations with their homelands, most Southeast Asians maintain an integrated communal life at the local level, interacting regularly with friends, relatives, and neighbors. As a group, Southeast Asians endured an especially traumatic exit from their homelands and have experienced considerable difficulty in adjusting to what is, for them, a strange new setting. Still, Southeast Asians have made many impressive accomplishments. For example, 1992 witnessed the flight of Eugene H. Trinh, a Vietnamese-born space shuttle astronaut, as well as the election of Choua Lee to the St. Paul, Minnesota, school board, making her one of the first two Southeast Asians to hold elective office in the United States (along with Tony Lam). Their struggles and accomplishments notwithstanding, as a recently arrived group, the broader history of Southeast Asians is yet to be written.

BIBLIOGRAPHICAL REFERENCES

There are a wide variety of publications dealing with many aspects of the Southeast Asian refugee experience. Some useful and up-to-date overviews include: Rubén G. Rumbaut's "A Legacy of War: Refugees from Vietnam, Laos and Cambodia," in *Origins and Destinies: Immigration, Race and Ethnicity in America*, edited by Silvia Pedraza and Rubén G. Rumbaut (Belmont, CA: Wadsworth, 1996) pp. 315–333; and Jeremy Hein, *From Vietnam, Laos and Cambodia: A Refugee Experience in the United States* (New York: Simon and Schuster, 1995). An official government publication, the annual *Report to Congress of the Refugee Resettlement Program* (Washington, DC.: U.S. Department of Health and Human Services, 1994), offers a wealth of statistics and policy information. The following are in-depth studies of particular Southeast Asian groups: Sucheng Chan, ed., *Hmong Means Free: Life in Laos and America* (Philadelphia: Temple University Press, 1994); Usha Welaratna, *Beyond the Killing Fields: Voices of Nine Cambodian Survivors in America* (Stanford, CA: Stanford University Press, 1993); and James A. Freeman, *Hearts of Sorrow: Vietnamese–American Lives* (Stanford, CA: Stanford University Press, 1989). Nazli Kibria's *Family Tightrope* (Princeton, NJ: Princeton University Press, 1993) offers a detailed examination of Vietnamese family adaptation, whereas Nathan Caplan, John K. Whitmore, and Marcella H. Choy's *The Boat People and Achievement in America: A Study of Family Life, Hard Work and Cultural Values* (Ann Arbor: University of Michigan Press, 1989) draws on survey data collected throughout the United States to demonstrate the family-based educational achievement of Southeast Asian refugees. Finally, Steven J. Gold's *Refugee Communities: A Comparative Field Study* (Newbury Park, CA: Sage, 1992) compares the experience of Vietnamese refugees with that of Soviet Jews and pays special attention to the formation of communal structures, such as political organizations and small businesses.

David W. Haines's edited volume *Case Studies in Diversity: Refugees in America in the 1990s* (Westport, CT: Praeger, 1997) includes the following excellent chapters on the major Southeast Asian Refugee groups: "Vietnamese," by Nguyen Manh Hung and David W. Haines (pp. 34–56); "Lao," by Pamela DeVoe (pp. 107–126); "Hmong," by Timothy Dunnigan, Douglas P. Olney, Miles A. McNall, and Marline A. Spring (pp. 145–166); "Khmer," by Carol A. Mortland (pp. 167–193); and "Chinese from Southeast Asia," by John K. Whitmore (pp. 223–243). Jo Ann Koltyk's *New Pioneers in the Heartland: Hmong Life in Wisconsin* (Needham Heights, MA: Allyn and Bacon, 1997) offers an ethnographic look at refugees' lives in the Midwest. Since the 1970s, the *International Migration Review* has published a wide array of articles about the experiences of Southeast Asians in the United States. Finally, annual data on refugees are available from the U.S. Office of Refugee Resettlement. Here, reference was made to its *1989 Report to Congress: Refugee Resettlement Program* (Washington, D.C.: U.S. Department of Health and Human Services, 1989).

WEST INDIANS/ CARIBBEANS

Philip Kasinitz and Milton Vickerman

A growing number of Americans can trace their ancestry to immigrants from the nations and territories of the West Indies.[1] Yet although they have immigrated to the United States since colonial times, and although they have come in substantial numbers since the turn of the century, West Indian immigrants are relatively understudied. Indeed, they have been frequently described, most notably by Roy S. Bryce-Laporte, as the "invisible immigrants." This is in large part due to the racial identity of most West Indian immigrants. As "blacks" (at least in the terms that race is thought of in the United States), West Indian immigrants are rarely seen as a distinct ethnic group apart from African Americans. Most scholarly and popular attention that the group has received has focused either on how West Indians construct their racial identity or on West Indians' economic "success" (or lack thereof) in light of what this might imply about African Americans. In recent years press descriptions have often pointed to the "discipline," "family values," and "work ethic" of a community that could produce a Colin Powell. That the same milieux could produce a Louis Farrakhan is only rarely noted.

In this essay we will present a discussion of three distinct but interrelated Caribbean ethnic groups, each of which has immigrated to the United States in large numbers since 1965: Anglophone West Indians, Haitians, and Dominicans. "West Indians" come from the largely African-descended[2] former British and Dutch colonies of the Caribbean basin, including the mainland CARICOM (Caribbean Community and Common Market) member nations of Guyana, Belize, and Surinam. Each of these nations is in some ways culturally distinct, but in the United States their immigrants—especially those from the Anglophone Caribbean who, by far, comprise the bulk of the West Indian population (see Table 8)—tend to form a single ethnic community. They live in the same neighborhoods, have similar employment patterns, and think of themselves as a common group ("one nation divided by water"). Moreover, prior to migrating, West

Table 8
West Indian Immigrants to the United States, 1956–1995

Country of Birth	1956-1960	1961-1965	1966-1970	1971-1975	1976-1980	1981-1985	1986-1990	1991-1995	Total
Antigua	298	866	1,729	1,969	4,014	8,081	1,762	—	18,719
Bahamas	1,646	1,203	1,132	1,609	2,498	2,660	4,648	3,563	18,959
Barbados	1,514	1,992	7,312	7,878	12,603	9,406	8,076	5,366	54,147
Dominica	219	432	1,767	1,182	3,294	2,818	3,626	3,572	16,910
Grenada	216	602	1,907	2,388	5,182	5,254	5,325	3,832	24,706
Jamaica	6,518	8,335	62,676	61,445	78,476	100,560	136,222	90,731	544,963
Montserrat	253	531	877	932	959	700	651	---	4,903
St. Kitts	283	870	3,132	1,960	4,220	7,096	3,513	--	21,074
St. Lucia	116	481	884	1,305	3,560	2,964	3,146	2,906	15,362
St. Vincent	199	559	1,384	1,613	3,040	3,673	3,880	---	14,348
Trinidad	1,497	2,149	2,236	33,278	27,297	17,018	22,515	33,708	139,698
Guyana	896	1,239	5,760	14,320	32,040	37,271	52,649	34,134	178,309
Belize	677	1,213	2,945	2,591	4,646	13,204	10,320	5,848	41,444
Other W.I.[a]	2,731	650	3,031	2,919	4,243	2,416	3,156	11,962	31,108
Haiti	3,265	9,889	27,648	27,130	30,294	43,890	96,273	95,977	334,366
D. Republic	4,675	35,372	58,744	67,051	78,403	104,663	147,140	218,495	714,543
Total	**25,003**	**66,383**	**183,164**	**229,570**	**294,769**	**361,674**	**502,902**	**510,094**	**2,173,559**

[a]Includes Anguilla, Aruba, British Virgin Islands, Caymans, Guadeloupe, Leeward Islands, Martinique, Netherland Antilles, Turks, and Windward Islands.

Source: U.S. Bureau of the Census, *Statistical Yearbook of the Immigration and Naturalization Service* (Washington, D.C.: Government Printing Office, 1992–1996).

Indians share several features in common: history, political traditions, language, educational system, and diversions.

Anglophone West Indians often share these neighborhoods and economic niches with Haitian immigrants and their descendants. Hailing from the poorest nation in the Western Hemisphere, Haitian immigrants bring to the United States a unique history stemming from early independence from France following the Haitian revolution of 1804 and Haiti's subsequent long period of political and economic isolation. Haitians are also linguistically distinct from other Caribbean immigrant groups. Almost all arrive in this country speaking Haitian Creole, even though a substantial minority (particularly the middle class) also speak French. Nevertheless, once in the United States, Haitian occupational and residential patterns have come to resemble those of West Indian immigrants.

The third major Caribbean immigrant group includes those from the Dominican Republic, whose homeland shares the Island of Hispaniola with Haiti. Spanish speaking and largely of mixed race, Dominicans culturally resemble Puerto Ricans and Cubans more than other Caribbean immigrants and thus will be dealt with only in passing in this chapter. Although very few Dominicans came to the United States prior to 1965, since that time they have become the largest foreign-born population in New York City, where they are overwhelmingly concentrated. Originally settling in communities dominated by Puerto Ricans, Dominicans have become the dominant group in several New York neighborhoods, most notably Washington Heights in upper Manhattan. Dominicans from this area have been recently elected to the New York City Council and the New York State Assembly, and in 1996 Leonel Fernandez, a former Washington Heights resident and graduate of the New York City public schools, was elected president of the Dominican Republic.

CARIBBEAN IMMIGRANTS IN THE UNITED STATES

One fact that clearly emerges about West Indians is that they travel. Faced with the limits of the small, insular economies and perennially high rates of unemployment, they have, for generations, utilized emigration as a means of obtaining a better life. The Anglophone Caribbean in particular has long sent its sons and daughters abroad—to Panama to build the Canal, to Cuba and the Dominican Republic to cut sugar cane early in the century, to Costa Rica to grow bananas, to Britain, and throughout most of this century, to the United States.

Although West Indians have migrated to the United States since colonial times, large-scale migration dates primarily from the beginning of the twentieth century. Before that time non-Hispanic Caribbean migration affected only a few regions in the United States.[3] There has, for example, been a long tradition of both circular labor migration and permanent settlement migration between the Bahamas and south Florida. During the mid-nineteenth century most of the black population of Key West, the major port city in southern Florida at that time, was Bahamian, and to this day the "Bahamian"-style houses of that city's historic district are highly prized. Southern Louisiana also saw an early influx from the Caribbean, as white and mulatto Haitians, sometimes accompanied by their black slaves, fled the 1804 revolution.

However, as in the twentieth century, the most significant impact of Caribbean migration in the eighteenth and nineteenth centuries was not felt in the regions of the United States closest to the Caribbean but rather in those northeastern American cities linked to the Caribbean region by trade, most notably New York City. Colonial and early postindependence New York was primarily a trade city, with substantial connections to the English and French colonies of the Caribbean, as well as a center for processing both Caribbean-imported sugar and coffee. Not surprisingly, white, mixed-race, and black immigrants from the region sometimes settled in New York during the eighteenth century. Prominent early New Yorkers of Caribbean origin included Alexander Hamilton (born on Nevis), Samuel Fraunces (the owner of the famed Fraunces Tavern and steward of President Washington's household in New York), and Pierre Toussaint (the Haitian-born former slave hairdresser, who, after buying his freedom, became a successful entrepreneur and philanthropist and who has recently been beatified for his charitable works). As the nineteenth century progressed, however, Europe vastly outpaced the Caribbean as New York's primary trading partner and source of immigrant labor, and migration from the Caribbean slowed to a trickle.

While some West Indian migration to the United States, particularly from Haiti, has been politically motivated, economic considerations have been primarily important. West Indians entered the country in three distinct waves, with the present being the largest and most protracted. The first wave, lasting from the turn of the century to the late 1920s, resulted from several overlapping factors. By the end of the nineteenth century, migration had become a solidly entrenched aspect of the culture of the various West Indian territories, with many West Indians driven from their small resource-poor and overpopulated islands to seek opportunities elsewhere. The initial movements occurred within the region. Following the abolition of slavery in 1834, blacks in larger territories, such as Jamaica and Guyana, adapted to the changed socioeconomic climate by withdrawing from plantations and becoming peasant farmers. However, in many of the smaller islands of the eastern Caribbean, the ex-slaves found this route closed to them since most of the productive land remained in the hands of plantation owners. Whereas blacks in Jamaica and the Windwards retreated to the hillsides to eke out a living on small plots, most eastern Caribbean blacks with similar aspirations had to look outward. As early as 1837, former slaves from Antigua were immigrating to Guyana to look for work; and chronic labor shortages in that territory, as well as in Trinidad, continued to attract freedmen for several decades. Such movements—both seasonal (i.e., freedmen moving to labor-short territories during sugar season) and permanent—occurred throughout the whole Caribbean. For instance, from the 1860s onward, the sugar cane industries of the Dominican Republic, Puerto Rico, and St. Croix received seasonal migrants from eastern Caribbean islands. Meanwhile, Barbadians were to be found in the Bahamas employed as schoolteachers and Jamaicans in Haiti serving as coachmen.

These interterritorial movements became more organized with the introduction of steamships and, especially, after the surge in demand for labor in Central America. A series of large-scale construction projects pulled in large numbers of West Indians. These included the construction of the Panama railway linking the Atlantic and Pacific Coasts in the 1850s; the Costa Rican railway in the 1870s; the first attempt at the construction of the Panama Canal in the 1880s; and the second, an American-led effort, in Panama in 1904. While these and subsequent events (e.g., the opening of oil refineries in Aruba) pulled thousands of West Indians toward other Caribbean territories and toward Central and South America, still other events pulled them in the direction of North America. Most important in this regard was the development of the banana industry and, with it, the growth of organized tourism. By 1879, American steamships were taking tourists to such islands as Cuba, Haiti, and Jamaica. On their return voyage to New York City (and Boston) they transported both produce and West Indians seeking their fortunes in the United States. This northern migration helped cement New York City as a center for West Indian immigration. In addition, numerous West Indians found their way to the United States through the Central American countries to which they had migrated as contract laborers. Panama is particularly important in this regard, for work on the Canal and later in the Canal Zone brought many thousands of English-speaking West Indians (as well as a smaller number of Haitians) into direct contact with American employers. Thus, while the ''Panama money'' sent home by workers transformed many an insular village in the Caribbean, the experience of working in Panama was a first step for many who would migrate to the United States during the first three decades of this century.

West Indian immigration mushroomed between 1900 and the mid-1920s. In his seminal work on these immigrants, Ira Reid shows that in the years 1889–1890, only 1,126 West Indians immigrated into the United States. However, by 1908, this number had reached 9,861; 13,677 by 1918; and 19,797 in 1924. Thereafter, numbers fell dramatically because of a combination of immigration restrictions and the Great Depression. Indeed, the latter event not only ended the first wave of West Indian migration but also actually reversed the flow of immigrants. Reid shows that whereas 1,685 West Indian immigrants entered the country in 1926, this number had declined by 1937 to 237. During the first third of this century, 40,000 Afro-Caribbean immigrants settled in New York City, mostly in Harlem. A minority within New York's black community, and a small immigrant group in a city of immigrants, this immigration would have an impact on American society, and particularly on New York's black community, far out of proportion to its numbers. The immigrants included people who would go on to comprise the bulk of mid-twentieth-century New York's black political and cultural leadership as well as the parents of Colin Powell, Shirley Chisholm, Harry Belafonte, Kenneth Clarke, and Louis Farrakhan.

The second wave of West Indian immigration began in the late 1930s. Largely male, it consisted chiefly of young professionals coming in on student visas, many of whom stayed on after completing their degrees; agricultural workers; and individuals migrating to join their families. The third—and present—period of immigration began with the 1965 Hart-Celler Immigration Act and has been characterized by much larger numbers than either of the previous two periods of immigration. This has resulted from several overlapping factors. Following World War II, the United Kingdom became the primary destination for Anglophone West Indians. However, in 1961, that country severely curbed immigration from the region. The Hart-Celler Immigration Act strongly attracted this migratory stream into the United States by shifting immigration policy away from considerations of immigrants' country of origin and toward the principle of family reunification. Since a sizable West Indian community already existed in the United States, larger numbers of naturalized and permanent resident West Indians were able to file for relatives. Moreover, several of the larger West Indian countries (notably Jamaica and Trinidad) had gained political independence from Britain in the early 1960s and, as fully fledged countries, were, under the 1965 act, able to send much larger numbers of people than had been the case previously. Additionally, the 1965 act allowed West Indians to enter the United States through sponsorship by Americans desirous of their services, which, in practice, meant women coming in as domestics for white families.

Together, these factors dramatically swelled immigration from the West Indies (see Table 8).[4] For instance, whereas only 2,149 Trinidadians officially migrated to the United States between 1961 and 1965, between 1966 and 1970, 22,367 did so. By the period 1986–1991, the number had increased to 27,379. Similarly, only 8,335 Jamaicans officially migrated to the United States between 1961 and 1965. However, between 1966 and 1970, 62,676 did so, and in the period 1981 to 1985, this number increased to 100,560. That this high rate of migration continues is shown by the fact that Jamaicans ranked as the ninth largest group (16,398 arrivals) admitted in 1995. In the New York City core region of settlement, they ranked fifth (with the Guyanese sixth) among all countries contributing immigrants to that city. To understand the significance that this number has for Jamaican society, it is only necessary to recall that Jamaica's total population is approximately 2.6 million. The "immigration rate" for these countries (i.e., the number of legal immigrants coming from a particular country divided by its population) underscores the significance of this process for West Indians. West Indian countries rank significantly higher on this index than do other countries sending large numbers of immigrants to the United States. For instance, in 1992, Guyana's immigration rate stood at 113 per 10,000 of population and Jamaica's at 75.7. In contrast, according to David Heer, the Philippines stood at 9.6, Taiwan at 7.86, and China at 0.33.

Compared to Anglophone West Indians, Dominicans and Haitians have been relative latecomers to the United States, but, as shown in Table 8, they have rapidly gained ground. In 1995, Haitians, with 14,021 arrivals, ranked fourteenth among America's immigrant-sending countries. Dominicans, with 38,512 immigrants in 1995, ranked fourth. As is the case with other Caribbean immigrants, the largest numbers settled in New York City and its suburbs, although significant numbers also went to south Florida and the Boston metropolitan area. Like other immigrants from the Caribbean, economic pressures provide the essential push factor impelling Haitians and Dominicans to migrate to the United States. For instance, Haiti's 1994 per capita income was $817, and unemployment stood at an estimated 50 percent; meanwhile, the Dominican Republic recorded a per capita income of $3,070 and an unemployment rate of 30 percent. Unlike other West Indian countries, however, political pressures also figure significantly among the factors pushing Haitians (especially) and Dominicans to migrate. In the 1980s and early 1990s thousands of Haitians, fleeing repression, attempted to enter the United States (in south Florida) as refugees. Casualties among these "boat people," and the overlapping of their arrival with refugees from Cuba— especially during the 1980 *Mariel* boatlift and again during the height of the *balseros* (the raft people) episode in 1993–1994—drew national attention. Much of this focused on the disparate treatment accorded the two groups by the American government. For instance, until May 1995, Cubans who reached American soil were routinely granted asylum. On the other hand, adopting a tough stance toward Haitians, the Reagan administration in the 1980s sought to intercept Haitian refugees and prevent them from reaching American soil. The Bush administration followed the same policy, as did the Clinton administration in its early years. Although candidate Bill Clinton had criticized the preceding Republican administrations for their Haitian policy, as president, he faced a crisis when the September 1991 overthrow of Jean-Bertrand Aristide led to a renewed outflow of Haitian boat people. The Clinton administration subsequently pursued a dual policy of returning some Haitians to Haiti and holding others at Guantánamo Bay, while seeking to restore Aristide to power. Following the occupation of Haiti in September 1994 by an American-led multinational "peacekeeping" force and the restoration of Aristide to power the next month, the bulk of the Haitians who had been detained at Guantánamo Bay were returned to Haiti. In recent years, American policy toward Haiti has sought to limit the flow of immigrants from that country by improving social and political conditions there.

Although not as dramatic, political turmoil has also contributed to Dominican migration to the United States by perpetuating social and economic inequalities. Dominican migration started in earnest during the unrest that followed the assassination of the dictator Rafael Trujillo in 1961 and the U.S. invasion in 1965– 1966. Early migrants were often political opponents of the repressive Balaguer regime, who, ironically, often found themselves forced to flee to the same United States whose troops had kept that regime in power. Later migrants were less likely to be political refugees per se but rather people who had found their opportunities for upward mobility stunted. In such a social atmosphere, the middle class in particular has felt threatened, and this has led to the large-scale migration of urban Dominicans. Since the 1980s, the deteriorating economic situation of the Dominican Republic has spurred a wider spectrum of Dominicans to migrate. While most travel legally, many have found illegal migration into nearby Puerto Rico to be a relatively easy way into the United States since travel between that island and the American mainland does not usually require immigration documentation. (Over 28,100 applied for amnesty under the 1986 Immigration Reform and Control Act [IRCA] program, more than 15,000 of whom had entered without documents.)

Today, Anglophone West Indians have continued their historic tendency to concentrate in large cities along the East Coast. Ancestry data from the 1990 census indicate that 56 percent of all individuals claiming (Anglophone) West Indian ancestry live in the Northeast; 34 percent in the South; 6 percent in the West; and 4 percent in the Midwest. In fact, West Indians' residential patterns are even more concentrated than these data indicate, as the tristate region of New York, New Jersey, and Connecticut accounts for 50 percent of all individuals claiming West Indian ancestry. Most of these are concentrated in New York City (where they constitute 25 percent of the black population)[5] and, more specifically, central Brooklyn (Crown Heights, Flatbush, and East Flatbush), southeastern Queens (Cambria Heights, Laurelton, Queens Village, and St. Albans), and the North Bronx. Outside of New York City, other large suburban concentrations are to be found in Mount Vernon, New York—whose mayor for most of the 1980s, Ronald Blackwood, was a Jamaican American—Bridgeport and Hartford in Connecticut, and East Orange and Montclair in New Jersey. In the South, Florida (especially the Miami metropolitan area) now accounts for the bulk of Anglophone West Indian immigrants in that region. However, sizable concentrations are also to be found in Atlanta, Richmond, and the suburbs surrounding Washington, D.C.

Haitians display a similar distribution, often living in the same neighborhoods as Anglophone West Indians. In 1990 some 55 percent of those claiming Haitian ancestry lived in the Northeast—mainly in New York City—and 41 percent lived in the South, primarily Florida. Indeed, in Miami, one neighborhood dominated by recent immigrants has come to be known as "Little Haiti," although as Haitians become upwardly mobile they will often leave the area for neighborhoods in which they live alongside Anglophone West Indians and middle-class African Americans. In recent years, a significant Haitian enclave has also developed in Summerville, Massachusetts, a suburb of Boston. Like Anglophone West Indians, Haitian residential patterns are partially shaped and complicated by racial discrimination. For these groups, "assimilation" out of the immigrant ghetto and into mainstream America may well mean assimilation into *black* America.

Dominicans exhibit an even more skewed spatial distribution, with 86 percent of those claiming such ancestry in 1990 residing in the Northeast, again primarily in New York City. Dominicans, however, rarely share neighborhoods with Anglophone West Indians or Haitians. They are far more likely to live among other Latinos, particularly Puerto Ricans. This is especially true of the earlier and poorer Dominican immigrants, who settled in such communities as East Harlem and the South Bronx. More affluent Dominicans settled alongside Cubans and South Americans in the central Queens neighborhood of Corona. However, over time, a more distinctly Dominican enclave has emerged in Washington Heights in upper Manhattan, and more middle-class Dominican neighborhoods have started to form in the nearby northern New Jersey suburbs.

MATERIAL CULTURE

Although West Indian immigrants[6] are to be found in every occupation, they tend to concentrate in the health care, service, and construction industries, with the relative degree of concentration varying by gender and, to a lesser extent, by region. Overall, West Indians and their children—particularly females— show high levels of labor force participation and low rates of public assistance use. The high numbers of wage earners per household has led to relatively high household incomes among both Anglophone West Indians and Haitians. However, West Indians, like African Americans, report very low rates of self-employment. According to the 1990 census, the rate for the entire United States was 7 percent. Whites exhibited a rate of 7.6 percent, and some immigrant groups—for example, the Taiwanese at 9.8 percent—had even higher ones. However, the rate for Trinidadians was only 4 percent, 3 percent for Jamaicans, and 2 percent for the Guyanese. In this respect, they resemble African Americans, who exhibited an overall self-employment rate of 2 percent. Further, as with African Americans, West Indian employment is disproportionately located in the public and not-for-profit sectors. While this concentration may have been advantageous during the 1970s and 1980s, it may have turned into a marked disadvantage as government employment declined in the 1990s. Despite well-developed niches, West Indians have not formed "ethnic enclaves" and, therefore, have little real control over the sectors in the economy in which they are concentrated.

Analysis of the 1990 census reveals that, overall, the health care field claims the highest concentration of West Indians. Approximately 9 percent of these immigrants work in the lower levels of this industry as nursing aides, orderlies, and attendants. Another 3 percent are employed as registered nurses. Other areas of relative concentration include such service industry occupations as maids, housemen, and janitors. Higher-level service industries, for example, cashiers and secretaries, also see concentrations of West Indians. Women comprise the bulk of the immigrants employed in these fields. West Indian males tend to exhibit less occupational concentration. Many gravitate to the construction industry, the skilled trades (e.g., boilermakers and mechanics), and the operation of motor vehicles (e.g., bus drivers). The latter is particularly evident in areas of high ethnic concentration (notably Crown Heights and Flatbush in Brooklyn). In those areas, West Indian immigrants (almost all males) have carved out a niche for themselves by exploiting the relatively poor transportation system: They have gone into business—in a pattern that is a transference from their Caribbean homelands—as unlicensed transportation operators, ferrying passengers more cheaply and quickly than does the publicly run transportation system.

The socioeconomic status of West Indians has taken on larger significance because their presence in the United States speaks to an enduring question: the extent to which the socioeconomic status of African Americans is determined by their race. Since West Indians, like African Americans, are largely of African descent, their achievement of a high socioeconomic status would seem to cast doubt on the notion that race particularly hinders the upward mobility of African Americans. Along these lines, several writers (e.g., Dennis Forsythe, Nathan Glazer and Patrick Moynihan, and Thomas Sowell) have argued that, measured in a variety of ways, West Indians have achieved "success" in the United States. For instance, Thomas Sowell, referring to New York City, has pointed to a disproportionate number of highly placed West Indian officials (e.g., federal judges and borough presidents) as evidence of this. He also notes that in the late 1960s the incomes of West Indians exceeded that of New York–based African Americans by 28 percent and that of African Americans nationally by 52 percent. These results have been attributed to a combination of structural factors (e.g., hailing from black-dominated societies) and cultural values that emphasize discipline, hard work, deferral of gratification, and greater faith in the American social system to treat blacks fairly. This has led writers, such as Forsythe, to argue that these characteristics allow West Indians to act as role models for African Americans.

Research among West Indians has shown that, subjectively speaking, they do perceive themselves as possessing many of these traits, and some do agree that they can be role models for African Americans. However, the evidence suggests that the socioeconomic status of West Indians is not so easily interpreted as refuting the notion that race continues to play a significant role in shaping the life chances of blacks in the United States. On several criteria, West Indians score significantly above African Americans. In fact, they tend to hover around various averages for the nation as a whole, whereas African Americans fall below these averages. On the other hand, they fall noticeably below the white and Asian populations on several key indicators of social standing. This is particularly obvious with respect to self-employment and the attainment of higher education.

With an eye to these ambiguous results, other writers have taken a more cautious stance in evaluating the extent of West Indian "success" in the United States. Reynolds Farley and Walter Allen, for instance, after an analysis of 1980 census data, concluded that although West Indians outpaced African Americans in certain areas (namely, family income and levels of education), overall both groups more closely resembled each other than either resembled whites or Asians. Utilizing the same data set, Suzanne Model arrived at broadly similar conclusions but showed that comparisons of West Indians and African Americans need to account for gender since West Indian females somewhat outperform their male counterparts. A later comparison of 1970 and 1990 data by the same writer underlined the caution with which these intraethnic comparisons must be made. She found that while West Indians' labor force participation rate exceeded that of African Americans, the income of the latter tended to exceed that of foreign-born West Indians. These West Indians eventually catch up with African Americans, but this takes several years. On the other hand, American-born West Indians, while outpacing African Americans in income, have been exhibiting less of a tendency to do so. Still another analysis of 1990 census data has concluded that West Indians' advantage over African Americans is limited and does not give them parity with white men. Similarly, Roger Waldinger has argued that even though West Indians have managed to establish themselves in certain ethnic niches (e.g., construction), discrimination continues to constrain both this group and African Americans to the degree that their fates only partially diverge. He concludes that such ethnic niches provide little shelter from racial discrimination and that West Indians are just as likely as African Americans to perceive and complain about it.

The Haitian communities in New York, Boston, and Miami are all largely internally divided between a middle-class group that arrived as political refugees in the 1950s, 1960s, and early 1970s and recent immigrants who have tended to come from impoverished backgrounds. The former group, which includes many professionals, largely shared the upward mobility of the African-American middle class during the 1970s and 1980s. More recent immigrants commonly arrive with lower levels of education and without the linguistic advantages of Anglophone West Indians. Nevertheless, they have also tended to congregate in the service sector. While self-employment is more common among Haitians than among Anglophone West Indians, most Haitian entrepreneurs operate on a very small scale, typically working as tailors, barbers, and taxi drivers. A 1985 Miami study by Alex Stepick found that less than 1 percent of Haitians were employed by other Haitians (interestingly, 45 percent were employed by Cubans).

Dominicans display somewhat higher rates of self-employment, particularly in retailing and restaurants. Indeed, in New York today many of the restaurants and ''bodegas'' (corner grocery stores) that serve Puerto Rican clienteles are actually owned by Dominicans. At the same time and unlike the other Caribbean groups, Dominicans are heavily represented in manufacturing. On the whole, Dominicans report significantly lower incomes than other Caribbean immigrants. In New York City the 1990 census found one third of Dominican households with incomes below the poverty level (as opposed to 21 percent of Haitians and 11 percent of Jamaicans). Dominicans reported far higher rates of unemployment than do other Caribbean immigrants and far lower rates of female labor force participation. Indeed, the higher poverty rate among Dominican households may well be due less to differences in wages than in the lower number of wage earners per household, with Dominican women far less likely to work outside of the home than Haitian or Anglophone West Indian women.

THE RACE ISSUE IN THE WEST INDIES AND THE UNITED STATES

Racial discrimination, as well as West Indians' perception that it is a serious problem, is one of the largest stumbling blocks facing the argument that race is *not* an issue in the lives of these immigrants or that they can easily surmount whatever racial difficulties they encounter to achieve upward mobility. In reality, West Indians encounter a great deal of difficulty dealing with racial discrimination in the United States. These problems have long complicated their assimilation into American society. Difficulties relating to race stem, primarily, from the tendency of West Indian societies, compared to American society, to deemphasize ascribed factors (especially race) in evaluating individuals. For decades, this relative difference has forced West Indian immigrants to grapple—often for the first time—with the question of racial/ethnic identity and how such an identity affects life chances.

European colonization of the Americas bequeathed the West Indies and the United States a common history of slavery. The two regions, along with western Europe, formed two of the three points of the triangular slave trade, which saw agricultural products being taken from the Americas to Europe, European products to Africa, and slaves back to the Americas. Therefore, both the United States and the West Indies drew slaves from the same source. Moreover, both regions developed ethnic hierarchies that placed Europeans firmly in control of political power, the economy, and the culture of the respective regions. African ancestry came to be associated with a wide variety of negative stereotypes.

Despite this, the African slaves who were imported into the United States and the West Indies found themselves inserted into very different structural contexts. In the former country, they became a distinct minority but in most West Indian societies a majority. This basic difference has had far-reaching consequences in the development of the respective regions. In the United States, blacks, being a classic minority population, have experienced much discrimination. While blacks have also experienced similar discrimination in the West Indies, their status as demographic majorities constantly worried the European elites governing those societies. Some writers have advanced the notion that this has given West Indian blacks greater self-confidence than African Americans. While that issue awaits empirical testing, it seems likely true that West Indian blacks' majority status prevented them from undergoing some of the more extreme experiences endured by African Americans. For instance, the rigid racial segregation and violence of the Jim Crow South never really took root in the post-slavery West Indies. Moreover, slavery in the British West Indies ended approximately thirty years (in 1834) before the abolition of slavery in the United States. In the

West Indies, their status as demographic majorities eventually (in the twentieth century) translated into blacks dominating politics in several West Indian countries. Another significant effect of demographic majority status in the modern-day West Indies is that blacks routinely encounter others like themselves in a wide range of roles, ranging from social failures to ministers of state. For the individual West Indian this tends to delink his or her life chances from race/ethnicity.

Two other factors, along with the history of slavery/colonialism and demographic majority status, have shaped West Indians' views on race: the existence of ideologies downplaying its importance and the absence of strict rules—such as the American "one-drop rule"—for defining "blackness." Typically, these ideologies portray West Indian societies as places in which several racial/ethnic groups live together in harmony. This is seen, for instance, in the national motto of Jamaica: "Out of Many, One People." Similarly, Trinidad's states: "Together We Aspire, Together We Achieve." And Guyana's is: "One People, One Nation." These mottoes advance the reality that, compared to the United States, racial/ethnic tension in most West Indian societies exists at a rather low level. (Trinidad and Guyana, with their conflict between blacks and East Indians, are exceptions to the rule.) However, in societies emerging from centuries of slavery and colonialism, in which Europeans abrogated privileges for themselves while denying them to individuals of African ancestry, race and ethnicity inevitably become issues. For instance, the twentieth century has seen the growth in pride of African ancestry through the development of Garveyism and Rastafarianism. The latter, through reggae music, speech patterns, and styles of dress, has had wide impact on Jamaica (its birthplace), other West Indian countries, and throughout the world. Some writers have suggested that the various ideologies downplaying racial conflict have, in fact, originated in reaction to the continued overlap between race and privilege in the West Indies. These ideologies justify the status quo by hiding the fact that nonblack elites dominate the economies of many West Indian countries. Despite this, many West Indians accept that their societies are free of racial conflict and, more important, that race/ethnicity plays little part in upward mobility. Instead, emphasis is placed on factors that are viewed as being within the control of the individual West Indian, especially education. Thus, while issues of race and ethnicity are potentially important, in practice they rarely become subjects for public debate.

West Indians' definition of race has also significantly affected their views on the subject. The tendency in the United States is to define as black any individual with even remote African ancestry. However, West Indian societies have traditionally relied on a wider range of criteria in defining race. These include ancestry, physical appearance, and socioeconomic status. The use of multiple criteria probably reflects the fact that widespread miscegenation has taken place in the West Indies between Europeans, Africans, East Indians, and Middle Easterners.

From the perspective of West Indians' encounter with American racism, the most important consequence of the factors outlined in the preceding discussion is that they downplay racial issues. This is especially true of West Indians of the post-independence generation, who, having grown up with blacks in charge of the political system, are unaccustomed to dealing with overt racial discrimination. However, being primarily of African ancestry, in the United States they must contend with the society's more overt racialism and tendency to view all individuals of African ancestry as being the same. These contradictions subject West Indian immigrants to strong cross-pressures, which, in turn, determine their adaptation to the country's ethnic hierarchy. West Indians often distance themselves from African Americans, seeking to establish a distinctive identity as "West Indians" that combines positive views of African ancestry with conservative social values and a focus on achieving "success" (defined educationally, occupationally, and materially). For instance, observers of early West Indian immigrants have noted that they strongly resented being discriminated against because of their color and often retorted by claiming allegiance to the British empire. Similarly, it has been said that the Pullman Coach Company refused to hire West Indians as stewards because they would not accept racial insults from white passengers.

Despite these sentiments, West Indians have found it difficult to escape strong societal pressures on individuals of African ancestry to identify as "black." They have encountered the same discrimination faced by African Americans and, over time, have come to accept that they share commonalities with the latter. This contradictory response of distancing and identification with African Americans is a long-standing trend, which is shaped by such factors as time of entry into the country, length of residency, social class, and age. Thus, the first two waves of West Indian immigrants, though bridling at racial discrimination, found themselves as subject to residential segregation as were African Americans. Living in largely African-American communities, many West Indians eventually intermarried with them and entered politics as representatives of the black community.

Although many of the overt manifestations of racial discrimination aimed at blacks have apparently declined, present-day West Indian immigrants still encounter racial discrimination and still coalesce with African Americans around such racially charged issues as police brutality, media representations of blacks, and the election of black candidates to higher office (e.g., New York City's first black mayor, David Dinkins). The most significant change being faced by the present wave of West Indian immigrants is that the apparent decline in overt displays of racial discrimination has coincided with the large post-1965 influx of immigrants, giving West Indians the possibility of creating, for the first time, distinct neighborhoods and, consequently, a distinctive identity in the New York City core area of settlement. However, it is still an open question whether this increased space for the creation of ethnic identity can effectively counter the historically powerful norm of viewing all individuals of African ancestry as being one and the same.

COMMUNITY ORGANIZATIONS

Caribbean immigrants have formed networks of community and church groups, fraternal organizations, and mutual assistance societies in addition to participating in groups organized by African Americans. Anglophone Caribbean groups tend to be organized by country of origin and by profession (or former profession: e.g., the associations of former police officers from Jamaica and Grenada). The alumni associations of various Caribbean high schools are also active in North America. These groups, and the umbrella organizations of various groups from particular nations, play a significant role in the politics of the home nations (for whom they frequently raise money) and sometimes play a less formal role in U.S. politics, as well. For example, two of the oldest such groups, the Sons and Daughters of Barbados and the Jamaica Progressive League,[7] have at times lobbied the U.S. Congress on immigration issues. While other groups have more purely social agendas (e.g., the large Trinidadian fraternal organizations and Carnival groups), they too are increasingly courted by both North American politicians and counselor representatives of the "home countries" eager to tap the political and financial support of the immigrant communities.

Haitian community organization groups are most frequently organized around refugee assistance and social service issues. The best known of these is Miami's Haitian Refugee Center, a multiservice group led by Father Gerard Jean-Juste, who was previously active in the Haitian community in Boston. Other Haitian groups include professional associations, branches of Haitian political parties, and in Miami, a Haitian American Chamber of Commerce. In New York a Caribbean American Chamber of Commerce represents both Anglophone West Indian and Haitian business owners. Haitians and West Indians have also come together in one national umbrella group, the Caribbean Action Lobby (CAL), which attempts to voice the common concerns of Caribbean immigrants. Internal divisions, however, have often undercut CAL's effectiveness.

Early Dominican migrants, many of whom were political refugees, formed hometown clubs similar to those of Puerto Ricans and political groups directly concerned with affairs in the Dominican Republic (frequently keeping intense Dominican political rivalries alive in exile). Dominican political parties continue to be active in the United States, and Dominican groups in New York and Boston have come to play an increasingly important role in raising money for development projects in the Dominican Republic. However, in recent years Dominican service organizations, bringing together Dominicans of various political stripes, have become more prominent. While ostensibly providing medical, legal, and social services, these groups have also formed the basis of a political infrastructure, particularly in New York, where they have also promoted naturalization. The most prominent, Alianza Dominicana, was crucial in the mobilizing effort that led to the election of a Dominican to the New York City Council in 1991.

POLITICS

Anglophone Caribbean immigrants have a long history of political mobilization in the United States, particularly in New York City. As in the economy, the group has no doubt benefited from its use of the English language and its relationship to the larger African-American community. At the same time, as in the economy and social life, the Anglophone Caribbean immigrant's political opportunities have also been sharply circumscribed by race.

Beginning in the 1930s West Indian immigrants and their children emerged as a major force in black Democratic Party politics in New York. As the African-American vote switched from Republican to Democratic during the New Deal, West Indian Democrats came to positions of power both in the party organization and, particularly after 1945, in elected offices as well. These included Hulan Jack (the first black Borough President of Manhattan, elected in 1954), Raymond Jones (the first black to head "Tammany Hall"—the Manhattan County Democratic Organization), Bertram Baker (the first black from Brooklyn to serve in the New York State Assembly), and Shirley Chisholm (in 1968, the first black woman elected to the U.S. Congress).

During the 1970s the leadership of New York's black politics would pass from West Indian hands to those of African Americans with roots in the civil rights and Black Power movements. When West Indian political figures would again emerge in the 1990s, they would be representatives of the newly formed West Indian neighborhoods of central Brooklyn. While earlier West Indian politicians would speak for largely African-American constituencies, this new generation would draw its support to a large degree from the post-1965 immigrants. Prominent among them are Jamaican-born Una Clarke, elected to the New York City Council in 1991, her fellow Jamaican Nick Perry, elected to the New York State Legislature in 1993, and Belize-born Lloyd Henry, who joined Ms. Clarke on the city council in 1993. Interestingly, in all of these cases, the Caribbean candidates may have benefited from the group's general lack of integration into the broader society. As victims of racial discrimination in housing, West Indians are the most residentially concentrated of new immigrant groups in New York. This has, however, produced a number of electoral districts with Caribbean majorities. Thus, West Indians are also the new immigrant group with the greatest political representation in the city.

Outside of the New York metropolitan area, West Indian and West Indian–descended politicians generally represent African-American constituencies. Prominent among them is Los Angeles Congressman Mervyn Dymally. However, the most renowned Caribbean American figures in U.S. politics today are those who never held elected office, especially former General Colin Powell (whose parents were from Jamaica), black power leaders Stokely Carmichael (born in Trinidad) and Malcolm X (whose mother was from Grenada), and Nation of Islam leader Louis Farrakahn (whose parents emigrated from Barbados).

Dominicans have a far shorter history of participation in U.S. politics, in part because of their relatively recent arrival and in part because many early Dominican immigrants were political exiles who concentrated on bringing about changes in their homeland. However, the group's overwhelming concentration in New York, particularly in upper Manhattan, has given the Dominicans a growing degree of influence in local politics. In 1991 a Dominican was elected to represent Washington Heights in the New York Council, and in 1996 the neighborhood sent another Dominican to the New York State Assembly. At the same time, the U.S. Dominican community has an increasing degree of influence on politics in the Dominican Republic. The major Dominican political parties have offices in New York and Boston, and in 1996 a longtime New Yorker, Leonel Fernandez, was elected president of the Dominican Republic.

Haitians have thus far had little involvement in U.S. politics, probably because of the Haitian community's focus on the politics of Haiti and the involvement of many prominent Haitian Americans in exile politics. Several Haitian activists who have been longtime residents of New York and Florida have played prominent roles in post-Duvalier governments in Haiti. However, the controversies and rivalries of Haitian politics may well have kept Haitian political organizations from forming a united front and representing the "Haitian community" in the United States. Haitian organizations within the Democratic Party were founded in New York in the early 1970s and in Miami in 1980. Haitians have also been involved in mass protest politics: A confrontation with a Cuban shopkeeper led to a disturbance between Haitians and police in Miami in 1990, and a similar dispute between a Haitian shopper and a Korean shopkeeper led to a controversial boycott of Korean stores along Brooklyn's Church Avenue in 1991. In both cases Haitian protestors worked closely with African-American leaders. In 1997 the beating and sexual torture of Haitian immigrant Abner Louima, allegedly by police officers in the Flatbush section of Brooklyn, unified and mobilized the Haitian community and again brought Haitians together with African Americans in mass protests against police brutality.

CULTURAL CONTRIBUTIONS

In recent decades Caribbean Americans have come to play a prominent role in the cultural life of the United States. For instance, several noteworthy literary figures have emerged. These include the St. Lucian–born Nobel Prize–winning poet and playwright Derrick Walcott, Grenadian-born poet Audre Lorde, and novelists Michael Thellwell (born in Jamaica) and Paule Marshall (born in Brooklyn of Barbadian parents). In another sphere of the arts, the popularity of Caribbean music—particularly Jamaican reggae and dance hall, Trinidadian calypso and soca, and Dominican meringue (along with the long popularity of Afro-Cuban music and its New York–derived offspring salsa)—has created opportunities for Caribbean and Caribbean American entertainers. This music has also influenced American popular music, jazz, and musical theater. On stage and screen, Caribbean actors, including Harry Belafonte, Brock Peters, and Sidney Poitier, have probably given most Americans their clearest positive image of Caribbean immigrants.

Nevertheless, despite the increasing likelihood of seeing West Indian characters in films (as well as the frequency of West Indians playing African Americans), Hollywood's depiction of Caribbean Americans has often been stereotypical and contradictory. This results from that medium's desire to draw as wide an audience as possible by focusing on the more exotic aspects of Caribbean life by merging the cultures of individual islands into a mishmash. A key aspect of this stereotype is that Rastafarians, though only a small portion of the population, are often presented as typifying Caribbean immigrants. In practical terms this means that films either present them as criminals or as buffoons. The former portrayal has tended to draw upon media reports of the late 1980s regarding the growth of Jamaican ''posses,'' which were said to be making strong inroads into the distribution of illegal drugs. Examples of films promoting such portrayals include *Predator II* (1990), *New Jack City* (1991), and *Only the Strong* (1993). However, *Marked for Death* (1990) is the best example of the genre since it presents a full-length treatment of West Indians that is so sharply drawn that some reviewers have termed it racist. Also, in having the Jamaican Rastafarian ''villains'' of the film practice Cuban Santeria as a means of avoiding capture, it well illustrates the tendency of such films to conflate the cultures of various Caribbean islands.

On the other hand, West Indians are also likely to be presented as objects of ridicule—a theme that seems to draw upon their status as immigrants from relatively underdeveloped countries placed in the context of a developed society. Thus, in *Trading Places* (1983), in a scene recalling the ''coon'' stereotype, a white actor dons black face, a Rastafarian wig, and a fake Jamaican accent to outwit a murderer. And the 1993 film *Cool Runnings*, by using stereotypes, mines the comedic possibilities inherent in the fact that a Jamaican bobsled team entered the 1988 Winter Olympics. Nor have non-Anglophone Caribbean immigrants escaped such stereotyping. *The Believers*, a 1987 film, presents Hispanic neighborhoods of New York City as being overrun by a homicidal Santeria/voodoo cult. Relatively few films have attempted to give positive portrayals of West Indians. Two exceptions to this have been *Clara's Heart* (1988), which attempts to depict the lives of Jamaican immigrants in Baltimore, and the curious *The Adventures of Buckaroo Banzai across the Eighth Dimension* (1984), which presents a Rastafarian in a highly unusual setting: as a member of an alien race attempting to prevent the conquest of the Earth by rival aliens.

Within West Indian immigrant communities probably the clearest expression of the groups' cultural creativity comes in the form of public celebrations. West Indians now hold annual carnivals—modeled loosely on the Trinidad Carnival—in New York, Hartford, Maryland, Boston, and Miami. In each case the event has become a focal point of the group's ethnic identity and perhaps the key in distinguishing West Indians from African Americans. New York's event features a week of concerts and custom fetes and climaxes with a procession down Brooklyn's Eastern Parkway on Labor Day. This "West Indian–American Carnival Day Parade" (as it is officially known) is now the city's largest ethnic celebration, surpassing St. Patrick's Day and the Puerto Rican Day Parade. Its revelers include Haitians and some African Americans as well as Anglophone West Indians. Dominicans also hold an annual parade in Washington Heights, modeled closely on the Puerto Rican event.

CONCLUSION

The development of Caribbean communities in some of the largest cities of the United States is one of the most significant consequences of the 1965 Hart-Celler Immigration Act. Although, in the case of immigrants from the Anglophone Caribbean, these communities actually predated that act by many decades, the Hart-Celler Act dramatically enlarged these communities by facilitating the entry of many more Caribbean immigrants than had previously been the case. In the case of Haitians and especially Dominicans, the act, coinciding with key political events in their home countries, facilitated the growth of new communities where none had existed before. These communities have had an impact on American cities in significant ways—especially New York City and Miami. First, the Caribbean immigrants have contributed to demographic changes that are resulting in the gradual enlargement of various minority populations at the expense of the formerly more numerous white majority. New York City has become a "majority-minority" city since, collectively, Latinos, West Indians, Asians, and other minority groups now outnumber whites. This is of economic import since "new" minorities are providing the necessary manpower for some of the city's most important industries (e.g., particularly the garment industry).

More problematically, some immigrants, as they have become overrepresented in certain industries (ethnic niches), have shouldered aside African Americans and benefited disproportionately from upward mobility as whites have migrated out of whole industries as well as out of New York City itself. This upward mobility appears to be true, to some extent, even of West Indian immigrants. However, in the long-standing debate over how well these immigrants do relative to African Americans and the role played by race in all this, caution is in order. In some areas they appear to perform better, whereas in others they appear to match the profile of African Americans closely. The latter is especially true with respect to their perceptions of and experiences with racial discrimination. Politically, Caribbean immigrants are also important since they are steadily gaining the representation to voice their own particular interests (e.g., issues centering on immigration), and they tend to constitute more of a swing vote than do African Americans. The impact of Caribbean immigrants also extends into the social sphere, for their expanded presence has influenced everything from cuisine to popular culture. Caribbean immigrants' influence on American society seems destined to continue and, perhaps, even increase, as large cities, such as New York City and Miami, continue to act as magnets for these people who are close neighbors and who are constantly seeking to better their lives.

NOTES

1. The exact definition of *West Indian* varies. Generally, writers have taken one of three perspectives: In the broad view, *West Indies* is coterminous with all the countries in the Caribbean, as well as those in Latin America that abut the Caribbean sea. The American government has often taken this view. In the narrow view, *West Indies* includes only the Anglophone countries in the Caribbean sea and those nations in South America (e.g., Guyana) and Central America (e.g., Belize) with strong historical and cultural affinities. The intermediate view also focuses on the Anglophone countries but adds, as well, Dutch and French possessions. The tendency in the literature is to rely on either the narrow or intermediate view, thereby placing the Spanish-speaking territories with the culturally similar nations of Central and South America. In this essay, the term *Caribbean* refers to both West Indians and non–West Indians (in this case, Dominicans).

2. Although in two of these nations, Trinidad and Guyana, the descendants of Asian Indians now outnumber the descendants of Africans.

3. Unless, of course, one considers the large numbers of slaves imported into the American South between the early seventeenth century and the cessation of the trade in the early nineteenth century. While many of these slaves were Africans who spent only a short time in the West Indies, it is probable that a fair number had actually been born in the islands. There was also a small flow in the seventeenth century of white emigrants from the eastern Caribbean (particularly Barbados) to the thirteen colonies and Canada.

4. Actually, these data underestimate the West Indian presence since they exclude illegal immigrants. Immigration and Naturalization Service data for 1992 place five Caribbean countries among the top twenty countries sending illegal immigrants. These are listed below in rank order and number of immigrants: Haiti (number 7—8,800), the Bahamas (number 8—7,100), Jamaica (number 14—4,200), the Dominican Republic (number 15—4,000), and Trinidad and Tobago (number 16—3,900).

5. This figure is derived from the 1990 census calculation of the percentage of the black population that is foreign-born. The figure is even higher for individual New York boroughs. For instance, approximately 31 percent of the black population of Brooklyn is of West Indian origin.

6. The following discussion is based on a combination of Bureau of the Census, *1990 Census of Population. The Foreign-Born Population of the United States*, 1990 CP–3–1 (Washington, D.C.: Government Printing Office, 1993), and *U.S. Census of Population and Housing, 1990. Public Use Microdata Samples* (Washington, D.C.: Bureau of the Census, 1992), using a 1 percent sample of foreign-born West Indians. The latter data set contains 8,507 cases and, unless otherwise noted, includes all individuals born in that region (including the Guyanese and Belizians), except those hailing from Cuba, Santo Domingo, and Puerto Rico.

7. The Jamaica Progressive League, founded in New York in the 1930s, played an important role in Jamaica's struggle for independence and helped establish one of Jamaica's two leading political parties, the People's National Party.

BIBLIOGRAPHIC REFERENCES

The most comprehensive study of pre–World War II Caribbean immigration to the United States is Ira Reid's *The Negro Immigrant* (New York: Columbia University Press, 1939), which covers West Indian, Haitian, and Latino Caribbean communities. A more recent historical account of the same period is provided by Irma Owens-Watkins's *Blood Relations* (Bloomington: University of Indiana Press, 1996). Useful discussions of West Indian immigration are also to be found in Bonham Richardson, *Caribbean Migration* (Knoxville: University of Tennessee Press, 1983); Barry B. Levine, ed., *The Caribbean Exodus* (New York: Praeger, 1987); and David Heer, *Immigration in America's Future* (Boulder: Westview Press, 1996). Two edited collections that cover various aspects of Dominican, West Indian, and Haitian life in New York are Nancy Foner, ed., *New Immigrants to New York City* (New York: Columbia University Press, 1987), and Constance Sutton and Elsa Chaney, eds., *Caribbean Life in New York City* (New York: Center for Migration Studies, 1987). For examples of works attempting a comprehensive coverage of the contemporary Caribbean per se, see David Lowenthal, *West Indian Societies* (London: Oxford University Press, 1972); Susan Craig, ed., *Contemporary Caribbean: A Sociological Reader* (Maracas, Trinidad and Tobago: The College Press, 1982); and Gordon Lewis's *The Growth of the Modern West Indies* (New York: Monthly Review Press, 1968).

For an overview of West Indian immigration to the United States, with an emphasis on their economic performance, see Ransford Palmer, ed., *In Search of a Better Life* (New York: Praeger, 1990), and Palmer's *Pilgrims from the Sun: West Indian Migration to America* (New York: Twayne, 1995). Much of the work in this area has focused on comparing West Indian immigrants' economic performance with that of African Americans. The older literature tends toward the view that these immigrants outperform African Americans because of their cultural attributes. Key examples of this view are Nathan Glazer and Daniel P. Moynihan, *Beyond the Melting Pot: The Negroes, Puerto Ricans; Jews, Italians, and Irish of New York City*, 2nd ed. (Cambridge, MA: MIT Press, 1970); Dennis Forsythe, "Black Immigrants and the American Ethos: Theories and Observations," in *Caribbean Immigration to the United States*, edited by R. S. Bryce-Laporte and Delores Mortimer (Washington, D.C.: Smithsonian Institute, 1976); several of the works of Thomas Sowell, for example, *Ethnic America: A History* (New York: Basic Books, 1981), *Markets and Minorities* (New York: Basic Books, 1981), *The Economics and Politics of Race: An International Perspective* (New York: Quill, 1983); and Oscar Glantz, "Native Sons and Immigrants: Some Beliefs and Values of American Born and West Indian Blacks at Brooklyn College," *Ethnicity* 5 (1978): 189–202.

Writers who have addressed the issue more recently view structural factors (e.g., racial discrimination and ethnic concentration in the economy) as being relatively more important. Furthermore, they see less clear-cut evidence that West Indians outperform African Americans. Two early works that belong in this camp are Lennox Raphael, "West Indians and Afro-Americans," *Freedomways* (Summer 1964): 438–445; and Roy S. Bryce-Laporte, "Black Immigrants, the Experience of Invisibility and Inequality," *Journal of Black Studies* 3.1 (1972): 29–56. Among more recent writers, proper, noteworthy works would include Reynolds Farley and Walter R. Allen's *The Color Line and the Quality of Life in America* (New York: Oxford University Press, 1987); Suzanne Model, "Caribbean Immigrants: A Black Success Story?" *International Migration Review* 25

(Summer 1991): 249–275; Model, "West Indian Prosperity: Fact or Fiction?" *Social Problems* 42.4 (November 1995): 535–552; Mattijs Kalmijn, "The Socioeconomic Assimilation of Caribbean Blacks," *Social Forces* 74.3 (March 1996): 911–930; and Roger Waldinger, *Still the Promised City? African Americans and the New Immigrants in Post-Industrial New York* (Cambridge, MA: Harvard University Press, 1996).

Some recent works have focused more closely on racial formation among West Indians and their political behavior. For examples of the former, see Milton Vickerman, *Cross Currents: West Indian Immigrants and Race* (New York: Oxford University Press, 1998), and Mary C. Waters, *"Black Like Who?" West Indian Immigrants Confront American Race Relations* (Cambridge and New York: Harvard University and Russel Sage, 1999). A good example of a work that analyzes the political behavior of West Indian immigrants is Philip Kasinitz, *Caribbean New York: Black Immigrants and the Politics of Race* (Ithaca: Cornell University Press, 1992).

For an overview of Haitians in New York City, see Michel Laguerre, *American Odyssey: Haitians in New York* (Ithaca: Cornell University Press, 1984). Good discussions on Haitians in Miami are to be found in Alex Stepick's 1992 essay, "The Refugees Nobody Wants: Haitians in Miami," in *Miami Now! Immigration Ethnicity, and Social Change* edited by Guillermo Grenier and Alex Stepick (Gainsville: University Press of Florida, 1992), pp. 57–82, as well as Alejandro Portes and Alex Stepick, eds., *City on the Edge: The Transformation of Miami* (Berkeley: University of California Press, 1993). For a work on Haitian racial identity, see Tekle Woldemikael, *Becoming Black American* (New York: AMS Press, 1989); and on Haitian religious practices in the United States, see Karen Brown, *Mama Lola* (Berkeley: University of California Press, 1991). For an exploration of the emerging "transnational" culture of Haitians in the United States and Haiti, see Nina Glick–Schiller and George Fouron, "Everywhere We Go We Are in Danger: Ti Manno and the Emergence of Haitian Transnational Identity," *American Ethnologist* 17.2 (May 1990): 329–347. The earliest major work on Dominicans in New York City is Glen Hendricks's *Dominican Diaspora* (New York: Teachers College Press, 1974), which, while now far out of date, continues to be interesting as a historical account of the early days of Dominican settlement. More recent studies of Dominicans include Eugenia Georges, *The Making of a Transnational Community* (New York: Columbia University Press, 1990), and Sherri Grasmuck and Patricia Pessar, *Between Two Islands* (Berkeley: University of California Press, 1991).

For a recent account of Dominican political and social groups in Boston, see Peggy Levitt, "Transnationalizing Community Development: The Case of Migration between Boston and the Dominican Republic," *Non-Profit and Voluntary Sector Quarterly* 26 (1997): 509–526. For an excellent overview comparing various Caribbean immigrant groups, see Sherri Grasmuch and Ramón Grosfoguel, "Geopolitics, Economic Niches and Gendered Social Capital among Recent Caribbean Immigrants in New York City," *Sociological Perspectives* 40.3 (Fall 1997): 339–386.

Appendix: Immigration Tables, 1820–1996, and Naturalization Tables, 1907–1996

Table A.1
Immigrants Admitted to the United States from the Top Five Countries of Last Residence, 1821–1996

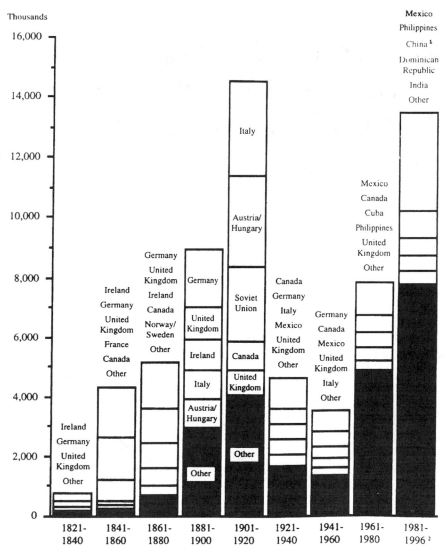

¹Includes People's Republic of China and Taiwan.
²Sixteen-year period.

Source: U.S. Bureau of the Census, *1996 Statistical Yearbook of the Immigration and Naturalization Service* (Washington, D.C.: Government Printing Office, 1996), Chart B.

Table A.2
Immigration to the United States: Fiscal Years 1820–1996

YEAR		SUBTOTALED AMOUNT	TOTAL NUMBER OF IMMIGRANTS
	1820		8,385
	1821-1830		143,439
	1831-1840		599,125
	1841-1850		1,713,251
	1851-1860		2,598,214
1831-1860		*4,910,590*	
	1861-1870		2,314,824
	1871-1880		2,812,191
	1881-1890		5,246,613
	1891-1900		3,687,564
	1901-1910		8,795,386
	1911-1920		5,735,811
1881-1920		*23,465,374*	
	1921-1930		4,107,209
	1931-1940		528,431
	1941-1950		1,035,039
	1951-1960		2,515,479
	1961-1970		3,321,677
	1971-1980		4,493,314
	1981-1990		7,338,062
	1991-1996		6,146,213
1961-1996		*21,299,266*	
1996			**63,140,227**

Source: Adapted from the U.S. Bureau of the Census, *1996 Statistical Yearbook of the Immigration and Naturalization Service* (Washington, D.C.: Government Printing Office, 1996), table 1.

Table A.3
Immigrants by Selected Region and Country of Last Residence, Fiscal Years 1821–1965

Country of Origin	1821-1840	1841-1860	1861-1880	1881-1900	1901-1920	1921-1940	1941-1960	1961-1965	1821-1965
TOTAL	742,564	4,311,465	5,127,015	8,934,177	14,531,197	4,635,640	3,550,518	1,450,312	43,282,888
Europe	594,478	4,050,019	4,337,066	8,290,836	12,377,927	2,810,760	1,946,874	533,002	34,940,962
Austria	*	*	70,133	460,119	1,121,858	36,431	91,966	6,638	1,787,145
Czechoslovkia (1)	*	*	*	*	3,426	116,587	9,265	1,005	130,283
Denmark	1,232	4,288	48,865	138,363	107,268	34,989	16,377	4,987	356,369
France	54,072	153,620	108,192	81,234	135,276	62,233	89,930	24,431	708,988
Germany	159,215	1,386,293	1,505,650	1,958,122	485,443	526,260	704,343	118,945	6,844,271
Greece	69	47	282	18,287	351,720	60,203	56,581	19,290	506,479
Ireland	258,105	1,694,838	872,649	1,043,898	485,246	222,207	68,151	27,844	4,672,938
Italy	2,662	11,101	67,484	959,202	3,155,401	523,343	243,152	78,893	5,041,238
Netherlands	2,490	19,040	25,643	80,459	91,980	34,098	67,137	22,218	343,065
Norway (2)	*	*	95,323	271,601	256,900	73,271	33,035	10,301	740,431
Poland (3)	385	1,269	14,997	148,526	4,813	244,760	17,556	32,889	465,195
Romania (4)	*	*	11	19,098	66,319	71,517	2,115	1,158	160,218
Sweden (2)	*	*	115,922	439,548	344,608	101,209	32,362	10,095	1,043,744
United Kingdom	100,889	691,018	1,154,939	1,078,895	867,358	371,142	342,130	88,730	3,345,461
USSR (former Soviet Union)	352	1,008	41,796	718,572	2,518,507	63,112	1,242	872	4,695,101
Yugoslavia (1)	*	*	*	*	1,888	54,899	9,801	5,305	71,893

546

Table A.3 (Continued)

Country of Origin	1821-1840	1841-1860	1861-1880	1881-1900	1901-1920	1921-1940	1941-1960	1961-1965	1821-1965
Asia & the									
Middle East (5)	**85**	**41,679**	**188,919**	**144,804**	**570,779**	**128,654**	**190,277**	**107,032**	**1,372,229**
China	10	41,432	187,502	76,510	41,883	34,835	26,366	8,156	416,694
India	37	79	132	337	6,795	2,382	3,734	2,602	16,098
Japan	*	*	335	28,212	213,634	35,410	47,805	19,759	345,155
Turkey	27	142	535	34,207	291,435	34,889	4,317	4,330	369,882
Canada (6)	**15,901**	**101,032**	**537,518**	**396,615**	**921,411**	**1,033,042**	**549,670**	**243,400**	**3,798,589**
Mexico (6,7)	**11,416**	**6,349**	**7,353**	**2,884**	**268,646**	**481,606**	**360,400**	**228,401**	**1,367,055**
Caribbean (8)	**16,135**	**24,188**	**23,003**	**62,108**	**230,972**	**90,401**	**172,816**	**119,596**	**739,219**
Central America	**149**	**817**	**252**	**953**	**25,351**	**21,630**	**66,416**	**52,182**	**167,750**
South America	**1,387**	**4,803**	**2,525**	**3,379**	**59,179**	**50,018**	**113,459**	**138,052**	**372,802**

[1] 1901–1920 includes data for 1920 only.
[2] Beginning in 1871.
[3] 1899–1919 not separately available.
[4] Beginning 1880.
[5] Philippines: 1941–1960: 23,998; 1961–1965: 12,327.
[6] Incomplete prior to 1908.
[7] No data 1886–1994.
[8] Cuba: 1961–1965: 45,567; Dominican Republic: 1962–1965: 32,151; Haiti: 1962–1965: 8,085; Jamaica: 1962–1965: 12,766.

Sources: U.S. Bureau of the Census, *1996 Statistical Yearbook of the Immigration and Naturalization Service* (Washington, D.C.: Government Printing Office, 1997), table 2; for 1961–1965, *Annual Report: Immigration and Naturalization Service* (Washington, D.C.: Government Printing Office, 1961–1965), table 6A.

Table A.4
Immigrants Admitted by Selected Region and Country of Birth,
Fiscal Years 1966–1996

	1966-1975	1976-1985	1986-1995	1996	1966-1996
TOTAL	**3,807,646**	**5,421,439**	**9,703,969**	**915,900**	**19,848,954**
Europe	**1,067,168**	**688,606**	**1,111,756**	**147,581**	**3,015,111**
Austria	7,768	4,089	5,492	554	**17,903**
Czechoslovakia	18,716	8,951	11,746	1,389	**40,802**
Denmark	7,066	5,264	6,165	608	**19,103**
France	23,328	19,069	26,824	3,079	**72,300**
Germany	101,614	68,124	72,476	6,748	**248,962**
Greece	128,924	51,497	24,426	1,452	**206,299**
Ireland	20,671	11,451	75,855	1,731	**109,708**
Italy	217,053	54,856	27,253	2,501	**301,663**
Netherlands	14,326	11,373	13,029	1,423	**40,151**
Norway (1)	5,933	3,774	4,721	478	**14,906**
Poland	49,567	59,208	175,566	15,772	**300,113**
Romania	16,739	27,005	50,642	5,801	**100,187**
Sweden	9,525	8,063	11,637	1,251	**30,476**
United Kingdom	157,184	142,249	151,812	13,624	**464,869**
USSR (former Soviet Union) (2)	14,498	73,573	321,652	62,777	**472,500**
Yugoslavia	62,741	21,285	30,941	11,854	**126,821**
Asia & The Middle East	**944,239**	**2,398,289**	**3,075,182**	**307,807**	**6,725,517**
Bangladesh (3)	*	7,300	38,253	8,221	**53,774**
Cambodia (3)	*	77,888	57,204	1,568	**136,660**
China (4,5)	101,393	243,707	370,709	41,728	**757,537**
Hong Kong	43,714	51,638	82,426	7,834	**185,612**
India	100,771	223,505	333,749	44,859	**702,884**
Iran	20,369	95,199	160,663	11,084	**287,315**
Israel	18,316	33,027	36,353	3,126	**90,822**
Japan	43,204	41,945	57,143	6,011	**148,303**
Korea	138,111	325,484	268,812	18,185	**750,592**
Laos (3)	*	119,711	83,263	2,847	**205,821**
Lebanon	15,698	40,556	50,136	4,382	**110,772**
Pakistan	*	44,811	93,448	12,519	**150,778**
Philippines	238,890	428,128	566,699	55,876	**1,289,593**
Syria	8,857	17,413	24,601	3,072	**53,943**
Taiwan (4,5)	*	53,955	127,506	13,401	**194,862**
Thailand	25,491	49,290	69,837	4,301	**148,919**
Turkey	18,744	20,865	21,473	3,657	**64,739**
Vietnam	20,038	398,306	442,297	42,067	**902,708**
Canada	159,665	122,571	138,526	15,825	**436,587**
Mexico	538,264	654,173	2,806,023	163,572	**4,162,032**

Table A.4 (Continued)

	1966-1975	1976-1985	1986-1995	1996	1966-1996
Caribbean (3)	*	**806,641**	**1,059,753**	**116,801**	**1,983,195**
Cuba	290,760	225,075	168,749	26,466	**711,050**
Dominican Republic	125,795	185,628	365,635	39,604	**716,662**
Haiti	54,778	75,465	192,250	18,386	**340,879**
Jamaica	124,121	181,110	203,976	19,089	**528,296**
Trinidad & Tobago	55,645	45,516	56,223	7,344	**164,728**
Central America (3)	*	**210,989**	**634,162**	**44,289**	**889,440**
El Salvador	18,058	66,710	301,466	17,903	**404,137**
Guatemala	18,712	36,461	129,482	8,763	**193,418**
Nicaragua	7,179	23,589	73,363	6,903	**111,034**
South America	**215,915**	**362,653**	**554,217**	**61,769**	**1,194,554**
Colombia	64,427	100,045	140,240	14,283	**318,995**
Ecuador	42,968	49,327	70,752	8,321	**171,368**
Guyana	20,080	75,936	96,787	9,489	**202,292**
Peru	15,099	42,406	96,428	12,871	**166,804**
Africa	**59,392**	**133,537**	**275,344**	**52,889**	**521,162**
Oceana	**28,436**	**40,868**	**47,862**	**5,309**	**122,475**

[1]Total is for 1966–1971, 1976–1996.
[2]1992–1996: Armenia: 20,849; Russia: 70,413; Ukraine: 92,220.
[3]Total is for 1976–1996.
[4]1966–1975: Taiwan and China combined. 1976–1981: Taiwan and China combined total: 142,680.
    1982–1985: China: 101,027 and Taiwan: 53,955.
[5]Total data for Chinese Mainland: 1982–1996: 513,464; for Taiwan: 1982–1996: 194,862 and over-
    all China and Taiwan: 1966–1996: 952,399.

Sources: 1975 Annual Report: Immigration and Naturalization Service (Washington, D.C.: Gov-
    ernment Printing Office, 1976), table 14; U.S. Bureau of the Census, *1985 Statistical Yearbook
    of the Immigration and Naturalization Service* (Washington, D.C.: Government Printing Office,
    1986), table IMM 1.3, and *1996 Statistical Yearbook of the Immigration and Naturalization
    Service* (Washington, D.C.: Government Printing Office, 1997), table 3.

Table A.5
Persons Naturalized, Fiscal Years 1907–1996

Years	Number of Persons Naturalized
1907-1910	111,738
1911-1920	1,128,972
1921-1930	1,773,185
1931-1940	1,518,464
1941-1950	1,987,028
1951-1960	1,189,946
1961-1970	1,120,263
1971-1980	1,464,772
1981-1990	2,214,265
1991-1995	1,785,186
1996	1,044,689
TOTAL 1907-1996	**15,338,508**

Source: U.S. Bureau of the Census, *1996 Statistical Yearbook of the Immigration and Naturalization
    Service* (Washington, D.C.: Government Printing Office, 1997), table 44.

Table A.6
Persons Naturalized by Selected Country or Region of Former Allegiance, Fiscal Years 1966–1996

	1966-75	1976-85	1986-95	1996	1966-96
Total (1)	1,138,349	1,806,911	2,969,814	1,044,689	6,959,763
Europe	**516,773**	**420,578**	**428,078**	**108,966**	**1,474,395**
Austria	6,673	2,981	1,497	347	11,498
Czechoslovakia	6,885	9,013	7,424	613	23,935
Denmark (2)	2,984	1,869	1,417	279	6,549
France	12,757	9,850	12,008	2,257	36,872
Germany	93,337	36,895	26,209	4,245	160,686
Greece	40,480	47,812	22,458	2,769	113,519
Ireland	22,344	9,183	10,211	3,010	44,748
Italy	90,207	59,088	30,158	4,617	184,070
Netherlands	17,120	6,509	5,061	1,015	29,705
Norway (2)	3,426	1,233	2,506	217	7,382
Poland	34,922	25,370	51,417	13,200	124,909
Romania	5,986	9,841	25,953	4,451	46,231
Sweden (2)	3,015	1,470	1,723	335	6,543
USSR (former Soviet Union)	7,509	24,996	57,930	36,265	126,700
United Kingdom	80,178	85,990	95,943	20,052	282,163
Yugoslavia	20,692	22,526	18,547	3,785	65,550
Asia & the Middle East	**236,429**	**753,430**	**1,368,611**	**267,334**	**2,625,804**
Bangladesh (3)	*	1,812	7,446	5,120	14,378
Cambodia (3)	*	3,005	29,453	5,077	37,535
China (4)	55,464	110,678	144,054	30,656	340,852
India	8,538	74,456	131,205	28,932	243,131
Iran	4,590	16,419	67,645	17,326	105,980
Israel	18,688	33,534	23,149	3,577	78,948
Japan	19,727	13,677	9,382	1,803	44,589
Korea	26,678	131,427	122,816	24,693	305,614
Laos	*	4,283	36,887	7,845	49,015
Lebanon	4,417	16,830	30,668	4,978	56,893
Pakistan (3)	*	13,137	32,212	10,278	55,627
Philippines	67,036	200,695	298,711	45,210	611,652
Syria	2,109	6,770	11,405	2,148	22,432
Taiwan (4)	*	10,458	70,358	12,431	93,247
Thailand	1,713	13,308	13,117	3,399	31,537
Turkey	4,732	7,559	12,291	1,885	26,467
Vietnam	4,530	70,263	244,623	47,625	367,041

Table A.6 (Continued)

	1966-75	1976-85	1986-95	1996	1966-96
Canada	59,531	33,220	47,769	10,324	150,844
Mexico	57,866	110,636	273,099	217,418	659,019
Caribbean	**164,733**	**281,986**	**377,025**	**155,178**	**978,922**
Cuba	136,146	146,356	116,905	62,168	461,575
Dominican Republic	7,811	39,793	76,914	27,293	151,811
Haiti	7,334	20,697	45,063	24,556	97,650
Jamaica	8,068	50,793	76,118	24,770	159,749
Trinidad and Tobago	3,528	11,941	28,994	8,619	53,082
Central America	**23,281**	**47,028**	**124,897**	**72,034**	**267,240**
El Salvador	2,251	10,499	37,027	33,240	83,017
Guatemala	2,213	7,321	17,822	13,383	40,739
Nicaragua	3,067	6,233	16,826	10,614	36,740
South America	**47,877**	**108,206**	**221,785**	**79,918**	**457,786**
Colombia	10,296	29,819	70,787	26,115	137,017
Ecuador	5,935	12,424	24,578	14,206	57,143
Guyana	1,991	17,528	43,053	10,618	73,190
Peru	4,723	12,937	30,461	12,073	60,194
Africa	**10,787**	**30,420**	**98,889**	**21,842**	**161,938**
Oceana	**4,614**	**7,289**	**10,954**	**2,676**	**25,533**

[1] In 1984, 23,000 files were missing.
[2] Data not available for 1986 for Norway, Denmark, and Sweden.
[3] Total is for 1976–1996.
[4] China and Taiwan: 1976–1981, 70,505, and overall total, 1966–1996: 444,557. For China alone: 1982–1985, 40,173, and for 1982–1996, 214,883. For Taiwan alone: 1982–1985, 10,458, and for 1982–1996, 103,705.

Sources: *1975 Annual Report: Immigration and Naturalization Service* (Washington, D.C.: INS, 1976), table 39; U.S. Bureau of the Census, *1985 Statistical Yearbook of the Immigration and Naturalization Service* (Washington, D.C.: Government Printing Office, 1986), table NAT 1.3; and *1996 Statistical Yearbook of the Immigration and Naturalization Service* (Washington, D.C.: Government Printing Office, 1997), table 47.

SELECTED GENERAL
BIBLIOGRAPHY

A number of fine works dealing with the debates over multiculturalism as well as with its inclusion in school curricula have already been cited in the references to the introduction of this volume. One other very new one by individuals central to the controversy is *History on Trial: Culture Wars and the Teaching of the Past*, by Gary B. Nash, Charlotte Crabtree, and Ross E. Dunn (New York: Alfred Knopf, 1997). I here wish to focus on works that treat ethnic groups in general and important ones that deal with particular groups but that are representative of the kinds of multicultural materials now available.

Since many of the essays here rely on U.S. Bureau of the Census and Immigration and Naturalization Service data, that is a good place to begin. It is worth noting that although they are imperfect (in terms of the undercount of the censuses, especially in 1990) and incomplete (many useful questions are not asked of immigrants and prospective citizens in terms of, for example, education, income, family size, original versus current occupation, etc.), they are still the most comprehensive sources of statistical data available, notably the specific census subject reports. See *1990 Census of Population. Supplementary Reports. Detailed Ancestry Groups for States*, 1990 CP-S-1–2 (Washington, D.C.: Government Printing Office, 1992); *1990 Census of Population. The Foreign-Born Population of the United States*, 1990 CP-3–1 (1993); *1990 Census of Population. Ancestry of the Population in the United States*, 1990 CP-3–2 (1993); *1990 Census of Population. Persons of Hispanic Origin in the United States*, 1990 CP-3–3 (1993); *1990 Census of Population. Asian and Pacific Islanders in the United States*, 1990 CP-3–5 (1993); and *1990 Census of Population. General Population Characteristics for American Indian and Alaska Native Areas*, 1990 CP-1–1A (1992). The INS annual reports prior to 1979 were entitled, for example, *1975 Annual Report: Immigration and Naturalization Service* (Washington, D.C.: Government Printing Office) and since then as, for example, *1995 Statistical Yearbook of the Immigration and Naturalization Service*. Many other periodic government publications are available as well as reports from various Senate and House committees. One of the most famous was the *Reports of the Immigration Commission* [the Dillingham Commission], 41 vols. (Washington, D.C.: Government Printing Office, 1911; reprinted by Arno Press, 1970). The Selection Commission on Immigration and Refugee Policy issued its nine-volume report in April 1981, the supplement to which was *U.S. Immigration Policy and the National Interest*. The most recent U.S. Commission on Immigration Reform issued its second interim June 1995 report, *Legal Immigration: Setting Priorities*. Its final report was submitted in September 1997. Several examples of the excellent use of census data are James Paul Allen and Eugene James Turner, *We the People: An Atlas of America's Ethnic Diversity* (New York: Macmillan, 1988), with its outstanding multicolored maps; Turner and Allen's very impressive new study, *The Ethnic Quilt: Population Diversity in Southern California* (Northridge CA: California State University, 1997), which is likewise a masterful use of census data, mapping, and historical analysis; and Frank D. Bean and Marta Tienda's *The Hispanic Population of the United States* (New York: Russell Sage, 1987) and Stanley Lieberson and Mary C. Waters's *From Many Strands: Ethnic and Racial Groups in Contemporary America* (New York: Russell Sage, 1988), two important and very informative works in a series for the National Committee for Research on the 1980 Census.

As noted at the outset, the major source of information on about 100 groups as well as key themes related to immigrant and ethnic experiences is the *Harvard Encyclopedia of American Ethnic Groups*, edited by Stephan Thernstrom, Ann Orlov, and Oscar Handlin (Cambridge: Harvard University Press, 1980). But it is now nearly two decades old and was put together when the newest (post-1965) wave of immigrants was still in its first stages; the end of the great civil rights era was apparent but the full consequences only partially evident; the wars in Southeast Asia had just ended and the waves of refugees were just beginning; and many other tumultuous events had not yet taken place, notably the fall of the shah of Iran, the Central American civil wars, and the end of the cold war. A work that somewhat bridges the old and the new with a model series of essays that have broad application, although they focus chiefly on one state, is *Peopling Indiana: The Ethnic Experience* (Indianapolis: Indiana Historical Society, 1996). A half dozen other rather recent works that provide valuable comparative approaches to broad spectrums of groups, immigrant and native (in most cases), are Lawrence H. Fuchs, *The American Kaleidoscope: Race Ethnicity, and the Civic Culture* (Hanover, NH: Wesleyan, 1990); Roger Daniels, *Coming to America: A History of Immigration and Ethnicity in American Life* (New York: HarperCollins, 1990); James S. Olson, *The Ethnic Dimension in American History*, 2nd ed. (New York: St. Martin's Press, 1994); Peter Kivisto, *Americans All: Race and Ethnic Relations in Historical, Structural, and Comparative Perspectives* (Belmont, CA: Wadsworth, 1995); Leonard Dinnerstein, Roger L. Nichols, and David M. Reimers, *Natives and Strangers: A Multicultural History of Americans* (New York: Oxford, 1996); and Elliott R. Barkan, *And Still They Come: Immigrants and American Society, 1920 to the 1990s* (Wheeling, IL: Harlan Davidson, 1996). Remaining yet one of the most thorough accounts of immigration legislative history is Edward P. Hutchinson's massive *Legislative History of American Immigration Policy, 1798–1965* (Philadelphia: University of Pennsylvania Press, 1981). Although marred by the quality of the reproductions, a tremendous source of materials, particularly on nineteenth- and early twentieth century European immigration, is the twenty-volume collection of articles assembled by George E. Pozzetta and collectively entitled *American Immigration and Ethnicity* (New York: Garland, 1990–1991). The volumes, all of which were reviewed individually in the *Journal of American Ethnic History*, 13.3 (Spring 1994): 51–88, covered general themes of ethnicity, emigration, ethnic communities, agricultural and small-town life, immigrant organizations, immigrant labor, businesses, and unions, politics and radicals, education, family patterns, women, acculturation and mobility, Americanization programs, nativism, identity and language maintenance, law and crime, folklore, religion, and a final volume focusing on the period since World War II. Another collection of original essays presents valuable overviews on a number of particular broad topics that overlay the essays included here. In the new *Encyclopedia of the United States in the Twentieth Century*, edited by Stanley Katz et al., 4 vols. (New York: Scribner, 1996), are, in volume 1, essays by Lizabeth Cohen and Mark Tebeau, "Gender Issues"; Earl Lewis, "Race"; Rudolph J. Vecoli, "Ethnicity and Immigration"; and Olivier Zunz, "Class." In volume 4 are essays by Richard Wrightman Fox, "Protestantism"; Patrick W. Carey, "Catholicism"; Catherine L. Albanese, "Nontraditional Religions"; Deborah Dash Moore, "Judaism and Jewish Culture"; and Kenneth W. Warren, "African American Cultural Movements." A most useful collection of essays on a rather extensive array of ethnic groups is *Origins and Destinies: Immigration, Race, and Ethnicity in America*, edited by Silvia Pedraza and Rubén Rumbaut (Belmont, CA: Wadsworth, 1996). Another useful one focuses on people of color in the West. Although its regional coverage is very specific in these terms, the scope of the articles is quite interesting, covering as they do a region far less often treated holistically: *Peoples of Color in the American West*, edited by Sucheng Chan, Douglas Henry Daniels, Mario T. Garcia, and Terry P. Wilson (Lexington, MA: D. C. Heath, 1994).

In addition, two publishers have recently come out with a series of excellent volumes on a wide variety of ethnic groups. They are not as academic as those produced twenty-five years ago by Random House and Prentice-Hall, but they are quite informative, based on direct community observation, and very accessible in their writing style: from Allyn and Bacon, in the first group (Needham Heights, MA, 1995–1997): James M. Freeman, *Changing Identities: Vietnamese Americans, 1975–1995*; Steven Gold, *From Workers' State to the Golden State: Jews from the Former Soviet Union in California*; Johanna Lessinger, *From the Ganges to the Hudson: Indian Immigrants in New York City*; Sarah J. Mahler, *Salvadorans in Suburbia: Symbiosis and Conflict*; and Patricia R. Pessar, *A Visa for a Dream: Dominicans in the United States*. The second series (1998) includes Jo Ann Koltyk, *New Pioneers in the Heartland: Hmong Life in Wisconsin*; Maxine L. Margolis, *An Invisible Minority: Brazilians in New York City*; Pyong Gap Min, *Changes and Conflict: Korean Immigrant Families in New York*; Alex Stepick, *Pride against Prejudice: Haitians in the United States*; and Bernard Wong, *Ethnicity and Entrepreneurship: The New Chinese Immigrants in the San Francisco Bay Area*. Oxford University has produced a delightful series of ten amply illustrated volumes, all entitled *Family Album* and all by Dorothy and Thomas Hobbler (New York, 1996). They include African, Chinese, Cuban, German, Irish, Italian, Japanese, Jewish, Mexican, and Scandinavian Americans.

Among the many volumes of works on immigration, several classics are worth noting because they do contain materials not always found in later studies, such as Carl Wittke's *We Who Built America: The Saga of the Immigrant*, rev. ed. (Cleveland, OH: Case Western Reserve, 1967 [1939]); Oscar Handlin's poetic depiction of immigrant struggles, *The Uprooted: The Epic Story of the Great Migrations That Made the American People*, 2nd ed. (Boston: Little, Brown, 1973 [1951]); Alan M. Kraut's very readable *The Huddled Masses: The Immigrant in American Society, 1880–1921* (Arlington Heights: Harlan Davidson, 1982; rev. ed. forthcoming); Thomas J. Archdeacon's very scholarly and comprehensive *Becoming American: An Ethnic History* (New York: Free Press, 1983), which, despite its title, largely concentrates on immigrants; John Bodnar's seminal response to

Handlin, *The Transplanted: A History of Immigrants in Urban America* (Bloomington: Indiana University Press, 1985); Maxine Schwartz Seller's *To Seek America: A History of Ethnic Life in the United States*, rev. ed. (Englewood, NJ: Jerry Ozer, 1988), which covers many topics not dealt with in other works; *Immigration Reconsidered: History, Sociology, and Politics*, edited by Virginia Yans-McLaughlin (New York: Oxford, 1990), an outstanding collection of essays on various dimensions of the immigrant experience; Ivan Chermayeff, Fred Wasserman, and Mary J. Shapiro, *Ellis Island: An Illustrated History of the Immigrant Experience* (New York: Macmillan, 1991), a marvelous compendium based on the remodeled Ellis Island Museum collection; David M. Reimers, *Still the Golden Door: The Third World Comes to America*, 2nd ed. (New York: Columbia University Press, 1992), yet the principal study of the recent immigration and the policies that have shaped it; and Walter Nugent, *Crossings: The Great Transatlantic Migrations, 1870–1914* (Bloomington: Indiana University Press, 1992), an eloquent study of the forces that drove Europeans to the New World. A good companion volume of essays to Nugent's work is *A Century of European Migrations, 1830–1930*, edited by Rudolph J. Vecoli and Suzanne M. Sinke (Urbana: University of Illinois Press, 1991), as well as Mark Wyman's *Round-Trip to America: The Immigrants Return to Europe, 1880–1930* (Ithaca, NY: Cornell University Press, 1993), one of the better—and most recent—works to analyze the forces impelling immigrants to return home and their impact in those homelands. Ronald Takaki's very beautifully written *A Different Mirror: A History of Multicultural America* (Boston: Little, Brown, 1993) thematically treats both immigrants and native populations (Indian and African Americans) but principally up to World War II, although a last chapter deals rather sweepingly with the more contemporary decades. Finally, still the most brilliant treatment of the Americans' response to both immigrants and African Americans is John Higham's *Strangers in the Land: Patterns of American Nativism, 1860–1925* (New Brunswick, NJ: Rutgers University Press, 1992 [1955]), while a very comprehensive volume on a related aspect would be Leonard Dinnerstein's *Antisemitism in America* (New York: Oxford University Press, 1994).

Many works have appeared during the past two decades focusing on women and their experiences. Representative of this exploding newer field are *Unequal Sisters: A Multicultural Reader in U.S. Women's History*, edited by Vicki L. Ruiz and Ellen Carol DuBois, 2nd ed. (New York: Routledge, 1994), a collection of thirty-six essays on a wide variety of women, representing the cross section of racial groups, as well as selected bibliographies on each; Maxine Seller, *Immigrant Women* (Philadelphia: Temple University Press, 1981), a collection of essays on women of a number of different groups; Donna Gabaccia, *From the Other Side: Women, Gender, & Immigrant Life in the U.S., 1820–1990* (Bloomington: Indiana University Press, 1994), a challenging thematic approach to the European immigrant women's experiences; Paula S. Rothenberg, ed., *Race, Class, and Gender in the United States: An Integrated Study*, 3rd ed. (New York: St. Martin's Press, 1995), an ambitious, multidisciplinary approach with a variety of perspectives; and *Peasant Maids—City Women: From the European Countryside to Urban America*, edited by Christine Harzig (Ithaca, NY: Cornell University Press, 1997), a new series of essays examining women's experiences in the old country and the new. Illustrative of the newer waves of migrants are *Daughters of Caliban: Caribbean Women in the Twentieth Century*, edited by Consuelo López Springfield (Bloomington: Indiana University Press, 1997), and *Puerto Rican Women and Work: Bridges in Transnational Labor*, by Altagracia Ortiz (Philadelphia: Temple University Press, 1996).

Needless to say, there have been a huge number of volumes on the European immigrant experience. The following ones can only illustrate the scope of the more recent materials available: Gary B. Nash's *Red, White, and Black: The Peoples of Early America*, 3rd ed. (Englewood Cliffs, NJ: Prentice-Hall, 1992), is an outstanding effort to provide a detailed yet sweeping analysis of the interaction of Europeans with the Africans they imported and with the Native Americans they encountered, whereas Bernard Bailyn provides most useful information, insights, and interpretations of the early white settlers in *Voyagers to the West* (New York: Alfred Knopf, 1986). Kerby A. Miller presented a superb analysis of the mind-set of nineteenth-century Irish in *Emigrants and Exiles: Ireland and the Irish Exodus to North America* (New York: Oxford, 1985) and should be paired with Hasia Diner's acclaimed *Erin's Daughters in America: Irish Immigrant Women in the Nineteenth Century* (Baltimore: Johns Hopkins University Press, 1983). Richard D. Alba offered a provocative analysis of assimilation and ethnic identity changes among Euro-Americans in *Ethnic Identity: The Transformation of White America* (New Haven, CT: Yale University Press, 1990), which should be read along with Mary Waters's quite fascinating sociological study of identity changes: *Ethnic Options: Choosing Identities in America* (Berkeley: University of California Press, 1990). John J. Bukowczyk edited an overall distinguished set of essays on Poles that brings their story to the present in *Polish Americans and Their History: Community, Culture, and Politics* (Pittsburgh: University of Pittsburgh Press, 1996); and Ronald H. Bayor and Timothy J. Meagher likewise edited an outstanding array of essays that spanned the breadth of the Irish-American experience in *The New York Irish* (Baltimore, MD: Johns Hopkins University Press, 1996). Steven Gold's very revealing and perceptive account of contemporary Soviet Jews, especially compared with Vietnamese refugees, appears in *Refugee Communities: A Comparative Field Study* (Newbury Park, CA: Sage, 1992); and Anny Bakalian presented an insightful case study of contemporary immigrants and their modes of adaptation to America in *Armenian Americans: From Being to Feeling Armenian* (New Brunswick, NJ: Rutgers University Press, 1993). The number of works on American Jews is quite considerable, and key ones are cited by Edward Shapiro in his essay in this volume. A few to keep in mind (besides Dinnerstein's, cited above) are Arthur Hertzberg's *The Jews in America: Four Centuries of an Uneasy Encounter* (New York: Simon and Schuster, 1989) or Gerald Sorin's new survey, *Tradition Transformed: Four Centuries of an Uneasy Encounter* (Baltimore: Johns Hopkins University Press, 1997); Jack Fischel and Sanford Pinsker, eds., *Jewish-American History and Culture: An Encyclopedia* (New York: Garland, 1992); and the beautifully written five-volume history of American Jews, edited by Henry Feingold (New York: American Jewish Historical Society, 1992): Eli Farber, *A Time for Planting: The First Migration, 1654–1820*; Hasia Diner, *A Time for Gathering: The Second Migration, 1820–1880*; Gerald Sorin, *A Time for Building: The Third Migration, 1880–1920*; Feingold, *A Time for Searching: Entering the Mainstream, 1920–1945*; and Edward Shapiro, *A Time for Healing: American Jewry since World War II*. Finally, regarding women, there are numerous works; see, for example, Joyce Antler's study that focuses on the lives of specific women, *The Journey Home: Jewish Women and the American Century* (New York: Free Press, 1997).

Many works have been published on the Asian experience in America. Among the more comprehensive ones are the following: Ronald Takaki's captivating and very eloquent study of the major Asian groups, principally during the century following the coming of the Chinese (for it is weakest on the period since 1965), *Strangers from a Different Shore: A History of Asian Americans* (Boston: Little, Brown, 1989). Sucheng Chan's *Asian Americans: An Interpretive History* (Boston: Twayne, 1991) offers a valu-

558 SELECTED GENERAL BIBLIOGRAPHY

able overview that is in some respects more detailed than Takaki's and more fully covers the recent decades. An excellent set of essays that remain a solid contribution is *Pacific Bridges: The New Immigration from Asia and the Pacific Islands*, edited by James T. Fawcett and Benjamin V. Cariño (Staten Island, NY: Center for Migration Studies, 1987). Several volumes have focused particularly on the legal history of Asians and their long struggle for equality: Bill Ong Hing, *Making and Remaking Asian America Through Immigration Policy, 1850–1990* (Stanford: Stanford University Press, 1993); a very fascinating collection of documents and first-person statements in *Racism, Dissent, and Asian Americans from 1850 to the Present: A Documentary History*, edited by Philip S. Foner and Daniel Rosenberg (Westport, CT: Greenwood Press, 1993); Hyung-chan Kim's thorough analysis in *A Legal History of Asian Americans, 1790–1990* (Westport, CT: Greenwood Press, 1994); and Kim's prodigiously edited collection of documents and essays, *Asian Americans and Congress: A Documentary History* (Westport, CT: Greenwood Press, 1996). The essays in this present volume, of course, offer ample listings of other specific works on individual groups.

While there is as yet no entirely satisfactory history of Latino/Hispanic immigration and their ethnic experience, Joan Moore and Harry Pachon attempted to modify their earlier work on Mexicans into a broader survey in *Hispanics in the United States* (Englewood Cliffs, NJ: Prentice-Hall, 1985). Besides the Bean and Tienda work, cited above, Edna Acosta-Belén and Barbara R. Sjostrom edited a useful set of essays in *The Hispanic Experience in the United States* (New York: Praeger, 1988), whereas a new collection that is even broader in its sweep of Latino experiences is *Challenging Fronteras: Structuring Latina and Latino Lives in the U.S.*, edited by Mary Romero, Pierrette Hondagneu-Sotelo, and Vilma Ortiz (New York: Routledge, 1997). Still astonishing for its sweep and comprehensiveness is Edward Spicer's *Cycles of Conquest* (Tuscon: University of Arizona Press, 1961), a history of the interaction of Native Americans, Mexicans, and Anglos in the Southwest across nearly four centuries. While Carey McWilliams's *North from Mexico* (Westport, CT: Greenwood Press, 1990 [1948]) remains the most fascinating study of Mexican immigration, Rudy Acuña provided more angry perspectives in the three editions of his history *Occupied America*, 3rd ed. (New York: Harper and Row, 1988), albeit more mellow with each succeeding edition. Matt S. Meier and Felicxiano Ribera presented a less detailed treatment, which, though revised, is still better on the earlier period, *Mexican Americans/American Mexicans: From Conquistadors to Chicanos*, rev. ed. (New York: Hill and Wang, 1993 [1972]). Again, important group-specific works are in the various essays.

The literature on African Americans is now vast, and only a few will be noted here, supplementing what Juliet Walker has included in her essay. Only John Hope Franklin's *From Slavery to Freedom*, 7th ed. (with Alfred A. Moss, Jr.) (New York: Alfred Knopf, 1994), has remained current as a history of the African-American experience. Lerone Bennett's *Before the Mayflower*, 6th ed. (New York: Penguin, 1990), has also been revised several times but is shaped by a pronounced interpretation and is marred by some errors. A relatively brief but useful overview entitled *African Americans and Civil Rights: From 1619 to the Present* was written by Michael L. Levine (Phoenix, AZ: Oryx Press, 1996). Quite useful for their perspectives and interpretations as well as much interesting detail—but somewhat dated now—are Marion Francis Berry and John Blassingame's *Long Time Memory: The Black Experience in America* (New York: Oxford University Press, 1982) and August Meier and Elliot Rudnick's *From Plantation to Ghetto*, 3rd ed. (New York: Hill and Wang, 1976). Still a classic on the early period is Winthrop D.

Jordan's brilliant *White over Black: American Attitudes toward the Negro, 1550–1812* (Chapel Hill: University of North Carolina Press, 1968). Donald Wright's syntheses of the colonial and early Republic eras are quite masterful: *African Americans in the Colonial Era: From African Origins through the American Revolution* (Arlington Heights: Harlan Davidson, 1990) and *African Americans in the Early Republic* (Arlington Heights: Harlan Davidson, 1993).

A number of other works that convey some sense of the breadth of works on African Americans are Joseph E. Holloway's edited volume *Africanisms in American Culture* (Bloomington: Indiana University Press, 1990); Ira Berlin, *Slaves without Masters: The Free Negro in the Antebellum South* (New York: Pantheon, 1974); Elizabeth Fox Genovese, *Within the Plantation Household: Black and White Women of the Old South* (Chapel Hill: University of North Carolina Press, 1988); Herbert G. Gutman's very original *The Black Family in Slavery and Freedom, 1750–1925* (New York: Vintage, 1976); Eric Foner's comprehensive study *Reconstruction: America's Unfinished Revolution, 1863–1877* (New York: Harper and Row, 1988); William Loren Katz, *The Black West: A Pictorial History*, 3rd ed. (Seattle: Open Hand, 1987); Nicholas Lemann's acclaimed work *The Promised Land: The Great Migration and How It Changed America* (New York: Random House, 1991); Joseph William Trotter, Jr., ed., *The Great Migration in Historical Perspective: New Dimensions of Race, Class & Gender* (Bloomington: Indiana University Press, 1991); Kathy Russell, Midge Wilson, and Ronald Wall's candid exploration entitled *The Color Complex: The Politics of Skin Color among African Americans* (New York: Harcourt Brace Jovanovitch, 1992); Harvey Sitkoff's *The Struggle for Black Equality, 1954–1980* (New York: Hill and Wang, 1981); David R. Goldberg's well-written (though somewhat uneven) study *Black, White, and Southern: Race Relations and Southern Culture, 1940 to the Present* (Baton Rouge: Louisiana State University Press, 1990); and William J. Wilson's two pathbreaking studies, *The Declining Significance of Race* (Chicago: University of Chicago Press, 1978) and *The Truly Disadvantaged: The Inner City, the Underclass, and Public Policy* (Chicago: University of Chicago Press, 1987). Three recent, outstanding examples of studies on the often overlooked roles of African-American women are Jacqueline Jones's poignant *Labor of Love, Labor of Sorrow: Black Women, Work, and the Family from Slavery to the Present* (New York: Basic Books, 1985); Darlene Clark Hine's *Hine Sight: Black Women and the Reconstruction of American History* (Bloomington: Indiana University Press, 1994); and Glenda Elizabeth Gilmore's *Gender and Jim Crow: Women and the Politics of White Supremacy in North Carolina, 1896–1920* (Chapel Hill: University of North Carolina Press, 1996).

For many years, standard works on Native Americans included such overviews as Harold E. Driver's *Indians of North America*, 2nd ed. (Chicago: University of Chicago 1969), and Wendell Oswalt's *This Land Was Theirs: A Study of the North American Indian*, 2nd ed. (New York: Wiley, 1973). The Smithsonian then commenced a series of volumes, each of which was to be a highly detailed *Handbook of North American Indians*. Not all volumes were realized, but two, for example, volume 8 on California, edited by Robert F. Heizer (Washington, D.C.: Author, 1978) and volume 9 on the Southwest, edited by Alfonso Ortiz (1979) are excellent resources. There is an immense number of volumes of collections of scholarly articles, treatments of individual tribes, and anthologies of statements and accounts by Native Americans themselves. Alice B. Kehoe, author of the essay on American Indians in this volume, has a widely used text, entitled *North American Indians: A Comprehensive Account*, 2nd ed. (Englewood Cliffs, NJ:

Prentice-Hall, 1992). Among his many renowned works covering the span of American Indian history, largely concerning policy-related issues, are Francis Paul Prucha's invaluable *The Great Father: The United States Government and the American Indians*, 2 vols. (Lincoln: University of Nebraska Press, 1984), *Atlas of American Indian Affairs* (Lincoln: University of Nebraska Press, 1990), and *American Indian Treaties: The History of a Political Anomaly* (Berkeley: University of California Press, 1997). Valuable for its treatment of an important theme traversing the centuries is Robert F. Berkhofer, Jr., *The White Man's Indian: Images of the American Indian from Columbus to the Present* (New York: Alfred Knopf, 1978). For a number of years a very useful compendium of articles has been Roger Nichols, ed., *The American Indian, Past and Present*, 4th ed. (New York: McGraw-Hill, 1992). Among the works illustrative of the more sophisticated and Indian-sensitive research on the earlier period are William Cronon, *Changes in the Land: Indians, Colonists, and the Ecology of New England* (New York: Hill and Wang, 1983); James H. Merrell's outstanding *The Indians' New World: The Catawbas and Their Neighbors* (Chapel Hill: University of North Carolina Press, 1989); *Powhatan's Mantle: Indians of the Colonial Southeast*, edited by Peter H. Wood, Gregory A. Waselkov, and M. Thomas Hatley (Lincoln: University of Nebraska Press, 1989); and James Axtell, *Beyond 1492: Encounters in Colonial North America* (New York: Oxford University Press, 1992). A few general works that cover a number of tribes in the later half of the nineteenth century are Philip Weeks, *Farewell My Nation: The American Indian and the United States, 1820–1890* (Arlington Heights: Harlan Davidson, 1990); Robert M. Utley, *The Indian Frontier of the American West, 1846–1890* (Albuquerque: University of New Mexico Press, 1984); and Frederick E. Hoxie, *A Final Promise: The Campaign to Assimilate the Indians, 1880–1920* (Lincoln: University of Nebraska Press, 1984). Illustrative of the many studies concerning the twentieth century are: Donald L. Parman, *Indians and the American West in the Twentieth Century* (Bloomington: Indiana University Press, 1994); Donald L. Fixico, *Termination and Relocation: Federal Indian Policy, 1945–1960* (Albuquerque: University of New Mexico Press, 1986); C. Matthew Snipp, *American Indians: The First of This Land* (New York: Russell Sage, 1989), another volume in the 1980 research project cited at the outset; John Wunder's highly sophisticated *"Retained by the People": A History of American Indians and the Bill of Rights* (New York: Oxford University Press, 1994); and two quite interesting works on the contemporary resurgence of identity and activism among Native Americans—Joane Nagel, *American Indian Ethnic Renewal: Red Power and the Resurgence of Identity and Culture* (New York: Oxford University Press, 1996), and Ward Churchill, *Since Predator Came: Notes from the Struggle for American Indian Liberation* (Littleton, CO: Aigis Publications, 1996). Finally an excellent study of urban Indians is Joan Weibel-Orlando's *Indian Country, L.A.: Maintaining Ethnic Community in Complex Society* (Urbana: University of Illinois Press, 1991).

One of the more interesting avenues for multicultural materials is the focus on urban areas, where most newcomers have been settling, a field that was much inspired by Oscar Handlin's pathbreaking study of the early Irish, *Boston's Immigrants, 1790–1865: A Study in Acculturation*, rev. ed. (New York: Atheneum Press, 1972); Nathan Glazer and Daniel P. Moynihan's *Beyond the Melting Pot: The Negroes, Puerto Ricans, Jews, Italians, and Irish of New York City*, 2nd ed. (Cambridge, MA: MIT Press, 1970); John Higham's *Send These Unto Me: Immigrants in Urban America*, rev. ed. (Baltimore: Johns Hopkins University Press, 1984); and Herbert Gans's now-classic study of Italians, *Urban Villagers: Group and Class in the Life of Italian Americans*, rev. ed. (New York: Free

Press, 1982). A small sampling of particularly good works includes: Ronald H. Bayor's very balanced and highly regarded study entitled *Neighbors in Conflict: The Irish, Germans, Jews, and Italians of New York City, 1929–1941*, 2nd ed. (Urbana: University of Illinois Press, 1988); Frederick M. Binder and David M. Reimers, *All the Nations under Heaven: An Ethnic and Racial History of New York City* (New York: Columbia University Press, 1995); *New Immigrants in New York*, edited by Nancy Foner (New York: Columbia University Press, 1987); *Ethnic Chicago: A Multicultural Portrait*, edited by Melvin G. Holli and Peter d'A. Jones (Grand Rapids, MI: Eerdman, 1995), a new edition of an excellent collection of essays; Alejandro Portes and Alex Stepick, eds., *City on the Edge: The Transformation of Miami* (Berkeley: University of California Press, 1993); Gary Mormino and George E. Pozzetta's very informative multiethnic study entitled *The Immigrant World of Ybor City: Italians and Their Latino Neighbors in Tampa, 1885–1985* (Urbana: University of Illinois Press, 1987); and in addition to Turner and Allen's census-based portrait of the Los Angeles region, cited above, a most exceptional contemporary set of essays edited by Roger Waldinger and Mehdi Bozorgmehr, *Ethnic Los Angeles* (New York: Russell Sage, 1996). In addition, a very informative series of studies illustrating diverse cases of in-depth, urban community studies is Louise Lamphere, ed., *Structuring Diversity: Ethnographic Perspectives on the New Immigrants* (Chicago: University of Chicago Press, 1992), and a new collection of essays, *The New African American Urban History*, edited by Kenneth W. Goings and Raymond A. Mohl (Thousand Oaks, CA: Sage, 1996), covers regional developments and a number of specific cities, particularly in the South.

Two other areas, among many, to consider from a multicultural perspective concern citizenship and race mixing. Three particularly valuable works treating the first are James H. Kettner's masterful *The Development of American Citizenship, 1608–1870* (Chapel Hill: University of North Carolina Press, 1978); Kenneth L. Karst, *Belonging to America: Equal Citizenship and the Constitution* (New Haven, CT: Yale University Press, 1989); and the enormous, statistically based analysis by Guillermina Jasso and Mark Rosenzweig, *The New Chosen People: Immigrants in the United States* (New York: Russell Sage, 1990). Three especially good works illustrative of the latter theme of race mixing are Paul Spikard, *Mixed Blood: Intermarriage and Ethnic Identity in Twentieth-Century America* (Madison: University of Wisconsin Press, 1989); Maria P. P. Root, ed., *Racially Mixed People in America* (Newbury Park, CA: Sage, 1992); and Jon Michael Spencer, *The New Colored People: The Mixed Race Movement* (New York: New York University Press, 1997).

Finally, two recently published texts provide very comprehensive treatments of many multicultural issues touched on by the essays in this volume and are good resources: Joe R. Feagin and Clarence Booher Feagin, *Racial and Ethnic Relations*, 5th ed. (Upper Saddle River, NJ: Prentice-Hall, 1996); and Richard T. Schaefer, *Racial and Ethnic Groups*, 7th ed. (New York: Longman, 1998). There are, too, a multitude of works focusing on issues of racism and race conflict, three of which will provide a start: Alden T. Vaughan, *Roots of American Racism: Essays on the Colonial Experience* (New York: Oxford University Press, 1995); Fred L. Pincus and Howard J. Ehrlich, eds., *Race and Ethnic Conflict: Contending Views on Prejudice, Discrimination, and Ethnoviolence* (Boulder, CO: Westview, 1994); Joe R. Feagin and Hernán Vera, *White Racism: The Basics* (New York: Routledge, 1995); and a collection of essays offering a different perspective on the issue, *Critical White Studies: Looking Behind the Mirror*, edited by Richard Delgado and Jean Stefancic (Philadelphia: Temple University Press, 1997).

Equally voluminous is the literature on ethnicity (in the United States and worldwide), some of which works are cited in the introduction and various chapters. A good starting point for an overview is a new work, William Petersen's *Ethnicity Counts* (New Brunswick, NJ: Rutgers University Press, 1997), along with one other, dealing with a theme also running through the various essays, Charles H. Mindel, Robert W. Habenstein, and Roosevelt Wright, Jr., eds., *Ethnic Families in America: Patterns and Variations*, 3rd ed. (New York: Elsevier, 1988), which is a strong collection of essays on seventeen different ethnic groups.

INDEX

A Nation of Peoples, America as, x–xi, 4

ABOUT THE CONTRIBUTORS

ELLIOTT ROBERT BARKAN has focused his professional career on developing an interdisciplinary, comparative approach to American ethnic issues. He has written and lectured extensively on topics related to contemporary immigration, race relations, and patterns of naturalization and has lectured in ten countries on a variety of contemporary and historical themes. Along with two dozen articles, his books include *Asian and Pacific Islander Migration to the United States: A Model of New Global Patterns* (1992) and *And Still They Come: Immigrants and American Society, 1920–1990s* (1996). His application of a multifaceted perspective to the adaptation and integration of ethnic groups was presented in "Race, Religion and Nationality in American Society: A Model of Ethnicity—From Contact to Assimilation" in the *Journal of American Ethnic History* (1995). Barkan has also been Book Review Editor for the *Journal of American Ethnic History* since 1985 and is currently a member of the Executive Board of the Immigration History Society as well as Professor of History and Ethnic Studies at California State University, San Bernardino. Greenwood Press will also soon publish his co-edited *Gateways to America: A Documentary History of the Immigration and Naturalization Laws of the United States*. He is presently working on a history of immigration into the American West in the twentieth century.

JAMES M. BERGQUIST is Professor of History at Villanova University. He has degrees from the University of Notre Dame and Northwestern University, where he received his doctorate. His writings have ranged across various subjects of American social history, including German Americans, their political life, and their newspaper press. He has served on the board of the Immigration History Society and edits the Society's newsletter.

CARLOS B. CORDOVA is Director of the Central American Research Institute and Professor of La Raza Studies at San Francisco State University. He has been teaching at San Francisco State University since 1974. A native of El Salvador, he has lived in the San Francisco Bay area since 1965 and has been actively involved in the Latino community in the Bay Area since then. His research includes the migration dynamics and acculturation experiences of Central Americans in the United States. Other research interests are popular religions and spirituality in Central America and the Caribbean.

JON CRUZ is a second-generation Filipino American. He received his doctorate in sociology at the University of California at Berkeley. He is currently Associate Professor in the Department of Sociology at the University of California at Santa Barbara. He has written on Filipino Americans' multiculturalism, mass media, and African-American music.

STEVEN EPPERSON taught American Religious History at Brigham Young University and was History Curator at the Museum of Church History and Art. From 1995 to 1997 he was a Young Scholar in American Religion at the Center for the Study of Religion and American Culture. He is the author of the award-winning *Mormons and Jews: Early Mormon Theologies of Israel* (1992).

STEVEN J. GOLD is Associate Professor of Sociology at Michigan State University, Senior Fellow at the Wilstein Institute of Jewish Policy Studies, and the past president of the International Visual Sociology Association. The author of *From the Workers' State to the Golden State: Jews from the Former Soviet Union in California* (1995), he has done extensive fieldwork with several immigrant and refugee communities in the United States. Gold has published articles on immigrant adaptation, ethnic self-employment, and community development in *Ethnic and Racial Studies, International Migration Review, Asian and Pacific Migration Review, Diaspora*, and *Western Journal of Medicine* as well as in several edited volumes. His first book, *Refugee Communities: A Comparative Field Study* (1992), was a finalist for the Robert Park Award in 1993. He is currently writing a book about ethnic economies.

GUILLERMO J. GRENIER is the Director of the Florida Center for Labor Research and Studies and Associate Professor of Sociology at Florida International University, the Florida State University at Miami. Born in Havana, Cuba, he received his undergraduate education at Emory University and Georgia State University in Atlanta. He received his Ph.D. from the University of New Mexico. He is the author of *Inhuman Relations: Quality Circles and Anti-Unionism in American History* (1988). His other books include *Employer Participation and Labor Law in the American Workplace* (1992); *Miami Now!: Immigration, Ethnicity, and Social Change* (1992); *Newcomers in the Workplace: Immigrants and the Restructuring of the U.S. Economy* (1994); and *This Land Is*

Our Land: Newcomers and Established Residents in Miami (forthcoming). He has written numerous articles on labor and ethnic issues in the United States and conducts yearly surveys on the attitudes of the Cuban-American community toward Cuba. Dr. Grenier has recently completed one year as a Fulbright Scholar researching his next project, the transition process of unions in Eastern Europe.

DAVID G. GUTIÉRREZ is a member of the History faculty and Co-director of the Southwest History Project at the University of California at San Diego (UCSD). Educated at the University of California, Santa Barbara, and at Stanford University, Gutiérrez has taught at the University of Utah, Stanford, and UCSD. Gutiérrez's research interests include immigration history, ethnic politics, and the history of citizenship in the United States. Recent publications include *Between Two Worlds: Mexican Immigrants in the United States* (1996) and *Walls and Mirrors: Mexican Americans, Mexican Immigrants and the Politics of Ethnicity* (1995), which was awarded the W. Turnentine Jackson Prize by the Western History Association in 1997. He is currently at work on a history of citizenship in the United States since World War II.

PHILIP KASINITZ teaches sociology at the Graduate Center and Hunter College of the City University of New York. He is the author of *Caribbean New York: Black Immigrants and the Politics of Race* (1992) and the editor of *Metropolis: Center and Symbol of Our Times* (1995). He is currently working on a project on poverty and urban space in the Red Hook section of Brooklyn as well as planning an extensive survey of second-generation immigrants in New York City.

ALICE B. KEHOE is Professor of Anthropology, Marquette University (Milwaukee, WI), where she has taught since 1968. She has been President of the Central States Anthropological Society and on the Board of Directors of the American Anthropological Association. Among her publications are the widely used textbook *North American Indians: A Comprehensive Account* (1981; 2nd ed. 1992) and *The Ghost Dance: Ethnohistory and Revitalization* (1989). Her introductory anthropology textbook *Humans* and her *Land of Prehistory: A Critical History of American Archaeology* were both published in 1998. Kehoe's current academic interests include American Indians and the history of archaeology. Her recent research includes ethnographic fieldwork in an Aymara village in Bolivia, historical research at the Institute for Advanced Studies in the Humanities, Edinburgh University, and continued collaboration with the Piegan Institute and Blackfeet Community College on the Blackfeet Reservation, Montana.

KWANG CHUNG KIM is a Professor of Sociology at Western Illinois University. His research interests include occupation and work, family relations, racial/ethnic group relations, and Korean and other Asian Americans. With Won Moo Hurh, Kim received two large two-year research grants (1978–1980, 1986–1988) from the National Institute of Mental Health. They have published *Korean Immigrants in America* (1984) and more than twenty articles on Korean immigrants and other Asian Americans. With Marilyn Fernandez, Kim coauthored two articles on intragroup differences in business participation rates among various Asian immigrant groups. He has recently edited *Koreans in the 'Hoods* (1999).

PAULINE NAWAHINEOKALA'I KING was born in Hawaii and educated in Honolulu and Washington, D.C. A graduate of Sarah Lawrence College, she received her doctorate degree from the University of Hawaii in history. She has written and edited works on the history of Hawaii and is currently the historian of the Hawaiian Islands in the History Department of the University of Hawaii.

GEORGE A. KOURVETARIS was educated both in Greece and in the United States, where he received his Ph.D. in 1969. He is currently a Professor of Sociology at Northern Illinois University. His major academic and research interests include political sociology, social theory, intergroup relations, and civil-military relations. He has authored, coauthored, or coedited twelve books. They include *First and Second Generation Greeks in Chicago* (1971) and, most recently, *Social Thought* (1994), *Political Sociology* (1997), and *Studies on Greek Americans* (1997). He has also authored and co-authored over sixty articles on such topics as political clientelism, electoral politics, class identification, political power, political participation, civil-military relations, intergroup relations, and ethnicity. He is also editor of the *Journal of Political and Military Sociology*, which he founded in 1973.

BRUCE LA BRACK is a Professor of Anthropology and International Studies in the School of International Studies, University of the Pacific, Stockton, California. He has published extensively on overseas South Asians, particularly the Sikhs in North America. He has held an American Institute of Indian Studies (New Delhi) Language Fellowship and been awarded Fulbright grants for study in India and research in Japan. Professor La Brack has conducted over twenty years of research on the impact of the South Asian American Diaspora on India and America, concentrating most recently on reciprocal political consequences of separatist movements.

DAVID C. MAUK is Associate Professor at the Norwegian University of Science and Technology in Trondheim, Norway, where he directs the English Department's program in American Civilization and teaches American immigration and ethnic history and U.S. politics. The coauthor of *American Civilization, An Introduction* (2nd ed. 1997), he has also published *The Colony That Rose from the Sea: Norwegian Maritime Migration and Community in Brooklyn, 1850–*

1910 (1997) and co-edited two volumes of *Norwegian-American Essays* (1993, 1996). A board member of the Norwegian Branch of the Norwegian-American Historical Association (NAHA), the Norwegian Emigrant Museum, and the American Studies Association in Norway, he has published articles on Norwegian-American labor leader Andrew Furuseth as well as on Norwegian communities in New York City: their maritime origins, welfare and religious institutions, socioeconomic conflicts, depression experience, and contemporary inter-ethnic relations. He is currently engaged by NAHA as a research director of the Twin Cities Project, which will result in an interethnic interpretation of Norwegian Americans' roles in the history of Minneapolis–St. Paul by the year 2000.

TIMOTHY J. MEAGHER is Archivist, Museum Director, and Adjunct Associate Professor of History at the Catholic University of America. He has edited two collections of essays on the Irish in America: *From Paddy to Studs: Irish American Communities in the Turn of Century Era* (1986) and, with Ronald Bayor, *The New York Irish* (1996). He has also written articles on Irish-American history for the *New England Quarterly*, the *Journal of Social History*, and the *U.S. Catholic Historian*.

DOMINIC A. PACYGA received his Ph.D. from the University of Illinois at Chicago in 1981. He has coauthored two books concerning Chicago neighborhoods and has published *Polish Immigrants and Industrial Chicago: Workers on the South Side, 1880–1922* (1991). Pacyga is a member of the faculty of the Liberal Education Department of Columbia College, Chicago. He is currently working on a study of Chicago and the United States in 1959.

LISANDRO PÉREZ is Associate Professor of Sociology and Director of the Cuban Research Institute at Florida International University (FIU). He received his Ph.D. in Sociology from the University of Florida. His first teaching position was at Louisiana State University, where he was promoted to Associate Professor and Coordinator of Graduate Studies. In 1985 he accepted the position of Chair of the Sociology and Anthropology Department at FIU. During his six-year term as Chair, he led the Department in the establishment of M.A. and Ph.D. degree programs. In 1991 he founded the Cuban Research Institute, dedicated to the study of Cuba and the Cuban-American community. He has published on Cuban demographics, society, and culture, as well as on the dynamics of the Cuban-American community. He was born in Havana, Cuba, and arrived in the United States at the age of eleven.

RAQUEL PINDERHUGHES is Associate Professor of Urban Studies at San Francisco State University. She is the co-editor, with Joan Moore, of *In the Barrios: Latinos and the Underclass Debate*. Her research areas and interests include urban restructuring, urban poverty, the socioeconomic position of the

Latino population in the United States, environmental equity, environmental justice, community organizing around local environmental issues, urban sustainable development, and green city planning. She recently completed studies on poverty and social inequality in San Francisco and on barriers to community organizing around small-source air polluters.

JOHN RADZILOWSKI is a Ph.D. candidate in History at Arizona State University (ASU) and also holds a certificate in scholarly publishing from ASU. He works as a freelance writer and editor and is the author of three books and the co-author of four others, which include *Prairie Town: A History of Marshall, Minnesota, 1872–1997* (1997) and (with Joseph Amato et al.) *To Call It Home: The Immigrants of Southwestern Minnesota* (1996). He writes a regular column on ethnicity and history for Polish-American newspapers with a combined circulation of 60,000.

THADDEUS C. RADZILOWSKI was born and raised in Hamtramck, Michigan. He received his M.A., a certificate in Russian and East European Studies, and a Ph.D. in History from the University of Michigan. He taught for twenty-five years at Southwest State University, in Marshall, Minnesota, where he also held the positions of Director of Rural Studies and Assistant Vice President for Academic Affairs. In 1995 he became President of St. Mary's College in Orchard Lake, Michigan. He has served in such positions as special adviser to the director of the National Endowment for the Humanities (NEH), as president of the Polish American Historical Association, and as acting director of the Immigration History Research Center at the University of Minnesota. He is the author of *Feudalism, Revolution, and the Meaning of Russian History: An Intellectual Biography of Nikolai Pavlovich Pavlov Silvanskii* (1994) and numerous articles on East European Americans and on ethnicity.

BRUNO RAMIREZ is Professor of History at the Université de Montréal (Canada). A specialist in labor and immigration history in North America, Ramirez is the author of *When Workers Fight: The Politics of Industrial Relations in the Progressive Era* (1978); *Les premiers Italiens de Montréal* (1984); *On the Move: French Canadian and Italian Migrants in the North Atlantic Economy, 1860–1914* (1991); and *Crossing the 49th Parallel: Canadian Emigration to the USA, 1900–1930* (1996).

PAOLA A. SENSI-ISOLANI has been educated in Italy, England, and the United States and has a Ph.D. in Anthropology from the University of California at Berkeley. She is a Professor of Anthropology and Chair of the Anthropology and Sociology Department at Saint Mary's College of California. Professor Sensi-Isolani has edited two books, *Italian Americans Celebrate Life: The Arts and Popular Culture* (1991), and *Struggle and Success: An Anthology of the Italian Immigrant Experience in California* (1993), and is the author of numerous articles on Italian Americans and on Italian immigration to the United States.

EDWARD S. SHAPIRO is a Professor of History at Seton Hall University in South Orange, New Jersey. His publications include *A Time for Healing: American Jewry since World War Two* (1992). Professor Shapiro is a member of the Academic Council of the American Jewish Historical Society and a member of the Editorial Board of American Jewish History.

SUZANNE M. SINKE is an Assistant Professor of History at Clemson University. She is co-editor, with Rudolph J. Vecoli, of *A Century of European Migrations, 1830–1930* (1991) and author of several articles on immigrant women, including "Give Us This Day: Dutch Immigrant Women in Two Protestant Denominations" in *Amerikastudien* (1993) and "The International Marriage Market: Theoretical and Historical Perspectives" in *People in Transit: German Migrations in Comparative Perspective, 1820–1930* (1995). She is currently working on a book based on her dissertation on Dutch immigrant women.

EILEEN H. TAMURA is director of history projects at the Curriculum Research and Development Group, University of Hawaii, and graduate faculty at the College of Education, University of Hawaii. She authored *Americanization, Acculturation, and Ethnic Identity: The Nisei Generation in Hawaii* (1994) and coauthored two textbooks, *A History of Hawai'i* (1989), which received an award from the American Association for State and Local History, and *China: Understanding Its Past* (1998). Her essays have appeared in *Journal of American Ethnic History, Pacific Historical Review, History of Education Quarterly, Pacific Educational Research Journal, The Social Studies, Social Education, New Issues in Asian American Studies*, and the *Asian American Encyclopedia*.

WILLIAM E. VAN VUGT is Professor of History at Calvin College, Grand Rapids, Michigan, where he teaches English History and United States Economic History. He earned his Ph.D. at the London School of Economics and Political Science. He has published articles in various journals, including the *Economic History Review*, the *Journal of Social History*, and the *Welsh History Review*, and has contributed chapters to several books on the history of American immigration. He recently published *Britain to America: The Mid-Nineteenth Century Immigrants to the United States* (1999).

MILTON VICKERMAN was born in Jamaica and migrated to the United States as a young adult. He took his advanced degrees at New York University. Presently, he is an Assistant Professor in the Department of Sociology at the University of Virginia. His primary research interests center around the issue of race, especially as viewed theoretically and historically; immigration, particularly as it pertains to West Indians; religion; and culture. He recently published *Cross Currents: West Indian Immigrants and Race* (1999).

LINDA S. WALBRIDGE was a Fulbright Scholar in Indonesia for the 1997–1998 academic year and is now a Visiting Research scholar at Indiana University–Purdue University in Indianapolis, in the Anthropology Department. She holds a Ph.D. from Wayne State University. Her doctoral research among the Lebanese Shi'i community in Michigan was the basis for her book *Without Forgetting the Iman: Lebanese Shi'ism in an American Community* (1997). She was the assistant director of the Middle East Institute at Columbia University from 1991 to 1993.

JULIET E. K. WALKER, a Professor of History, teaches at the University of Illinois at Urbana-Champaign. Walker has been a Research Associate at Harvard University's Du Bois Institute, a Fellow at the Princeton University Shelby–Cullom Davis Center for Historical Studies, and a Berkshire Fellow at Harvard-Radcliffe Bunting Institute. Walker is the author of the first comprehensive history of African-American business, *History of Black Business in America: Capitalism, Racism, Entrepreneurship* (1998), and editor of the *Encyclopedia of African American Business History* (1998) as well as author of *Free Frank: A Black Pioneer on the Antebellum Frontier* (1983; paperback ed., 1994), *War, Peace, and Structural Violence: Peace Activism and the African American Experience* (1992), and more than forty articles, essays, and reviews. She has won awards for her publications and teaching, and her fellowships include a Rockefeller and one from the National Endowment for the Humanities, as well as a Fulbright at the University of Witwatersrand, Johannesburg, South Africa.

FRANÇOIS WEIL is an Associate Professor of American History at the Ecole des Hautes Études en Sciences Sociales in Paris. Among other books, he is the author of *Les Franco-Americains* (1989) and is currently at work on a book on French migrants and ethnics in Latin and North America in the nineteenth and twentieth centuries.

CARMEN TERESA WHALEN is an Assistant Professor in the Puerto Rican and Hispanic Caribbean Studies Department and the History Department at Rutgers University in New Brunswick, New Jersey. She is currently working on a book on Puerto Rican migration to Philadelphia in the post–World War II era.

JUDY YUNG is a second-generation Chinese American born and raised in San Francisco's Chinatown. She has served as a public librarian, as a community journalist, and as director of both the Chinese Women of America Research Project (Chinese Culture Foundation of San Francisco) and the Asian American Women's Book Project (Asian Women United of California). She received her

Ph.D. in Ethnic Studies from the University of California at Berkeley and is presently an Associate Professor in American Studies at the University of California at Santa Cruz. Professor Yung is the coauthor, with Him Mark Lai and Genny Lim, of *Island: Poetry and History of Chinese Immigrants on Angel Island, 1910–1940* (1980, 1991) and the author of *Chinese Women of America: A Pictorial History* (1986) and *Unbound Feet: A Social History of Chinese Women in San Francisco* (1995).